Secularism in the Arab World

Based at the Aga Khan Centre in London, the Aga Khan University, Institute for the Study of Muslim Civilisations is a higher education institution with a focus on research, publications, graduate studies and outreach. It promotes scholarship that opens up new perspectives on Muslim heritage, modernity, religion, culture, and society. The Institute aims to create opportunities for interaction among academics and other professionals in an effort to deepen the understanding of pressing issues affecting Muslim societies today.

In Translation: Modern Muslim Thinkers

Series Editor: Abdou Filali-Ansary

This series aims to broaden current debates about Muslim realities which often overlook seminal works produced in languages other than English. By identifying and translating critical and innovative thinking that has engendered important debates within its own settings, the series seeks to introduce new perspectives to the discussions about Muslim civilisations taking place on the world stage.

Available titles:

Islam: Between Message and History
Abdelmadjid Charfi

Islam and the Foundations of Political Power
Ali Abdel Razek

The Sorrowful Muslim's Guide
Hussein Ahmad Amin
Translated by Yasmin Amin and Nesrin Amin

Secularism in the Arab World: Contexts, Ideas and Consequences
Aziz al-Azmeh
Translated by David Bond

Forthcoming titles:

Islam and Human Rights
Mohsen Kadivar
Translated by Niki Akhavan

edinburghuniversitypress.com/series/tmmt

Secularism in the Arab World

Contexts, Ideas and Consequences

AZIZ AL-AZMEH

EDINBURGH
University Press
IN ASSOCIATION WITH

THE AGA KHAN UNIVERSITY
INSTITUTE FOR THE STUDY OF MUSLIM CIVILISATIONS

The opinions expressed in this volume are those of the authors and do not necessarily reflect those of the Aga Khan University, Institute for the Study of Muslim Civilisations.

Edinburgh University Press is one of the leading university presses in the UK. We publish academic books and journals in our selected subject areas across the humanities and social sciences, combining cutting-edge scholarship with high editorial and production values to produce academic works of lasting importance. For more information visit our website: edinburghuniversitypress.com

Edinburgh University Press Ltd
The Tun – Holyrood Road
12 (2f) Jackson's Entry
Edinburgh EH8 8PJ

First published in hardback by Edinburgh University Press 2019

Typeset in 10.5/13 Adobe Garamond by
IDSUK (DataConnection) Ltd,

A CIP record for this book is available from the British Library

ISBN 978 1 4744 4746 1 (hardback)
ISBN 978 1 4744 4747 8 (paperback)
ISBN 978 1 4744 4749 2 (webready PDF)
ISBN 978 1 4744 4748 5 (epub)

Contents

Foreword by Gilbert Achcar vii
Preface to the English Translation xi
1992–2018 xi
Negative Authority xxii
Keywords: Vitalism, Historism xxv
Secularism and the Sociology of Fate xxx
One Post-colonialist Standard xlii
Acknowledgements l
Preface to the Second Arabic Edition li

Introduction 1

1 Religion and the World in Historical Perspective 7
1 On the Term "Secularism" 7
2 Religion and Public Life in Christian Commonwealths 9
3 Islam and the World 34

2 The Reformist State and the Universalist Orientation 85
1 The State and its Society: Education and Secular Culture 96
2 The Secularisation of Daily Life 126
3 The State: From the *Millet* to the Secular State 153

3 Intellectual Transformations and Elusive Reconciliation 181
1 Evolutionism and Salafism 184
2 Translation and Equivocation 204
3 Explicit Secularism and Accord with Reality 225

4 Sites of Secularism in the Twentieth Century 245
1 Secular Legislation and Social Dynamics 251
2 Intellectual Secularism and Reformist Retrogression 286
3 Secularism and Politics 329

5 The Nationalist Era and the Future Besieged 351
1 The Flowering of Secularism and its Social Dynamic 353
2 State, Religion, and the Beleaguered Future 384

6 Secularism at the Turn of the Millennium in the Context of its Adversaries 407
1 The Discourse of Exceptionalism and its Auxiliaries 422
2 Islam, Politics, and Society 431
3 The Context of Secularism 446

Bibliography 451
Index 511

Foreword by Gilbert Achcar

In the long view of our global political and intellectual history, the last quarter of the twentieth century will remain as the period when the whole set of beliefs that were dominant in that century's third quarter, in the wake of the Second World War, started to crumble along with the political–social–economic regimes that underpinned them.

Hitherto dominant beliefs consisted, in short, of three variants of the faith in a future guided by rationality reigning supreme, in direct filiation from the eighteenth century's Age of Enlightenment through the universalist positivism and the democratic emancipatory aspirations of the nineteenth century, and in sharp reaction to the massive and extremely tragic backlash against those values that peaked with the rise of totalitarianism during the first half of the twentieth century.

One of the three post-war variants emerged in the Soviet Union after Stalin and was shared by the worldwide mass of Moscow's partisans and admirers: it was a belief in a socialist future rid of the worst features of Stalinism and predicated upon successful economic competition with the capitalist West. The second was the Western response to the first: the belief in the uninterrupted development of a form of capitalism that benefits all spheres of society. The third was constituted by imitations of the first two variants in the Global South, consisting, in essence, of two types of developmentalism: one based on private-sector participation and the other on state monopolisation.

The last quarter of the twentieth century saw this tripartite ideological configuration come under attack and start unravelling, or even collapse altogether in the case of the Communist component. A neoliberal social-Darwinist ideological onslaught prevailed over all three ideological beliefs, buttressed by the discardment of the idea of collective universal emancipation. There was nonetheless a short-lived attempt to provide a neoliberal version of the emancipatory ambition of past epochs. Heralding the "end of history" and trying to reconcile the idea of welfare with an enterprise that consisted fundamentally in the dismantlement of actual welfare progresses achieved during the previous decades, that attempt ended in ridicule.

The reactionary onslaught was accompanied in its early stage by the postmodernist deconstruction of the very idea of progress. This went along with the resurgence of premodern systems of values and the replacement of the perspective of advance towards a rosy future with that of return to a no less rosy past. The convergence of postmodern with premodern in the rejection of modernity was most powerful in the Global South where modernism became increasingly lambasted as an ideology made in the Global North, and with equal zeal whether detractors were upholders of some brand of "post-colonial" views or upholders of archaic traditional values.

This convergence took a very acute form in the Arab world where it centred on the issue of religion. The shift from the Nasserist to the Saudi era during the 1970s led to a wide-ranging offensive against secularism, which had been from the start a key target of the Saudi-sponsored and US-backed attack against "Arab Socialism" and Communism. Unlike other parts of the world, the main anti-Communist ideology deployed by the United States in the Arab world during the Cold War had not been liberalism, but indeed Islam – particularly its fundamentalist interpretation.

This unholy alliance between the United States and Islamic fundamentalism culminated in the war against the Soviet occupation of Afghanistan in the 1980s. It ended in a tragic iteration of the tale of the sorcerer's apprentice, whose first climax on 11 September 2001 was to be followed by several others. Thanks to an unexpected "cunning of reason", Islamic fundamentalism managed in its expansion to extend to both ends of the spectrum of political attitudes towards the United States. In 1979 already, in counterpoint to the Saudi–US alliance, Iran's "Islamic Revolution" offered a fiercely anti-US populist variety of Islamic fundamentalism, thus enabling religious ideologies to complete their prevailing over secular left-wing ones in the Arab world. Nationalists who had hitherto resisted the Saudi-sponsored Islamic ideological drive in the name of anti-imperialism abandoned their secularist claims in fascination with anti-Western Khomeinism.

It is in the context of this creeping Islamisation of the full spectrum of regional politics that Aziz al-Azmeh published in Arabic in 1992 his *Secularism from a Different Perspective*. The author of the critically acclaimed *Islams and Modernities*, published in English the year after and in two further editions since then, thus established his reputation as the foremost thinker and defender of secularism and modernity against Islamic fundamentalism and the postmodern–premodern nexus in the Arab world.

There indeed, the present book is perceived as the main cornerstone of Aziz al-Azmeh's intellectual edifice in the pursuit of his defence of reason against the new historical attempt at destroying it. Writing in Arabic, the author conceived this work primarily as a major intervention in the Arab intellectual debate, of course. However, it is not for that matter a work whose interest is essentially limited to the region to which it was addressed, as one could legitimately believe. The reasons for that are threefold.

First, this book is not one of vulgarisation: on the contrary, it is a demanding read, fully respectful of its initial readers – Arab intellectuals – by presuming that they share the author's high standards of cultural requirement. Not that Aziz al-Azmeh has some elitist conception of intellectual intercourse: on the contrary, he has patiently disseminated his views in Arabic in countless didactic interventions in different formats and media.

Second, the topic of this book only gained in importance since its first publication in Arabic. The religious reaction has meanwhile carried on engulfing the Arab world in various forms, gaining in intensity, and producing ever more violent avatars that spilled over increasingly from the Muslim-majority world into the West. So much so that Muslims' secularisation, an issue that Western governments had earlier dismissed as pertaining to cultural identity in the hypocritical pretence of not interfering in such matters, has become a major concern of these governments with regard to Muslim migrants, and therefore to their source countries as well.

Last but not least, due to the above, but also due to the expansion of political currents upholding reactionary interpretations of Christianity in Western countries, including those Eastern European countries that do now belong politically to the West, and due as well to the ostentatious use made of religion by the post-Communist Russian government since the turn of the century, secularism has become anew a key topic of the intellectual and political debate in the Global North. This book's contribution to the discussion certainly goes beyond its immediate concern with Islam and the Arab world: its methodological approach is relevant to different cultural spheres, including the Western one.

For all these reasons, it is excellent news that the present book is finally made available to the English-language readership. It is high time indeed for this most sophisticated and stimulating discussion of secularism to transcend the confines of its original language and join the global discussion.

Preface to the English Translation

The Arabic original of this book was published twenty-six years ago. In times such as ours, that is, times of accelerated history and rapid change, half a generation is a long time indeed. The Arab World has in many ways and in the lifetime of one generation changed almost beyond recognition. This book aimed to understand historical change in the religious field, and the central cognitive purpose of this book remains unchanged. It was originally intended as a cognitive and cultural intervention in a constellation of specific political and cultural conjunctures arising from the end of the Cold War, and its purposes have clearly not been exhausted.

The book's purpose revolves around the capacity for recognition of fact and for discrimination: centrally between fact and fiction, however fiction might be generated, by complacency, hope, fantasy, disillusion, passion, resentment or fatigue, and, equally centrally. It strives for recognition of the distinction between cause and effect. It sought discriminating clarity in the histories of modernity and of secularisation, and in the circumstances and trends of relevance to its themes that were gathering at the moment of writing. It will be asked quite naturally if the tendential analyses provided in the book were borne out by subsequent developments or vitiated by them. This preface will problematise this question, and then take up the reasons why the terms in which it has been posed are inadequate to reality, including issues arising from recent critical analyses of the secularism thesis. It will end with considering one distinctive but not untypical case.

1 1992–2018

Like European societies in the past half century, like India and many other places as well, the Arab World has witnessed developments barely conceivable not long ago. Once marginal ideological, cultural, and political forces are moving to the centre and rapidly setting future agendas for themselves as for others – the reference here is primarily to forces fired by nativism, like the extreme Right in Europe, Hindu and Buddhist nationalism in south and south-east Asia, and Trumpism and the alt-right in the United States. In this global flow the Arab World has become manifestly more religious than it was in 1992, sometimes ostentatiously, as indicated by personal appearance no less than in political and social vocabularies used. Once marginal with respect to the main thrust of the public sphere in the way described in this book, religion pushed towards centre stage; once marginal forms of religion, Salafism, crowded out median, lived religiosity. Veiled women had by the 1980s – Arabia excluded – come to be commonly regarded as an embarrassing anachronism in the broadest of social circles. In subsequent decades veiling gained social admissibility in most milieux, and became indeed a token of conformist respectability. It even spread to the rural population, in the uniform guise now widely marketed as the international "traditional Muslim headscarf", made all the more rigorous in recent years by the double head scarf, possibly invented by Turkish cloth merchants, and by the veiling of very young girls and infants, as well as by effacement of countenance in black. This uniform is quite different to traditional, very local female garb, including the custom of covering the head by both men and women. And, if anything, the hostility to secularism had grown in parallel, or at least the impression that it is so is strong, as the word is not infrequently used as an imprecation.

What in 1991 was perceived as a gathering menace has since flourished in many instances where explicitly anti-secularist forces have attempted to move from the sub-cultural, political, and social margins to the centre. Jihadist Salafism has since represented an especially nightmarish experiment in Islamist social engineering. The Muslim Brethren tried their own version in Egypt, succumbing fatally to their avid craving for power bolstered by claims to historical entitlement, as they attempted, with an almost fevered impulse, to *ikhwanise* the country precipitately and on the hop – *akhwana, ikhwanisation*, is a term in Arab political vocabulary, derived from *ikhwan*, brethren, as in Muslim Brethren, meaning literally "brotherification". It is used to describe Muslim Brother policies of imposing their social, cultural, and political norms on others, including the bureaucracy, the armed forces, civil institutions and movements, major cultural organisms, and so forth – during Muhammad Morsi's tenure of the Presidency, with the aim of state capture by the party (June 2012–July 2013). The apparent ascendancy of these forces overall had conveyed a strong sense of inevitability, until fatigue with religious claims to political power started to gather pace and to become explicit in recent years.

This sense of inevitability arose from the idea that an Islamic order must be the solution to the myriad crises and impasses besetting the Arab World, an argument that was served up together with another, that Islamists were the legitimate answer to decades of tyranny, injustice, neglect, dispossession, and state capture by private, often patrimonial, interests and networks. One might understand how religious motifs might be appealing in inconsolable situations compounded by generalised anomie and social and socio-geographic disaggregation, and how logistical resources, providing supply, can generate a need for the emotional gratification of religious goods, symbols, motifs, and traditions newly invented. One can also appreciate how this would work in countries like Syria, voided of a public sphere, its body politic dismantled. Yet it needs to be said that legitimacy here is an unfortunate choice of word and sentiment. Islamist forces were clearly a symptom of the crisis, not a possible solution, not least as they offer imaginary answers compounded with tyrannical and exclusivist impulses, thereby begging the issue of legitimacy altogether, and conflating a sociological and mass-psychological understanding of Islamist appeal in a moment of crisis with the artless justification of Islamist drive and use of democratist vocabularies.

While politically some of the religious assault on political power has been blunted recently, the residue of social, cultural, and cognitive effects precipitated by Islamist social and ideological expansion have become rooted. It was spawned, often with state help, and has been in gestation for more than three decades, and it has come to constitute a palpable social undertow. While some might like to claim that this could invalidate the analytical itineraries of this book, written from a robustly secularist perspective, closer consideration will show that developments over the past twenty-six years in fact tend to confirm the book's analyses, and can be interpreted most cogently in terms of the book's analytical tools.[1]

Readers of this book will find that a consistent line of analytical argument, accompanied by a narrative, are pursued throughout. The procedure is historical, tracing the ways in which secularisation, implicit or explicit, took root, unevenly, in central regions of modern Arab history over a century and a half, and in the political, social, legal, cultural, institutional, and cognitive spheres.

1 See Aziz Al-Azmeh, *Islams and Modernities*, 3rd edn (London: Verso, 2009), chs 2, 3, 4, 10; 'Azīz Al-'Aẓma [Aziz al-Azmeh], *Sūrīya wa'ṣ-ṣu'ūd al-uṣūlī*, ed. Ḥammūd Ḥammūd (Beirut: Riyad al-Rayyis Books, 2015).

It does so with attention to structures and trends no less than to sometimes granular detail concerning matters such as intellectual orientations, legal reforms, gender relations, ambivalences, the unevenness of the social distribution and regional and socio-spatial disposition of relevant developments discussed, time lags, ambiguities, and successes. It is to be expected that such a book will address historical realities without bowdlerisation, and would not mince words or use euphemisms, such as using adjectival and related attributive forms, "secularity" or "the secular", to obscure reality or attempt by verbal magic to keep secularism at bay; nor does it use inverted commas redundantly, as an expression of vacuous sarcasm and rebuke and disparagement, and apart from what is appropriate to quotation or parody.

The developments addressed in this book include the rise of Islamism in the last third of the twentieth century. This can be explained as a result of processes of uneven social differentiation, which defined modernity globally, whereby the religious field was in many crucial instances differentiated out, and was consequently open to cultivation as a stand-alone instance at the margins, with its own subculture. Under certain circumstances of disaggregation and crisis, this, abstracted from social relations, can become the locus of proposing a counter-society, and a socio-political project for moving to the centre, under the signature of rolling back the very history, that of modernisation and her sister phenomenon, secularisation, which had relegated it to the margins and created it as a specific instance, enabling its later quest for hegemony. The differentiation of the religious sphere betokens a degree of autonomisation of religion, but, in a secular order, in terms of a system whose guiding ideas and motifs are not religious and not derived from religion or justified by it. This necessitates accommodations of a normative and cognitive kind, and administrative, legal, and other levels of regulation by a state-administrative order. The common idea that secularism implied the separation of state and religion is pertinent to some instances and functions, but not others.

The other topic treated throughout is the quite distinct issue of secularism as an ideal, a programme, a state ideology. Readers will find traced the way in which secularism became an issue of controversy, first defined by budding Islamist forces as a polemical and social foil as they came to elaborate themselves at the margins. This was reinforced institutionally in the course of the Cold War, with Islamism contra secularism defining the cultural plank of the "containment of Communism" strategy, one not confined to the Arab World, but also active in Italy, and Poland, and Indonesia and Malaysia where it expressed itself in tremendous bloodshed. This development is discussed in the final chapter.

In all instances, a primary thesis and conceptual premise of this book is that events and trends occur in history, and that historical dynamics and conjunctures trump putative origins, which are clichés used as emblems of combat rather than historical realities. Secularism and secularisation are objective historical processes, accompanying the differentiation of societal functions attendant upon the equally objective global forces of modernity. An analysis of secular historical, social, and cultural itineraries is therefore one that would seek to achieve knowledge of the object of study commensurate with and adequate to reality – this, the cognitive task of discrimination, is what this book has sought to do, as has been well noted by ʿAzmī Bishāra in a major – and massive – recent book on religion and secularism.[2] Bishāra's book is cognate with this one in seeking cognitive discrimination and in finding that it is impossible historically to understand religion in the modern world without a clear understanding of secularism. Its first two volumes sketch in systematic and comprehensive compass the range of possible parameters connecting religion and secularism, going on to a discussion of the intellectual, social, and political histories across European history into the twentieth century. The volume concerning the Arab World is yet to come, but there is enough critical discussion of Arab circumstances to reveal that many perspicacious questions asked (some briefly brought together in the final chapter) resulted from and were enriched by determined reflections upon the Islamist surge and its contexts, and the cognitive assimilation of this surge, at the peak of which the book was conceived and written.

Yet my book was not a general argument for secularism, albeit written from a secularist position, in recognition of secularisation as a systemic objective dynamic. Arabic letters are replete with assertions of secularism and political, ethical, social, and cognitive pleas for it, rarely well developed. The most elaborate philosophical argument for secularism in Arabic, appearing in the same conjuncture as this book and sharing some of its concerns, is a technical epistemological critique of religious turns of thought by the philosopher ʿAdil Dahir. It develops rigorously what he called "hard" as opposed to "soft",

2 ʿAzmī Bishāra, *Al-dīn wa'l-ʿalmāniyya fī siyāq tārīkhī*, 2 vols in 3 parts (Doha: Arab Center for Research and Policy Studies, 2012–2015), 2/1: 88, n. 47.

complaisant secularism,[3] whose various aspects are discussed in the chapters that follow this preface.

As a consequence of the emphasis on history, one cannot take seriously the common repertoire of explanations on offer, which propose explanations for the rise and spread of anti-secular forces in terms of the "return of religion" to its supposedly rightful place long repressed, in spite of history. This in turn is seen as the reassertion of Arab ethnological energies and predispositions, ultimately an ethnological destiny, temporarily obscured by colonialism and elitist secularism. Constantly on offer also, especially in more politicised discourses, are disquisitions upon the failure of secularism, modernity, and nationalism, indeed on the failure of "the Arab state" as such, with vocabularies that indicate contempt, odium, and malediction. The argument from historical failure is as common as it is specious, and generally operates by taking effect for cause, and by turning criticism of defects, incompleteness, and deficits into an argument for invalidation, illegitimacy, even for the altogether fictitious character of secularism or whatever else is being thereby degraded polemically, reality chased away by inverted commas. Such arguments are premised ultimately on impressionistic statements about the piety of the Arabs, that they really be Super-Muslims, a view propagated in tandem by Islamists and outside observers, including academic experts. Such arguments are brought to bear in order to take the recession and attrition of secularism for what insurance companies might call Acts of God, independent of human action, and to argue for the artificiality of social transformations associated with it, as if societies and histories were facts of nature resistant to change. This theme shall be revisited below.

I would expect that readers of this book would not, upon reflection, be attuned to mystical outlooks ascribing occult causes such as "the repressed" for the extraordinary, even exhibitionistic forms of religiosity that spread in the Arab World in the lifetime of one generation. Such explanations are really justifications and apologies in the guise of explanation, which extrude both history and the transformations of society from the picture. If occult explanations in terms of the return of the dead were put aside, the widening force of religious phenomena would need to be conceived in terms other

---

3 ʿĀdil Ḍāhir, *Al-Usus al-Falsafiya li'l-ʿIlmānīya* (Beirut: Dār al-Sāqī, 1993) – the public role of the two positions has been fruitfully discussed: see Bishara, *Ad-Din*, 2/1: 83–85.

than "return", for religion had never departed nor was it ever buried in order for it to be resurrected. Religion has been reconfigured, and the spread of this Wahhabi-embossed, Petro-Islamic reconfiguration of the religious field, which has come in recent years to colour what is known as "moderate Islam" as well, is not the efflorescence of an ethnological nature and the reassertion of destiny in abeyance, but a dynamic social and cultural contrivance that would not have been possible without political direction and logistical capacity.

It was the Cold War that provided the initial impulse to build well-funded world-wide institutions of devotions, education, communications, culture and political and civic organisation, all of which served as primary agents of what eventually became large-scale and fairly homogenising re-socialisation into Wahhabi sensibilities, cognitive turns, social mores, grafted upon a Muslim Brother core of infrastructure, political experience, sensibility and ideological orientation – at first piecemeal, from the late 1970s with greater and more concerted intensity. This was accompanied by the spread of a number of perceptible tokens: personal appearance, manners of dress increasingly bizarre, turns of phrase, tones of voice, facial expressions. The role of the Cold War in refashioning cultures, including religion, is a topic that has been producing a rapidly growing bibliography, and the Crown Prince of Saudi Arabia has himself avowed the link between the Cold War and the spread of Wahhabism.[4] Somewhat idle for long, except in response to local needs of limited proselytism or polemic (as in anti-secular activity in the Arab World), but sustained by Islamist political parties, this very considerable logistical and institutional infrastructure came to life under the impulse of the Rushdie Affair of 1988–1989, and became a global logistical resource. That was the point at which transformations effecting dress, voice, expression, views, and sensibility started with growing intensity to build an internal dynamic of re-socialisation. This fed upon the cultivation of rage, of a habitus of distemper, an eagerness to take offence, exhibitionistic self-stigmatisation by increasingly eccentric looks and manners, expressed in terms of, and inculcating habituation into, a culture of special

4 Karen Young, interview with Crown Prince Muḥammad b. Salmān in *The Washington Post*, 22 March 2018. See the broad-ranging studies in Philip Muehlenbeck (ed.), *Religion and the Cold War* (Nashville: Vanderbilt University Press, 2012), and, for a Euro-American focus, Dianne Kirkby (ed.), *Religion and the Cold War* (Basingstoke: Palgrave, 2003).

pleading and of denunciation, well-suited to the uncontrolled stridency of political controversy in the United States, reflected in the temper of many a post-colonialist institution. The rest of the story is well known. Similarly, the increasing religious conservatism observable in Turkey over the past fifteen years needs to be correlated to the fortunes of the ruling political party and the attendant, deliberate intellectual archaisation (including retrogressive revision of school curricula) and expansion of the state religious organ Diyanet, whose budget has increased at least fourfold since 2006.

This "return" to religion is explainable by the same concepts and analytical instruments used to analyse secularism in this book, with no recourse needed to mystical or meta-historical and meta-social explanations. Just as secularism is not interpretable in terms of itself, or conceivable as simply a check list of features existing or lacking, but requires to be seen in terms of historical and social science categories, and as mutually constitutive with the religious field, so also is deliberate reverse social and political engineering by means of Islamisation not amenable to analytical approach in terms of itself, as a sui generis "culture", but with reference to the process's moorings in social and political dynamics, in terms of long-term, uneven, complex social and political processes. Islamisation is an active, complex process, not simply the revelation of a hidden societal nature prior to society, history, and conjuncture.

Revisionist work on secularism by social scientists has not always been exercised by ideas of occult reanimation or resuscitation. It emerged in reaction to empirical evidence that religion had not disappeared under modern conditions. Unsurprisingly, such work flourished especially as fundamentalism, first in the United States, later the Islamic variety,[5] came into its own and became mediatically interesting and politically significant. It could have emerged earlier, as religion was never absent, but it did not, and seemed uninteresting; this is not irrelevant and would require explanation. The tenor of some of this work is distinctly apologetic. The growing visibility of religion was often put forward polemically to invalidate classical secularisation theory,[6] taken by some more for a "sacralised" ideal and an ideological

5 For connections between the two, see Sadiq J. Al-Azm, *On Fundamentalisms* (Berlin: Gerlach Press, 2014), ch. 2.

6 For which see the classic work of David Martin, *A General Theory of Secularization* (Oxford: Basil Blackwell, 1969/1978).

position than a sociology properly speaking.[7] This, despite the fact that the waning away of religion is not a matter required by classical secularisation theory, as distinct from the thesis of privatisation, which is constitutive of it. It is overall clear that anti-secular polemics have simplified the basic thesis and conflated its elements,[8] a thesis related to functional differentiation under conditions of modernity.[9] It is commonly the case that discussions of secularisation start with ideological constructions of what it is supposed to be ideally, with historical reality then read in this light and found wanting or imperfect. It shall be seen below that there is also a strong seam of political and academic denial: not only denial that secularism actually occurred, and that it is an objective historical dynamic often independent of individual or collective volition and not always perceived by those who undergo it, but also of denial by social scientists of their own social science craft, as some of them turn secularisation into a morality play. The reconfiguration of the religious field, it is being suggested here, is attributable to the differentiation of religion in the context of a far broader global trend of functional differentiation that structured much of the social and cultural developments of the Arab World over the past century. Such reconfigurations in a broader extent have been studied most productively in recent work.[10]

These matters are clear enough in this book, but are also sustained by one highly revisionist sociologist.[11] Correlatively, what might arguably be seen as the re-enchantment of the world can also be accounted for adequately by the very Weberian thesis of differentiation and disenchantment.[12] The decline of religious belief, and the social practice of religion, are distinct analytically and may not be, as is often the case, conflated.[13] Matters are such that the

7 Jeffrey K. Hadden, "Toward desacralizing secularization theory", *Social Forces* 65/3 (1987): 587–611, 588, and passim.

8 David Yamane, "Secularization on trial: In defence of a neosecularization paradigm", *Journal for the Scientific Study of Religion* 36 (1997): 109–122.

9 On differentiation, especially Bishāra, *Ad-Dīn*, 2/2, 181–245.

10 See especially Bryan S. Turner, *Religion and Modern Society. Citizenship, Secularisation and the State* (Cambridge: Cambridge University Press, 2011), 277–279, and passim.

11 José Casanova, *Public Religions in the Modern World* (Chicago: University of Chicago Press, 1994), 15–21.

12 Especially Richard Jenkins, "Disenchantment, enchantment and re-enchantment: Max Weber at the millennium", *Max Weber Studies* 1 (2000): 11–32, at 12–13.

13 Cf. José Casanova, "A reply to Talal Asad", in *Powers of the Secular Modern. Talal Asad and His Interlocutors*, eds D. Scott and C. Hirschkind (Stanford: Stanford University Press, 2006), 12–30, at 16.

social enracination of religion, even when privatised, does not allow a ready answer to the question as to whether belief might be belief in a specific creed or in the social necessity of religious affiliation: the two are often conflated in tendentious arguments directed against secularisation theory.[14]

There is no scope in this preface to take account systematically of the enormous scholarly and other type of literature on issues raised by this book. Some recent scholarship enhanced and strengthened the points made, in many cases adding nuance and refinement; some of these have been added to the footnotes, where appropriate, to bring them up to date. But there is scope for trying to explain why the common explanations signalled in the previous paragraphs are so very common, and why contrary arguments are often resisted and disregarded, despite works showing clearly, in temperate language, the overwhelming salience and reality of secular transformations in societies from Egypt though India to Japan, looked upon through the lens of social differentiation.[15] Unsurprisingly, given the polemical and ideological nature of much that is said in this regard, analyses critical of secularisation tend to ignore the state, transnational flows, market forces and elements that precipitate secular transformations,[16] thereby standing the world upon its head. What can be done here and now is to offer an analysis of what might metaphorically be termed broadly a political economy of misrecognition and cognitive distortion, a critique of critical critique.

Arab discussions have generally sumnambulated in the apologetic moulds that were analysed in the final two chapters of this book, in almost elegiac tonalities, moulds of socio-cognitive misrecognition that have come to assume the character of common sense, and have not usually been supported by empirical work, historical or social.[17] This has become all the more grievous as social media

14 Bishāra, *Ad-Dīn*, vol. 1, ch. 2, section 4, at 237. See Loek Halman and Veerle Draulans, "How secular is Europe?", *British Journal of Sociology* 57 (2006): 263–288.

15 For instance: David N. Gellner, "Studying secularism, practising secularism. Anthropological perspectives", *Social Anthropology* 9 (2001): 337–340, and Gudrun Krämer, "Secularity contested: Religion, identity and the public order in the Arab Middle East", in *Multiple Secularities beyond the West,* eds Marian Burchart, Monika Wohlrab-Sahr, and Matthias Middell (Berlin: De Gruyter, 2015), 121–137.

16 See among others the comments of Krämer, "Secularity contested", 124.

17 Azīz Al-ʿAẓma, "Bayn al-tārīkh wa'l-istikāna li'l-qadar", *Bidāyāt* 14 (2016): 104–111. On ideological transformations accompanying impasses of recognition and analysis, see Michaelle L. Browers, *Political Ideology in the Arab World. Accommodation and Transformation* (Cambridge: Cambridge University Press, 2009).

and instant, unreflected, comment virally transmitted, tend to produce cultural effects conducive to summary modes of expression discussed below, contributing to the culture of misrecognition, including the conflation of real and virtual communities.[18] Much of the work that has tried to go beyond these moulds, and much of this followed the broad wave of revulsion at political Islam since 2011 – there is even a trend of apologetic re-interpretation inside Saudi Arabia seeking to reformulate Wahhabism in moulds of secular reasonableness[19] – has been characterised by much the same features of impressionism, inattention to empirical detail, and a breath-taking apologetic schematism.

Much of this exercise in misapprehension occured in the flow of anti-state and the anti-secularist motifs associated with it, at a time when the premises of Islamist political discourse, internalised by many of their erstwhile adversaries, were gaining wide purchase, almost by default. Both relayed ideological goods, often at second hand, from the closing stage of the Cold War and the neo-liberal restructuring that followed immediately thereafter. All such was salient to "transition", as it is called in Eastern Europe, later from the "end of history" triumphalism of the winning party; the social Darwinism of the Neo-Liberal order was matched by a social Darwinist view of societies, nations, and communities. Fired by a schematic and almost angelical view of "civil society",[20] defined negatively as that which is not the abominated state, or positively in terms of supposedly cosy, ancestral identities inimical to the state, these discourses formed part of a rather artless, talismanic view of democracy, which voided this concept of politics and viewed it in terms of abstract rights, a matter evident in the Damascus Spring of 2000–2001, and manifest in many aspects of the Arab Spring of 2010–2011. Democracy was viewed as correspondence of society and the state, a sociological absurdity of grandiose tonality, ideologically populist, almost tailor-made to fit Islamist aspirations to the exclusive representation of society.[21]

---

18 See, most suggestively, "Community", "Culture", and "Memory" in *Digital Keywords: A Vocabulary of Information, Society and Culture*, ed. Benjamin Peters (Princeton: Princeton University Press, 2016), s.v.

19 Khālid Al-Dakhīl, *Al-Wahhābīya bayn ash-shirk wa taṣaḍḍu' al-qabīla* (Beirut: al-Shabaka al-'Arabiyya li'l-Abḥāth wa'n-Nashr, 2013); Khālid Al-Dakhīl, "Al-Wahhābīya: Murāja'a ukhrā", *Al-Ḥayāt*, 20 February 2016.

20 On this concept, including aspects of its usage in Arab political discourse: 'Azmī Bishāra, *Al-mujtama' al-madanī* (Beirut: Markaz Dirāsāt al-Waḥda al-'Arabīya, 2000).

21 Aziz Al-Azmeh, "Populism contra democracy: Recent democratist discourse in the Arab World", in *Democracy without Democrats*, ed. Ghassan Salamé (London: I. B. Tauris, 1994), 112–129.

Ultimately, this was an attempt by many members of the Arab intelligentsia to offer an apology for political Islamism, expecting thereby to ride the Islamist tiger with varying degrees of reluctance. This has to some extent become defanged, and elements within it are considering it prudent, albeit not without internal conflict, to divide the religious from the political, to the extent of the Tunisian Nahda putting forward unveiled women for election (one became the Mayor of Tunis in early July 2018); the future itineraries here and in incipient similar trends within the Moroccan Justice and Development party are yet difficult to predict. This apology, and its anti-secular and anti-modern motifs, has come to be conducted with post-colonialist and postmodernist vocabularies and motifs, rarely at first hand. To this very considerable extent, it belongs to a global trend of anti-modernism and anti-secularism, one that is particularly strong in Anglophone countries. It is to this that we now turn.

2 *Negative Authority*

A fairly simple contention involving a number of interconnected themes and propositions related to these themes is being suggested. None of these propositions is particularly novel.[22] But the issues raised have been insistent, and some points made, against the flow, more than two decades ago, now stand out more cogently than ever, and are revisited or rediscovered by many.

The simple contention is that Islamism, which is habitually taken for a vitiation of modernist claims made for modern Arab history and other histories as well, has been made possible rhetorically and conceptually primarily by a standard global repertoire of anti-modernist motifs and concepts of late eighteenth- and nineteenth-century vintage, emergent with modernity. The same would apply to other self-consciously retrogressive identitarian motifs, ideas, sensibilities, and moods that sustain and are sustained by a differentialist culturalism. The specific concern in these pages is Euro-American, but it needs to be said that, in the Arab World (India and other places are comparable, with chronological variation), anti-modernist tropes and metaphors had

22 See Aijaz Ahmad, *In Theory* (London: Verso, 1992); Aijaz Ahmad, "Post-colonial theory and the 'post' condition", *The Socialist Register* 33 (1997): 353–382; Arif Dirlik, *The Postcolonial Aura* (Boulder: Westview Press, 1997); Al-Azmeh, *Islams and Modernities.*

under Cold War impulse migrated from social, ideological, and political margins in the direction of centre stage, at first incrementally from about 1967, later epidemically from 1979, and settled pandemically since 1989. These tropes have seeped into the interstices of nationalist, liberal, and left-wing discourses, and have, with their culturalist and populist templates, in effect blunted political and analytical capacity.[23] They became all the more strongly rooted after the attack on the Twin Towers in New York on 9/11, becoming an item of common sense; it was at that point that was consolidated the definitive recasting of German Turks and French Arabs and British Pakistanis into uniform "Muslims", and that a great many of them internalised this, genuinely or defensively.

In the Euro-American context, these apologetics for obscurantism have not been the work of conservatives only (including practising Muslims), but also of representatives of postmodernist and post-colonialist currents to whom the left has largely devolved, and who take themselves, oddly enough, to be avant-garde. That they present mirror-images of present afterlives of classic ultra-conservative conceptions, now reconditioned rather luridly, often with the strident and hectoring tonalities characteristic of anti-modern polemics historically,[24] seems to generate little curiosity or to occasion self-reflection. It is this vindication of postmodern obscurantism that needs to lie at the core of the discussion. These issues will now be discussed; the work of Talal Asad will be called up to sample many of these conveniently.[25]

The promotion and cultivation of sentimentalist nativism and cognitive relativism, associated with postmodernist and post-colonialist currents, generally enunciated in a polemical mode broadly termed critical theory or deconstruction, is now firmly established in universities, particularly in the United States, and indeed in many international organisations and foundations as well. This dragon-slaying type of critique is largely enthralled by hostility to greater proportions of its object of study as approached by others, and had

23 This book, chs 5 and 6; 'Azīz Al-'Azma, *Dunyā al-dīn fī ḥāḍir al-'arab*, rev. edn (Beirut: Dār al-Ṭalī'a, 2002), chs 1–4; 'Azīz Al-'Azma, 'Bayn at-tārīkh'.

24 For the rhetoric of vituperation, see especially Antoine Compagnon, *Les Antimodernes. De Joseph de Maistre à Roland Barthes* (Paris: Gallimard, 2006), ch. 6

25 Asad's knowledge of and views on Islam and secularism have recently been clearly and comprehensively sketched and respectfully put down: Hadi Enayat, *Islam and Secularism in Post-Colonial Thought. A Cartography of Asadian Geneaologies* (London: Palgrave Macmillan, 2017).

been especially appealing to feminists, cultural studies types, queer theorists, and other latecomer niches of the academy. It had petrified all too rapidly on acquiring institutional grounding, and developed into an institutional paradigm, with the usual political economy of a regnant academic orthodoxy,[26] fostering a doctrinaire, in principle rigid and often formulaic output.

The resulting rhetoric of suspicion is of a type with nineteenth-century phrenological criminology, psychoanalysis, and the detective novel, all based, like medieval inquisitorial procedures, on reading signs. It favours disciplinary-juristic terms such as "interpellation" and "interrogation", and "negotiation" as well, in an attitude of hermeneutical hubris powered by negative energy, employing a number of standard rhetorical devices so well brought out recently.[27] Of particular pertinence to issues of post-colonialism's unfriendly attitude towards secularism and to the related work of Asad is the way in which Subaltern Studies keeled over towards neo-nativism and sentimentalism. This came with a decided anti-modern mood, once Ranajit Guha departed from the helm and a crop of younger, gifted Indian academics at US universities came to appropriate the label and decide its direction, paralleling mutations in other fields,[28] moving from anti-colonialism[29] to post-colonialism. Post-colonialist discourse is parasitical on anti-colonialism, towards which it is related only rhetorically.

Two consequences attend the overdetermination of this mode of academic practice by the adversarial mood. The first is that, with few exceptions, its cognitive harvest is slight generally, despite the persistent claim that it is closer to the ground, and that modernists are too much given to abstraction, a position very often associated with anti-intellectualism,[30] here paraded by intellectuals as anti-elitism. Those works that do rest on empirical research tend to oscillate between elementary empirical description and

---

26 Michael Billig, "Towards a critique of the critical", *Discourse and Society* 11 (2000): 291–292.

27 Rita Felski, "Suspicious minds", *Poetics Today* 32 (2011): 215–234.

28 Perry Anderson, *The H-Word. The Peripeteia of Hegemony* (London: Verso, 2017), 100–102; Sumit Sarkar, "The decline of the subaltern in Subaltern Studies", in *Mapping Subaltern Studies and the Postcolonial*, ed. Vinayak Chaturvedi (London: Verso, 2000), 300–323.

29 Exemplarily: Eric Robert Wolf, *Europe and the People without History*, 2nd edn (Oakland: University of California Press, 2010).

30 Zeev Sternhell, *The Anti-Enlightenment Tradition* (New Haven: Yale University Press, 2010), 28–29; Judith Shklar, *After Utopia: The Decline of Political Faith* (Princeton: Princeton University Press, 1957/2015), 241–244.

meta-theoretical imperatives, the imperatives of transposing the normative into the cognitive, such as advocacy for representing an egalitarianism of "voices" rather than establishing facts and analytical itineraries. This feature is palpable in Asad, with pronouncements based on sparse empirical material and slight reading overall, the two commensurate with what is evidently an extraordinary economy of effort and curiosity. Overall, the mid-level, sociological or historical element, analytically crucial, is dislodged. The perspective of the subject-position blunts the basic distinction between observer and observed, scientific practitioner and her material and object of study. The second consequence is that this mode of academic practice is impelled by negative energy, a choleric indignation that is inculcated as an institutional habitus. Analysis is in the service of activism.

Anti-modernism is of course complex, and has for more than two centuries spoken in a variety of tonalities, genres, and conceptual languages. It is often forgotten, even by sociologists, that anti-modernism has not been primarily or indeed solely a matter of discourses, moods, and motifs, of "interpretative frames", or a phenomenon that belongs to the realm of "meaning", whatever the word may mean beyond the evocation of something enticingly occult and by default of conveying a more concrete indication. "Meaning" is generally deployed to proclaim a knowing eye and ear, intimating the ineffable, and perhaps more importantly to convey pathos. It is not often enough remembered that anti-modernism has always been a social, political, and cultural dynamic, reflecting far more than inertial energy or a flowering of meaning, and has been asserted with a variety of instruments including profuse bloodshed. The Iranian revolution is a clear case in point here: it was not only an archaising harking back of the spirit to deep meaning, but also a social engineering project with the use of state violence.

3 Keywords: Vitalism, Historism

Post-colonialist and postmodernist directions in the social and human sciences can be characterised by a number of conceptual features, none of which is novel or post-anything really. A primary feature is a vitalist and organismic concept of society, society being viewed metaphorically in biological terms. This is complemented by a constructivist and relativist epistemology, where knowledge comes to be taken for a form of collective instinct, and where discourse and other forms of enunciation are merely redactions of indigenous sentiment and disposition. Issues of truth and falsity, when raised at all, are of secondary interest. This yields, of necessity, a cognitive relativism, ultimately nihilistic, expressed in terms such as incommensurability, *Verstehen*, or the reducibility of knowledge to power. The package is overdetermined by the terms of a polemic against positivism and other politico-cognitive iniquities, generally reduced to a schematic representation with little correspondence to actual positions or practices.[31]

The other primary feature is a deterministic, historist conception of time and history.[32] Historism – distinct from universalising historicism – conceives history as that of generically different stocks, enclosed within predetermined characteristics, containing "identities" in common parlance today. Historism presupposes abiding morphological elements in any given collectivity – Herder's *Kräfte*, national spirit, collective personality, national character, culture, civilisation, religion, life-forms, world views, and so forth – that are impermeable to history. In this scheme, neither conjuncture nor future are history in any significant way; they are rather redactions of ethnological destiny. Secularisation and modernisation are pronounced illusory because they do not form part of the narrative of destiny.

Returning to where we started: apart from historist polemic, what has been witnessed in recent decades is not so much a return to religion as recourse to religion, alongside a reconfiguration of the religious field, globally, over the lifetime of the past generation. Not a return, nor a resurrection, but a recasting, because of history and not in spite of history. What is commonly seen as the return of religion, with spectacular and sanguine force since the end of the Cold War,[33] has had a history of repetition, reflecting long-term tensions, connecting its various moments in complex ways,[34] in phase with

---

31 See especially the discussion of an analogous phenomenon, constructivist sociology of science, in Larry Laudan, "The pseudo-science of science", *Philosophy of Social Science* 11 (1981): 173–198.

32 A very clear synoptic characterisation of historism is in Georg Iggers, "Historicism: The history and meaning of the term", *Journal of the History of Ideas* 56 (1995): 129–152, at 135–136, and passim; Sternhell, *The Anti-Enlightenment Tradition*, 19–24. One of the clearest synoptic statements of the entire doctrine is by a Patristic figure in post-colonialist and postmodernist circles: Hans Georg Gadamer, "Herder et ses théories sur l'Histoire", *Cahiers de l'Institut Allemand, II: Regards sur l'histoire*, ed. Karl Epting, Paris, 1941, 9–36.

33 Al-Azmeh, *Islams and Modernities*, ch. 2; Aziz Al-Azmeh, "Civilisation as a political disposition", *Economy and Society* 41 (2012); 501–512.

34 See the comment of Richard Shorten, "Reactionary rhetoric reconsidered", *Journal of Political Ideologies* 20 (2015): 179–200, at 188–196.

broader developments beyond the world of the mind. The putative return is in this respect part of a cyclical global anti-modernist, anti-Enlightenment counter-revolution surge, repeating previous performances that involved laggard nationalism, relativism, anti-rationalism, entailing meditations on decadence, degeneration, resurrection, and the dawn and twilight of nations and communities, together with a cult of the popular soul. The present phase of globalisation is the last in a series to date; a globalising dynamic is implicit and explicit in all the analyses of this book.

The first phase of this constellation of topoi and sentiments crystallised following the collapse of an older world with 1789 (leading intellectual lights: Herder, de Maistre, Burke), the second following 1848, boosted in 1870 (leading lights: Carlyle, Savigny, von Stein, Gobineau, Le Bon, Pope Pius IX's *Syllabus of Errors* of 1864) with the eruption of "the people". Such moods continued in various forms into the morbid malaise of the fin de siècle consolidated in the third phase following 1917 and 1918, crystallising in various forms of fascism broadly defined (some leading lights: Maurras, Spengler, Schmitt, Heidegger, Hassan al-Banna, Madhav Sadashiv Golwalkar). The fourth built upon the mobilisation of religion during the Cold War, conjugated with earlier tropes of disenchantment, and followed upon the consequences and exemplarity of the Iranian Revolution. It also built upon a right-wing liberalism nurtured by anti-Communism, on an impasse in political thinking with triumphalist declamations, however short-lived, of the End of History, and on revisionist historiographies of all movements that had once held historical promise such as the French and Russian Revolutions.[35] There is an ideological continuum that traverses all these currents, continuing through the interwar period in movements with fascism in the variety of its forms, the Muslim Brothers and the Indian RSS and militant strands of romantic Arab, Turkish, and Iranian nationalism.[36] One crucial difference between political Romanticism in its first post-1789 phase and in the present one is that in the earlier one, the defeat of Zeus betokened the

35 Cf. ʿAbdallāh Al-ʿArwī, *Mafhūm al-ḥurrīya* (Casablanca: al-Markaz al-Thaqāfi al-ʿArabī, 2008), 71, 90; Shklar, *After Utopia*, 235–239.

36 Traction is being added to this view from more recent work: Georges Corm, *Pour une lecture profane des conflits. Sur le «retour du religieux» dans les conflits du Moyen-Orient* (Paris: La Découverte, 2015), 51–57 and Sternhell, *The Anti-Enlightenment Tradition*, 14–17, and ch. 8 for right-liberal Cold War anti-Enlightenment declamations.

triumph of Prometheus, while from the middle of the twentieth century the death of God meant the defeat of his creature as well.[37]

Culture is the overarching topos for this trend in the present phase of this by-now global cycle, with culturalism being the meta-social and meta-historical template that has been adopted as the carrier of anti-modernism, its grand narrative.[38] Culture has come to play the role that race had previously had in the analysis of collectivities. Contrary to what transpires from its own voices, culturalism is strongly foundationalist, standing on a grand narrative of the singular, the subject, the self-identical substance, the pre-colonial and pre-modern, the prelapsarian. It makes stout assumptions of homogeneity and homeopathy in its concept of society, and of essential continuity in its concept of time as mere passage, thus vitiating history and extruding the historical from the historist narrative.[39]

At the close of the twentieth century these conceptual modules were, in the academy, taking on a character of incontestability and self-evidence, the common sense of the post-Cold War era, well-worn, familiar, predictable, formulaic, and effortlessly repeatable. In academic output, this sought inspiration from the pathos of Heidegger and Nietzsche, and sought sustenance from the irrationalism of the Frankfurt School's aversion to the Enlightenment. With this came also Benjamin's partiality to mystical concepts and vocabularies, much of which was inspired by the masterpieces of fin-de-siècle German pessimistic irrationalism, always the most interesting: Klages' Magical Philosophy and Stefan Georg's *Denkbilder*. The impact of both on critical theory has been underestimated, or indeed gone unnoticed.[40] Alongside this, much was owed to American cultural anthropology, important for the shaping of culturalism that fed into post-colonial scholarship. This constellation of references was, in

---

37 So Shklar, *After Utopia*, 111 – see ibid., 114–120.

38 Al-Azmeh, *Islams and Modernities*, ch. 1.

39 Al-Azmeh, *Islams and Modernities*, 25–26, 30–31; Judith Schlanger, *Les métaphores de l'organisme* (Paris: Vrin, 1971); "Organismus", in *Geschichtliche Grundbegriffe*, s.v.

40 Axel Honneth, "Anthropologische Berührungpunkte zwischen der lebensphilosophischen Kulturkritik und 'Der Dialektik der Aufklärung'", in *21. Deutscher Soziologentag 1982: Beiträge der Sektions- und ad hoc Gruppen*, eds Friedrich Heckmann and Peter Winter (Wiesbaden: Westdeutscher Verlag, 1983), 786–792, at 786–789; Georg Stauth and Bryan S. Turner, "Ludwig Klages (1872–1956) and the origins of critical theory", *Theory, Culture and Society* 9 (1992); 45–63, at 45; and now Jason Josephson-Storm, *The Myth of Disenchantment: Magic, Modernity and the Birth of the Human Sciences* (Chicago: University of Chicago Press, 2017), ch. 8 and p. 238.

some settings, attuned to American cultural anthropology, decisively inseminated by Franz Boas, both directly and through Ruth Benedict's "patterns of culture" and through Margaret Mead, with the fare of nineteenth-century German ethno-psychology and ethnology, historism, folklore studies, and the Brothers Grimm, bringing ideas of nativism against civilisation, the ethnographer all the while dutifully receiving from native informants what the latter thought they might like to hear.[41]

These anti-modernist, culturalist, and nativist directions of thought, academic and political, concur that there is a mystical core that is lost to modernity and because of it, which can be resuscitated when trans-historical essences return. The corollary has often been, since Herder, that there be a prelapsarian, uncorrupted condition that the time of modernity had sullied, bringing us to the lamentable condition of the present. All seek to evoke "meaning", which devolves to a social version of the innate ideas concept, of a knowledge indistinct from Life, being life's poetry to modernity's prose, a condition of authenticity, a culture of Volksgeist, a psychologistic metaphor taken for a fact.[42] Ostensible meaning and the various topoi and figures that stand for it are the equivalent of what in the first, romantic phase of anti-modernism was known as the Sublime, expressive of pathos. In any generic characterisation of anti-modernism, as that most perceptively offered by Compagnon,[43] the Sublime is cast as the aesthetic figure, alongside other component figures in anti-modernist discourses. These comprise the historical figure, what I would prefer to designate as the political figure of counter-revolution (the post-1989 instantations are manifest and nameable); the philosophical figure of anti-Enlightenment, what I would call culturalism encompassing historism, vitalism, and cognitive relativism; the moral or existential figure, what I would designate as the sentimentalist figure of pessimism, to which I would add nostalgia; the religious figure of original sin, which I would reformulate as a fall from a prelapsarian, now identified as a pre-colonial and pre-modern state of grace; and a stylistic figure of

41 See especially Tessel Pollmann, "Margaret Mead's Balinese: The fitting symbols of the American Dream", *Indonesia* 49 (1990): 1–35; Derek Freeman, *Margaret Mead and the Heretic. The Making and Unmaking of an Anthropological Myth* (Harmondsworth: Penguin Books, 1996); Adam Kuper, *The Invention of Primitive Society* (London: Routledge, 1988), ch. 7.

42 Al-Azmeh, *Islams and Modernities*, 28–31.

43 Compagnon, *Les Antimodernes*, 17 and passim.

tone, voice, and timbre, with an accent on imprecation and vituperation, and dependence on the use of ethos and pathos articulated by tonality rather than on conceptual precision.

4 Secularism and the Sociology of Fate

In a gentler version of Carl Schmitt's decisionism, post-colonialist academic work, in some of which Schmitt assumes oracular status, transposes what it sees as moral or political imperatives into cognitive ones. Correlatively, it privileges identity, understood in terms of culturalist differentialism, as a category of analysis and as the locus of irreducible value and voice conjoined. The sociological redactions of destiny and fate to be found in work on Islamism are of this type: Islam, which overdetermines societies nominated as Muslim, being their ethnological nature, becomes ineluctable destiny. In this perspective, sociology is the least of inputs. Note the discursive precipitation of decisionism here: this sociology of fate is primarily an apologetic discourse for special pleading, and primarily rhetorical, its sociologistic facet being related to the residual language of the academic milieu in which it is communicated. Discussions of secularism are particularly apt here, as Islamism and secularism appear as a contrastive pair. Charles Taylor opens his grand and vastly learned *A Secular Age* with an explicitly contrastive reference to Islam,[44] suggesting that the issue of secularism in Europe has to a large extent come to be relevant because Islam is perceived as a recalcitrant and bothersome presence, an impression to which many Muslim organisations and individuals have been contributing amply and enthusiastically.

The sociologistic redaction of destiny is the outcrop of historist vitalism: the idea that societies are held together by trans-historical dispositions that trumps actual historical dynamics, except in so far as it deranges the authentic nature of society. Historist discourse here typically involves topics of decline, often conflated with change overall, taken for disease, senescence, infection, estrangement of essence, decomposition, de-specification. The result of such diremptions of essence will, according to this perspective, inevitably be an inauthentic grotesque, what Spengler termed a Pseudomorph. Note that the

44 Charles Taylor, *A Secular Age* (Cambridge, MA: Harvard University Press, 2007).

conceptual morphology of vitalism here is metaphysical, and more specifically Neo-Platonic, one of substance, plenitude of being, and privation of being.

Civilisations[45] and similar figures of organism do not change in real ways, but can be adulterated, soiled, and, indeed, defiled by forms of derangement – such are modernity or secularisation, both in this perspective, conditions of inauthenticity and heteronomy. One may well note the way in which organismic metaphors lend themselves to sonorities of pathos. The diseased and unnatural humour is treatable homeopathically, with the restoration of tradition, by return to roots, carried by nostalgia and identitarian reaffirmation. Thus, the idea that Arab societies, being in essence on this reading Islamic societies rather than societies that contain actual Muslims, need to and will inevitably return to an initial condition of purity after confrontations, challenges, and periods of contamination with extraneous agents, colonial regimes, and modernising elites, that had deranged the body politic and the body social, but did not sully the fastness of origins.

What is missing here is the concrete: that traditions and practices are plural and arranged in a system of internal distribution and relations domination in any given social unit; that judgements upon the activity or inactivity of cultural elements and upon analytical utility of culture is dependent on the precise object of analysis; that tradition and the appeal to tradition under the aspect of culture is here rather, as in atavism and primitivism, more a politico-discursive resource for those who invoke it than an actually identifiable entity. If tradition were to be taken for an entity, it would rather be an object of anthropological study in so far as it is a hypothesis put forward to account for observed repetition, rather than to be this repetition itself [46] – this last point is especially pertinent to any comment on Asad. In contrast: Clifford Geertz, often referred to as a patriarch of culturalism, was nevertheless an anthropologists' anthropologist and could therefore not be a cultural determinist of this or any other stripe. His

45 Aziz Al-Azmeh, *The Times of History: Universal Topics in Islamic Historiography* (New York and Budapest: Central European University Press, 2007), ch. 2.

46 As in conservative discourse generally, classically expressed by Edward Shils, "Tradition", *Comparative Studies in Society and History* 13 (1971): 122–159 – but see Al-Azmeh, *Islams and Modernities*, 32–34; Pascal Boyer, *Tradition as Truth and Communication. A Cognitive Description of Traditional Discourse* (Cambridge: Cambridge University Press, 1990), 2–4, 32–37, 79–86; Marc Augé, *Le sens des autres. Actualité de l'antropologie* (Paris: Fayard, 1994), 28–29 ; Adam Kuper, *Culture: The Anthropologist's Account* (Cambridge, MA: Harvard University Press, 1999), ch. 7.

ethnographic work, which is of the highest possible order, impelled him to question very seriously and in practice the analytical value and operationalist use of the notion of culture. With reference to Bali, he highlighted "the tendency for the divisive effect of social institutions to predominate over the unifying power of cultural ones", affirming that "few political elites can have as intensely sought loyalty by means so ingeniously designed to produce treachery as did the Balinese".[47]

The sociological redaction of destiny would have things otherwise. Arab societies, and Iranian society as well, being congenitally predisposed to an ethnological destiny expressed in what is generally known as Islamic culture or Islamic civilisation, are captive to – and, to some, protected by – a congenital cultural incapacity for change of real consequence. The changes undergone by these societies over more than a century had been heteronomous, and in the final analysis a charade. Abidance is captive to the parameters of origin, of the initial condition.[48] We have here a notion of culture as a prison of social instinct rather than as a field of human action, including improvement, culture being regarded as a self-subsistent thing rather than a property of individuals and groups,[49] a sui generis, irreducible subject rather than an attribute, overdetermining history, society, and change.

To recapitulate: all revivalist and thus vitalist movements, and their associates and adjuncts within the academy, speak of a return to unadulterated origins, and of the ontological impossibility of departure therefrom. All invoke redactions of destiny, considered as inevitable forces of nature, compelling societies to regress to initial conditions prevailing before the Fall, now called colonialism or rule by secularising elites, invoked in their turn as clichés. Such are, for instance, the invocation of traditions with no regard to its social topography and on an impossible assumption of social and cultural homogeneity, or indulgence in "civilisational analysis" or "civilisational dialogue" rather than addressing history, again on an assumption of internal homogeneity for each unit involved. My assumption is that civilisation is

47 Clifford Geertz, *Negara: The Theatre State in Nineteenth-Century Bali* (Princeton: Princeton University Press, 1980), 45.

48 This concept is very well thought through by Sudipta Kaviraj, "Outline of a revisionist theory of modernity", *European Journal of Sociology* 46 (2005): 497–526.

49 Dan Sperber and Nicolas Claidière, "Defining and explaining culture (comments on Richerson and Boyd, *Not by genes alone*)", *Biology and Philosophy* 23 (2008): 283–292, at 291–292.

not an invariant and homogeneous social form but, in the most suggestive phrase of Marcel Mauss, a hyper-social system of social systems. Civilisation in recent civilisationist discourse acts as a rhetorical figure of historist continuity, rendering "civilisational analysis" an endless elaboration of clichés intended to represent an essence of congenital predispositions – all playing on vitalist and organismic metaphors in the sub-Spenglerian versions current today, with Huntington as a prime example.

At present, invocations of identity and native voice proffer a programme of what Taylor called, rather delicately, a politics of recognition – a politics that, when performed on the ground, at points of concrete application, has generally devolved more often than not to a politics of self-affirmative identitarian bluster, generally unmannerly to degrees that must surely challenge anyone's appetite for recognition. Advocacy of recognition in these terms yields a communalist template premised on the self-enclosure of human collectivities, and their cultivation of origins, expressed in traditions, spawning particularistic and exclusivist claims to ethics and politics. Culture is here beyond the reach of sociological and historical analysis. Often counterposed to what is taken for a teleology of the Enlightenment, this is a reverse, an oddly retrojective teleology that seeks the future in the ineluctability of the past.

Among other things, this decorous perspective yields nominal pluralisation and multiplication quite commonly, seemingly without end, with multiple modernities and multiple secularities emerging effortlessly and recognisably. If underdeveloped countries, including those identified as Islamic, cannot in this perspective really be said to have modernised or secularised but that they had rather been disfigured, or that they be unwilling and incapable congenitally of improvement, they can nevertheless condescendingly be included in the conversation politely, and said to have modernised or secularised multiply and in their own particular ways. This is all seemingly innocent, straightforward, and matter-of-fact, but adrift conceptually. I used the term Islams, which has often been misread without the intended irony, and placed in the flow of reclamations of voice and the cognitive Saturnalia of Difference and so forth. Yet this usage sought to reinstate and encourage a critical, properly historical analysis of the themes generally treated simplistically and stereotypically, not to dissolve a category – here, Islam – into senseless plurality, nor to dissolve the categories of Islam and of Modernity into skittish revelry, or a redemption of authenticity.[50] *Islams and Modernities* and other works were intended, in contrast, to reaffirm the purely nominal character of the category "Islam", and to argue against its use as a classificatory, analytical, or causal concept.

What was most explicitly intended is not the effacement of general analytical concepts, but the reinstatement of history against culturalist claims for abidance. Multiplying secularities or modernities, and other targets of this rhetoric of categorical deflation, cannot free historical reality from either secularisation or modernity as objective historical dynamics.[51] Such multiplications are unmistakably impelled less by the need to take due conceptual note of empirical findings than by a culturalist agenda. Infirming secularisation in "the longue durée of civilisational history", such thinking in terms of "cultural diversity", appealing to such matters as "spiritual ontologies" and searching for "cultural meanings", yields, it is claimed, a "cultural sociology of secular modernities".[52] But such a procedure, it has been well noted, will have a scattering effect, depriving concepts of analytical utility,[53] in effect effacing the concept entirely by the overlay of respectful multiplication. There is in this kind of advocacy a blanket reduction of social process and of history to culture; one cannot, it is claimed, see secularisation as occurring "outside culture",[54] whatever it is that may be understood from "outside" and inside, or from an entity that is so bounded.

These terms of the discussion perforce carry the semantic energy of the keywords just mentioned as they are used politically today, and carry the drift of a Spenglerian/Huntingtonian/Dugin orientation, judging matters in terms of predeterminative origins or persistences rather than by dynamic process. It works in terms of ethnological destiny, rather than by empirical considerations from sociology. It inflects undeniable empirical variety and unevenness towards vitalism and historism, and causes the fact of variety to drift semantically to the sheer multiplicity of thin empirical wedges, each sui generis. For quite apart from empirical concerns, it seems incontestable

---

50 Compare the historiographic multiplication of the Enlightenment in the most perceptive analysis of Jonathan Sheehan, "Enlightenment, religion and the enigma of secularization: A review essay", *The American Historical Review* 108 (2003): 1,061–1,080, at 1,066–1,069, 1,075–1,076.

51 Al-Azmeh, *Islams and Modernities*, xiii–xiv.

52 Marian Burchardt and Monika Wohlrab-Sahr, "Multiple secularities: Religion and modernity in the global age", *International Sociology* 28 (2013): 605–611, at 605–607.

53 Sheehan, "Enlightenment", 1,075.

54 Burchardt and Wohlrab-Sahr, "Multiple secularities", 606.

that much of the intent propelling multiplicationism can be understood in terms of a protocol of intercultural courtesy reminiscent of "interfaith dialogue", and a token of adherence to the celebration of diversity by means of conceptual diplomacy – a manifest case in point of transposing normative interest into cognitive propositions, the ought transmuting into an is. The term "multiple" here is itself the performance of an ethos, of belonging to a particular politico-cultural place rather than another, supporting particular constituencies against others in a conflictual environment, changing the valence of a statement from negative to positive, from the lack of advancement to multiple forms of development. Such multiplication amounts ultimately to mincing words, like saying gosh and golly, darn and sugar, to euphemistic usage, a socio-linguistic phenomenon of evasion and circumvention, a rhetorical figure of attenuation, belonging together with the apotropaic to a common class of quasi-magical enunciations.[55]

Yet concepts and categories, and these include modernity and secularism, are by definition general, pertaining to the whole class of phenomena that they organise, and cannot, as is sometimes charged, be "monolithic": they can become monolithic only when voided of conceptual sense and rendered into fetishes, like the notion of identity in its various redactions as culture or religion and so forth. Concepts deployed comparatively cannot be held captive to nominal multiplication, each a multiple sui generis, but must rest on generic commonality: comparison between elements of a category indicates an analytical grid of variations in which differences are regarded as variant members of the class of phenomena constituting the category, not as sui generis individuals. Similarities and differences are variations rather than signals of the generic specificity of each term of comparison. In conceptual terms, variations indicate particular instances that mediate the general and the individual.[56] Regarded thus, multiplicationism is a variant of nativisim and identitarianism. One had better either use a concept in its generality, or drop it.

55 Émile Benveniste, "Euphémismes anciens et modernes", in *Problèmes de linguistique générale* (Paris: Vrin, 1966), 308–314; "Euphemismus", in *Handbuch religionswissenschaftlicher Grundbegriffe*, eds H. Cancik et al. (Stuttgart: Kohlhammer, 1988–2001), s.v.

56 A recent book written in this spirit and attentive to the weight of empirical detail is that of Murat Akan, *The Politics of Secularism: Religion, Diversity, and Institutional Change in France and Turkey* (New York: Columbia University Press, 2017).

There is clearly in these discussions a fundamental confusion between the modernity/secularism package of analytical categories, and normative recognitions, misrecognitions, ambivalences, resistances, or denials of these processes. Both modernity and secularism are objective processes, correlative with each other, global, instantiations of which are related by a process of combined and uneven development, as sketched in this book. As long as the discussion is misrecognised when pitched at the level of normative perception by actors or victims, and the actual process described in terms of triumph, disquiet, or grievance, the chances of a productive discussion are reduced substantively. Such a pitch has become quite normal, with secularism in India egregiously reduced to "a credo",[57] ignoring actual social and political processes and transformations, or, in a study of the German Democratic Republic, defined, with a lowering of the sociological gaze, as "an interpretative frame",[58] or, finally, as with Asad, pronounced with grandiose pathos to be a "regime of truth".[59] Truth itself is in this perspective multiple, voided of cognitive implication, with no reference to any regime of ascertainability and verifiablity, thus used indifferently for any sort of bunk or fantasy: this is a regime of alternative facts.

Being general by definition, concepts are quite naturally applicable outside the immediate circumstance of their emergence and initial use. One is surprised that few post-colonialists have had qualms about using, outside Western Europe, the concepts of the economy and of society, which were made possible, named, and articulated in Europe in the eighteenth and nineteenth centuries respectively,[60] yet declare loud reserve when the discussion pertains to the categories of secularism and religion, while often extolling Foucault as Weber is simultaneously declared to have been snarled by European conditions. Secularism in a world of solipsistic multiplicity and incommensurability is required conceptually to be entrapped in the frame of its conceptual emergence. Thus, we find secularism, very commonly today,

---

57 T. N. Madan, "Secularism and the intellectuals", *Economic and Political Weekly* 29/18 (1994): 1,095–1,096, at 1,095.

58 Monika Wohlrab-Sahr, Thomas Schmidt-Lux, and Uta Karstein, "Secularization as conflict", *Social Compass* 55 (2008): 127–139.

59 See the discussion of Enayat, *Islam and Secularism*, ch. 2.

60 On economy: Louis Dumont, *From Mandeville to Marx: The Genesis and Triumph of Economic Ideology* (Chicago: University of Chicago Press, 1977); on society: Wolf Lepenies, *Between Literature and Science: The Rise of Sociology* (Cambridge: Cambridge University Press, 1988).

defined as post-Christian, a sort of "Christianity in sheep's clothing",[61] and denied in other settings, at best relegated to one among many multiple and sui generis secularities. In parallel, the applicability of the category of religion to Islam is denied, on the specious presumption that it emerged in post-Reformation Europe.

This last point shall be revisited below. Secularism is in this perspective construed as a movement within religion (one notes that culture and religion are often used interchangeably in this type of discourse, especially with regard to Islam), rather than what it was historically, part of a broader process of societal and cultural differentiation. There is an assumption not only of the overdetermination of society and of history by religion, but also of societal homogeneity. Correlatively, it is noteworthy that the grafting of secularism onto the history of Christianity is much in vogue now; like many others, including the majority of secularism's Islamist critics, Asad concurs entirely.[62] This is a variation on an older trope of denigration directed at the Enlightenment, of the French Revolution, later at Marxism, and now at secularism. This is in the long tradition of denigrating all of these in their turn by construing them as eschatological movements, from Herder and de Maistre to Carl Schmitt, taking in the Frankfurt School, with a period of special flourishing in anti-Communist Cold War polemics that continue to thrive today.[63] Secularism as post-Christianity continuous with its Christian parent is a facile and impressionistic meta-historical position that collapses before historical investigation, not least given the pseudo-historical historicist readings of the relation between state and Church in Europe, which are exceedingly complex and by no means uniform, and cannot accommodate this assumption of continuity and internal emergence. It rests on superficial

61 Jonathan Sheehan, "Thomas Hobbes, D.D.: Theology, orthodoxy, and history", *The Journal of Modern History*, 88 (2016): 249–274, at 251.

62 It is appropriate here to indicate that Asad's ideas in this respect and in many others have for long been common in the Arab World, with a variety of inflections and in a variety of idioms. The post-colonial position is stated with greater penetration and sustained by broader reading, albeit without the emblematic authorities invoked in Europe and the US, by, for instance, the late, ex-Marxist culture-Islamist 'Abd al-Wahhāb Al-Masīri in a wide-ranging debate towards the end of his life: 'Abdalwahhāb Al-Masīrī and 'Azīz Al-'Aẓma, *Al-'ilmānīya taḥt al-mijhar* (Beirut: Dar al-Fikr, 1990).

63 Richard Shorten, "The Enlightenment, communism and political religion: Reflections on a misleading trajectory", *Journal of Political Ideologies* 8 (2003): 13–37; Sternhell, *The Anti-Enlightenment Tradition*, ch. 8.

associations, including ones between psychological states that characterise revolutions and messianic stirrings.[64]

In this historist and vitalist regard, secularisation is taken in a rather cavalier manner for the subtraction of religion, curiously with its continued existence under another, spuriously secular signature, as Enlightenment or Communism. Subtraction in these discussions often refers to institutional transformations whereby religious institutions were turned around and taken over, but such transformation within is slight overall, differentiation having spawned different types of institution, and the subtraction argument is anchored more firmly in the anti-modern figure of nostalgia for the sublime than in empirical realities of history. Secularisation (and modernisation: the two are often interchangeable in many discussions) is thereby construed as a form of loss,[65] of alienation, what Taylor regretted poignantly and eloquently as the "excarnation", of "buffeted" selves, in the secular "wasteland".[66] This is the consequence of "immanence" – hence the "immanent frame" web facility that many readers of this book will be familiar with – that had set aside transcendence with its sense of "fullness",[67] a usurpation of the authentic, a privation of essence, a state of unwholesomeness, a disnature. All of these terms are nebulous and mystifying, emanating from anti-modern Romanticism, and convey pathos rather than determinate sense. In counterpart to this is generally suggested the mystique of reaffirmation – a premise for "recognition" – and, often enough, restoration of an idyll obscured by history, including that of an Islamic prelapsarian utopia or life taken for an Islamic discursive tradition. All of these are poetical terms redolent of the occult, once one subtracted the pop-psychological aspects and vocabularies that one encounters often in these types of utterance.

In the final analysis, the specious character of the subtraction and persistence model is that it posits a morphological continuity between historical formations that does not obtain in the real world, and extrudes all consideration

64 Cf. Judith Shklar, "The political theory of utopia: From melancholy to nostalgia", *Daedalus* 94 (1965): 367–381, at 373, 375. For an excellent discussion, Shorten, "The Enlightenment".

65 This point stressed by Blumenberg, in his defence of modernity: Hans Blumenberg, *The Legitimacy of the Modern Age*, trans. R. M. Wallace (Cambridge, MA: MIT Press, 1985), 116–120, 533, and passim.

66 Taylor, *A Secular Age*, 613–614, 772, 37–42, 138, 307–321, 448–490, 770.

67 See the comments of Craig Calhoun, "Review of Taylor, *A Secular Age*", *European Journal of Sociology* 49 (2008): 455–461.

of historical breaks, structural transformations, innovations, and functional differentiations that came with modernity, which are central to this discussion and to this book. The fact is that the anachronism of the subtraction thesis is based on a prior, underlying analytical premise, that of the relation between secularism and Christianity, and this will bring us back to deterministic historism, culturalism, and traditionalism, and their joint rhetorical trope, that of the return of religion as to an initial condition of authenticity and fullness to which history is irrelevant.

This prior analytical premise is conducted in the form of pseudo-historical narrative. I shall refer here to two types of analysis, influential in broadly different disciplinary academic milieux. One is in the broadest sense historical in orientation, represented in sociological analysis and in psycho-conceptual history, best represented respectively by the major work of Casanova and Taylor. The other type is distanciated from history by a distrust expressed in the name given to the undertaking, called geneaological, with only a very remote claim to anthropology, represented here by various widely quoted essays by Talal Asad. Claiming to be an insider's – "emic" is a common term – recasting of the past in light of the present, geneaologists compose pedigrees, virtual histories of ethos positive and negative.

We are told, yet again, that secularisation is "identified with a particular civilizational trajectory",[68] one that is described by Taylor at length with reference to the North Atlantic region, to which he adds psycho-historical factors of the embedding and disembedding of individuals in quite mystifying terms, full of pathos but eluding concrete sense, some that were highlighted already. This amounts to a comprehensive disapproval of modernity in the tragic mode, often without reference to the overarching and pessimistic Roman Catholicism of this position.[69] Reference to criticisms of capitalism by Marx, when speaking of fetishism of the commodities, of alienation, and of religion,[70] would have enriched considerably discussions of this attitude of discontent and disenchantment with civilisation, and taken it in a more constructive direction.

---

68 Taylor, *Secular Age*, 36.

69 See Matthew Rose, "Tayloring Christianity", in www.firstthings.com/article/2014/12/tailoring-christianity (accessed on 27 April 2018).

70 These are much more nuanced and complex than is usually admitted – see Alberto Toscano, *Fanaticism: On the Uses of an Idea* (London: Verso, 2010), ch. 5.

Yet for all the high-grade philosophical skills one receives from Taylor habitually, his discussion of separate civilisational trajectories remains meta-historical, guided by the conflation of historical dynamics with an essentialist ethnology of the West as overdetermined by Christian traditions understood monolithically, and in a view of progress and of the Enlightenment blurred by melancholy aversion. The unstated assumption is that Europe's had been "societies of faith", a cliché that historical research has moderated very considerably and nuanced beyond the proportions that would make this supposition serviceable for the sort of argument discussed here. Casanova, some of whose arguments also stand on this silent presumption, is yet enough of a robust sociologist to state that the assumption that pre-modern Europeans were more religious than today is one "in need of confirmation";[71] the same will extend to super-Islamisation of Muslims both today and yesterday. Yet Casanova perpetrates a similar, common conflation, when he claims that secularism is the product of a specifically Western modernity, and that it is therefore "fundamentally and inevitably post-Christian"[72] – the postist locution having the effect rhetorically of disclaiming a break with previously regnant forms of Christianity, and discursively of extruding history, both as tendential dynamic and as conjuncture, and eliminating the weight of historical breaks. Casanova insists generously that the multiplication of secularism, like that of modernity, should "open the possibility that other religions may also play a role in institutionalizing their own patterns of secularization",[73] thus locating these processes within religion, with an unspoken assumption that religion, presumably taken for a culture in the sense of historist culturalism, overdetermines the development of a particular historical formation.

Casanova claims further that secularism first arose as a Western theological category.[74] This conveys a close fit with the traditionalist and civilisational – culturalist – discourse here proffered, but its meaning is, on closer examination, uncertain. I am not aware of secularism as a Christian theological category as such, although secularisation in canon law applies to persons

71 Casanova, *Public Religions*, 16.

72 José Casanova, "The secular, secularizations, secularism", in *Rethinking Secularism*, eds Craig Calhoun, M. Juergensmeyer and J. van Antwerpen (Oxford: Oxford University Press, 2011), 54–74, at 63.

73 Casanova, *Public Religions*, 234.

74 Ibid., 61.

and properties removed, temporarily or permanently, and in various proportions, from Church control, by dispensation or by force. Dubbing whatever is related to religion or the Church as "theological" is unhelpful, mystifying, and allows for impressionistic affirmations. I am not aware of secularism as a specifically Christian category either. Clearly quotation of New Testament fragments about giving to Caesar what is Caesar's, wrenched out of context, and overinterpreted as the first and last word on Christianity and politics, is a show as poor as it is common. What one is left with is a drift that can be seen more clearly when Islam is spoken of, namely, the drift, presented as self-evident common sense, towards identifying past with future, and identifying culture, civilisation, and religion, and, indeed, towards rendering religion the defining element of both, the arbiter of destiny.

In this way, the idea that secularism, one outgrowth of social differentiation occurring with global modernity, might involve a common trans-geographical social dynamic, however uneven and varied, and have common global characteristics, both graspable by an overarching concept, is made to devolve to an illusion or a lie, at best a colonial or elitist imposition or instrument of manipulation and justification. It is trumped by the inexorable march of sociological destiny. There is, with Casanova, and as a clear consequence of historism, a meta-historical assumption of incommensurable historical itineraries, multiple modernities, denominated by him as post-Hindu, post-Confucian, and post-Muslim.[75] Post-Muslim modernity in this register would be vulnerable to the view, becoming increasingly more common and emerging from similar assumptions, that Islam – without qualification – according to one historian working with the same meta-historical template, be necessarily at odds with modernity, which is incompatible with Islam's "ontological and theological commitments".[76] This is a specious and often contra-factual type of historical argument that Casanova shares with very many others – and these include Hindu and Muslim culturalists of various hues, cultural nationalists, and fundamentalists, who have been putting forward this point for a long time now.

Patronising multiculturalist impulses apart, the global dynamic of ideological post-colonialist vitalist historism is one of European origin and impulse,

75 Ibid., 64.

76 Michael Alan Gillespie, *The Theological Origins of Modernity* (Chicago: University of Chicago Press, 2008), 292.

one that was internalised and made local everywhere, in a variety of forms and to varying extents. It would be pertinent to stress here that the polemics against Eurocentrism are often incoherent in that they use the various possible senses of the term interchangeably, often misconstruing Euro-centred historical analyses as ideologically Eurocentric. This is why ideas about "provincialising Europe" are so manifestly delusional, for Eurocentrism in regarding modern history has solid empirical foundations, and is surely more than just an ideological gloss. There may well be ethical or political foundations for such postures of denial, but it is clearly illegitimate to transpose these imperatives into cognitive propositions, and to correct political asymmetries by a kind of cognitive decisionism and the assertion of cognitive nativism.

5 One Post-colonialist Standard

Talal Asad complements the sorts of arguments just discussed with what appears to be the oracular definitiveness of native voice. His is an apology for nativism and relativism, not untypical of post-colonialists with a "cosmopolitan impulse" sitting in New York and London.[77] His apology is grounded in a rhetoric of attachment, investment, and reverie, consistently transposing what are perceived to be ethical and sentimental imperatives into cognitive goods. His apology slides thereby from the sociology of politics to sentimentalist psychopolitical self-indulgence, implying the sort of decisionism evoked above. It comes from a side of the multicultural spectrum in which disenchantment with Europe upon discovering that it is imperfect slips, if not entirely into the all-too-common pathetic judgement of historical invalidation, at least into a posture of definitive disenchantment and desire for provincialisation.

Not unexpectedly, Asad suggests that one should learn to treat Enlightenment assumptions as belonging to "specific kinds of reasoning" and, therefore, in the perspective of relativism and the vitalist, social-instinct mode of cognition, not as the ground from which the understanding of the non-Enlightenment traditions must begin.[78] Much concerned with the operations of power and ideology in what is known as cultural translation,

77 Enayat, *Islam and Secularism*, 90.

78 Talal Asad, Talal, "Responses", in *Powers of the Secular Modern. Talal Asad and His Interlocutors*, eds D. Scott and C. Hirschkind (Stanford: Stanford University Press, 2006), 206.

what he does is appeal to hermeneutical notions, wielded in such a way as to yield ultimately much patterning, sympathy, and antipathy, but little analytical understanding. Witness, for instance, his disciple, one might in all fairness say his late ethnographic persona, the late Saba Mahmoud, who pleaded that hyper-pietist practices by some Egyptian women should be seen as "technologies of the self".[79] The term comes from Foucault referring to antique ethics, and is not emic, not being one used by these women, but nevertheless apt in a banal way, sounding dispassionately technocratic, yet in the pathos of self-grooming it evokes, is misleading. For this involves, structurally, technologies of selves constituted through compliance, which would in scientific terms qualify as processes of re-socialisation and the inculcation of a habitus of compliance by an authority, of such wrenching violence as to involve the induction of fear, weeping, and elation, hysterical conditions which Mahmoud's objects of study avow.[80] This redaction is inattentive to process and context, which are the basic conditions of anthropological analysis; it devolves to advocacy. The task of the anthropologists is thereby confined to apologetic description of matters irreducible to analysis, with analytical discourse often taken, with assertive tremulousness, for intrusive.[81]

Now for more specific comment, through the sinuous and engaging casuistics of Asad's reservations, nuances, and caveats, whose overall effect, and whose tones suggesting Solomonic sagacity, might enchant and thereby disorient a certain type of reader. Asad questions the notion of the secular and the related notion of religion. He endorses famously the curious contention, common today and no longer quirky, that religion be a notion that is irretrievably manacled to its European conditions of emergence.[82] This position is odd not only because the Islam to which Asad refers and takes as normative is the one that, building on possibilities to be found in Muslim religious texts,

---

79 Saba Mahmoud, "Rehearsed spontaneity and the conventionality of ritual: Disciplines of *ṣalāt*", *American Ethnologist* 28 (2001): 827–853.

80 Ibid., 839–845.

81 Such post-colonialist anxieties are limpidly described by Clifford Geertz, *After the Fact. Two Countries, Four Decades, One Anthropologist* (Cambridge, MA: Harvard University Press, 1995), 128–130.

82 But see Brian C. Wilson, "From the lexical to the polythetic: A brief history of the definition of religion", in *What is Religion? Origins, Definitions, and Explanations*, eds Thomas A. Idinopoulos and Brian C. Wilson (Leiden: Brill, 1998), 141–162.

has been profoundly Protestantised, like reform Judaism and Buddhism,[83] but also because the Qur'anic text itself, quite straightforwardly, has available, like Christianity, a clear and distinct notion of logolatrous and doctrinal religion that corresponds to the one that Asad attributes to the Reformation. The Qur'an is a text that Asad would have been well advised to consider as he pronounced summarily upon "Muslim discursive traditions".[84] More important than the Qur'an is of course the history of the distinction of religion in political and institutional practices that might be termed Islamic, including the distinction *dīn/dunyā*, *sharī'a/siyāsa*, of *siyāsa shar'iyya*, politics and law *more religio*, much vaunted today by fundamentalists.[85] This is ubiquitous: one need mention only in passing the Sanskritic *agāma* as religion, and distinctions between *shūkyō* and *sezoku* in Japanese history, *artha* and *dharma/dhamma* in Hindu and Buddhist polities.

Like other concepts subject to anxieties of approach on the grounds of origin, this scepticism about the concept of religion and the category of religious phenomena is fully subject to criticism from "the fallacy of partial description", that since concepts may emerge from social activity, they are reducible to these conditions.[86] This is quite apart from crude simplification of Foucault's pronouncements on knowledge and power used to signal an ethos rather than any meaningful analytical procedure, and relating more to the reading of Foucault's late, post-Californian period. This is a persistent drift in postmodernist and post-colonialist writing, where operations of causality are displaced, and the very notion of causality, when used at all, taken to apply only to the constructivist attribution of causality, for what commonly goes by

---

83 See 'Azīz Al-'Aẓma, "Al-iṣlāḥiyūn al-nahḍawiyūn wa fikrat al-iṣlāḥ fī al-majāl ad-dīnī", *Al-Mustaqbal al-'Arabī* 455 (2017): 75–99; Reinhard Schulze, "Islam und Judentum im Angesicht der Protestantisierung der Religionen im 19. Jahrhundert", in *Judaism, Christianity and Islam in the Course of History: Exchange and Conflicts*, eds Lothar Gall and Dietmar Willoweit (Munich: Oldenbourg, 2010), 139–164; Richard Gombrich, *Theravada Bhuddism. A Social History from Ancient Benares to Modern Colombo* (London: Routledge & Kegan Paul, 1988), ch. 7.

84 For the Qur'an, a start might be made with Q 5:3, 2:132, 3:19, 85, and see D. Marshall, *God, Muhammad and the Unbelievers* (London: Curzon, 1999). For Asad's "discursive traditions", Enayat, *Islam and Secularism*, ch. 4. For broader pertinent comment on Asad in relation to what is known from the history of religion Bishāra, *al-Dīn*, 2/1, 804.

85 Aziz Al-Azmeh, *Muslim Kingship: Power and the Sacred in Muslim, Christian and Pagan Polities* (London: I. B. Tauris, 1997), 181–188.

86 Laudan, "Pseudo-science", 194–195.

the term "geneaology".[87] It is incontestable that new religions have been constructed to suit colonial and post-colonial conditions, generally along lines broadly congruent with what with the Reformation became a standard pattern, as in Bali and New Zealand, for instance.[88] But this is something quite distinct from a dead weight of origin rendering the analytical category of religion itself irrelevant. As Casanova rightly maintains, to dissolve religion and secularism into geneaology and archaeology – another metaphorical term used by Foucault, conveying mystifying pathos to its users – would leave us analytically impoverished and without adequate conceptual tools.[89]

This is all culturalist solipsism par excellence. Building upon this position, Asad proposes a nativist rhetoric of attachment. The Islamic religion, he declares solemnly, is the result of a discursive process,[90] apparently without roots in a general historical and anthropological category of religion, or in its own complex actual history. An anthropology of Islam should begin where Muslims begin, he alleges, with the concept of a discursive tradition relating to the Muslim canon, and the practice of what he calls, appropriately, "apt performance" driven by the canon.[91] Islam, which Asad rightly maintains is not a distinctive social structure, is made to escape sociological and anthropological scrutiny – social structure and process are irrelevant to the anthropologist become geneaologist. Clearly, discursive traditions here are stand-alone objects, with little to mediate between discursive traditions and the denial of Islam as a social structure: questions about practices are made invisible, and it is unclear if the persons performing aptly can be defined socially or anthropologically in any other terms at all.

---

87 Bruno Latour, "Ramsès II est-il mort de la tuberculose?", *La Recherche*, 307, March 1998, 84–85, for instance, commenting on the death from tuberculosis of Ramses II as revealed by an autopsy of his mummified remains, asserted that the Pharaoh could not conceivably have died of TB, the bacillus being unknown at the time of his death in BC 1213, and concluding that this attribution of disease was ananachronistic, retrospective causality, and, as such, illegitimate.

88 Michel Picard, "What's in a name? Agama Hindu Bali in the making", in *Hinduism in Modern Indonesia*, ed. Martin Ramstedt (London and New York: Routledge Curzon, 2004), 56–75; Jonathan Z. Smith, *Imagining Religion* (Chicago: University of Chicago Press, 1982), ch. 5.

89 José Casanova, "A reply to Talal Asad", in *Powers of the Secular Modern. Talal Asad and His Interlocutors*, eds D. Scott and C. Hirschkind (Stanford: Stanford University Press, 2006), 12–30.

90 Talal Asad, *Genealogies of Religion* (Baltimore and London: Johns Hopkins University Press, 1993), 29.

91 Talal Asad, *The Idea of an Anthropology of Islam* (Washington, DC: Georgetown University Press, 1986), 14–15.

Islam is thus liberated from the social moorings of its practices and their political economy, and becomes mystified as Tradition, that is, discourses appealing to a historist ideal that give correct form to given practices precisely because they are claimed to have been established by history.[92] Asad's Islam is a mentalist construct with associated performances, in effect a psychodrama. What is it, apart from the tendentious use of general impressions, that impels Asad to speak of "strongly held traditions"[93] without indications of who it is who holds to what traditions strongly, and when and under what circumstances, and with what sense given to strength here? This kind of impressionistic statement is a very common cliché in popular journalism no less than in scholarship and in Islamophobic discourses. Clearly, what Asad and Mahmoud are describing in tandem are Muslim beings who are "pre-eminently and determinatively religious",[94] in fact, super-Muslims, as they exist in the self-orientalising imagination.

We are back to homeostatic, incommensurable traditions, engaged in the polite protocol of recognition (Asad sounds combative but pessimistic overall) between untranslatable registers, expressing themselves in indigenous voices, which are ultimately affective, aesthetic, and political choices, unrelated to cognitive categories. Being matters of political, ethical, or traditionalist choice, all voices but the native are liable to corrosion, including the voice of scientific reason that expresses itself in terms of categories of the social and human sciences, and nothing remains admissible but to take discourses on their own terms. Thus, for instance, Saba Mahmoud, building upon Asad's scepticism about the notion of religion as she studied networks of feminine piety in Egypt minutely and illuminatingly, with its rituals, reflections, habit-formations, and corporeal discipline, insisted virtuously that, instead of conceptualising her material and turning her subjects into objects as a researcher must, her work should lead, rather, to parochialising the researcher's assumptions.[95] Calls to self-reflexivity are always welcome. But this would need to be a conceptual self-reflexivity, rather than counterposing an ethical discipline of subjectivity

92 Ibid., 14.

93 Asad, *Genealogies*, 267.

94 Enayat, *Islam and Secularism*, 92. Curiously, Enayat (at 27) seems not to disagree entirely, perhaps under the impress of the persistent clamour by sections of the Muslim population in Britain.

95 Saba Mahmoud, *Politics of Piety. The Islamic Revival and the Feminist Subject* (Princeton: Princeton University Press, 2004), 36.

to cognitive purpose, to the detriment of the latter, analogous in many ways to contrition, penance, and confession in medieval Latin Christianity that had elicited Asad's curiosity in the past.

Clichés, including self-parodic ones, described but not interpreted, come to have greater salience than sociological reason. We are, after all, squarely in the domain of metaphors and other figures of the organism. Similarly, in a long discussion of Saudi *naṣīḥa* (advice) texts offered to royal authorities by a group of then younger, *ikhwanised* Wahhabi ulama, Asad holds that any analytical expectation of a uniform rationality guiding analysis must be regarded as an imposition. He interprets limitations of *naṣīḥa* materials and attitudes to be due, not to incapacity for contemplating change, nor to an intrinsic contradiction between reason and religion, but as arising from a "particular discursive tradition" and its associated disciplines.[96] *Naṣīḥa* appears thus unrelated to clerical politics, or to hegemonic claims and processes or repressive and patrimonial relations and positions, but arises primarily from officious assumptions of a moral order of virtuous individuals partly responsible for one another's moral condition.[97] Any qualification or analysis in terms of political and institutional anthropology, or thinking about what it might be that impels and empowers one to claim the right to be meddlesome, seems irrelevant, and impertinent.

The distinction between the "anthropology of modernity", as Asad calls it, which is in fact an anti-modernist pseudo-historical polemic, and apology for Tradition, is nowhere apparent. Saba Mahmoud took this apologetic pathway further in an explicit apology for obscurantism.[98] Speaking, like Asad, against the secular notion of religion, which, she maintains with a pathos-full of implications, is "abstract",[99] excoriated certain advocates of Muslim reform (Nasr Abu Zayd, Hasan Hanafi, and others) for pleading for the historicity of Koranic interpretation, on the grounds that this procedure "disenfranchises" traditional modes of interpretation. I will not go into the historical facts of the matter, including who it is that disenfranchises whom, and whether what she terms traditional is in fact traditional by any proper historical descrip-

96 Asad, *Genealogies*, 232.

97 Ibid., 233.

98 Saba Mahmoud, "Secularism, hermeneutics, and empire: The politics of Islamic reformation", *Public Culture* 18 (2006): 323–347.

99 Ibid., 341.

tion and how. These will not be relevant to Mahmoud's argument, which is rounded off politically by suggesting that these Muslim reformists were just tailoring their work to an imperialist agenda, in effect, agents of imperialism: alleged agents "demonised" by Mahmoud for undermining what she liked to suppose were authentic inherited narratives,[100] which would have been soiled by reformist motifs. Asad's tonalities while pleading the case for mobs baying for Salman Rushdie's blood are altogether less strident,[101] but in both cases it seems unnecessary to check whether what they have convinced themselves were matters of tradition were in fact any more than very recent and group-specific, sub-cultural reconstitutions of the Muslim religion, along lines quite precisely analogous to those of exigent Calvinism.

This irrationalist doctrine, attendant upon vitalism, is in this case tailored to an apology for contemporary identitarian Islamism, and its obscuranist expressions apparently favoured by Asad, on grounds of authenticity, one would presume, and as a consequence elevated pars pro toto to Islam in general past and present. Yet Asad uses the very conception of religion he decries so much to speak of Muslims in Europe, or rather, to reconstitute them as a homogeneous and coherent bloc driven by a discursive tradition, one way of traducing the notion of faith. He advocates a society of *Staende* (Estates), something on the analogy with a confederation of *millets*, without relations dominance (that is, a polity without politics), a contiguity of minorities, informed by a notion of religion that is not only that of the Reformation, but is also Qur'anic.[102] For, he maintains, Muslim immigrants (he prefers this term to that of citizens, irrespective of generation), cannot be satisfactorily represented in Europe, given Europe's ideological construction.[103] That they are represented as citizens like other citizens, and without special pleading, seems irrelevant, at best uninteresting. To Muslims Asad attributes ways of life and practices articulated by bookish traditions: it is these, rather than really existing Muslims, that need political institutions to represent them, an image harking back to practices of medieval Christendom and medieval Islam.[104]

---

100 Ebrahim Moosa and Sher Ali Tareen, "Revival and reform", *The Princeton Enyclopedia of Islamic Political Thought*, ed. Gerhard Boewering (Princeton: Princeton University Press, 2013), 462–470, at 468.

101 Asad, *Genealogies*, chs 7 and 8.

102 Asad, *Formations*, ch. 5.

103 Ibid., 159.

104 Ibid., 178.

It is manifest that this whole argumentative edifice is geared towards a form of identitarianism articulated in traditionalist (as distinct from traditional) terms. The politics of recognition involves not so much the apprehension of reality as categorisation and stereotypification, and a considerable degree of re-socialisation and the inculcation of false memories. The result is socio-dramatic, "apt performance". One wonders if Asad extended his reflections to propose that his own advocacy of Tradition might not be apt performance of neo-conservative, anti-modern ideology.

*****

So also are social and cultural Islamisation, and salafication in the Arab World in recent decades. With exceptions, these are not in substantive continuity with the past, and this applies most specifically to fundamentalism and stringent pietism or social salafication. Identity, it must be stressed, is less an indicative concept than a performative one,[105] and hence a dynamic political designation. In the context discussed here, and to return to the discussion of modernisation and social differentiation, the identitarian conception of Islam as a total socio-political and ethical superstructure corresponding to the nature of society makes perfect sense. It is, after all, the secularisation thesis, with its stress on social differentiation, that is able to account for the emergence of religion as an independent instance that makes total claims on representing society. The question of secularism is not one that defines the relation between Islam and the West, whatever they may designate; it is in actual fact a struggle within Muslim-majority countries themselves.

This is the setting of this book: a quest for clarity, the recognition of reality, including the reality of apologetic presumptions of ethnological destiny that take themselves for pristine voice. This preface left off from where the book ended, and closed this particular circle with considering a cautionary case in point. The translation of the book was substantially revised by the author, who added indications for updates in the text as well as in the notes.

105 Aziz Al-Azmeh, "Identity in the Arab world", in *Keywords: Identity*, ed. Nadia Tazi (New York: The Other Press, 2004), 47–64.

Acknowledgements

Earlier versions of various sections and arguments of this preface were presented as part of the Globalisation Lecture delivered at the University of London's School of Oriental and African Studies in 2015, and a paper to a conference on the Critique of Modernity held in 2018 at Leipzig University. My sincere thanks to my hosts, Gilbert Achkar and Monika Wohlrab-Sahr, and to lively audiences. I should also like to express my sincere thanks to Charlotte Whiting of the Aga Khan University, Institute for the Study of Muslim Civilisations for the meticulous hard work she put into ensuring that the complex and difficult manuscript of the translation, revisions of the translation, bibliography, transliteration, and much else were seen into the production stage with unfailing accuracy and courtesy.

Preface to the Second Arabic Edition

I shall not add in these few words to previous comment, having already offered comment on what has been written and said about this book. The book provoked numerous reactions, questions, and criticisms and also enjoyed a considerable degree of endorsement and support. I have expended much effort in examining and probing inaccurate, irrelevant subjective criticisms and in rectifying the blemishes that appeared in the original. I also responded to issues that may have been caused by misconception. I delivered my replies, additions, and clarification in a series of discussions, lectures, and articles the most pertinent of which were published in my collection of essays *Dunyā al-dīn fī aḍir al-ʿarab* (The World of Religion in the Arab World Today). The first edition was published in Beirut in 1996 by Dar al-Ṭalīʿa, and further editions have appeared since.

I have no fundamental points to add to what I have mentioned regarding the subject matter of this book and the intellectual and cultural context that has narrowed the horizons of comment upon it, except that the spread of retrograde forces over the Arab cultural sphere as it exists today necessitated a different perspective, one adopted in this book: one of history, which has no completion or full accomplishment, which does not recognise origins as much as historical periods and mutations. History is constant movement and the secularism both actual and implicit of the Arabs in the last century is not a special case. It has been a basic constituent element even of the currents of thought that oppose secularism. Critical reflection must pursue the demonstration of truth on the basis of history while contending with irrational and baleful tendencies.

It only remains for me here to thank my readers and the Centre for Arab Unity Studies, who pressed for this new edition and for the correction, in the second edition, of typographical errors.

Introduction

The Arabs entered modernity with the entry of the modern world – soldiers, merchants, diplomats, and capitalism – into Arab lands. Modern history removed Arabs from the cultural and civilisational continuity that they came to think had persisted for centuries, and impelled them to changes and breakthroughs in all domains of society, culture, and political structures. These changes traversed these domains and sectors, provoking new developments unevenly, articulated by a structural connection between the Arabs and world history with its centre first in Europe, and then the Atlantic, and finally in the Atlantic and East Asia, with a dispersed geographical centre uniting the world into the single temporal unit of today's advanced capitalism.

Modernity is a general indication of a historical evolution that took place in the context of modern world history. It indicates modalities of connection with and entry into global history: a centralised state whose influence penetrates society, relying on means of communication and the dissemination of a centralised culture, new means of organising production and reproducing labour power through the market and unevenly freeing the operations of production from domestic, patriarchal, and family environments.

To these one can add the increasing use of industrial and quasi-industrial methods and the educational and technical skills that these methods engender, instead of artisanal work practices, as well as the spread of cultural and political associations with modern characteristics such as political parties and societies, while rational models of administration and its structures are introduced in the institutions of the state. This necessitates conceiving implicitly or explicitly a linear temporality that seeks to impose itself on the operation of production in general. The values of global rationality spread and in fact achieved primacy in public output. The associated desiderata included a view of truth based on science or even scientism, an anthropocentric conception of the political system, whether in terms of the Left or of the Right, with ideas of popular organisation, concepts of nationalism, democracy, and socialism, veneration of political leaders, party-political life, and information and educational output. Finally, these signs of entry into modernity were closely connected with marked social changes affecting both urban and rural social groups that had moved to cities. These changes manifested themselves in processes of social promotion and decline and, positively or negatively, in the position of women in society where these wider changes were reflected in a summary and emblematic way.

Integration into capitalist globalisation was the historical context of secularism in the history of the modern world. This integration had positive and negative features, and was partly a voluntary process and partly arising from the force of circumstance. It constituted the conditions that made secularisation a historical reality as well as a concept, although the former does not necessarily require a secular ideology or deliberately secular thinking or social engineering. Indeed, secular thought in the modern history of the Arabs – as in the histories of most European countries – was integrated in socio-political thought and practice without special theorisation or delimitation. Secularism arose from reality and has been a register of modern Arab historical reality that will not be understood adequately without this concept.

The reality of secularisation does not only derive from the fact that the world rather than religion is the decisive element in social life. Secularism in Arab life and thought, the subject of this book, reflects the emergence of modern political, administrative, and cognitive notions and practices, and, concomitantly, the marginalisation of the religious institution with its intellectual wherewithal. Over centuries of Arab history this institution dominated the formal, public face of culture, education, and law. The reaction of this institution to change was vigorous, with the support of political groups that sought its assistance, and solicited sentiment, to advance their political and democratic – and undemocratic – contestation. Undoubtedly the entry of the Arabs into the temporality of modernity was uneven and took varied forms and rhythms, distinct in character and orientation according to relevant parameters of geography, politics, social and educational conditions, and the character of the state in which the various aspects of modernity converged and were united.

Thus, the attack on secularism and the failure to recognise its preponderance, largely undeclared, in modern Arab history arose from traditional religious voices, the weight of social blockages, and structural inequalities, as well as the crisis in national liberation that prompted some Arab states to move from leading society to taking shortcuts by pandering to a religious character ascribed to society. This crisis took various pathological forms in obsessive imaginings and inventions of Heritage (*turāth*), a massive social, political, and lucrative industry. Secularism was in these circumstances set up to signal something woefully foreign, there being no awareness that secularism, like globalisation, had become in the last century a structural element internal to politics, economics, culture, and society. This is especially true at the end of the twentieth century, when places distant from one another had come to occupy the same temporal dimension in real time, and distant time zones were brought into proximity in a functional unity structured by disparities and internal unevenness across geographical units. The Arab world is similarly characterised by unevenness, where realities of very disparate vintages coexist in the same time, a temporal balkanisation that also mirrors the internal unevenness of world metropolitan centres.

Secularism only emerges as a coherent view of history, society, and cognitive operation when, as an overwhelming reality, it encounters resistance grounded in the ways of thinking of parties that seek to monopolise cultural and social authority, and consequently political power, in the name of a heritage that is antithetical to actually existing reality and imagined to have preceded it. In Arab lands secularism was represented intellectually by the universal heritage of bourgeois thought – without an effective bourgeoisie – based on rationality in thought, utilitarianism in society and politics, and nationalism in ideology. Opposition to secularisation was officiated in the name of an authenticity prior to secularism and in the form of denial. As in France, the history of secularism was also a history of contrarianism – in the name of religion – to the world as reality and as apprehension of reality. A religious perspective considers the actual world as contrary to the truth represented by the opinion of the religious party. Secular thought was therefore always a riposte to the impulse to flee from and resist reality.

The different perspective from which the subject of secularism in Arab life and thought is treated in this book is, therefore, that of historical reality and the recognition of temporality as a qualitative transformative force. This runs contrary to the construal of modern history with reference to longing and nostalgic imaginings. The first criterion adopted here was broadly Khaldunian, the recognition of what is implausible and impossible, and recognition of the alien nature of the past, its propensity to recede away. The second guiding principle was to consider history as a constellation of different itineraries, none of which – European, Arab, or any other – enjoys an ontological singularity that precludes its integration into the globalising forces of modern history. Europe is not a homogeneous unity to which we can oppose the Arab world but a historical reality, one that is subject to change. Europe is not the model and measure of what the Arabs must be, but is a historical dynamic, the product of economic and political supremacy, extending to the social, cultural, and intellectual fields characteristic of globalisation with its attendant disparities and unevenness. Indeed, Europe herself is not the measure or a perfect example of secularism but represents, as we shall see, inconsummately secularised spaces with varied historical trajectories weaving the mutually constitutive relationship between religion and the world. It is clear that secularism is a historical category whose constitution can vary with different contexts, and that is exposed to different types and measures of resistance. Europe is not an example of perfection, but is nevertheless the dynamic centre from which modern history emerged, acquiring a global dimension that encompassed Europe and all the rest. Yet the Arabs are not hostages to the European historical experience. The Arabs are not confined by Europe's historical experience but are part of a universal dynamic transcending the borders of the West. A complex of inferiority towards the West is therefore the contrary of secular thought, as such a complex is one characteristic of a political and socio-cultural parochialism, arising from a baleful sense of backwardness. Westernisation does not entail alienation from the present; true alienation is flight from the reality of universalisation, carried by phantasms of authenticity and historical continuity. These illusions underlie claims that cultural renaissance involves extracting cultural individuality from the recesses of the past that are imagined to thrive in the present, while nothing is said about the reality of a world where any call to cultural revival necessarily derives its internal preconditions and constituent elements from universal civilisation.

This book is a historical, social, and intellectual study of secularism in Eastern and Western Arab lands in the context of the course of modern Arab history and of modern world history. It begins with a discussion of pertinent moments of European history in order to highlight the broad and varied nature of secularism and its actual connections to state and religion. It then moves to study moments of the Arab past, highlighting the realities of the relationship between religion and the world, in politics, law, and the construction of religious institutions and their role.

The second chapter moves on to the reformist and *dirigiste* state that developed from the nineteenth century. It will be shown how this state was the central dynamic in the history of Arab modernity, laying institutional, cultural, intellectual, and social bases that have underpinned modern Arab history up until well into the final part of the twentieth century. This type of state is taken up in some detail as its effects were lasting and persisted into later periods. The *dirigiste* state represented a break with the past, and integration into the rhythm of world history, especially in law, education, politics, thought, and in the creation of new categories of secular intellectuals. The historical contours of this state and the involvements and roles of those secular intellectuals are discussed in Chapter 3, where the secularisation of thought is dealt with, in both its overt terms and its implicit forms that we witness in the translation of modernity into an Islamic idiom by Arab and Turkish thinkers associated with the Islamic reform movements.

The second and third chapters study the secular contribution to modern state-building represented by the Kemalist revolution in post-Ottoman Turkey as Arabs detach themselves from this process in favour of a contrary historical course, breaking away in ideological terms from Ottoman history while prolonging it in political, social, and legal terms. The fourth chapter deals with the unfolding of the modern state in the construction of heritage, the revision and reform of the legal systems, and social change. The bases of the religious reaction to these initiatives are assessed, and the conditions for the reconciliation between elements of Arab liberalism and religion.

In the fifth chapter, examples of overt secularism in the fields of literature, thought, and the study of heritage are scanned, as is the subsequent confusion that characterised the position of the national states in Arab lands with regard to religion in the context of internal Arab political antagonisms that echoed the international struggle between the capitalist and socialist blocs.

The sixth chapter is a summary overview that draws in lines of argument and adds some conclusions on the requirement for secularism in Arab lands that, buffeted by economic backwardness and wracked by civil conflicts, will only achieve long-term stability oriented towards the future through an accommodation with history, reliance on democratic forms, and the assimilation of pluralism as a means of organising political, social, and cultural life.

It is superfluous to point out that the subject treated in this book is broad, multi-faceted, and highly complex. Some topics dealt with subjects hitherto unexamined in scholarship. This work is one of exploration and reconnaissance in the first instance. Inevitably, not all aspects of the topics covered could be examined in all their dimensions. Focus was placed on the principal elements that were essential in the analysis of others. For example, legal reforms of al-Sanhuri in Egypt were taken up with some detail as they were the most thoroughgoing and paradigmatic, while other, congruent developments in other countries were treated in more restricted compass. As much of what is said in this book goes against historical tropes and stereotypes, abundant documentation has been provided.

There is no doubt that it would not have been possible to complete a book such as this without the help of other colleagues in various ways. First, I wish to thank the Centre for Arab Unity Studies and its General Director, Dr Haseeb, for ensuring that I obtained many of the required materials from the holdings of the Egyptian National Library and Archives in Cairo and the library of the American University of Beirut. I wish to express my gratitude to the staff of the libraries who smoothed the path of my research and furnished the resources I required. These include the al-Assad National Library in Damascus; the Bodleian Library, the Oriental Institute, and Middle East Centre in Oxford; the School of Oriental and African Studies Library and the British Library in London; the Bibliothèque nationale de France and the library of the École nationale des langues orientales vivantes in Paris; and the Library of Congress in Washington, DC. During the 1989/1990 academic year, St Antony's College and the Middle East Centre in Oxford extended to me hospitality that enabled me to finish this work in an ideal atmosphere. I am grateful to Derek Hopwood, the Centre's Director. I am also grateful to Albert Hourani, Baber Johansen, Kheireddine Hasīb, Rashid al-'Inani, Sami Zubaida, Şerif Mardin, Abdallah Laroui, Farouk Mardam-Bey, and Magda Baraka for their contribution to this book through offering advice and engaging in discussion by various means, both direct and indirect. Last but not least, I wish to make special mention of Bashir al-Da'uq, Rim Sa'ad, and Fawwaz Trabulsi who read the manuscript text of this book and who gave their opinions, amended superfluous material, identified shortcomings and also ways of reconciling overall conformity and the requirements of objectivity.

1
Religion and the World in Historical Perspective

1 On the Term "Secularism"

It is not known exactly when the term "secularism" (*'ilmāniyya*) entered the Arabic language and how it spread in contemporary Arabic political, social, and historical writing. Mention had been made of the expression "civil" (*madaniyya*) as a quality and as an adjective with reference to institutions with a non-religious basis, as we see in the writing of Farah Antoun on the separation of civil and religious powers, for example.[1] This is also found in the characterisation by Muhammad 'Abduh of the caliph as a "civil ruler" in every respect.[2] The expression subsequently continued in use until recent times and in the 1920s one finds mention of calls for a civil legal system in the 1920s.[3] The term "secularism", *'ilmāniyya*, in its contemporary meaning entered into common use at that time designating then what it means today.[4] The term became established in the work of Sati' al-Husri and others after him.[5] The form *'almāniyya* has come to acquire greater purchase usage in recent decades, accompanied by pointless debates.

1 Faraḥ Anṭūn, *Ibn Rushd wa falsafatuhu ma' nuṣūṣ al-munāẓara bayna Muḥammad 'Abduh wa Faraḥ Anṭūn*, with an Introduction by Adūnīs al-'Akrā (Beirut: Dār al-Ṭalī'a, 1981), 144.

2 Muḥammad 'Abduh, *Al-a'māl al-kāmila*, collected, edited, and introduced by Muḥammad 'Amāra, 6 vols (Beirut: al-Mu'assasa al-'Arabiyya li'l-Dirāsa wa'l-Nashr, 1972–1974), vol. 3, 278.

3 Fahmī Jad'ān, *Usus al-taqaddum 'ind mufakkirī al-islām fī al-'ālam al-'arabī al-ḥadīth* (Beirut: al-Mu'assasa al-'Arabiyya li'l-Dirāsāt wa al-Nashr, 1979), 340.

4 See, for example, Salāma Mūsā, *Al-yawm wa al-ghadd* (Cairo: al-Maṭb'a al-Miṣriyya, 1927), 12.

5 Sāṭi' al-Ḥuṣrī, *Al-a'māl al-qawmiyya li Sāṭi' al-Ḥuṣrī: Silsilat al-turāth al-qawmī*, 3 vols (Beirut: Markaz Dirasāt al-Waḥda al-'Arabiyya, 1985), 1,390–1,391.

The French term *laïcité* expresses some of the past echoes of what secularism has meant in history. There is the term *sécularisme* derived from the Latin word "saeculum", which linguistically means a generation of people. In Church Latin the term took on a particular meaning, alluding to the temporal as opposed to spiritual world. This term has been current in Protestant countries generally while in Catholic countries the term of *laïcité* has been employed, one adopted in Turkish through the expression *laiklik*. This is derived from two Greek expressions, *laos*, people, and *laikos*, laity, as distinct from clerics.

A broad conclusion from these two expressions is that one indicates the spiritual and intellectual dimensions of secularism, while the other intends aspects connected with the religious institution as a socio-political unit. But this is no ground for the classification of secularism into two families. The meanings of these terms have not been stable, and do not correspond historically to their narrow lexical meanings or to their etymologies. There were specific distinctions between secularism in Catholic and Protestant regions although both shared a common feature: that religion as a source of authority in social and intellectual questions is not privileged over other sources of authority in societies internally differentiated. Intellectual, political, and social affairs and their regulation are thus not subject to religious authority, in its institutional, intellectual, or symbolic aspects, and this authority is not considered the fundamental source of authority in social life. Religion becomes part of the sphere of personal worship. Religious associations, such as churches and denominations, are, like other voluntary associations, integrated into the sphere of general freedoms. As religious freedom is a form of personal freedom, none of its legal obligations may contravene civil law that has a positive, secular foundation. This general feature of secularism holds in all of the situations in which secularism has existed. It is valid in Britain where there is an official Church (the Anglican Church) headed by the monarch, as it is also valid in France where a formal constitutional separation exists between state and Church and their respective institutions.

The modalities of connection between religion and the world in secular societies are by no means uniform. One can observe that in countries such as France, with a Catholic majority, the secular state, supported by a robust collection of institutions and currents of thought, exists in a society with a not inconsiderable but by no means majoritarian or hegemonic rate of religious conviction, underpinned by strong religious institutions. In countries like the Netherlands and in Britain, we witness lower rates of religious belief and observance and a very marked marginalisation of religious institutions and ideas.[6] In the United States we find a civil form of religiosity with marked internal differentiations, one distinct from the state and the system of education, but that is at the same time an important and visible component of social life and codes of behaviour.[7] Secularism is therefore highly complex and varied and it is impossible to discuss it without recourse to concrete histories. It cannot be described summarily, derived, for instance, from its so-called foundations in Christianity[8] or from religious authority, without further specification.[9] This idea is common in contemporary Arab discourse about secularism, which sees the Arabs' putative individuality as a mirror image of the supposed individuality of the other, secular Christian Europe. The purportedly simple history of Europe is a mere counterpart to the summary finality that the proponents of this type of pseudo-history ascribe to their own, Arab societies.

2 Religion and Public Life in Christian Commonwealths

Some Arab authors ascribe secularism to an ahistorical other, supposedly unique as Arabs too are presumed to be unique, no matter how improbably. Some even claimed that secularism was a way of organising life commanded by Christianity, using the famous expression attributed to Jesus in the Gospels, affirming that to God should be given what is God's, and to Caesar what is Caesar's, implying the separation of Church and state.[10] This line of thought is characterised by a grave misconception of historical reality, presuming to amalgamate the Gospels with Christian life, in the same way that it seems desirable to suppose a mutual reducibility of Islamic texts and the history of

6 For a general description see Martin, *Theory of Secularization*, 5–7, 18–55.

7 William Herberg, *Protestant, Catholic, Jew* (New York: Doubleday, 1955), 82–83, 222–223, and passim.

8 Aḥmad Kamāl Abū al-Majd, *Ḥiwār lā muwājaha: Dirasāt ḥawl al-islām wa al-'asr* (Kuwait: Majallat al-'Arabī, 1985), 129.

9 Muḥammad 'Amāra, *Al-dawla al-islāmiyya bayn al-'ilmāniyya wa al-ṣulṭa al-dīniyya* (Beirut, Cairo: Dār al-Shurūq, 1988), 63.

10 There is no doubt that Sāṭi' al-Ḥuṣrī, as was often the case, was a significant exception to the failings of the ahistorical view prevailing in modern Arab thought. See, for example, his commentary on this very subject in al-Ḥuṣrī, *Al-a'māl al-qawmiyya*, 1,926–1,927.

Islam, with egregious disregard of the highly complex reality of the relation between normative texts and historical realities, and the extremely anomalous nature of cases where they might be wished to correspond really.

This approach supposes that for each historical entity it sets up as a category for delimitation or description, such as Christianity, there is one definitive and in essence invariant character set at the outset, in the same way as it assumes that Paleo-Islam in Medina was in its essentials born complete, such that historians would need only to set out the successive manifestations of an essential Islam in the light of this model, either to prove continuity or to claim that a subsequent state was a departure from the firm foundation of what had come before. In other words, this approach assumes that history is merely a collection of circumstances that undermine its origins only by deviation from ends predetermined by beginnings. History does not change meaningfully, and all appearance of change is parsed as a departure from the origin, to be followed by a resumption of this origin, essentially unchanged, as in all discourses on "awakening" or "the return to Islam".

But metahistorical considerations and metaphysical evaluation need to be left aside in order to consider the realities of Christian history before we consider aspects of Islamic history. Until recent periods Christianity, when connected to politics, followed the pattern common to monotheist religions in its use of doctrinal concepts to enframe intellectual and spiritual authority. The same might be claimed for Zoroastrianism in Sassanid Iran and for Christianity in its Byzantine form, then for the Papacy in the West and for Islam in many periods of its histories. These religions differ clearly from ancient religions linked to states and empires and in particular from Roman paganism.[11] Ancient empires did not impose doctrinal homogeneity on their public legislatures. Their religions were "weak" in terms of doctrinal content and dense with ritual practices that, among other things, facilitated

11 We rely here on detailed, careful, and reliable work that Arab writers on secularism and the relation between state and religion in Europe and Islam have often disregarded. Jūrj Qurm [Georges Corm], *Taʿaddud al-adyān wa anẓimat al-ḥukm: Dirāsa sūsiyūlūjiyya wa qānūniyya muqārana* (Beirut: Dār al-Nahār li'l-Nashr, 1979). Two works by the present author treating these matters in detail appeared after this book, and contain ample reference to specialised literature: *Muslim Kingship: Power and the Sacred in Muslim, Christian and Pagan Polities* (London: I. B. Tauris, 1996) and *The Emergence of Islam in Late Antiquity: Allah and His People* (Cambridge: Cambridge University Press, 2014), chs 2 and 3.

the integration of the deities of defeated groups into the divine economy of victorious peoples. In the late Roman Empire formal religious requirements were limited to sacrifice to the Emperor, which in practice meant worship of the state without doctrinal consequences. Paganism is a form of religion that, at a deep level, integrates and adapts diverse elements to one another.

Integration took place therefore on the basis of a supervening general practice that assimilated specificities as provincial peculiarities. These existed on the fringes of the empire, and were not necessarily linked to religion; they were local codifications for customary practices adapted to local conditions. Roman law in its details was not generally imposed on those regions, the *limes*, as it was in provincial centres, where Roman-style economic and social relations prevailed. The absence from pagan devotions of monopolistic divinities opened the way to the peaceful coexistence of different religious groups within a single political framework.[12]

With the change from the pagan Roman Empire to the Christian Roman, or Byzantine, Empire there was a return to one of the earlier forms of social solidarity (similar to ancient Judaism) with a common pattern of devotional practice as a condition of citizenship and law and as its guarantee.[13] Devotional practice acquired restrictive doctrinal associations that consigned people who did not accept official doctrine – by the fact of their belonging to another religion – to a position outside the general legal framework. Doctrine required them to be confined to civil and religious conditions that were restrictive politically and socially, and governed by special laws. Thus, relations between confessions were politicised and religious conviviality became hostage to inter-state relations and adhesion to the majority faith, amid a climate charged with religious animosity and scorn, fuelled by socio-cultural differentiations that assigned primacy to one group over another because the rulers had sacrificed the universality of law to doctrinal adhesion, inflicting harm on social stability and peace. Some Catholic authors still see Byzantine Caesaro-papism as a Christian ideal.[14] In this system, the state did not merely proclaim and sponsor – through the person of the Emperor – the formulation of doctrine (as in the doctrinal councils in Nicaea and elsewhere) and support and propagate the true form of doctrine.

12 Qurm, *Taʿaddud al-adyān wa anẓimat al-ḥhukm*, 138.
13 Ibid, 139.
14 Ibid.

The state also relied on religion and its ultimate purposes as the basis for state and laws and sought to adapt social realities to the demands of Christian interpretation as exercised by clerics.

Religious authority laid the officially legitimising foundations for civil authority and adjudicated in many civil affairs. None of the matters mentioned were ever definitive and unchanging. History admits no finalities. The use of religious symbolism by Constantine, pagan and Christian, was constant. When he transferred the imperial capital to Constantinople (Istanbul after the Ottoman conquest of 1453), the city was consecrated to the Virgin Mary.[15] He then convened the Council of Nicaea in 325 CE, converting to Christianity only on his deathbed, having also promoted pagan cults in a context where Christianity enjoyed forms of primacy. It later absorbed previous sources of authority and Christianised them, conferring on them its own characteristics, and its name. The pagan state was the first to protect the Church and bring it into the structure of government. This beginning did not prevent the Church from setting its seal on the new state, and it was the state itself that actually sought this change to a political theocracy. The Byzantine state embodied the ideal of a Christian state. It is in fact odd that Arab intellectuals and researchers in Islamic religious history and caliphate ignore the political and religious heritage of the pre-Islamic Levant.

Thus, the decisions of the Councils entered the field of public and private law. In the Code of Justinian (483–565 CE), these took on a weight equal to that of other sources of law.[16] Roman law was blended with ecclesiastical concepts in such a way as to preserve a legal heritage that detached itself ultimately from religion and was integrated into distinct modern European legal systems. In so far as the Church was operating under the patronage of a great state with strong structures in Byzantium, it became in Rome the sole coherent authority in times of great instability precipitating and following what are known as Barbarian invasions. Rome became thereafter the spiritual patron of the Holy Roman Empire, established when Pope Leo II crowned Charlemagne Emperor on Christmas Day of the year 800. The Church only acquired effective political and military power equalling the power of kings and notables at the time of Gregory VII (r. 1073–1085), a power that

15 Alistair Kee, *Constantine versus Christ: The Triumph of Ideology* (London: SCM, 1982).

16 With regard to church laws in general, see the highly useful texts in J. M. Buckley, et al., "Canon Law", in *New Catholic Encyclopaedia*, 15 vols (New York: McGraw Hill, 1967), vol. 3, 29–53.

increased and diminished with the passing of centuries and changes of inter-state and royal-imperial relations in Europe and beyond. This power – be it political or religious – was always linked closely to the state, the state as patron and the Church as guide, given that its personnel were the literate element of power. The legal function of the Church was limited to deciding legal matters pertaining to the Church, its internal relations and organisation and the field of worship; but this was extended into many areas of life, especially in the golden age of Canon Law from the eleventh century to the thirteenth. This coincided with the control of the Church over the rite of passage known as baptism. Usury was banned and marriage was regulated: where marriage had been based on local and tribal practices, such as those of the Franks that allowed marriage of brothers and sisters, marriage became a sacramental bond transcending society and supervised by the Church.[17] The Church then, in a highly complex and conflictual history, codified the rules of war and political authority, and adopted the principle of papal primacy and sponsored political theories that made kings into images and imitations of Christ and political thought into a political Christology. This later became the theory of the divine right of kings and government by grace of God.[18]

This concern with social relations and politics in addition to worship was not the only element that rendered Christian legal and intellectual traditions comparable to those of Islam. The conceptual logical and para-logical mechanisms that were used in Western Christian thought were comparable to those of Islamic jurisprudence and its fundamental principles, such as abrogation, analogy, and the attribution of the power of interpretation to the legislator, then to doctrine and customs. All of this indicates in legal terms common Roman and Middle Eastern conditions of development, in addition to the convergence of the two religions in the context of the two monotheist religions and the resulting concepts of power and authority and text.

We must lastly mention a basic point in the history of Christian thought and jurisprudence in their relation to different societies. It is clear that the extent to which certain requirements of canon law were applicable varied with time and place. Its more uniform application developed with the

17 Georges Duby, *The Knight, the Lady and the Priest: The Making of Modern Marriage*, trans. Barbara Bray (Harmondsworth: Penguin Books, 1985).
18 Ernst H. Kantorowicz, *The King's Two Bodies: A Study in Medieval Political Theology* (Princeton: Princeton University Press, 1957), 16, 47–48, and passim.

spread of the major religious orders and their implantation in European rural areas, especially following the Reformation, Protestant as well as Catholic. As for European cities, these retained a large degree of legal independence, enabling them later to develop capitalism and a new class of civil jurists who crafted civil laws and produced secular thought, often in collaboration with elements from the clergy of the Italian cities that were bound by family connections to the urban patricians.[19]

The thirteenth century was a decisive moment of transition in the emergence of a self-consciously Latin Christianity – Christendom. That century witnessed the beginning of the activities of the Dominican Order in 1216 of which Thomas Aquinas was a member, as well as of the Franciscan Order. The Dominicans specialised in doctrinal formation, countering heresy and carrying out inquisitorial activities, starting in the year 1233, while the Franciscans concentrated on evangelisation in the countryside. The rhythms of feudal society were, however, slow, with difficulties in communication and centralisation. It was legally fragmented and rested on feudal foundations in which the Church and the monarchy shared legal power with princes without this necessarily meaning a diminution in prerogatives, variously claimed, of political centralisation. In this separation between political and legal centralism lies one of the conditions of the separation of powers to which democracy later gave a legal framework. Liturgical practice did not have the density of organisation that it was later to possess. It seems, for example, that from the eleventh to the sixteenth centuries male and female religious and pious lay people took communion only three or four times a year. European rural areas retained a collection of beliefs in a variety of supernatural beings, elves and sacred streams and much else. These competed for the loyalty of peasants with a belief in one God and in the unicity of supernatural power.[20] In sum, this period was one of doctrinal and institutional preparation of the intellectual and organisational structures that were to emerge and yield real and general homogeneity in European societies when later linked to the

---

19 Lucien Paul Victor Febvre, *The Problem of Unbelief in the Sixteenth Century: The Religion of Rabelais*, trans. Beatrice Gottlieb (Cambridge, MA: Harvard University Press, 1982), 322.

20 See, in particular, the third chapter of Aron Gurevich's *Medieval Popular Culture: Problems of Belief and Perception*, trans Janos Bak and Paul Hollingsworth, Cambridge Studies in Oral and Literate Culture 14 (Cambridge: Cambridge University Press and Paris: Éditions de la Maison des sciences de l'Homme, 1988).

emergence of centralised European states with the Protestant and Catholic reforms and its later development.

We shall see that claims made about the conflict between state and Church are greatly exaggerated. The Church only enjoyed independence in feudal society in which the Church was a feudal power, monarchical or quasi-monarchical like other powers. In the sixteenth century churches were integrated – conflictually, and incompletely – into European polities and their structures, functioning within them as religious entities related to the state and often regulated by it, and supporting state ideology, after the Peace of Augsburg in 1555. As a result of that the spread of the effect of religious authority into public life became one of the bases of royal rule and a major instrument in imposing legal and ideological homogeneity in the absence of educational structures and instruments of communication and administration that was later to characterise the modern state. Thus, excommunication from the Church became in the sixteenth century one penalty for defaulting on debts. France abounded in liturgical celebrations with a religious character; there were sixty days of festivals according to the Church calendar, in addition to Sundays.[21]

Martin Luther's attack on the sale of indulgences by the Church in 1516 and his ninety-five theses are celebrated events, and need little explanation. Luther, a former Augustinian monk, soon married a former nun and unleashed the Protestant Reformation in alliance with some German princes.[22] The Reformation, a hugely complex historical phenomenon that can be approached only very approximatively here,[23] opened an era of European wars that subverted the European balance of power system, and led to the emergence of a state system based on two elements, namely royal or princely absolutism, and churches subordinated to these absolutist systems, especially in Spain, France, and Britain. In Germany, however, religious reform was an opportunity for the independence of some German principalities from the imperial system, with principalities supported by dynamic local economies, with local churches operating in German into which Luther translated the Bible.[24] This translation had a decisive impact on the modern German literary

21 Febvre, *Problem of Unbelief*, 339, 347, n. 22.

22 Perry Anderson, *Lineages of the Absolutist State* (London: Verso, 1979), part 1.

23 For an indication, see C. Scott Dixon, *Contesting the Reformation* (Oxford: Wiley-Blackwell, 2012).

24 Lucien Paul Victor Febvre, *Martin Luther: A Destiny*, trans. Roberts Tapley (London and Toronto: J. M. Dent and Sons, 1930), 99–123.

language. Protestantism in certain regions – French Huguenot Calvinist Protestantism in the south and Scottish Presbyterianism – was an expression of autonomist tendencies among local aristocracies resisting the attempts at centralisation.[25] The same is true of Dutch Protestantism that was led by the bourgeoisie of the Dutch trading cities against Habsburg-Spanish imperial domination. Protestantism was linked with an important element that would long characterise Church–state relations, namely a high degree of state secularisation of Church property. This was especially true in the case of the German principalities and in the case of Britain under Henry VIII.

Protestantism combatted heresy pitilessly and worked on imposing ideological, spiritual, and devotional uniformity, with stress on personal conduct and personal conscience, that is to say, cultural centralisation in the face of forms of non-conformist radical Protestantism that supported revolutionary movements of which the best known was the peasant revolt led by Thomas Müntzer, initially a disciple of Luther, who was executed in 1525. Catholicism did not remain on the sidelines but began working with great enthusiasm and energy on legislating and canalising the tremendous religious and spiritual energies unleashed by Protestantism on the battlefield, in intellectual life, and in sensibilities across the European continent. Catholic Reform – some call it the Counter-Reformation – in its turn was an element in the creation of states that were religiously and confessionally homogenous, with non-Catholics disenfranchised, persecuted, or removed from Catholic territory, perhaps most famously in France with the revocation of the Edict of Nantes in 1685. The Catholic Church did not lack experience in these matters. The Spanish monarchy had been zealous in ensuring religious uniformity in its lands. In 1479 it set up an inspectorate to examine families of Jewish and Muslim origin upon whom baptism was imposed to ensure that their Christianity was not a mere subterfuge, before expelling them from the country. The Pope founded an inquisitional office attached to the Vatican in 1542 to persecute Protestants, and the Council of Trent assembled in three stages from 1523 to 1545 to decide on doctrine and law and the organisation of the Church, and to put in place the bases of the campaign against local popular religions – that is to say what religions call heresy – and creating cultural uniformity in towns and the countryside.[26] One

---

25 Anderson, *Lineages*, 92, 136.

26 Robert Mandrou, *From Humanism to Science, 1480–1700*, trans. Brian Pearce (Harmondsworth: Penguin Books, 1978), 162–250.

of the means of imposing this uniformity was new emphasis on personal morality and pressure on individual conduct. The organisation of daily life in Catholic Bavaria in the time of Albrecht V (1550–1579) was almost a mirror image of Calvinist Geneva.[27] Pressure was exerted on rural regions in various ways, of which the hysteria of witch-persecution and burnings at the stake was one of the most important. This operation extended over two centuries in both Protestant and Catholic lands to an equal extent. It seems that it was one of the means of eliminating concentrations of local religions and social organisations that rebelled against uniformity and centralisation. Violence took terrifying forms of which the St Bartholomew's Day massacre of Protestants in France of 24 August 1572 was among the most important. The religious wars and the massacres aimed at producing confessional homogeneity only ceased with the Treaty of Westphalia in 1648, which introduced Europe to a new international system through its recognition of the independence of the German states, Holland and Italy. It also put an effective end to the all-but-nominal existence of the Holy Roman Empire and put France in a central position in the European system at the expense of Spain. In addition, the Treaty of Westphalia further enshrined the principle of *Cujius regio ejus religio* whereby subjects were to conform to the denomination of their princes.

The Protestant and Catholic reformers therefore consecrated the principle of confessional uniformity and gave added force to the submission of Church to state. Although the Catholic Church retained margins of independence because of the existence of the Roman papacy and the possibility of playing off nations one against the other within Europe by popes who were in effect kings of large parts of Italy. This Ultramontanism was linked to an agreement between the French kings and the Catholic Church that gave the kings the right to appoint the holders of high office in the Gallicanist (French) Church while the kings dispensed the Church from paying taxes, contrary to the situation in Spain where Church property was subject to high rates of taxation. In Italy, however, the Papal office acted as a central Italian kingdom and its power was part of the web of relations between the different Italian states and was part of the links between aristocratic families. In Britain the religious sphere was recast as Henry VIII proclaimed himself head of the Church in 1534 and dissolved the monastic orders and seized their property, and by the

27 Ibid., 164.

Civil War, which led a century later to the formation of a national Church and the taming of radical Protestant denominations, after the absorption of some elements of Protestantism into the Anglican Church.

The outcomes of the European sixteenth and seventeenth centuries, with their eventful, accelerated history, ran counter to the images disseminated by some Arab intellectuals on the relation between Church and state in Europe. These are images based generally on scanty readings, or on vestigial memories of history lessons in primary or secondary school. These two centuries produced a broader presence of Protestant and Catholic Christianity in European societies, and their transformation from nominally Christian societies to societies that became Christian in practice and daily outlook. This involved states whose centralisation required making their societies culturally uniform to the extent permitted by the existing means of communication and administration. A feature of those states was the role played by the clergy as agents of cultural and legal unity.

The state represented political, secular, and civil power and the Church was a cultural and ideological structure as well as a secular and civil structure controlling immense properties and propelling some of its senior figures, such as Cardinal Richelieu (1585–1642), to the highest offices of the state. The aristocracy entwined itself with the leadership of the Church, with great families usually sending one of their sons into the Church with the expectation that he would very quickly rise to the highest position. The link between Church and state was therefore a link of partnership and convergence in an overarching socio-political system whose strongest element in political terms was the monarchy, which governed in virtue of divine right, in various redactions, which the Church had invented for it without this preventing conflicts between religious and state institutions. The primacy of king over Church was always mitigated, and often conflictual. These conflicts were not, however, general, and primacy did not extend to every area. Primacy was not permanent but changed according to social and political and cultural transformations; Christianity was an official doctrine of the state in which citizenship, religious practice, and confessional belonging were united. Non-Catholics were deprived of civil rights in Catholic countries and non-Protestants were deprived of civil rights and the possibility of entering educational establishments or government service in Protestant countries, until well into the nineteenth century. The Church condemned heretics, and then handed them over to the civil authorities for the execution of sentence, as in the classical Muslim legal system. Thus, we find one of the proponents of religious tolerance among liberal thinkers, John Locke, limiting this tolerance to Protestant sects, and excluding Catholics and atheists. A leading sceptic such as Voltaire insisted on the need for a state religion as a means of social control of the broad mass of people, and on the necessity to restrict posts in public administration to those adhering to state confession.[28] What was then political common sense recognised the link between religion and politics. It is perhaps unsurprising that, later, Protestants in France were rather more inclined to radicalism (and membership of the Socialist party) than non-Protestants, and that the same may be said of Catholics of Great Britain.[29]

Since there were yet few serious cultural, intellectual, or ideological pressures on the Church as an institution (apart from the religious pressure from rival denominations) it is unsurprising that clerics often led the way in natural scientific research in Europe; it is often forgotten that Copernicus himself was a Church canon. Basic facts are often disregarded. One is that the nominalist school in Schlolastic philosophy was closely connected to the emergence of the first experimental concepts in natural sciences and mathematic studies that led to the new scientific methods of Galileo and Newton. Those studies were in good measure based on Arabic science that had been transmitted to Europe,[30] including the mathematics that went into the Copernican system. The Jesuit Order was founded to be the educational and intellectual arm of the Catholic Church and research indicates that the Jesuits were highly active in natural, experimental, and mathematical sciences, and that many of them were closely linked to Copernicus's astronomical research. Copernicus's research itself did not necessarily affect strategically placed doctrinal matters. This becomes apparent in the light of the archives of Galileo's trial discovered recently in the Vatican.[31] A Jesuit conspiracy appears to have been hatched in Rome against Galileo with the aim of eliminating him and a cultural aristocratic circle with which he was linked,

28 Rāndāl, Jūn Hermān [John Herman Randall], *Takwīn al-ʿaql al-hadīth*, trans. of *The Making of the Modern Mind* (1926) by Georges Ṭuʿma, 2 vols (Beirut: Dār al-Thaqāfa/Mu'assasat Franklin, 1965–1966), vol. 1, 561, 563.

29 Martin, *Theory of Secularization*, 19.

30 A. C. Crombie, *Robert Grosseteste and the Origins of Experimental Science* (Oxford: Clarendon Press, 1953), 294, 36–37, 77–80, and passim.

31 Pietro Redondi, *Galileo Heretic*, trans. Raymond Rosenthal (London: Allen Lane, The Penguin Press, 1988).

operating under the patronage of the Pope. The long-term aim of the conspiracy was to bring influence to bear on the power of the Supreme Pontiff. Initially, the accusation levelled at Galileo was much more serious than the mere adoption of the Copernican theory of planetary orbits, which he only did with studied reserve and in a technical sense. The substance of the accusation against him was the adoption of an atomic physical theory expressly prohibited by the Council of Trent, because it denied the philosophical and magical bases of the eucharistic rite as this Council had defined them. These maintain that wine and bread are in fact changed into the blood and flesh of Christ when they are consecrated (transubstantiation), while the theory of atoms would yield the conclusion that this was impossible, and that claims for transformation of substance are to be interpreted in an allegorical fashion (such was close to the Reformed Church of Zwingli in Zurich). The Pope felt constrained to go along with the Jesuit plan, but nevertheless intervened in the trial's frame of reference, in specifying its procedure, and in shaping the charge that he succeeded in diverting from an accusation of a capital offence to one that did not incur the death penalty. The Pope succeeded in protecting Galileo, and in defending himself against the accusation that he was patron of a person condemned to the stake as a heretic. Galileo was not imprisoned but was obliged to reside in his country house.

We might conclude that the Church was neither systematically nor necessarily an obstacle to scientific research, and that secularism is not as is often claimed necessarily linked to scientific activity. The history of the conflict between religion and science has generally been oversimplified, and recent decades have seen a growth area of scholarship in this field, energised by renewed sympathy for religion in many circles. Scientific activity can remain confined to matters of technical detail without leading necessarily to an attitude inimical to religion, on the condition that, first, scientific activity does not lead to a general application of scientific facts and associated methods across the different fields where reason is applied to doctrine and that, second, religion be considered a domain distinct generically from scientific knowledge. This clearly appears in the religious beliefs of the majority of early natural scientists. Robert Boyle was strongly opposed to atheism and to scepticism in matters of religion and saw in science proofs of the incoherence of atheism. Newton, whose own private Christianity was highly heterodox, was obsessed with the Bible, believed in alchemy and magic, and considered the rotation of the planets and their velocities as elements – because of their regularity – put in place by God and in this specific respect not open to human enquiry.[32] Giordiano Bruno believed in magic numbers and letters[33] while most natural scientists in the nineteenth century believed in God.[34] Until the end of the eighteenth century, French Catholics accepted the natural sciences and only the Jansenists, with strong affinities to Protestantism and among whose number was Blaise Pascal, himself a great mathematician, were opposed to the natural science and their results.

It was only after the clashes that followed the French Revolution that the French Gallicanist Church adopted a position of hostility to science. The Jesuits tended to see in the sacred texts a re-modelling of the natural law.[35] The role played by science was nevertheless doubtless a strong factor in the emergence of domains of science beyond the control of scripture and the religious institution; the impact of Newtonian science on freethinking and the Enlightenment was enormous. One effect of fundamental scientific discoveries – especially the new astronomical sciences and the mathematisation of nature by Galileo and Descartes – was the collapse of the image of the world as a finite normative and natural hierarchical structure, based on a vision of heaven and earth and planets. This image was replaced by one of an infinite domain, governed by laws rather than animated by innate substantive natures. These discoveries also rendered irrelevant the idea of a qualitative space, replaced with a notion of space that was abstract, uniform, and geometrical.[36] Nature was no longer conceived as governed by an external purpose. Humans were no longer the centre of the universe. Although Newton believed in the continuous divine providence, to the

---

32 Alexandre Koyré, *Newtonian Studies* (London: Chapman and Hall, 1965), 201, 203–204. See now Rob Iliffe, *Priest of Nature: The Religious Worlds of Isaac Newton* (Oxford: Oxford University Press, 2017).

33 Frances Yates, *Giordiano Bruno and the Hermetic Tradition* (London: Routledge, 1964).

34 A. Eymien, "Science et religion", in *Dictionnaire apologétique de la foi catholique*, eds A. d'Alès, et al., 4 vols (Paris: Gabriel Beauchesne, 1923), vol. 4, 1,242–1,254.

35 Robert L. Palmer, *Catholics and Unbelievers in Eighteenth-Century France* (Princeton: Princeton University Press, 1939/1971), 28, 34–35, 165, 203–205; and Owen Chadwick, *The Secularization of the European Mind in the Nineteenth Century: The Gifford Lectures in the University of Edinburgh for 1973–74* (Cambridge: Cambridge University Press, 1975), 122. On this matter, see the excellent recent account of David Wootton, *The Invention of Science. A New History of the Scientific Revolution* (London: Penguin Books, 2016), ch. 13.

36 Koyré, *Newtonian Studies*, 6–9; A. E. Burtt, *The Metaphysical Foundations of Modern Physical Science* (London: Routledge, 1932), passim.

extent of holding that the solar system would necessarily collapse around its centre if this were suspended,[37] this conviction did not necessarily entail belief in divine ends beyond the cosmos itself.

God's role therein was no more than that of a diligent overseer,[38] much like a retired engineer. This view was linked to the experimental and mathematical precision that characterised the way that Newton practised science,[39] in addition to a basic principle that no causes may be recognised, unless they were both true and adequate to explaining the phenomena under discussion.[40] God thus became an unnecessary explanatory hypothesis in the study of nature, as Laplace said to Napoleon, famously.[41] Newton's theory of the role of divine intervention in the maintenance of the cosmos was subject to the mockery of other scientists, many, like Leibniz, not given to religious scepticism, who saw in the hypothesis of divine providence a diminution of the divine capacity to create a complete and perfect instrument requiring no maintenance.[42] The position of Newton and the comments made about it represented a medial position between a vision of the world based on Christian providence, teleology, and miracles, and a tendency that crystallised subsequently, in the example of Laplace, which saw the rational organisation of nature as divinity itself, that is to say, in what we call natural religion.[43]

In pursuing secularism, therefore, one would be advised to resist the temptation of resorting to militant slogans, and assert the expectation of a melodramatic contest between science and religion – this was to come later, after the French Revolution and the Napoleonic wars, by a besieged papacy, with the declaration by Pope Pius IX of the Syllabus of Errors that denounced the modern age and its new cognitive regime wholesale.[44] Science is a collection of precise elements of knowledge and religion is an imaginative structure with an evaluative dimension that is not subject to reason. A situation of

37 Burtt, *The Metaphysical Foundations*, 291.

38 Ibid., 294.

39 Koyré, *Newtonian Studies*, 25–52.

40 Ibid., 265–266. Compare Burtt, *The Metaphysical Foundations*, 283–286.

41 Alexandre Koyré, *From the Closed World to the Infinite University* (Baltimore: Johns Hopkins University Press, 1957), passim.

42 Burtt, *The Metaphysical Foundations*, 289–290.

43 Ibid., 297.

44 See conveniently Eamon Duffy, *Saints and Sinners: A History of the Popes* (New Haven and London: Yale University Press, 2006), 286–304.

contradiction between these two generically distinct products of the human spirit cannot be postulated legitimately even if religion sought, with its claim to possess the ultimate truth of the cosmos, to invalidate scientific activity: under discussion here is a period of time when concepts based on scientific activity were broadening their remit to areas outside the sphere of nature and competing with religion in interpretative authority. Science, combined with social and political authority, which later acquired ideological and cultural dimensions, marginalised religious modes of cognition and deliberation, limiting them to a sphere of life with an increasingly restricted definition, namely religious practice. This became possible with the convergence between the generalisation of scientific modernity and the discovery that a historically situated world was the realm of change and transformation, often then redacted as evolution and elevation, and that social change could be made possible and reflected in modern political forms, including democracy.[45]

In other words, the rational bases for secularism were sufficient to reveal that the presumption of permanence of the past was an illusion, allied to the dominance of social and intellectual authorities sustained by such an illusion. This realisation came associated with a political and cultural condition upheld by a secular grouping of new cultural actors – antiquarians, lawyers, physicians – with non-religious occupations, linked to the political rise of non-aristocratic classes, the bourgeoisie and its allies, whose pressure, both social and political, led to political change, including revolutionary transformation. Undoubtedly the new educational establishments and their social extensions and associations exercised considerable effect on the development of thought outside the bounds of the religious imagination. The seed had been sown in Italy in the first half of the fifteenth century, the period of the humanist Renaissance that was an expression of the culture of aristocratic and new professional social groups independent of the royal and imperial system, and based on urban classes enriched by trade. Humanist literature and its culture was multiform and boundless in variety, and its high reputation in the context of these cities was a sign of the cultural distinction of particular social classes, without this implying that its major figures were irreligious. This can be compared with the *adab* in the Abbasid period, a

45 Lauro Martines, *Power and Imagination: City-States in Renaissance Italy* (Harmondsworth: Penguin Books, 1983), 262.

token of social distinction emblematised by secular and literary sensibility and knowledge, good conduct, and elevated taste. Clerics were not alien to this process, and as mentioned previously, they were closely connected with the social workings of the Italian cities and the higher echelons of the Church. Alongside secular cultural actors, they were responsible for restoring prestige to Roman legal and medical and philosophical – including Ibn Rushdist – knowledge on which the repute of Italian universities (notably Bologna and Padova) was based.[46] Fine arts developed and spread to religious and secular architecture under the patronage of clerical princes and laymen alike. In music great aesthetic capacities flowered, encompassing liturgical music after the removal of the interdiction on musical instruments in church. Monteverdi (1567–1643), flourishing in Venice, represented music's crowning breakthrough for the aesthetic of the Catholic Reform and, some time after him, Schütz (1585–1672) and Bach (1685–1750) came to occupy similar positions in Protestant Germany and beyond. In the rest of Europe there were new higher educational institutions not confined to theological studies and taking up newer directions in the production of knowledge, established under royal patronage: Germany saw the foundation of many after the Reformation, and the Royal College in Paris was founded in 1530 (known afterwards as the Collège de France), and various scientific societies were founded under royal patronage like the Royal Society in England. These institutions were active in the production of scientific knowledge and, together with independent antiquarians, of the linguistic and historical knowledge necessary to study legal texts and the Bible. These institutions led European culture, already separating out into different linguistic cultures, to distance itself from the exclusively Latinate culture of traditional clerics, and to produce new literary forms dealing with profane subjects, of which the novel, a product of the late seventeenth century, was to be perhaps the most noted. Concomitantly, new forms of awareness emerged, in the form of new techniques of perception and visual representation, building upon the use of medieval Arabic geometry of perspective in recasting the technique of painting in Renaissance Italy.[47] A new world was emerging,

46 Compare Mandrou, *From Humanism to Science, 1480–1700*, 23–25.

47 Ibid., 25–27; Hans Belting, *Florence and Baghdad: Renaissance Art and Arab Science*, trans. D. L. Schneider (Cambridge, MA: Harvard University Press, 2011). See also Pierre Francastel, *Peinture et société: Naissance et destruction d'un espace plastique de la Renaissance au Cubisme* (Lyon: Audin, 1951).

initially limited to enlightened individuals and groups. In the sphere of the imagination, for many centuries such groups continued to be closely aligned with political deference and social deference to public worship and in some cases the personal discipline imposed by religion.

The link with religious belief was not a stumbling block to the emergence of the legal and theoretical bases of new political ideas, what were to eventually become ideas of popular representation (including democracy), and thus to secularism. These ideas were erected on the vestiges of the theory of natural law that ecclesiastical legal theories assumed was a law preceding civil laws, and based on the will of God. The new theory, in its classical form represented by the Dutch scholar Hugo Grotius (1583–1645), was based on reverting to the sense that natural law had had in Roman law: that all law was civil law based in human nature, a view that bears comparison to some classical perspectives on the relationship between Muslim jurisprudence and human interest. Although Grotius considered that this law came to exist through divine will in the last analysis, he held that the basis of civil law arose from imperatives of the civil nature of humans.[48] It became evident therefore, in view of this political and legal orientation, that human nature should be linked with what was appropriate for the period of the beginnings of European capitalism, based on cities freed, at an institutional level, from princely and clerical control, and in need of legal structures appropriate for property ownership and trade. Laissez-faire theories emerged on a basis of economic liberties, stressed by John Locke; to these, political liberty might or might not be added.[49] In this perspective, it became possible to define justice quite simply as the fulfilment of a contract,[50] without external factors. The high point of this separation of the economy from politics was its establishment as a particular discipline under the name of political economy in the eighteenth century by French Physiocrats such as Quesnay (1694–1774) and Turgot (1727–1781). This was not possible without breaking the link between the possession of immovable property and the control of people, giving free rein to movable wealth that became the paradigmatic

48 Richard Tuck, *Natural Right Theories: Their Origin and Development* (Cambridge: Cambridge University Press, 1979), 17–20, 40, 59–76.

49 Ibid., 77–79, and chs 4 and 5; C. B. MacPherson, *The Political Theory of Possessive Individualism* (Oxford: Oxford University Press, 1964), 268–269.

50 Christopher Hill, *The Intellectual Origins of the English Revolution* (Oxford: Clarendon Press, 1965), 268–269.

form of a new and uniform definition of wealth, giving rise to the science of economics.[51] This was closely related to the abstract quantitative terms that had become the founding concepts for natural sciences. This also entailed the emergence of an important new concept, the freedom of civil society and the independence of its internal relations from the state and from all the other institutions such as the Church. In Hegel's famous later expression, society is a "kingdom of ends", a society that can be discovered by political economy, leading in the late nineteenth century to an awareness of the separation of the sphere of society from the sphere of economy. Society then became the topic of distinct science, sociology. Whereas classical social theories, such as the geometrical-mechanistic theory of Hobbes or the individualism of Locke, considered society to express a stable human nature, progressive French thought in the eighteenth century and Rousseau's critique of ahistorical theories of society that preceded this led to history taking the place of stable nature as a basis for rights.[52] To these were later added Hegelian philosophy, and later the developments embodied in the important work of Karl Marx.

These broad trends, distinct from those associated with religion and beyond the control of religious authority, were connected to an expanding intellectual and cognitive atmosphere that spread due to the perceived independence of the laws of nature from supernatural finalities. It was clear that the inevitable result of the independence of society and its new, differentiated instances and fields of action, and the emergence of new classes of cultural actors freed cognitively from conditions imposed by religious institutions, would be exposure of this older cognitive system to questioning and doubt, in intellectual, cultural, as well as symbolic terms. It was only a matter of time before questioning was to reach the premises of religious doctrine. The cautious and outwardly pious Descartes was a sceptic in spite of himself.[53] His philosophical project in its broadest terms provided parameters for the beginning of critical scrutiny of the Bible. But there is no doubt that the founder of historical criticism as a motif of broader reach than that of specialised work was Spinoza in his historical study of the Old Testament, inasmuch

51 Dumont, *From Mandeville to Marx*, 5–7, 35–36, and passim. See also Karl Polanyi, *The Great Transformation* (Boston: Beacon Press, 1957).

52 Andrejz Rapaczynski, *Nature and Politics: Liberalism in the Philosophies of Hobbes, Locke and Rousseau* (Ithaca: Cornell University Press, 1979), 219–221, 263–291.

53 Richard Popkin, *A History of Scepticism from Erasmus to Spinoza* (Berkeley and Los Angeles: University of California Press, 1979), 193 ff.

as he showed that this text does not contain intellectual matter subject to criteria of veracity or rejection, but consists of a mythical discourse of morals and virtue.[54] Spinoza emblematised the broader implications of philological research, which was historical and linguistic in character, and distinguished between "the truth" as religion and religious traditions perceived it, and the historical meaning of the text and its content as revealed by factual evidence.[55] Attention was turned to the possibilities afforded by philological research. The Jesuit Richard Simon in the last quarter of the seventeenth century carried out a critical study of the Old Testament and demonstrated the incoherence of the text. He was met with a religious reaction of such violence that it ended research in this subject in France until the middle of the nineteenth century. Protestant researchers resumed research, influenced by German Protestant Higher Criticism of the Bible.[56]

But the rise of the historicist spirit in the nineteenth century liberated reason and enabled it to study the foundations of sacred books, all of which, it emerged, had editors, histories of composition and textual layers of different origins, linked to the events of their times and the myths of those periods, rather than being linked to absolute truths as religious institutions would claim.[57] Perhaps the most significant indication of the atrophy of religion as the ultimate authority is the perception that scientific research into religious texts came from within the religious institution itself. This was especially true with the beginning of historical research on the life of Christ by the Protestant theologian David Friedrich Strauss (1808–1874), and with Feuerbach's (1804–1872) subversive philosophical transcendence of Christian doctrine and religion generally, outlined in his *Essence of Christianity* (1841).

54 Ibid., 230–239. See also Spinoza, *Theological-Political Treatise*, ed. Jonathan Israel (Cambridge: Cambridge University Press, 2007). See *Spinoza's Theological-Political Treatise: A Critical Guide*, eds Yitzhak Malamed and Michael A. Rosenthal (Cambridge: Cambridge University Press, 2010) and Steven Nadler, *A Book Forged in Hell: Spinoza's Scandalous Treatise and the Birth of the Secular* (Princeton: Princeton University Press, 2011).

55 See especially the observations of Tzvetan Todorov, *Symbolism and Interpretation* (London: Routledge & Kegan Paul, 1983), 128–142.

56 Hans Frei, *The Eclipse of Biblical Narrative* (New Haven: Yale University Press, 1980); Paul Hazard, *The European Mind, 1680–1715* (Harmondsworth: Penguin Books, 1964), ch. 3; Philip Spencer, *The Politics of Belief in the 19th Century France* (London: Faber and Faber, 1954), 178–179; W. J. S. Sparrow, *Religious Thought in France in the Nineteenth Century* (London: George Allen and Unwin, 1935), 29–88; and Popkin, *A History of Scepticism from Erasmus to Spinoza*, 236–237.

57 See the analysis in Arabic by Ḥasan Ḥanafī, "Qirā'at al-naṣṣ", in Ḥasan Ḥanafī, *Dirasāt falsafiyya* (Cairo: Maktabat al-Anglo-Miṣriyya, 1988), 523–549.

Feuerbach had had a religious education and was influenced by Hegelian historicism.[58] In the twentieth century, such historical criticism as practised by Rudolf Bultmann (1884–1976), for instance, resulted in the stripping away of myth from the text whose contents were seen as being insulated from history, as moral and affective doctrinal beliefs operating symbolically with no relation to any reality other than that of the mythical imagination prevailing when scripture was generated. That was naturally linked to the fading away of religious authority if projected against modern scientific knowledge, long after the origins of humans in history were revealed to reside in a lower rung of the ladder of evolution.

The origins of humans on the ladder of animal evolution began from primitive creatures that evolved into different species, leading to primates from which humans were descended. Marx discovered, in parallel and on the basis of the historicity of humans and of their relations of power and production, that historical forms have bases in the economy and in the relations of social forces. One could say that, on the basis of these new developments in human history, while nations and civilisations had claimed descent from heroes or prophets or gods, modern civilisation is the only one that claimed that its present is superior to its beginnings, beginnings marked by bestiality and savagery.[59] These strands of thought combined into a trend with others that were to varying degrees complementary or contradictory in relation to them. These included the current of declarative and satirical atheism represented in the eighteenth century by the materialist d'Holbach (1723–1789) and the current of natural religion that has been mentioned before and that, in its more daring redactions, considered the revealed religions and their scriptures as fairy tales based on idolatry.[60] These currents led to religion being assigned by important and central elements in the new intellectual classes the status of a marginal culture, associated with certain social groups

58 See John Edward Toews, *Hegelianism: The Path towards Dialectical Humanism 1805–1841* (Cambridge: Cambridge University Press, 1980), 165–199. See too Ḥasan Ḥanafī, "Al-ightirāb al-dīnī 'inda Fuyirbāch", in Ḥanafī, *Dirasāt falsafiyya*, 400–445.

59 Compare the observations around the concept of nature in liberal thought in Marshall Sahlins, *Culture and Practical Reason* (Chicago: University of Chicago Press, 1976), 52–53.

60 Perhaps the best and most eloquent and elevated expression regarding this question is, as usual, that of Kant: Immanuel Kant, *Religion Within the Limits of Reasons Alone,* trans J. M. Green (Chicago: n.p., 1934), 142–143, 166–167.

or with a history on the wane, a culture that, although it might have breadth, has little authoritativeness left.

The convergence of these trends was not isolated from a set of more important connections that determined the course of European history, as it became the hub of global history in the nineteenth century. Marx expressed these connections in a famous text on the historically cumulative and complementary link between British political economy (civil society) and German philosophy (historicism and criticism of religion) and French politics (revolutionary democracy). These combined to orient European history in the direction of liberty based on violent popular and social revolutions (1789, 1830, 1848, 1870). France was in this process the pioneer in reconfiguring and clarifying the relation between the world and religion. Outside France the situation was less clear, characterised by objectively secular developments without this being integrated into anti-religious or anti-clerical turns of thought. Atheism in Germany, for example, was restricted to left-wing fringes and materialist positivist thinkers such as Feuerbach, Karl Vogt (1817–1895) and Jacob Maleschott (1822–1893), who sought to present arguments showing that science led necessarily to the rejection of religion, insisting on the eternal nature of matter and the absence of finality in nature.[61]

In Britain secularism was an intellectual school that arose from natural religion and was correlated with utilitarian and positivist philosophies that saw in the improvement of material life a sufficient condition for human happiness.[62] In both cases secular proposals were met with a certain degree of institutional resistance, without bloodshed:[63] the last execution for blasphemy in Britain took place in Edinburgh in 1697.[64] Both the production of knowledge and public life in Britain and Germany had, however, embarked upon a direction independent of religion, despite the insistence of many

61 Chadwick, *The Secularization of the European Mind in the Nineteenth Century*, 165–172. See Frederick Gregory, *Scientific Materialism in Nineteenth Century Germany* (Dordrecht: D. Reidel, 1977).

62 Eric Waterhouse, "Secularism", in *Encyclopædia of Religion and Ethics*, 13 vols (Edinburgh: T. and T. Clark, 1920), vol. 11, 348.

63 Nicolas Walter, *Blasphemy Ancient and Modern* (London: Rationalist Press Association, 1990), 44–55.

64 Ibid., 26. See now Michael F. Graham, *The Blasphemies of Thomas Aikenhead* (Edinburgh: Edinburgh University Press, 2008).

politicians (as also happens in Arab countries) that Christianity is a basic element of the law. It is noteworthy that, in England, such statements emanated from laypeople with the parliamentary power to determine the official creed and having the prerogative of rejecting decisions taken by councils and organs of the Church. There were no serious clashes and indeed the history of Darwinism shows that this scientific doctrine's effects on religion were absorbed by the religious establishment through engagement with some of its basic themes after a period of virulent resistance, thereby adapting to the spirit of the time and engaging with what was and was no longer held to be acceptable by prevalent culture.[65]

In France the conflict was more intense and the Church was under pressure from the state, even before the Revolution, when the state sought twice (and failed) in the eighteenth century to tax Church property, and expelled the Jesuits from the realm in 1762 because of their ultramontane position that spiritual authority had primacy over temporal authority, thereby emphasising the authority of the Pope at the expense of the authority of the king. The state replaced clerics with lay teachers in the educational establishments previously run by the Jesuits. The state had also lifted the proscriptions against Protestants that had deprived them of political and general civil rights until 1787, when the state recognised the principle of religious tolerance.[66] That principle was not recognised in Britain with regard to Catholics before 1829, Jews in 1842, and the irreligious in 1888.

In France the state had legislated in 1757 for the death penalty for anyone expressing an anti-religious opinion, a law that had remained without practical effect[67] – note that this was state law, not a Church judgment. With the French Revolution and the seizure of Church property and the institution of a civil law that also governed the clergy, Robespierre initiated a cult of reason and the worship of the Supreme Being, and made the Cathedral of Notre Dame in Paris its temple. The Revolution inaugurated many secular forms of social and political ritual in which Rousseau located the base of society, forms of which continued to develop with Auguste

65 James R. Moore, *The Post-Darwinian Controversies: A Study of the Protestant Struggle to Come to Terms with Darwin in Great Britain and America, 1870–1900* (Cambridge: Cambridge University Press, 1979), chs 9–12.

66 Palmer, *Catholics and Unbelievers in Eighteenth-Century France*, 9–10.

67 Ibid., 17.

Comte and the Saint-Simonians.[68] Napoleon came to a concordat with the Church, granting it reparations for some of the losses incurred in the secularisation and nationalisation of Church properties. The nineteenth century was marked throughout by a bitter struggle between Church and state as the Church sought to recover the material, ideological, and moral position it had previously held, especially its monopoly of the education system and marriage, which Napoleon had made a civil institution.[69] The Church succeeded, for instance, in lobbying to prevent the nomination of Ernest Renan to the Collège de France in 1862 because of his denial of the divinity of Jesus in his historical-critical biography of Jesus (1863). The work of Renan was in fact the point on which the Church's efforts had concentrated in constructing defensive positions to which believers could adhere. The Church was active on many fronts to save its doctrine and its connection with the natural sciences, seen by French positivism as the intellectual Achilles heel of religion.[70]

The success of the Church remained dependent on political conditions and the link between the French state and Rome in the context of relations within the concert of the European powers, as well as the political formation of the state. The French bourgeoisie hesitated in its attitude to the Church. Prior to 1848 much of it was firmly opposed to the Church although French society had been cleft, with the emergence of a religious and monarchist tendency with an Ultramontane orientation, supporting the Papacy and its primacy over the Gallican (national) Church founded in 1682 and a rival secular current. This assumed its fullest form in the 1870 Paris Commune that, accompanied by a massacre of the clergy, abolished financial support for the Church and separated it from the state.

This bitter enmity was not surprising. Catholicism represented one aspect of the attempted intervention of European powers against revolutionary France and also sponsored rural monarchist movements of extreme reactionary character. Catholicism adopted a position of almost complete support of

68 Donald Geoffrey Charlton, *Secular Religions in France, 1815–1870* (London and New York: Oxford University Press, 1963), 4–6.

69 On this important question see Roger Henry Soltau, *French Political Thought in the 19th Century* (New York: Russell and Russell, 1959), 66–78, 170–171.

70 G. K. Malone, "Apologetics", in *New Catholic Encyclopedia*, vol. 1, 671, 669–677, and S. A. Metczek, "Fideism", in *New Catholic Encyclopedia*, vol. 5, 908–909.

the Papacy, especially during the tenure of Pope Pius IX mentioned earlier, who led an ideological and political campaign of determined hostility to science, liberal ideologies, secularism, and nationalism. He declared his independence and opposed attempts to unify Italy and Germany and emphasised the Church's political primacy, its fundamental political role, and its cultural and normative primacy. This led to the emergence of an ideological, national-Catholic, and monarchical political tradition that has marked important trends of the French Right up until the present day.[71]

The Church adopted an official position of opposition to major tendencies of thought central to the nineteenth century, characterised by political liberalism, and the theory of social evolution that saw the course of history as a progress from initially primitive to civilised and evolved forms. Central lines of thought in this century regarded religion characteristic of periods preceding modernity and rationality, periods enthralled to supernatural and other irrational beliefs, rather than to rationality. The persistence of the Church in the nineteenth century in trying to roll back that century, in retreat from and in opposition to historical reality, led to the ferocious anti-clericalism of the Paris Commune, to the decisive institutionalisation of secular education by the Minister of Education Jules Ferry from 1882 to 1886, and finally the official complete separation between Church and state in the law of 9 December 1905, with the Church considered a private association. Clearly the history summarised here unfolded in a very complex web of relations and political, social, and intellectual clashes resulting from conflict, negotiations, compromise, and bargaining around myriad matters of detail.[72] Only in 1946 was there a textual stipulation of secularism in the French constitution, after a brief period when, under the Vichy regime, reference to Christianity was reintroduced into school curricula.

Only in the Soviet Union was the French Jacobin example pursued to its full implication. Marxism took the evolutionary view of history to its fullest extent, blending historical determinism and Jacobin politics in changing society from backwardness to progressive modernity. The Soviet Union

71 With regard to this dense and rich history see Soltau, *French Political Thought*, 176–188, and Spencer, *The Politics of Belief in the 19th Century France*, 21–28, 83, 145–146, 192–195, 237–239.

72 See the discussion of this in Theodore Zeldin, *France 1848–1945: Politics and Anger* (Oxford: Oxford University Press, 1979), 324–334. See Jean Baubérot, *Histoire de la laicité en France*, 4th edn (Paris: Presses Universitaires de France, 2007).

proclaimed itself an atheist state, and pursued an aggressive atheism in social, cultural, and educational terms. It also used social engineering to strike at the key social links that assured religious authority in Russia and adjoining territories, being the Church and aristocracy. In the Muslim-majority republics, in addition to the Muslim clergy, these key elements were the social structures preserving the traditional position of women and their subaltern status. The Soviets treated women there as a "surrogate proletariat",[73] a social fulcrum.

Elsewhere in Europe the French condition of secularisation became effective in practice without its secularist ideological impulses.[74] In united Germany today, the Church is a private entity like other associations, one to which individuals belong and express their adhesion by paying taxes destined to it, as though they were membership subscriptions – collected and disbursed by the state. Other citizens express their separation from the Church by choosing to withhold taxes. Britain is in real terms a thoroughly secularised country, albeit formally presided over by monarchs who are also heads of the state Church.[75] France and the Soviet Union were distinguished from other historical itineraries in the intensity of the confrontation and its bitterness. In France, the displacement of religion as a fundamental point of reference for history and public life in general was officially proclaimed, its place taken by the republicanist legacy of the French Revolution.

Secularism is clearly neither univocal nor simple or uniform, and allows for no summary description. It involves a number of historical, political, social, cultural, intellectual, cognitive, and ideological transformations, and is part of a broader context of distinction and opposition between religion and world, arising from the differentiation of societal functions arising in modernity. Secularism is an objective social and political process that is multi-faceted and is not a ready-made formula that can be applied, rejected, or spoilt. Cognitively, secularism entails the refusal of explanations that transcend natural or historical phenomena and determinedly affirms change

73 G. J. Masell, *The Surrogate Proletariat. Moslem Women and Revolutionary Strategies in Soviet Central Asia, 1919–1929* (Princeton: Princeton University Press, 1974).

74 See Hugh McLeod, *Secularisation in Western Europe, 1848–1914* (London: Palgrave Macmillan, 2000).

75 See Callum G. Brown, *The Death of Christian Britain: Understanding Secularisation, 1800–2000* (London: Routledge, 2000).

within history. Institutionally, secularism sees religious institutions as voluntary organisations not unlike clubs and other assemblies, and, in political terms, it sees religion as distinct from the state. In terms of morals and values, secularism links morals to social realities, and moral restraint with the individual conscience, rather than with compulsion and fear induced by fear of punishment in this world or the next. All these dimensions of secularism had different forms and were related to the wider historical realities. Secularism is therefore never complete and fully accomplished. It consists of forms and pathways dependent on context. Secularism has a real history and is not ideological histories describing contests between knights and demons. Can the histories of Islam and Muslims evade history, complexity, multiplicity, inner distinctions, and differentiation?

3 Islam and the World

The general parameters of analysis valid for the histories sometimes known as "Christian history" discussed in the previous paragraphs apply to so-called Islamic histories. These include alertness to real change and transformation, and the link between scriptures – the Gospels in Christianity and the Qur'an for Islam – and history: a link in which history does not perform the text, and pass or fail in doing so, but one in which it is rather historical reality that imposes meanings on the text, through a process of interpretation that redacts the relationship as if it were one in which the text determines reality. No text is pristine and unsoiled by history and immune at any point to the attribution of sense that it cannot convey by itself; a text has readers and receivers, without which it is empty. The original meanings of scripture are accessible only to precise philological research once the veil of doctrine is lifted from readers' eyes and once they shake off its claims. Historical mastery of scriptural texts is only one of the necessary requirements of the approach to history adopted here, requiring that one not be complicit with the text as a doctrinal document. When scripture is situated in actual history, the attractions and ease of anachronism, which cause many to suppose that original scripture may be given meanings that are possible only in later historical periods, are mitigated by historical reason.

This chapter will therefore not discuss Qur'anic verses connected with matters relevant to power and government. Islamist politics derived indications of legitimacy from these verses, which were quoted plentifully. But neither politics nor a social model can be derived from scriptural verses. Qur'anic enunciations can be read to sustain diverse and contradictory positions. More than ninety years ago 'Ali 'Abd al-Raziq (1888–1966) presented conclusive textual demonstration that there is in the Qur'an no clear political model, even if his arguments can be complemented with additional material, and despite the circumstances of his famous book's composition and the doctrinal considerations that he adopted in forming his view of early Islamic history.[76]

Therefore, this present discussion of Islamic government will be directed towards the realities of historical practice without entering the confusion and cross-purposes mentioned by a leading Islamic thinker:

> What usually happens when reading about old customs or the laws of past generations is that each faction chooses part of the events of the past, its legacy, and its precedents which supports the faction's own views or at least deduces from those events the proof which confirms their aims. Thus present-day commentators judge others as departing from the traditions, customs, practices and ways of the preceding generations.[77]

The focus will not be on early history that includes the Qur'an and Paleo-Muslim history, later mythologised and patterned, but rather on actual history; there is no question here, as is often the case, of taking the Qur'anic beginnings for an imaginary history of an ideal Islam that never existed. Beginnings are less interesting than the unfolding of actual historical events, and outcomes are certainly not inherent in beginnings, neither can beginnings be understood from outcomes.

---

76 'Ali 'Abd al-Raziq, *Al-islām wa uṣūl al-ḥukm, baḥth fī al-khilāfa wa al-ḥukūma fī al-islām*, 2nd edn (Cairo: Maṭba'at Miṣr, 1965), 14–17, 71–73, translated into English by M. Loutfi as Ali Abdel Razek, *Islam and the Foundations of Political Power*, ed. A. Filali-Ansary (Edinburgh: Edinburgh University Press in association with the Aga Khan University Institute for the Study of Muslim Civilisations, 2012). Compare the observations of Kamāl 'Abd al-Laṭīf, *Al-ta'wīl wa al-mufāraqa: Naḥwa ta'wīl falsafī li'l-naẓar al-siyāsī al-'arabī* (Casablanca: al-Markaz al-Thaqāfī al-'Arabī, 1987), 88–89. See now Aziz al-Azmeh ['Azīz al-'Aẓma], "Islamic political thought: Current historiography and the framework of history", in *The Times of History: Universal Topics in Islamic Historiography* (New York and Budapest: Central European University Press, 2007), ch. 7.

77 Ṭāriq al-Bishrī, *Al-muslimūn wa al-aqbāṭ fī iṭār al-jamā'a al-waṭaniyya* (Beirut: Dār al-Waḥda, 1982), 88–89.

In his narration of events of the year 369/979–980, Abu al-Faraj ibn al-Jawzi related the following account of the relations between the mighty Buyid prince, overlord of Baghdad, and the 'Abbasid caliph al-Ta'i':

> 'Adud al-Dawla asked al-Ta'i' on his second arrival to Baghdad that he add *tāj al-millah* [Crown of the Community] to his honorific title and repeat his grant of robes of honour, to crown him and adorn him with finery studded with jewels. Al-Ta'i' acceded to his request. Al-Ta'i' sat on the dais of the Caliphate in the al-Salam courtyard. Around him were his personal retainers to the number of one hundred, with waistbands and swords and embellished clothes. Before the Caliph's stood the *muṣhaf* of 'Uthman and a screen sent by 'Adud al-Dawla which he requested should be placed so as to conceal Al-Ta'i from view, so none of the soldiery would see al-Ta'i before he did. The Turks and the Daylamites entered, none bearing swords. The nobles and officials stood on either side. As 'Adud al-Dawla arrived, al-Ta'i was informed and he gave permission for him to enter, whereupon he entered. The order was given that the screen be lifted. 'Adud al-Dawla was told: "he has caught sight of you," whereupon 'Adud al-Dawla kissed the ground which none of his companions did, submitting his neck to the Caliph. One of [his] commanders, Ziyad, was alarmed at what he saw, and said to him in Persian: "What is this, O king, is this Almighty God?" 'Adud al-Dawla turned to Abu al-Qasim 'Abd al-'Aziz b. Yusuf and said: "make him understand and tell him that this is the Caliph of God on earth." Then 'Adud al-Dawla continued advancing and kissed the ground nine times as he did so. al-Ta'i' turned to Khalis his steward and said to him: "Bring him closer." 'Adud al-Dawla rose up and kissed the ground twice and al-Ta'i' said to him: "Approach me." He approached and knelt and kissed the Caliph's foot, and the Caliph placed his right hand on him. His seat stood in front of him, on the right side of the Caliph's, and 'Adud al-Dawla did not sit down. The Caliph said to him again "Sit down." He nodded but did not sit down. Al-Ta'i' said to him "I swear that you shall sit down," whereupon he kissed the seat and sat down . . . then al-Ta'i' said "I have seen fit that I shall delegate to you the affairs of the subjects which Almighty God has put in my charge, in east and west, and administration in all regions, except for my entourage and

> my wealth and what is behind my door. So take possession of this, asking God for guidance." 'Adud al-Dawla said to him: "Almighty God will help me to obey our master and serve him and I wish . . . that the chief commanders who entered with me should hear the word of the Prince of the Believers." Al-Ta'i' repeated the delegation of authority to 'Adud al-Dawla and his reliance on him.[78]

It is clear from this remarkable text that the relationship between the caliph and the princes was not as simple as many imagine it to have been. It is undoubtedly the case that 'Adud al-Dawla was in fact the caliph's benefactor, but he nevertheless chose to abase himself publicly and kiss the ground before him and kiss his foot, without regard to the actual balance of forces between them. The caliph returned to this fact when he delegated to 'Adud al-Dawla "the affairs of the subjects which Almighty God has put in my charge, in east and west, and administration in all regions, except for my entourage and my wealth and what is behind my door". 'Adud al-Dawla also wanted the formula of delegation to be pronounced openly in hearing of court officials and the military. The effective delegation by the caliphs, through the order that caliphs issued to those given control over their lands directly, came to constitute law according to the principle of legitimation of usurpation elaborated by al-Mawardi (975–1058) and Abu Ya'la Ibn al-Farra', contemporary of al-Mawardi and one of the leading Hanbalites of his time. But this delegation was not confined to usurpers. Abbasid caliphs delegated authority in Sijistan and India and Khurasan to Mahmoud of Ghazni and to Saladin and his successors in Egypt, Syria, and Yemen and all territory they conquered by the sword.[79] At the time of the Mamluks the Abbasid caliphs delegated power to the sultan and transferred authority to him, repeating the following formula: "I have delegated to you all affairs of the Muslims and I entrust

78 Abū al-Faraj 'Abd al-Raḥmān ibn 'Alī ibn al-Jawzī, *Al-muntaẓam fī tarīkh al-mulūk wa al-umam*, ed. F. Krenkow, 10 vols (Hyderabad: Dā'irat al-Ma'ārif al-'Uthmāniyya, 1357–1358/1938–1939), vol. 7, 98–99.

79 Taqī al-Dīn Abū al-'Abbās Aḥmad ibn 'Alī al-Maqrīzī, *Al-sulūk li ma'rifat duwal al-mulūk*, eds Muḥammad Muṣṭafā Ziyāda and Sa'īd 'Abd al-Fattāḥ 'Āshūr, 3 vols (Cairo: Dār al-Kutub al-Miṣrīya, 1956–1971), vol. 1, 60, 242, 247, 268. For this theme, and for other aspects of the Caliphate and for Muslim political conceptions and practices, see now Al-Azmeh, *Muslim Kingship*, 170–177.

to you all my prerogatives in the affairs of religion." Then the sultan would order the authorities to pronounce the Friday sermon in the name of the caliph and would send him a thousand dinars and the Alexandrian fabrics.[80]

The caliphs were sovereign, although one cannot claim this for all after al-Mu'tasim. The caliphate was after that period a multiplicity of shifting elements in which some caliphs secured measures of autonomy and sovereignty by playing on the antagonisms between competing outside forces. It is true that the Mamluk sultan Abu Sa'id Barquq, for example, had the title "Guardian of the Prince of the believers" because one base for Mamluk authority was dominance of the caliphate.[81] This was not a detraction from the authority of the caliphate. "If a rule is undermined, this rule itself is not thereby invalidated" according to the expression of al-Mawardi.[82] The rule required preserving the imamate in terms of the caliphate, and the preservation of the Shar'ist order. This was what led, as Abu Ya'la Ibn al-Farra' rightly saw, to the necessity of delegating authority to newly emergent powers, this delegation being the "manifestation of obedience which brings about the disappearance of obstinacy and of the vice of contradiction".[83]

While new powers could act without reference to the caliph, this did not prevent them from having recourse to the institution of the powerless caliphate to confirm their authority, adopting the caliph's sovereignty. This means that, in historical terms, caliphal office can be held and maintained with or without executive authority. The caliphate is an office that can be temporal, entailing military command and control over subjects and their fortunes. It can have a juridical character and may combine the executive and juridical dimensions together. In any case the legal status of the caliphal office is enduring while its political dimension has been transient, the office

80 Abū al-'Abbās Aḥmad ibn Aḥmad al-Qalqashandī, *Ma'āthir ināfa fī ma'ālim al-khilāfa*, ed. 'Abd al-Sattār Aḥmad Farrāj, 14 vols (Kuwait: al-Majlis al-Waṭanī li'l-Thaqāfa wa al-Funūn wa al-ādāb, 1964), vol. 2, 241–244.

81 Ibn Khaldūn, *Al-ta'rīf bi Ibn Khaldūn wa riḥlatuhu gharban wa sharqan*, ed. and annotated by Muhammad ibn Tāwīt al-Ṭanjī (Cairo: Lajnat al-Ta'līf wa al-Tarjama wa al-Nashr, 1951), 283, 296. See also Ibn Khaldūn, *Prologomènes d'Ebn Khaldoun*, texte arabe d'après les manuscrits de la bibliothèque impériale, ed. M. Quatremère, 3 vols (Paris: Institut impérial de France, 1858), vol. 1, 3.

82 Abū al-Ḥasan 'Alī ibn Muḥammad al-Māwardī, *Al-aḥkām as-sulṭāniyya wa al-wilāyāt al-dīniyya*, 3rd edn (Cairo: Maktabat wa Maṭba'at al-Bābī al-Ḥalabī, 1973), 258–259.

83 Muḥammad ibn al-Ḥusayn ibn Muḥammad ibn Khalaf Abū Ya'lā ibn al-Farrā', *Al-aḥkām al-sulṭāniyya*, ed. Muḥammad Ḥāmid al-Fīqī, 2nd edn (Cairo: Maktabat wa Maṭba'at Muṣṭafā al-Bābī al-Ḥalabī wa Awlāduhu, 1966), 37–38.

being greater than the man who occupies it. This political function can cease to exist with its delegation to a new potentate who exercises it in the name of the caliph and in the name of the possession by the potentate of political power formerly attributed to the caliph, now stripped of authority. The potentate, with the capacity to act, does so as the agent of the caliph, who is unable to act. The reason for delegation is held to derive from incapacity, which nevertheless legally confers political power on another agent. Juridical capacity confers legality on the person holding power.

What was this capacity from which overpowering potentates derived their power? It was doubtless a single authority in which the caliph and the potentate participated. Delegation does not convey the idea of differentiation between legal and political authority or between a legislative and an executive structure. Sovereignty is like God, singular and indivisible, as the word sultan, according to one of its clearest and most eloquent theoreticians, means both capacity and the ultimate point of appeal. This scholar uses a familiar scholastic justification for the one-ness of God used by Arab political writing to demonstrate by analogy the one-ness of power. This theoretician inverses the analogy and instead of demonstrating the one-ness of power through the one-ness of God, he demonstrates the unicity of God Himself by analogy with the indivisibility of temporal power.[84] The uninterrupted link from God to holders of power has its structural equivalent in the pyramidal structure leading from the caliph to his subordinates. On that basis the holder of royal or princely power relates to God as his subordinates relate to him, as the ruler acts according to God's law and therefore by divine delegation, and subordinates act by delegation from the caliph.[85]

There is a continuum of authority around which the delegation of power is articulated, without there being any generic differences of nature in authority in every one of its stations. The axis of Arabo-Islamic discussion has revolved

84 Abū 'Abd Allāh Muḥammad ibn Ibrāhīm ibn Jamā'a, *Taḥrir al-aḥkām fi tadbīr ahl al-islām*, ed. Hans Kofler, in *Islamica* 6 (1934): 364–365. With regard to the argument used by Ibn Jamā'a, see, for example, Abū al-Ḥasan 'Alī Ibn Ismā'īl al-Ash'arī, *Kitāb al-luma' fi al-radd 'alā ahl al-zīgh wa al-bida'*, ed. Ḥammūda Gharāba (Cairo: Matba't Miṣr, 1955), 20–51; Muḥammad ibn Muḥammad ibn Maḥmūd Abū Manṣūr al-Māturīdī, *Kitāb al-tawḥīd*, ed. Fatḥ Allāh Khulayf (Beirut: Dār al-Mashriq, 1970), 20; Ibn Rushd, *Al-muqaddimāt al-mumahhidāt li bayān ma iqtaḍathu rusūm al-mudawanna min al-aḥkām al-shar'iyyāt wa al-taḥṣīlāt al-muḥkamāt al-shar'iyyāt li ummahāt masā'il al-mushkilāt* (Cairo: n.p., n.d.), 8.

85 Ibn Jamā'a, *Taḥrir al-aḥkām fi tadbīr ahl al-islām*, 363.

around the source of power from which it emerges. This source is an absolute authority that imposes its demands and infuses them with its charisma in a descending series of posts and offices whose only specificity from the point of view of the hierarchical authority is that they are appended to this supreme authority. This authority is connected to its societal material of subjects only by hierarchy, by superordination in which authority is the sole decisive element, precluding any notion of reciprocity.[86] One encounters the common people in Arab political discourse only in so far as they are the object of this one superordinate sultanic subject. Mention or discussion of the common people is almost invariably negative in tone; it has no specific consistency, its sole capacity being to obey.[87] This hierarchical system is abstract and based exclusively on distanciation. Society, the body of power, is merely elemental stuff that acquires quality only as material for control and restraint, the inchoate for action by power.[88] The state is merely the temporal itinerary of the power exercised by the historical element that is the absolute ruler.[89]

God, we are told, only called the ruler a king (*malik*) because he called himself king, and the relation of authority is no other than the relation between the stations of the ruler and the ruled connected by obedience.[90] The hierarchy, from its most sublime point represented by God and the ruler, to its lowliest echelon represented by the populace, is an absolute hierarchy in which the only positive instance is the apex. The only positive element is the active agent, endowing form to lower being. Power is therefore related to society as the spirit is to the body, and order exists only with a superordinate authority working to bring form to human assembly.[91] This is a notion of

86 Compare ʿAzīz al-ʿAẓma [Aziz al-Azmeh], "Al-siyāsa wa al-lāsiyāsa fī al fikr al-ʿarabī al-islāmī", in *Al-turāth bayn al-ṣulṭān wa al-tarīkh* (Beirut: Dār al-Ṭalīʿa, and Casablanca: Manshūrāt ʿUyūn, 1986/1990), 46–47. See now al-Azmeh, *Muslim Kingship*, chs 6 and 7.

87 ʿIzz al-Dīn al-ʿAllām, "Mafhūm al-ḥāshiya fī al-adab al-siyāsī al-sulṭānī", *Abhāth* (Rabat) 4/13 (1986): 101.

88 Waḍḍāḥ Sharāra, "Al-malik, al-ʿāmma, al-ṭabīʿa, al-mawt", *Dirasāt ʿArabiyya* 16/12 (1980): 19–46. See Al-Azmeh, *Muslim Kingship*, ch. 6.

89 Aziz al-Azmeh, *Ibn Khaldun: An Essay in Reinterpretation* (New York and Budapest: Central European University Press, 2003), 26–7.

90 Abū al-Faraj ʿAbd al-Raḥmān ibn ʿAlī ibn al-Jawzī, *Al-miṣbāḥ al-muḍī' fī khilāfat al-musṭaḍī'*, ed. Nājia ʿAbd Allah Ibrāhīm, Silsilat kutub al-turāth 19, 2 vols (Baghdad: Wizārat al-Awqāf, 1976), vol. 1, 143.

91 Abū Bakr Muḥammad ibn Walīd al-Ṭurṭūshī, *Sirāj al-mulūk* (Cairo: n.p., 1319/1901), 34, 39. See also Abū Hāmid ibn Muḥammad al-Ghazālī, *Mīzān al-ʿamal*, ed. and intro. Sulaymān Duyā, Dhakhā'ir al-ʿArab 38 (Cairo: Dār al-Maʿārif, 1964), 235–236.

power as an expression of categorical separation and compulsion, as a structure that creates society just as the power of God creates the orderly cosmos and humanity. It combines the different genres of writing power in classical Arab and Muslim traditions: works of *ahkām al-ṣultaniyya* (jurisprudence of public authority), works of Shar'ist politics (*siyāsa shar'iyya*), and books of advice to princes.

This political theology is complemented by a hierarchical understanding of the cosmos and a metaphysical assumption that all composition, natural or human, is induced by compulsion. This is one of the metaphysical foundations and structural features of Arabo-Islamic thought and episteme more broadly conceived, which, regrettably, cannot be explored. Thus, to Ibn Khaldun, for instance, the body-social is attained only by internalised sanction. Only through an all-powerful ruler can any social structure be constructed and its stability preserved, according to all Islamic thinkers almost without exception; a body is unsound without a head and for that reason it was often repeated that the "sultan is the shadow of God on earth".[92] Thus, revolt against the sultan is unconscionable unless he were to depart from Islam. In this respect the statement attributed to Ahmad ibn Hanbal is the most eloquent in this regard: "Hearing and obeying are due to the Prince of the Believers and the imams, the virtuous and the wicked, and to whoever has assumed the Caliphate and secured consensus, and whoever attained the Caliphate by the sword and became Prince of the Believers."[93] And as the forging of individuals into sociality is only attainable by restraining authority, the social structure given form by the shari'a is only rendered complete through an all-embracing authority that renders the existence of this structure possible.

The two systems of authority, temporal and religious, are combined in the caliphate or in the authority delegated by the caliph. They are structurally equivalent and mutually serviceable, and can stand for each other. It is therefore unnecessary to distinguish generically between the caliphate and the sultanate as forms of rule and of statecraft in relation to the body-social; both are natural forms of authority, the difference between which is technical

92 Taqī al-Dīn Aḥmad ibn 'Abd al-Ḥalīm ibn Taymiyya, *Al-siyāsa al-shar'iyya fī iṣlaḥ ar-rā'ī wa al-ra'iyya* (Cairo: al-Maṭba'a al-Khayrīya, 1322/1904), 77–78.

93 Muḥammad ibn al-Ḥusayn ibn Muḥammad ibn Khalaf Abū Ya'lā ibn al-Farrā', *Tabaqāt al-ḥanābila*, ed. Muḥammad Ḥāmid al-Fīqī, 2 vols (Cairo: Maṭba'at al-Sunna al-Muḥammadiyya, al-Tafsīr al-'Ilmi, 1952), vol. 1, 26.

in the juristic sense and in historical manifestation. The first was based on the ancestral transmission of charisma linking it to both prophecy and nobility of descent, just as in the Shi'ite imamate. If anything, the Shi'ite imamate might be seen as historically – but not generically – distinct from the caliphate in that it accentuates the claims for absolutism by its emphasis on absence during the Occultation. The caliphate, like the sultanate and the imamate, is an absolute authority linked to its body (society) by a relation of vertical hierarchy and coercion. This is not unusual given the long heritage of absolute power in the Near East, which passed through Byzantine and Sassanid forms in addition to early influences from Southern Arabia that introduced a royalist and priestly heritage to early caliphal politics. This understanding of power and its exercise continued for as long as states thought themselves in terms of religion and of their history as Islamic history. These hierarchies were interconnected by the separation of orders attributed to particular categories of persons: differentiation in legal capacity (adult/minor/free/slave/man/woman/Muslim/*dhimmi*), as well as between professions, some territorially defined, distinguished between noble callings such as scholarship and trade, intermediary professions, and lowly activities such as dyeing and other trades, many marked by Sufi association, adherence to specific legal schools, and particular forms of group-specific dress and sociolects. The daily instruments of state power, such as ministers and chamberlains, were transient, exposed at every instant to confiscation and elimination by the prevailing and invariant structure, one that was based, inevitably, in Ibn Khaldun's expression, on the privatisation of power and glory, and on the correlation between wealth and rank.[94]

The caliphate's technical distinction mentioned already relates to the differing sources of charismatic energy conveyed by holders of this august office. Legal scholars disagreed about the permissibility of giving the caliph the title of "Caliph of God" and a great many refused this. The title preferred by many legal scholars was "Caliph of the Prophet of God", appointed to pursue the Prophet's mandate, exact divine rights, and defend the territory of Islam, but this did not mitigate but ran parallel to vicarage of God.[95] The juristic approach not unnaturally emphasised the legal status of the caliphate as formulated by scholars in the Abbasid period. They were neither historians

---

94 Al-Māwardī, *Al-Aḥkām al-sulṭāniyya wa al-wilāyāt al-dīniyya*, 15.

95 Al-Azmeh, *Muslim Kingship*, 74–77, 160–162, 203–205.

nor sociologists and, based largely on precedent but also on other forms of law making, they described and specified the way that the caliph exercised the power and prerogatives attributed to him by Muslim jurisprudence. The caliph was Muslim law's chief executive, and for this capacity it was held to be a requirement for office that the incumbent be knowledgeable to the degree required for holding a judgeship.

One clearly sees in the opening lines of Mawardi's famous legal treatise that he establishes the necessity of the caliphate by a traditionalist-jusristic argument as well as on one relating to the nature of kingship. The legalistic redaction of the caliphate is not sufficient to describe its powers. In addition to its foundations in human nature – namely the instruments and mechanisms of political power in terms of soldiers and officials, and the foundation of social power upon a Baghdadi aristocratic class – there were also popular imaginings of the caliphate of which jurists themselves partook. The caliph had a divine or spiritual breath infused into him, which could bring fortune and misfortune, and the robe of the caliph brought blessing on the person who touched it.[96] When Ibn al Jawzi mentioned that the justice of the caliph brought fertility to the earth, he did not mean, if we read the text carefully, a metaphorical declaration and an economic link between justice and the flourishing of agriculture, but intended a magical connection between them.[97]

This vision of power and its holders was not foreign to the heritage of the region. The relation between power and the gods had always been direct, although it bore a variety of forms and expressions. This had not been foreign to Europe either, where the power of curing scrofula by touch was attributed to the monarchs of France (less so in Britain) until the early nineteenth century.[98] It is only to be expected in a civilisation such as medieval Arabo-Islamic civilisation when the worlds of cognition and imagination were populated by supernatural and miraculous forces and beings, by jinns, demons, and auspicious and inauspicious stars and various forms of action at a distance as in magic. Caliphs and sultans employed astrologers who played a role analogous to today's think-tank consultants.

96 For example, Abū Ya'lā ibn al-Farrā', *Tabaqāt al-ḥanābila*, vol. 2, 340.

97 Ibn al-Jawzī, *Al-miṣbāḥ al-muḍī' fi khilāfat al-mustaḍī'*, vol. 1, 289–291.

98 Marc Bloch, *Les Rois thaumaturges: Étude sur le caractère surnaturel attribué à la puissance royale particulièrement en France et en Angleterre* (Paris: Armand Colin, 1961).

Stringently pietistic scholars represented only a highly placed yet thin sliver of society. That caliphs were God's caliphs is not a fact that is difficult to accept. What would seem odd is if this were not the case. There is no proof that the culture of the jurists and of other ulama dominated society.[99] As previously mentioned, 'Adud al-Dawla affirmed that the caliph al-Ta'i a was Caliph of God. We find this expression frequently in historical texts and throughout *One Thousand and One Nights* in addition to court poetry that gave the title Caliph of God and its associated meaning to the caliphs from an early period in the history of Islam.[100] This charismatic dimension took a highly specific and clear form at the beginning of the Abbasid regime, with echoes of an eschatological spiritual guide or Mahdi, then again with the caliph Al-Nasir li-Din Allah (r. 1180–1225) who combined the *futuwwa* young men's association with the aristocracy of Baghdad, thus making him, unusually for an Abbasid, a Baghdadi king, belonging to the social fabric of the city.[101]

Al-Nasir combined, in the words of his spiritual and ideological adviser Shihab al-Din Abu Hafs al-Suhrawardi in the book *'Adālat al-a'yān 'alā al-burhān*, the caliphate, *futuwwa*, and Sufism, making his charisma (*baraka*), his spirituality, and his link with divinity perceptible to his subjects, having incorporated Sufism and the hallowness associated with it.[102] It is noteworthy that Sufi sainthood was not alone in being capable of miracles. Historical sources are full of accounts of miracles performed by pietistic ulama, including Ahmad ibn Hanbal (780–855 CE) who seems to have felt constrained to deny that blessings could be had from touching his body.[103] He was nevertheless able to cure with water in which a hair of the Prophet had been dipped. He would mutter over water and then use it to cure the lame. His tomb

99 On the *ulama* much research has been done in recent years and the field is being transformed beyond the usual clichés. See, for instance, Muhammad Qasim Zaman, *Religion and Politics under the Early Abbasids* (Leiden: Brill, 1997) and Daphna Ephrat, *A Learned Society in a Period of Transition: The Sunni 'Ulama' of Eleventh-Century Baghdad* (Albany: State University of New York Press, 2000). See Al-Azmeh, "God's caravan".

100 Patricia Crone and Martin Hinds, *God's Caliph* (Cambridge: Cambridge University Press, 1986; Al-Azmeh, *Muslim Kingship*, 74–77, 160–162, 203–205.

101 Claude Cahen, "Notes sur le début de la futuwwa d'Al Nāṣir", *Oriens* 6 (1953): 18–23, 20, passim.

102 Angelika Hartmann, *An-Nasir li Din Allah, 1180–1225: Politik, Religion und Kultur in der späten Abbāsidenzeit,* Studien zur Geschichte und Kultur des Islamischen Orients, n.f., Bd; 8 (Berlin: Walter de Gruyter, 1975), 112–116 and 233 ff.

103 Abū Ya'lā ibn al-Farā', *Ṭabaqāt al-ḥanābila*, vol. 1, 228.

had a sweet fragrance. His drawers, the thread of which had snapped while he was being whipped during the *mihna* persecution initiated by the caliph al-Ma'mun (lasting from 833 to 851), were inexplicably restored and hid his nudity after he muttered something under his breath.[104] Others would heal the sick by reading the Qur'an and then spitting on the person requiring a cure (a very ancient remedy, practised also by Jesus and Muhammad); heads severed during the *mihna* were able to recite the Qur'an.[105]

It is clear that the religious aspect of the caliphate was complex and significant. Its magical inflection was sometimes linked to the millenarian charismatic movements to which Abbasid propaganda was not unrelated. This persisted in such movements as the Fatimids, the revolt of Ibn Qasi, based at Mertola in Algarve in 1144–1150, and the significant Mahdist dimension at the beginning of the Almohad state in the early twelfth century CE.[106] It is also true that this effectively magical charismatic dimension was transferred to the sultanate that was linked to religion, not through magic, but through the legal order, itself becoming infused with charisma. In reality this order linked the caliphate and overpowering otherwise independent sultanates. The caliphate was not pristine, according to Ibn Khaldun, except at the time of the Shar'ist caliphate of the first four successors to Muhammad (to which he added Mu'awiya), which was only of short duration.[107] It was confined to prophetic action and to matters of the hereafter, not to worldly kingship.[108]

---

104 Abū al-Faraj 'Abd al-Raḥman ibn 'Alī ibn al-Jawzī, *Manāqib al-imām Aḥmad ibn Ḥanbal* (Beirut: Dār al-Afāq al-Jadīda, 1973), 186–187, 483, 513.

105 Abū Ya'lā ibn al-Farrā', *Tabaqāt al-ḥanābila*, vol. 1, 81–82, and vol. 2, 256.

106 See with regard to this point Ibn Khaldūn, *Prologomènes d'Ebn Khaldoun*, vol. 2, 51 and Ibn Khaldūn, *Tārīkh al-'alāma Ibn Khaldūn*, ed. Yūsuf As'ad Dāghir, 15 vols (Beirut: n.p., 1956), vol. 2, 562 ff.; Aḥmad Ibn Ḥusayn ibn 'Alī ibn al-Khaṭīb, *Al-fārisiyya fi mabādī' al-dawla al-ḥafṣiyya*, eds Muḥammad al-Shādhlī Nayfar and 'Abd al-Majīd al-Turkī, Nafā'is al-makhṭuṭāt, al-Maktaba al-Tarīkhiyya 5 (Tunis: al-Dār al-Tunisiyya li'l-Nashr, 1968), 100–101; 'Abd al-Wāḥīd al-Marrākishī, *Al-mu'jib fi talkhīṣ akhbār al-Maghrib al-kitāb al-thālith*, ed. Muḥammad Sa'īd al-'Aryān (Cairo: Lajnat Iḥyā' al-Turāth al-Islāmī, 1963), 247, 500–506. See also Dominique Urvoy, "La Pensée d'Ibn Tumart", *Bulletin des études orientales* 27 (1974), 38–39; J. Dreher, "L'Imamat d'Ibn Qasi à Mertola (automne 1144–été 1145): Légitimité d'une domination soufie?", *Mélanges de l'Institut Dominicain d'Études Orientales* 18 (1988), 195–210, and D. R. Goodrich, *A Sufi Revolt in Portugal* (unpublished PhD thesis, Columbia University, 1978).

107 Ibn Khaldoun, *Prologomènes d'Ebn Khaldoun*, vol. 2, 249.

108 Muḥammad ibn 'Alī ibn Ṭabātabā ibn al-Ṭiqṭaqā, *Al-fakhrī fi al-ādāb al-sulṭāniyya wa al-duwal al-islāmiyya* (Cairo: n.p., 1926), 60.

Outside these exceptional circumstances, Muslim thinkers – practical men, jurists, rather than phantasiasts, for the most part – did not admit any pure form of justice and righteousness, but rather saw a state constituted legally, that is to say a natural state that took Muslim jurisprudence as its legal system.[109] The "perfect Caliphate" dispensing "pure justice" was a divine system, with precedents at the time of Adam, during some short prophetic periods culminating in Muhammad's prophecy. It would be re-enacted at the time of the appearance of the Mahdi, when the affairs of the world would return to their original condition according to a theology of history usually called salvation history, characteristic of monotheistic views of history.[110] While awaiting the End of Times the caliphate or rather the Muhammadan and Medinan models of exemplarity were in practical terms an unrepeatable golden age and a myth of beginnings in theoretical and legal terms, among others.[111] People living in later times of imperfection can only approximate what has been handed down insofar as circumstances allow. As in *imitatio christi* for pious Christians, the person and practice of the Prophet represented the ultimate, unattainable authority in terms of personal conduct. Recalling the Prophet's words and deeds brought prophetic blessings (public recitals from Bukhari and Muslim were and are occasionally still religious rites that solicit benedictions). There is no doubt that the transformations of the image of the Prophet in the heritage of the Salafiyya, especially by Ibn Taymiyya, bore very considerable influence of Shi'ite conceptions of the semi-divine infallible and impeccable imam, even if this attribution of influence was regarded with horror.[112]

---

109 'Abd Allāh al-'Arwī [Abdallah Laroui], *Mafhūm al-dawla* (Casablanca: al-Markaz al-Thaqāfī al-'Arabi, 1981), 123, and ch. 4.

110 For more details see 'Azīz al-'Aẓma, *Al-kitāba al-tārīkhiyya wa al-ma'rifa al-tārīkhiyya, muqadimma fī uṣūl ṣinā'at al-tārīkh al-'arabī* (Beirut: Dar et-Ṭalī'a, 1983), ch. 3. See now Aziz Al-Azmeh, *The Times of History: Universal Topics in Islamic Historiography* (New York and Budapest, Central European University Press, 2007), chs 1, 2 and 5 and Al-Azmeh, *Muslim Kingship*, 41–54.

111 al-'Arwī, *Mafhūm al-dawla*, 118 and ch. 4. See the detailed discussion of this point in Aziz al-Azmeh, "Utopia and the state in Islamic political thought", *History of Political Thought* 11 (1990): 9–20 – reprinted in al-Azmeh, *Islams and Modernities*. See now al-Azmeh, *Muslim Kingship*, 101–114.

112 Henri Laoust, *Essai sur les doctrines morales et politiques de Taki-d-Din Ahmad B. Taimiya* (Cairo: IFAO, 1939), 186–195.

It is certain that this change in the way of imagining the Prophet occurred at the same time as the beginning of the celebration of his birthday. This new feast was associated with the response in Baghdad to the celebration of 'Ashura under Buyid patronage, when the caliph al-Muti' (946–974) commanded his judge formally to pronounce the Prophetic *sunna* as a public example.[113] One should not forget in this regard the highly important role of Ali ibn Abi Talib and al-Husain ibn 'Ali in Sufi lineages as well as in the lineages of urban guilds and young men's associations (*fityan*, *futuwwa*), as well as the wide prevalence of non-Twelver Shi'ism (Ismaili, Nusayri, Druze) in major parts of Syria, including the city of Aleppo through Ayyubid and Mamluk times, and well into the Ottoman period.[114] It is not surprising that the Salafiyya sought to remake the image of the Prophet on the model of Ali and the rest of the Shia imams.

In the domain of legislation for everyday life, religious charisma flowed through sultanic rule in the medium of Shar'ist politics whose first theoretician was without doubt al-Mawardi (972–1058 CE) in his famous *Ordinances of Government*.[115] Religious communities are unlike schools of jurisprudence or types of polity, and prophecy is not just "one type of just policy instituted for the general benefit of the people in world". Such a view, according to Ibn Taymiyya, is idolatrous.[116] Religious communities, when a Prophet is absent, need a person who can lead them and can act within them as the analogue of the caliph, whether or not this person be a caliph in technical terms.[117] On this basis, the sultanate or a military-regional command can be regarded as "a statement of commitment or offering through which one approaches God".[118] For rulership was "one of the highest obligations of religion and indeed there is no religion without rulership", and one must throughout adhere completely to the content of revealed legislation to which

113 Ibn al-Jawzī, *Al-muntaẓam fi tarikh al-mulūk wa al-umam*, vol. 7, 65.

114 Muḥammad Jamāl Bārūt, *Al-Ṣirā' al-'Uthmānī-al-Ṣafawī wa āthāruhu al-shī'iya fī shamāl Bilād ash-Shām* (Doha: Arab Centre for Research and Policy Research, 2018), 1–46.

115 Henri Laoust, "La pensée et l'action politiques d'al-Mawardi", in idem, *Pluralismes dans l'Islam* (Paris: Geuthner, 1983), 192. See now al-Azmeh, *Muslim Kingship*, 163–188.

116 Taqī al-Dīn Aḥmad ibn 'Abd al-Ḥalīm ibn Taymiyya, *Minhāj al-sunna al-nabawiyya fī naqḍ kalām al-shī'a wa al-qadariyya*, 9 vols (Cairo: al-Maṭba'a al-Amīriyya, 1322/1904), vol. 1, 3.

117 Ibn Khaldoun, *Prologomènes d'Ebn Khaldoun*, vol. 1, 415.

118 Ibn Taymiyya, *Al-siyāsa al-shar'iyya fī iṣlaḥ ar-rā'ī wa al-ra'iyya*, 76–77.

nothing must be added or removed in the name of politics, shari'a being the consummate politics.[119] Shar'ist politics is not shari'a according to politics, but is an incontrovertible body of judgments on the basis of shari'a that does not admit departures in the name of politics or custom and usage.[120] Shar'ist politics in the writings of al-Mawardi and Ibn Taymiyya and others was a distillation of centuries of positive law and legal practice and of application by the ulama, the shari'a's guardians, who often exercised pressure on the state, sometimes successfully, to abolish illegal taxes, forbid drinking and prostitution, and reform the financial system in order to prevent interest-bearing loans and other matters.[121]

In the caliphate, shari'a and politics converged, along with charismatic and magical force. Some medieval Muslim thinkers, as previously noted, referred politics to shari'a and made politics an exercise of shari'a. Analogies between the political husbandry of subjects and the divine government of creation were often made, as already mentioned, and analogies whose middle terms were ideas of unilateral and unilineal hierarchy between gods, kings, and subjects were common. The Islamic attributes and characterisations of the caliphate were not specific to any doctrine. There were, however, instances of the adoption by the state of particular theological doctrines in a situation that had for long not had a regnant orthodoxy. The most famous of these was the attempt of al-Ma'mun and al-Mu'tasim to make Mu'tazilism, and specifically its doctrine that the Qur'an was created in time, into official state theology in the ninth century.[122]

Perhaps the most important such attempt in later history was the attempt of the Abbasid caliph al-Qadir Billah (991–1031) to compel subjects to adhere to his Creed (*'aqida*) of 1117 that affirmed a Ḥanbalite position with Asha'arite inflections, and instituted a persecution of the Mu'tazilites and

119 Ibn al-Jawzī, *Al-miṣbāḥ al-muḍī' fi khilāfat al-muṣtaḍī'*, vol. 1, 298–299.

120 Ibn Jamā'a, *Taḥrīr al-aḥkām fi tadbīr ahl al-islām*, 395 and passim.

121 For example: Ibn Rajab, *Al-dhayl 'alā ṭabaqāt al-ḥanābila*, ed. Muḥammad Ḥāmid al-Fiqī, 2 vols (Cairo: Maṭba'at al-Sunna al-Muḥammadiyya, 1952), vol. 1, 18. See also, on wine and prostitution taxes and their farming out in the Ayyubid and Mamluk periods and their great economic importance, Hassanein Rabie, *The Financial System of Egypt, AH 564–741, 1169–1341 AD* (London and New York: Oxford University Press, 1972), 119–121.

122 See Dominique Sourdel, "La politique religieuse du calife abbaside al-Ma'mūn", *Revue d'études islamiques* 30 (1962): 27–48. See most recently John P. Turner, *Inquisition in Early Islam* (London: I. B. Tauris, 2015), chs 1 and 6.

the Shi'a.[123] The prominent Hanbalite Abu Ya'la Muhammad Ibn al-Farra', qadi of the caliphal harem, a theologian much influenced by Mu'tazilism, nevertheless had an important part in formulating the creed of al-Qadir Billah.[124] One should not overlook the reliance of the Ottoman state on 'Ash'ari theology as official state doctrine.[125]

The caliphate represented an integral authority and was an emblem of good order. It was the lynchpin of order and the medium of assertions of historical continuity and integrity in which individual sovereigns were but moments of passage. The caliphate was permanent while the sultanate was contingent. If the caliphate ceased to function, or the caliph were declared inept, or if a despot blinded a caliph and subdued the office, the continuity of the general system of order and civilisation persisted due to the persistence of shari'a as emblematic of order in general, whereby shari'a comes to stand for prophetic and caliphal charisma and comes to inhabit sultanic charisma – so at least for official ideological output purveyed tirelessly and interminably by the ulama.[126]

When Ibn Khaldun took over the direction of the al-Qamhiyya *madrasa,* he said in his oration of acceptance that God had made the ulama "guardians and backbones" for the community, "stars by which the follower is guided and luminaries who bring the community closer to knowledge".[127] One qadi in al-Andalus declared that there is no honour in this world – after the caliphate – greater than the office of judge.[128] This made the ulama the legatees of the caliphate and expressed a recurrent opinion to the effect that the ulama had become legatees of the prophets. Ibn Taymiyya, in an expression more closely aligned with the reality of juridical practice, said that the righteousness of subjects depended on that of those in charge of them, and

---

123 Ibn al-Jawzī, *Al-muntaẓam fī tarīkh al-mulūk wa al-umam*, vol. 7, 65, 109–111, 161, 268, 277, 287–289.

124 Abū Ya'lā ibn al-Farrā', *Ṭabaqāt al-ḥanābila*, vol. 2, 197, 199. On the effect of Mu'tatazilism on Hanbalites in the fifth century of the Hijra see al-Azmeh, *Arabic Thought and Islamic Societies*, 216–217.

125 Taşköprüzāde, *Miftāḥ al-sa'āda wa miṣbāḥ al-siyāda fī mawḍū'āt al-'ulūm*, eds Bakrī and Abū Nūr, 4 vols (Cairo: n.p., n.d.), vol. 1, 411.

126 Al-Azmeh, *Muslim Kingship*, 181–188.

127 Ibn Khaldūn, *Al-ta'rīf bi Ibn Khaldūn*, 281.

128 Al-Nubāhī, *Tarīkh quḍāt al-Andalus aw al-marqaba al-'ulyā fī man yastaḥiqq al-qaḍā' wa al-futyā* (Beirut: n.p., n.d.), 2.

that those in charge consist of two groups: rulers and scholars. Their unity brings goodness and their separation, corruption.[129]

Such statements highlight a matter that requires discussion before moving on to deal with shari'a's connection to the world. The matter is that of the existence of a specific socio-professional group, a sodality, which is an estate-type form of organisation and a specific form of a social estate, that of the ulama. It can be inferred from the statements already quoted that this group was an entity of social action dependent upon social relations of authority, with a strong sense of self-awareness. To the common claim that "our Islam" denies constituted religious authority, and the concurrence of religious and political authority was not part of "our resplendent reality or our pure heritage",[130] the following can be said. This is the result of a wishful fantasy rather than a deliberative reading of history, with the added presumption that wishes projected onto the past must represent reality in the most truthful and just fashion. Rashid Rida maintained that Islam knew no religious authority and that historical examples of such authority are only imitative of Christian clericalism.[131] This contention is beside the point. Islam is a religion like others, and cannot exist or persist without a religious institution because the absence of this institution is a departure from the social nature of religion. A specialist class of religious professionals manned the religious institution and provided it with continuity in specific places and times, in itself and in relation to cultural, intellectual, political, and social institutions. Religious professionals made the production and dissemination of religious goods – creeds, symbols, rituals, and beliefs – a continuous and constant process to the extent that changing historical circumstances allowed.[132] The growth of religions in complex societies takes place only with the emergence of priesthood,[133] in the institutional and sociological sense of a sodality that

129 Ibn Taymiyya, *Al-siyāsa al-shar'iyya fī iṣlaḥ ar-rā'ī wa al-ra'iyya*, 75, 79.

130 'Amāra, *Al-dawla al-islāmiyya bayn al-'ilmāniyya wa al-ṣulṭa al-dīniyya*, 63–64.

131 Muḥammad Rashīd Riḍā, *Shubuhāt al-naṣārā wa ḥujaj al-islām* (Cairo: Maṭba'at al-manār, 1322/1904), 73.

132 Writing on religious sociology is extensive. As such, only the two following works are indicated in particular: Pierre Bourdieu, "Une interprétation de la religion selon Max Weber", *Archives européennes de sociologie* 12/1 (1971): 3–21 and "Génèse et structure du champ religieux", *Revue française de sociologie* 12 (1971): 293–334.

133 Max Weber, *Economy and Society: An Outline of Interpretative Sociology*, trans. C. Roth and C. Wittich (Berkeley and Los Angeles: University of California Press, 1968), 400, 424–426, 432 and Kant, *Religion Within the Limits of Reason Alone*, 163–164.

guards boundaries and assures the continuity of that which constitutes religion in practice, ideas, dogmas, rituals.

Historical study has not taken enough account of these matters and the study of the social and cultural history of Muslim polities is only in its early stage. There are, however, ample social indications of the existence of a class of specialist professionals in religion and related matters, namely the law and devotions. There were families of such professionals that persisted over long periods, indicating a convergence between social estates and the institution of religion, namely the presence of the former in the folds of the latter. One historian of the Maliki school made reference to the Al Hammad b. Zaid family that led the Maliki school both in wealth and in jurisprudence in Iraq from the middle of the second century to the end of the fifth century of the Hijra.[134] We have accounts of the al-Shahrazuri family who were in charge of the administration of the law in Syria and Arabia in the fifth and sixth centuries.[135] The Banu Sasra family transmitted from generation to generation knowledge, jurisprudence, and offices in Damascus from the middle of the fifth century to the end of the eighth century.[136] The Banu Jama'a were the principal aristocrats of religious knowledge and legal offices in Egypt and Syria during the Mamluk period.[137] In Damascus the Banu Qudama and Banu al-Munajja played a similar role.[138] The Maghreb did not lag behind these developments and the Banu Marzuq are perhaps one of the best examples of this transmission of knowledge and religious authority within families, while mention should also be made of the al-Shaykh in Saudi Arabia and its predecessor Wahhabite polities.[139] Detailed study of medieval Nishapur, the principal commercial city of Khurasan and one of

134 Burhān al-Dīn Ibrāhīm ibn Farḥūn, *Al-dībāj al-mudhahhab fī ma'rifat a'yān 'ulamā' al-madhab* (Cairo: n.p., 1351/1932), 96.

135 Shams al-Dīn Abū al-'Abbās Aḥmad ibn Khallikān, *Wafayāt al-'ayān wa anbā' ahl al-zamān*, ed. Iḥsān 'Abbās, 8 vols (Beirut: Dār al-thaqāfa, 1967), vol. 4, 68 ff.

136 William Brinner, "The Banu Ṣaṣrā: A Study in the transmission of scholarly tradition", *Studia Islamica* 7 (1960): 167–195.

137 Kamal Salibi, "The Banu Jamā'a: A dynasty of Shāfi'i jurists in the Mamlūk period", *Studia Islamica* 9 (1958): 97–109.

138 Henri Laoust, "Le Hanbalisme sous les mamlouks Bahrides", *Revue d'études islamiques* 28 (1960) : 1–71, 38 ff.

139 M. Hadi-Sadok, "Ibn Marzuk" in *The Encyclopedia of Islam*, eds B. Lewis, V. L. Ménage, C. Pellat, and J. Schacht, with C. Dumont, E. van Donzel, and G. R. Hawting, 2nd edn, 12 vols (Leiden: Brill, 1954–2005), vol. 3 (1971), 865–868.

the principal centres of Islamic learning, brings out well a situation in which two aristocratic groups monopolised law, government, and religious knowledge in a context of intense, often violent competition.

Such knowledge (*ʿilm*) was one of the basic specialities in Nishapur, which produced some of the most important developments in Muslim theology and in the theory of mysticism. This aristocratic class, divided between Shafiʿis and Hanafis, supported its legal and spiritual power with large landholdings that were the basis of its relations with the state and with the rest of society.[140] The coming of the Seljuk period put an end to this freelancing position enjoyed by the religious institution within society and the religious-intellectual institution was attached to the state, with schools being set up and the production of cultured scholars directly by the state. This had the effect of at once broadening and restricting the link between scholars and society. It was broader in the sense that the *madrasas* covered students' living expenses from the revenues generated by *awqāf*, thus enabling many students of modest or poor social origin to study and enter the devotional and legal institutions. The link became more restricted because the *madrasas* made the social – sodality – institution of *ʿilm* – a field covering worship and administration of *fiqh* – an institution-based professional training through a set itinerary, thanks to the *madrasas*, excluding whatever may have emerged outside the framework of these schools.[141] There is much unclarity, as detailed research is only patchy. What is certain is that after the Seljuk period and the foundation of the *madrasas* – the first was in Nishapur and the most famous was the Nizamiyya school in Baghdad – religious and scientific institutions were state sponsored, established outside the web of social relations. But their workings nevertheless integrated elements of kin networks. Some examples of this family-centred institutionalisation have been indicated. Prior to the Seljuk period *ʿilm* had been, to a greater extent, a private institution with the family as its basic institutional framework outside the administration of the law, and state patronage as its organising principle.

140 Richard W. Bulliett, *The Patricians of Nishapur: A Study in Medieval Islamic Social History*, Harvard Middle East Studies 16 (Cambridge, MA: Harvard University Press, 1972), 25–16, 62.

141 al-Azmeh, *Arabic Thought and Islamic Societies*, 211 ff. See now, among others, Ephrat, *A Learned Society* and al-Azmeh, *Muslim Kingship*, 102–5. See now the comments of Al-Azmeh, "Islamic political thought", at 220–235.

Whatever studies are available indicate that there was a hierarchical division in the religious and intellectual institution, with higher echelons of the legal system monopolised by patricians, appointed by the sovereign. Those who occupied lower ranks, such as district judges and imams in small mosques, were appointed by the qadi and faced a glass ceiling rarely breached.[142] This hierarchy continued, especially in Syria, and to a lesser extent in Egypt, throughout the Ottoman period. Egyptian scholars were connected to the countryside and to trade guilds, more than their colleagues in Syria, who were further removed from the lower orders.[143]

One of the leading jurists of the Mamluk period distinguished between ulama strictly speaking, and office-holders.[144] Among the former he counted experts on Prophetic traditions and grammarians and others, while judges (qadis) and market inspectors (*muḥtasib*) and *madrasa* instructors were to be regarded as office-holders. There is no doubt about the accuracy of this technical distinction, which appears to have had an evaluative purpose. Among other things, office-holders were distinguished by special dress.[145] High office was accompanied by great economic power accruing from access to *waqf* resources, wealth and prestige, in addition to cultural and legal authority, and the accumulation of social capital. Ibn Khallikan (d. 1282) held the office of qadi in Syria from al-'Arish to the Euphrates, and was inspector for all the *awqāf* of Syria and an instructor in seven *madrasa*s at once, each endowed with a stipend.[146] His contemporary Ibn bint al-A'azz accumulated the posts of chief qadi in Egypt, preacher at al-Azhar, inspector of the Treasury and the *awqāf*, *shaykh al-shuyukh* (inspector of Sufi orders), and supervisor of the bequests of al-Zahir Baybars, in addition to a number of

142 Bulliett, *The Patricians of Nishapur*, 54 ff; C. F. Petry, *The Civilian Elite in Cairo in the Later Middle Ages* (Princeton: Princeton University Press, 1971), 226, 229, and passim; John E. Mandaville, "The Muslim judiciary in Damascus in the late Mamluk period" (unpublished PhD dissertation, Princeton University, 1969), 8, 10–13, 41.

143 André Raymond, *Artisans et commerçants au Caire au XVIIIe siècle,* 2 vols (Damascus: IFEA, 1973–1974), 419–424.

144 Tāj al-Dīn Abū Naṣr 'Abd al-Wahhāb ibn 'Alī al-Subkī, *Mu'īd al-ni'am wa mubīd al-niqam*, ed. D. O. Myhrman (London: Luzac, 1908), 94 ff, 145 ff. New impression as *Herrn D. W. Myhrman's Ausgabe Des Kitāb Mu'id An-Ni'am Wa-Mubid An-Niqam: Kritisch Beleuchtet*, ed. K. V. Zettersteen (London: Forgotten Books, 2018).

145 Abū al-'Abbās Aḥmad ibn Aḥmad al-Qalqashandī, *Ṣubḥ al-a'shā fī ṣinā'at al-inshā*, 14 vols (Cairo: Dār al-Kutub al-Miṣriyya, 1913–1919), vol. 4, 41–43.

146 Al-Maqrīzī, *Al-sulūk li ma'rifat duwal al-mulūk,* vol. 2, 362, 442–443, vol. 3, 241–242, 319.

teaching posts.[147] Badr al-Din ibn Jama'a was the first to accumulate the posts of *shaykh al-shuyukh*, chief qadi, and chief preacher.[148] Office-holders also benefited from the tax concessions that continued until the end of the Ottoman period.[149] A qadi in Fès in the period of Ibn Khaldun chose for his emolument the duties to be collected on the sale of wine.[150] There are as many examples of probity and of individual ulama standing up to authority as there are examples of collusion and complicity between ulama and those close to authority in order to sell *awqāf*, and other illegal matters.[151] While it is true that scholars and office-holders in the legal and devotional systems of the state were distinct groups, it is certain that all these office-holders were drawn from the ranks of the ulama. This sodality did not emerge only from social interaction but from functionally differentiated official institutions of learning distinct from social relations. These institutions trained the ulama from whom office-holders were selected by state functionaries on the basis of social and political considerations.[152] By any historical and social measure, the administrative structures for the religious and legal institution constitute what was in effect a state Church or at least a state-sponsored priestly hierarchy, with the chief qadi at its head, and members including judges of all ranks, and the appointees of the chief qadi or his representatives: holders of devotional offices such as imāms and preachers, holders of posts in *awqāf* administration and related tax collection, administration of the property of orphans and minors as well as the maintenance and service of *awqāf* properties. In addition, there was the supervision of the educational establishments linked to the *awqāf* institution, such as madaris and hadith teaching units, their administration and finance, and the appointment of professors and repetitors. One can also include the supervision of Sufi devotional

147 Ibid., 773.

148 al-Nu'āymī, *Al-dāris fi tarīkh al-madāris*, ed. Ja'far al-Ḥusaynī (Damascus: al-Majma' al-'Ilmī al-'Arabī, 1948), vol. 2, 156.

149 Raymond, *Artisans et commerçants*, 425–426.

150 Ibn Khaldun, *Prologomènes d'Ebn Khaldoun*, vol. 2, 300.

151 Al-Maqrīzī, *Al-sulūk li ma'rifat duwal al-mulūk*, vol. 2, 362, 442–443, vol. 3, 241–242, 319; al-Subkī, *Mu'īd al-ni'am wa mubīd al-niqam*, 145–146.

152 For a somewhat schematic but synoptic account of growing professionalisation and technocratisation of the legal corps, with different emphases to those here, see recently Lena Salaymeh, *The Beginnings of Islamic Law: Late Antique Islamicate Legal Traditions* (Cambridge: Cambridge University Press, 2016), 148–157.

institutions, such as the brotherhoods, buildings connected to the brotherhoods, such as *ribāts* and *khanqāhs*, and the ratification of the election of shaykhs for the brotherhoods.

The legal and religious establishment therefore supervised the systems of education, worship, and law in just the same way as the Church controlled the former two in Europe until European states started setting up their own educational and legal domains. One needs also to mention formal normative and mythographic hegemony, irrespective of the degree to which this corresponds to practices and realities. This complete or quasi-complete control, with antecedents in a somewhat less formal structure of state patronage, began in earnest in the Seljuk period in Baghdad, spreading westwards and consolidated in the Mashreq during the Mamluk period with decisive support from the state and its high officials. It continued in the Ottoman state with increased official control and more elaborate organisation under *şeyhülislam*. In the Maghreb these developments occurred at a somewhat slower rate. The Hafsid and Merinid periods saw a decisive turn towards laying the bases of control by the religious establishment of education, worship, and law, although this did have scattered beginnings in the early Almoravid and Almohad periods before continuing in two distinct forms, on the Ottoman (in Tunisia and Algeria) and Sherifian (in Morocco) models.[153]

The point of departure of the Arab present or, rather, the recent Arab past, one taken by modernity unawares, is not to be found in the Medina of the Rightly-Guided Caliphs or the Damascus of ʿUmar II, but with an Ottoman or Mamluk heritage in terms of religion, law, and education and, politically, with the heritage of the figure of the sultan, not of the Muhammadan Prophet-King. This is why previous pages made special mention of the Mamluk and late Abbasid periods involving caliphs and sultans, because it was these periods, not some imagined early Islam, that saw the the points of departure of the period of Arab modernity. The early period of Islam is a

153 On the beginnings of *madrasas* in Morocco and policies related to them, see ʿAbd Allāh ibn Marzūq, *Al-Musnad al-ṣaḥīḥ al-ḥasan fī maʾāthir mawlānā Abī al-Ḥasan*, ed. Évariste Lévi-Provencal, *Hespéris* 5/4 (1925): 19–20, and comments; Shihāb al-Dīn al-ʿUmarī, *Waṣf Ifrīqiya wa al-Andalus*, ed. Ḥusayn Husnī ʿAbd al-Wahhāb (Tunis: n.p., n.d.), 907; Maya Shatzmiller, "Les premiers Mérinides et le milieu religieux de Fès", *Studia Islamica* 43 (1976): 109–118, 115–116 and Robert Brunschwig, *La Berbérie orientale sous les Hafsides dès origines à la fin du* xv*e siècle*, 2 vols (Paris: Adrien-Maisonneuve, 1940–1947), vol. 2, 287 ff.

period of imaginary beginnings, illusory or hoped-for beginnings, although it is a period whose actual history is quite well known. Any discussion about "authenticity" must consider actual historical beginnings, not virtual ones. Arab roots, the roots of today's Arabs, when found not in global modernity, are to be found in the Ottoman system. At the close of the twentieth century and the beginnings of the next, seams of salafisation that intensified during the Mamluk period were mined vigorously.[154]

The devotional, ideological, doctrinal, and legal institution functioned according to social and economic mechanisms. Its control was not only administrative in character but also had, as was the case in the history of European Church history, a moral element based on the role of this institution as representative of two closely connected sources of authority:

1 State authority. The state appointed the senior members of these institutions such as the qadi, and executed the judgments emanating from these institutions, as in medieval and early modern Europe.
2 Charismatic religious authority represented by the members of the religious and legal establishment as they bandied the shari'a – the emblem and title of charisma – in its different practical instantiations, legal, devotional, and educational. *Madrasas* and similar institutions and more specialised entities such as hadith colleges had proliferated in Damascus, especially since the Ayyubid period. It was these institutions that educated the members of the priestly and legal corps.

These institutions made the knowledge disseminated by their members into institutionally perpetuated traditions on the one hand, and actualised high literate culture on the other.[155] It was the *madrasas* that made this tradition an official tradition for society, an obligatory habitus of public rectitude exercising an official compulsion that may not have been in conformity to actually existing cultures. Within the *madrasas* the educational process reproduced the absolute vertical hierarchy that was previously noted as one of the aspects of authority. The downward link between professor, repetitor,

154 M. J. Bārūt, *Ḥamalāt kisirwān fī al-tārīkh al-siyāsī li fatāwī Ibn Taymiyya* (Doha: Arab Center for Research and Policy Studies, 2017), 222–255.
155 The following section is based on the analysis in Al-Azmeh, *Arabic Thought and Islamic Societies*, 223 ff.

student, or acolyte was conjoined with symbolic distinctions expressed in an etiquette of deference, bearing, and bodily comportment, intended for the social confirmation of pyramidal hierarchy and, in practical terms, its discursive reproduction. If one turned to works on education, for example, it would be clear that the pedagogic practice rested on a simple structure of delivery and reception and assimilation of knowledge. Pedagogical technique was premised upon the reaffirmation of rank in live pedagogical settings – such as seating arrangements, and manners of dress. It emerges also that the inability properly to receive knowledge effectively was attributed not to the pedagogy but to factors associated with magic, such as eating fresh coriander, looking at a man crucified, or throwing live lice to the ground.[156] It does not seem that the criticisms made by Ibn Khaldun and others of pedagogic techniques had any noticeable effect. Education was a constellation of conventions of behaviour that had no intrinsic connection to the content of the material being delivered and received, but resided rather in the social and cultural hierarchies that related the operations of teaching and learning. Teaching implied the transfer of material – specific texts – from one location to another. This meant that pedagogy was grounded in the control of transferring cognitive goods. Such control had strong technical justifications in epochs before printing, when the integral transcription and the careful copying of manuscripts were of great importance. This technical context was not the sole factor involved. Oral modes of communication often attached less practical importance to mechanical accuracy of repetition than to stable genre-defining elements and patterns of discourse that could lead to the production of texts that varied while preserving fundamental formal and structural elements. Such was pre-Islamic poetry, popular poetry, epics, and other works.[157] The insistence on textual precision was a component of the exercise of authority with a textual definition: the foundational textual canon (Qur'an and hadith) and the canon of tradition erected in the name of foundational text and of fidelity to the canon: jurisprudence, exegesis, commentary, and other genres. Ibn Khal-

156 For example, Abū Sa'ad 'Abd al-Karīm ibn Muḥammad al-Sam'āni, *Adab al-imlā' wa al-istimlā'*, ed. M. Weisweiler (Leiden: Brill, 1952) and Burhān al-Islām al-Zarnūjī, *Ta'līm al-muta'allim ṭarīq al-ta'llum*, ed. Marwān Qabbānī (Beirut: al-Maktab al-Islāmī, 1981), 75–133.

157 Michael Zwettler, *The Oral Tradition of Classical Arabic Poetry: Its Character and Implications* (Columbus: Ohio State University Press, 1978), and Eric Alfred Havelock, *Preface to Plato* (Oxford: Basil Blackwell, 1963). See now Aziz al-Azmeh, *The Arabs and Islam in Late Antiquity: A Critique of Approaches to Arabic Sources* (Berlin: Gerlach Press, 2014), especially chs 5, 6 and 7.

dun was entirely right when he compared education to learning a trade, where the individual progresses step by step from apprentice to master. What this involves is the acquisition of a habitus.

In both cases one underwent training to acquire a technical capacity, and not to acquire a capacity for advancing the material received.[158] In the end the student obtains a collection of licences (*ijaza*) that confirm his memory and grasp of the text or texts covered by these licences, that is to say a certificate that he acquired a collection of skills or a particular skill enabling proper repetition and further transmission. It is noteworthy here that the licence was granted on the basis of tuition in the live audition of a written text. This is significant in a number of ways, of which the most important is perhaps the relationship of authority between learner and teacher, a relationship consolidated by live supervision, a matter analytically separable from the substance of the original text. The supervision of accurate textual transmission is not that of a neutral authority external to transmission, but is the very authority of transmission, guaranteeing the integrity of the text. The supervision is not that of a nameless authority but that of a very specific one, one with an energetic presence in the form of the master (*shaykh*) interposed between the original text and its receiver. The master confirms the primacy of the text, which is the subject of the act of reception, as well as the foundational authority of knowledge (*'ilm*) itself. This also means that the master is the guardian of the text's foundational authority, his presence representing the religious and legal establishment in its scholarly garb (which was also coded sartorially), bearing witness to this primacy, reproducing and maintaining tradition. The prepotency of canonical texts and related traditions as obligatory points of transit, served up as beginnings, vanishes in the absence of an institution to confirm it, safeguard it, and save it from corruption and atrophy. For this reason, the discursive forms common in Muslim traditions (and in the Christian and Jewish as well) of marginal notes, commentaries, glosses, scholia, and the extensive commentaries upon commentaries were not supplements without value, but were acts of *aggiornamento*, the forms of the presence of knowledge of the foundational texts in moments subsequent to their redaction. Beginnings, as points of reference for traditions, are rarely real beginnings, and every

158 Ibn Khaldūn, *Prologomènes d'Ebn Khaldoun*, vol. 2, 376.

alleged beginning has a contemporary characteristic at which we only arrive though exegesis and pedagogy, designed to efface difference between times and assert anachronism, devouring time in the process.[159] Even if the past, in terms of significance or principle or ritual, had priority over the present, the present has an effective primacy in relation to the past represented by the master, who represents the social and institutional establishment of tradition, and the religious and legal institution that has effective political authority in the present.

The pedagogical process was therefore validated ritually by two inseparable authorities serving as points of reference and of passage: the nominal authority of the founding text and the effective power of the religious, legal, and priestly establishment. Here priestly power was also the mediator between the present and its alleged textual origins: canon and principles of jurisprudence. Teaching and learning was a link enabling successive historical moments to know the foundations of this knowledge located in the Qur'an, hadith, and the Arabic language. The judgment reached in court linked the imperfect realities of today to putative origins, and restored to them the order inherent in what is known as shari'a.

What is this shari'a and how were its judgments to be arrived at? And how is the world linked with these exemplary origins that bring the world to a possible degree of completeness? And how, from these exemplary origins, is a legal system generated whose integrity is invigilated by the religious and legal institution?[160]

An observer attentive to prevailing discourse on shari'a today, but unwary of conceptual and historical complexity, can have the impression that the shari'a is a determinate collection of rulings that can be applied or neglected, or that it is a collection of rules with clear features that can be recognised intuitively or by native intelligence, as if it were a code of law or at least a collection of general principles, the keys to which can be obtained from the

159 See Aziz al-Azmeh, "Chronophagous discourse: A study of the clerico-legal appropriation of the world in an Islamic tradition", in *The Times of History*, ch. 3.

160 The following section is based on al-Azmeh, *Arabic Thought and Islamic Societies*, 86–95 and Aziz al-Azmeh, "Islamic Legal Theory and the Appropriation of Reality", in *Islamic Law: Social and Historical Contexts*, ed. Aziz al-Azmeh (London and New York: Routledge, 1988), 250–265. See now Baudouin Dupret, *What is the Sharia?* (London: Hurst in association with Aga Khan University Institute for the Study of Muslim Civilisations, 2018).

guardians of shari'a, of which there are many today, formal or informal, and in competition, the ulama. Historical reality, however, does not show that there was original shari'a material, but practices remembered to various extents and in various ways become shari'a material by tradition. Shari'a has a history. Perhaps its first histories concerned the relations between portions of the Qur'an. The regulation of inheritance and temporary marriage in the Qur'an were not the result of the changes from one interpretation of the text to another, but the result of political and social changes that led to a change in the qualities and senses ascribed to the text. Different and contradictory Qur'anic verses were used as a justification for contradictory judgements about the status of conquered lands that in the days of the Prophet were considered war booty and as *fay'* (what by right belonging to God and consequently to Muslims collectively) in the days of 'Umar.[161] This is a natural development in the social and political constitution of texts. The early history of shari'a accounts for only a small part of the rulings that were to accumulate in the fullness of time – not all unambiguous – relating to punishment, family, devotions, contracts and much more. The social history of Muslim law is still in its early phases of research, but there has been much progress in recent decades.[162] Much of this actual history related itself discursively and historically to hadith, which remained effectively outside the scope of historical criticism. It is true that, as Ibn Khaldun said, al-Bukhari and Muslim collected hadith that had achieved practical recognition in legislation, while al-Tirmidhi and the authors of the six books of canonical hadith collected the traditions that were actionable.[163] Fakhr al-Din al-Razi quite correctly

161 For instance, David S. Powers, *Studies in the Quran and Hadīth: The Formation of the Islamic Law of Inheritance* (Berkeley and Los Angeles: University of California Press, 1986). With regard to temporary marriage, compare Muḥsin Al-Amīn, *Al-ḥuṣūn al-manī'a fi radd mā awradahu ṣāhib al-manār fi ḥaqq al-shī'a*, 2nd edn, 2 vols (Cairo: Dār al-Zahrā', 1985), 48 ff. Concerning lands conquered by force see Abū 'Ubayd al-Qāsim al-Harawī ibn Sallām, *Al-amwāl*, ed. Muḥammad Khalīl Harrās (Cairo: Maktabat al-Kulliyāt al-Azhariyya, 1968), 85–86.

162 See now, among others, M. Holmes Katz, *Body of Text: The Emergence of the Sunni Law of Ritual Purity* (Albany: State University of New York Press, 2002); Arthur Gribetz, *Strange Bedfellows: mut'at al-nisā' and mut'at al-ḥajj: A Study Based on Sunnī and Shī'ī sources of tafsīr, ḥadīth and fiqh* (Berlin: Klaus Schwarz Verlag, 1994).

163 Ibn Khaldun, *Les Prolegomènes d'Ebn Khaldoun*, vol. 1, 399. See Jonathan Brown, *The Canonization of al-Bukhari and Muslim: The Formation and Function of the Sunnı Hadıth Canon* (Leiden and Boston: Brill, 2007) and Asma Helali, *Étude sur la tradition prophétique: La question de l'authenticité du Ier/VIème au VIème/XIIème siècle* (unpublished doctoral thesis, École Pratique des Hautes Études [Vème Section: Sciences Réligieuses], Paris, 2004).

noted that al-Bukhari and others had no access to knowledge of the unseen, and collected traditions using judgments to the best of their abilities. The most that one could do, so it was held, was to think well of the hadith collectors and of the Companions of the Prophet, who sometimes bitterly, and on occasion mortally, undermined one another.[164] These statements highlight one of the most important facts connected to hadith when considered as source of shari'a: the authenticity of hadith texts and the binding quality of rules that might derive from their exemplarity are not internal properties of these enunciations premised on probatively verifiable historical authenticity, but rather from their attestation through what Muslim traditions term consensus (*ijmā'*), which was basically a political rather than cognitive certification.[165] Attestation to the validity of hadith is derived from an attestation to the validity of its transmission. The veracity of hadith therefore attests to the authority controlling heritage, based on a self-attesting and self-authorising past consensus, without this *ijmā'* itself being authenticated historically.

For this reason, Razi added that he rejected accounts that contradict what he presumes must be true about the Prophet and related figures.[166] The Prophet thereby becomes a figure of prophecy as determined theologically and doctrinally, rather than a figure of history. For the same reason the ulama, including the leading hadith critics, indicated the need to privilege certification of witnesses (*ta'dil*) over their censure (*jarh*): "were we to open this chapter or to prioritise censure without limit, no master [imam] would emerge intact."[167]

The authentication of hadith is based upon the self-authentication of a tradition and this heritage is embodied at every moment in those who bear and transmit it: the religious and legal institution that exists in the forms of *madrasas*, legal schools (*madhāhib*), and the legal and devotional offices occupied by the ulama sodality collectively. This is the intermediary between God and the sources of shari'a, exercising authority by virtue of

164 Fakhr al-Dīn Muhammad ibn 'Umar al-Rāzī, *Asās al-taqdīs* (Cairo: Maṭba'at Kurdistān al-'Ilmīya, 1967), 85–86.

165 See C. Mansour, *L'Autorité dans la pensée musulmane. Le concept d'ijmâ consensus et la problématique de l'autorité* (Paris: Vrin, 1975), and al-Azmeh, *Arabic Thought and Islamic Societies*, 162–164.

166 al-Rāzī, *Asās al-taqdīs*, 209–210.

167 Tāj al-Dīn Abū Naṣr 'Abd al-Wahhāb Ibn 'Alī al-Subkī, *Ṭabaqāt al-shāfiyya al-kubrā*, eds Maḥmūd Muhammad al-Tanāḥī and 'Abd al-Fattāḥ Muḥammad al-Hilu, 6 vols (Cairo: n.p., 1964), vol. 2, 9 ff., and Abū al-Khayr Muḥammad ibn 'Abd al-Raḥmān al-Sakhāwī, *Al-i'lān bi al-tawbīkh li-man dhamma ahl al-tarīkh* (Damascus: Nashr al-Qudsī, 1349/1930), 68–69.

knowledge of shari'a, and controlling shari'a by its continuous acts of verification and authentication: a ritual of repetition, with devotional reward. Perhaps the inflexible position of Abu Hanifa (d. Baghdad 767) in questions of hadith and his reluctance to accept its texts indicated not only his preference for considered opinion over attested hadith, but more generally indicated proof of the congenital weakness of hadith as a root of shari'a whose rulings were in reality based on considered opinion, preference, custom, and other practices.[168] Subsequently legislation was reformulated as shari'a with a prime basis in hadith, having the authority to override the Qur'an – this was the signal and lasting contribution of al-Shafi'i (d. Cairo 767) to the principles of Muslim jurisprudence. In the case of this latter, the principles of jurisprudence were in their relative generality and abstraction congruent with the legal and cultural unity arising from conditions of the emergent Abbasid imperial context. Jurisprudence had been made up previously of Syrian, Iraqi, and Medinan practices, ad hoc rulings, and a Prophetic Sunna in the process of construction. Local traditions became hadith, and consensus confirmed this ascription, hadith thereby becoming a legal tradition, redacted in the canonical and pre-canonical collections (*sihah* and *masanid*).[169]

Just as Qur'an-based legislation has a history, like legislation on the basis of hadith, two histories obscured from jurisprudence that ascribe their traditions to beginnings posited as such, so also is the history of Muslim jurisprudence construed to be based on these beginnings, connected by analogy (*qiyās*), between individual legal judgments and their ostensible origin, construed as binding norm, norm in Qur'an and hadith. Analogy is not a demonstrative logical operation based on general principles, discussions of which are to be found in the jurisprudential epistemology that normally preface, at length, works of the Principles of Jurisprudence ('ilm usūl al-fiqh). *Qiyās* involves connecting an ostensible origin called *asl*, be it a normative principle, exemplary precedent, or a maxim, with a specific case ("branch": *far'*) and transferring

---

168 Ibn Khaldun, *Prologomènes d'Ebn Khaldoun*, vol. 2, 399. On the reputation of Ibn Hanifa, see Abū 'Amr ibn Yūsuf ibn 'Abd Allāh ibn 'Abd al-Barr, *Al-intiqā' fī faḍā'il al-thalātha al-a'imma al-fuqahā'* (Beirut: Dār al-Kitāb al-Jadīd, n.d.), 149 ff.

169 There has been a growing amount of research on these topics in the last twenty years. See now Benjamin Jokisch, *Islamic Imperial Law: Harun al-Rashid's Codification Project* (Berlin and New York: Walter de Gruyter, 2007).

judgments derivable from the former onto the latter. This discussion will not address the logical assessment or the ways in which these two elements are not a logical connection.[170]

The analogical link is, rather, a demonstration of the transfer of a judgment between two elements, based on an indicative sign of connection – the connection is indexical and rhetorical, and involves the "submission", in the words of al-Ghazali, of the latter specific case to the prior normative element. This eliminates the specificity of the derivative and connects it with the primacy of the precedent or origin, a renewal in repetition.[171] Shari'a judgment is not based on establishing proof, but on the legal decision to affirm the connection on the part of the authorised instance represented by the person speaking in the name of shari'a. The point is subtle, but legists were at pains to assert that the connection is symbolic and involves the affirmation, almost ritual, of submission to the origin: that the correlation between inebriation and the prohibition on drinking alcoholic beverages (not all – Hanafi jurisprudence knew distinctions) is not based on the material causality that connects the two, but on their correlation carried over into specific cases as correlation, the index (the technical term is *'illa*, which also means "cause") – but not the material cause – of which is inebriation, irrespective of the *ratio legis*, of why such should be prohibited.

The legal judgment thus remodels a particular life-situation and restates elements arising from it in terms of legal discourse and its technical vocabularies, such that realities to which reference is made are translated from the natural, social, or historical registers of reality to that of legal language.[172] The transfiguration of reality from experience to law is analogous to the change of nouns from the literal to the metaphorical. The meanings of nouns are classified as lexical, conventional, and legal.[173] Indices of correlation and juristic

---

170 See al-Azmeh, *Arabic Thought and Islamic Societies*, 90–93.

171 Abū Ḥāmid ibn Muḥammad al-Ghazālī, *Miḥakk al-naẓar fī al-manṭiq*, eds Badr al-Dīn al-Na'sānī al-Ḥalabī and Muṣṭafā al-Qabbāni al-Dimashqī (Cairo: al-Maṭba'a al-Adabiyya, n.d.), 33 and Bahā' al-Dīn 'Abd Allāh ibn 'Abd al-Raḥmān ibn 'Aqīl, *Kitāb al-jadal 'ala ṭarīqat al-fuqahā'*, ed. Georges Makdisi, in *Revue d'études orientales* 20 (1967), para. 42.

172 Sayf al-Dīn Abū al-Ḥasan 'Alī al-'Āmidī, *Al-iḥkām fī uṣūl al-aḥkām*, 4 vols (Cairo: n.p., 1914), vol. 1, 82 and 'Abd Allāh ibn 'Amr ibn Muḥammad ibn 'Alī al-Shīrāzī, Nāṣir al-Dīn al-Bayḍāwī, *Minhāj al-wuṣūl ilā 'ilm al-uṣūl* (Cairo: n.p., 1326/1908), 78.

173 Abū Ḥāmid ibn Muḥammad al-Ghazālī, *Al-muṣṭasfa min 'ilm al-uṣūl*, 2 vols (Cairo, n.p.: 1356/1937), vol. 1, 322ff., and Al-Bazdawī, *Kanz al-wuṣūl*, on the margins of 'Abd al-Azīz al-Bukhārī, *Kashf al-asrār* (Constantinople: Maktabat al-Ṣanāyi', 1889), 1014.

analogies are causes of judgments only metaphorically: "a legal judgment is not equivalent to the matter to which causality is ascribed, but the ascription of causality by legal discourse (*shar'*)."[174] The obligation entailed by a legal judgment is not entailed by the legal causes or indices of correlation in themselves, but by the legal judgment that they are causes, in the virtual sense delineated: "[causes] were posited to lighten matters for humans. Since obligation arises from an unseen agency, it was attributed to the causes that have been posited, while it was affirmed by a foreordinance in which the creature has no choice." The cause is identified not because an effective causality is attached to it, but rather because the judgment is attributed to it.[175]

As a consequence, legal causes do not in themselves engender obligation; this is engendered by the legislator. Drinking wine was not subject to prohibition prior to its interdiction by the legislator. Chastity and the preservation of family lineages are not real legal causes for proscribing fornication; both existed before the coming of shari'a.[176] The legal indication of judgments is therefore an index of authority, a judgment with a hidden origin with no clear justification for it except that of command – it is not excluded that a material explanation is present, but this is irrelevant for legal purposes. This view of legal judgment, which came to predominate among Sunnis, is contrary to the Mu'tazilite theory that saw in legal rulings elements that conformed to the nature of things and were not at variance with them, on the assumption that since the benevolent God was persistent in positing what was best and most apt.[177] Sunni jurisprudents agreed generally that the legal judgments were "the discourse of Law and not a description of an act, neither goodness nor iniquity. Reason played no part in it and there were no legal rulings before the coming of Shar'."[178]

The human mind is incapable of judging independently the affairs of this world or the next, they being confined in these matters to knowledge

---

174 al-Āmidī, *Al-iḥkām fī uṣūl al-aḥkām*, vol. 1, 182.

175 al-Bazdawī, *Kanz al-wuṣūl*, 661, 663.

176 Ibn 'Aqīl, *Kitāb al-jadal 'alā ṭarīqat al-fuqahā'*, para. 42; Ibn Rushd, *Al-muqaddimāt*, 23; Abū al-Fatḥ 'Uthmān Ibn Jinnī, *Al-khaṣā'iṣ fī falsafat al-lugha al-'arabiyya*, ed. Muḥammad 'Alī al-Najjār, 2nd edn, 2 vols (Cairo: Dār al-Kutub al-Miṣrīyya, 1952–1956), vol. 1, 50–51.

177 Abū al-Ḥusayn Muḥammad ibn 'Alī al-Ṭayyib al-Baṣrī, *Al-mu'tamad fī uṣūl al-fiqh*, eds Muḥammad Ḥamīd Allāh, et al. (Damascus: al-Ma'had al-'Ilmī al-Faransī li'l-Dirasāt al-'Arabiyya, 1964), 177–179.

178 al-Ghazālī, *Al-Muṣṭasfā min 'ilm al-uṣūl*, vol. 1, 7. Compare 55 ff.

imparted by God.[179] It is the shari'a itself that instructs us to the way of inferring that it is posited in the human interest.[180] There is no good reason why the obligation of prayers should be tied to specific times, nor is there a good reason to correlate stoning with fornication. It is not clear why the Hajj rituals are prescribed as they are, or why a specific number of prayers have been performed daily or the justifications for divorce regulations.[181] The theory of *maṣālih mursala*, the consideration of human interest generally conceived, of Mu'tazilite origins and with a history that included al-Ghazali, Ibn Rushd, and Shatibi, did not go beyond these limits. It broadened the domain of jurisprudence rather than broadening its conceptual horizons, by assimilating new legal conditions and developments. The concept of the five legal categories of interest (the preservation of religion, life, wealth, progeny, and sanity) encompassed by Muslim jurisprudence tidied up the legal system conceptually by means of these categories, but did not innovate. Nor did it abrogate preceding legislation from the Qur'an and other sources. It hesitated between a notion of a mutable natural law that it could have yielded conceptually, and the reliance on an unseen authority that has once and for all decided the basic repertoire of immutable rules. In the final analysis, therefore, the indicative sign of correlation facilitating legal judgment by means of analogy is the link between an origin asserted by the Law, and a derived judgment arrived at a distance by force of command. The only means for action at a distance is a magical conception of affect, or else by the charismatic authority (the jurisprudents) carrying out this magical effect.

Muslim law (*fiqh*) was therefore "knowledge [of legal judgments] or knowledge of them as obligations and practices, based on an apprehension of certainty, even if, in themselves, these judgements are not categorically certain".[182] Muslim law, like hadith, based itself on the presumption that its contents (judgments – narrative reports in the case of hadith) were true,

179 Abū Isḥāq Ibrāhīm ibn Mūsā al-Shāṭibī, *Al-i'tiṣām*, ed. Muḥammad Rashīd Riḍā, 2 vols (Cairo: n.p., 1332/1913), vol. 1, 46.

180 Abu Isḥāq Ibrāhīm ibn Mūsā al-Shāṭibī, *Al-muwāfaqāt fī uṣūl al-aḥkām*, ed. Muḥammad Munīr, 4 vols (Cairo: n.p., 1922), vol. 2, 3–4.

181 al-Ghazālī, *Al-mustaṣfā min 'ilm al-uṣūl*, vol. 1, 93 and Ibn Jinnī, *Al-khaṣā'iṣ fī falsafat al-lugha al-'arabiyya*, vol. 1, 48.

182 al-Āmidī, *Al-iḥkām fī uṣūl al-aḥkām*, vol. 1, 7.

without this conviction being of a general nature or being a cognitive judgement of certitude. This enables the extension to the field of jurisprudence in general of the analysis previously applied earlier in this chapter to hadith. In the absence of real as distinct from indexical and virtual causality in jurisprudence, in the absence of concrete *ratio legis*, as in the absence of actual history from the domain of hadith, one sees indications that actual history, the historical link between the principles and the derived judgments of jurisprudence, emerged only subsequent to the prior historical stabilisation of what was later construed as derived judgment. These judgments (*furū*ʿ) emerged from various historical experiences that finally came together in legal networks of tradition such as the Awzaʿiyya, the Zahiriyya, and the Jaririyya, all of which became extinct, and the Hanafiyya, the Shafiʿiyya, the Malikiyya, and, at a later date, the Hanbaliyya. The science of the Principles of Jurisprudence developed later than did the basic repertoire of judgments (*furū*ʿ) that were to become classical Muslim law, and was the locus of their systematic and genre-specific integration as traditions, providing systematic post factum reconstruction, substantive integration, and jurisprudential justification.[183]

The Principles of Jurisprudence was thus in effect not so much a method of legislative practice as much as a theoretical epistemology for jurisprudence retrospectively systematised as elaborations of tradition. Later developments of jurisprudence do not seem to have been incorporated into later works of the Principles of Jurisprudence, whose concerns seem to have concentrated on post factum considerations of the more classical bodies of judgments.[184] Only in a very restricted fashion did later works seek to generate the new judgments (*furū*ʿ).

Before concluding this chapter with an examination of the highly important question of ideology, it would be appropriate to consider the realities of legal practice, having considered shariʿa in relation to its origins and metalegal elaboration. It was noted earlier that shariʿa is historically heterogeneous, that its rulings and alleged principles were juxtaposed by authority rather

183 See recent work: Ahmed El Shamsy, *The Canonization of Islamic Law* (Cambridge: Cambridge University Press, 2015); *The Oxford Handbook of Islamic Law*, eds Anver M. Emon and Rumee Ahmed (Oxford: Oxford University Press, 2018).

184 Chafik Chehata, "Logique juridique et droit musulman", *Studia Islamica* 23 (1965): 5–25, 16–17 and Wael B. Hallaq, "Was the gate of Ijitihad closed?" *International Journal of Middle East Studies* 16 (1984): 3–41, 19.

than the one emerging from the other. Shari'a was constructed ideologically in the form of a cognitive discipline that was sustained by the devotional and legal institutions. This is why the four Sunni law schools (in fact, networks and traditions) that remained and that absorbed the jurisprudence handed down from the period before them, recognised one another mutually, despite sometimes ferocious enmity arising from vested interests.

Many jurisprudents dealt with contradiction between legal arguments and came to say that, if it were impossible to reach agreements between two arguments due to contradiction, either it was a question linked to textual abrogation (*naskh*), the use of another argument, or the decision of a judge.[185] Many legal treatises, such as Mawardi's *al-ahkām al-sulṭāniyya*, worked through different possible interpretations of canonical proof texts without stating a preference or coming to a clear opinion of what might or might not be certain.

This gave effective authorities – in the case of al-Mawardi, the caliph – the options of reaching a preference or indeed the possibility of making a judgment independent of previous legislative traditions (*ijtihād mutlaq*) and with general applicability.[186] Juristic disagreements were ascribed by the legists to different conclusions drawn from the same textual sources. But it would be more accurate to say that the schools of jurisprudence formed distinct collections of traditions, despite their insistence on shared textual origins.[187] The important point to be made is that jurisprudential judgments were ultimately not judgments enacted on the basis of religion or according to shari'a in a general and abstract way, as is often claimed, but on the basis of the judgments produced by the highly technical discipline jurisprudence. Matters considered sinful in religion are not necessarily subject to legal prohibition, not least in the law of contracts pertaining to *hiyal*, casuistical stratagems: for instance, the construal of payment of interest as a contact of virtual sale followed by resale at a higher price.

Iniquity is reprehensible but it is not forbidden.[188] Careful study of Hanafi jurisprudence indicates that legal liability is something quite distinct

185 al-Ghazālī, *Al-muṣṭaṣfā min 'ilm al-uṣūl*, vol. 2, 139–140.

186 Al-Māwardī, *Al-aḥkām as-sulṭāniyya wa al-wilāyāt al-dīniyya*, 66–67.

187 Compare Chafik Chehata, "L'*Ikhtilāf* et la conception musulmane du droit", in *L'Ambivalence dans la culture arabe*, ed. J.-P. Charnay (Paris: Éditions Anthropos, 1967), 259–263, 266.

188 See the material examples and the opinions contained in Chafik Chehata, "La religion et les fondements des droits en Islam", *Archives de philosophie de droit* 18 (1973): 17–25, 18–21.

from religious liability, the former a matter for the legal system, the latter for God. It also indicates that shari'a judgments are not concerned with matters of religion, and that morals – as distinct from infractions legally defined – are not subjects for judgments of jurisprudence. These are technical in character and concern practical matters that have been transferred to the field of technical legal terminology, into which these matters were integrated, and in which they acquire an objectivity specific to jurisprudence. This was distinct from the religious and moral considerations covered by the institution of *responsa*, or fatwa, rather than the administration of justice.[189]

It is not odd, therefore, in these conditions, that jurisprudence should be described in practical terms as characterised by a realism mitigating an attachment to tradition, and that it accommodates a pluralism in practice restrained by considerations of probity and discretion in application.[190] In practical terms, it is constituted of cases and individual solutions to particular questions, with a dominant concern for practicality – the Principles of Jurisprudence were hugely ideological, but ulamas when they exercised their legal capacity as judges or legislators tended to be very practical men, like legal professionals in all ages. The centre of gravity in the legal operation always involved a slippage from the rule to the application of the rule.[191] This description was given in an allusion to the Maghrebi practice of jurisprudence in the 1940s, but it appears applicable to the exercise of legal judgment as a whole in the Mashreq up until the period of the Ottoman reforms in the nineteenth century. The Maghrebi collections of legal precedents and statutes seem to have retained their realistic stamp with their foundation in particular cases, opinions, and practice that characterised Maghrebi jurisprudence before the Principles of Jurisprudence stamped its concerns on practical jurisprudence. In general the evolution of the Principles of Jurisprudence was weak in the Maghreb, and the Malaki school after Malik seemed not to have had major jurisprudential figures before Abu al-Walid al-Baji (d. 1081).[192] The application of discretion

189 Baber Johansen, "Die sündige, gesunde Amme: Moral und gesetzliche Bestimmung (hukm) im Islamischen Recht", *Die Welt des Islams* 28 (1988): 271–273, 277–279.

190 See recently: Ahmed Fekry Ibrahim, *Pragmatism in Islamic Law* (Syracuse: Syracuse University Press, 2017).

191 Jacques Berque, *Essai sur la méthode juridique maghrébine* (Rabat: M. Leforestier, 1944), 21–22, 51.

192 al-Azmeh, *Arabic Thought and Islamic Societies*, 209–211 and Abdelmadjid Turki, *Polémiques entre Ibn Hazm et Bājī sur les principes de la loi musulmane: Essai sur le littéralisme Zahirite et la finalité Malékite* (Alger: Études et documents, n.d.), 48–51.

and the relaxation or suspension of established rules was reflected in the analysis of al-Shatibi (relying on al-Ghazali) of the five general categories of the public-interest purposes of shar' outlined already (preservation of life, religion, progeny, wealth, and sanity).[193] In this systematic theoretical enterprise there is a considerable amount of historical and practical realism. It was the cognitive complement to the reality of continuous juristic and legal practice. Therefore, this theorisation was presented by Shatibi in effect as a confirmation of the customs and practices considered as public interest, assimilated to the framework of law construed in terms of Principles.[194] It was difficult to link discretion and juristic preference to the Principles because, in its Hanafite form, discretion and preference involved the abandonment of formal analogy in favour of what conformed better with the situation at hand. This application of discretionary reasoning was not deemed proper by the Shafi'ite jurists, and the Hanbali jurists remained undecided. But this procedure of preference (*istiḥsān*) seemed very often to be a practical necessity, used without use of this or related technical terms.[195]

A concrete illustration of this can be sought in Shatibi's discussion of loans. Although loaning a dirham at interest constituted usury, it is licit usury because of the benign facility it accorded to the borrower, who was thereby rendered a service. This follows the legal principle of giving preference to a particular benefit over the prescription of a contrary general argument.[196] The casuistic stratagems of jurisprudence fall under a similar mode of reasoning. Shatibi, for example, declared these to be invalid if they contravened a basic principle or a legal benefit, but declared them licit if they did not, such as the sales of goods not yet produced,[197] a type of sale on which considerable difference of opinion existed and had been generally considered illicit. Other legists who did not proscribe casuistic stratagems agreed with this position,

193 As we said, al-Shāṭibī's theories relied to a certain extent on the work of al-Ghazālī. See al-Ghazālī, *Al-Muṣṭasfā min 'ilm al-uṣūl*, vol. 1, 286.

194 al-Shāṭibī, *Al-muwāfaqāt fī uṣūl al-aḥkām*, vol. 2, 211–212.

195 Muḥammad Sa'īd al-Būṭī, *Ḍawābiṭ al-maṣlaḥa fī al-sharī'a al-islāmiyya*, 4th edn (Beirut: Mu'assasat al-Risāla, 1982), 368–383; Abū al-Ḥasan 'Alī ibn Muḥammad al-Māwardī, *Adab al-qāḍī*, eds Muḥyī Hilāl al-Sirhān Iḥyā' al-turāth al-islāmī (Baghdad: Maṭba'at al-Irshād, 1971), 650–654; Abū 'Abd Allāh Muḥammad ibn Abū Bakr ibn Qayyim al-Jawziyya, *I'lām al-muwaqqi'īn 'an rabb al-'ālamīn*, revised by Ṭaḥa 'Abd al-Ra'ūf Sa'd (Beirut: Dār al-Jīl, n.d.), vol. 1, 339–342.

196 al-Shāṭibī, *Al-muwāfaqāt fī uṣūl al-ahḥkām*, vol. 4, 135, 134–138.

197 Ibid., vol. 2, 287–288.

and considered stratagems to be limited to those that lead to the achievement of licit aims without sophistry.[198] Al-Sarakhsi, the leading Hanafi legist (d. 1090), considered in a casuistical text that all transactions are characterised by casuistic stratagems. He proscribed stratagems designed to negate the rights of others, but preferred stratagems to lies.[199]

There is no doubt that al-Sarakhsi's equivocal position conformed to the interests of the Khurasani trading aristocracy whose trading and financial activities formed the context for the formation of much of Hanafi law of commercial transactions. This was based on a situation in which vigorous trade required legal and other instruments facilitating financial and fiscal flexibility, with an emphasis on profit. Historical data shows that the form of Hanafi commercial jurisprudence was based on the maintenance of Khurasani legal practices connected with trade and that the modification undergone by these laws when they were Islamised was marginal. The Hanafi formulation of this legal repertoire was the most developed form of commercial law in the Middle Ages. The concept of legal capacity in Hanafi *fiqh* generally – that is to say, the notion of legal person – was based on the capacity to exercise ownership or the capacity to dispose freely of one's property and exercise one's rights.[200] In the same way that Hanafi commercial law was based on worldly requirements, it was signalled earlier that Qur'anic legislation for inheritances had similar bases. Modern scholarship has shown how laws relating to agricultural taxation in the Mamluk and Ottoman periods changed greatly, due to the historical and economic transformation in which the world was involved, a process that began in the fifteenth century.[201]

To sum up, Muslim laws of transaction were law in practice and shari'a in name. It was civil legal activity, religious in its public articulation and

---

198 Ibn Qayyim al-Jawziyya, *I'lām al-muwaqqi'īn 'an rabb al-'ālamīn*, vol. 3, 181–182, 335–336.

199 Muḥammad b. Aḥmad al-Sarakhsī, "*Min kitāb al-mabsūṭ*", annex to al-Shaybānī, *Al-makhārij fī al-ḥiyal*, ed. Joseph Schacht (Leipzig: Heinrichs, 1930), 85, 88, 90–91.

200 With regard to legal capacity in Hanafi jurisprudence, see: Baber Johansen, "Secular and religious elements in Hanafi law: Function and limits of absolute character of government authority", in *Islam et politique au Maghreb*, eds Ernest Gellner and Jean-Claude Vatin (Paris: Éditions du CNRS, 1981), 283–285. On the historical and economic context for jurisprudence relating to business partnerships and loans and other matters, see Abraham L. Udovitch, *Partnership and Profit in Medieval Islam* (Princeton: Princeton University Press, 1970). See also Maxime Rodinson, *Islam and Capitalism* (London: Saqi Books, 2007), chs 3 and 4.

201 Baber Johansen, *The Islamic Law of Land Tax and Rent* (London: Croon Helm, 1988).

general outward form. Shari'a cannot be understood historically apart from this: judgments take place in terms of positive law, *fiqh*, in the envelope of an ideological emblem of good order that is the shari'a. What is referred to as shari'a never covered all legal activity in the histories of Muslims. The system of secular state-regulated courts, the *mazālim*, aimed to go beyond the "narrowness of obligation to the breadth of licence".[202] The *mazālim* and their junior version, the *hisba* or market inspection, were based on the "fear associated with the power of the sultans and the force of severity".[203] The *mazālim* are a form of sovereign power applied in the sense of jurisdiction between adversaries through judgments based on the discretionary powers of the ruler.[204]

The *mazālim* were courts where a form of litigation were practised with regard to matters that were not directly regulated by formal Muslim law, and were subject to sultanic-administrative rather than legal system jurisdiction. The *mazālim* were concerned with matters that political authorities considered to require particular and sometimes expeditious resolution of the kind that formal Muslim law did not allow for: thus homicide, for which jurisprudence depended on a complaint issued by the victim's family, was also seen as litigation involving particular types of discretionary punishment, or decisions on the validity of particular types of witness. Only in the Ottoman *qanun namehs* were certain procedures and provisions of the *mazālim* given a codified form, especially with regard to taxes and punishments.

The Ottoman state complemented customary and civil, sultanic laws with Muslim law, by entrusting the application of civil law to formal shari'a courts. There is here a sign of a rationalising administrative direction in the regulation of the Ottoman sultanate, and to the formal consolidation by the Ottoman state of the setting up of a state "Church" initiated by the Seljuks, Mamluks, and Ayyubids. The Ottomans broadened its area of activity and brought it into the heart of the operation of legislative statecraft. All the laws promulgated by the Ottoman sultan were accredited by *şeyhülislam* – now the head of the entire imperial legal, devotional, and educational hierarchy – and sealed with his ring. It is not known to what extent the *şeyhülislam*

202 Al-Māwardī, *Al-aḥkām as-sulṭāniyya wa al-wilāyāt al-dīniyya*, 83.
203 Abū Ya'lā ibn al-Farrā', *Al-aḥkām al-sulṭāniyya*, 286.
204 Al-Qalqashandī, *Ma 'āthir ināfa fi ma'ālim al-khilāfa*, vol. 1, 78–79.

was able to exert influence in disallowing the legislative will of the sultan, but it is known that disputes existed and that the will of the sultan did not always prevail.[205] Thus, the Ottoman state finally absorbed the institutions of public life into the framework of the legal institution. In the Muslim polities that had preceded the Ottomans, these institutions had been distributed among the shari'a courts, chartered by the sultan and the caliph, and under the control of the chief judge. The administration of justice was dispersed among the courts of the *mazālim*, the violence of the sultan, and the prosecuting authority of the *muḥtasib* – all of these mechanisms, quite apart from the normal social mechanisms of sanction, control, and informal mediation, whose extent must have been very extensive indeed, geographically as well as socially, but hardly at all studied by historians. All the legal operations were then integrated into the framework of the shari'a courts, which was under the supervision of an organised institution headed by the *şeyhülislam*, chief judges and other judges as well sent by the state to the main regional capitals: Cairo, Damascus, Alexandria, Aleppo, and others, although this administrative integration under the banner of the shari'a did not produce a codification of the substantive law and jurisprudence in the modern sense of legislation arranged in separate chapters integrated into a single code. Courts remained divided according to legal schools, and litigants found great benefit in this. The study of documents from the shari'a courts in seventeenth-century Cairo, for example, shows that women seeking to initiate divorce preferred to petition the Hanbali judge given the greater leeway in Hanbali jurisprudence for women to divorce men in comparison to Hanafi jurisprudence.[206] The Ottoman state succeeded in unifying the legal systems and integrating them into a structure that was relatively independent of state administration, operating according to the formal requirements of justice. The Ottomans completed the advanced administrative rationalisation of their state by integrating the elements of urban administration such as the municipalities, which had remained outside traditional legal regulation. These elements were added to the tasks allocated to deputies of the judge.[207]

205 Richard Repp, "Qanūn and Shari'a in the Ottoman Context" in *Islamic Law: Social and Historical Contexts*, ed. al-Azmeh (London and New York: Routledge, 1988), 128–130 and passim.

206 Galal el-Nahal, *The Judicial Administration of Ottoman Egypt in the Seventeenth Century* (Minneapolis and Chicago: Bibliotheca Islamica, 1979), 47.

207 Ibid., 52–54, 57–59, 61–62. See now overall, James Baldwin, *Islamic Law and Empire in Ottoman Cairo* (Edinburgh: Edinburgh University Press, 2017).

A municipal system had existed in the Roman and Byzantine periods and had survived in the form of local practices about which Muslim law remained silent generally. Some such customs were integrated systematically in a formal legal way.[208] With the Ottomans, only rural areas remained outside the scope of public Ottoman law and it is unlikely that the authority of the administrative institution of the *şeyhülislam* had spread in outlying regions, except the regions in which armies were stationed (a parallel here with the Roman *limes*). The Ottoman state's aptitude for constant supervision and administrative centralisation was limited by the means of communication in the pre-industrial world. Roads and telegraph lines were among the first measures of modernisation of the Ottoman state in the nineteenth century. Rural areas will have remained under the authority of local customs and notables, even in matters of personal status that were at variance with what is usually known as Muslim laws of personal status.[209] Mountainous regions remained under the power of their chiefs and notables such as the Anatolian *beylerbeys*, and the *muqāṭaʿjjīya* in Mount Lebanon who dealt with all matters except personal status, which Church custom entrusted to clerics.[210] However, within the limitations of the technical possibilities of the time, the Ottoman judge held sway. He was entrusted with the mission of transmitting *firmāns* – which appointed and dismissed Ottoman governors – and transferring power from one governor to another,[211] acting as a chief notary. The representative of the shariʿa was the representative of the continuity of state and of order in general, as we saw previously with regard to the caliph in the late Abbasid period. In the same way the qadi represented the system, with his application of *fiqh* in the framework of the system of jurisdiction that inherited the charisma of the classical caliphate, later deposited in the shariʿa and its symbols.

It is clear from the preceding pages that the shariʿa symbolising the legal system achieved its mature form and comprehensive purview in later rather than earlier histories of Muslims. Substantive law emerged from specific histories, followed schools of jurisprudence, administrative techniques, and the

---

208 Claude Cahen, "Mouvements populaires et autonomisme urbain dans l'Asie musulmane du Moyen-Âge", *Arabica* 5 (1958): 225–250; 6 (1959): 25–56, 223–265.

209 Al-Subkī, *Muʿīd al-niʿam wa mubīd al-naqam*, 76.

210 Hānī Fāris, *Al-nazaʿāt al-ṭaʾifiyya fī tarīkh Lubnān al-ḥadīth* (Beirut: al-Dār al-Ahliyya li'l-Nashr wa al-Tawzīʿ, 1980), 24.

211 El-Nahal, *The Judicial Administration of Ottoman Egypt*, 65.

institutionalisation of transmitted legal material, both new and renewed, from many regions of the empire.

Legal practices from Iraq became Hanafi and Ja'fari while material from Medina and Kairouan became Maliki.[212] Material from Khurasan of commercial character was integrated into Hanafi jurisprudence. Islamic legal heritage was founded on developing legislation, Arab custom, and local practice. Thereafter this material was classified topically, its secular conditions of emergence obscured, later systematised into the Principles of Jurisprudence, as we saw. Islam constituted itself from its social and legal environments, duly recast and branded as shari'a, and called Islamic.

It will not escape the alert observer that these developments occurred when the Muslims in Iraq and Syria began to settle into the position of a majority – in the year 888 the proportion of Muslims in these regions did not exceed 50 per cent. Egypt was slower than Iraq and Syria in mass conversion, while Iran was the swiftest.[213] When Sunni Islam emerged as a form of Islam distinct from the types of imami Shi'ism that crystallised at the same period (the tenth and the eleventh centuries), it emerged (ideologically represented in Hanbalite utopia, first in Baghdad and later in Damascus), under the patronage and protection of the Seljuks and their successors, who sponsored the Muslim priestly class represented by the four legal schools and rooted, institutionally, in the common educational itinerary of *madrasas*. Islam, as a general sign of the good order, had not succeeded in absorbing all the customs that existed in territories where it predominated. These customs coexisted with the institutions of the *mazālim* and the *ḥisba,* both of which had Byzantine counterparts. The superintendent of markets (*muḥtasib*) had been termed *agoranomos.* The legal content and the administrative procedure for both the *mazālim* and the *ḥisba* were codified in the framework of the shari'a with the coming of the Ottoman state. Shari'a, therefore, in the complete and comprehensive meaning that it took on in the Ottoman state, represented a resumption, after a long interruption, of the alliance of religion and government that prevailed in Byzantium – it being noted that extreme care must

212 There is still only one detailed study of the interaction between Islam and its wider context (social, legal, religious, cultural, political, and economic), namely Michael Morony's excellent *Iraq after the Muslim Conquests* (Princeton: Princeton University Press, 1984). More recent work has been cited in foregoing footnotes.

213 Richard W. Bulliett, *Conversion to Islam in the Medieval Period* (Cambridge, MA: Harvard University Press, 1979), figs 5, 15, 17, 19.

be taken to stay at a distance from clichés about Byzantium, or to disregard the extreme complexity of the situation as it developed over the centuries.[214] In the Ottoman state the sultan and the *şeyhülislam* formed the different elements of this alliance.[215]

It might be said that if the Arab armies had not occupied Syria and Iran and then established there and elsewhere an empire that distinguished itself with a religious appellation, legal evolutions that in crucial ways might have paralleled Muslim law might well have occurred and would have been characterised as Christian and Zoroastrian. Shariʿa represented a recasting of the affairs of the world in a sharʿist language with its repertoire of historical and politico-theological references. As previously noted, this recasting was first a link between legal maxims, practices, and judgments, and ostensible lineages connecting them to high-octane precedents attributed to the beginnings of Islam. These maxims, practices, and judgements were later synthesised into the systematic system of the Principles of Jurisprudence, whose principles were then posited as legal origins. This discipline developed when judgments, individually and collectively, were linked by meta-legal necessity to Sunni Islam erected in the name of shariʿa and its prophetic and patristic precedents. From an ideological point of view, this discipline affirmed attributes of sanctity to legal practices and customs that were old, renewed, and revived. Shariʿa became a general title for good order and a sign of the continuation of this order in private and public life. Other histories, in the same way, used other general titles to designate the order and organisation of the affairs of the social world: *themis* for the Greeks and *dharma* and its many cognates in Indic and Buddhist polities and social systems.

The multiplicity of legal institutes – or indeed their contradictory nature – which shariʿa contains is not evidence for the flexibility of shariʿa, as is often asserted. It is not a readily identifiable and recognisable entity with clear boundaries susceptible to being stretched, tempered, manipulated, and

214 See Averil Cameron, *Byzantine Matters* (Princeton: Princeton University Press, 2014); Gilbert Dagron, *Empereur et prêtre. Étude sur le "césaropapisme" byzantin* (Paris: Gallimard, 1996); al-Azmeh, *Muslim Kingship*, chs 2 and 3.

215 The viewpoint adopted here is that of the Ataturk-era Minister of Education Halide Edib, that Ottoman civilisation was the inheritor of the Byzantine Empire even though Islam played a major role. We nevertheless disagree with her starting point even if our conclusions are similar. Halide Edib, *Turkey Faces West. A Turkish View of Recent Changes and their Origin* (New Haven: Yale University Press, 1930), 30, 33–34.

shaped. Shari'a is a loose container whose unity is derived only from its name as attributed by social actors capable of decreeing a certain concrete element of thought or practice to conform with or disjunct from the shari'a, what Hegel might have termed a "bored [otiose] concept". Vastly divergent places and times and histories and laws can only be united in a way that is nominal. The shari'a is capacious; it names concrete elements as it appropriates them. It is a charismatic title, a sign and a token of rectitude. The creation of tradition overall is only accomplished by an institutional structure able to decide upon and enforce tradition. This institution is no other than the priestly sodality, the authority armed by the state power, a state in its turn declaring itself to be in the name of the shari'a: it constitutes itself with reference to a sign signifying sanctity, and derives sanctity from this sign.

On this basis shari'a is in fact a collection of discrete legal decisions and customary regulations and practices that emerged in the course of time. Its alleged stability signals its symbolic status: this requires completeness, self-sufficiency, and closure, so that its claim for primacy and authoritativeness of reference and appeal with regard to its content can be confirmed. There was not in historical reality a closing of the gate of *ijtihād*, the continuous declaration of this closure notwithstanding.[216] This myth has been part of the claim to completeness, one contemporaneous with the recasting of Muslim law in the form of a principles-structured jurisprudence discussed previously. Shari'a consumes histories voraciously, and engenders Islam from history and transfigures history into the history of Islam. Shari'a recasts the affairs of the world as parts of its own being, bearing its Islamic name. This consumption of history, effacing its multiple specificities and distinctions, and its different times as well, is characteristic of all authority with universalist aspirations. Such authority inclines towards symbolic centralisation in terms of foundational doctrine and law, as in the case of two metahistorical categories widely called Islam and the modern West. In the same way that the West sees history preceding its own as its own pre-history and otherwise hardly history at all, Islamic discourse centres the pattern of history around the genealogies associated with it alone, the rest being false starts or dead ends.

In both cases this situation leads to the development of a historist discourse involving an implicit ethnology that attributes wholesome characteristics to

---

216 Hallaq, "Was the Gate of Ijitihad Closed?", passim.

those in control of the centre, while other peoples come to be marked with savagery and various forms of defectiveness and derangement, as in certain egregious forms of Orientalism and its medieval Arabo-Islamic analogue,[217] and among contemporary civilisation warriors.

In the case of medieval Muslim polities, this orientation was, like that of others, connected to a strong tendency to the centralisation of resources – of commerce, trade, monetary facilities. It was also connected to a trading economy based on the realisation of enormous profits from long-range external trade during the history of the unified Muslim empire and later in the politically fragmented successor states. This orientation was only possible due to its strong material foundations, the most important of which was techniques of ideological authority based on a structure for material and cultural (written and verbal) communication that made Baghdad, later Cairo, Istanbul, and other cities, global metropolises in terms of the historical geography of these times. These techniques and their underlying capacities also united a region with expanding frontiers in the heyday of Abbasid imperialism through a network of trading connections that extended from China to the frontiers of northern Europe.[218] This unification, as noted earlier, was based on the adaptation and further development of a long heritage of techniques associated with authority, ideology, and economy left by the Romans, East-Roman Byzantium, and the Sassanians in regions that later became Umayyad and Abbasid heartlands.[219] These techniques, in their horizontal and vertical extensions (from the centre to the edges and vertically down the hierarchy of power) were transmitted by caliphate and the sultanate and reproduced in various forms and with adjustments down the line. Apart from the crucial role of courtly society, often with cosmopolitan leanings and using the oecumenical vehicle of Arabic, and its profuse literary and

217 al-ʿAẓma, *Al-kitāba al-tārīkhiyya wa al-maʿrifa al-tārīkhiyya: Muqadima fi uṣūl ṣināʿat al-tārīkh al-ʿarabī*, ch. 3 and ʿAzīz al-ʿAẓma, *Al-ʿarab wa al-barābira* (London: Riyad al-Rayyis li-l-nashr, 1991) – an English summary of some main conclusions in Aziz al-Azmeh, "Barbarians in Arab eyes", *Past and Present* 134 (1992): 3–18.

218 For an outstanding description see Maurice Lombard, *The Golden Age of Islam*, trans. Joan Spencer (Amsterdam: North Holland Publishing Company and New York: American Elsevier, 1975), vol. 2.

219 The concept of these techniques and their description is derived from Michael Mann, *The Sources of Social Power*, 4 vols (Cambridge: Cambridge University Press, 1986), vol. 1, *A History of Power from the Beginning to* AD *1760*, ch. 10 and 11. See now also al-Azmeh, *The Emergence of Islam in Late Antiquity*, chs 1 and 8.

other cultures, these techniques were produced and reproduced by a class with an equally important basic role in this universalist and cosmopolitan structure, namely, the ulama, who evolved corporatively, as we saw, into what resembles a state Church. Shari'a was the emblem under which this production and reproduction of ideological authority was officiated. The claim for totalising wholesomeness attributed to shari'a is in effect the presence of authority in the discourse of and on the shari'a. Just as the caliphal and sultanic systems of rule appropriated individual and collective wills as their own, so also does shari'a appropriate minds, representations, and rationalities into a singular unit with claims to exhaustive rationality upon which it embosses its stamp, with exclusive authority in the domain of sacred goods. Let it be emphasised that, all this notwithstanding, there is no reason to hold that shar'ist culture was any more central than secular and courtly cultures before Ayyubid and Mamluk times.

Shari'a, which sought by social and political means to stamp its name on politics, ideology, and many features of public morality, indicates putative origins, and blends present and past indifferently, submitting the present to exemplary origins. Juristic analogy, discussed above, is emblematic of this. Shari'a signals purity of origins and betokens of the continuation of right order.[220] In just the same way as the *'illa* (indicative sign of correlation) in jurisprudence is a sign that integrates different cases into a presumed general category, shari'a, by calling things Islamic, is a fundamental element in a system of classification that defines culture and civilisation – classification and its elementary form, binary classification, is a basic element in ideological enunciations. There is little doubt that separation between inside and outside and the erection of emblems classifying things with reference to origins are fundamental operations in all ideological activity, as indicated by modern anthropology and semiotics.[221] The Islamic appellative "shari'a" functions as a metonym for reality, and assigns uniform characteristics to the individual elements of this changing reality. This name reshapes reality in its image, imposing on reality its presumed characteristics and removing its actual multiplicity and endows it with virtual unity that requires public announcement

220 See Aziz Al-Azmeh, "Registers of genealogical purity in classical Islam", in *Discourses of Purity in Transnational Perspective*, eds M. Bely, N. Jaspert, and S. Köck (Leiden: Brill, 2015), 387–405.

221 'Azīz al-'Aẓma, "Al-dīn wa al-idiyūlūjiya", in *Al-turāth bayn al-sulṭān wa al-tārīkh*, 2nd edn (Beirut: Dār at-Talī'a, Manshūrāt 'Uyūn, 1990), 83–112.

and repetition – this is how fundamentalism functions as a system of politics and social engineering. It consumes the present as it consumes history, separating the authentic from the intrusive, nature from disnature, homeopathic from allopathic, indicating the exclusive genealogy of that which comes to be incorporated into the vast if nevertheless nominal ambit of shari'a.

In the same way, ruling dynasties perceived their beginnings to be in their putative origins and construed their present on their genealogies, in such a way that these, which see the past in light of the present, take the place of history, which works with a preference for keeping the past in the time to which it belongs. While historical thinking looks at subsequent events in the light of preceding ones, genealogical thinking has a positional logic and looks at past in terms of the present. For this reason "the defamation of the origin of a thing defames the thing itself".[222] Similarly, as Ibn al-Khatib said, "the relationship of grandfather to the grandfather is that of grandson to grandson".[223] It is not the social and cultural purpose of genealogy to provide cognition of the past as much as establishing relative positions in hierarchies of the present.[224] And for that reason the histories of Muslims were full of imaginary genealogies and the invention of Quraishi lineages of which Ibn Khaldun included countless examples. And, for that reason, historical and political literature was much concerned with origins. The concern to create lineages and connect things with their origins was a matter that determined the structure of jurisprudence and theology and political and social life, literary genres and social culture in their various forms. Among other things, this included the etiquette of drinking; in assemblies the cup passed from the left to the right in imitation, according to the author of a compendious book on drinking and frolicking, of the style of the Prophet, who in his social gatherings passed the cup of milk clockwise – perhaps a parody, at least tongue in cheek, but indicative nevertheless.

222 Taqī al-Dīn Aḥmad ibn 'Abd al-Ḥalīm ibn Taymiyya, *Muwāfaqat ṣarīh al-ma'qūl li ṣaḥīḥ al-manqūl*, eds Muḥammad Muḥyī al-Dīn 'Abd al-Ḥamīd and Muḥammad Ḥāmid al-Fiqī, 2 vols (Cairo: Maṭba'at al-Sunna al-Muḥammadiyya, 1950–1953), vol. 1, 10.

223 Abū al-'Abbās Aḥmad ibn Muḥammad al-Maqqarī, *Nafḥ al-ṭīb min ghuṣn al-Andalus al-raṭīb*, ed. Iḥsān 'Abbās, 8 vols (Beirut: n.p., 1968), vol. 5, 121.

224 Julio Caro Baroja, *Estudios Mogrebies* (Madrid: Consejo Superior de Investigaciones Cientificas, Instituto de Estudios Africanos, 1957), 30–31; Pierre Bourdieu, *Esquisse d'une théorie de la pratique, précédée de trois études d'ethnologie kabyle*. Collection "Travaux de sciences sociales", vol. 92 (Geneva: Droz, 1972), 88; Abū Isḥāq Ibrāhīm al-Raqīq al-Nadīm, *Qutb al-surūr fī awṣāf al-khumūr*, ed. Aḥmad al-Jundī (Damascus: Majma al-Lūgha al-Arabiyya, 1966), 279.

Knowledge of history and lineage occupied a prominent position in all fields of Islamic discourse, from words and deeds on which analogies and beliefs were constructed to historical events from which lessons were to be learnt. Matters of religious exhortation and reminder are also involved in this, as were rituals such as the pilgrimage and the circumambulation of the Kaaba for which Abrahamic or post-Abrahamic lineages were created. This historical knowledge associated with shari'a formed a vertical top-down source of authority that evaluated contemporary affairs in the name of their prestige on the scale of genealogy (nobility and distance), and indicated absolute beginnings and unique truths followed only by their reproduction and the completion of their foundational operation. All the beginnings are gathered together in one decisive moment, which is that at which discourse commences.[225]

Shari'a thus shares with other areas of discursive, ideological cultural output in the creation of myths of origins. All civilisations create for themselves mythical beginnings in events that are attributed to history or derived from it, events of inauguration and beginnings in which the heroic role is played by mythical or mythified personalities that have become the subject of legend, who may be gods or human heroes or, in modern civilisations, ideas of general will or popular sovereignty. Without a myth of beginnings, no civilisation can have sound foundations in its cultural symbolism, and Islamic civilisation does not depart from this feature of human history overall, finding in certain foundational historical events and in the link with the canonical texts the means of connecting any moment of the present with a founding event – or making a judgement of unwholesome absence.

Islamic civilisation distinguished itself – and the past tense is used here as this is an historical reality belonging to past times, present today as bookish memories, much like Roman civilisation – by two basic features connected with its myth of origin. The first is that foundational events are not limited to occurrences in western Arabia in the seventh century, but encompass also texts to which is endowed a foundational efficacy. The second is that Muslim disciplines of formal knowledge (*ʿilm*), which work to

225 al-ʿAẓma, *Al-kitāba al-tārīkhiyya wa al-maʿrifa al-tārīkhiyya: Muqaddima fi uṣūl ṣināʿat al-tārīkh al-ʿarabī*, 133–140, and Muhammad Arkoun, *Al-fikr al-ʿarabī*, trans. ʿĀdil al-ʿAwwā (Beirut: Manshūrāt ʿUwaydāt, 1982), 47–51. See now al-Azmeh, *The Times of History*, ch. 1.

maintain genealogies and have reference to founding events as structural features, constitute the framework for the making of the myth. Myth is not confined to narratives that resemble fairy tales, but includes a considerable quantity of objective knowledge-related content, patterned and narrated in ways characteristic of myth, and accessible to mythographic analysis. Myth is not just a fairy tale or a legend of origins, but a form of transferring real or imaginary origins from a beginning – real or imaginary – to a present characterised by a direct genealogical link. In addition, there are not myths of origin without rituals that retell its story and confirm its memory and vouch for its authority. The books of *'ilm* and the occasions of reading and study of it and laying the foundations of *'ilm* in Islamic civilisation were the rituals of the Islamic myth of origins, irrespective of what practical or pragmatic purposes they satisfied and functions they performed; such, for instance, are ritual readings of *hadith* works in devotional settings. Such is also of course pilgrimage at Mecca.

Thus, Muslim religious, devotional, and legal institutions, later developing into the analogue of state churches, were the setting for the transmission and the circulation of this self-referential founding myth for the genealogical ideology. This myth names, and by naming constitutes an apparatus of the symbolic imagination that is one of the supports for the self-perpetuation of any civilisation or other form of ideological order. There is no continuity without the illusion of continuity. The reality of continuity can only be founded on the illusion of persistence through the imposition of an imaginary form of reality, and civilisations, extremely complex categories and historical phenomena, act summarily and nominally as rhetorical figures for continuity over time. This is only possible if the operation of naming were reinforced by the compulsion of certitude premised on credibility claimed and maintained by two sources of authority: the power of naming – naming things as Islamic – on the one hand and its power as an institutional apparatus linked to political authority on the other.

The reality of Islam has been mutable, heterogeneous, distinct in its elements. The official public consciousness related to the shari'a has not necessarily prevailed in any exclusive way among all groups and at all times. Cultural homogenisation (including homogenisation in the name of shari'a) was possible only in modern times with the possibilities of communication and administration proper to modern states. Officious piety was often mocked, in medieval Arab as in medieval European societies. This is abundantly clear in Arabic as well as in Persian literature.[226] Parodies of the Qur'an continued after al-Ma'arri (d. 1057) while the mystically possessed poets, in subsequent eras, had an important role, employing a definitely revolutionary tone.[227] Those controlling shari'a continued to deny commoners access to theology, and proscribed unlicensed preaching.[228] In general the history of the homogeneity ascribed to Islam remains an unwritten chapter in social and cultural history. But there are no grounds for accrediting the claims to homogeneity as anything but an ideological trope; among other historical evidence, this is clear from continuous polemics against miscreants. What one is more likely to expect is that cultures as forms of daily practice in Muslim lands were common to the members of all confessions; Jewish holy men, for example, in the Atlas Mountains and in Yemen were venerated by Muslims and the Muslim mausolea of saints in Egypt were visited by Christians for benediction and miracle-making.[229] At a level of formal culture, a convergence in the dominant intellectual structures is witnessed. Works of canon law in Arab countries, Maronite and others, are marked by a definite Islamic character in organisation and content, and there

226 See, for instance, Aziz al-Azmeh, "Freidenkertum und Humanismus. Universelle Stimmungen, Motiven und Themen im Zeitalter der Abbasiden", in *Humanismus, Reformation, Aufklärung*, eds Hubert Cancik and Hubert Schöpner (Berlin: Humanistische Akademie, 2017), pp. 15–31 (an earlier version of the same: "Abbasid Culture and the Universal History of Freethinking", *Critical Muslim* 12 [2014]: 73–88); Zoltán Szombathy, *Mujun: Libertinism in Medieval Muslim Society and Literature* (London: Gibb Memorial Series, 2013).

227 For example, the *ṣuwar* al-shaykh Sha'bān al-Majdhūb in Abū al-Mawāhib 'Abd al-Wahhāb ibn Aḥmad al-Sha'rānī, *Al-ṭabaqāt al-kubrā al-musammāt lawāḥiq al-anwār fī ṭabaqāt al-akhyār*, 2 vols (Cairo: Maṭba'at al-Bābī al-Ḥalabī, 1954), vol. 2, 185–186. A *majdhūb* (mystic or one possessed) is the person drawn towards God without a spiritual guide; the same word is used in colloquial Arabic for an idiot or a fool. See also Ibn Khallikān, *Wafayāt al-'Ayān*, vol. 7, 256; al-Nu'āymī, *Al-Dāris fī tārīkh al-madāris*, 213; Taqī al-Dīn Abū al-'Abbās Aḥmad ibn 'Alī al-Maqrīzī, *Al-mawā'iẓ wa al-i'tibār bi dhikr al-khiṭaṭ wa al-āthār al-ma'rūf bi al-khiṭaṭ al-maqrīzīya*, 2 vols (Cairo: Maṭba'at Bulāq, 1270/1853), vol. 2, 435.

228 Abū al-Faraj 'Abd al-Raḥmān ibn 'Alī ibn al-Jawzī, *Kitāb al-quṣṣāṣ wa al-mudhakkirīn*, ed. M. S. Schwartz (Beirut: al-Matba'a al-Kāthūlīkiyya, n.d.), paras 24, 200–273; Ḍiyā' al-Dīn Muḥammad ibn Muḥammad ibn al-Ukhūwwa, *Ma'ālim al-qurba fī aḥkām al-ḥisba*, ed. R. Leakey, revised and trans. Reuben Levy (Cambridge: Cambridge University Press, 1938), 179–181; Al-Subkī, *Mu'īd al-ni'am wa mubīd al-niqam*, 162–163. Al-Subkī (at p. 205) wanted to prohibit "fabricated books", popular literature such as *Sīrat 'Antara.*

229 On the absorption by the Church of local customs in Europe, see Jacques Le Goff, *Time, Work and Culture in the Middle Ages*, trans. Arthur Goldhammer (London and Chicago: University of Chicago Press, 1982), 157 and passim. See especially Richard F. Green, *Elf Queens and Holy Friars: Fairy Beliefs and the Medieval Church* (Philadelphia: University of Pennsylvania Press, 2017).

is no doubt that this is a reflection of a common social circumstance, and not necessarily due to the influence of Muslim jurisprudence.[230] Medieval Jewish theology is permeated with kalam.[231]

What is the sense, therefore, of speaking of an "Islamic" history? Is the totalising form in which Islam appears in this context not a categorical error? The inevitable conclusion is that the Islam of historical self-fashioning and tradition was a nominal Islam, from which history has been extruded except for specific elements reconfigured in a narrative with purposes approaching those of myth. The characterisation holds only through the voice of authority, and its capacity to impose assent. If Arab Islam was Byzantine in many of its characteristics, and Arab Christianity was Islamic in many of its features, and if Persian and Hebrew literature used similar Arabic poetic metres, what of origins and historical primacy?

230 For example, Abū Sayf Yūsuf, *Al-aqbāṭ wa al-qawmiyya al-ʿarabiyya: Dirāsa istiṭlāʿiya* (Beirut: Markaz Dirāsāt al-Waḥda al-ʿArabiyya, 1987), 96 and Shafīq Shiḥāta [Chafik Chehata], *Aḥkām al-aḥwāl al-shakhṣiyya li-ghayr al-muslimīn min al-miṣriyīn*, 8 vols (Cairo: Jāmiʿat al-Duwal al-ʿArabiyya, Maʿhad al-Dirasāt al-ʿArabiyya al-ʿĀliya, 1958–1963), vol. 1, *Fī maṣādir al-fiqh al-masīḥī al-sharqī wa fī al-khuṭba*, 41, 43–44, 47. See Salaymeh, *The Beginning of Islamic Law*, ch. 6, for aspects of Muslim and Jewish divorce.

231 See, for instance, Harry A. Wolfson, *Repercussions of the Kalam in Jewish Philosophy* (Cambridge, MA: Harvard University Press, 1978) and Daniel J. Lasker, "The Jewish critique of Christianity under Islam in the Middle Ages", *Proceedings of the American Academy for Jewish Research* 57 (1990–1991): 121–153.

2
The Reformist State and the Universalist Orientation

Secularism, as described in the previous chapter, emerged as an integral component to the course and effects of modern European historical development: secularism understood as the centrality of non-religious elements in the intellectual equipment of the age, its normative regulation, and its symbolic apparatus. European, or more precisely, Western European, history was not confined to Europe, but transported its economic, political, intellectual, organisational, and imaginative wherewithal wherever it expanded after the first period of financial and commercial expansion based on sheer plunder, one that involved principally Spain and her colonies, later Holland and England. This continued as Europe settled into a phase of long-term, organised exploitation of the world. North-west Europe's eruption of energy and its spread set up a global system driven initially by early forms of capitalism, mercantilism, and international trade from the sixteenth century onwards. This system was based on satisfying the developing economic interests of Europe by subordinating the rest of the world and yoking its economies to Europe. There followed pressure by military might and colonial expansion, direct and indirect, aimed at transforming the societies and political systems of the non-European world in ways that conformed to the subaltern condition to which their economies were now reduced.[1]

1 Perhaps the best description of this world system from the point of view of subordinate and dependent continents is Eric Robert Wolf's, *Europe and the People without History* (Berkeley and Los Angeles: University of California Press, 1982). This book has as its starting point the dependent non-European world, in contrast to Amsterdam and London in the better known and more influential work of Immanuel Wallerstein. For an exemplary recent study of the East Indies in this period, informed by a perspective similar to the Wolfian, see Romain Bertrand, *L'Histoire à parts égales* (Paris: Seuil, 2011).

The expansion of Europe led to the eventual collapse of many political structures across the world. However, large states – such as the Ottoman Empire and the Alaoui sultanate in Morocco – were able to withstand European pressure in various ways that preserved their integrity to the degree possible. Initially, such states had been compelled to respond to monetary inflation in the sixteenth century and the steady expansion of commercial concessions (the so-called "Capitulations") that had spread around the Mediterranean from the Middle Ages onwards.

But these responses, such as they were initially, tended to lack overall coherence, taking the limited form of piecemeal administrative and military arrangements. They did not involve an overall strategy of systemic transformation in the face of an expanding global economy seeking hegemony, and European military and diplomatic pressures were ultimately to prevail. Istanbul did, however, emerge to be far ahead of others in pondering these issues, it being the capital city of the cosmopolitan imperial state, and the hinge of diplomatic and cultural links between the principal cities of the sultanate – Cairo, Aleppo, Damascus, and Tunis, later Beirut – with European countries. Indications suggest that systematic consideration of the weakness of the Ottoman state commenced in the early eighteenth century with the report of Çelebi Mehmet, Ottoman envoy to the court of Louis XV in 1720. The work *Usul el-hikem fi nizam el-ümem* (from the Arabic *Uṣūl al-ḥikam fi niẓām al-umam*) by Ibrahim Müteferrika, published in 1731, included a detailed presentation of the bases of government in Europe. The author, a Hungarian convert, suggested an overall reorganisation of the armies of the Ottoman state on modern foundations. Despite the fierce opposition from military and Anatolian feudal interests as well as the state administration that opposed reform, the first engineering school was set up in Istanbul in 1769. Foreigners were brought in to train the army and continual Russian attacks on the territory of the Ottoman state were used to justify these reforms. These first reforms reached their peak with the foundation of the Nizam-i cedid army at the time of Selim III. These were interrupted completely when the janissaries and other parties revolted against the sultan Selim III in 1807, and thwarted the new military system as well as initiatives to re-establish state control of finances and to end favouritism in appointments to the religious and scholarly establishment.[2]

2 Niyazi Berkes, *The Development of Secularism in Turkey* (Montreal: McGill University Press, 1964), 33–34, 42–43, and 56–60 and Stanford J. Shaw, *Between Old and New: The Ottoman Empire under Selim III, 1789–1807* (Cambridge, MA: Harvard University Press, 1971). See now

The Ottoman response unfolded at the level of state organisation, both in Istanbul and in its Arab provinces that possessed a sometimes considerable degree of local autonomy in an imperial state framework (Cairo and Tunis – Mount Lebanon fared differently). The Ottoman state initiated institutional and associated reforms and related them to society and the economy in ways more deliberate than hitherto, and more responsive to the demands of the imperial centre. As part of this process, Selim III attempted to control more closely the workings of the Capitulations system, with strong opposition from European powers.[3] The reforms of Selim III were enacted by royal edict and were unconnected to specific institutions and administrative instruments linked to the reform process, with little regard for the internal political moorings of these reforms. The more fundamental Ottoman reforms known as "the Benevolent Institutes", the *Tanzimat*, initiated by the edict of Gülhaneh in 1839 – and other initiatives in the Egypt of Muhammad Ali Pasha (r. 1805–1848) then in the period of Ismail (r. 1863–1879) and in the Tunis of Muhammad Bay (r. 1855–1859) – were therefore enacted after the elimination of opponents to reform. Examples include Muhammad Ali's notorious banquet massacre of almost the entire politico-military elite in the Citadel of Cairo 1811, and the bloody elimination of thousands of janissaries and their allies in Istanbul in 1826. These reforms occurred in the context of what might be described as the political culture of the *Tanzimat*.

The unfolding of events related to reform in Istanbul, Egypt, and Tunis followed different rhythms and took on distinct aspects. These were not entirely separate nor entirely country specific, as their causes and their guiding ideas were linked. In Istanbul this operation, in its historical unfolding, came with a certain coherence from the start. Administrative, legal, and educational reforms were accompanied by new understandings of the state, its structures and functions. In Egypt the initial phase of the reforms under Muhammad Ali Pasha blended the personalised, patrimonial Mamluk state – based on the appropriation of revenue and military service regarded as corvée – together with a new style of state administration and its dependent institutions such as the staggered beginnings of a new educational system.[4]

Baki Tezcan, *The Second Ottoman Empire. Political and Social Transformation in the Early Modern World* (Cambridge: Cambridge University Press, 2010).

3 Berkes, *Development of Secularism*, 178–179.

4 See in general, with emphasis on the army, Khaled Fahmy, *All the Pasha's Men* (Cambridge: Cambridge University Press, 1997).

In Tunis the reforms were enacted and implemented rather more integrally, much like in Istanbul, although they came slightly later and, like reforms emanating from Istanbul, were uneven in their implementation in terms of geography and demographic group. Tunisia after 1881 was exposed to even more rapid evolution under the effect of French colonisation, engaged at that time in bringing about far-reaching and highly disintegrative change in the neighbouring French territory of Algeria. These changes had placed Algeria on a distinctive path of development after the state of the Prince Abdelkader had been vanquished in 1847.

The situation in Morocco was a blend between military resistance and a revived spirit of centralised Makhzen power in part actuated by a Salafi orientation – similar in some basic motifs to Wahhabism, but intellectually better developed – which did not lead to any notable changes. The reformist policy of Makhzen authority in Morocco was limited to undercutting Sufi fraternities, restriction of the social and political privileges of some elements among the ulama (such as the Idrisids), and consolidation of the sultan's power over the judiciary and the Qarawiyyin Mosque. An alliance of Salafi character developed between the sultan Abdelhafiz (r. 1908–1912 – author of the heresiographic and rigourist *Kashf al-qināʿ ʿan iʿtiqād ṭawāʾif al-ibtidāʿ*, published in Fès in 1326/1908) and some of the ulama headed by Abu Shuʿayb al-Dukkali (1878–1937), an alliance that led to harsh sanctions against those contravening the demands on behaviour imposed by this Salafi tendency. Muhammad ʿAbduh described this as "exaggerated fanaticism and punishments such as amputation of limbs for smoking and drinking".[5] This gave state and society the character of an embalmed mummy.[6] This backward-looking Moroccan resistance was closer to that of Abdelkader in Algeria than it was to the headlong entry into modernity and the opening up to the future that took place in Istanbul, Cairo, and Tunis.

---

5 ʿAbduh, *Al-aʿmāl al-kāmila*, vol. 3, 313; Yūsuf Ilyān Sarkīs, *Muʿjam al-maṭbūʿāt al-ʿarabiyya wa al-muʿarraba*, 2 vols (Cairo: Maṭbaʿat Sarkīs, 1927–1931), 1,271, and Edmund Burke III, "The Moroccan Ulama, 1860–1912: An introduction", in *Scholars, Saints and Sufis: Muslim Religious Institutions in the Middle East since 1500*, ed. Nikki R. Keddie (Berkeley and Lost Angeles: University of California Press, 1972), 107–114.

6 The expression is Abdallah Laroui's [ʿAbd Allāh al-ʿArwī]. See his *The History of the Maghreb: An Interpretative Essay*, trans. Ralph Manheim, Princeton Studies on the Near East (Princeton: Princeton University Press, 1977), 326, 367.

There is no doubt that the new reforms, in their economic, administrative, financial, and legal aspects, were rooted in the structure of the global system centred in Europe. They had been a response to the demands of this system based on the primacy of European interests in the East. These included financial interests in the form of the debts owed by Istanbul, Cairo, and Tunis. The circumstances were not very different from the pressures, both administrative and structural, by the World Bank today. These interests also included legal concessions made to the European communities and those local Christian and Jewish communities that had been placed under European protection. While European consuls intervened directly in the political and legal affairs of the Ottoman Empire, foreign intervention was not the only factor driving the *Tanzimat*. These reforms under their different names had been carried out in response to internal organisational necessities. They needed to be addressed if the structures of the Ottoman and the Egyptian states were to survive in the context of modernity towards which the prevailing economic and political system in the nineteenth century had driven them.

Other reform movements that developed in outlying regions and on the frontiers of the empire reinforced obsolete social structures and economic links. The Senoussi in Cyrenaica defended clan networks and reinforced them with religious sanction and alliance, while the Wahhabis employed clan networks buttressed by religion, in the service of centralisation and independence for Najd in the Arabian Peninsula as required by its position in the local markets developing under British impact and that of the British–Ottoman contention in the region. The Mahdi in Sudan used religiously reinforced clan networks and appeal to charismatic sanctity to defend slave-trading routes and sources and the social and political networks that lent dynamism to them. These movements were in consequence reformist according to the self-perception of those involved, and to the traditional sense of the term "reform" in the history of religion: return to the past from a present considered decadent. Such reform manifested itself as withdrawal and retreat.

In the Ottoman state and its dependencies, the *Tanzimat* reforms were a voluntary move towards integration into the global political and economic system based on a balance of forces that favoured European interests, and on a new statist political culture. This culture entailed a constellation of political and social concepts that underpinned calls for political reform – including, very furtively, forms of limited participation – alongside ideas of rational and positive legislation, a new intellectual and cultural formation that was implicitly secular. All this occurred under the auspices of the *Tanzimat* state. These changes were accompanied by educational, cultural and legal innovations fashioned by this state. The Egyptian state, without local parties and associations, constructed a national concept of political association, and from this concept emerged both modernity and, later, Egyptian nationalism.[7] In Istanbul the state carried out the same mission on a wider front than merely the Turkish provinces of the empire.

The *Tanzimat* state sought to reshape itself in the form of the European state as conceived both by the *Tanzimat* state and by modern European states themselves. The pre-modern state had been minimalist, subordinating social groups and classes without penetrating them, linking them to itself primarily by the tributary relation of taxation and legal privilege. In contrast, the *Tanzimat* state sought societal penetration, through its attempt to engineer individuals for social as distinct from strictly jurisprudential purposes as relatively autonomous entities rather than as members of a collectivity, however defined, and, several moves down the line, as citizens.

The *Tanzimat* state was, therefore, through its political culture, tendentially at the vanguard of universal political thought as it existed in Europe, based on principles of nationalism and citizenship. This was situated at the intersection of political, technical, and social change and relied on an official culture of political supervision and direction, a culture marking, ideally, the state and its personnel.[8] The *Tanzimat* state relied on principles of administrative rationality that potentially implied the removal of the sultanic personalisation of executive authority. It also sought to eliminate the intermediate entities – craft guilds, ethnic communities, and so on – which were the nodal points of collective as distinct from individual subordination to the sultanic state. Henceforth the state – represented by the sultan – sought to administer individual subjects whose relations with the state was to have a direct character, distinct from the ascription of collective character

7 al-Bishrī, *Al-Muslimūn wa al-Aqbāṭ fī iṭār al-jamā'a al-waṭaniyya*, 11–12. See now Adam Mestyan, *Arab Patriotism. The Ideology and Culture of Power in Late Ottoman Egypt* (Princeton: Princeton University Press, 2017). More broadly: Şükrü Hanioğlu, *A Brief History of the Late Ottoman Empire* (Princeton: Princeton University Press, 2010).

8 Ernest Gellner, *Nations and Nationalism, New Perspectives on the Past* (Oxford: Basil Blackwell and Ithaca: Cornell University Press, 1983), 48, 58, and passim; Eric J. Hobsbawm, *Nations and Nationalism since 1780: Programme, Myth and Reality* (Cambridge: Cambridge University Press, 1990), 10–11.

of ethnic communities, villages, and craft and Sufi order-based groupings.[9] Such units of subordination were at the heart of the system that the obsolescent pre-*Tanzimat* order had sought to protect, through its maintenance of corporate distinctions between schools of *fiqh* and confessions, distinctions that determined their respective social locations and the connections between them. Another system of collective control and separation govering the movement of women in public space – how, when, and where – had been determined by detailed administrative provisions in a system that surpassed in the detail of its regulation the organisation of other social distinctions.[10] The reforming state enacted laws in its capacity as the fundamental law-making instance, in contrast to the traditional Muslim jurisprudential system that had, as we have seen, reclaimed local customs and regulations labelling them "Islamic" or even used these as the basis of legal generalisation as in the *'amal* in Fès and other initiatives in Morocco.[11]

The *Tanzimat* state was not entirely successful in all its plans and in every domain. It had variable degrees of success in implementing new legislation and the new administrative and legal logic connected to it. There were variations and considerable unevenness in depth and extent of transformation according to a variety of parameters, geographical, ecological, socio-economic, communitarian, and educational. The late Ottoman state faced a number of internal impediments linked to administrative personnel as well as objective social and financial obstacles.[12] These affected the implementation of reforms, which varied from the relatively comprehensive in western Anatolia and parts

9 On intermediary bodies and the relationship of the Tanzimāt state with them, compare Wajīh Kawtharāni, *Al-sulṭa wa al-mujtama' wa al-'amal al-siyāsī: Min ta'rikh al-wilāya al-'uthmāniyya fī bilād al-shām*, Doctoral Thesis Series, 13 (Beirut: Markaz Dirasāt al-Waḥda al-'Arabiyya, 1988), 50, 77–90.

10 Nora Seni, "Ville ottomane et représentation du corps féminin", *Les Temps Modernes* 456–457 (1984): 66–95, 66–74, 83.

11 For an excellent analysis of the importance of engagement with local customs and the ways that they could be used, see the fundamental text of one of the most important jurisprudents of the Syrian provinces in the nineteenth century, Muḥammad Amīn ibn 'Ābidīn (d. 1836), Superintendent of *fatwā* in Damascus, "Nashr al-'urf fī binā' ba'ḍ al-aḥkām 'alā al-'urf", in Muḥammad Amīn ibn 'Ābidīn, *Majmū'at rasā'il Ibn 'Ābidīn*, 2 vols (Istanbul: Maṭba'at al-Sharika al-Ṣuḥufiyya al-'Uthmāniyya wa Muḥammad Hāshim al-Kutubī, 1325/1907), vol. 2, 114–147. With regard to a specific Moroccan case (al-Saksāwa in the High Atlas) see Jacques Berque, *Structures sociales du Haut-Atlas*, bibliothèque de sociologie contemporaine, série B. Travaux du centre d'Études sociologiques (Paris: Presses Universitaires de France, 1955), 244–245, 323–397.

12 Kawtharāni, *Al-sulṭa wa al-mujtama' wa al-'amal al-siyāsī*, 118–122.

of Ottoman Syria, to slower procedures and a narrower range in the Ottoman provinces of Iraq. In Yemen and Hejaz reforms were extremely fragmentary.[13]

In Egypt, there was an incipient whiff of administrative rationality and proto-nationalist concepts spread by Napoleonic propaganda. The reformist work of al-Tahtawi (1801–1873) was admired by Muhammad Ali Pasha to the extent that he ordered that it be read aloud in his palaces and translated into Turkish.[14] Nevertheless, Muhammad Ali's state seems to have given primary importance to its function as an instance of surveillance and control. The state's educational role was limited to what was required to set up these systems and the technical needs of ther army.[15] Al-Tahtawi himself remained a theoretician of political despotism. Despite the relative success achieved in Egypt, the important point for this discussion is the constellation of the principles, theoretical as well as practical (administrative and political) on which the *Tanzimat* were based. These constituted a vague orientation of action, destined, like all other such programmes, to have had very uneven achievement. The most important aspect of this orientation was the primacy of the state apparatus over other entities of a social and religious character. The operation of this state apparatus implied a number of principles with, in first place, the submission of this apparatus, from its lowest ranks to the sultanate at its summit, to a general law that should go beyond the sultan's personal power over all ranks of the administration. The *Tanzimat* state was thus part of the global trend that characterised modernist developments and their related ideologies, associated with modernism and positivism, in Europe and elsewhere – in Ottoman domains, south-east Asia, and Latin America. It was therefore unsurprising that Auguste Comte considered in his open letter to Reşid Paşa (1800–1858), one of the leading reformers, that the reformist Ottoman state was inclining towards positivism in a way impossible in the

---

13 Sāṭiʿ al-Ḥuṣrī', *Al-bilād al-ʿarabiyya wa al-dawla al-ʿuthmāniyya: Muḥāḍarāt alqāhā ʿalā ṭullāb maʿhad al-dirāsāt al-ʿarabiyya al-ʿāliya* (Beirut: Dār al-'Ilm l'il-Malāyīn, 1960), 93–94.

14 Aḥmad Ḥusayn al-Sāwī, *Fajr al-ṣaḥāfa fī Miṣr: Dirāsa fī iʿlām al-ḥamla al-faransiyya* (Cairo: al-Hay'a al-Miṣriyya al-ʿĀmma li'l-Kitāb, 1975), ch. 2; Louis ʿAwaḍ, *Al-muʾāththirāt al-ajnabiyya fī al-adab al-ʿarabī al-ḥadīth*, 2 vols (Cairo: Jāmiʿat al-Duwal al-ʿArabiyya, Maʿhad al-Dirāsāt al-ʿArabiyya al-ʿĀliya, 1962), part 1, *Min al-ḥamla al-faransiyya ilā ʿahd Ismāʿīl*, ch. 1, 147 ff. See also Jurjī Zaydān, *Tarājim mashāhīr al-sharq fī al-qarn al-tāsiʿ ʿashar*, 2 vols (Beirut: Dār Maktabat al-Ḥayāt, 1970), 33.

15 Timothy Mitchell, *Colonising Egypt* (Cambridge and New York: Cambridge University Press, 1988), chs 2 and 3 and ʿAbduh, *Al-aʿmāl al-kāmila*, vol. 1, 725.

states of Europe, benighted, in Comte's opinion, by revolution and chaos.[16] Unsurprisingly, the followers of Comte and the Saint-Simonians were active on a broad scale in the Arab lands and notably in Egypt and Algeria. Many of these taught in Muhammad Ali's schools and brought with them ideas of control and social homogenisation.[17]

In this course of things, basic political legislation was accompanied by guarantees from the rulers, not hitherto subject to constitutional regulation. The Gülhaneh Edict of 1839 was described by one late Ottoman official as an "abbreviated version of the fundamental law on the basis of which realms are administered according to consultation in the hope of broadening its scope in the future". It was issued together with a handwritten undertaking by the sultan Abdülmecit that he would respect the content of the Edict, and that he would promulgate no laws contradicting the Edict or enact anything that would invalidate it. As for the Tunisian *'Ahd al-Amān* (Pledge of Security) issued by Muhammad Bay in 1857, this was complemented in 1861 with a Fundamental Law issued by Muhammad Sadiq Bay, which held him personally and his legatees bound by the provisions of the Pledge and the laws that derived from it. Such adhesion to the Pledge was a condition for the Bay of Tunis to receive the allegiance of his subjects.[18]

The basic legislation of the *Tanzimat* clearly did not establish a democratic system or institute a secular order linked to democracy such as to liberate the individual from any authority save that of individual conscience. The process nevertheless sowed the seeds that subsequently led to the constitutional trends in Istanbul and Cairo. Crucial to these reforms is that they led to the emergence of a new class of intellectuals linked to political and administrative modernisation, and initially arising from the administrative and operational needs of those reforms. Tunisia had a somewhat distinctive position. It had been set on a distinctive path by the French occupation of 1881, although she did resemble the Ottoman regions in the long-term historical trajectory that made the Tunisian evolutions closer, overall, to those of the Middle East than to those of the Maghreb. Although the Ottoman sultans at the time of the

16 Auguste Comte, *Système de politique positive* (Paris: Chez l'auteur, 1853), xlviii, xlil.

17 Mitchell, *Colonising Egypt*, 39–40. See now Osama Abi-Mershed, *Apostles of Modernity: Saint Simonians and the Civilizing Mission in Algeria* (Stanford: Stanford University Press, 2010).

18 'Abd al-'Aziz al-'Azma, *Mir'āt al-shām: Tarikh dimashq wa ahluhā* (London: Riyad al-Rayyis li'l-Kutb wa al-Nashr, 1988), 175.

Tanzimat declared their adhesion to an impersonal system of law and called it Islamic law (as stipulated in the Gülhaneh Edict), they imposed no limit, constitutionally or practically, on their supreme administrative and executive power, and on their oversight of the religious and legal institution, represented by the *şeyhülislam* whose appointment was the gift of the sultan. The relationship between the sultan and the religious institution underwent a significant change in favour of the former, deepening his historical but not absolute pre-eminence. The Gülhaneh Edict was issued, for the first time in the history of the Ottoman state, without a supporting fatwa from the *şeyhülislam*.[19] The reason for that was not opposition on the part of Ahmad Arif Hikmet Bey, who occupied this position at the time and was a supporter of the *Tanzimat*.[20]

The Gülhaneh Edict affirmed the power of the sultan to issue laws without reference to any other authority. Sultan Mahmud II had ordered the *şeyhülislam*'s to draft a treatise providing a basis for the sultan's legislative authority, affirming it and justifying it.[21] It was under this sultan that the greater part of the arrangements for the promulgation of the Gülhaneh Edict were completed, although the Edict was issued five months after his death accompanied by the signature of his son and successor, sultan Abdülmecit. This is unsurprising considering that the elimination of the janissaries had, as a consequence, the retreat of the religious institution and the strengthening of the state at the expense of all the other institutions. Indeed, the *şeyhülislam*'s direct link and access to the person of the sultan was removed, and he became, with the formation of the first council of Ministers under sultan Mahmud, one of the members of this council, subordinate in the administrative hierarchy to the Prime Minister, known as the Grand Vizier. Developments at the centre of the Ottoman state and its core regions (notably Syria) played a decisive role in the separation of religious and political authority at the level of exercise of authority and direct legislation. In Egypt, however, this separation was enacted in operational rather than legal terms, and depended less on definite administrative regulation than on the

19 Berkes, *The Development of Secularism in Turkey*, 147.

20 Khayr al-Din al-Tūnisī, *Aqwām al-masālik fī ma'rifat aḥwāl al-mamālik*, ed. Muḥammad al-Munṣif al-Shanūfī, 2nd edn (Tunis: al-Dār al-Tūnisiyya li'l-Nashr, 1972), 142.

21 Berkes, *The Development of Secularism in Turkey*, 146 and Şerif Mardin, *The Genesis of Young Ottoman Thought: A Study in the Modernisation of Turkish Political Ideas*, Princeton Oriental Studies, vol. 21 (Princeton: Princeton University Press, 1962), 149.

will of individual rulers of Egypt, from Muhammad 'Ali Pasha to the Khedive Ismail. The instruments of this separation were state control of the income accruing from *awqāf* and a direct financial dependence on the Egyptian state by the Azhar and the wider religious institution.[22]

In Tunis, Kheireddine (1820–1890) treated the religious institution – intertwined with the Tunisian Maliki and Hanafi patriciate – with great circumspection and finesse.[23] His general intellectual orientation gave primacy to religious considerations and regarded worldly matters to be practical arrangements essential for the stability of religion.[24] He sought to justify Ottoman reforms by claiming that the reforming Ottoman sultans associated the ulama with the state ministers in the affairs of state.[25] In general, Kheireddine sought to widen the scope of Muslim jurisprudence so as to include politics, as had been the case in Islamic history – a subject covered in the preceding chapter – rather than the contrary, which was the overall direction elsewhere.[26] In these conditions, it is unsurprising that Kheireddine was considered in Istanbul to have been reactionary, and his appointment to the post of Grand Vizier by the sultan Abdülhamid II was therefore seen as quite apt.[27]

The ideas of Ottoman reform did not therefore involve or imply any notion of the separation of power, even though the independent and impersonal legal authority of Muslim jurisprudence had been announced. This does not indicate disorder so much as the transitional nature of Ottoman reforms. It would have been surprising if the decisive separation of powers occurred when such a separation was still uncertain in Europe itself. The Ottoman sultan committed himself to consultation without there being mechanisms that governed the operations of such a process, and before the functions of the state Consultative Council were better organised. These developments led to the formation of a new Ottoman constitution in 1876 and the election of the first Ottoman parliament in 1877.

---

22 Daniel Crecelius, "Non-ideological responses in the Egyptian Ulama to Modernization", in *Scholars, Saints and Sufis: Muslim Religious Institutions in the Middle East since 1500*, ed. Nikki R. Keddie (Berkeley: University of California Press, 1972), 181–182.

23 Arnold Harrison Green, *The Tunisian Ulama, 1873–1915: Social Structure and Response to Ideological Currents* (Leiden: Brill, 1978), 117–118.

24 Khayr al-Dīn al-Tūnisī, *Aqwām al-masālik*, 82–83, 142–143, 154–155 and elsewhere.

25 Ibid., 137–138.

26 al-Laṭīf, *Al-ta'wīl wa al-mufāraqa*, 11–15.

27 Mardin, *The Genesis of Young Ottoman Thought*, 385–387, 390–391.

This was destined to be an abortive constitutional attempt, as only a few months passed before the sultan Abdülhamid II dissolved the state Consultative Bureau and suspended the Constitution in 1879, the very same Constitution that established the sultan as caliph and pronounced the Constitution a shar'i document. In the period between the official proclamation of the principle of citizenship independent of religious affiliation in 1869 and the removal of the *şeyhülislam* and his associated institution from the central position in the state on the one hand, and the constitutional movement in the Ottoman state on the other, was a short period rich in events, during which educational establishments independent of religious institutions were founded and legal reforms were enacted by the state. A new class also emerged, composed of secular intellectuals, a development that was significantly to alter the link between religion and affairs of the world in the Ottoman state and in key sectors of the Arab lands. This led to a new approach to fashioning the relationship between religion and the wider world, namely Islamic reformism. The next section of this chapter studies these developments in more detail.

1 The State and its Society: Education and Secular Culture

Unlike earlier state forms, that of the *Tanzimat* sought to penetrate society to the measure possible rather than hold its various collective units in a tributary and patrimonial connection to it. Economic and administrative methods existed to achieve this, principally the registration of land and the confirmation of private ownership under state supervision. This state also aimed to put in social engineering expedients to change society according to concepts of the newer state form, culturally hegemonic and politically *dirigiste*, when politics as distinct from administration entered the picture at all. The way forward was to refashion education and law on new bases that largely disconnected, except when necessary, from preceding institutions that had been the purview of the traditional ulamaic legal and religious establishment.

In place of the systems of law and culture that confirmed distinctions within the social structure controlled by the state, the objective import of these reforms was to generate forms of horizontal cultural homogeneity underwriting state cultural hegemony. This enabled the state authorities to extend their control without recourse to intermediary levels of social authority. At the beginning of the reforms this had, naturally, not yet become possible; it would only be implemented within certain narrow social limits. The process remains incomplete up until the present day, and is of such complexity as to be incomplete everywhere and remain a tendential dynamic rather than a fully accomplished condition. Educational systems everywhere are grounded in their foundational elementary level. The organisation and management of primary education at this stage was one of the most difficult tasks to accomplish. Universal primary education requires an organisational, administrative, and financial capacity that the early *Tanzimat* state possessed only in small measure. Thus, large numbers entered intermediate and secondary education with a prior traditional formation that made modern education difficult to digest, and lacking adequate cultural and intellectual resources that might have been offered by the modern primary state sector.[28]

Primary education still took place largely in the rudimentary schools run according to the traditional method imparting elementary literacy and numeracy, and Qur'an memorisation or that of the Gospels in Christian schools, such as those of the Copts.[29] This included a surfeit of traditional otherworldly religious lore instead of modern knowledge.[30] The expanding need for persons with elementary education in Egypt led to a large increase in the number of such rudimentary schools from 1,319 with 44,095 pupils in 1871 to 5,730 establishments with 137,553 pupils in 1878.[31] Although the Ottoman state ordered free primary education to be provided in 1868, its ability to realise this was very limited.[32]

Primary education was not itself therefore an environment that nurtured a culture adapted to the modern world, from which secular notions implicit or explicit might emerge and evolve, fulfilling the social and cultural purposes of the reforming state. Emphasis was placed on setting up educational establishments to produce middle-ranking and senior personnel required by the state administration and the military. Most immediately relevant, therefore, were schools of translation, administration, and law, such as the Languages School in Cairo, and military engineering and medical schools. The Ottoman state thus

28 The most comprehensive study is Selçuk Akşim Somel, *The Modernization of Public Education in the Ottoman Empire, 1839–1908* (Leiden: Brill, 2001).

29 Aḥmad 'Izzat 'Abd al-Karīm, *Tārīkh al-ta'līm fī Miṣr min nihāyat ḥukm Muḥammad 'Alī ilā awā'il ḥukm Tawfīq, 1848–1882*, 4 vols (Cairo: Wizārat al-ma'ārif al-'umūmiyya, 1945), vol. 2, 833.

30 Compare with Berkes, *The Development of Secularism in Turkey*, 101, 174.

31 'Abd al-Karīm, *Tārīkh al-ta'līm*, vol. 2, 316.

32 Berkes, *The Development of Secularism in Turkey*, 174, 180.

pursued, at an accelerating rate, the establishment of educational institutions, broadening them to include preparatory (*Rüşdiye*) – intermediate – schools from 1838 onwards, to supply military and other colleges with pupils with appropriate skills. There was also an attempt to set up a university in Istanbul called Darülfünun (College of Arts) in 1870, which lasted only two years for political and technical reasons. Training schools for male and female teachers were founded in 1848 and 1870 to provide specialised teaching personnel associated with the state rather than importing this personnel from the network of religious schools.[33] The official state schools were spread through many provinces of the empire especially in the main cities of Syria and Anatolia.

In Egypt when the Egyptian state ended its wars, and government monopolies were abolished, and when the factories built by Muhammad 'Ali to meet his needs were closed, the number of educated people with higher qualifications surpassed the number of vacant posts. Many of these became a burden to the government and when 'Abbas Pasha came to power in 1848, he abolished higher educational establishments, except for the military school.[34] During the reign of Isma'il (1863–1879), who, despite his flaws, was an active moderniser, a new educational policy was adopted, with the removal of the military character from schools that had come to take on the semblance of barracks. A school of administration and languages was founded, and free schools financed by the *awqāf* were set up. Some government primary and preparatory schools were opened in Cairo and other cities and Ali Mubarak (1823–1893), as director of the Schools Department, worked on the founding of Dar al-'Ulum, a tertiary-level institution intended for training education personnel from outside the institutions of al-Azhar. All these plans stumbled, mainly for financial reasons, in their ambitions of extension across the whole of Egyptian territory. The Egyptian state eventually encouraged the establishment of private schools.[35] In Tunisia, all education had remained under the control of the religious establishment until the founding of the Sadikiya College in 1875. From 1894 onwards France sought to spread a centralised education system across the primary sector of education.

---

33 Ibid., 175, 180, 185.

34 Jurjī Zaydān, *Tārīkh adāb al-lugha al-'arabiyya*, 2 vols (Beirut: Dār maktabat al-ḥayāt, 1984), 385.

35 'Abd al-Karīm, *Tarīkh al-ta'līm*, vol. 2, 42, 46–47, 58–59, 171–173, 196–209, 346–347, 546, 548, and passim.

State schools were distinguished from the religious schools by their clear political point of reference – the state – and the cultural and intellectual resources on which they drew in modern disciplines such as the natural sciences, history, European languages, and law. The opposition of the religious factions to these schools throughout the nineteenth century was characterised by attacks against geography, geology, and astronomy in particular. Tahtawi and others undertook the defence of the "sciences of wisdom and useful knowledge" on which accuracy and discernment depend, "coming next only to the sovereign". Tahtawi quoted the interest of some Egyptian religious scholars in these sciences, such as, he claimed, Shaykh Ahmad al-Damanhuri (1690–1778), shaykh of al-Azhar, and also pointed to the collection of books on natural sciences that seem to have been produced during the relative intellectual revival that Istanbul saw in the eighteenth century.[36] Highly cultured and intellectually open groups of religious scholars existed up until the 1760s in Istanbul, after which date they dwindled away.[37] The new disciplines involved in education – that took no account of religion as a system of thought or education – had independent bases that gave religious culture a marginal appearance or at most something that had its own particular field and did not overlap with the new fields of knowledge. This character still marks education in the Arab countries today (with only marginal exceptions). Yet this process of modernist induction through education, like many others, was not fully and integrally accomplished for a number of reasons of which the most important was, perhaps, the fact that government schools were not universal and continued to rely to a large extent on drawing students from the religious elementary establishments. Government schools were also obliged to lower the level and demands of studies in order to cater for such students and to give them remedial instruction in arithmetic and other subjects.[38] Things did not always go according to the principles of education and organisation that had been originally envisaged, and the situation was an image of wider

36 Rifā'a Rāfi al-Ṭahṭāwī, *Al-a'māl al-kāmila li Rifā'a Rāfi' al-Ṭahṭāwī*, ed. Muḥammad 'Amāra, 5 vols (Beirut: al-Mu'assasa al-'Arabiyya lil-Dirāsāt wa al-Nashr, 1973), vol. 1, 533, 534, 536. See now Khaled El-Rouayheb, "Was there a revival of logical studies in eighteenth-century Egypt?", *Die Welt des Islams* 45 (2005): 1–19; Bekir Harun Küçük, *Early Enlightenment in Istanbul* (unpublished PhD dissertation, University of California, San Diego, 2012).

37 Mardin, *The Genesis of Young Ottoman Thought*, 216 ff.

38 'Abd al-Karīm, *Tarīkh al-ta'līm*, vol. 2, 62, 312.

Egyptian society with its vast inequalities. Many schools outside Cairo were rudimentary and squalid; teachers were in often conflict with one another and beat their pupils severely.[39]

The situation overall shifted often due to administrative and budgetary uncertainties. Reliance was placed on religious schools to provide teachers of Arabic and religious studies, subjects that were not neglected but somewhat marginalised in Egypt, Turkey, and Syria. Yet in Egypt the religious institution was reintroduced into the government education service when the *kuttāb*s were removed from oversight of the ministry of education in the late nineteenth century and placed under the authority of the *awqāf* department.[40] The power of the state was thus removed from a highly strategic and sensitive sector, that of the primary education of generations of Egyptians, who were handed over to the domination of religious interests, as huge numbers still are today.

The hostility of Lord Cromer (British Consul-General in Egypt from 1883 to 1907) to the education of Egyptians is well-known. The British administration was responsible for the abolition of free education (limited henceforth to the religious institution), the closure of the Language School and a narrowing of the scope of education under state responsibility. In line with an approach to colonialism in the nineteenth century shared with the Dutch and other colonial powers (and ambivalently the French), the British encouraged reactionary tendencies in society, on the pretext that Egypt needed to retain its authenticity and traditions. The British headmistress of the only girls' primary school in Cairo insisted that pupils – who had scarcely reached the age of eleven – be veiled.[41] Foreign missionary schools contributed to the ideological attack on state secular education, although these schools did follow methods based on the then-current state of knowledge in modern human and natural sciences. One of the effects of this, and a consequence of the pressure of missionary schools, was that the Coptic Church, especially in the reign of Pope Cyril IV (1806–1861), founded schools of a modernising character, in parallel to the state's modernisation of the education system. This came after the number of pupils in Protestant schools rose to 600 in 1875, 1,265 in 1895, and to 29,000 in 1904.[42] These schools in particular received financial aid from the Khedives

39 Ibid., vol. 2, 239.
40 Ibid., vol. 2, 345–346.
41 Salāma Mūsā, *Mukhtārāt Salāma Mūsā* (Beirut: Maktabat al-Ma'ārif, 1963), 150.
42 al-Bishrī, *Al-muslimūn wa al-aqbāṭ fī iṭār al-jamā'a al-waṭaniyya*, 34–38, and 'Abd al-Karīm, *Tarīkh al-ta'līm*, vol. 2, 833, 836.

Sa'id (r. 1854–1863) and Isma'il and in 1878 contained 25 per cent of the total number of Egyptian pupils.[43]

The effects of Christian denominational schools, and their use of knowledge for religious or political ends, will be discussed elsewhere in this book. But mention needs to be made of one particular institution, the Syrian Protestant College (established in 1866 – in 1920 de-denominationalised and renamed the American University of Beirut) that worked, despite its initial religious goals, to spread scientific and rational thought, and came to play a significant role in the development of progressive tendencies in modern Arab thought.[44] One major opponent of foreign education, the highly influential Muslim reformist and later Wahhabite propagandist Rashid Rida (1865–1935), considered, in a 1908 address to Muslim students at the Syrian Protestant College, that compared with other foreign institutions, American institutions taught more effectively, were better disciplined, and the most independent and the least partisan towards those of different religious or political loyalties (this statement can be applied generally to Protestant institutions in Ottoman Syria).[45] The possible political aims of missionary schools did not, however, dissuade Ottoman Turks, Syrians, and Egyptians from sending their children to them. People did not refrain from criticising the sorry condition of the official schools and from affirming, sometimes but not always regretfully, the scientific and pedagogical superiority of the foreign schools. These schools did not achieve notable success in converting Muslims, and their net effect was, in the final analysis, a positive one: modern sciences and other cognitive resources and methods were disseminated in a context that was, for practical purposes, a secular one, as the religious element in the missionary schools was excluded as far as Muslim pupils were concerned. For Christians, however, the political consequences were far from positive: the missionary schools kindled sectarian and denominational competition and conflicts among Christians and fanned separatist political trends, especially in Lebanon. Some of these schools also stirred

43 'Abd al-Karīm, *Tarīkh al-ta'līm*, vol. 2, 826, 828.

44 See Ada Porter (ed.), *Lead, Innovate, Serve: A Visual History of the American University of Beirut's First One Hundred and Fifty Years* (Beirut: American University of Beirut Press, 2016) and Betty S. Anderson, *The American University of Beirut: Arab Nationalism and Liberal Education* (Austin: University of Texas Press, 2012).

45 Muhammad Rashīd Riḍā, *Mukhtārāt siyāsiyya min majallat al-manār*, ed. Wajīh Kawtharānī (Beirut: Dār al-Ṭalī'a, 1980), 118, and Berkes, *The Development of Secularism in Turkey*, 103–104.

up anti-secular and anti-Ottoman sentiments, with consequences for the development of Arab autonomism in Syria.[46]

These schools, however, produced a corpus of cognitive goods associated with the needs and ethos of state civilian and military functionaries in Syria and other areas of the Ottoman sultanate. The number of books written by state officials and teachers in government schools multiplied, on subjects such as language, literature, travel, engineering, medicine, geography, and, to a lesser extent, European and African history, as well as constitutional, administrative, and commercial law, together with the natural sciences. The majority of these books were printed in Egypt, with a smaller number in Syria, with a concentration of printing activity in Beirut and secondarily in Damascus. Such works seem to have been entirely absent in North Africa.[47] Most of the authors were teachers or civil servants, some engaged in incipient journalism, and many were enthusiastic autodidacts. The works of Nawfal Nawfal Trabulsi (1812–1887) exemplify this trend. He was author of *Zubdat al-ṣahā'if fī uṣūl al-ma'ārif* ("the cream of writings on the fundamentals of knowledge"), which included material on the history of learning among different peoples, and the foundations of philosophical, natural, and linguistic sciences. Another example is the work of Shafiq Mansur al-Misri (1856–1890) who wrote works on mathematics and civil law and applied European notation to Arabic music.[48] These and other works indicate the existence and spread of an encyclopaedic or quasi-encyclopaedic culture, doubtless lacking depth and precision, but it included modern human and natural knowledge with bases in which religion played no part. This culture was concerned with matters of development and progress on the basis of European models.

These cognitive goods and the network of intellectuals associated with them, intellectuals connected to the state in the first instance, led to the founding of small-scale scientific societies, such as the Syrian Scientific

46 For example, one of the Syrian deputies to the Ottoman Assembly of Deputies: see Anonymous [As'ad Dāghīr], *Thawrat al-'Arab ḍidd al-Atrāk: Muqaddimātuhā, asbābuhā, natā'ijuhā*, Biqalam aḥad a'ḍā' al-jama'iyyāt al-sirriya al-'arabiyya, ed. 'Iṣām Shbāru (Beirut: Dār Miṣbaḥ al-Fikr, 1987), 126 and see also the comment of George Khiḍr in Markaz Dirāsāt al-Waḥda al-'Arabiyya (ed.), *Al-turāth wa taḥadiyyāt al-'aṣr fī al-waṭan al-'arabī: Al-aṣāla wa al-mu'āsara. Buḥūth wa munāqashāt al-nadwā al-fikriyya allatī nazẓamhā markaz dirasāt al-waḥda al-'arabiyya*, 2nd edn (Beirut: Markaz Dirāsāt al-Waḥda al-'Arabiyya, 1987), 355.

47 Sarkīs, *Mu'jam al-maṭbū'āt al-'arabiyya wa al-mu'arraba.*

48 Zaydān, *Tarājim mashāhīr al-sharq fī al-qarn al-tāsi' 'ashar*, vol. 2, 210, 220, 221.

Society founded in Beirut in 1847, whose members included Muslims and Christians, with a majority of the latter. Many senior officials, notables, and intellectuals in Beirut, Istanbul, Damascus, Cairo, and the rest of the cities of Syria joined the society. The interests of the Society were oriented towards issues of progress, backwardness, the education of women, natural laws, and the history of European civilisation, questions that were reflected in the lectures organised by the Society. These interests reflected an appropriation by Arab intellectuals of general terms associated with European progress from the Renaissance until the nineteenth century, as well as an emphasis on science as the road to progress.[49]

Societies and books were not the only means of spreading the new secularising culture. The second half of the nineteenth century, and particularly the last quarter of the century, saw in Egypt and Syria the spread of magazines. In Syria, newspapers were known as *qarzaiṭa* (an Arabisation of *gazette*), and there was much discussion in this new medium of Japan and its rapid progress.[50] Graduates of the Syrian Protestant College founded journals in Egypt where they were able to publish more freely, most notably *al-Muqtaṭaf* and *al-Hilāl*, both of which played a significant role in the dissemination of scientific, humanistic, secular, and rationalist culture and its cognitive goods in Egypt and other Arab lands, and putting into general circulation the works of European authors, abridged or translated.[51]

Finally, while discussing the spread of knowledge and secularism, mention should be made of the schools set up with a secular orientation from the very start. The first of these schools was the National School that Butrus al-Bustani set up in the year 1863 in Choueifat just outside Beirut. The school still exists with several branches in the Arab World. Its declared aim was aversion of sectarianism, preservation and promotion of the Arabic language, and the acquisition of modern sciences and foreign languages, with a basic affirmation of two fundamental principles, religious freedom and

49 Kawtharāni, *Al-sulṭa wa al-mujtama' wa al-'amal al-siyāsī*, 143–144.

50 'Anbara Salām al-Khālidī, *Jawla fī al-dhikrayāt bayna lubnān wa filasṭīn* (Beirut: Dār al-Nahār li'l-Nashr, 1978), 32–33.

51 See now Dagmar Glass, *Der al-Muqtaṭaf und seine Öffentlichkeit. Aufklärung, Räsonnement und Meinungsstreit in der frühen arabischen Zeitschriftenkommunikation*, 2 vols (Würzburg: Ergon Verlag, 2004); Thomas Philipp, *Jurji Zaidan and the Foundations of Arab Nationalism* (New York: Syracuse University Press, 2014); Nadia al-Bagdadi, *Vorgestellte Öffentlichkeit: Zur Genese moderner Prosa in Ägypten* (Wiesbaden: Reichert Verlag, 2010).

Ottoman national community.[52] This school was followed by the Galata Lycée in Istanbul, created by the state in 1868 with a secular programme, to educate 150 Muslim and 150 non-Muslim pupils. It was confronted with fierce opposition from religious circles: the Pope in Rome issued a ban on Christians from enrolling in this school, with the *şeyhülislam* making a parallel pronouncement; Russia urged Orthodox Christians to boycott it while the Rabbinate also opposed the school. Nevertheless, it proved to be an outstanding success.[53]

In Egypt, a French notable from Alexandria set up the first free and non-denominational school in Cairo in 1873, without this achieving the reputation of the two previously mentioned schools.[54] One other institution should be mentioned as secular education is discussed, one that was later to have an important influence: the Egyptian University, opened in 1908 after local efforts at fundraising carried out by a group headed by Sa'd Zaghloul, the chief figure in Egyptian liberal reformist nationalism (1859–1927). Qasim Amin (1865–1908) worked as the group's secretary, collecting contributions from individuals and government departments, under the patronage of the Khedive.[55] The history of what later became Istanbul University, the Darülfünun, had a checkered history from its foundation in 1863, with moments of restriction and closure under Abdülhamid. Other cities such as Damascus acquired tertiary institutes piecemeal; the Syrian University in Damascus was set up in 1923 as a merger of the older colleges of medicine (1903) and law (1913).

It can, therefore, be said that in milieux that had received a secular education, across the Ottoman state, modern sciences and other cognitive goods, separated from religious authority, came with state patronage to attain the primacy of the cognitive norm over other types of knowledge available. The discussion of Islamic reformism to follow in the next chapter will show that

52 Zaydān, *Tarājim mashāhīr al-sharq fī al-qarn al-tāsi' 'ashar*, vol. 2, 37–38 and Na'īm 'Aṭiyya, "Ma'ālim al-fikr al-tarbawī fī al-bilād al-'arabiyya fī al-mi'at sana al-akhīra", in Al-Jāmi'a al-Amīrikiyya fī Bayrūt, Hay'at al-Dirasāt al-'Arabiyya (ed.), *Al-fikr al-'arabi fī mi'at sana: Buḥūth mu'tamar hay'at al-dirāsāt al-'arabiyya al-mun'aqida fī tishrīn al-thānī 1966 fī al-jāmi'a al-amīrikiyya fī bairūt*, ed. Fu'ād Ṣarrūf and Nabīh Amīn Fāris (Beirut: al-Jāmi'a al-Amīrikiyya, 1967), 480.

53 Berkes, *The Development of Secularism in Turkey*, 189–191.

54 'Abd al-Karīm, *Tārīkh al-ta'līm*, 862–864.

55 Zaydān, *Tārīkh adāb al-lugha al-'arabiyya*, vol. 2, 393. See Donald Reid, *Cairo University and the Making of Modern Egypt* (Cambridge: Cambridge University Press, 1990).

many religious figures assumed the task of learning and mastering these branches of knowledge, or at least sought confirmation from these sciences. In these circumstances it is unsurprising that Muhammad Rashid Rida, product of a purely traditional religious education, sought to "introduce some of the modern concepts into his poetry" while, as a young man, he was a pupil of mildly reformist Shaykh Husayn al-Jisr (1845–1909) and a reader of the journals *al-Muqtaṭaf* and *Al-'Urwa al-Wuthqā*. He composed a poem on gravity, and conversed with "free Christian literary figures".[56] Much the same might be said of persons with a religious formation who had joined state service. Attention will be given later to the most important example of such figures, and Rashid Rida's early mentor, Shaykh Muhammad 'Abduh.

In a similar way the graduates of the Sadiqiyya College in Tunis, of whom the liberal nationalist Bashir Sfar (1856–1917) was the most prominent, joined with some liberal reformist Zeitouna – the local analogue to Cairo's Azhar – graduates, headed by Salim Buhajib (1827–1924), in support of the minister Kheireddine and his methods.[57] Kheireddine had been obliged to rely on Zeitouna scholars and adopted a policy of trying to win them over, when the needs of the state for administrative personnel became evident. This was particularly the case in Tunis when the traditional sources for such personnel, the slave markets, had dwindled with the official abolition of slavery in 1846. The relationship with the Zeitouna remained tense nevertheless, despite the success of Kheireddine in introducing modern subjects into its curriculum – history, geography, and arithmetic – and in achieving a degree of reform in its administration. The majority of the patrician families among the Malikites stood aloof from cooperation with Kheireddine in contrast with the Hanafis from the families of Bayram, Bin Khuja, and others. This meant that he had to rely increasingly on Zeitouna scholars of rural or modest urban origins.[58] In the minds of such early members of the new class of intellectuals, and especially the Zeitouna graduates, two worlds were juxtaposed, one secular and the other supernatural, a juxtaposition some of whose results will be studied in a discussion of Islamic reformism and the fluctuating nature of its authority later in this book.

56 Shakīb Arslān, *Al-Sayyid Rashīd Riḍā aw ikhā' arba'īn sana* (Damascus: Maṭba'at Ibn Zaydūn and Cairo: Maṭba'at Dār al-Kutub al-Miṣriyya, 1937), 113–114, 130.

57 Muḥammad al-Faḍl ibn 'Āshūr, *Al-ḥaraka al-adabiyya wa al-fikriyya fī Tūnis* (Cairo: Jāmi'at al-Duwal al-'Arabiyya, Ma'had al-Dirāsāt al-'Āliya, 1956), 45–47.

58 Green, *The Tunisian Ulama, 1873–1915*, 118, 120, 122.

In regions that were later to become Turkey, mention should be made of some of the enlightened religious scholars who saw fit to write works on psychology and the concept of natural law. Such members of the ulama supported both sultans Selim III and Mahmud II in their reforms and then supported the *Tanzimat* in their first period. There is no doubt that the most famous of these was Ahmet Cevdet Paşa (1822–1895). Apart from being counsellor to Reşit Paşa mentioned earlier in connection with Auguste Comte, he was the author of a famous history and other chronicles of the Ottoman state, as well as a translator of Ibn Khaldun. He participated actively in the reform of education and headed the commission for the *Mecelle* of judicial ordinances (1869–1876), the first modern-style codification of Hanafi commercial jurisprudence, after having exchanged the distinctive attire of the ulama for civil dress of a modern office-holder, in shirt, suit, and a fez (tarbush).[59] Rifaʿa Rafiʿ al-Tahtawi had preceded him in changing from the *jubba* and turban to European dress and fez while in government service some time after his return from Paris.[60]

In Syria the interconnection between the leading ulama and the families of notables certainly had an effect on the decline of the social foundations of the religious institution. Patrician families, instead of educating their sons in the religious schools in preparation for assuming leading positions among the ulama, switched to the Ottoman state schools in Damascus, Aleppo, and Istanbul, paving the way to entry to the new civil service and the officer corps.[61]

The state, therefore, and the circles of senior functionaries linked to it, was a patron of new ideas and conceptions that were pushing aside religious modes of thought from the public centrality previously occupied, and replacing them with new points of reference. This started in military schools, continued in institutes specialised in the production of bureaucrats, and took root in the

59 Richard Chambers, in *Scholars, Saints and Sufis: Muslim Religious Institutions in the Middle East since 1500*, ed. Nikki R. Keddie (Berkeley and Los Angeles: University of California Press, 1972, 38–43.

60 Zaydān, *Tarājim mashāhīr al-sharq fī al-qarn al-tāsiʿ ʿashar*, vol. 2, 32–33. See the excellent studies in Elizabeth Özdalga (ed.), *Late Ottoman Society: The Intellectual Legacy* (London, Routledge Curzon, 2005).

61 Albert H. Hourani, "Ottoman reform and the politics of notables", in *The Beginnings of Modernisation in the Middle East: The Nineteenth Century*, eds William R. Polk and Richard Chambers, Publications of the Center for Middle Eastern Studies 1 (Chicago: University of Chicago Press, 1968), 60–64.

work procedures of government institutions, where it flowered variously. It also spread with the educational system, in translations and general technical works, as well as associations, newspapers, and magazines. Then came the writings of the Young Ottomans and those Arabs who adopted a similar approach, such as Ali Mubarak, ʿAbdallah al-Nadim (1843–1896), Faris – later Ahmad Faris – al-Shidyaq (1805–1887), Francis Marrash (1836–1873) and Adib Ishaq (1856–1885). Their writings were expressions of aspiration to advancement, progress, technical and social organisation, and the acquisition of sciences and secular knowledge, as well as criticisms of superstitions, social and intellectual passivity and indolence, and the reactionary social and intellectual condition of the ulama.

Shaykh Muhammad ʿAbduh (1849–1905), a key figure in modern Muslim reform in the Arab World and beyond, adopted a comparable orientation in his writings in *al-Ahrām* and subsequently in the *al-Waqāʾiʿ al-Miṣriyya* (Egyptian Official Gazette) and in his history of the ʿUrabi Revolution (1879–1882) and its preludes. He called for the state to be guided and built upon solid institutional and rational supports, as well as for political participation, patriotism, reform, and equity. He, an Azharite and a lifelong member of the ulama, adopted in these writings a tone and vocabulary from which religion and religious discourse in any form was absent and also produced writings on religious topics as well.

These journalistic writings were of a generally political, nationalist, and modernist approach and theme, deriving their authority, not from scriptural citations, but from the secular concepts considered pivotal at that time, concepts that were linked usually to the French Revolution and its heritage: enlightenment and rationality, political participation and equity. The revolutionary tone of these concepts was downplayed, and a degree of gradualism and caution was put in their place, as they became softened by English Whig political ideas.[62]

All these orientations of thought accompanied the emergence of a new class of cultural actors, distinct from more traditional figures linked to the religious institution, and socially encoded by different manners of dress, general

62 Ra'īf Khūrī, *Al-fikr al-ʿarabī al-ḥadīth, athar al-thawra al-faransiyya fi tawjjuhihi al-siyāsī wa al-ijtimāʿī* (Beirut: Dār al-Makshūf, 1943), 126, 132, 135–136; Anṭwān Ghaṭṭās Karam, "Fī al-adab al-ʿarabī al-hadīth", Al-jāmiʿa al-amīrikiyya fī Bayrūt, hay'at al-dirasāt al-ʿarabiyya, *Al-fikr al-ʿarabi fi mi'at sana; buḥūth mu'tamar hay'at al-dirasāt al-ʿarabiyya al-munʿaqida fi tishrīn al-thānī 1966 fi al-jāmi'a al-amīrikiyya fi bairūt* (Beirut: al-Jāmiʿa al-Amīrikiyya fī Bayrūt, 1967), 194.

comportment, vocabularies used and circulation in different social spaces. The new cultural actors had as a base a new institutional authority, the state, which, prior to the *Tanzimat* state, had been culturally ineffective and lacked any intellectual character or vocation. These new cultural actors also had a basis in intellectual and political authority linked to the broad orientation of the *Tanzimat* state, declared or undeclared, and formed part of a global history whose keyword was progress, parsed as science and social transformation from a state of decadence and historical senescence to a condition of advancement. This was to be achieved by means of education and the administrative and rational organisation of public life that these new cultural actors considered to have been tested and proven in the site of historical authority represented by Europe, seen as the driving force of the nineteenth century. The origins of this class of cultural actors varied: the children of Muslim city notables, Christian graduates of missionary institutions in Syria, intellectuals of rural origins of whose aspirations the 'Urabi Revolt in Egypt (1879–1882), for instance, was an expression, or a mixture of these elements as we saw previously in Tunis.[63] The final result was not connected so much with social origins as with the social and intellectual context of subsequent careers, in which these intellectuals were the instrument of the state in its attempts at the moral and intellectual penetration of society, in its quest for hegemony.

These considerations hold in a general way also for the Maghreb to the west, although development here was later and slower, and followed distinct but related trajectories, with much regional differentiation within the Maghreb itself. The Mashriqi concern with concepts of progress supported by the early signs of a liberal conception of politics sustaining a modern conception of state were not as central in the Maghreb countries during the period we are concerned with here.

In Morocco, reforms of the sultanic institutions did not lead to the development of a novel and unfamiliar ideological and intellectual field, despite the glimmerings of liberal influence deriving from the Syrian press in the late nineteenth century and early twentieth among certain business and intellectual circles in Tangiers and Fès who had assisted sultan 'Abd al-Hafiz (r. 1909–1912) in his unsuccessful attempt to promulgate a constitution.[64]

---

63 Jacques Berque, *Egypt and Revolution*, trans. Jean Stewart (London: Faber and Faber, 1972), 113–118.
64 Laroui, *The History of the Maghreb*, 363–363.

In Tunisia and Algeria French colonialism acted quickly to hasten the induction of this stratum of the social elite into the pathways of global culture as it existed at that time, in terms of the self-declared civilising mission. In Tunisia, primary education was put under the control of the state from the year 1894 through the founding of the 'Asfuriyya school to train teachers. The Sadikiya College was reorganised under the French administration and French was made the basic language for education. The relationship of this modernised elite to the ulama patriciate was based on the same links of mutual disqualification that had existed between this ulamaic upper crust and Kheireddine Pasha with one difference, namely that the Hanafis joined the Malikis in opposing the new French-impelled educational reforms.[65] French authorities in Tunis continued this policy until 1907 when they began to operate on the basis of a politics of the notable families. They restricted educational reforms and supressed the Young Tunis party founded by the *évolués* (mention has already been made of Buhajib and Bashir Sfar) as the French called them: persons strongly influenced by the political and intellectual foundations of global civilisation represented for them by France. This led them to advance demands that were considered "unreasonable" when the Young Tunis called on French liberals fully to apply liberal principles in Tunisia as they were in France, to all citizens without exception or distinction.[66] It would not have been possible to set up the Young Tunis party without the alliance that developed between liberal French administrators in Tunis and the Tunisian reformers (who included some ulama). This alliance produced the newspaper *al-Hadira* and the Khaldouniyya association, founded in 1896 with the encouragement of the French authorities. A number of religious scholars opposed to France participated in these efforts promoting enlightened learning, and the opening lecture in the Khaldouniyya association, delivered by Salim Buhajib, dealt with the subject of science, as a reason for pride, and the reason why God had appointed humanity as His vicars in this world.[67] Nevertheless the majority of ulama considered the matter from a narrow institutional point of view: the corporate interests of the Zeitouna prevailed over the public

---

65 Green, *The Tunisian Ulama, 1873–1915*, 139–142, 171,173.

66 Ibid., 199–201; Laroui, *The History of the Maghreb*, 346–347.

67 Muḥammad al-Fāḍl Ibn 'Āshūr, "Dhikrā Ibn Khaldūn fī Tūnis", *al-Fikr* 6 (1961): 516–517.

interest of new cognitive needs, to which they closed their eyes and ears on the pretext of defending Islam. As soon as the French authorities decided to try to win over the leading families after 1907, and to prohibit Young Tunis, the ulama greeted the development favourably and displayed complete readiness to cooperate with the French, under the banner of loyalty to the Bay.[68] It is hardly surprising that Tunisian nationalists had no special fondness of the religious institution.

Algeria witnessed a not incomparable development, albeit a comparability much complicated by difference in scale and internal complexity, and in a situation where the pressure of colonialism was far more intense, and the structure of the local Algerian religious and political institutions too fragile to withstand it effectively. Apart from Jews, rapidly and proactively assimilated (and granted French citizenship in 1870), Algerians were categorised by French colonial authorities into two components. One was a marginalised majority excluded from the colonial state's attempt to refashion society, immobile in an indigenous Islamic or Berber specificity forced on it by colonial authority. The other was a group of *évolués* with liberal and progressive ideas, which subsequently became nationalist. These followed the approach of Young Tunis in forming the Young Algerians association on similar political and intellectual bases as in Tunis.[69]

The *évolués* of Algeria and Tunisia were therefore cultured individuals broadly comparable in their intellectual and ideological formation and goods to the modern intelligentsia in other Arab regions. The differences were nevertheless significant. While cultural actors in Egypt and Istanbul were associated with the state and were striving to induce this state into the framework of global modernity, intellectuals under French tutelage in North Africa were active in a situation in which colonial educational policies sought to separate them from a broader society, assigned by colonialism to an incurable particularity and a congenital incapacity for development. Colonialism had shut out this indigenous society from entry into the movement of universal modernity that it regarded as a civilising mission, save through the highly restrictive avenue of economic and geo-strategic dependence. One consequence was withdrawal to a particularity constructed in the

---

68 Green, *The Tunisian Ulama, 1873–1915*, 165–168, 201, 221–222, 224.

69 Ali Merad, *Le Réformisme musulman en Algérie de 1925 a 1940: Essai d'histoire religieuse et sociale* (Paris and The Hague: Mouton, 1967), 47, 51–52.

process described, and expressed by the framing of French policies towards what were taken for Muslim Jurisprudence and local Berber custom, in the literal sense of an attempt to return to the past.[70] The whole regime was underwritten by the deployment of violence and disruption of extraordinary amplitude, to the extent that the colonial state in Algeria had been termed "a permanent state of exception".[71]

The universalist horizon of culturally Francophile cultural figures in Tunisia and Algeria, although it developed in a context of a highly rapid and comprehensive transmission of and assimilation to a culture, produced in its early stages a highly specific form of attachment to France. This was rapidly dissipated and led to local Francophone cultural actors splitting into two parties with similar progressivist cultures and liberal (later socialist) values: those associated with the coloniser, and those secular nationalists who laid the groundwork for the later nationalist movements aiming for independence. Nationalist intellectuals were imbued with progressivist, nationalist values and particularly those of the French Revolution, and called for the generalisation of modern education, while hesitating between open opposition to France and indirect opposition to French policies.[72]

Unsurprisingly, a particular image emerged of local intellectuals as a cultural vanguard standing uncertainly in the broader societal context. Intellectuals with a relatively modest formation, such as teachers and ulama, were inclined to separate culture from politics and to follow a conciliatory policy with regard to colonialism. This was the case of the Association of Ulama in Algeria,[73] who sought a policy of double subalternity, guarding indigenous society culturally from the colonial state while confirming political dependence. This is the content of the separation made by the major figure in this movement, the Zeitouna-educated reformist Shaykh 'Abd al-Hamid Ibn Badis (1889–1940), between ethnic nationality and political nationality.[74]

70 Cf. Laroui, *The History of the Maghreb*, 325.

71 Olivier Le Cour Grandmaison, *Coloniser, exterminer: Sur la guerre et l'état colonial* (Paris: Farard, 2005), ch. 4. See also Nicolas Schaub, *Représenter l'Algérie. Images et conquête au XIXe siècle* (Paris: Comité des Travaux Historiques et Scientifiques, 2015).

72 For example, in Algeria, Abū al-Qāsim Sa'ad Allāh, *Al-ḥaraka al-waṭaniyya fī al-jazā'ir*, 3 vols (Cairo: al-Munaẓẓama al-'Arabiyya li'l-Thaqāfa wa al-'Ulūm, Ma'had al-Buḥūth wa al-Dirasāt al-'Arabiyya, 1977), vol. 2, 149–154, 173–190.

73 Merad, *Le Réformisme musulman en Algérie*, ch. 8

74 Ibid., 397.

Modern intellectuals under the French colonial state in its early phase were distinguished by linguistic and cultural competences, and by access to cognitive goods and tools that deliberately set them apart from the remainder of society. In contrast, the reforming state of the *Tanzimat* type propagated modern culture and cognitive goods as broadly as was logistically possible, quite deliberately, to varying degrees that depended on administrative, financial, and social capacity: to its greatest extent in littoral regions (including Istanbul of course) and to its least in Egypt under Cromer. Yet in the *Tanzimat* state as in the colonial state, intentions notwithstanding, global modern culture gave rise to a divergence between a cultured minority with a reasonable level of accomplishment and a mass of the population who were variously illiterate, captive to a mental universe suffused with the supernatural and the irrational, and confined to traditional religious education.

This distinction intersected, in the territories of the Ottoman state and in Egypt, with a visible class distinction: parts of the upper classes emerging from modern education, particularly those linked to state service both civilian and military, differentiated from the rest of society – both higher up the soci-economic scale and lower – in the adoption of cultural goods and vocabularies for public affairs, buttressed by visible tokens relating to personal and corporate styles: manners of dress, taste, sensibility, table manners, home furnishings, modes of conviviality, and much else that their detractors dubbed *tafarnuj* (Frankism), commonly known as Westernisation. This would become, as will be shown subsequently, an element connected with the cleavage between religious and secular cultures. The political culture of the educated class associated with the modern state that stood in the first instance on French principles, and on notions of evolution, attainable, and verifiable objective knowledge, public and administrative regulation, with an element of the notion of political participation that varied widely with different times, circumstances, locations, and groups. These concepts that betoken an emphasis on rationalisation were not commonly shared across society. The incipient transformation of subjects into a people was affected by the press and the system of new education, limited, in the period under examination, in its means of circulation and uneven in its distribution, but nevertheless not entirely confined to a state elite and a few educated people from specific milieux.

The civil vehicles and organisms that could bring together elements of the new intelligentsia – intellectuals (teachers, journalists, translators, littérateurs), politicians, and state officials – were still very weak at the end of the nineteenth century. The societies of the Ottoman state were embarking upon a laborious and hesitant exit from the framework of a patrimonial state based on tributary relations of subjects corporately conceived, to one tendentially generative in its socio-political and historical trajectory of individual citizens. It was not yet habitual for people of different backgrounds and sects, and of varying professional status, to come together in the context of private voluntary institutions. Masonic lodges at that time formed such a context and offered a link "stronger than the link of solidarity by birth because it was based on the linking of individuals of different races and language and religious confessions by unity of purpose, truthfulness, charity and and fidelity".[75] For a rational and historical view of Arab history and the history of other nations, one needs when speaking of Freemasonry to eschew the habitual statements of panic and horror based on conspiracy theories widely disseminated in the Arab world and elsewhere in the second half of the twentieth century, even linking Freemasonry and purported international Jewish and Communist conspiracies. This link has its origins, it seems, in Jesuit anti-masonic writing,[76] duly generalised to a broader swathe of the political and ideological Right.

Freemasonry in Europe emerged in opposition to absolutist authorities in order to confer power to the people:[77] such was the starting assertion of Muhammad Rashid Rida in his *responsum* or fatwa (legal opinion) delivered in 1911, before his political alliances dissipated the rationality he had acquired in his younger days and under Muhammad 'Abduh. Freemasonry, he added, developed in Ottoman Syria and Egypt for literary and social purposes with a political dimension, aiming to bring together influential persons from different origins, increase their numbers, strengthen their common bond at the expense of their religious connections, and prepare them to remove religious and personalised forms of authority and to replace shari'a

75 Shāhīn Makāriyūs, *Al-ādāb al-māsūniyya* (Cairo: Maṭba'at al-Muqtaṭaf, 1895), 138. See Dorothé Sommer, *Freemasonry in the Ottoman Empire. A History of the Fraternity and its Influence in Syria and the Levant* (London: I. B. Tauris, 2015).

76 Muḥammad Rashīd Riḍā, *Fatāwā*, 6 vols (Beirut: Dār al-Kitāb al-Jadīd, 1970), no. 745, and Shāhīn Makāriyūs, *Faḍā'il al-māsūniyya* (Cairo: Maṭba'at al-Muqtaṭaf, 1899), 121. On the Christian roots of the anti-Masonic controversy, see Fr. Louis Cheikho S. J., *Al-sirr al-maṣūn fī shī'at al-farmasūn*, 6 fascicles (Beirut: al-Maṭba'a al-Kāthūlīkiyya, 1910–1911). Riḍā, *Fatāwā*, no. 365.

77 Riḍā, *Fatāwā*, no. 365. Compare no. 745 of 1927.

with a modern code of law.[78] This is equally true of Ottoman, Egyptian, and European Freemasonry which emerged in Europe in association with the doctrine of natural religion. Masons tended to believe in God as a concept rather than as a person, and were generally hostile to the religious institution, and generally thought of society as being subject to secular regulation, rational consideration, and a utilitarian orientation. Freemasonry in Europe of the eighteenth century (where it exercised a definite influence on the French Revolution) was the domain in which liberal aristocratic and the bourgeois literati assembled in a grouping that opposed the separation of society into estates, with special hostility to the clerical estate, as was the case in Ancien Régime France. Among their number were Voltaire, King Frederick II, Montesquieu, Goethe, Herder, Lafayette, Franklin, Condorcet, and others. Masonic lodges were based on enlightenment concepts such as reason, progress, political participation, and criticism of religious authority and were the filter for currents of thought in general linked with the French Revolution and pragmatic utilitarianism in Britain.[79]

Just as the Masonic movement developed outside the ambit of the state in eighteenth-century Europe, heralding the emergence of individuality unbound from contexts of birth and the influence of religious regulation, freemasonry in Ottoman domains adopted similar outlooks, setting up a locus of conviviality and sociality outside the framework of subordination to religious confessions and other social units prescribed by birth. In the Ottoman state the Masonic movement was linked generally with progressive and radical ideas.[80]

Freemasons participated in Egypt in the work of what Jamal al-Din al-Afghani (1838–1897) called, without much specification and perhaps optimistically, *The Free Party*, and took part in the effort to overthrow Isma'il.[81] Al-Afghani, Muhammad 'Abduh, Sa'd Zaghlul, the nationalist politician and autodidactic historian Muhammad Farid (1868–1919), Has-

78 Ibid., no. 431 of 1912. Riḍā issued another fatwa allowing a Muslim to be called "Fāris al-Haykal [Knight of the Temple]" in a non-religious association (he intended by this Masonic societies) as long as no harm was done (Fatwa 383 of 1911).

79 Georges Gusdorf, *Les principes de la pensée au siècle des lumières, Les sciences humaines et la pensée occidentale*, 14 vols (Paris: Payot, 1971), vol. 4, 402–411.

80 Paul Dumont, "La Franc-maçonnerie ottomane et les 'idées françaises'", in *Les Arabes, les Turcs et la Révolution françaises*: special issue of *Revue du monde musulman et de la Méditerranée* 52–53 (1989): 150–159.

81 'Alī Shalash, ed. *Jamāl al-Dīn al-Afghānī, silsilat al-a'māl al-majhūla* (London: Riyad al-Rayyis li'l-Kutub wa al-Nashr, 1981), 248.

san Youssef, proprietor of the nationalist newspaper *al-Mu'ayyad*, and the nationalist lawyer and newspaper editor Mustafa Kamil (1874–1908) were Freemasons. Leading Ottoman officials were also among the society's members: Midhat Paşa, author of the Ottoman constitution, Namık Kemal, leader of the Young Ottomans, a number of notables and officials from Damascus and Beirut, and statesmen such as Lord Kitchener, Boutros Ghali, Reşit Paşa, *vali* of Damascus who opened the first masonic lodge of his time in Beirut in 1866, in addition to the Khedive Tawfīq, who joined in 1881 and was elected Grand Master in 1887, a post he occupied until 1891 when a senior civil servant was elected to the post.[82] The Khedival family exercised control over Freemasonry in Egypt; its meetings in Ottoman Syria concluded with prayers for the sultan whose image was displayed in the meeting hall – although this did not protect them from closure in 1891.[83] Despite the control exercised by the Khedive, the watchwords of the Masonic movement were those of the French Revolution: liberty, fraternity, equality.

Overall, Freemasons were progressive legitimists, not revolutionaries. Freemasons of the English tendency (the Scottish rite) gave change a vague general meaning without any revolutionary implications. As for freedom, it was according to one Freemason "a term which we have only heard employed in its now-customary meaning only since the presence of Freemasonry as an institution in Egypt and with the appearance of newspapers and scientific publications". It had a restricted meaning in Muslim jurisprudence, a capacity to act contrasted to the condition of slavery. It was parsed by the same author as "a capacity in the soul which enables the realisation of righteous intentions without fear of criticism".[84]

The division of Masonic lodges into a French branch (Turkey, Ottoman Syria, and Egypt) and, in Egypt, another, Scottish branch aligned to Britain, bespoke a distinction within the new cultural and administrative elites. Lodges aligned with Britain generally included cotton merchants and elements loyal to Britain. One of these lodges became the famous Gezira Club in Cairo. There

82 Karim Wissa, "Freemasonry in Egypt, 1798–1921: A study in cultural and political encounters", *Bulletin of the British Society of Middle East Studies* 16/2 (1989): 143–161, 143–146. Makāriyūs, *Faḍā'il al-māsūniyya*, 34, 119,121, 124, 192 and Makāriyūs, *Al-ādāb al-māsūniyya*, 195, 197 and Al-'Aẓma, *Mir'āt al-shām: Tarīkh dimashq wa ahluhā*, 183; Sarkīs, *Mu'jam al-maṭbū'āt al-'arabiyya wa al-mu'arraba*, 413–444.

83 Makāriyūs, *Faḍā'il al-māsūniyya*, 62.

84 Ibid., 122–123.

was no lack of intellectuals, in particular graduates of the Syrian Protestant College with a scientific culture and of a positivist, utilitarian orientation such as Ya'qub Sarruf and Jurji Zaydan and others. Freemasonry, in its French branch, was distinguished by its hostility to British colonialism and the strength of its antipathy to missionaries.[85]

The element that united both varieties of Freemasonry was the reception and assimilation of universal bourgeois culture, including its spectrum of attitudes to religion. Like Masonic writings, lodge meetings opened with expressions of European concepts of eighteenth-century natural religion, invoking the "Great Architect of the Universe". A natural quality was ascribed to the Deity, unconnected to specific revealed religions and the clergymen guarding over them. The expression can be interpreted in the Newtonian way, discussed in the previous chapter, or in a Deistic or Voltairian manner. It was apt for the Masonic movement to request that its brethren believe in God and treat all religions equally, reconfigured as moral action in the first instance, from which temperate and sound civilisation develops. This is accompanied by Masonic insistence on freedom of conscience and mutual respect between the members of different religions.[86] While the growing influence of positivism on the Grand Lodge of the East (the French branch) led to dropping mention of the existence of God and the eternity of the soul, and made the divinity merely a Deistic cosmic principle, the effect of positivism on the Masonic lodge in Beirut, for example, was limited to abolishing belief in God as a condition of membership, without requiring individual brethren to subscribe to this position.[87]

Thus, the Masonic lodges in the last third of the nineteenth century were a repository of incipient bourgeois culture with its secular orientation and the marginal place of religion within it. This was not least the case as there had been strong opposition to Freemasonry from the European religious establishment, without the religious institutions among Arabs and Turks being party to this at the beginning.[88] The reaction of the ulama to the spread of Freemasonry was slow and scattered. The Western churches had been the

85 Wissa, "Freemasonry in Egypt, 1798–1921", 152–153.
86 Makāriyūs, *Al-ādāb al-māsūniyya*, 6–11, 20–21, 23.
87 Makāriyūs, *Faḍā'il al-māsūniyya*, 125–162.
88 Cheikho, *Al-sirr al-maṣūn fī shī'at al-farmasūn*, fascicle 4, 16–24, 26–32, and Riḍā, *Fatāwā*, no. 365.

first to combat it, followed by the Eastern churches. Freemasonry was therefore a source of enlightenment for the intellect and tended to counter zealotry (*taʿaṣṣub*), "the plague of civilisation". It was an environment where early moves were made towards considering religious affiliation a private matter with no necessary implication for public life.[89] Religion was seen as a moral form of piety and a belief in the rational organisation of the affairs of the world, without this implying specific supernatural doctrines binding on the Freemasons.

Interesting in this context is the emergence of a marginal social phenomenon congruent to what was emerging in Europe also, namely, spiritualism and occultism, involving belief in a supernatural realm without any specific religious or institutional location. This rendered a social disposition for belief in unseen entities born of habit. It is not clear if spiritualism was linked to Middle Eastern Freemasonry, as it certainly had an influence on European Freemasonry in the Romantic period at the end of the eighteenth century and the beginnings of the nineteenth century.[90] Dar al-Muqtaṭaf published in 1896 an Arabic translation of one of the most important spiritualist figures of the eighteenth century, the Swedish visionary Emanuel Swedenborg (1688–1772), under the title *Heaven and Hell and the intermediate state or the World of the Spirit*,[91] published in 1758. Books on spiritiualist séances (invocation of spirits of the dead) began appearing in Arabic at the end of the nineteenth century, at the time that this movement developed in Europe.[92] This led to condemnation by the Vatican in 1898 and an interdiction on Catholic membership of Freemasonry.

All this notwithstanding, there is no reason to suppose that the acculturation of the new intellectuals into the bourgeois culture of global modernity was complete, nor that such intellectuals were representative of the entire intelligentsia. It might well appear dissonant to speak of a bourgeoisie in such a general sense: what is important to outline is that, classical definitions in terms of class notwithstanding, the term is used here in the sense that German historians generally adopt for social strata emerging from education, bearing

89 Makāriyūs, *Al-ādāb al-māsūniyya*, 53–54.

90 Gusdorf, *Les principes de la pensée au siècle des lumières*, 412–414.

91 Sarkīs, *Muʿjam al-maṭbūʿāt al-ʿarabiyya wa al-muʿarraba*, 1,036.

92 Ibid., 1,138, 1,294, 1,330, 1,239 and elsewhere.

and producing the high culture that is attributed to the bourgeoise, and engaged in the intellectual professions and in state service: the Bildungsbürgertum, a bourgeoisie by education and learning if not by economic position, with historically an outsize role.

The key point is the emergence of new intelligentsia who operated by conceptual and cognitive means in a context of which religious manners of thought and expression were not involved when matters of public life were considered, without this implying an express intention to set religion aside or to adopt a hostile attitude towards it. This objective distanciation of religion was part of a modular package of cognitive and public values that appeared irresistible to those concerned with public responsibility and the common good. The institutional and organisational vehicle of the new cultural and cognitive regimes, the state as a secular entity, stepped onto terrain that the religious institution had claimed previously as its domain, and, more important, carved out for itself new spaces arising from the needs of objective social, economic, and institutional developments. This applies irrespective of the condition of incipience that marked much of the nineteenth century.

Contradiction and the incompatibility between modern intellectuals and the older body of intellectuals – the ulama – emerges most clearly if one considers that, in Egypt, for instance, whereas new-style intellectuals were drawn from journalists, officials, and military officers who participated in the revolt of 'Urabi Pasha, the participation of ulama in this revolt was largely confined to readings of devotional material – the *Ṣaḥīḥ* of al-Bukhari – in the mosques of al-Azhar and al-Husain, hoping that this would precipitate magical effect that would help 'Urabi Pasha and his army against the British. Meanwhile, Shaykh al-Abyari, the Khedive's chaplain, rallied to 'Urabi, then resumed urging the people to obey the Khedive when he was returned to power after 'Urabi's defeat.[93] In light of this one grasps how al-Azhar's introversion and enmity to the modern world and, indeed, to all change, reached such a degree that its students hurled stones at the police when the latter sought to enter the mosque to check the implementation of the sanitary precautions required by the plague in 1896.[94]

93 'Abduh, *Al-a'māl al-kāmila*, vol. 1, 460–461.

94 al-Ittiḥād al-ishtirākī al-'arabī, *Al-Azhar, tārīkhuhu wa taṭawwuruhu* (Cairo: al-Ittiḥād al-Ishtirākī al-'Arabī, 1964), 247.

One sympathises with the former Azharite, Muhammad 'Abduh, when he wrote of himself: "Should I possess any part of sound knowledge . . . I obtained it only after having spent ten years cleansing my mind of what had adhered to it of the squalor of al-Azhar. Up until now my mind has not attained the degree of clarity I would like."[95] The reason is not, as the prominent Moroccan religious reformer and nationalist 'Allal al-Fasi (1910–1974) rightly saw, that al-Azhar relied on rural students rather than urban ones, for an institution is not entirely governed by the origins of its members since it acts to blend them within its own framework to ensure its self-perpetuation.[96] This is understandable in the context of an attitude of denial and a retreat from reality that bedevils every strong institution with a long history when it suffers humiliation or marginalisation in an unexpected way for which it does not have a framework of comprehension. It can only resist negatively, by withdrawal and retreat to elementary defensive postures. Al-Azhar and similar institutions were nevertheless obliged to accept reforms, which were limited for a long period to administrative and organisational measures related more to the needs of an absolute ruler such as Muhammad 'Ali or the sultans of Morocco than to the concepts of the reforming state.[97]

The first reform programme of Shaykh al-'Arusi, appointed Shaykh of al-Azhar by the Khedive Isma'il in 1865, was aimed ostensibly at combatting intellectual incompetence, indiscipline, corruption, and deficiencies in organisation, administration, and financial control. This was in addition to physical squalor, perceived sodomy, and the use of musical instruments after Qur'an recitation. A number of reforms were suggested that were implemented only under al-'Arusi's successor. These included examining the students in specific subjects, for the first time in the history of al-Azhar.[98] Al-'Arusi suggested introducing some modern linguistic or scientific (*ḥikmiyya*) subjects.[99] This was in addition to the more basic reform in the methods of teaching Islamic sciences contained in the curricular reform programme of Muhammad 'Abduh.[100] Both

95 'Abduh, *Al-a'māl al-kāmila*, vol. 3, 179.
96 'Allāl al-Fāsī, *Al-naqd al-dhātī*, 2nd edn (Tetouan: Dār al-Fikr al-Maghribī, n.d.), 16.
97 See Indira Falk Gesinck, *Islamic Reform and Conservatism: Al-Azhar and the Evolution of Modern Sunni Islam* (London: I. B. Tauris, 2014).
98 'Abd al-Karīm, *Tarīkh al-ta'līm*, vol. 2, 796–797, 811, 815–816, vol. 3, 158–182.
99 Ibid., vol. 3, 175.
100 Muḥammad Rashīd Riḍā, *Tarīkh al-ustādh al-imām al-shaykh Muḥammad 'Abduh*, 3 vols (Cairo: Maṭba'at al-Manār, 1350/1931), vol. 1, 440.

reforms, however, came much too late, which rendered the al-Azhar reforms quite disconnected from and out of phase with the emergent new cultural forms, dispositions, and sensibilities. Al-Azhar, on the contrary, remained a bastion for the production of a particular culture for a corporate group that for long came to occupy a wilfully marginal position in relation to the state and its new culture as well as to the course of world history. There remained a certain regard for this group in the setting of popular religiosity among simpler folk, a religiosity that perceived ulama as possessing a charismatic capacity and magical efficacy. This popular piety, partial to magical engagement with life's difficulties (but also with a very keen sense of reality), relied on ulama to provide amulets, spells, and exorcisms, and the knowledge to use Qur'anic texts in a magical and talismanic way.[101] Simpler ulama and rural folk were not the only ones to resort to this magic activity. Muhammad Rashid Rida, no less, believed in healing by amulets and in the wonders of the saints, treated the sick with amulets and believed that he was able to perform wonders, even as he attacked what he took for diabolical inspiration and charlatans who deceived ordinary folk with such matters.[102]

The influence of al-Azhar was raised to another level when the institution became the ally of the Khedives in their struggle with nationalist forces on the one hand and with the British administration on the other. It remained allied to the Egyptian Khedival-royal family until it was ousted from power in 1952. It was this new situation that strengthened the authority of al-Azhar and made it a centre of power that allowed it to extend beyond its local Egyptian social, political, and cultural base – its importance before that time is exorbitantly exaggerated. Its alliance with the Khedive shielded it to a considerable extent from the reforms pioneered by Muhammad 'Abduh. One might also mention the political animosity and poor relationship between Muhammad 'Abduh and the Khedive, and Lord Cromer's well-known support for 'Abduh the Mufti of Egypt.[103]

101 On the talismanic and magical uses of the Qur'an in daily life see Jacques Jomier, "La place du Coran dans la vie quotidienne en Égypte", *Revue de l'Institut des belles-lettres arabes* 15 (1952): 131–165. See more generally K. Malone O'Connor, "Popular and talismanic uses of the Qur'an", in *Encyclopedia of the Qur'an*, ed. J. Dammen McAuliffe, 5 vols (Leiden: Brill, 2004), vol. 4, 163–182.

102 Arslān, *Al-Sayyid Rashīd Riḍā aw ikhā' arba'īn sana*, 63–67, 76–77.

103 Riḍā, *Tarīkh al-ustādh al-imām al-shaykh Muḥammad 'Abduh*, vol. 1, 500–502, 558, 571–575, 630–635. See Mark Sedgwick, *Muhammad Abduh* (Oxford: Oneworld, 2014).

In Tunis the situation was scarcely different even if the Zeitouna had preceded al-Azhar in integrating mathematics into its curriculum. The reforms were, however, very limited despite the pressure of the movement of Young Tunis, the students, and some reformist ulama. The hostility to Muhammad ʿAbduh in the Zeitouna accounts for the frosty reception that greeted him when he visited Tunis in 1903, and the hounding of his followers, with the ultraconservatives of the Zeitouna prevailing.[104] The reactionary and defensive ulama in Istanbul, Cairo, and Tunis were popularly influential, because of their purported resources in magic and their promotion of a comforting sense of continuity.

The new intellectuals were influential because of their link to the state and to the dynamic of the nineteenth century. While the number of ulama in Egypt was greater, with 9,441 students at al-Azhar in 1872 (the number of students of languages did not, in the same year, exceed thirty) most students, nevertheless, oscillated between religious and non-religious scholarship, and blended and absorbed elements from both,[105] deployed singly or together, according to circumstance. State authorities had unleashed cultural and political forces in the Ottoman constitutional movement, in Egypt and in the Young Tunis movement, and then reined them in, relying instead on the forces of religious reaction. On this basis, the increased roles of religious notables in the Egyptian state and the reliance of French colonialism on religious figures in Tunis and elsewhere was a phenomenon that complemented the reliance of the sultan Abdülhamid on religious reactionaries in Anatolia and Ottoman Syria. When he suspended the constitution in 1878, he came to rely culturally and ideologically on a reinforced religious institution with newer forms of activity, at the same time as pursuing the implementation of the educational and administrative reforms. Indeed, his modernising educational policy was vigorous if conducted in a spirit of traditional authoritarianism.

Sultan Abdülhamid set about dissolving all voluntary associations, and permitted only charitable associations that were confessional in character.[106] He sought to limit the growth of civic currents in society and reinvigorated

104 Riḍā, *Tarīkh al-ustādh al-imām shaykh Muḥammad ʿAbduh*, vol. 1, 874 and Green, *The Tunisian Ulama, 1873–1915*, 178–190, 214–218, 178–190, 214–218.

105 Berkes, *The Development of Secularism in Turkey*, 142; ʿAbd al-Karīm, *Tarīkh al-taʿlīm*, vol. 2, 549, 719.

106 Sulayman al-Bustānī, *ʿIbra wa dhikrā: Aw al-dawla al-ʿuthmāniyya qabla al-dustūr wa baʿduhu* (Cairo: Maṭbaʿat al-Akhbār, 1908), 55–57.

older patrimonial arrangements. He placed special emphasis on censorship, and set up a rigorous system of internal espionage. This was a drift that loyalists in the state administration described as a lesser evil: "How many things governments have recourse to under duress lest they be obliged to implement even more grievous measures!"[107] This was doubtless an allusion to mounting European pressure on the Ottoman sultanate and European sponsorship of separatist movements within the territory of the Ottoman state, such as the increasing separatist activity among Armenians and other ethnic groups, and the founding in 1882 of the Ottoman Public Debt Administration, mortgaging state finances to European powers.

It seems clear that fear of further fragmentation of state territory was one primary reason for the quarrel between Abdülhamid and Midhat Paşa around the clauses of the Ottoman constitution. The first aimed at directly strengthening the centre while the latter considered participation and decentralisation a way of fusing together the nationalities and confessions of the Ottoman state.[108] Abdülhamid came to rely on elements in the state that he considered socially and politically conservative, especially Arabs and the Albanians, instead of the Istanbul Turks whom he seems to have considered corrupt. He formed the Sultan's Guard from Arabs and increased the proportion of Arabs in the military schools, founding a special school attached to the palace to instruct the sons of Arab and Kurdish tribal leaders. It was said that he wanted to make Arabic an official language alongside Turkish.[109] But, as Abdülhamid was a product of his time, he did not see reactionary religion as the only effective factor in strengthening the centre and rather concentrated on the expansion of education. A tally of books published during Abdülhamid's reign indicates a clear concentration on scientific works.[110] The sultan's priorities led rather haphazardly to continuing preparatory intellectual groundwork that led ultimately to a reconnection with the intellectual outlook of the bourgeois world and the *Tanzimat* period.[111] The Young Turk party confirmed this link and the revolution of Mustafa Kemal brought it to completion.

---

107 al-ʿAẓma, *Mirʾāt al-shām*, 207.

108 Berkes, *The Development of Secularism in Turkey*, 230–231.

109 al-ʿAẓma, *Mirʾāt al-shām*, 192–193, 210. See also Halide Edib, *Turkey Faces West*, 92–93 and Philip Mansell, *Sultans in Splendour* (London: André Deutsch, 1988), 23.

110 Şerif Mardin, *Religion and Social Change in Modern Turkey: The Case of Bediüzzaman Said Nursi* (Albany: State University of New York Press, 1989), 137, and 126n.

111 See now François Georgon, *Abdulhamid II, le sultan caliphe* (Paris: Farard, 2003).

In cultural and political terms the reactionary tendencies of Abdülhamid were based on two elements, one related to jurisprudence and the other to Sufi fraternities.[112] Activity among Sufis was delegated to Shaykh Abu al-Huda al-Sayyadi (1850–1909), who hailed from a village outside Aleppo and worked to broaden the influence of the Rifa'iyya fraternity, especially in Ottoman Syria and in Iraq, and to control the rural Sufi fraternities[113] and compete with the Kaylaniya fraternity for prestige.[114] Narratives circulated Syria and Iraq that the great saints of Damascus, Muhyeddin Ibn 'Arabi (1165–1240) and Shaykh 'Abd al-Ghani al-Nabulsi (1641–1731) had received mystical foreknowledge that Ottoman rule would last until the Hour of Resurrection.[115]

Abu al-Huda emphasised piety, trust in God, and obedience to the sovereign.[116] A number of religious and impious writers mobilised their pens to give renewed prestige to the medieval juristic theory of political power. Abdülhamid became, through Abu al-Huda's writings: "*khalīfat al-ḥaḍra al-nabawiyya*" ("successor to the Prophetic presence") and emphasised the "necessity to submit to God's epiphany bestowed upon the Sultan and his subordinates".[117] Shaykh Husayn al-Jisr, the teacher of Muhammad Rashid Rida, wrote the *Al-risāla al-ḥamīdiyya fi ḥaqīqat al-diyāna al-islāmīya wa ḥaqqīyat al-sharī'a al-muḥammadiyya* ("The Hamidian Treatise on the Truth of the Islamic Religion and the Rightfulness of the Muhammadan Path") in 1888, in which breaking allegiance to the imam and rebellion against him were proscribed, the book being dedicated to "Abd al-Hamid Khan *khalīfa* (vicar) of God on earth".[118] Jamil Sidqi al-Zahawi (1863–1936), the Iraqi poet and sceptic, had previously criticised the sultan Abdülhamid in a poem and had been condemned to house arrest.[119] He then wrote a book

112 See Selim Deringil, *The Well-Protected Domains: Ideology and the Legitimation of Power in the Ottoman Empire, 1876–1909* (London: I. B. Tauris, 1998).

113 Butros Abū Manneh, "Sultan Abdelhamid II and Shaikh Abdulhuda Al-Sayyadi", *Middle Eastern Studies* 15/2 (1979): 138–139.

114 Arslān, *Al-Sayyid Rashīd Riḍā aw ikhā' arba'īn sana*, 124.

115 Riḍā, *Mukhtārāt siyāsiyya min majallat al-manār*, 194.

116 Abū al-Hudā al-Ṣayyādi, *Dā'ī al-rashād li sabīl al-ittiḥād wa al-inqiyād* (Istanbul: al-Maṭba'a al-Sulṭāniyya, n.d.), 3–4.

117 Ibid., 20.

118 Ḥusayn al-Jisr, *Al-risāla al-ḥamīdiyya fi ḥiqqīyat al-diyāna al-islāmīyya wa ḥaqīqat al-sharī'a al-muḥammadiyya*, ed. Khālid Ziyadā (Tripoli: Jarūs Press, al-Maktaba al-Ḥadītha, n.d.), 44, 89.

119 Hilāl Nājī, *Al-zahāwī wa dīwānuhu al-mafqūd* (Cairo: Dar al-'Arab, 1964), 30–31. Zahawi's life and his relations with the British and King Faysal I of Iraq were marked by contradictions. Ibid., 34–37.

refuting the arguments of the Wahhabis, which opened with a chapter on the imamate. On its cover page was a poetic encomium by the Iraqi poet al-Rusafi (1875–1945), the author of a vast sceptical, critical, and irreverent biography of Muhammad the Apostle, written in al-Falluja in 1933 and published posthumously.[120] Al-Zahawi affirmed in this book, relying on various Qur'anic proof-texts, that the imamate was an imperative, and so too was obedience to it, and that the indivisibility of the sultan's authority is the analogue to the indivisible oneness of God. He affirmed that "the inhabitant of Yildiz Palace [Abdülhamīd]" was the "Imām of the Islamic *Umma* in an absolute sense, and defender of the Hanifi community [Muslims] across the world, God's authority upon earth, the executor of the commands of religion, obligatory and supererogatory. His elevated commands remain the path of righteousness and his imperial decisions are a glowing light in the heavens of glory."[121]

In the period from 1880 to 1907 Abu al-Huda and his followers published some ten books annually, and this ideological, or rather publicity, offensive was intended to win over the most conservative elements in the religious establishment.[122] This became clear through an all-embracing, integralist, and fundamentalist understanding of the application of shari'a that has become familiar in recent decades. All of its provisions were imperative and all required application. These included stoning and slavery, for which shari'a provided even as it enjoined manumition.[123] Shari'a on this understanding also made obligatory holy war, jihad, against non-Muslims "when an opportunity presents itself in order to bring them to Islam or assure their obedience to the Sultan".[124]

Reformist movements within Islam were persecuted and the famous incident of the *mujtahidūn* occurred in Damascus in 1895 when a number of reformist religious figures – reformist, but generally pietistic and socially conservative, inflecting 'Abduh's Salafism in that direction – were accused of *ijtihād*, independent judgment with the abandonment of accrued traditions as Salafism would have required. The political situation in the city and the

120 Ma'rūf al-Ruṣāfī, *Al-shakhṣiyya al-muḥammadiyya* (Cologne: al-Kamel Verlag, 2002).
121 Jamīl Ṣidqī al-Zahāwī, *Al-fajr al-ṣādiq fī al-radd 'alā munkirī al-tawassul wa al-karāmāt wa al-khawāriq* (Cairo: Maṭba'at al-Wā'iẓ, 1333/1914), 3–4, 7–8.
122 Abū Manneh, "Sultan Abdelhamid II and Shaikh Abdulhuda Al-Sayyadi", 140.
123 al-Jisr, *Al-risāla al-ḥamīdiyya*, 102, 118, 314, 230.
124 Ibid., 114–115.

balance of forces contributed to absence of any noteworthy results from this incident.[125] Some of Abu al-Huda's followers sought to forbid the teaching of geography, languages, and contemporary sciences. Schools associated with reactionary scholars were founded that excluded these subjects even if they were obliged shortly afterwards to integrate them in compliance with state educational policy.[126]

The press in the Ottoman Syrian provinces was forbidden, by order of the sultan, from mentioning the death of Muhammad 'Abduh.[127] These forces came together after the 1908 revolt by the Committee for Union and Progress that ushered in the second constitutional period. They aided the restoration of the sultan's authority during the counter-coup of 31 March 1909, until his deposition on 10 July 1909. The party of the Muhammadan Union (al-Ittihad al-Muhammadi), which was founded in Istanbul and extended as far as Damascus, had as its basic demand the application of shari'a and stigmatised the post-1908 constitution as contrary to it. This party brought together ulama and Sufi shaykhs with soldiers and subalterns promoted on the trot without being graduates of military schools that would have imparted elements of modern secular education.[128] This union had opposed the results of the enlightened, scientific, evolutionary, and universalist education embodied in the Committee of Union and Progress (CUP), against whom it had mounted a *Kulturkampf*. The struggle between Abdülhamid and his adversaries was one between two conceptions of the constitution: the sultan's view based on a perception of the constitution as an administrative means for control by the sultan and caliph, who exercised sovereignty as one appointed vicar of God, and a modernist conception of vaguely conceived popular sovereignty. The sultan's concept saw the constitution as an aspect of shari'a and subsumable under it, while the modernist conception saw the constitution as the source of all legislation. Indeed, the plan of the constitution prepared by

---

125 Ẓāfir al-Qāsimī, *Jamāl al-Dīn al-qāsimī wa 'aṣruhu* (Damascus: Maktabat Aṭlas, 1965), 44–69 and Kawtharāni, *Al-sulṭa wa al-mujtama' wa al-'amal al-siyāsī*, 149–150. See in general: David Dean Commins, *Islamic Reform: Politics and Social Change in Late Ottoman Syria* (Oxford: Oxford University Press, 1990).

126 al-Qāsimī, *Jamāl al-Dīn al-qāsimī wa 'aṣruhu*, 17.

127 Riḍā, *Tarīkh al-ustādh al-imām al-shaykh Muḥammad 'Abduh*, vol. 1, 7.

128 Al-Ḥuṣrī', *Al-bilād al-'arabiyya wa al-dawla al-'uthmāniyya*, 110–113 and David Commins, "Religious reformers and Arabists in Damascus, 1885–1914", *International Journal of Middle East Studies* 18 (1986): 405–425, 414–416.

Midhat Paşa before its institution did not mention a state religion at all, nor conceive a position of *şeyhülislam* – which had become redundant – contrary to what was contained in the constitution after its modification.[129]

2 The Secularisation of Daily Life

Speaking about the secularisation of life can appear to restate the obvious because life is of its nature worldly. Yet life does come to acquire a secular stamp when religious interests pass polemical judgements characterising social changes that escaped their grip as being in contradiction with religion. When such interests found themselves adopting defensive positions, they resorted to describing social transformations from which they excluded themselves as contrary to religion, and themselves as religion's true representatives. The issue of women's location in society was (and still is) in this sense a strategic battleground both symbolically and socially. Issues concerning dress (including veiling), barring females from proper education, male tyranny, preference for marriage with parallel cousins, and prayer in segregated spaces in houses of worship were not specifically Muslim religious matters but social customs that applied to both Christians and Muslims in Ottoman Syria and Egypt, very similar to the aversion – common to Christians and Muslims – to the consumption of swine.[130] This may go back to ancient local customs that Islam and Judaism adopted. When, therefore, Jurji Zaidan reproved the "immoderate" mixing of the sexes in activities such as dancing, he referred to "our Eastern customs".[131] When Muhammad 'Abduh approved the abolition of polygamy, he based his argument on a kind of natural law that works through the sane human understanding (*al-fiṭra*) and not only on Muslim jurisprudence.[132] It is clear that polygamy in Arab cities is linked not

129 Mardin, *The Genesis of Young Ottoman Thought*, 124.

130 Salāma Mūsā, *Tarbiyat Salāma Mūsā* (Cairo: Mu'assasat al-Khānjī, 1958), 16; Jurjī Zaydān, *Mukhtārāt Jurjī Zaydān*, 3 vols (Cairo: Maṭba'at al-hilāl, 1919–1921), vol. 1, 141–142; Naẓīra Zayn al-Dīn, *Al-fatāt wa al-shuyūkh: Naẓarāt wa munāẓarāt fī al-sufūr wa al-ḥijāb wa taḥrīr al-mar'a wa al-tajaddud al-ijtimā'ī fī al-'ālam al-islāmī* (Beirut: al-Matba'a al-Amīrikiyya, 1929), 115; Wedad Zenié-Ziegler, *In Search of Shadows: Conversations with Egyptian Women* (London: Zed Books, 1988), 23, 37, ch. 2, and passim; Aḥmad Fāris al-Shidyāq, *Al-sāq 'alā al-sāq fī mā huwa al-fāryāq aw ayyām wa shuhūr wa a'wām fī 'ajam al-'arab wa al-a'jām* (Beirut: Dār Maktabat al-Ḥayāt, 1966), 229.

131 Zaydān, *Mukhtārāt Jurjī Zaydān*, vol. 1, 146.

132 'Abduh, *Al-a'māl al-kāmila*, vol. 2, 84, 94.

to religious practice but to social class, as polygamy and divorce were rare higher up the social scale.[133] It was not unusual that Muslim women from the lower classes should sit unveiled outside their houses[134] in the same way that sociological research on marriage in a Lebanese Christian community indicates that social norms prevailed over religious norms when the two were in contradiction.[135] This is likely to be the case in all communities.

Things come to be characterised as secular, therefore, when their sheer worldliness comes to be construed by specific socio-political interests as being in contradiction to sacred values of which these interests claim to be the voice. A case in point is the temporal regime of global modernity. When the Gregorian anno domini calendar became the calendar of reference used in all regions of Europe at the end of the eighteenth century, transmuted from being one specific Church calendar to a calendar in general use, societies that followed its rhythms changed to the rhythm of global time centred on Europe (even Saudi Arabia came to adopt it for practical purposes in 2016).[136] In 1790, the Ottoman state adopted a new financial calendar – although it did have administrative precedents especially in the agricultural field – based on solar months counted within the Hijra year.[137] The temporality of the state diverged from the rhythms of religious ritual, which had divided up time according to divisions that govern the rhythm of the succession of ritual moments: Ramadan, and the two feasts in addition to the Prophet's birthday, the Night of Destiny in Ramadan and other calendrical stations. While it appears that the Gregorian calendar was adopted by the Maronite Church in 1606 without difficulty, its introduction into the practices of the Eastern Catholic Church in Damascus in 1860 led to much discord.[138] Opposition to moving from a local to a universal temporality was not restricted to Muslim clerics. It seems that arguments also arose about considering Friday to be a day of rest, in accordance with the novel institution of weekly days of rest globally congruent with novel ways of organising labour. Some ulama proscribed it,

133 al-Khālidī *Jawla fī al-dhikrayāt*, 53 and Ḥalīm Barakāt, *Al-mujtama' al-'arabī al-mu'āṣir: Baḥth istiṭlā'ī wa ijtimā'ī* (Beirut: Markaz Dirāsāt al-Waḥda al-'Arabiyya, 1984), 209–210.

134 Aḥmad Amīn, *Ḥayātī*, 3rd edn (Cairo: Maktabat al-Nahḍa al-Miṣriyya, 1958).

135 Barakāt, *Al-mujtama' al-'arabī al-mu'āṣir*, 127.

136 "The prince's time machine", *The Economist*, 17 December 2016.

137 Berkes, *The Development of Secularism in Turkey*, 420–422.

138 Sarkīs, *Mu'jam al-maṭbū'āt al-'arabiyya wa al-mu'arraba*, 1,138, 1,207–1,208, 1,331, 1,318 and elsewhere.

dubbing it illicit in religious terms. Problems arose with the cessation of work on Sundays by some Muslims in Beirut and Cairo.[139] The Gregorian calendar eventually became the standard method of calendrical reckoning in most places, and became written into law as the legally prescribed way of registering births and other matters – as in the third article of the Egyptian civil code.

Resistance of the ulama was also provoked by the introduction of printing, another disturbing sign of change. Printing was authorised by an Ottoman fatwa in 1727 on the condition that no copy of the Qur'an or religious books be printed.[140] The first *mushaf* was printed and distributed in 1924 (the Cairto edition). Similarly, as in Europe some centuries earlier, dissection in medical instruction faced strong opposition that was only overcome by an edict of the sultan in 1841.[141] In Egypt things took a more gradual course: first came permission to dissect canine carcasses, then the cadavers of Christians and slaves, and, in the end, the authorisation of the dissection of dead humans in general.[142]

The adoption of what were seen as European ways, *tafarnuj*, was one indicator taken by spokesmen for religious interests as signalling the collapse and perdition of religion. This adoption by sections of society of expanding global habits of sociality became a sign of secularisation and was an indication of social incorporation into a new temporality, introduced by the *Tanzimat* state and sustained by translations of Western novels that provided concrete indications of how life was lived in European countries. Translations of Sherlock Holmes novels were available in railway stations on the route between Beirut and Damascus in the early part of the twentieth century.[143]

The availability of books accelerated, and the types of publication revealed rapid social changes. The rapidity of social transformation meant that those caught up in it were in need in some social milieux for orientation that society

---

139 Riḍā, *Fatāwā*, no. 474.

140 Berkes, *The Development of Secularism in Turkey*, 40–41. On resistance to printing, see Geoffrey Roper (ed.), *Historical Aspects of Printing and Publishing in Languages of the Middle East* (Leiden: Brill, 2014) and Nadia Al-Bagdadi, "Introduction", to *Sacred Texts and Print Culture: The Case of the Qur'an and the Eastern Bible*, ed. Nadia al-Bagdadi (New York and Budapest: Central European University Press, forthcoming).

141 Ibid., 115–116.

142 Zaydān, *Tārīkh adāb al-lugha al-'arabiyya*, vol. 2, 379.

143 Al-Khālidī, *Jawla fī al-dhikrayāt bayna lubnān wa filasṭīn*, 46.

was no longer providing as a matter of course in daily life. There were cook books, books of social etiquette, as well as books that claimed to provide keys to success in an incipient capitalist society with a specific form of organisation, such as *How to Prevail in the Battlefield of Life* (1902), *The Secret of Success* (1880) and others, as well as books that, as their authors claimed, provided people who had become individuals with the ability to establish spousal relations of a new type independent from its old frameworks. Of these might be mentioned *Advice for the Young on Chastity or the Law of Marriage: Its Natural Laws and its Correct Physiological and Other Conditions.*[144] Self-help books at the end of the twentieth century represented an accentuated phase of this type of need.

Among the basic indications of life beyond the confines of living tradition hallowed by religious interests at moments of its passing was manner of dress. Significant transformation began with obliging state officials in the Egypt of Muhammad ʿAli Pasha to adopt a distinctive form of dress, closely related to the European military uniforms adopted for the Ottoman and Egyptian armies – similar developments occurred all around the globe, from Hawaii to Thailand and India as well. This uniform was adopted for use in Istanbul in 1826. The fez became obligatory in place of the turban. In the period from 1860 to 1870 the modern uniform spread in Ottoman Syria beyond the framework of state officials to all the sectors of society that were aligned with the reforms. Foreigners in Damascus meanwhile were obliged to wear local dress until 1832, when this started to become the object of scorn and to be associated with the lower classes at the beginning of the twentieth century.[145] Religious attacks on these changes were relentless, to the extent that Muhammad ʿAbduh was obliged to issue a fatwa that those wearing European-style hats may not be declared unbelievers.[146] Rashid Rida authorised wearing a hat "for its own sake" but proscribed it inasmuch as, according to him, it weakened religious solidarity.[147] In this allusion to Kemalist Turkey, Rida identifies the practical and objective consequences of

144 Sarkīs, *Muʿjam al-maṭbūʿat al-ʿarabiyya wa al-muʿarraba,* 1,138, 1,207–1,208, 1,331, 1,418 and elsewhere.

145 R. Tresse, "L'Evolution du costume syrien depuis un siècle", *Renseignements coloniaux: Supplément au bulletin du Comité de l'Afrique Française* (1938), 47.

146 ʿAbduh, *Al-aʿmāl al-kāmila,* vol. 3, 515.

147 Riḍā, *Fatāwā,* no. 30, 665.

vestimentary transformation, namely the integration into a universal global habitus of sociality, rejected by historically defunct social groups, with the religious class in prime position among these. Not only Muslims criticised the adoption of European dress and attire; such criticism was widespread among Syrian Christians as late as the post-First World War period, with mockery directed at those who maintained no moustaches, and at modern clothes, especially women's clothes, considered exorbitantly expensive as well as implying unbelief and debasement.[148]

There is no doubt that the severe attacks launched by Rashid Rida on Europeanisation, including the trimming of beards – whose origins he saw to reside in effeminacy – was part of a wider attack on newer developments. The early Arab theatre came under attack; the playwright Abu Khalil Qabbani (1835–1902) was compelled to continue his career in Cairo following the closure of his Damascus theatre by the authorities.[149] The theatre was a danger to traditions that Rashid Rida designated as Islamic, a danger also associated with the mingling of men and women on stage.[150] A vast polemical literature in Arabic against *tafarnuj* was produced, invoking Islam.[151] There was much congruent Turkish writing as well, condemning and mocking Europeanisation, taken as an abstract sign of an attack on moribund social arrangements rendered marginal by the development of new global forms of sociality, with indications of social hierarchies involved.[152] This also betokened a parallel disjunction between sources of religious authority and the points of reference for secularism. The less dramatic and everyday changes in urban topography did not attract criticism: new state-sponsored as well as private architectural styles, and the loss by public baths of much of their custom, attendant upon newer modes of habitation and modernising public works, including more extensive networks of water canalisation. A

148 J. Lecerf, "La crise vestimentaire d'après-guerre en Syrie d'après la littérature populaire", *Renseignements coloniaux: Supplément au bulletin du Comité de l'Afrique Française* (1938): 45–47.

149 Riḍā, *Fatāwā*, no. 116.

150 Ibid., no. 210.

151 See 'Abd al-Raḥmān al-Kawākibī, *Umm al-Qurā*, in *Al-a'māl al-kāmila*, ed. Muḥammad 'Amāra (Beirut: al-Mu'assasa al-'Arabiyya li'l-Dirāsāt wa al-Nashr, 1975), 329–331. This author is much praised for his alleged democratist positions, and generally interpreted with considerable anachronism and tendentiousness.

152 Şerif Mardin, "Super Westernisation in urban life in the Ottoman Empire in the last quarter of the nineteenth century", in *Turkey: Geographic and Social Perspectives*, P. Benedict, et al. (Leiden: Brill, 1974), 403–446.

related development was the recession of older practices of personal hygiene, often associated with the public bath, including depilation of the armpit (both sexes), shaving of the pubic region (both sexes), and of the head (for men) and legs (women). The celebration of the beginning of the Hijra year in Egypt (starting in 1908) was considered an imitation of the Christian New Year, but not much came of the opposition.[153]

In the same way, the question of women's education, their unveiling and mixing with men – developments that had begun to impose themselves on public life from the end of the nineteenth century – was basically a question of social conservatism that religious figures turned into a religious issue, and, consequently, in the contexts of polemic and contestation, into the surest emblem of godless secularism. The issue is still with us in much the same terms today. The principal cities in the Anatolian littoral, especially Istanbul, were at the forefront of places in which women began to make gains. In 1881, for the first time, a woman from Istanbul was allowed to give an address to school students on the occasion of a graduation ceremony. In 1883, the appointment of female civil servants in government departments began, initially in the Department of Education.[154] Women from the upper classes in Cairo were starting to debate women's education and to attend opera, where they sat in reserved boxes.[155]

Women's debates in the Arab provinces were largely confined to patrician mileux. The education of girls in the nineteenth century started with the opening by missionaries of the first girls' school in Egypt in 1836, which was in effect a charitable endeavour designed for poor girls and orphans who were to be prepared for domestic service, or to be workers or wives. Girls from more prosperous backgrounds studied at home under the supervision of European governesses and Muslim ulama teachers.[156] These girls were taught French, piano, and other skills required for their social position as this was being buttressed by newer tastes and forms of sociality.[157] It might be noted that in 1832 Muhammad Ali instructed Clot Bey (Antoine Clot, 1793–1868)

153 Muḥammad Muḥammad Ḥusayn, *Al-ittijāhāt al-waṭaniyya fī al-adab al-mu'āṣir*, 2 vols (Beirut: Dār al-Irshād, 1970), vol. 1, 319.

154 Berkes, *The Development of Secularism in Turkey*, 176.

155 Huda Shaarawi, *Harem Years: The Memoirs of an Egyptian Feminist*, trans. Margot Badran (London: Virago Press, 1986), 62, 62n, and 80.

156 'Abd al-Karīm, *Tarīkh al-ta'līm*, vol. 2, 356, 361, 373–376.

157 Ibid., 356.

to establish a school to train female paramedics and midwives. Recruitment was a serious problem and resort needed to be made to inducting slave girls into this kind of service.

In the provinces of Ottoman Syria, where the British founded the first school for girls in Beirut in 1860, the education of girls was broadly comparable to that prevailing in Egypt. Education seemed freer in relative terms and girls higher up the social scale studied in foreign schools from an early period, in addition to the practice of study at home. In the later part of the century, they would read *al-Muqtaṭaf, al-Hilāl,* and, later, Jirji Baz's bi-weekly *al-Ḥasnā' al-Bayrūtiyya* (1909–1912), a women's magazine published in Beirut, preceded by quite a few short-lived ones such as *al-Fatāt* in Alexandria (1892) or *Al-Sayyidāt wa'l-Banāt* (Ladies and Girls) of Rose Antun, Farah Antun's sister and collaborator, in 1902, and followed by many. Many girls' schools had a charitable character as in Egypt, intended to train poorer girls.[158] The progress of women in Ottoman Syria was closely linked to the rise of bourgeois sensibilities, sociality and values brought by modern education; it involved Christian women of modest status and Muslims higher up the social scale – more modest Muslim women needed to wait some decades.[159]

Reality on the ground was, however, in advance of mentalities, as the notion of the inferiority of women was widely spread across different religious confessions and intellectual orientations, sometimes aggressively mysogynistic. Veiling was a token of this prevailing attitude, emphasising women's subalternity and taking this as a sign of robust social order. 'Abd al-Rahman al-Kawakibi, considered by some the pioneer of Arab nationalism, believed that the Chinese custom of foot-binding was a splendid one, "so that it may be difficult for them [women] to wander about and seek to corrupt an honourable life".[160] Shibli Shumayyil, physician, graduate of the Syrian Protestant College, Darwinist, atheist, and pioneer of secularism, in a text of 1886, claimed that scientific knowledge demonstrated that women were weaker than men in body, mind, and morals, and their position in society

158 Zaydān, *Tārīkh adāb al-lugha al-'arabiyya,* vol. 2, 397; al-Khālidī, *Jawla fī al-dhikrayāt bayna lubnān wa filasṭīn,* 66, 122–115.

159 Muḥammad Jamīl Bayhum, *Al-mar'a fī'l-islām wa fī al-ḥaḍāra al-gharbiyya,* introduced by Georges Ṭarābīshī (Beirut: Dar al-Ṭalī'a, 1980), 87–88.

160 al-Kawākibī, *Al-a'māl al-kāmila,* 329.

declined further in relation to men as society progressed. He thought that whenever women were closer to a primitive social condition, the greater the measure of equality and of superiority they had as against men. This accords well with Darwin's own views, and with an impressionistic reading of certain trends in nineteenth-century anthropology (Bachofen, Tyler) that take matriarchy to be the primitive stage of humanity.[161] Jurji Zaydan expressed in his European travelogue of 1912 his distaste for the amount of freedom women enjoyed there, and their lassitude concerning religious observance, considering that this offended the Oriental sense of decency.[162]

The gradualist approach towards the advancement of women was not confined to Muslim authors but was shared by Christian intellectuals as well.[163] Nor were timorous moral suspicions arising from gynophobic attitudes limited to those Muslims who found in veiling a guarantee of chastity and a thwarting of possible misconduct.[164] The view of women as deficient, and therefore not in need of more than a modicum of education appropriate to their condition and simple role as child-rearers, was not one on which conservative Muslims or Christians differed. This applies equally to opposition to women's work outside the home and to the mixing of the sexes.[165]

A woman appearing in public unveiled was not common during the period of concern to this discussion. Girls were veiled from an early age, under strong social pressure. Some protested discretely. Some engaged in discussions concerning veiling and the lot of women in general, and some read Qasim Amin, perhaps for consolation. Women in Ottoman Syria envied Egyptian women for their presumed liberties.[166] Only few people were inclined to an untroubled position with regard to women. Some ulama in Beirut were opposed to girls learning to play the piano and did not wish them

---

161 Shiblī al-Shumayyil, *Majmūʿat al-duktūr Shiblī al-Shumayyil*, 2 vols, 2nd edn (Cairo: Maṭbaʿat al-Maʿārif, 1910), 97–98. See Gerald Bergman, "The history of the human female inferiority idea in evolutionary biology", *Rivista di Biologia*, 96 (2002): 379–412.

162 Jurjī Zaydān, *Al-riḥla ilā Urubba*, ed. Qāsim Wahhāb (Abu Dhabi: Dār al-Suwaydī, 2002), 51.

163 Fahmī Jadʿān, *Usus al-taqaddum*, 481–482; Zaydān, *Mukhtārāt Jurjī Zaydān*, vol. 2, 167.

164 al-Jisr, *Al-risāla al-ḥamīdiyya*, 116; and Ṭalaʿat Ḥarb, *Tarbiyat al-marʾa wa al-ḥijāb* (Cairo: Maṭbaʿat al-Taraqqī, 1899), 60.

165 al-Shumayyil, *Majmūʿat al-duktūr Shiblī al-Shumayyil*, 103–104; Jamāl al-Dīn al-Afghānī, *Al-aʿmāl al-kāmila li Jamāl al-Dīn al-Afghānī*, ed. Muḥammad ʿAmāra (Cairo: al-Muʾassasa al-Miṣriyya al-ʿĀmma, n.d.), 525, 529; Zaydān, *Mukhtārāt Jurjī Zaydān*, vol. 2, 357, 360 and Faraḥ Anṭūn, *Mukhtārāt* (Beirut: Dar Ṣādir, 1950), 22, 25–27.

166 al-Khālidī, *Jawla fī al-dhikrayāt bayna lubnān wa filasṭīn*, 37–38, 73–74.

to drift to what they considered the excessive freedom of Damascene women who had adopted Turkish, that is, Istanbuli – ways.[167] The same attitudes motivated the criticism of Turkish education policies and the appointment of Halide Edib (1884–1964) – who later became the Minister of Education under Atatürk, and who was one of the most distinguished feminine figures in Turkish letters and public life during her lifetime – to the post of inspector of schools in Damascus, Beirut, and Mount Lebanon and director of a teacher-training school for girls in Beirut.[168]

Prevailing progressive views about women were not, it must be said, boldly progressive, but belonged to a generally moderate reformist approach composed of two tendencies: on the one hand, bourgeois, liberal, and Westernising thought represented by Murqus Fahmi, author of the play *Women of the East* (1894),[169] and Islamic reformist thought represented by Muhammad 'Abduh and Qasim Amin. Rare were clear feminist calls for the equality of women such as that made by Shidyāq in the pages of his Istanbul newspaper *al-Jawā'ib*.[170] The consolidation of the principle of the education of women in the early twentieth century derived from the converging influence of the two above-mentioned currents of thought, and their interfaces with social transformations.

There is, however, considerable difference between the principle of education for women in itself, which does not seem to have encountered serious opposition once a dynamic was established. More serious differences arose with regard to the liberties of women and to what they should be allowed to learn.[171] The prevailing justification for education was uncontroversial, and raised few thorny issues, as, for example, in the general statement by Muhammad 'Abduh:

> As for women, a veil has been positioned between them and what they should know of their religion and of their world, and we do not know when it will be lifted. It does not occur to anyone to instruct

167 Muḥammad Rashīd Riḍā, *Riḥlāt al-imām Muḥammad Rashīd Riḍā*, ed. Yūsuf Ibish, 2 vols (Beirut: al-Mu'assasa al-'Arabiyya li'l-Dirāsāt wa al-Nashr, 1971), 244.

168 Ibid., 246 and Khālidī, *Jawla fī al-dhikrayāt*, 110.

169 Margot Badran, "Introduction", in Shaarawi, *Harem Years*, 14–15.

170 'Imād al-Ṣulḥ, *Aḥmad Fāris al-Shidyāq āthāruhu wa 'aṣruhu* (Beirut: Dar al-Nahār li'l-Nashr, 1980), 314–315, and cf. Nājī, *Al-zahāwī wa dīwānuhu al-mafqūd*, 163–165.

171 'Awaḍ, *Al-mu'aththirāt al-ajnabiyya fī al-adab al-'arabī al-ḥadīth*, vol. 1, 82, 84.

> them in a creed, or that they should perform any devotional act bar fasting. What chastity that they preserve is due to custom and a sense of modesty, or perhaps minimal awareness of what is permissible and forbidden. With a very few rare exceptions – one can count them all in under a minute – their minds are full of superstition and their talk is mostly drivel.[172]

Qasim Amin's views developed over the short time between the publication of his two famous books on the woman question, in 1899 and 1900,[173] inspired by the attitude of 'Abduh and not really going beyond it. But his thoughts on unveiling concerned a move to what he considered shar'i headwear, whatever that might have meant then, revealing the feminine face whose masking would deter women's knowledge of the world.[174] He was far more conservative than Tahtawi in his view that broader personal liberties would lead to rashness and libertinism and arrived at the conclusion that a limitation on personal freedom was essential for social stability.[175] Qasim Amin was thus at one with critics who believed that the fundamental result of the liberation of women was degradation, decline, and social collapse:[176] a view much criticised at the time, with claims that the purportedly corrupt morals of women were linked to the coercion and restrictions and disabilities they experienced, and that the veil could itself be a factor in causing moral corruption, given its basis in suspicion of and low regard for women.[177] Yet despite his caution and his relatively conservative positions, Qasim Amin received fierce criticism.[178] It is unsurprising that Qasim Amin, in the words of one commentator, went

172 'Abduh, *Al-a'māl a-kāmila*, vol. 3, 229.

173 Both are available in English translations by Samiha Sidhom Peterson: Qāsim Amīn, *The Liberation of Women and The New Woman* (Cairo: American University of Cairo Press, 1992). A meticulous and most enlightening analysis of the two works and their relationship: Muḥammad al-Ḥaddād, *Ḥafriyyāt ta'wīliyya fī al-khiṭāb al-iṣlāḥī al-islāmī* (Beirut: Dār al-Ṭalī'a, 2002), 156–192.

174 Qāsim Amīn, *Al-a'māl al-kāmila*, ed. Muhammad 'Amāra, 2 vols (Beirut: al-Mu'assasa al-'Arabiyya li'l-Dirāsāt wa al-Nashr, 1976), 43ff.

175 'Awaḍ, *al-mu'āththirāt al-ajnabiyya fī al-adab al-'arabī al-ḥadīth*, vol. 1, 17, 19.

176 See Ḥarb, *Tarbiyat al-mar'a wa al-ḥijāb*, 26ff. One can compare the Tunisian author Muḥammad b. Muṣṭafā ibn al-Khūja, *Al-iqtirāth fī ḥuqūq al-ināth* (Algiers: n.p., 1895), and *Al-lubāb fī aḥkām al-zinā wa al-libās wa al-iḥtijāb* (Algiers: n.p., 1907), both of which dwell on purportedly bad intentions and morals of women: Jad'ān, *Usus al-taqaddum*, 460–464.

177 See Zaydān, *Mukhtārāt Jurjī Zaydān*, vol. 1, 143–144, vol. 2, 167.

178 On this subject and on the various reactions see Jad'ān, *Usus at-taqaddum*, 463–465.

into rebound and embraced Western liberal bourgeoisie positions between his first book, which attracted criticism, and the second, just as bitterly criticised in its turn.[179] It was not so much an extension and development of Amin's position as the clarity in his thought that brought upon him the controversy provoked by his book. Qasim Amin proposed minimalist ideas that modern universalist culture, and the society envisaged by this culture, saw as self-evident and natural ideas that emerged from the evolution of society and history in the course of the nineteenth century. The novelties thereby becoming apparent were taken for evidence of extreme iniquity in the minds of Qasim Amin's critics. His worldly critics presented change gleefully as a disaster for religion, while others used religion as a resource from which they drew self-righteous armament.

Some commentators who have to be seen as progressive by the standards of the time deployed religious arguments, and while they agreed with Qasim Amin's call for the education of women within certain limits, criticised his call for unveiling. Tala'at Harb (1867–1921), the prominent nationalist economist and banker, was among them.[180] An absolute contradiction was posited between the liberal and the religious position and the one supported by religious arguments, with the veil figuring as the emblem of distinction between the two. In the rhetorical figure of the veil, and the restrictive view of gender disability in general, was deposited a vein of sanctity, while the liberation of women, on the contrary, became emblematic of secularisation. Women became a field of semantic and semiotic competition between signs of the sacred and the profane or worldly, between a world fed by the sacred and its opposite.

This contest began with the affair of Qasim Amin and continued to be interpreted as a primary token of contrariety and field of contestation between religious and secular people for a long period. Mustafa Sabri (1860–1940) was the last *şeyhülislam* in the Ottoman state, who took refuge in Egypt after the abolition of the caliphate, and there exercised extensive cultural activity characterised by an uncompromisingly traditionalist, indeed reactionary religious position for which he had been known since his youth, expressed with extraordinary competence and erudition. His book on the subject of women

179 Ibid., 464.
180 Ḥarb, *Tarbiyat al-mar'a wa al-ḥijāb*, 44–45, 56–57, 60–61.

might be regarded as the broadest and most competent and comprehensive exposition of the conservative religious viewpoint on the subject.[181] But this, too, was no longer sufficient to rein in the forward movement of society. The late nineteenth century and early twentieth saw the rise of early women's associations of a cultural and charitable type, essentially in Egypt, with a decided political nationalist turn after the First World War, and especially with the 1919 Egyptian Revolution against British occupation. In Damascus during the First World War, the Red Star association was founded (which later became the Red Crescent) at the initiative of Nazik al-'Abid (1898–1959). Its members took an active part in the national movement and some were present at the famous Battle of Maysalun on 24 July 1920, when French troops under General Gouraud started their invasion of Syria. They treated the wounded, and tended Yusuf al-'Azmeh (1884–1920), the minister of war in the independent Arab kingdom of Syria, who succumbed to his wounds, subsequently becoming Syria's national hero, while the Syrian Arab forces were in flight. In Beirut other associations of cultural and charitable character were set up, such as the Association for Awakening of Young Arab Women (*jam'iyyat yaqẓat al-fatāt al-'arabiyya*), with the accord of the Ottoman governor and the support of Ahmad Mukhtar Bayhum (1878–1922), a prominent progressive patrician.

It was therefore clear that a new world was taking shape, based on intellectual, social, and cultural foundations that were outside the control of religious authorities and constituencies, but without positioning itself against it. This world developed in circumstances that saw the state acting to transfer as much social authority as possible from intermediate entities – religious confessions included – to itself as it sought to penetrate society through individual citizens fashioned by social change and legal transformations to be discussed presently. In this world, religious institutions were at a respectful distance, having been removed fairly rapidly, without the intent of this removal being openly announced or indeed seeming to be pressing, from erstwhile positions of figuring as the prime authority in education, overtaken by newer institutions but by no means eliminated. Faced with this prospect of marginalisation and irrelevance, religious institutions and their individual members came to ally themselves with retrograde social forces. In a defensive strategy,

181 Muṣṭafā Ṣabrī, *Qawlī fī al-mar'a wa muqāranatuhu bi aqwāl muqallidat al-gharb* (Cairo: al-Maṭba'a al-Salafiyya, 1354/1975).

one that is still active and has not completely failed but is indeed in a state of revival in the past three decades, they created, in the flow of social differentiation brought about by modernity, a religious sector differentiated like others, along with new vested interests.

Was it social and educational marginalisation that made ulama frequently the subject of mockery, lampooned as narrow-minded and prim, boorish, uncivilised, greedy, rapacious, clinging to reactionary attitudes? Ahmad Amin (1886–1954), a major figure in Egyptian letters, describes his difficulty in finding a bride while he was a turbanned *'alim* in his earlier life. The turban, he informed his reader, is respected only outwardly and as a matter of form while actually being held in low regard. Especially in cities, turbanned persons were generally held in contempt until they demonstrated that they were worthy of respect.[182] Similarly it is uncertain if, in previous periods, ulama enjoyed the regard they claimed was accorded to them ceremoniously despite the sneering mockery directed at them throughout the ages, as mentioned in the previous chapter. This applied not only to the Muslim priesthood. Shidyaq drew on a long satirical heritage as he noted that, of churchmen, one heard only "things that are a disgrace to honour and to reason", and that it was rare to encounter a virtuous cleric; as for learning, "it was forbidden them". He poked fun at a bishop, entitling an imaginary book of his *al-hakāka fi al-rakāka – The Leavings Pile Concerning Lame Style.*[183]

Law was and remains a realm in which public life is subject to regulation. A form of control of the rhythm of the social and economic changes that came over Arab regions in the nineteenth century was reflected in the details of legal change. Important for the concerns of this book is to signal the emergent secularisation of legal conceptions, procedures, and institutions. The governing trend in legal change throughout late Ottoman lands under the *Tanzimat* state was the establishment of legal structures external to the institutional and social networks of control, and beyond the technical and intellectual competence of the ulama and their institutions. The promulgation of crucial laws with bases and points of reference that are in practical terms detached from those used in Muslim jurisprudence were not often declared as such, and were

182 Amīn, *Ḥayātī*, 183–222.

183 al-Shidyāq, *Al-Sāq alā al-sāq*, 138–139, 497. Translation of the title: al-Shidyāq, *Leg Over Leg*, trans. Humphrey Davies, 4 vols (New York: New York University Press, 2014), vol. 2, para. 2.3.5, vol. 4, para. 4.19.1.

often said apologetically to derive from the shari'a or said to be in conformity with it. This is not surprising, as for the most part ulamaic institutions opposed these codifications actively in Istanbul and Tunis, and in other places adopted a policy of grudging boycott. No wonder, given that these codifications and their overall system did not only elude the control of the corporate body of the ulama, but in many of their clauses were in contradiction with the text and the spirit of what had been received from the long and profuse traditions of Muslim jurisprudence.

The Ottoman Penal Law of 1840 (with the Penal Code of 1810 as one of its sources) adopted the principle of "no penalty without explicit stipulation", thus contradicting the practice of discretionary punishments decided by political authorities allowable in Muslim jurisprudence (*ta'zīr*), and setting penal law on firmer bases.[184] The Ottoman Penal Law also abolished the penalties of stoning for fornication and severing hands for theft. The Ottoman Penal Law of 1858 abolished apostasy as a crime, granting, for the first time in the history of Islam, one of the necessary guarantees for the establishment of fundamental freedoms.

The implementation of these legal codes was entrusted to secular courts called *maḥākim niẓāmiyya* (administrative courts) or the *maḥākim 'adaliyya* (courts of justice) – as distinct from shari'a courts. In the Syrian provinces new types of court were known as *majlis al-jināyāt* (criminal council) or *majlis al-ḍabṭiyya* (police court). These operated under a new state institution, the ministry of justice, without relying on shari'a judges. Yet despite the importance of the penal laws and in particular their symbolic link to prescriptive and Qur'anic imperatives of classical Muslim juriprudence, new commercial laws were codified earlier, a natural development given novel economic conditions in both their local and colonial dimensions. These codifications were created to regulate and accommodate new developments. Mixed commercial councils existed from earlier times, and in 1840 these were organised under the name of *majlis al-tijāra*, or the commercial council. The first commercial code was elaborated in 1850 on the basis of French laws, and the form of application of these laws was rearranged, this being

184 On the general legal changes see Shafīq Shiḥāta, *Al-ittijāhāt al-tashrī'iyya fī qawanīn al-bilād al-'arabiyya* (Cairo: Jāmi'at al-Duwal al-'Arabiyya, Ma'had al-Dirāsāt al-'Arabiyya al-'Āliya, 1960); Berkes, *The Development of Secularism in Turkey* and Norman Anderson, *Law Reform in the Muslim World* (London: Athlone Press, 1976).

entrusted to commercial courts sponsored by the ministry of commerce, then known as the Agency of Utilities (*wikālat al-'umūr al-nāfi'a*). These courts were the first judicial institutions that were outside the control of the shar'i court system, and it was the first judicial system to consider the testimony of a non-Muslim *dhimmī* equal to that of a Muslim. This important precedent spread quickly across the different parts of the judicial system. The Ottoman Nationality Law of 1869 considered non-Ottoman Muslims to be foreigners, another crucial step in the move to socially engineer society along lines of modern notions of national sovereignty, territory, and nationality, and, ultimately, on a bourgeois model of citizenship.[185]

Egyptian developments, in both content and form, were congruent with those occurring in the Ottoman capital. Just as in Anatolia and in the Syrian provinces, new laws aimed to establish complete individual ownership rights over agricultural land and in other areas. This was congruent with circumstances of integration into the global capitalist system and received traction from the individuation of legislative conceptions. But Egypt remained for a while a situation apart. It was noted previously that the state of Muhammad Ali was more classically sultanic than reformist. The penal regime was extremely harsh, even primitive; sanctions varied according to the status of the perpetrator and penalties were not confined to individual perpetrators. It was stipulated that a village headman could be punished if a theft was committed in his village by an intruder who then fled. Muhammad Ali Pasha's penal regime was based on the discipline required by the state administration as well as, perhaps, local customs. The situation changed after later modifications (of French origin) from 1876 to 1883, when primitive punishments such as flogging and public humiliation were abolished, replaced by forfeiture of liberty (imprisonment). The principle of the individual character of a sanction was confirmed.

With regard to commercial matters, Egyptians and foreigners had been subject to the Capitulations enacted after the Anglo-Ottoman Treaty of 1838, required to settle disputes in consular courts that operated on the basis of the Ottoman Commercial Law of 1850 and remained in force until 1875. In that year the Mixed Courts were set up, which guaranteed the "desire of the

---

185 See now Avi Rubin, *Ottoman Nizamiye Courts: Law and Modernity* (London: Palgrave Macmillan, 2011).

Egyptians" – it is more likely the desire of the reforming state in Egypt – to present a "local legal system corresponding to the needs of the Capitulations while recovering the legislative sovereignty of the Egyptian state". This was a preparation for the establishment of a civil justice system in 1880 whose point of substantive reference was French laws that, since al-Tahtawi and others translated French – Napoleonic – civil code into Arabic during the reign of Isma'il Pasha (r. 1863–79), had become part of the legal culture of Egyptian jurists. From 1880 onwards Copts were appointed as judges for the first time, in a highly significant step.[186]

As in Turkey and the Syrian provinces, a legal system was set up in Egypt with bases in secular substantive law and with a secular apparatus. Neverthless, issues of scale and logistical capacity disallowed this system from carrying out out its purposes adequately. Village headmen were delegated to adjudicate in certain disputes to the degree that, of all people, Muhammad 'Abduh felt constrained to suggest that the field of competence of shari'a courts be widened to include some civil matters with which the new legal system was as yet unable to deal.[187] This despite 'Abduh's scathing criticism of shari'a courts in his famous report of 1899: their buildings were ramshackle, with substandard equipment to a degree insulting to the legal profession, with incompetent and inadequately paid judges complaisant to political authority, unable to guarantee the execution of more than a tenth of their sentences.[188]

The new laws suggest two ideological sources, secular and religious, and their substantive content indicates secular positive law. The first article of the Ottoman Penal Law of 1858 stipulated that codification could not be construed as an abolition of the sanctions of shari'a, but as a codification within the bounds of the discretionary power entrusted to political authorities. Bloodwit (blood money) or indemnity for injury was not abolished but was removed to outside the domain of civil courts, relegated to local arbitration, thus removed from the domain of law to that of local practice. The text was ambivalent: it gestured towards religion as a point of reference, and resorted to a well-established principle of Muslim jurisprudence – the ruler's discretionary authority – to enact non-shar'ist laws that had their points of

186 al-Bishrī, *Al-muslimūn wa al-aqbāṭ fī iṭār al-jamā'a al-waṭaniyya*, 30–31.

187 Riḍā, *Tarīkh al-ustādh al-imām shaykh Muḥammad 'Abduh*, vol. 1, 615.

188 'Abduh, *Al-a'māl al-kāmila*, vol. 2, 222–224, 227–230, 278.

reference elsewhere. This was congruent with the de facto marginalisation of shari'a, relegated to a parallel system. The relationship between shari'a and law became one of social and political struggle over authority within a composite legal system. While the secular judicial system was better suited to the time and circumstance and with a greater degree of executive capacity, there is no doubt that there were technical, administrative, and financial limits to its spread outside the urban centres and other large centres of habitation. Limits were thereby set to its exemplary capacity and normative consequence.

The same may be said of the famous *Mecelle* or code of commercial transactions, promulgated from 1869 to 1876 in Turkish, translated into Arabic by Ahmad Faris al-Shidyaq, who published it at his *al-Jawā'ib* press in Istanbul. Despite the Muslim juristic language of its opening paragraphs and its reliance on major collections of Hanafi jurisprudence, being in this sense not unprecedented, the very fact of being a deliberate and highly selective codification made it the first major legal code in modern form, acquiring thereby a significance that made it greatly influential in Arab legal culture.

In its codification of commercial transactions, the *Mecelle* did not rely on consistent and systematic legislative arguments and procedures using general legal categories. It was rather an arrangement and topical classification of certain positive rulings occurring in Hanafi works and appropriate for conditions of the moment. This did not inhibit the chief consequence: the transformation of law-making into the framing of statutes promulgated by the state in the form of a code. That the positive content of these rulings was not new but continued older practices, and that the personnel who drafted it were ulama in the main, acquires novelty in this material being treated precisely for what it is, positive legislation removed from its sources or justifications in Muslim Principles of Jurisprudence, that is, desacralised.[189] *Fiqh* was thereby nationalised, or rather "statified", whereas previously law promulgated by political authorities or arising from practice had been Islamised in the best tradition of Ottoman *kanun*; shari'a was thereby made civil whereas previously civil law had been shar'ified. It was not difficult to translate Hanafi jurisprudence of transactions, or basic elements

189 See Shiḥāta, *Al-ittijāhāt al-tashrī'iyya*, 19 and Ṭāriq al-Bishrī, "Al-mas'ala al-qānūniyya bayn al-sharī'a al-islāmiyya wa al-qānūn al-waḍ'ī", in *Al-Turāth wa Taḥaddiyāt al-'Asr fī al-Waṭan al-'Arabī*, ed. Markaz Dirāsāt al-Waḥda al-'Arabiyya (Beirut: Markaz Dirāsāt al-Waḥda al-'Arabiyya, 1985), 625.

of it, into a form suitable to the circumstances of the nineteenth century. From the Transoxianian al-Sarkhasi (d. 1096) to the Damascene Muhammad Amin Ibn ʿAbidin (1783–1836), the general character of Hanafi transactions jurisprudence was secular in impulse and rationale (if not of sharʿi rationalisation). It rested on a conception that identified legal personality with the capacity for ownership, and saw in legal capacity a locus for action with legal consequence and the acquisition – and discharge – of rights.[190]

Egyptian legal developments, when they came, were diffferent in character to the *Mecelle*, although in Egypt there were no codifications deriving from *fiqh* despite the famous text of Muhammad Qadri Pasha (1821–1888), a graduate of the Languages School and Minister of Education, entitled *Murshid al-ḥayrān fī maʿrifat aḥwāl al-insān fī al-muʿāmalāt al-sharʿiyya ʿalā maḏhab al-imām Abī Ḥanīfa mulāʾiman lī ʿurf al-diyār al-miṣriyya wa sāʾir al-umam al-islāmiyya* ("Guide for the Perplexed to the Knowledge of the Condition of Humanity According to Hanafi Law of Sharʿist Transactions Appropriate to the Customs of the Lands of Egypt and Other Muslim Nations"), published in 1890 and close in spirit to the preamble to the *Mecelle*. Egyptian laws did adapt material from Muslim jurisprudence eclectically and according to established legal usage. Egyptian and Ottoman legists were practical men, taking from available sources – French, custom and use, of which *fiqh* had long become a part – what seemed most suitable. Egyptian penal law recognised both the avowal of guilt as a legal requirement and the principle of financial indemnity for fatal injury, in continuity with both traditional jurisprudence and tribal custom. It made it obligatory to consult the *mufti* before carrying out death sentences, and the first Egyptian civil law code of 1883 integrated many principles and rulings from Muslim jurisprudence: rulings concerning mediation, gifts, inheritance and testaments, incorporated into the law code chapter and verse.

It is clear that these developments were neither coherent nor followed a plan, although they did accumulate tendentially in congruence with modernising and secularising social and administrative transformations of which they were part. Multiple complex circumstances and multiple groups with

190 See Baber Johansen, "Secular and religious elements in Hanafite law: Function and limits of absolute character of government authority", in *Islam et politique au Maghreb*, eds Ernest Gellner and Jean-Claude Vatin (Paris: Éditions du CNRS, 1981), 283–284, 296.

sometimes opposing interests made for the political, social, and legal contradictions that accompanied these changes. For instance, Ottoman commercial law, drawing on French law, stipulated the shared financial responsibility of wife and husband in case of death or insolvency of the husband, that contradicted the prevailing *fiqh* provisions of personal status.[191] In all, these codifications were hardly sufficient to keep up with global legal and economic developments. Legislation in Turkey and Egypt was derived from French law, and French legists were the mainstay of instruction in law schools. French law was thoroughly codified, as opposed to English law, which was and remains close in this respect to Islamic jurisprudence, in its rather inchoate, aggregative structure and reliance on precedent and case law. According to the major legist of modern Egypt, Dr Abd al-Razzaq al-Sanhuri (1895–1971), a graduate of the Paris law faculty and a jurist of great importance to modern civil legislation in the Arab World, much confusion, contradiction, and vagueness occurred in these codifications, citing even linguistic infelicities and translation errors, in addition to the absence of a statute of limitations and neglect of personal status legislation in the areas of gifts and inheritance. Nevertheless, these new codes constituted progress, compared with the confusion that preceded them, especially as they set up legal institutions on stable and, with time, durable foundations.[192]

Legal reforms in Tunisia before the French occupation were more cautious than in other principal Ottoman lands. In 1855, Muhammad Bay decreed that notaries should be subject to authorisation by the state, in the first step of tweaking legal institutions. In 1857, a special court to hear criminal cases was set up, although the scope for its activity was very limited to the extent that criminal justice became the preserve of the Bay, who then delegated this authority to provincial governors and sitting qadis.[193] French occupation of Algeria and Tunisia brought rapid and comprehensive change in the judicial and legal spheres. One could say that the communities of foreign settlers played a role analogous to that of an incipient bourgeoisie elsewhere, in bringing about a significant modernist legal transformation, at a time when the higher-level instances of local society had been eliminated in Algeria and mar-

191 Shiḥāta, *Al-ittijāhāt al-tashrī'iyya*, 21; al-Bishrī, "Al-mas'ala al-qānūniyya", 624.

192 'Abd al-Razzāq Aḥmad al-Sanhūrī, "Darūrat tanqīh al-qānūn al-madanī al-miṣrī wa 'alā ayy asās yakūn hadhā al-tanqīh?", *Majallat al-qānūn wa al-iqtiṣād* 6/1 (1936): 3–144, 14–42.

193 Green, *The Tunisian Ulama, 1873–1915*, 33, 52, 143–144.

ginalised in Tunisia. Algerians who remained subject to traditional institutes and institutions of Muslim jurisprudence were treated in a way analogous to the *dhimma* collectivities under Muslim jurisprudence.[194] Economic and military pressure accompanied legal violence and clove Algerian society into a society of the colonial state whose affairs were regulated by the new laws and their attendant legal system, and another part composed of the natives, *les indigenes*. These latter resorted to modern courts in matters relating to agrarian issues, including tenure, but deferred to local custom in outlying regions and retained specific and *fiqhi* rules of personal status. French citizenship in Algeria (for Algerians and European settlers) was associated with complete transfer to the jurisdiction of secular judicial authority. The majority of Algerians remained under an ostensibly decentralised customary regulation, although in application this was managed by the French legal apparatus.

In Morocco, during the first part of the Protectorate period (1912–1956), meaningful legal changes were introduced, intended to fit in with the economic interests of colonialism and the settlers.[195] Under French sponsorship, the sultan issued the so-called Berber *dhahīr* (decree) of 1914, which gave judicial authority to local groups in addition to local powers, outside the jurisdiction of the authorities of the Makhzen (the royal court's patrimonial network and its institutions), on an assumption of Berber customary specificity. Muslim authors charged that this measure was intended to remove the status of shari'a as a point of reference.[196] Most importantly, this decree struck at the very notion of a Moroccan national community by removing regions from central authority and linking them directly to France. This is analogous to the way in which European states successfully sought to deal with the Ottoman state on the basis of the so-called "mosaic model" of contiguous but separate communities, a policy transferred to Morocco with the aim of creating – and then managing – minorities.

The authorities of reforming Ottoman and post-Ottoman states refrained from interfering with regulations of personal status. These remained in the orbit of traditional Muslim jurisprudence and its legal system of application. This was not only due to the force of social conservatism and to resistance to

194 Laroui, *History of the Maghreb*, 305–6, 313, 324, 340.

195 See details in 'Allāl al-Fāsī, *Difā' 'an al-sharī'a*, 2nd edn (Beirut: Manshūrāt al-'aṣr al-Ḥadīth, 1972), chs 13–15.

196 Ibid., 49.

introducing changes to regulations attributed directly to the holy writ. This applies especially to regulations of inheritance.[197] *Waqf* endowment regulations were the only ones belonging to personal status regulation that were exposed to effective reform, carried out in tandem with transformations in patterns of land ownership. The key element of this reform entailed the divisibility of family endowment (*awqāf dhurrīya*), first in Algeria and later in Ottoman territories. In the same vein, laws of testament – inexistent in classical Muslim jurisprudence – were applied in Egypt to *kharaj* land, as part of legal reforms that were inconsistent and complex over a long period of time. When, in 1896, for instance, landholdings were added to this provision, family endowments were reconfirmed as indivisible, in a move of private appropriation. This movement of legal change led in the end to the consolidation of large agricultural estates that were the background for the majority of the social and economic changes and the political class in nineteenth- and twentieth-century Egypt.[198]

Changes affecting family endowments were a component in the freeing of land and estates from communal family ownership, and the consolidation of private holdings. The retention of elements from classical Muslim jurisprudence worked to consolidate individual ownership as these tended to fragment property down the generations, which devolved to private hands, although these could be and were recycled by a variety of social mechanisms (including marriage strategies) to shifting collective benefit. The important unit is the social unit in which property circulated, and the mechanisms of demographic reproduction and the broader division of labour. The important element is the character of rights accruing from inheritance; property dispersed through death is liable to re-composition by marriage, sale, or donation to relatives. Lands in the Arab world know several types of such rights, depending on ecological conditions, mode of production, and social structure.

---

197 See the important contributions by Martha Mundy, "The family, inheritance and Islam: A re-examination of the sociology of Farā'id law", in *Islamic Law: Social and Historical Contexts*, ed. Aziz al-Azmeh (London and New York: Routledge, 1988), 1, 10–12, 16, 49–55, 56–65 and Abdelwahab Bouhdiba, *Sexuality in Islam*, trans. Alan Sheridan (London and Boston: Routledge, 1985), 114–115.

198 See now Richard A. Debs, *Islamic Law and Civil Code: The Law of Property in Egypt* (New York: Columbia University Press, 2010), chs 2–4.

The maintenance of Muslim jurisprudence was simultaneously one of the elements in the freeing of property from communal ownership and the individualisation of ownership, and also an element in extending the reach of the state into the process of production of which the family had been a basic component. Thus, it is unsurprising in an earlier time that the Copts of Egypt should join Muslims in clinging to the Muslim inheritance regulations and resist Napoleon's attempt to change it.[199] This law postulated a conception of ownership linked to the family as a basic unit of production. The subtle legal devices applied to women in questions of inheritance involving wills and the restriction of property to male instead of female descendants represented only one way in which the precepts of shari'a were adapted to social relations and social structure.

The codification of personal status received hardly any attention by the early reformist state, even though some Arab Christian confessions sought to codify their personal status laws at different points in time.[200] The Law of Family Rights of 1917 was the first Ottoman attempt to codify personal status laws, and resulted from social changes brought by the First World War. Precedents to this are not known in the work of Ottoman ulama, even if some of Muhammad 'Abduh's proposals seem to have been either adopted or paralleled in the reform of marriage regulations in the 1917 law. According to the principle of *talfiq*, the adoption of the legal precedents adjudged best in the circumstances and irrespective of their *madhhab* (law school) provenance, Muhammad 'Abduh issued a responsum (fatwa) giving women the right to petition a judge, at their initiative and of their accord, to divorce them from husbands who harmed, beat, or reviled them without justification in law, or who abandoned them without legal cause.[201] He also empowered a woman legally to stipulate in her marriage contract her capacity to initiate a divorce.[202] 'Abduh also held polygamy to be inadmissible legally, describing it as a social custom and removing it from the domain of shari'a.[203] He also stipulated the necessity for the intended couple to be acquainted with one

199 Yūsuf, *Al-aqbāṭ wa al-qawmiyya al-'arabiyya*, 101.

200 Shiḥāta, *Aḥkām al-aḥwāl al-shakhṣiyya*, 47–50.

201 'Abduh, *Al-a'māl al-kāmila*, vol. 6, 384.

202 Ibid., 393. On the prior development of relevant jurisprudence, see Lena Salaymeh, *The Beginnings of Islamic Law: Late Antique Islamicate Legal Traditions* (Cambridge: Cambridge University Press, 2016), ch. 6.

203 'Abduh, *Al-a'māl al-kāmila*, vol. 2, 94–95.

another before marriage, citing, apparently without irony, a Prophetic hadith that one did not buy a mule before having inspected it.[204]

Yet reformed Ottoman family law in 1917 was marked by considerable timidity and fell short of what might have been expected by 'Abduh. It codified selected classical provisions, in the manner of the *Mecelle*, without departing from them or drawing on other sources. It did – and this was a considerable departure informed by the principle of *talfiq* – adopt from the Ja'fari (Twelver Shi'ite) school the admissibility of testaments, limited to a third of a legacy, and made no allusion to the Shi'i source other than reference to "some scholars".[205] The law also adopted from the Hanbali school the possibility of the marriage contract including a clause providing for divorce if the husband were to take another wife. The law did not abolish polygamy but prescribed restrictive conditions.

The most important element in these ad hoc modifications for the purposes of this argument (and the codification of the regulations of non-Muslim confessions in the same law) was the shift in the authority empowered to formalise marriages and divorces. This code required the contracting parties to register marriages in the records of the civil authorities, and divorce was entrusted to civil courts. This initiative faced fierce opposition from the religious authorities who saw, rightly, that one of the most important ways in which their authority was articulated was in jeopardy. When the Allied troops occupied Constantinople after the First World War, the churches intervened so that the Allies would abolish this code, with control of personal status laws reverting to the different religious communities in 1921. Five years later modern Turkey was to have a comprehensive civil law of personal status that abrogated previous regulation.[206]

It has been indicated that religious institutions adopted positions of active or passive resistance to the changes that, to a large extent, removed the shar'ist character of many forms of social and economic transaction and made the judicial apparatus an authority independent of religious institutional authorities. To some extent one can agree with Rashid Rida's view that civil courts in Egypt would not have been set up were it not for the reactionary character of the al-Azhar scholars and their refusal to codify penal law,

204 Ibid., 72–73.

205 Anderson, *Law Reform in the Muslim World*, 55.

206 Berkes, *The Development of Secularism in Turkey*, 418–419.

and for the fact that their Muslim legal system was less able to render justice than civil courts.[207] Enlightened bearers of turbans, headed by Muhammad 'Abduh and Rashid Rida in the first phase of his career, when he was still under the positive influence of his teacher, had tried as much as possible to adapt Muslim jurisprudence and reform its provisions in a way that would have preserved its primacy symbolically. A case in point was the way that some provisions were modified within the framework of shari'a, reformed "from the inside". Muhammad 'Abduh praised the Ottoman *Mecelle* and actually taught it to students in Beirut when he was in exile from Egypt.[208] More important than this – and this point will be dealt with in the discussion of Islamic Reformism below – is the removal of laws of commercial transactions from the fetters of religion. Muhammad 'Abduh recognised the principle of commendable innovation (*bid'a mustaḥsana*) in customs, food, drink, lodging, and everything that would lighten difficulty, bring benefit, or prevent harm, as long as it was not forbidden explicitly in a Qur'anic text.[209] Rashid Rida went back directly to Hanafi legal heritage (Ibn 'Abidin, drawing on al-Sarakhsi) in a situation when relations with foreign countries were of great importance, and recognised the validity of dealings not governed by shari'a outside Muslim lands. In a fatwa authorising the insurance of goods he added:

> Conditions established by the jurisprudents for the validity and invalidity of contracts, for the observance of this or that commitment, for the validity or invalidity of judgments: such are not devotional matters through which one approaches Almighty God, such that a defective contract would constitute a sin on the part of the contracting parties, if it were to be by their explicit mutual agreement and choice. No. These matters were prescribed to regulate legal provisions, safeguard rights and facilitate the arrival by judges at just judgements. They do not deprive people of their freedom to dispose of their property as they see it beneficial to themselves, by preserving their property or by making it grow. This along with abiding by God's statutes in his gracious Book and by the Sunna of the Prophet,

207 Riḍā, *Tarīkh al-ustādh al-imām al-shaykh Muḥammad 'Abduh*, vol. 1, 620–621.

208 'Abduh, *Al-a'māl al-kāmila*, vol. 2, 295.

209 Ibid., vol. 6, 260.

> Praise and Blessings Upon Him: forbidding dishonesty, trickery, forcible expropriation and so on. This is what the jurisprudent Ibn Hajar meant when he admitted legally taking and giving by mutual agreement and consent in matters contrary to the sound conditions of the contract (of sale and other matters), as if he were saying: these sound conditions and provisions of validity of contracts are those that the judge would impose upon parties in dispute. But if they agree among themselves otherwise, there can be no objection raised. [Ibn Hajar] considered such matters on which legal authorities were silent to be matters perceived intuitively. It is clear that the person of sound mind is free to dispose of his property as he sees fit as long as he does not commit something illicit . . . Legislation concerning transactions seeks the avoidance of harm, bringing benefit and the preservation of interests. If it is established through experience that these matters are harmful and wasteful of property with no benefit, they are forbidden. God is most knowledgeable.[210]

Muhammad Bayram of Tunisia (1840–1889) had a pioneering role in providing justification in traditional Muslim jurisprudence for modern social transactions, such as the ban on slavery and the legitimacy of buying what would today be called treasury bonds.[211] Thus, the way was opened to all types of transactions arising from new conditions of the time. The Qur'an was reconceived as a text of formal guidance without much by way of practical legal consequence, save in very limited contexts. This situation was not, however, entirely stable as the later discussion of Islamic reformism will show.

Such legal latitude came from Muhammad 'Abduh and Rashid Rida in response to requests for *responsa*, and it is known that such fatwas were consultative; they did not have the force of law and were not binding to judges. These requests may well have arisen from attempts to bring influence to bear on some judges by traders who could not obtain satisfaction from civil courts or who were in areas where there were no civil courts. Many requests for *responsa* came from India, Java, the Balkans, and Central Asia, or from pious

210 Riḍā, *Fatāwā*, no. 164.

211 Zaydān, *Tarājim mashāhīr al-sharq fī al-qarn al tāsi' 'ashar*, vol. 2, 290.

traders engaged in unfamiliar types of transaction. One might recall that, in many cases, traders were encountering a new commercial world, and that they might have sought help and assurance from a quasi-magical guarantee that a charismatic fatwa might infuse into transactions with an unknown world. In any case, the transactions authorised by the turbaned legislators were those that conformed to the economic conditions at that time, and in particular financial transactions. The famous fatwa of Muhammad ʿAbduh allowing investment in the post office savings bank in 1903 was justified by the argument that it did not fall within the ambit of the ground for the prohibition of usury, namely, the exploitation of another's need. As such, the profits of the savings bank were beneficial to both parties and came under the juristic category of sales.[212] Cromer, with his narrow world-view, not unnaturally considered this fatwa the most beneficial thing that ʿAbduh had ever done.[213]

Rashid Rida subsequently declared stock market operations to be legitimate in principle on the basis of the rule of "no harm received or inflicted" (*la ḍarar wa lā ḍirār*) arising in Muslim Principles of Jurisprudence, as well as the avoidance of deceit and gambling.[214] We do not know why this principle was not applied to lottery, which Rashid Rida considered an illicit game of chance.[215] This position may be traceable to a temper of guileful ambivalence whereby dogmatic positions that have become fragile and uncertain allocate points to be held stubbornly as a strategic reserve that maintains the semblance of the earlier dogmatic position while moving on other fronts. Rashid Rida kept pace with existing socio-political conditions with his issuing of a fatwa on the illegality of executing apostates. He considered that this old statute had been primarily political, relevant only to a specific period of Muslim history (the so-called apostasy or *ridda* wars, 632–633), which saw, for pragmatic reasons, the suspension of the Qur'anic principle of "no compulsion in religion".[216] When, later, his own positions had shifted towards those associated with Wahhabism, Rida asseverated the dire consequences of apostasy as a

212 ʿAbduh, *Al-aʿmāl al-kāmila*, vol. 1, 677.

213 Riḍā, *Tarīkh al-ustādh al-imām al-shaykh Muḥammad ʿAbduh*, vol. 1, 425. See the crisp description of Cromer's limited horizons in Berque, *Egypt and Revolution*, 149–150.

214 Riḍā, *Fatāwā*, no. 40.

215 Riḍā., *Fatāwā*, no. 215.

216 Ibid., 224. See too Muḥammad Tawfīq Ṣidqī, *Dīn Allāh fī kutub ʿanbiyāʾihi* (Cairo: Maṭbaʿat al-Manār, 1916), 211–213.

truism, for, he claimed, the treatment of apostates was well established, their lot harsher than that of idolaters.[217]

Slavery was another matter in which ulama intervened. In 1846, slavery was abolished in Tunisia, and in Egypt in 1877. By the early twentieth century only some Africans were still sold by Sudanese slave-traders in Jeddah for export, principally to Najd, but also to a lesser extent to Yemen.[218] Slavery was officially abolished in Saudi Arabia only in 1955. While Muhammad ʿAbduh was quite ready to say that there is nothing in Islam that stood against a complete abolition of slavery and that Islam condemned it fundamentally,[219] Rashīd Riḍā's position was less consistent with his own time and more consistent with Muslim heritage. He held that Islam had not abolished slavery because this would have been disadvantageous practically. At the same time, he condemned the kidnapping and sale of Africans and the purchase of Circassian girls from their families, but without touching upon the principle of slavery itself at all.[220]

Muslim reformers dealt with a broad range of other matters juristically, with a view to certifying the legitimacy of new usages and needs once they had spread in sections of society that mattered. Among these were photography and cinema, whose prohibition by adversaries was, according to Rida, related to aniconism arising from anti-idolatrous needs of early Islam.[221] The medicinal use of alcoholic beverages when necessary and the use of alcohol in medical treatment, paint, and perfumes were pronounced licit.[222] As for attempts by the ulama to try to revoke judgments passed by civil justice, incidents were very scarce. Muhammad ʿAbduh tended towards alignment with the orientation of modern history and the gains of social progress than was then the case of French law. He judged it licit for a woman to withdraw her shares from the Suez Canal Company without seeking her husband's prior permission, the company having prevented her from doing so in accordance with French law.[223]

---

217 Muḥammad Rashīd Riḍā, *Al-khilāfa aw al-imāma al-ʿuẓmā* (Cairo: Maṭbaʿat al-Manār, 1341/1922), 107.

218 ʿAbd al-Raḥmān al-Kawākibī, "Tijārat al-raqīq wa aḥkāmuhā fī al-islām", in *Al-aʿmāl al-kāmila*, ed. Muḥammad ʿAmāra (Beirūt: al-Muʾassasa al-ʿArabiyya li'l-Dirāsāt wa al-Nashr, 1979), 259–264.

219 Shalash (ed.), *Jamāl al-Dīn al-Afghānī, silsilat al-aʿmāl al-majhūla*, 59.

220 Riḍā, *Fatāwā*, no. 237.

221 ʿAbduh, *Al-aʿmāl al-kāmila*, vol. 2, 204; Riḍā, *Fatāwā*, nos 33, 280.

222 Riḍā, *Fatāwā*, nos 6, 607, 636, 638.

223 ʿAbduh, *Al-aʿmāl al-kāmila*, vol. 2, 265.

3 *The State: From the* Millet *to the Secular State*

The *Tanzimat* state sought, therefore, unsteadily but tendentially and cumulatively to reconfigure itself whereby its control would extend across society, according to the paradigm that the modern Napoleonic state experimented with in Europe, which saw the state engineering, deliberately or not, but in all cases objectively, increasing degrees of civic homogenisation, led culturally – and sometimes politically – by a bourgeoisie or by social and political agencies that stood for such a role. Such were the national states built in the course of the nineteenth century. Law and education were the two means used by the *Tanzimat* state to achieve this purpose, and to separate its present reformist temporality from a heritage of tributary obedience, building a society linked to the state through individuals now being reconstituted by law as individuals, without the intermediary associations of communities, religious confessions, and the craft guilds. Not all national states succeeded in transforming their citizens into political individuals; tributary habits persisted.

The reformist Ottoman state was no different in this respect, as within it there was vigorous constitutionalist movement even if it was aborted by the sultan Abdülhamid II in 1876. This notwithstanding, the constitutional movement sought to transform at least some Ottoman subjects into citizens in the legal and cultural sense, by educational and legal reforms, and by the involvement of notables in Istanbul and the provinces in regional councils known as the administrative councils. This change was not accomplished in the political sense that would have had democracy – in whatever form – as a condition. Neither was it accomplished in the social sense of succeeding in the dismantling of tribal and confessional structures. The *millet* organisation had been a pillar of the system of subordination on which the Ottoman state was based before its entry into the time of modernity.

The mechanisms of the *millet* system and their background in the confessional regulations in Islam cannot be taken up here.[224] Confessional groupings formed units of taxation, as did villages, quarters in cities, craft and trade guilds, as well as constituting social units based on networks of kinship. Craft specialisation is perhaps one of the most important indications of that link. In nineteenth-century Damascus, for example, most shepherds were Kurds, most musicians were gypsies, and knife-grinders were mostly

224 See Qurm, *Ta'addud al-adyān wa anẓimat al-ḥukm*, 229–261.

Afghans. The majority of rope-makers came from the district of Mizza to the west of the city, while most builders were Christians. Jews formed the majority of money changers, singers, traders in used articles, latrine cleaners, shoeshiners, and engravers, while all jewellers were Christian.[225] In the manner required by the system of tributary and patrimonial subordination, the leaders of these units were responsible for internal control and for managing their affairs according to specific standards, including the application of the canon law to the personal status of Christians within their communities, looking after welfare and performing functions of adjudication. The Greek Orthodox Patriarch of Constantinople disposed of powers that made him effectively representative of a mini-state within the state, with power to exile, imprison, and excommunicate parishioners. The state would provide military assistance to enforce the Patriarch's orders.[226] The same was true of the leaders of the other communities, who formed a subordinate part of the state framework, whose authority was sought by all the communities. One should not, however, imagine that this practical vertical segregation entailed cultural separations, as a common illusion would have it. Communities in Arab lands were entangled and intermingled, in regional, cultural, and religious continuities that do not admit the logic of political borders or that of the succession of states. Armenians and Greeks spoke Turkish dialects, and there was shared participation by communities in festivals. Patrimonial relations trumped those of religion or confession, as in the case of the Maronites and Druze on Mount Lebanon and the Kurds and Assyrians in Mesopotamia, occasional and sometimes extremely violent fissures notwithstanding. Food, dress, lodging, folklore, manners, myths, customs, traditions, and economic activities all bore strong resemblances between one confessional or ethnic community and another.[227] So too did marriage celebrations, rites of supplication and intercession, and beliefs in al-Khidr (Mar Jirjis/St George), as well as legends related to agriculture and much else.[228] There is no doubt of the

225 Muḥammad Saʿīd al-Qāsimī and Jamāl al-Dīn al-Qāsimī, *Qāmūs el-ṣināʿāt al-dimashqiyya*, ed. Ẓāfir al-Qasimī, 2 vols (Paris and The Hague: Mouton, 1960), vol. 1, 55, 90, 153, 264, vol. 2, 220, 230, 280, 366, 416; and Fakhrī al-Bārūdī, *Muḏakkarāt al-Bārūdī* (Beirut/Damascus, n.p., 1951), 62.

226 Qurm, *Taʿaddud al-adyān wa anẓimat al-ḥukm*, 273.

227 Ibid., 285–287.

228 Sami Zubaida, "Components of popular culture in the Middle East", in *Mass Culture, Popular Culture and Social Life in the Middle East*, eds Sami Zubaida and G. Stauth (Frankfurt: Campus Verlag and Boulder: Westview Press, 1987), 142–146 and Barakāt, *Al-mujtamaʿ al-ʿarabī al-muʿāṣir*, 262.

continuity between some pagan rituals and rituals carried out in the name of Islam in Egypt and in many regions of the Arab Maghreb, and on a larger scale, too. These are the types of continuity that indicate definite cultural continuation between communities across time and space.[229]

The reforming Ottoman state unburdened Christians of numerous impositions, such as the subordination of their craft corporations to the *shaykh al-mashāyikh* (syndic of syndics), and these corporations became independent, self-administered civil units.[230] The abolition of the law of apostasy came after strong resistance from the *şeyhülislam* and the Patriarchs of the Greek Orthodox and Armenian churches, at a time when many European countries (including Great Britain that, in the person of Stratford Canning, who served as British envoy to Constantinople from 1842 to 1858, pressed the Ottoman administration in this direction) were still to grant their Catholic and Jewish citizens complete rights of citizenship. The Maronite Church militated against Protestants in Lebanon, and the Greek Orthodox Church opposed Protestant activities in Ottoman Syria and elsewhere. Christian communities were competitive, querulous, and fractious, with disputes especially between communities of European loyalty and local communities. Eastern churches prohibited the reading of Protestant gospel translations.[231] There were also many Christian polemics against Islam and its doctrines. In Paris a journal was published under the name *Barjīs Bārīz*, which lampooned and calumniated Islam and its prophet.[232] Most confessional conflicts revolved around the advantages derived from belonging to

229 See Ḥusayn Aḥmad Amīn, *Ḥawl al-da'wa ilā taṭbīq al-sharī'a al-islāmiyya* (Beirut: Dār al-Nahḍa al-'Arabiyya, 1985), 95; 'Uthmān al-Ka''āk, *Al-taqālīd wa al-'ādāt al-sha'biyya aw al-fūlklūr al-tūnisī* (Tunis: al-Dār al-Qawmiyya li'l-Nashr wa-l-Tawzī", 1963), 55–56, 63–69; and Henri Renault, "Les survivances des cultes de Cybèle, Venus et Bacchus (Aissaoua, Ouled Nail, Karabouz)", *Revue tunisienne* (1917): 150–154.

230 I. Qudsi, "Notice sur les corporations de Damas", in *Actes du VIème Congrès international des orientalistes*, 2 vols (Leiden: n.p., 1885), vol. 2, 29–30.

231 Ignatius Hazīm, "Shawāghil al-fikr al-masīḥī mundhu 1866", in Al-Jāmi'a al-Amīrikiyya fī Bayrūt (ed.), *Al-fikr al-'arabi fī mi'at sana: Buḥūth mu'tamar hay'at al-dirasāt al-'arabiyya al-mun'aqida fī tishrīn al-thānī 1966 fī al-jāmi'a al-amīrikiyya fī Bairūt*, eds Fu'ād Ṣarrūf and Nabīh Amīn Fāris (Beirut: al-Jāmi'a al-Amīrikiyya, 1967), 378–382; 'Aṭīyya, "Ma'ālim al-fikr al-tarbawī fī al-bilād al-'arabiyya fī al-mi'at sana al-akhīra", 474; Sarkīs, *Mu'jam al-maṭbū'āt al-'arabiyya wa al-mu'arraba*, 862, 865, 874; Fāris, *Al-naz'āt al-ṭā'ifiyya fī tarīkh lubnān al-ḥadīth*, 134–135.

232 R. Edwards, *La Syrie, 1840–1862* (Paris: n. p., 1862), 171; Hazīm, "Shawāghil al-fikr al-masīḥī mundhu 1866", 371–375.

the denominations under European consular protection and sponsorship, and this competition – and overuse and indeed misuse of Capitulations – accentuated antipathies and worked to aggravate cleavages, all of which militated against the social and moral texture of what could have been an emergent fabric of citizens emerging from state policies. For example, in Aleppo in the middle of the nineteenth century, there were 1,500 official dragomen (officially translators, but in effect local all-purpose agents) in the service of foreign consuls. They enjoyed all the legal privileges of the Capitulations. The number of actual interpreters was six. One consul in Aleppo appointed a local wealthy gentleman as his cook, affording him thereby the enjoyment of the legal and commercial privileges that associated with foreign protection.[233] Britain pressed the Ottomans to recognise the Protestants as a new *millet*. Together with the Aga Khan, they encouraged the formation in Syria of another new *millet* – the Isma'iliyya – when a group in Salamiyyeh recognised the Aga Khan as their leader and imam in the 1880s. Thereafter a number of Isma'ili leaders were put on trial, charged with collusion with a foreign power against the Ottoman caliph.[234] All this took place while European propaganda was continually calling for more "justice" towards Christian communities, at a time when these communities, emblematised by their patricians, were elevated, privileged, enjoyed legal exemptions, and had a significant presence in the state apparatus, and exercised influence through European consuls.

The legal and educational reforms that worked tendentially to dissolve collective units of social subordination were, as previously noted, among the conditions for the setting up of the Ottoman state on new bases in accordance with the concepts of the reforms and in conformity with the regnant state model of the nineteenth century. These reforms faced fundamental difficulties of application – technical, administrative, and financial – in addition to political opposition from religious and communalist institutions. Resistance was not limited to the Muslim religious establishment. The opposition of the Christian religious institutions was fiercer in many cases, as these institutions were thriving in a competitive setting, sponsored

233 Edwards, *La Syrie*, 77–82.

234 Dick Douwes and Norman N. Lewis, "The trial of the Syrian Ismai'ilis in the first decade of the 20th century", *International Journal of Middle East Studies* 21 (1989): 215–232, 21–217, 218 ff.; Qorm, *Ta'addud al-adyān wa anẓimat al-ḥukm*, 281–282, 290–299.

or supported very openly by the different and competing European powers. Direct European pressure was among the important factors driving the Ottoman state to implement political and legal reforms. While economic interests impelled European powers towards increased secularising rationalisation of the Ottoman sultanate, political interest drove these powers to sponsor communal fragmentation. The result was that Muslims did not as a group directly benefit from the *Tanzimat* although as individuals many were beneficiaries of the progressivist and cultural policies of the *Tanzimat*. The cohesion of the Christian communities increased as a result of political pressure in the direction of increased communalisation of public life in association with privileges, strengthening communal leadership secular as well as clerical, the two often in conflict. Muslims became citizens of the Ottoman state in senses that in many urban milieux approached the modern meaning of citizenship. Ottoman reformers wanted the *millets* to become merely religious associations, and the *Tanzimat* sought to institute equality of legal status, the basis for the development of citizenship. Yet European consuls wanted Christians to be the only ones to enjoy equality, while at the same time enjoying the privileges of the Capitulations according to which they had an extraterritorial legal status, answerable to the authority of the *millets* and that of the European consuls, but not the Otoman state. Stratford Canning held that equality should be between communities, not between Ottoman citizens as individuals – the model would be called multiculturalist today. Ultimately, Canning did not want the Ottoman state to have a body politic, a body-national: the role of the Ottoman state would be to provide security, based solely on international guarantees and expressions within Ottoman domains of the balance of European power.[235] In short, Canning sought a weak and subordinate Ottoman state.

In other words, while the Ottoman state aspired to join the Zeitgeist with the transformation of Ottoman subjects into a body national capable of entering this global world according to the necessary political, social, and economic conditions, Europe only looked at the Ottoman state from a perspective of what was seen as margins necessary for capitalism's metropolitan development, and a terrain of geo-political contestation. Europeans

235 Berkes, *The Development of Secularism in Turkey*, 147, 153–154; al-Ḥuṣrī', *Al-bilād al-'arabiyya wa al-dawla al-'uthmāniyya*, 94.

wanted the Ottoman economy to be subordinate, incomplete, and incoherent, based on a trading and export sector linked to the global colonial economy, without structural and internal unity. Ottoman domains so conceived would function through social enclaves with few internal links or connections, any wider economic cohesion being through direct links to Europe. The Ottoman state would thus provide the legal and administrative facilitation of relations of subordination linking multiple enclave units in this periphery to European control. All these factors – European action aimed at political fragmentation, economic subordination, the absence of economic and productive cycles within the Ottoman state – were closely connected. They hampered the progressive potential of the Ottoman state and aborted its historical possibilities for a period that ended only after the First World War, with the establishment of the modern Turkish republic. Meanwhile, Arab lands continued to experience fissures along confessional lines, at the junction of emergent communal leadership and consular pressure, and remained hostage to the global balance of power. In the lands of the Ottoman sultanate, confessional cleavages converged with discriminatory treatment of workers of different origin in European-owned sectors; Armenians, for example were in some places remunerated better than Muslims. There were bloody clashes between workers of different religions and ethnicities, in a situation of competition and migration.[236] Competition in the labour market reinforced communal cleavages and the patrimonial character of employment, hampering the emergent abstract character of labour, which in turn forms one of the important bases for the birth of the individual and of a body-social on which citizenship is based.

Attempts to fragment and uproot, to accentuate distinctions and antagonisms, were not successful everywhere or in equal measure. Although the British tried to induce the Copts to adopt separatist positions and to reinvent themselves as a *millet* under new circumstances, only a small minority seems to have been seriously interested. The Coptic Church resisted the enticements of protection by the Vatican, defended the local education system, and, as would be expected, opposed missionary schools. The Coptic authorities supported the 'Urabi Revolt (1879–1882); the only Christian base of

236 Donald Quataert, *Social Disintegration and Popular Resistance in the Ottoman Empire 1881–1908: Reactions to European Economic Penetration* (New York and London: New York University Press, 1983).

support for the British in Egypt were Syrians, mainly of Lebanon, whose promotion in government circles was sponsored by Britain at the expense of the Copts. This took place after similar legal steps to those enacted in the rest of the Ottoman sultanate were implemented to limit communal fragmentation. These included the abolition of the *jizya* in 1855, opening military ranks to Copts in 1856, and eligibility for candidature for the parliament on the basis of Egyptian birth alone rather than religion. In Ottoman Syria, urban Christians were no less conservative than their Muslim neighbours. Catholicism's presence in Damascus went back to 1720, although Catholic priests needed disguise when visiting members of their flock in Bab Musalla, a suburb notorious for its turbulence. Statements attributed to the Greek Orthodox in Damascus show that some considered it permissible to shed the blood of Catholics[237] – more likely to be an indication of an irascible mood rather than of fact. When the Ottoman state sought to retaliate against the Greek Orthodox (known locally as *Arwām*, sg. Rūmī, Roman) on suspicion of having helped the nationalist Greek insurrection (1821–1832), Damascus notables gave evidence that the Orthodox of Syria were Arabs with no link to the Greeks, that they spoke a different language, and had given no financial assistance to the rustic Greeks. The state disregarded the incident.[238] It is not surprising therefore that the Greek Orthodox community in Ottoman Syria took a different orientation from that of many other Ottoman Christian groups elsewhere, Arabising their liturgy, formerly using Greek, as well as their clerical personnel following the election of the first ethnically Arab Patriarch of Antioch and All the East in 1899, with his seat in Damascus.[239]

Despite the resistance of the two Christian communities – Greek Orthodox in Ottoman Syria and Egyptian Copts – the *millet* policy was a major conduit for European policies inside the Ottoman territories, and underpinned the internal workings of what was called the "Eastern Question", or the question of emergent national communities in the Ottoman territories of Europe and Asia, territories of the Sick Man of Europe as the Ottoman state was known.

---

237 Yūsuf, *Al-aqbāṭ wa al-qawmiyya al-'arabiyya*, 97, 10–104, 113, 116–121 and elsewhere. Mikhā'īl al-Dimashqī, *Tārīkh ḥawādith al-Shām wa Lubnān (1197/1782–1275/1841)*, ed. Louis Ma'lūf (Beirut: n.p., 1912), 3ff.; Mikhā'īl Breik, *Tārīkh al-Shām 1720–1782*, ed. Qusṭanṭīn al-Bāsha (Harissa: n.p.,1930), 2–3; R. Thoumin, "Deux quartiers de Damas: Le Quartier chrétien de Bab Musallâ et le quartier Kurde", *Bulletin d'études orientales* 1 (1931): 113.

238 Al-'Aẓma, *Mir'āt al-shām*, 166.

239 al-Ḥuṣrī', *Al-a'māl al-qawmiyya*, 752–753.

The *millet* system was rejuvenated under European influence, which made it a cornerstone of international diplomacy. The lynchpin of European activity in Ottoman territories, the *millet* system was also the instrument used to stymie attempts made by the reformist Ottoman state to erode the socio-religious communalist structure that stood in the way of social evolution towards citizenship. This objective tendential outcome of such development, when unhampered, was effective secular change corresponding to the inherent logic of the *Tanzimat* state. Modernist cultural changes came to the Ottomans while the direct effect of European propaganda among Christian communities was to strengthen the convergence between communitarian isolationism and the expression of an ideology with a nationalist character, especially among Greeks and Armenians, some of it highly modernist, but divergent politically. As Halide Edib said, as the Ottomans adopted the concepts of democracy from the West, representatives of Christian communities moved towards nationalism.[240]

Such transfromations were attainable in geographically detachable parts of the empire: in the Balkan and Greek regions where new states developed on the basis of local aspirations and European wishes. In the eighteenth century, Empress Catherine of Russia (r. 1762–96) had suggested the establishment of a Greek state, a suggestion that met a warm reception in Europe. Important currents in Greek nationalism adopted this in the form of the "Great Idea", or "Ultimate Aim", the *megali idea*, an irredentist nationalism that involved, crucially, the capture of Constantinople and implied, to some, the recreation of the Byzantine Empire. Within Ottoman territory the situation was less promising, particularly in Anatolia and the Syrian provinces, but this did not prevent the emergence of secessionist movements, especially among the Armenians.

But activist secessionism was in general sublimated into isolationist education sustained by the churches. The results of these policies are visible up until the present day especially in Lebanon where it seems that the Civil War (1975–1990) took it back to the nineteenth century, a situation that has since been aggravated. The communal massacres and attempted imposition of confessional homogeneity – what has come to be called ethnic cleansing – over scattered areas, by violence or forced exile, were an important feature of the

240 Edib, *Turkey Faces West*, 75, 71–76. See too Kawtharāni, *Al-sulṭa wa al-mujtama‘ wa al-‘amal al-siyāsī*, 70–71.

consolidation of national states in the Balkans and Greece. In nineteenth-century Lebanon, a new communal awareness developed from the ruins of older socio-political arrangements, with the simultaneous collapse of the Shihab emirate in 1841 and the growing power of the Maronite Church at the expense of Maronite feudal princes, confessional and economic interests being played in tandem. When direct Ottoman rule was restored after the abolition of the Shihab emirate, and Ottoman administrative measures unrelated to sectarianism were put in place, confessional rivalry was given renewed salience. Local interest groups calling for a Christian, French-sponsored state were played together with other external interests, converging in the ultimate erasure of traditional feudal authorities while giving a confessional character to political affairs. A vicious civil war then produced the Mount Lebanon Mutasarrifiya system (1864–1914), consecrating confessionalism as a basis for political representation.[241] As is generally the case in such situations, this was accompanied by the production of a new historiography and historical geneaologies that postulated the Maronites a self-contained and independent community from the outset, thus forming the basis for the invention of a national history and a national society.[242]

This European move towards the sponsorship and nursing of nations out of religious confessions was not entirely successful in Arab lands. Some representatives of the Maronites of Lebanon were very receptive, and attempts and promises were made in Assyrian Christian regions of Iraq and Anatolia, and among smaller confessional groups. But none of these came to much. It is likely that one of the basic factors in this overall situation was that groups less receptive to Western intentions and blandishments were generally urban and educated, especially those that had acquired an Ottoman civic culture or a Protestant education.[243] Among Egyptian Copts, trends of this kind did gain some ground in certain milieux, foregrounding the idea of the Copts as a nation apart descended from the Ancient Egyptians. Short-lived newspapers were published advocating these views, such *al-Waṭan* (1877) and *Miṣr* (1895), although these do not seem to have represented a significant and

241 Ussama Makdisi, *The Culture of Sectarianism* (Berkeley: University of California Press, 2000); Engin Akarli, *The Long Peace: Ottoman Lebanon, 1861–1920* (Berkeley: University of California Press, 1993).

242 See Ahmad Beydoun, *Identité confessionnelle et temps social chez les historiens libanais contemporains* (Beirut: Université Libanaise, 1984).

243 Compare with al-Ḥuṣrī', *Al-aʿmāl al-qawmiyya li Sāṭiʿ al-Ḥuṣrī*, 751.

influential current. The overall tendency among the Copts was national in character, with secular currents appearing in the conflict between laity and clergy. Lay Copts evolved in their relation to the state while Coptic Orthodox Church reforms disappeared in the "folds of the cassock" of one Coptic Pope, Cyril V (*c.*1830–1927), who occupied the papal throne of Alexandria for about half a century.[244] The position of the Greek Orthodox in the Ottoman Syrian provinces was earlier noted, while perhaps the best example of an Arab Christian Ottoman intellectual and educationist is that of Butrus al-Bustani who saw the Ottoman bond as a national one – in the sense of the modern nation state of citizens – interwoven with local Syrian patriotism.

This connection between Syrian patriotism and Ottoman citizenship was the dominant characteristic of other Syrian Christian intellectuals such as Francis Marrash, Ahmad Faris al-Shidyaq, and Nasif al-Yaziji (1800–1871) and others of the first generation, as well as Salim 'Anhuri (1856–1933), Adib Ishaq (1856–1885), and Farah Antun (1872–1922) of the second generation. The only secessionist tendencies were among the Maronites of Mount Lebanon and parts of the coast. The overall tone of political discourse among this group of intellectuals was not different from that prevailing among Ottoman progressives: praise for the *Tanzimat* reforms and the principle of citizenship that they made conceivable, and praise for Midhat Paşa, for Ottoman constitutionalism and, subsequently, support for the Committee of Union and Progress when they overthrew the sultan Abdülhamid II in 1909.[245]

There is not therefore a link, direct or indirect, between Arab secularism and nationalism, and a purported Christian vanguard attempting to solicit protection through such an ideological commitment, as is commonly claimed, with implications of crude instrumentalisation, and imputations of insincerity and unreality. Arab nationalism did not yet exist and, and when it did it was not, as will be shown below, based necessarily on a secular vision. Only in connection with France was it advocated as such by certain Christian intellectuals, such as Najib 'Azuri (1873?–1916), a shady character and

244 Yūsuf, *Al-aqbāṭ wa al-qawmiyya al-'arabiyya*, 138–139; al-Bishrī, *Al-Muslimūn wa al-Aqbāṭ fi iṭār al-jamā'a al-waṭaniyya*, 373–380, 388.

245 For example, al-Bustānī, *'Ibra wa dhikrā: Aw al-dawla al-'uthmāniyya qabla al-dustūr wa ba'duhu*, 3, 6, 7, 90–94 and elsewhere. Compare with Salīm 'Anḥūrī, *Siḥr hārūt* (Damascus: al-Maṭba'a al-ḥanafiyya, 1302/1885), 205. See too Kawtharāni, *Al-sulṭa wa al-mujtama' wa al-'amal al-siyāsī*, 130–135.

author of *Le reveil de la nation arabe* (1905), who called for an Arab kingdom extending from the Euphrates and Tigris to the Suez Canal, a call that did not find echo.[246] There was no direct link yet between Arab nationalism, still very scarce, and secularism, nor a necessary connection between nationalism and particular religious confessions. When in 1919 a delegation of the League of Nations went to the Syrian provinces to listen to people's views and wishes, there was a majority consensus for Syrian independence, except for groups directly dependent, or perceiving themselves to be directly dependent, on outside powers: some Christians belonging to Western denominations, and the Algerian notability in Damascus, descendants of the Prince Abdelkader (1808–1883) – initially hero of anti-French resitance in Algeria from 1830 until his surrender in 1847, from 1855 Freemason, Sufi, and resident in Damascus on a French pension – and his followers.[247]

Only a minority of Syrian Christians who emigrated to Egypt were opposed to the Ottoman state or had an Arab political, as distinct from cultural, orientation. Salim Taqla (1849–1892), founder with his brother of the famous Egyptian newspaper *Al-Ahrām* in 1875, had Ottoman sympathies. So too did other very prominent literary figures, such as Khalil Mutran (1872–1949) and Jurji Zaidan, at least in the early period of the latter's journal *al-Hilāl* founded in 1892. So also Egyptian Muslim intellectuals and literary figures combining Egyptian patriotism with Ottomanism, such as 'Abdallah Nadim, the neo-classical poets Ahmad Shawqi (1868–1932) and Hafiz Ibrahim (1872–1932), Wali al-Din Yakan (1873–1928) who stood close to the Committee for Union and Progress, 'Ali Yusuf (1863–1913), editor of *al-Mu'ayyad* newspaper close to 'Abduh and Egyptian nationalists, and the inspiring nationalist firebrand Mustafa Kamil.[248] As for Muhammad 'Abduh, he believed that it was unconscionable for the Arabs to leave the Ottoman state, although they merited independence. 'Abduh opposed Cromer's attempt in 1899 to appoint a chief qadi for Egypt rather than accepting the official nominated by the sultan.[249] In a text from

246 Also Kawtharāni, *Al-Sulṭa wa al-mujtama' wa al-'amal al-siyāsī*, 161. See Eliezer Tauber, *The Emergence of the Arab Movements* (London: Routledge, 1993), ch. 6

247 al-'Aẓma, *Mir'āt al-shām*, 254.

248 Anīs al-Khūrī al-Maqdisī, *Al-'awāmil al-fa''āla fī al-adab al-'arabī al-ḥadīth*, Silsilat al-'Ulūm al-Sharqiyya, fasc. 15 (Beirut: al-Jāmi'a al-Amīrikiyya, n.d.), fasc. 1: *Fī al-'awāmil al-siyāsiyya* (Beirut: al-Jāmi'a al-Amīrikiyya, n.d.), 2–9.

249 Riḍā, *Tarīkh al-ustādh al-imām al-shaykh Muḥammad 'Abduh*, vol. 1, 576–578, 913–914.

1911, Ahmad Lutfi al-Sayyid (1872–1963) urged the Arabs to participate positively in the political affairs of the Ottoman state in order to maintain their standing within it and to maintain its internal harmony.[250] The link between Egypt and the Ottoman state was only severed when a British protectorate over Egypt was proclaimed at the beginning of the First World War, and the Khedive Abbas was deposed. Prince Hussein Kamil assumed the throne in his place and took the title of sultan, as a final sign of secession from the Sublime Porte. The Egyptian Council of Ministers then issued a decision abolishing the post of the chief qadi. Nevertheless, the manifestations of enmity towards Britain and of sympathy to the Ottomans were numerous.[251] Egyptian nationalists such as Mustafa Kamil saw the Ottoman state as a framework that protected Egypt from total British control, and were thus in an intermediate position between an Ottomanist and Islamist loyalty. But the effective base of the Egyptian nationalists was a distinction between national and religious solidarities. Their attitudes to the Egyptians of Turkish origin and to the Ottomans more broadly were also distinct.[252]

What has often been seen as the beginnings of Arab nationalism as expressed by al-Kawakibi and others was in fact only an association of the caliphate with Arabhood – as will be shown later in this chapter – and a restriction of the leadership of the Muslim state to Arab Muslims. This discourse was not national in tone, but religious. The aim of al-Kawakibi's book *Umm al-qurā* was to save the Islamic *umma* from indifference, the doctrine of fatalism, the temptations of doctrinal dissension, neglect of religion, idolatry, blind imitation, and inequality, a typical Muslim reformist agenda. The remedy suggested was for the Arabs to meet the needs of the Islamic *umma* and provide its leadership, due to what he judged to be their special virtues: religion, solidarity, pride, and moral vigilance.[253] Mustapha Kamil and others had long attacked the notion of an Arab caliphate, on the grounds that it was a British wile.[254] The idea of an Arab caliphate was not new; it had been debated in mid-nineteenth century France under Napoleon III, with 'Abd al-Qadir as the candidate, at a time when scenarios for the

250 Aḥmad Luṭfī al-Sayyid, *Al-Muntakhabāt*, ed. Ismā'īl Maẓhar (Cairo: Maktabat al-Anglo-Miṣriyya, 1937), 250–251.

251 Ḥusayn, *Al-ittijahāt al-waṭaniyya fī al-adab al-mu'āṣir*, vol. 2, 10.

252 Ibid., vol. 1, 20–39, 75–90.

253 'Abd al-Raḥmān al-Kawākibī, *Al-a'māl al-kāmila*, 318–319, 356–357.

254 Ḥusayn, *Al-ittijahāt al-waṭaniyya fī al-adab al-mu'āṣir*, vol. 1, 25, 39–43.

break-up of the Ottoman state multiplied.[255] In Egypt in the early twentieth century the only enemies of the Ottoman state were the newspapers *al-Muqaṭṭam* and *al-Muqtaṭaf*, both loyal to Britain. The situation in the Syrian provinces was not very different. There was no trace among Muslims of the tendency towards an Arab ethno-nationalism apart the fellow-feeling of cultural-linguistic as distinct from political nationality, similar to the position of the Christians discussed already.[256] This common sentiment did not extend beyond language to government, authority, political nationalism, or to a call to break away from the Turks, to use Rashid Rida's expression.[257] It seems rather that the ulama and notables of the Syrian provinces and Iraq were "more loyal to the Turks than the Turks themselves".[258] The opposition to the sultan Abdülhamid II was played out within an Ottoman frame of reference that united various political orientations whose common feature was not secular, as it combined liberals and Islamic reformers together.

It was even said that the Fraternal Arab Union (Jam'iyyat al-Ikha' al-'Arabi), which was set up in Istanbul at the time of Abdülhamid II, was created on the suggestion of the caliph himself, intended to draw support away from the Committee of Union and Progress. Forces ranged against Abdülhamid were secular and constitutionalist, and also Islamic reformist, proclaiming constitutionalism and calling for *ijtihād* along the lines of Muhammad 'Abduh, in an Ottoman political framework.[259] Such a framework was supported in Syria by intellectuals with political engagement: Rafiq al-Azm (1865–1925) and Rashid Rida as well as Abd al-Rahman al-Shahbandar (1879–1940), Shukri al-Asali (1868–1916) and other members of the Jam'iyyat al-Nahḍa al-'Arabiyya, the Arab Renaissance Society. The common discourse was one of an Ottoman nation, even when the idea of a Syrian people as a social and linguistic entity was aired, within the wider Ottoman community, without implications of a national entity entailing an autonomous state.[260]

255 Marcel Emérit, "La Crise syrienne et l'expansion économique française en 1860", *Revue historique* 20 (1952): 211–232. See the simplified view presented in Riḍā, *Mukhtārāt siyāsiyya min majallat al-manār*, 200.

256 Riḍā, *Mukhtārāt siyāsiyya min majallat al-manār*, 156–157.

257 Riḍā, *Mukhtārāt siyāsiyya min majallat al-manār*, 197–200.

258 Kawtharāni, *Al-sulṭa wa al-mujtama' wa al-'amal al-siyāsī*, 161–162, 167.

259 Riḍā, *Riḥlāt al-imām Muḥammad Rashīd Riḍā*, 25–26.

260 Berkes, *The Development of Secularism in Turkey*, 305–309; Mardin, *The Genesis of Young Ottoman Thought*, 40–41; Commins, "Religious reformers and Arabists in Damascus, 1885–1914", 410–412; al-Khālidī, *Jawla fī al-dhikrayāt bayna Lubnān wa Filasṭīn*, 62.

Only after 1910 was it possible for Arab nationalist associations such as the Young Arab Society (al-'Arabiyya al-Fatāt) to emerge, when Talat Paşa took over the Ministry of the Interior and proceeded to purge Arab officers from important positions and to Turkify the state apparatus, with the crystallisation of a purely Turkish nationalism. In Cairo, the Party for Decentralisation (Ḥizb al-Lamarkaziyya) was founded, led by Rafiq al-'Azm. The Literary Club (al-Muntadā al-Adabī) was established in Istanbul in 1908, and some of the members went on to found the Young Arab Society and the clandestine al-Jam'iyya al-Qaḥṭāniyya in 1909, a society named after Qahtan, a legendary ancestor of the Arab ethnos, possibly a riposte to growing Turanism. Other associations were also formed, conveying an atmosphere of great dynamism and instability: the Reform Association (Jam'iyyat al-Iṣlaḥ) in Beirut and the Basra Reform Association (Jam'iyyat al-Baṣra al-Iṣlāḥiyya) called for administrative and other forms of decentralisation, and for Arabic to be considered the official language in the Arab Ottoman provinces. This was accompanied by a reaffirmation of loyalty to the Ottoman state, in other words, Ottoman patriotism. This position was repeated in the 1913 First Arab Conference in Paris, which brought together Arab associations of different tendencies.[261] Many Arab movements emerged around the Committee of Union and Progress and a large number of Arab intellectuals joined the Committee in the Syrian provinces and Iraq.[262] Many sought to efface memory of this association after the First World War.[263]

This convergence between Arabs and Turks was not unnatural, as Turkish Unionists and Arab Unionists belonged to the same stratum of newer intelligentsia, which emerged from the culture of the reforming state, a stratum

261 Anonymous [As'ad Dāghīr], *Thawrat al-'Arab ḍidd al-Atrāk*, 79–102.

262 Riḍā, *Muktārāt siyāsiyya min majallat al-Manār*, 202; Khālidī, *Jawla fī al-dhikrayāt bayna Lubnān wa Filasṭīn*, 60; Najdat Fatḥī Ṣafwat, "Muqadimma" to Ma'rūf al-Ruṣāfī, *Al-a'māl a- majhūla*, ed. Najdat Fatḥī Ṣafwat (London: Riyad al-Rayyis lil-Kutub wa al-Nashr, 1988), 12–13. See Hasan Kayali, *Arabs and Young Turks. Ottomanism, Arabism and Islamism in the Ottoman Empire, 1908–1918* (Berkeley: University of California Press, 1998).

263 With regard to Sāṭi' al-Ḥuṣrī, the ranking Arab nationalist ideologue of his generation, and the CUP, he was a member of the CUP in its Macedonian stronghold. For documentary evidence see Tatiana Tikhonova, *Sāṭi' al-Ḥuṣrī: Rā'id al-manḥā al-'ilmānī fī al-fikr al-qawmī al-'arabi*, trans. Tawfīq Sallūm (Moscow: Dār al-Taqaddum, 1987), 21–24. For this generation before and after the First World War, see the most interesting work of Michael Provence, *The Last Ottoman Generation and the Making of the Modern Middle East* (Cambridge: Cambridge University Press, 2017).

composed of officers, lawyers, writers, and other professional figures. It was also to be expected that the leaders of the Committee for Union and Progress would negotiate with Arab intellectuals, such as 'Abd al-Hamid al-Zahrawi (b. 1855, hanged in 1916) after the 1913 Conference, that such figures were appointed to the Senate in Istanbul, and that the Ottoman authorities would respond to demands that included Arabic education in the Arab provinces through creation of the Arabic sultanic schools, the appointment of Arabs to important positions, the entrusting of *awqāf* administration to local authorities, and provision for Arab conscripts to serve in their home provinces.[264] The political culture for these Arabs and their Turkish counterparts was a common one, emerging from the new educational system and state service, sustained by a notion of Ottoman citizenship. Two Arab nationalists who grew up in this atmosphere, one from Syria and the other from Iraq, were fair in their assessment when they recognised that the Turks represented an exemplary model for them embodying the concept of national community.[265] It was the Ottoman context – and not the wider Arab context – that created the atmosphere in which the Unionists and the majority of the Arab nationalists came to conceive of political action, its possibilities, its framework, and its coordinates. It was not for nothing that the *Tanzimat* and its dynamics were conceived as a process of "re-Ottomanization".[266]

It was also not unnatural that those holding power in the Ottoman state should have inclined towards Turkish nationalism with increasing severity and determination. There was first the fragmentation to which the state had been brought by calls for nationhood, whether by Greeks, Armenians, or others. Then there is no doubt that the Turks – not a fully ethnic indicator then, but rather those inducted into the culture of new education and state service in the civil and military sectors, quite apart from Turkmen of the countryside – comprised a highly coherent class with a culture linked to state administration and other functions. The relative Turkification of education was an attempt

---

264 al-'Aẓma, *Mir'āt al-shām*, 212. See Anonymous [As'ad Dāghir], *Thawrat al-'arab ḍidd al-atrāk*, 119 and elsewhere.

265 'Abd al-Raḥmān al-Shāhbandar, *Al-qaḍāya al-ijtima'iyya al-kubrā fī al-'ālam al-'arabī* (Cairo: Maṭba'at Miṣr wa Matba'at al-Muqtaṭaf wa al-Muqaṭṭam, 1932), 7, and Sāmī Shawkat, *Hādhihi ahdāfunā: Majmū'at muḥāḍarāt wa maqālāt wa aḥādīth qawmiyya* (Baghdad: Wizārat al-Ma'ārif, 1939), 52–53.

266 Bruce Masters, *The Arabs of the Ottoman Empire* (New York: Cambridge University Press, 2013), ch. 6.

to reproduce an administrative cadre for a state apparatus in rapid expansion, and to acculturate populations in the manner normal in modernising states. This Turkification was in any case relative and the image that has been formed of its extent in the Arab lands is fundamentally polemical and greatly exaggerated. The Turkification of the administration was in its turn the result of demands for greater centralisation, especially under conditions of the First World War, leading to greater direct control, and the development of a coherent command cadre generated by common education, sensibility and professional and political experience. In reality, Arab secessionism – as distinct from administrative and linguistic autonomism – had only patchy incidence and consequence before the war, and there is little doubt that British policy and blandishments were important for its crystallisation. Secessionism must be judged a major factor in precipitating the decisive and uncompromising turn of Turkish Ottoman nationalists into Turkish nationalists, as Arab secessionism was the ultimate and perhaps most vexatious precipitate of the Eastern Question problem, intensified by conditions of war. War also brought about a shift from a constitutionalist temper to authoritarian Turkish nationalism, for which the groundwork had been laid by the writings of Ziya Gökalp (1876–1924). By origin an ethnic Kurd, Gökalp had been closely linked to Sati' al-Husri, and argued with him over this very issue in public discussions and exchanges that were among the most important intellectual and political debates of the pre-First World War period.[267]

Turkism was a specific redaction of Ottoman nationalism, since it concerned specifically the Turkish element or the element that had been Turkified in the manner indicated above – including persons like Gökalp, and the entire metropolitan and provincial elites. This Turkified element controlled the most cohesive element of the Ottoman state apparatus, namely the armed forces. Their task was to represent and defend the interests of the Ottoman state against European forces and internal threats of fragmentation. These included Armenian nationalism and the Arab rebellion of 1916 led by the *Sharīfs* of Mecca. A change took place in the Ottoman state perception of ethnic groups and denominations and other intermediary units between state and individual citizen. This change was accompanied by a shift in political

267 Berkes, *The Development of Secularism in Turkey*, 319–321, 405–410; Mardin, *The Genesis of Young Ottoman Thought*, 278.

vocabulary: the term *millet* began to be applied to citizens of the state, who became the Ottoman *millet*. Denominations became communities (*cemaat*) and ethnic groups became races (*unsur*).[268] The *millet* lost the communitarian character that had marked the earlier Ottoman tributary patrimonial system, and greater socio-spatial domains made open to even more vigorous central intervention with the aim of removing communal particularisms and constructing citizenship on secular foundations and, ultimately, without ascriptive privileges. This prepared the way for the Kemalist revolution and the completion of Turkish national liberation, which entailed the displacement or elimination of various ethnic groups as a Turkish people was created from heteroclite elements, including rural Turkomen – a bloody process, as is the nature of such historical phenomena and other forms of revolutionary transformation. This trend had been reflected in the programme of the Committee of Union and Progress, which abolished the economic and legal Capitulations at the beginning of the First World War. It was followed by the savage elimination of the Armenian and Greek trading bourgeoisie who had controlled much of the Ottoman economy, and by the creation of a Turkish or Turkified Muslim bourgeoisie. The ethnic cleansing of eastern Anatolia was largely an accomplished fact. Under war conditions, the Unionists drew unforgivingly and mercilessly upon the consequences of the regime of capitulations, privileges, and particularities promoted by European Consuls that had preempted the possibility of integrating Christian *millas* into Ottoman citizenship. Instead, as discussed above, Christian denominations were being confined to enclaves under foreign protection at a time when the modernising aspirations of the *Tanzimat* were applied to the Muslim majority of the Ottoman population.

The exemplary punishment meted out to some Arab nationalists during the First World War, hanged in public squares in Damascus and Beirut (still called officially Martyrs' Square in both capitals), was a peremptory action of a type with other defensive operations conducted by the Ottoman state at that time, this time targeting high-value individuals rather than resorting to extensive massacres, depopulation, and expropriation as was the case with Armenians and Assyrians in eastern and southern Anatolia. There is no doubt that these peremptory executions – Abd al-Hamid al-Zahrawi was

268 Berkes, *The Development of Secularism in Turkey*, 329–333; Edib, *Turkey Faces West*, 192–193.

one of the victims – were not entirely arbitrary acts. Reckless moves had been made against a state at war with other states, and relations of various kinds had been established with foreign consuls and other operatives of foreign powers. There is no evidence that more than a few people in the Syrian provinces were active against the Ottoman state to which the majority were, it seems, still loyal.[269] The identification of the state itself with the centralised Turkish or Turkified system was matched by an identification of Islam with the Arab cause, even in secessionist discourse that did not support notions of Pan-Islamism, as in the case of al-Zahrawi.[270]

Arab nationalist discourse at the time of the First World War had not developed clear contours, nor was it clearly articulated or entirely coherent in its direction. It revolved at that point around the idea of Arab independence, without having a clear further orientation. Arab nationalism started to acquire clarity as it acquired reality, when after the war two Arab states came into existence: independent Iraq and Syria, briefly independent and soon to be under the French Mandate. It is difficult to separate the polemical dimension in Arab nationalist discourse during the First World War, associated with the Arab rebellion of the Sharif Hussein of Mecca channelled by Britain, from its conceptual and ideological dimension. A central current in the call for Arab secession was put forth as opposition to tyranny on the one hand, and as objection to the CUP for their scorn of Islam and their preference for politics over shari'a and heedlessness of religion. There were discourses glorifying the virtues of the Sharif of Mecca, some by Christian authors.[271] Arab secessionist discourse deployed an Islamic sentiment, in the style of al-Kawikibi's book *Umm al-qurā* published in 1900. Like al-Kawakibi, Sharif Hussein of Mecca was well disposed to accepting the support and ideas of secession and the erection of an Arab caliphate proposed by Wilfred Blunt (1840–1922), the equine enthusiast, the imperialist grandee Lord Kitchener (1850–1916) and Kitchener's protégé Mark Sykes (1879–1919), whose name is associated with the Sykes–Picot Agreement of 1916.[272] Despite Rashid Rida's declared

269 al-'Aẓma, *Mir'āt al-shām*, 220–221, 230.

270 Jad'ān, *Usus al-taqaddum*, 280.

271 See, for example, the anonymous 1916 text (very likely to be by the Lebanese Maronite Arab nationalist As'ad Dāghir) *Thawrat al-'arab ḍidd al-atrāk*, 212–228, 269–270 and elsewhere. Compare Riḍā, *Mukhtārāt siyāsiyya min majallat al-Manār*, 233–236.

272 Martin S. Kramer, *Islam Assembled: The Advent of the Muslim Congresses* (New York: Columbia University Press, 1986), 80.

mistrust of the British, he concurred with the Sharif Hussein on a number of matters in 1916, including financial support he was to receive annually from the Sharif of Mecca.[273] The Sharif's sentiments had turned against the Unionists of the CUP, after they declined support for his 1909 proposal to set up a centre for religious propaganda and guidance in Istanbul.[274] One wonders in which world he thought he lived.

The attribution of secularism to anti-Ottoman Turkish Arab nationalism is therefore a questionable proposition. The proclamation of Sharif Hussein announcing the Arab Revolt justified this move by holding that the CUP undermined "the sole bond between the Gracious Ottoman sultanate and all the Muslims of the world, namely adherence to the Book and to the Sunna".[275] The Unionists, the proclamation added, allowed soldiers stationed in Mecca to abstain from fasting during Ramadan, and permitted equality between men and women in inheritance (an untrue claim). The Sharif declared that the aim of his secession was "succour for the religion of Islam" and "striving to elevate the lot of Muslims" on the basis of shari'a, "which is the only source of authority for us and it is the only basis for our judgments, and of justice in general and in detail". He declared readiness to adopt from the "arts of modern progress" and "conditions for sound progress", all that was compatible with the fundamentals of religion and its practices. The proclamation made no mention of Arabism, declaring that the revolt was a religious duty. Rashid Rida, proclaiming allegiance to Sharif Hussein (6 October 1916) in a speech addressed to all Muslims, declared that Islam is a religion in which authority to rule lay with the Arabs.[276] He went on to address the notables of Mecca and affirm the need for the caliphate to be entrusted to the Prophet's tribe of Quraysh of whom the Sharif was a descendant.[277] This did not prevent Rashid Rida, having subsequently shifted his allegiance to the Wahhabis after their victory in the Hejaz in 1925, from making a scathing attack on the Hashemites, charging them with loyalty to the British during the First World War and for their alliance with Britain. In this, a number of factors converged to eliminate the possibility of a choice for Arab independence: the First World

273 Ibid., 81; and Arslān, *Al-Sayyid Rashīd Riḍā aw ikhā' arba'īn sana*, 155–156.

274 Arslān, *Al-Sayyid Rashīd Riḍā*, 148.

275 See the text in Anonymous [As'ad Dāghir], *Thawrat al-'arab ḍidd al-atrāk*, 282–289.

276 Ibid., 320.

277 Riḍā, *Mukhtārāt siyāsiyya min majallat al-Manār*, 203.

War, generating the defensive actions of the Turkish Unionists, and British activity in the Arabian Peninsula. Secession was a wartime manoeuvre carried out under British and French protection, sponsored by the British Army and its intelligence services represented on the ground by Colonel T. E. Lawrence, Lawrence of Arabia (1888–1935).

Thus unfolded the campaign known as the Great Arab Revolt. The number of Arab participants from the Syrian provinces and Iraq is still unknown, as are the detailed circumstances that led them to desert the Ottoman army and join the Hijazi revolt and the campaign led by Lawrence. Most of the Arab participants had far stronger professional, political, and intellectual connections to the Unionist officers than to the Arabs of the Hijaz and to British intelligence officers.[278] Above all else, the Arab rebellion was a communitarian revolt. It was a revolt with a religious pretext, and it was a communitarian revolt according to the meaning that European powers gave to the term *milla* (community) within the parameters of the mosaic model. It was an ethnically Arab movement, without being an Arab nationalist movement; really more nativist. There is no doubt that many participants in the revolt had little political sophistication. This was combined with British chicanery, with the narrow clan ambitions of the Hashemites, and the exclusion of Syrian Christians.[279] A communitarian and confessional state during the First World War and its aftermath was an item of British policy, and the wartime demagogy of the Unionists helped to give it sustenance. In 1914 five fatwas calling for jihad were issued from Istanbul. Britain adopted a similar approach, with Mecca and its notables as its starting point, and French authorities produced fatwas from the ulama of Morocco, its religious notables, and the Moroccan sultan, in addition to shaykhs of the Sufi fraternities and the *muftis* of Algeria. These fatwas attacked those emanating from Istanbul and supported France in the war with the arguments that the Ottomans did not serve the interests of the Muslims, their caliphate was corrupt, and they were not descended from Quraysh.[280] Yet at the same time the Unionists worked to limit further the role of religious authorities in the affairs of state. In 1916 a number of reforms had been proposed by Ziya Gökalp. The

278 Compare with al-ʿAẓma, *Mir'āt al-shām*, 220, 231.

279 Compare with Riḍā, *Riḥlāt al-imām Muḥammad Rashīd Riḍā*, 255.

280 Mission scientifique du Maroc, "Les musulmans français et la guerre", *Revue du monde musulman* 8/29 (1914): 343–557.

most important of these was the removal of the *şeyhülislam* from ministerial rank and the placing of shariʿa courts under the authority of the Ministry of Justice instead of under the office of *şeyhülislam*. The *awqāf* were reorganised and placed under a newly created special ministry, an arrangement that persists in post-Ottoman Arab countries. Administrative responsibility for religious schools was transferred to the Ministry of Education.

Turkish reformers thus continued further the historical dynamic of the *Tanzimat*, and prepared the way for the definitive future direction for the completion of legal reforms, and the termination of the twin system of religious and secular responsibility for education.[281] The institution of the caliphate and its associated *şeyhülislam* were separated from that of executive secular authority. Under the control of Mustapha Kemal, a form of Islamic diplomacy became focused on calling for a caliphate independent of foreign control.[282] Kemal emerged as the leader of the Turkish national movement folllowing the fall of the Ottoman Empire on 30 October 1918. Kemal had led the successful bold and determined defence of Istanbul at Çanakkale (Gallipoli) in 1915 against Allied forces composed essentially of the British Army and Navy. He emerged as supreme Turkish commander, leading resistance to the Anglo-French plan to expand the Greek state at the expense of Turkish territory in Anatolia and in implementation of the clauses of the Treaty of Sèvres of 1920.

Kemal mustered the remaining Ottoman forces and during 1921 and 1922 repulsed the Greek and Italian attack launched from Izmir against western Anatolia, in conjunction with the Allies. He also successfully resisted the attempts of the French Army, advancing from Syria, to set up Armenian zones in the southern Anatolian region of Cilicia. When Britain occupied Istanbul in March 1920, Kemal and his supporters moved to Ankara, which was proclaimed temporary capital and seat of the National Assembly, founded on 24 April 1920. In the meantime, Britain refused to recognise the nationalist government in Ankara while the captive caliph and the *şeyhülislam* acted to stir up revolts in Anatolia against the national government. A fatwa was issued – distributed in the medium of leaflets dropped by Greek aircraft – authorising the shedding of Kemal's blood. In a ludicrous tragi-comic sequence of events, Kemal was demoted from general to major. The *mufti* of Ankara issued a fatwa

281 Berkes, *The Development of Secularism in Turkey*, 415–416; and Taha Parla, *The Social and Political Thought of Ziya Gökalp, 1876–1924* (Leiden: Brill, 1985), 39–40.

282 Kramer, *Islam Assembled*, 74–75.

calling for the liberation of the caliph from British sequestration. The caliph then placed himself under British protection, and left Istanbul on board a warship of the Royal Navy on 17 November 1922. The National Assembly responded by urging its own shari'a council to issue a fatwa, the last issued in Turkey, to remove the caliph from office and install in his place Abdülmecid II (1868–1944). This was in exchange for a written undertaking by the caliph that he recognised the authority of the National Assembly, abdicating the sultanate and confining himself to spiritual authority.[283] This chapter of Turkish history concluded with the proclamation by the National Assembly of the Turkish Republic at midnight on 29 October 1923 and the election of Mustapha Kemal as President. The caliphate was abolished on 3 March 1924, with the Ottoman royal family expelled from Turkey – it took decades of litigation for its descendants to recover some of their patrimony. The official body responsible for *awqāf* was abolished together with shari'a. Turkey was thus saved from policies and dynamics that had sought to fragment it and link its history to the doleful fate of the Arab Middle East.

The notion of a Muslim state was the sign of the complaisance of the Arab political movement of 1916 to British policy. The last sputter of this movement was the ceremony of allegiance to Sharif Hussein as caliph in eastern Transjordan in March 1924, a few days after the abolition of the Ottoman caliphate. Hussein adopted the plan of al-Kawakibi's *Umm al-qurā* for the establishment of an advisory council for the caliphate composed of thirty-one members: sixteen from the Hijaz, three from India, three from Sudan, two from Bukhara, two from Java, and one each from Syria, Turkey, Afghanistan, and Daghestan.[284] As is known, the Sharif Hussein ibn 'Ali abdicated his position in favour of his son 'Ali in October of the same year (1924). 'Ali ibn Hussein also abdicated from the caliphate and only a few days later the Wahhabi forces of Abd al-Aziz Ibn Saud occupied Mecca, without British objection. Philby of Arabia (Harry St. John Philby, 1885–1960) had already done much of the leg-work, and was already in place as an advisor to Ibn Saud.

The abolition of the caliphate, and the consequent establishment of a robustly secular state in Turkey, was a passage that was neither even, nor smooth. It had many twists and turns, and resulted from political processes,

---

283 Edib, *Turkey Faces West*, 201.
284 Kramer, *Islam Assembled*, 83–84.

one of whose basic elements – the formation of a national entity – had been brought up already. The founding National Assembly was traversed by tensions and differences, and was composed of tendencies with varied political and ideological orientations. It even issued a decision forbidding alcoholic drinks, card games and backgammon in 1920. The Assembly included an Islamic faction that opposed the proclamation of the Republic, considering it an atheistic and Communist concept. Its constitution stipulated that Islam was the religion of the state.[285] It prepared for the abolition of the sultanate (whose abolition, on the proclamation of the Republic in 1923, had preceded that of the caliphate) with a Muslim juristic text drafted by the ulama of Ankara and Anatolia, using traditional styles of Muslim argumentation. It proposed that the caliphate be merely a case of legal delegation on the part of the *umma*, that the legal representatives of the state do not lose their positions when a caliph dies. The caliphate can make no decisions concerning landholding or the grant of land. It also argued that the appointment of the imam was only for the sake of the public interest, and that this interest could well be served by a government. It argued finally that the caliphate, after the period of the Rightly-Guided Caliphs, was only a blameworthy sultanate and an unsound caliphate. This office therefore needed regulation, and its duties and privileges could be delegated to one individual or a national assembly. It was therefore permissible to separate the sultanate, or worldly power, from the caliphate.[286] The National Assembly, who delegated to the ulama the composition of this text, therefore saw fit to use the heritage of Islamic reformism (to be discussed in the next chapter) as a point of transition between traditional discourse about government and modern discourse that, with the abolition of the caliphate, was to become a tangible political and ideological reality.

After the abolition of the caliphate there followed a series of laws that became emblematic of the new Turkey. These laws built upon a dynamic that had for nearly a century been broadening the scope of state competence to law, education, and society. It allowed the formalisation of state supremacy over intermediate instances that had hitherto curbed state capacity to fulfil its modernising dynamic. The Kemalist state was a realisation of the modern

285 Berkes, *The Development of Secularism in Turkey*, 448, 456–457.

286 Anonymous, *Al-khilāfa wa sulṭat al-umma*, trans. ʿAbd al-Ghanī Sanī Bek (Cairo: Maṭbaʿat al-Hilāl, 1924), 4–6, 16–17, 28–29, 32–37, 39–41, 51–55.

state that the Ottomans had sought to create throughout the nineteenth century in the face of strong European opposition. Abdülhamid II in particular had sought to realise this plan by means that were no longer appropriate to the time. Under the Republic, the shari'a and the Ministry of *awqāf* were abolished, along with the closure of religious schools with the unification and consolidation of the education system into one directed by the state. All laws based on Muslim jurisprudence in every field were abrogated with the unification of the juristic and legal system into civil law. Provisions for Muslim marriage contracts were not abolished, and remained available for those who desired them, but after the conclusion of a civil marriage. The right of men to unilateral divorce was abolished as the matter was entrusted to the courts on modern legal bases. Polygamy was also abolished, but women enfranchised only in 1934 – in Britain in 1928, France in 1944 (for literate women only: universal suffrage came in 1965), in Switzerland only in 1971. Sufi fraternities were closed, and all associations founded on religious or confessional bases were forbidden. Anti-secular propaganda was forbidden in 1926 and the constitution became secular in 1928, although the secularism of state was only proclaimed constitutionally in 1937. Unveiling was made obligatory for school-girls and students; the wives of state functionaries were expected to attend official functions unveiled, in an operation of rapid Jacobin-style acculturation that included also the banning of turbans and other items of "outlandish dress".

The consolidation of a modern society was complemented by a sharp disengagement from the Arabs, linked, in the eyes of the Turkish nationalists, with the obsolete system of the caliphate, and with the Turks having been stabbed in the back by the Arabs during the First World War. The Qur'an was translated into Turkish in 1923 after very strong opposition, and muezzins were obliged to make the call to prayer in Turkish from 1931 onwards.[287] In 1927 the Latin alphabet was adopted, and the use of Arabic was prohibited.[288] The question of the alphabet was part of the need to create a distinction from the past through which the Turks could very rapidly be forged into a nation out of heteroclite

287 Brett Wilson, *Translating the Qur'an in an Age of Nationalism: Print Culture and Modern Islam in Turkey* (Oxford: Oxford University Press, 2014), ch. 5. For the arguments of those opposed, arguing that this would separate Turks from Islam, see the book by the last *şeyhülislam* Muṣṭafā Ṣabrī, *Mas'alat tarjamat al-qur'ān* (Cairo: al-Maṭba'a al-Salafiyya, 1351/1932)

288 Berkes, *The Development of Secularism in Turkey*, 195.

human material. Nations, as noted previously, are not eternal but created alongside nation states or aspiration towards nation states, and like all nations in the phase of political formation, this required quasi-historical or pseudo-historical legends and myths. The Turanian current had been present but not predominant in Turkey, but Mustapha Kemal supported two pseudo-historical propositions: that the Turks invented writing in what was called their Sumerian and Hittite phases, and that they invented vocal articulation and speech.[289]

Unsurprisingly, the formation of the Turkish nation entailed brutal actions not unlike those associated with Balkan nationalisms, namely, "population exchange". After the war of 1921–1922, from about 1.3 to approximately 1.5 million Greeks were expelled from Turkey to Greece. Most were descendants of Anatolia's original inhabitants, centuries before the Turks. In turn, 400,000 Turks were expelled from Greece. The state followed a vigorous policy of Turkifying non-Turkophone rural inhabitants such as Arabs, Kurds, remaining Greeks and Armenians, many, especially women and orphaned children, Islamised. The urban populations had adopted the Turkish language, although many were bilingual with Arabic, Greek, or Armenian. From 1934 Mustapha Kemal came to be called Atatürk, Father of the Turks.

Kemalism expressed the internal political victory of the late Ottoman Bildungsbürgertum, and most especially of its representation in the armed forces, a new cultural class produced by the Ottoman reforming state. The result of this victory was fundamental change affecting Turkish society and thought, in effect fashioning a national society anew by forced acculturation. The Committee for Union and Progress had provided the climate in which Mustapha Kemal and his comrades had evolved. To these cohorts belonged army officers, civil servants, and teachers, especially persons who defined themselves as Turks and came from the provinces and had grown up or been educated in the centre, the bastion of the state and its educational institutions; one might mention again two ethnic Kurds, Ziya Gökalp and Ismet Inönü (1884–1973), Kemal's fellow officer who succeeded him to the presidency of the republic. Many brought with them the influence of the developing provincial nationalisms, especially those of the Balkans. Thessaloniki (Selanik/Salonika) was especially important in this story; it was there that

289 Dankwart A. Rustow, "Politics and Islam in Turkey 1920–1955", in Richard Nelson Frye, ed., *Islam and the West* (Gravenhage: Mouton, 1957), 81–82.

CUP members such as Mustapha Kemal and Sati' al-Husri were highly active; Kemal was born there.[290]

All of these groups subsequently constituted a centre that obliged the heteroclite composition later to become known as the Turkish people to move out of a temporality of subordinate estates and millets and villages whose persistence would have compromised the historical promise of its evolution, and still does. The new post-war Turkish state imposed an integration into a temporality of independence, despite the opposition of the European powers. This meant an entry into social and intellectual modernity and a clear break with the social and intellectual forces that had led to defeat and to fragmentation, particularly the collapse of the southern front through Anglo-Hashemite collaboration. The relatively marginal status of many of the members of the CUP helped their revolutionary activity and their revolutionary disposition, as in the case of many avant-garde movements in history. The Kemalist revolution and the Hashemite revolt were fundamentally different: the Kemalist revolution broke with the *millet* state whose modernisation was put on definitive course by the complete secularisation of state and society, while the Hashemite revolt was a move towards a colonial system inaugurating a period during which secularist Arab thought developed and marked the nationalism spawned by the colonial system. Independent Arab states that emerged, liberal or authoritarian socialist, were not able to carry through reforms correlative with their emergence and the agencies of their emergence to the extent of breaking with the centuries of milletism: denominations, communities, and clans all were reinvented obstacles to the social conditions of progress and development. Perhaps the best testimony of the importance of the Kemalist example and its possible historical significance is the praise for Mustapha Kemal from one of the great Islamic reformist figures of the twentieth century, the Algerian Shaykh Abd al-Hamid Ibn Badis – in a text historically clear-sighted and just, despite being crafted in a language and a vocabulary with an Islamo-nationalist twist. On 4 November 1938 Ibn Badis wrote in the Algerian monthly journal *al-Shihāb*:

> On the seventeenth day of the holy month of Ramadan there passed away the greatest man humanity has known in modern history, and one of the greatest geniuses of the East to emerge ... at different moments of history, who change the course of history and create it anew. That

290 See Mark Mazower, *Salonika, City of Ghosts* (New York: Vintage, 2006), ch. 6 and part 2, passim.

man is Mustapha Kemal, hero of Gallipoli in the Dardanelles, Sakarya in Anatolia [near Ankara, August–September 1921, marking the definitive strategic reverse of the Greek push into Anatolia] and the reviver of Turkey from a state of near-death to her present condition of riches, glory and elevation. When we say "hero of Gallipoli" we mean victor over the British, the greatest naval power which Mustapha Kemal defeated in the Great War in the worst defeat which Britain had known in her long history. When we say "hero of Sakarya" we mean the victor over the British and their Greek, Italian and French allies after the Great War and the one who expelled them from the land of Turkey after the occupation of its capital and the absorption of its provinces and coasts. When we say, the reviver of Turkey, we say the reviver of the Islamic East as a whole. The position that Turkey occupied in the heart of the Islamic world for many centuries is her position and there is no surprise that the revival of the Islamic world is linked to Turkey's revival. Before the First World War Turkey was the front line of the East in the face of the Western attack and within range of the shells of colonialist evil and the Christian fanaticism of the Western nations. When the war ended and Turkey emerged, crushed and fragmented, the Western states dealt with the nations of the East as though they controlled them, under amiable colonial names. They occupied Turkey itself and the capital of the Caliphate and the Caliph became their plaything and subject to their action . . . Kemal, who assembled those scattered remnants and gathered around him his brothers from among the honourable sons of Turkey, and breathed out his spirit over the land of Anatolia where the root of noble Turkey is to be found. That noble people resisted the captive Caliph and his miserable government and his impostor sheikhs on the inside, and, on the outside, defeated the Western states with Britain at their forefront.

Ibn Badis added, in an allusion to his realistic assessment of history and conditions in Turkey, that the position of Mustapha Kemal in relation to Islam came as a result of the condition of the caliph and the *şeyhülislam*: Muslim nations, he maintained, which saw the Ottoman caliph as their leader, rose up against him, with a likely reference to the Arab revolt, whereupon Mustapha Kemal revolted against the Muslims and said to them: "Each of us to himself, there is no benefit in communication as long as you are in your present state. Be yourselves and then come, let us engage with one another and cooperate as do sovereign nations. As for Islam, Kemal translated the Qur'an for the Turkish nation into its language so that it could take Islam from its source and draw on it from its origin. He enabled the Turkish nation to perform the rituals of Islam and in its mosques Islam was manifest and year after year its festivals were more and more in evidence, culminating in the great manifestation of Islam on the day of Kemal's burial and the prayers over his grave."[291]

Atatürk did not abolish religion, rather he separated it from public life, enabled its rituals to be performed and censured those who wanted to use religion as a means to secure authority and power and to set up cultural and social centres of power that diminish the authority of the state and sought to consume it. Kemal's banishing of the caliphate and its associated elements of the religious establishment from the legislative domain was a modernisation of religion. This was carried out at a time when the supernatural and anachronistic elements in legislation were no longer tenable, especially at a time of rapid change and a new historical outlook. Kemalist secularism was the systemic integration of a new national community into global temporality, disallowing the imperialist West from maintaining its cultural superiority by maintaining the world's margins in a condition of cultural, intellectual, and scientific backwardness – which is precisely the direction to which the global multiculturalist and nativist regime of the early twenty-first century is reverting.[292] Kemalism and its secularism emerged at a rare historical moment when it succeeded in meeting the national and military challenges, and those of integration into a moment of avant-garde universalism, at a precious historical moment that preceded the stabilisation of the new colonial system that followed the First World War. Post-Ottoman Arab lands missed that particular train. The following chapters will show how religious institutions and forces had the opportunity, with political backing, to curb the global tendential process of advancement in Arab societies. To a large extent this institution and these forces succeeded in aborting the modernist globalising enterprise that had brought about the progress of Arab societies in many domains and indeed had managed to cover the central locations of these societies until recently. Even in Turkey itself religious institutions and forces, duly reconfigured, will go on the offensive against the modernist enterprise.

---

291 ʻAbd al-Ḥamīd ibn Bādīs, *Kitāb āthār ibn Bādīs*, ed. ʻImād al-Ṭālibī, 4 vols (Algiers: Dār Maktabat al-Sharika al-Jazā'iriyya li'l-Ta'līf wa al-Tarjama wa al-Ṭibā'a wa al-Tawzī' wa al-Nashr, n.d.), vol. 3, 130–133.

292 Aziz al-Azmeh, *Islams and Modernities*, ch. 2.

3
Intellectual Transformations and Elusive Reconciliation

The previous chapter focused on the new culture of practical global acculturation that swept across Arab lands and other Ottoman territories in the nineteenth and early twentieth centuries. Systems of education and law underwent change and there were intimations of a possibility for political change. There were changes in social life in its most visible manifestations, such as dress, styles of residence, transport and communications, work, and the presence of foreigners. These produced strategic fractures in older socio-cultural structures, and strategic departures that were not fully realised, but were incompletely and unevenly spread in social and geographical terms. This was due to the limitations of the material capacities of Arab societies as well as to foreign pressures. Moribund conservative classes, exemplified by the religious institutions, put up resistance as they fought to defend vested interests and positions held hitherto.

In form, the state was a transitional one. It was neither entirely modern in its institutions and modus operandi nor sultanic. But it did develop in the context of a clear break with its immediate past: an economic break brought by international capitalism that defined backwardness and subordination as a mode of contemporaneity and sought to perpetuate it, and a social break that followed the consequent atrophy of the previous urban and rural forces and relations of production. Some of these that persisted nevertheless were not absorbed in the reconfiguration of new social structures, but continued to exist in parallel. There were, in parallel, cultural changes, most clearly manifest in the retreat of religious culture, albeit with broadening content, to the margins of official state culture and the social centre. This latter relied on scientific impulses of European provenance, on schools and printed periodicals, and new intellectuals. State sponsorship gave an authoritative character to the output of this official culture, in addition to its obvious link to European points of reference that were manifestly and distinctively new as well as powerful. This official culture developed in the folds of disciplines with a technical bent and purpose. It was a child of its time: the nineteenth century with its positivism, optimism, and utilitarianism. It was a culture appropriate to the new bureaucracy that adopted, in practical terms, some of its ideas of administrative, legal, educational, and other reforms that became part of a new emergent cognitive habitus appropriate to the class of new bureaucrats, intellectuals, and officers. But there did not emerge a fully articulated ideological framework that might be called the "*Tanzimat* ideology". These new ideas emerged operationally and technically as a novel administrative rationality was being developed without, in most cases, an explicit theoretical, political, or social underpinning.

On the other hand, along with this new emergent rationality, habits of state authoritarianism continued and, in some respects, acquired modern organisational and technical instruments that rendered them effective. This made certain positivist concepts, such as that of social engineering, highly attractive to senior state functionaries since these concepts stressed central control over transformation in societies whose own internal dynamism was subjected to stresses. Positivism and the Saint-Simonian movement of the early nineteenth century did influence the *Tanzimat* and the reorganisation of aspects of Egyptian society under Muhammad Ali Pasha and his successors. The *Tanzimat* and the Egyptian reformers saw this as the means of reordering unstable societies, caused by revolution in Europe or uncertainties arising from the "oriental" character ascribed to the Orient by Orientals who mattered.[1]

These new ideas came to acquire a normative character in practice to the extent that they became a measure against which older concepts were retained or disregarded. As we shall see, Islamic learning – as distinct from

1 Robert Walker, "Saint-Simon and the passage from political to social science", in *The Language of Political Theory in Early Modern Europe*, ed. Anthony Pagden (Cambridge: Cambridge University Press, 1987), 334–336.

the institution as a whole – and its normative apparatus attempted accommodation to this emergent order that, tendentially and objectively, had the potential to invalidate the authority of Islam's traditional texts. Muslim points of reference, in turn, also had recourse to "French ideas" to formulate political concepts that would free those who adopted them from the power of the upper echelons of the bureaucracy.

It was under such conditions that emerged the Young Ottoman movement and its Arab variant, Muslim reformism. But the modernising formulation of Islamic symbolic authority central to both was not the only integrated discursive redaction of the *Tanzimat* period. There developed a secularising tendency that adopted the implicit secular consequences of new conditions as a token for its integration into the dominant global, universalising culture of the nineteenth century. This produced discourses in various measures of correspondence to the prevalent historical conditions, prospects, and realities without anachronism or a sense of captivity to a past in thrall to the supernatural, even if this subjection was taken to be entirely symbolic. Secularists with varying degrees of self-awareness came to acquire a perception of their age corresponding to reality as both status quo and the tendential promise of transformations in place, a perception related to a complex network of changes occurring during that period. Modes and degrees of change within society were varied and uneven, depending on region, class, social group, proximity, or distance to Istanbul, Beirut, and Cairo, integration into state education systems, and corresponding forms of intellectual and cultural transformation. In both cases, the new cultural actors evoked in Chapter 2, be they secularist or Islamic reformers, were, in the content of their thought, the product of the universal dimension of their culture and of their quest for concepts that were in circulation at their time, understood in its universal dimension.

It is superfluous to recall that the concepts involved in expressing this apprehension of reality and of historical promise were of European provenance. Their formulation, their historical and symbolic points of reference, and the socio-cultural, political, and even intellectual consequences of political discourses resulting, assumed varied forms. In the case of Muslim reformism, a reticence precluded an engagement with universalism in a way and to a degree that could have guaranteed coherence, balance, and credibility. Comprador culture was an outgrowth of immediate economic and political activity and did not acquire an intellectual character.

1 Evolutionism and Salafism

To sum up, the different intellectual tendencies that emerged under the *Tanzimat* state were underpinned by an attempt to deal with a number of questions that converged around the problematic of advancement – *nahḍa*, or renaissance, is a historiographic category generated to give a name and a title to this quest for advancement. Arab research on this subject has suffered from numerous problematic, apologetic, or ideological elements that have rendered it difficult to understand the heritage of the *nahḍa* and grasp its common historical character despite the split between a call for complete convergence with Europe, and a moment of retreat and retrogression, seeking to lie low in Islamic symbolism.[2] Were it not for the contributions of Abdallah Laroui and Waddah Sharara and from a small number of others, our understanding of modern Arab thought would have remained captive to simplifications and historical distortions arising from political passions or an elementary descriptive approach, to say nothing of blindness to comparable histories of marginalisation and subordination.[3]

There is no doubt that discourse associated with the *nahḍa* at the end of the late nineteenth century relied on the optimistic evolutionism of that century, linked to Darwinism and positivism. This discourse is thus positively distinguished from *nahḍa*-evoking discourse catering to the political and ideological tastes of the late twentieth century and early twenty-first, emblematised in an Islamist party calling itself Nahda, which will be examined in some respects in

2 One can commend wholeheartedly the observations put forward in this respect by ʿAbd al-Ilāh Bilqazīz in "Muqaddimāt li taḥlīl al-khiṭāb al-siyāsī al-ʿarabī: al-khiṭāb al-nahḍawī wa al-uṭur al-marjiʿiyya", *Al-mustaqbal al-ʿarabī* 123 (1989): 5, 9, 16. Younger scholars writing in European languages and outside the tropes of post-colonial historiography are starting to make a difference, such as Marwa Elshakry, *Reading Darwin in Arabic 1860–1950* (Chicago: University of Chicago Press, 2013) or Adam Mestyan, *Arab Patriotism. The Ideology and Culture of Power in Late Ottoman Egypt* (Princeton: Princeton University Press, 2017), or Nadia Al-Bagdadi, *Vorgestellte Öffentlichkeit: Zur Genese moderner Prosa in Ägypten* (Wiesbaden: Reichert Verlag, 2010), with their thick contextualisation. One would have wished and expected the overall direction of revisiting well-established analyses to have yielded more consistently enriching historical results that one finds in, for instance, J. Hanssen and M. Weiss (eds), *Arabic Thought beyond the Liberal Age* (Cambridge: Cambridge University Press, 2016).

3 For an excellent example of study of the term "renaissance" in the Third World and a probing examination of its mythology and its historical situation see V. C. Joshi, *Rammohun Roy and the Process of Modernization of India* (Delhi: Vikas Publishing House, 1975).

Chapter 6 of this book. Evolutionary positivism entails situating the *nahḍa* in a positivist context that assumed a degree of natural inevitability for human progress. Darwinism, understood in simplified terms as meaning the struggle for survival and elevation with time, leads to a naturalist and "scientific" image of predation between nations that began with the imperialist attack on the Ottoman state and other Eastern lands.

Muhammad 'Abduh, like the secularist Shibli al-Shumayyil (1850–1917), adopted the Comtean positivist schema of social evolution through three stages on an upward scale and numerous contexts.[4] 'Abduh, in 1881, found that there were three successive ages of humanity. The first was natural, the second social, and the third political.

> Humans start callow and instinctual, searching for food and shelter and the rest of their natural needs according to their capacities. An aspiration to protect the self leads them to preserve the species, and the multiplicity of needs leads them to seek help so they come together and gather with others, becoming socialised in a civil setting. They progress in this respect, consider matters themselves and take an interest in the affairs of their species, becoming political, which [defines] the accomplished civic human, with full rights and duties.

They then mandate a person consensually, such as the Khedive and the ministers chosen by people through the will of that elevated prince.[5]

'Abduh thus reclaimed evolutionism inasmuch as it is a positivist framework pointing to movement from the lower to the higher, in the setting of social organisation – 'Abduh, in the field of the history of religions, was evolutionist in a way particular to him, corresponding to the way that religion and education were seen at his time, especially by Herbert Spencer (1820–1903), the English evolutionary sociologist whom 'Abduh met while in Britain and whose book on education he translated into Arabic (he did not have this translation published). Adapting ideas of religion current in his time and arising from a number of Enlightenment thinkers, including David Hume, 'Abduh held that religious

---

4 Shiblī al-Shumayyil, *Ta'rīb li sharḥ Büchner 'alā maḍhab Darwin fī intiqāl al-anwā wa ẓuhūr al-ālam al-'uḍwī wa iṭlāq dhālika 'alā al-insān* (Alexandria: Maṭba'at jarīdat al-Maḥrūsa, 1884), ح – ط and *Majmū'at al-duktūr Shiblī al-Shumayyil*, vol. 2, 85–87.

5 'Abduh, *Al-a'māl al-kāmila*, vol. 1, 337.

evolution followed in degrees that of civilisation and society. Order based on force and coercion corresponded to the primitive stage of humanity, when the image of authority and the fear of death led the imagination to sanctify physically tangible idols and to worship them. Humans then evolved to a stage of prophecy, when humanity attains such mental maturity as to facilitate distinguishing right from wrong. Finally, in the third stage, people come to recognise the truth of prophecy that they had lost when following "the path of the demon of overlordship and submission to the allurements of politics".[6]

This specific context of the three-stage theory of history was not limited to the general religious history of humanity but also applied to the history of the monotheist religions as mentioned in Muhammad 'Abduh's *Risālat al-tawḥīd* (1897): monotheistic religions evolve from religions based on command, reprimand, and a demand for absolute obedience (Abduh intends Judaism here), to a religion of sentiment and inner feeling that addresses emotions (in the case of Christianity) and, in Islam, a religion addressing reason, associating this with sentiment in guiding humanity to felicity in both this and the other world.[7]

Abduh was not alone in following the evolutionary view of religion, which situated it, and therefore Islam, in the context of a positivist historical evolution for human progress, which would bring about convergence between progress and rightly guided behaviour. Jamal al-Din al-Afghani held that human fantasy evolved alongside the evolution of reason.[8] Primitive humans worshipped lower beings such as stones, and then evolved to worship fire, and then clouds and the heavenly spheres until they attained the worship of abstract entities pure of considerations of quantity and quality. Al-Afghani's position had particularities that will be studied later, although his ideas belonged to the broader context made possible by positivist ideas of history that underpinned a central strand of nineteenth-century culture, and that concurred with the ideas prevailing in the thought of Muhammad 'Abduh, 'Ali Yusuf, and others.[9]

Religion evolved therefore, in accordance with the pattern of human evolution. The divine chronology for inspiration and prophecy followed a

6 Ibid., vol. 4, 558–561, and compare vol. 1, 281–287.

7 Ibid., vol. 3, 447–450. Rashīd Riḍā adopted this concept in *Muḥāwarāt al-muṣliḥ wa al-muqallid* (Cairo: Maṭba'at Majallat al-Manār, 1334/1916), 2–3.

8 'Anḥūri, *Siḥr hārūt*, 177.

9 Jad'ān, *Usus al-taqaddum*, 167–183 and passim.

secular, earthly chronology. Religion was an instinctive awareness of supernatural creatures beyond the world, since humans are articulate animals and religious by nature.[10] One Muslim reformist went so far as to suggest that it was possible for animals to perceive that which transcends the realm of experience, and perceive directly the presence of the Creator and Provider.[11] The long-standing idea that religion is inherent in humanity was also taken up by the Aleppan intellectual Francis Marrash, in a text whose importance will be explored later in this volume. He found religious practice to be an instinctive tendency necessary to the preservation of the species, in the same measure as procreation.[12] Religion and perception of religion and the supernatural were based in nature, although this religious appropriation of evolutionism nowhere indicated the source and cause of this instinctive predilection.

Following ideas current at that time about the history of religions, Arab intellectuals in this secularising age held to the very old and common theory that religion arose from fear: fear of death, and fear of overwhelming, unintelligible natural forces, the appeasement of which is at the origin of religion.[13] Muhammad ʿAbduh and others, however, did not deal with this in discussions of religion and history. Religion, they held, was providential, resulting from divine mercy, and God's choice for that which is best. This, as is known, is a Mu'tazilite conception, reclaimed as it corresponded to the evolutionary theory adopted by ʿAbduh and others, without it being based in a secular view of religion. Its reliance on conceptions of prophecy and a prophetic dispensation was one that rendered the deployment of evolutionism a parallel argument to religious conceptions, external to the framework of historical discourse.

The idea that religion was a social necessity was deployed in another, more immediately political direction also, one with more far-reaching consequences for Arab social and political thought: religion as identitarian reclamation was proposed as a necessary element in the defence of a collective self, and an

10 ʿAbduh, *Al-aʿmāl al-kāmila*, vol. 3, 487.

11 Ibn Bādīs, *Kitāb āthār Ibn Bādīs*, vol. 2, 22.

12 Fransīs Marrāsh, *Shahādat al-ṭabīʿa fī wujūd Allāh wa al-sharīʿa* (Beirut: Maṭbaʿat al-Amīrkān, 1892), 43–44. On this figure, see Karam al-Ḥilū, *Al-fikr al-libirālī ʿinda Fransīs al-Marrāsh* (Beirut: Centre for Arab Unity Studies, 2006).

13 al-Shumayyil, *Taʿrīb li sharḥ Büchner ʿalā maḍhab Darwin*, ج and *Majmūʿat al-duktūr Shiblī al-Shumayyil*, 14.

indicator of religious solidarity that resembled racial solidarity in its "speaking with one voice and acquiring a unity of purpose and the quest for victory over opponents by force thus gathered", in the words of al-Afghani.[14] The moral justification of religion, as a force for curbing appetites, and that then works to organise society,[15] is a necessary preliminary to the politico-romantic discourse of the *nahḍa* with a para-nationalist character, which developed among the Young Ottomans, particularly in the case of Namik Kemal (1840–1888),[16] while al-Afghani was the most striking pan-Islamic example of this.[17] This type of moral justification is one of the bases of the Turkish nationalist position as exemplified by Ziya Gökalp,[18] and recurs in today's neo-Afghanist Islamist, culture-nationalist movements and ideologies, including Khomeinism.

This political discourse adopted another principle attributed to Darwinism, that of the struggle for survival, which was applied to society and politics, although Darwin himself refrained from taking the path of what was to be known as social Darwinism. Indeed, social Darwinism was a crude adaptation of Jean-Baptiste Lamarck's (1744–1829) early contribution to what later became the theory of evolution, which stressed the transmission of characteristics acquired in adaptation to an environment as adaptation continues.[19] Nationalist right-wing thought in Europe and racial theories had found the notion of the struggle for survival and survival of the fittest to be congenial in a colonial setting, a vision, they believed, in which virtue and force converged. Al-Afghani put forward the idea that humans are no different to animals, plants, and minerals in this respect: "strength is the manifestation of life and survival and weakness is the domain of dissipation and ruin . . . power appears and becomes concrete only by weakening and subduing others."[20]

Muhammad 'Abduh interpreted Qur'anic verse 2:251 ("Had God not driven back the people, some by the means of others, the earth would surely

14 Jamāl al-Dīn al-Afghānī, *Al-a'māl al-kāmila*, 312.

15 Ibid., 141–147, 181–183 and Marrāsh, *Shahādat al-ṭabī'a*, 3.

16 On the thought and activity of Namik Kemal see Berkes, *The Development of Secularism in Turkey*, 209–222 and Mardin, *The Genesis of Young Ottoman Thought*, ch. 10.

17 Berkes, *The Development of Secularism in Turkey*, 222.

18 Parla, *Social and Political Thought of Ziya Gökalp*, 29, 42, 46.

19 See H. L. Kay, *The Social Meaning of Modern Biology: From Social Darwinism to Sociobiology* (New Haven: Yale University Press, 1986); and M. Hawkins, *Social Darwinism in European and American Thought, 1860–1945* (Cambridge: Cambridge University Press, 1997).

20 al-Afghānī, *Al-a'māl al-kāmila*, 443–444.

have corrupted") by saying that this statement "is one of the general laws which scholars today call the struggle for survival, claiming that war is as natural to humans as it is a consequence of the general struggle for existence. Some of those who engage parasitically and dilettantishly in the study of social laws believe the struggle for survival, which they say is a general law, is due to the influence of the materialists in the present age, and that it is sheer injustice and oppression . . . contrary to the guidance of religion. Had those who say such things known the meaning of human life or known themselves they would not say what they said." As for natural selection and "the survival of the fittest" these are "consequent upon what preceded. Almighty God says that the human instinct for fending off each other and urging one another towards what is right and in the general interest, is the safeguard against corruption on earth, that is to say this human tendency is the reason for the survival of that which is right and salutary."[21]

The reclamation by Islamic Reformism of what was known as social Darwinism was conditioned by social Darwinist concepts, even if in Islamic Reformist discourse this took the form of commentary on Qur'anic verses. These verses were only occasions to link a novel, European intellectual resource of efficacious authority with the symbolic authority of Islam represented by the Qur'an. The discourse of reformism originated from and dwelt in two separate worlds and was integrated into two types of worldly condition: the one intellectual, the other socio-political. The discourse of politics was in fact objectively secular, in which religion was only the assembly of moral virtues. Its social description was of a type proposed in al-Afghani and 'Abduh's journal *al-'Urwa al-Wuthqā* (of which eighteen issues were published in Paris from March to October 1884), the title reclaiming the symbolic resonance of the Qur'an where occurs: "Virtues are the anchor of unity in the body social and the bond of unity between individuals. Virtues incline both individuals towards those like them so that the mass of the people are as one single individual, acting with a single will . . . one can say that the virtues in the human world are like the force of gravitation in the macrocosm, [regulating the planetary system] . . . by which God's wisdom is realised. So also are the virtues in human society by which God preserves individual existence until the appointed moment and confirms the survival of the species until God's

21 *Al-Manār* 64/7 (February 1906): 929–930. This text is not in 'Abduh's *Al-a'māl al-kāmila*, vol. 4, 720, where it should be.

purposes are fulfilled."[22] The intervention of divine providence is intrusive in this argument, agglutinated onto the nature of society, at best a remote final cause, but more importantly a rhetorical association. This is an association in which dogma is external to the secular socio-economic argument being made, but draws it to its orbit affectively. The notion of divine intervention does not differ from the role of the Deity as an external agent of conservation of the order of the universe as previously discussed in the context of scientific evolution in Europe. Social unity as discussed in *al-'Urwa al-Wuthqā* or in the work of the Syrian secularist Farah Antoun (1874–1922)[23] or Abd al-Hamid al-Zahrawi[24] is a political unity, a unity of force, abstract capacity for action arising from the convergence and interaction between moral resources and aggressive impulses. In this convergence is enacted a unity that is capable of entering into relations with similarly constituted external entities, units of potency and action. Here lies the secret of the attraction of Ibn Khaldun for al-Afghani, 'Abduh and al-Zahrawi, among very many others of their contemporaries. Personal virtues reinforced the sense of solidarity and, together with collective virtues, constituted religious or racial cohesion, and formed the basis for the survival of nations. For this reason, jihad was unlike war; it was a restoration of creation to a state of righteousness – clearly jihad is here used to lend a sense of distinctiveness, tapping into Muslim religious vocabulary. Turkish and Arab nationalists shared this moralistic and altruistic view of national action.[25]

Thus, nations are constituted by glory, by virtues, and by the bond of virtue uniting all their members, a bond represented by confessional membership. The religion that the nation adopts will be the element that unites it and the basic elements for its existence as an effective force. Were this structure to collapse "the nature of social existence requires that a foreign power will prevail over this nation and subdue it".[26] The predatory, biological model does not stop at this limit: "every nation which does not deploy its strength to overwhelm other nations and, through victory, to sap away from them that which

22 Jamāl al-Dīn al-Afghānī and Muḥammad 'Abduh, *Al-'urwa al-wuthqā wa al-thawra al-taḥrīriyya al-kubrā* (Cairo: Dār al-'Arab, 1958), 59–60.

23 Faraḥ Anṭūn, "Ṣawt min ba'īd", *al-Jāmi'a* 5/5 (1906), 186.

24 Jad'ān, *Usus al-taqaddum*, 212, 217.

25 Parla, *The Social and Political Thought of Ziya Gökalp*, 31.

26 al-Afghānī and 'Abduh, *Al-'Urwa al-wuthqā*, 63.

causes them to be nourished and be fortified, will one day be carved away and diminish, its traces effaced from the face of the earth. Mastery over nations is like nourishment in the life of a person . . . it is not possible for a nation to retain its substance and despoil those around it in order to extract from them the substance it needs for its growth unless this nation is united in obtaining what its constitution needs."[27] Religion is only one element in this savage world, which is modelled on both the animal kingdom and imperial relations, not so much a religion as socio-political bond. Religious partisanship (what might today be called identity) is analogous to racial partisanship, albeit purer and more beneficial. This partisanship is "a universal spirit, dwelling in the constitution and form of the nation, and in the spirits of the nation's individuals, in their senses and sentiments". Were this spirit to perish, partisanship will be enfeebled and "the nation's form [used in the Aristotelian sense] will be terminated even if its individuals did survive".[28] Solidarity involves "a longing for . . . perfection" in the context of a biological model for the nation, the various categories of its population coming together according to a biologistic model in which they resemble different parts and organs of the body, held together by a vital force that gives it form.[29]

There is little religion in this para-nationalist model. Its conceptual terms of reference belong to the nineteenth century, and are shared by very many, including the positivist and Darwinist Shibli Shumayyil in his image of society.[30] It was not a tradition-driven view of the nation, despite the plenty of terms originating in medieval Arabic natural philosophy, such as *hayūla* (*hyle*), *mizāj* (temper), *'aql* (intelligence), and so on. Yet these terms cannot be interpreted in terms of their original context. They are rather nativist gestures, and betray a formation received by al-Afghani in Iranian seminaries. The resulting organismic and vitalist discourse on society and polity was not as widespread in Qom or Baghdad in the tenth century as it was in Istanbul, Paris, Cairo, and Beirut of the nineteenth

27 Ibid., 74.
28 Ibid., 40–41, 45.
29 'Alī Shalash (ed.), *Jamāl al-Dīn al-Afghānī, silsilat al-a'māl al-majhūla* (London: Riyad al-Rayyis li'l-kutub wa al-nashr, 1987), 78 and compare al-Afghānī and 'Abduh, *Al-'urwa al-wuthqā*, 33 and elsewhere.
30 Waḍḍāḥ Sharāra, *Ḥawl ba'ḍ mushkilāt al-dawla fī al-thaqāfa wa al-mujtama' al-'arabiyyayn* (Beirut: dār al-Ḥadātha, 1980), 62.

century; any interpretation must read this discourse in the places where it was received. This Romantic discourse on society and polity finds its bearings in the ideologies of the European counter-revolutionary Right. They formed the implicit conceptual ballast of the utilitarian understanding of Islam conveyed by Muslim reformists in the context of the *nahḍa*. With an intellectual like Yusuf 'Ali, for instance, this discourse was merged with evolutionism to yield the idea that the more predatory the nation, the more condign and worthier, and the more advanced it was.[31]

In Arab lands it is not generally realised how widespread the concepts and motifs of right-wing European thought were in Arabic political thinking.[32] It is not surprising, since it has generally been left-wing Arabs who usually indicated their European intellectual sources. The right of the political spectrum, notably those of the religious Right today, have generally been either unaware of the strong connection between their thought and European thought, or in denial. There are certainly Romantic and nationalist echoes in the thought of Namik Kemal, related to the writings of Herder in the late eighteenth century.[33] It is equally certain that al-Afghani, building on a counter-revolutionary and indeed reactionary temper following the Paris Commune, attributed what he saw as the corruption of the French, and the iniquities of the Paris Commune, to Voltaire, Rousseau, and the French Revolution, in the same way that he attributed what he considered to be the corruption of the Ottomans to the *Tanzimat* reformers.[34] Overall, nationalist and racist right-wing ideologies in Europe sought to use assumptions of historical continuity and of the stable and homogeneous natures of nations as premises on which to construct conceptions of politics and society. This presumed stability and continuity accounted, in their eyes, for specific incommensurabilities between nations, on a model of biological speciation, dividing a national interior that was an integral subjectivity, and a pure alterity, as we shall see in the discourse on authenticity in Chapter 6 below. This approach was, in its historical circumstances, polemical above all. It regarded politics as essentially an attempt at "conservation of an entity

31 Jad'ān, *Usus al-taqaddum*, 394–395. On European ideologies, in this context, see Aziz al-Azmeh, "Culturalism", in *Islams and Modernities*, 3rd edn (London: Verso, 2009), 17–39.

32 Ra'īf Khūrī was an exception. See Khūrī, *Al-fikr al-'arabī al-ḥadīth*, 143–151.

33 Mardin, *The Genesis of Young Ottoman Thought*, 335–336.

34 al-Afghānī, *Al-a'māl al-kāmila*, 161–163.

against alien intrusion".[35] The impulse and point of reference of these views was conjunctural and political in the main, unrelated to religion, conjoining political concepts of the age of European empires and anti-imperialist resistance. These vitalist concepts were adopted with their sense reversed, in that the original "other", the Eastern colonised nations, became an assertive subject. The link of the East with modern universal history thus became one of separation and rejection as absolute and universal as the universality of the West. The relation of the nation's self to history became one of imagined recovery, resumption, and connection.

These rhetorical solutions generated an unrestrained drift. The journal *al-'Urwa al-Wuthqā* attacked the new culture of the press and education, seeing it only as imitation of foreigners and the elimination of "the reclusion and antipathy by means of which people protect their rights and safeguard their independence". Modern education was repudiated not because of the ideas it conveyed but because it did not arise from the nation, did not accord with its nature, and was rooted elsewhere.[36] Lineage and the integrity of descent – what later came to be designated as "authenticity" – became at once the measure of good order, rectitude, and guidance to the repositories of capacity. The peoples of the East were ill-prepared to consider the consequences of their actions, overwhelmed by fear, envy, oppression, treachery, the enslavement of the weak, and megalomania, all of which led to them losing their countries.[37]

If the Muslim in his present condition became "the unbeliever's argument for his unbelief", to use the expression in a letter by 'Abduh during his sojourn in Paris, the only solution was to return to the reserves of strength and to draw guidance from the past and revive what had existed previously.[38]

> What is recognised by the clear understanding and what is attested by the history of human society until the present moment is that great nations, if afflicted by weakness because of division of opinion, or of inattention to the consequences of unfortunate actions, or

35 'Abduh, *Al-a'māl al-kāmila*, 580.
36 al-Afghānī and 'Abduh, *Al-'urwa al-wuthqā*, 17–19.
37 al-Afghānī, *Al-a'māl al-kāmila*, 94, 98–99.
38 'Abduh, *Al-a'māl al-kāmila*, vol. 1, 597.

> of recourse to repose by nature impermanent, or of temptation by passing delight, and who then are overcome by a foreign power which roused such nations from their slumber, and if it were to be challenged by an aggressive external power, it will be first disturbed and somewhat alerted. When the afflictions of events persist, and when the distress of such afflictions is felt painfully, [the nation] hearkens forth to retain what has so far remained, and to retrieve what has been lost . . . It is then that the nation senses her true strength, which consists of nothing but the convergence and coalescence of her members. Divine inspiration, instinctual predisposition and religious instruction guides it to perceive that, beyond this union, it needs nothing.[39]

This discourse emerging during the *nahḍa* attributes the capacity for resistance to the national self; not to the earthly factors indicated as the causes of weakness, but to "divine inspiration, instinctual predisposition and religious instruction". The diagnosis of foreign occupation was realistic while guidance towards the future was poetical. Revival was only achievable by a rhetoric of advertence to the recollection of past glories, according to the words of al-Afghani[40] – and indeed to his deeds also: it seems that his instruction to disciples in Cairo was based, not on intellectual expositions, but at drawing out "a vital force permeating the soul and moving it to action".[41]

In this type of discourse, Islam figures as a singular indication of sites of resistance, and the primary agent in these rhetorical solutions that were to remain marginal for long. The problems of development and historical advancement, of economies and cultures and political systems, were thus reduced to the break of a continuous self with its past and the exposure of its present to external intrusions. Education and acculturation are repudiated, as the reformist yearns for origins and roots, and rejects innovation.[42] Reformers of this type present their disciples and the wider public a model of past strength – the classical Arab-Muslim state – and postulates its comparability to the modern nation state. They therefore skip over history, and

39 al-Afghānī and 'Abduh, *Al-'urwa al-wuthqā*, 2.

40 Shalash (ed.), *Jamāl al-Dīn al-Afghānī*, 81.

41 'Abbās Maḥmūd al-'Aqqād, *Muḥammad 'Abduh*. Silsilat a'lām al-'arab 1 (Cairo: al-Mu'assasa al-Miṣriyya al-'Āmma li'l-Ta'līf wa al-Tarjama wa al-Nashr, n.d.), 125.

42 al-Afghānī and 'Abduh, *Al-'urwa al-wuthqā*, 15–17, 20.

see in decline no more than an intrusive and transient factor that had no access to the essence of the Islamic self. Decline was the result of innovations introduced into Islam by atheists and foreigners. Degeneration was seen to be represented by Sufis.[43] History is then conceived in contrasts: interior and exterior, essence and accident, authentic and heteronomous, modelled on the image of Western nations although the authentic interior and true dimension of the national character was constituted by Islam "as it was in its beginnings". Political activity in this context became a call to maintain this firm bond, and the task of the reformer was to awaken inner energies and thus overcome history and its forces. "The germ of religion is, through inheritance, embedded in the spirit . . . and the person seeking to revive the nation needs only a single breath whose inspiration animates all spirits."[44]

This utilitarian understanding of Islam needed translation into a context or contexts that go beyond the simple repetition of the name as a slogan. The Islamist figures of the *nahḍa* had a political, social, and intellectual agenda, and these raised challenges and necessitated integration into real contexts that required answers to practical questions. It was not enough to hope that the Qur'an be the ruler,[45] or for the association of al-'Urwa al-Wuthqā to describe its long-term aim as the "return of Islamic government and the guidance of religion to the purity, justice and integrity of Islam in its first age".[46] It was not enough for al-Afghani to call on the example of Luther to affirm that every historical change needs to be enacted by a religious movement.[47] It was necessary for the *nahḍa* reformers to link the name of Islam to a body politic. Thus, 'Abduh described the association of al-'Urwa al-Wuthqā[48] as a "confessional association", although in the newspaper of the association it was stated that its defence of the Muslims and the occasional special pleading for their sake was not intended to "separate them from those of their neighbours in their own countries who are in accord with them on the interests of their countries and who have for generations shared its

43 'Abduh, *Al-a'māl al-kāmila*, 210–211 and al-Afghānī and 'Abduh, *Al-'urwa al-wuthqā*, 49 and elsewhere.

44 Al-Afghānī and 'Abduh, *Al-'urwa al-wuthqā*, 20–21.

45 Ibid., 72.

46 Riḍā, *Tarīkh al-ustādh al-imām al-shaykh Muḥammad 'Abduh*, vol. 1, 283.

47 Ibid., 72–73.

48 'Abduh, *Al-a'māl al-kāmila*, vol. 1, 586.

benefits. This is not part of our purpose and we are not so inclined and our religion and shari'a do not allow it. The aim is to warn Easterners in general and Muslims in particular against the dominance of foreigners over them and against corruption in their countries. We are concerned with Muslims because they are the dominant element in the regions which have been victims of foreigner treachery, regions whose populations have been humiliated and their resources plundered."[49]

Thus, Islam was construed as a fundamental nature for the society desired by these reformers. This was a comprehensive construct, faithfully reflecting the total image of conquering Europe. And why should this not be so, the reformers asked: after all, France calls herself the protector of the Catholics in the East while the Queen of England entitles herself the Queen of the Protestants. The Tsar of Russia is both monarch and head of the Church. Why should the sultan Abdülhamid not be allowed to take the title of Caliph of the Muslims or Commander of the Believers?[50]

This particular orientation leads directly back to the impasse of the *Tanzimat*, discussed in the previous chapter. This was connected with the way that Western policies contributed to the etiolation of the *Tanzimat*'s tendential orientation to the creation of abstract citizens and secular institutions. Islamic reformism appeared on the scene, first in Istanbul, and then in Paris and finally in Cairo and elsewhere as the features of this impasse were becoming clear, and the limits to the reformist capacity of the Ottoman state became manifest, in both subjective and objective terms, during the reign of Abdülhamid and with the abortion of the constitutional period.

In subjective terms, the deficits were due to the exclusivist authoritarian state represented by senior officials and ministers, who appropriated official positions for themselves and in effect erected a glass ceiling beyond which competent and cultured officials in the departments of state were not able to progress and enter the ranks of what was emerging as a body politic at the top of the social and administrative scale. A new hierarchy emerged, following the newer ranking order of the modernising state, reinforced by visible cultural distinctions emerging from wealth accruing from the prospects and opportunities of high office. These included manners of dress, bearing, etiquette, table manners, newer tastes

49 Al-Afghānī and ʿAbduh, *Al-ʿurwa al-wuthqā*, 272.
50 ʿAbduh, *Al-aʿmāl al-kāmila*, vol. 3, 234.

in cultural products such as novels, newspapers, and theatre as they emerged, house furnishings and much else. The Young Ottomans were generally drawn from groups of the state-generated intelligentsia – Bildungsbürgertum – whose social and institutional ascent and upward mobility had been arrested, and who had adopted an attitude of a puritanical moralism, including a moralised religion, as an emblem of their distinctiveness and a leitmotif of their programme.[51]

The Young Ottomans did not criticise the state's cultural project to which they owed much, including their education, but only some of its political consequences. Most did not take this criticism to the extent that is found in al-'Urwa al-Wuthqā, although the impulse was there implicitly. Young Ottoman criticism of the *Tanzimat* was nevertheless not especially clement. Like Islamist reformist Arabs, the Young Ottomans were the product of the civic culture of the state, although the Turkish reformers of that generation adopted this orientation in a more decisive fashion than did their Arab counterparts, whose position was characterised by an ideological instability.

This instability led to ideological oscillation and, ultimately, when practical consequences were in view and not just theoretical horizons, to the bifurcation of Islamic Arab reformism into two types of intellectual and politician. First, there was what Rida called 'Abduh's secular party, led by Sa'd Zaghloul. It will be shown later how this led to the integration of reformist discourse – in its social and intellectual dimensions, not the political – into significant parts of contemporary Arab conservative thought. Second, there was the religious party that produced the *salafiyya* of Rashid Riḍā and his followers, ultimately the Society of the Muslim Brothers.[52] The first party emerged in salons held in the residence of the patrician scholar Ahmad Taymur (1871–1930), and subsequently in that of Muhammad 'Abduh himself. Both fora were attended by Sa'd Zaghloul, Qasim Amin, the Damascene Rafiq al-Azm (1865–1925) and Rashid Rida, with guests such as the major Damascene erudite and politician Muhammad Kurd Ali (1876–1953), founder of the Arab Academy in Damascus.[53] The second party emerged around Rashid Rida in Egypt and in Syria from a milieu of religious scholars marginalised in professional and intellectual terms. These sought to carve out renewed positions of authority

51 Mardin, *The Genesis of Young Ottoman Thought*, 108–117, 124–131.

52 Riḍā, *Tarīkh al-ustādh al-imām al-shaykh Muḥammad 'Abduh*, vol. 1, 2.

53 Ibid., vol. 1, 774–775.

by practically grafting current political values upon Islam. They attempted to widen the scope of religious education to correspond to the requirements of the modern period, in competition with the secular and foreign schools.[54] One should note that Rashid Rida and others considered the reformers of the Syrian provinces such as Shaykh Tahir al-Jaza'iri and Jamal al-Din al-Qasimi to be conservative.[55]

In seeking to make Islam an emblem of resistance to the West, to the authoritarianism of high government officials as well as the uneven effects of the *Tanzimat*, Islamic reformism was an ideology of siege: its only option was to approve the new order, but without accepting its political results and repudiating its social consequences that led to the marginalisation of the social milieu where Islamic reformism was incubated. This was also the case of al-Afghani himself, who was expelled from Istanbul in 1871 when he was a partisan of educational reform, and was readily sacrificed to the attack by the *şeyhülislam* against that party.[56] The situation was one in which it was easy to equate the *Tanzimat* with concessions granted to foreigners and Christians generally, including the trading bourgeoisie of Istanbul and Izmir, composed primarily of Greeks and Armenians.

In Cairo and Alexandria a similar situation prevailed: unsurprisingly the cultural and political tendency with a nationalist character deployed religion as an indicator of Ottoman nationality. The prominent Young Ottoman Namik Kemal, "the leader of the new renaissance", as he was called by Rida,[57] based his

54 al-Kawtharānī, *Al-sulṭa wa al-mujtama' wa al-'amal al-siyāsī*, 145–149 and David Commins, "Religious reformers and Arabists in Damascus, 1885–1914", *International Journal of Middle East Studies* 18 (1986), 408.

55 al-Qāsimī, *Jamāl al-Dīn al-qāsimī wa 'aṣruhu*, 72. See Commins, *Islamic Reform*.

56 Nikki R. Keddie, *Sayid Jamāl al-Dīn "al-Afghānī": A Political Biography* (Berkeley and Los Angeles: University of California Press, 1972), 62–80. This book contains the biography of al-Afghani based on Persian, Turkish, and European documents, and revises the traditional narrative still generally accepted in the Arab world due to political and narrative fancies that were based on the narrative of al-Afghani himself, seconded by his disciple 'Abduh and also by Jurjī Zaydān. It seems odd that the traditional narrative survives despite its incoherence and the existence of many other sources, and even existing knowledge of the basic facts about al-Afghani. His contemporary and competitor for favour in Istanbul, Abu'l-Huda al-Sayyadi, knew, for example, that he was not Afghan but an Iranian. See Riḍā, *Tarīkh al-ustādh al-imām shaykh Muḥammad 'Abduh*, vol. 1, 90. When al-Afghani stayed in Afghanistan in 1866–1867, he described himself as being from Istanbul, before he ever visited Istanbul. For critical comment on the received, related biography of 'Abduh, coloured by Riḍā's self-serving framing, see al-Ḥaddād, *Ḥafriyyāt ta'wīliyya fī al-khiṭāb al-iṣlāḥī al-'arabī*, 193–202.

57 Riḍā, *Mukhtārāt siyāsiyya min majallat Al-Manār*, 165.

criticism of the secular nature of the *Tanzimat* on the distinction between the economic and technical-communication bases of progress (technology, education, and the press), and its cultural, intellectual, and social dimensions.[58] The Young Ottomans established and propagated the illusion, which became widely accepted in the Arab world, that development, progress, and independence can be made possible by merely embracing technical proficiency, without correlative transformations in the organisation of state and culture that are, after all, the vehicle that makes technical proficiency durable. They also claimed that a modern cognitive regime can be adopted without the creation of a new cultural framework for its reception and assimilation. Scientific disciplines and technology were seen as "mechanical skills which develop as civilisation develops. They have no religion or homeland and follow the unfolding of civilisation and historical change. As for the morals and spiritual faculties by which the life of nations is renewed, these vary as nations vary in their constitutions and their national and confessional personalities. These spiritual capacities maintain national temperaments and races' inherited characteristics."[59] Al-Afghani urged the Ottomans to imitate Japan, as he saw it, by adopting technology and only those institutions adjudged appropriate, and to reject the rest, conforming to the general interest and benefits accruing from the spread of technical skills, science, and objective knowledge.[60]

In addition, the Young Ottomans, perhaps unwittingly but objectively, laid the ideological bases for Hamidian despotism that stood, as noted earlier, on two main pillars: technology and modern education on the one hand, and reliance on religion and its associated solidarities on the other. Islamic Reformism accompanied the political call addressed by the sultan to Muslim leaders through the Reformist ideology of Islamic internationalism, and through the political activity of al-Afghani on the other, especially during the period of his second residence in Istanbul (1892–1897) and the period immediately preceding this. Arab Islamic Reformism accompanied the Hamidian cultural project with its attack on Westernisation and its support for Ottoman education.[61] The

58 For criticism of the *Tanzimat* by Nāmik Kemāl and the Young Ottomans see Mardin, *The Genesis of Young Ottoman Thought*, 163–164, and Berkes, *The Development of Secularism in Turkey*, 216–218.

59 Riḍā, *Riḥlāt al-imām Muḥammad Rashīd Riḍā*, 257.

60 al-Afghānī, *Al-a'māl al-kāmila*, 199–201, 228, and Shalash (ed.), *Jamāl al-Dīn al-Afghānī, silsilat al-a'māl al-majhūla*, 109.

61 See 'Abduh, *Al-a'māl al-kāmila*, vol. 3, 73 and Riḍā, *Tarīkh al-ustādh al-imām al-shaykh Muḥammad 'Abduh*, vol. 1, 45 and elsewhere.

organised base of support for sultan Abdülhamid was constituted by reactionary religious elements to the exclusion of reformists, whose support was limited and indirect. Religious reactionaries had sought to oppose Islamic reformers in Egypt, Ottoman Syria, and Istanbul.[62]

As suggested, Arab-Islamic reformism was separated into two moments that converged only in the encounter between al-Afghani and ʿAbduh in the association of al-ʿUrwa al-Wuthqā. Their alliance was somewhat adventitious. The first (political) moment arose from a particular historical conjuncture and stabilised in its natural historical environment, supporting the Pan-Islamic policy of the caliphate as followed by the sultan Abdülhamid; what for ʿAbduh was a sentiment was for Afghani a strategy. Arab-Islamic reformism was thus made open to transfiguration from its basic para-nationalist character into a call for rule by a religious authority. The properly nationalist dimension, obscured by developments, crystallised in Turkey first, and later, during and after the First World War, in Arab regions. It took the form of regional as well as extra-territorial, pan-Arab nationalism. These two moments only converged again in the last decades of the twentieth century, when Islamist politics came to acquire a para-nationalist dimension, energised by sheer xenophobia, in its bid for political and ideological expansion. The second moment, educational and intellectual, was based on a clear aversion to direct political involvement; ʿAbduh reproached al-Afghani for preferring politics over education and for precipitate action.[63] He believed that the service of Islam was best carried out through education that "unites the forces of the nation"[64] – a gesture towards the cultural hegemonic and homogenising tendencies of the modern type of state.

Politics, or perhaps intellectual differences, prevented ʿAbduh from eulogising his former mentor when al-Afghani died in 1897, as he refrained from writing an obituary requested by *al-Muqtaṭaf*.[65] Perhaps the more strongly indicative element in separating the two moments of Islamic reformism and integrating only one of them into the politics of Abdülhamid was the sultan's wish, as recounted by Rashid Rida, that no obituaries for al-Afghani be published in the Ottoman press. The Ottoman authorities confiscated Egyptian

62 al-Qāsimī, *Jamāl al-Dīn al-Qāsimī wa ʿaṣruhu*, 205–211.
63 ʿAbduh, *Al-aʿmāl al-kāmila*, vol. 1, 682.
64 Riḍā, *Tarīkh al-ustādh al-imām shaykh Muḥammad ʿAbduh*, vol. 1, 425.
65 ʿAbduh, *Al-aʿmāl al-kāmila*, vol. 2, 353 (note) and 344 (note).

newspapers and journals that published such obituaries.[66] While al-Afghani referred to Luther more often than 'Abduh and tried to emulate him more closely, it was to 'Abduh that a Lutheran-style reform was attributed.[67] Both seem to have had only a broad-strokes acquaintance with the Reformation.

Certainly in 'Abduh's educational and intellectual reform there were areas of close affinity to Martin Luther,[68] not least of which was that 'Abduh, like Luther (to use Karl Marx's expression relative to Martin Luther), broke the boundaries of religion by erecting the boundaries of faith, and broke faith in religious authority by returning authority to faith.[69] Questions pertaining to religion specifically apart, 'Abduh's programme was a continuation of the utilitarian current of thought that he and al-Afghani adopted from the Enlightenment's positivist outflows.[70] This assumed a correspondence between faith and this broad, universal modernist current of thought and of social organisation. The fundamentals of Islam were devotional-doctrinal on the one hand, including the interests of the afterlife and the protection of religion, and, on the other worldly principles, reflecting 'Abduh's time: access to belief through reason, the primacy of reason over the literal sense of shar'ist material when the two appear to be contradictory, precluding accusations of unbelief, and a consideration of God's ways expressed as the laws of nature and society.[71] 'Abduh approached ideas of natural religion when he recognised in *Risālat al-tawḥīd* that reason had primacy over authoritative dispensation and instruction (*tablīgh*), in the basic religious doctrines: "it is recognised among all Muslims, save those whose reason and religion cannot be trusted, that there are elements of religion in which one cannot believe save through reason, such as knowledge of God's existence, His power to send Prophets, His knowledge of what he communicates to them through inspiration, and His desire that they be elected for His mission, and the consequences of this, such as understanding the meaning of

66 Riḍā, *Tarīkh al-ustādh al-imām al-shaykh Muḥammad 'Abduh*, vol. 1, 91.

67 On the reception of 'Abduh, see Muḥammad al-Ḥaddād, *Muḥammad 'Abduh. Qirā'a jadīda fī khiṭāb al-iṣlāḥ ad-dīnī* (Beirut: Dār al-Ṭalī'a, 2002), 18, 49–66, among many other references.

68 On Muslim Reform and Protestantism, see al-'Aẓma, "Al-iṣlāḥiyūn al-nahḍawīyūn wa fikrat al-iṣlāḥ fī al-majāl ad-dīnī", and the references made there.

69 Karl Marx, in Karl Marx and Friedrich Engels, *Collected Works*, 50 vols (London: Lawrence and Wishart, 1975), vol. 3, 182.

70 See Abdallah Laroui, *Islam et modernité* (Paris: La Découverte, 1986), ch. 6.

71 'Abduh, *Al-a'māl al-kāmila*, vol. 3, 282–311, vol. 2, 318–319.

the [Muhammadan] message and believing in the message itself."[72] 'Abduh was careful to state that belief in God through the words of the Prophet and scripture alone is unsound.

He established bases for reaffirming the Mu'tazilite view that divine will and power corresponded only to that which is possible,[73] making divine actions conform to what nature permits without calling himself a Mu'tazalite, doubtless because this name had echoes liable to provoke further opposition from religious conservatives. Reason became the point of reference in matters of religion no less than in the affairs of the world – an idea that gained wide purchase. One Tunisian reformer, Salem Bouhajib, in a speech delivered at the opening of the Khaldouniyya association in 1896, considered that science was the very reason why God appointed Adam and his descendants as His Caliphs, and that the reason why Muslims were backward was because they lagged behind in universal sciences.[74]

Muslim reformism postulated a correspondence between authentic Islam and reason, and another between modernity and reason – "reason" being used emblematically, vaguely, and with no determinate content. This a priori notion of reason, unexamined and untested,[75] made possible a rhetorical identification of Islam and modernity in general, postulating Islam as the fount of a temperate civilization indistinguishable – except in terms of loftiness – from modern secular civilization that constituted the practical paradigm. In the reasoning of Muslim modernism, civilization was construed after the image of secular evolutionism.[76] However the requirements of political and class separation between social constituencies that accompanied the beginnings of the reformist discourse, as noted earlier, made for yet another of the paradoxes of Muslim modernism. The society that was practically and objectively taken for the paradigm was a society that was imperfect in principle. Conversely, society characterised as "Islamic" was in practical terms deficient, but it was in principle a perfect society, with perfect origins – the Qur'an and early Islam – that needed to be recovered. Islam came to differ from other religions, especially Christianity, in that Islam was an ally of the sciences. Christianity

---

72 Ibid., vol. 3, 357, 278–280 and compare with al-Afghānī, *Al-a'māl al-kāmila*, 173–179.

73 See Riḍā, *Shubuhāt al-naṣārā wa ḥujaj al-islām*, 54–57, 62–67.

74 Ibn 'Āshūr, *Al-ḥaraka al-adabiyya wa al-fikriyya fī Tūnis*, 54.

75 Jad'ān, *Usus al-taqaddum*, 338.

76 Ibid., 387–410.

followed an opposite trajectory, with people distancing themselves from it the closer they came to science.[77]

In this way, Muslim modernist reform restored credibility to Islam as a point of reference, redacted after the experience of the *Tanzimat* in a way that identified Islam – ideally, in its beginnings – and present conditions of modernity. As noted earlier, Muslim reform bifurcated. One of its parties pursued this reinterpretative redaction, the other, more consistently Salafist, embarked upon a retraction and a withdrawal from latitude in crucial domains (including legislation). The utilitarian Islam deriving from the secularising interpretation constituted – effectively, tendentially, without explicit articulation – the import imputed to normative Islam as reconfigured and recast in this process. This Islam symbolised the soundness of a national-denominational identification appropriate to conditions of the late Ottoman Empire as perceived by specific constituencies, and indicated simultaneously the legitimacy of many novelties. This reformism thus emerged as a political moment that persisted as a politico-cultural idea after the political moment itself had lapsed.

The juxtaposition within it of registers of fantasy and of reality that were presumed to be not only in accord but to coincide was to generate a debilitating habitus in many sectors of Arab political thought, ingraining a self-defeating potential within it, quite apart from creating opportunities for religious intervention in politics, first by the religious establishment, later by religious political parties. It was also a transitional intellectual moment seeking to broaden the remit of religious discourse to include the world of the nineteenth and twentieth centuries in a vain attempt to link the modern world and the religion of ages past. Its hallmark was the conflation of the objective and the normative,[78] and the oscillation between them under the same title. As noted earlier, the Islamic Middle Ages saw such a conflation whereby the objective and positive was reduced to the normative and redacted in terms of it. But this was characteristic of the context of an official culture in which religious discourse and its vocabularies were at least in principle presented as normative, in contrast to the far more complex configuration of the public sphere's points of reference, positivistic and religious, which emerged in the *Tanzimat* state, with its

77 Riḍā, *Shubuhāt al-naṣārā*, 16–17.

78 ʿAlī Umlīl, *Al-iṣlāḥiyya al-ʿarabiyya wa al-dawla al-waṭaniyya* (Beirut: Dār al-Tanwīr and Casablanca: al-Markaz al-Thaqāfī al-ʿArabī, 1985), 62.

scientistic, bureaucratic discourse on society and public interest. Nostalgia and sentimentalist longing replaced reality, and the rational guarantees for truth and objectivity were evaded. An old concept of Islam as an innate, natural religion re-emerged with modernism, under a new guise.

Islamic reformism emerged as a programme that aimed to marry the Islam resulting from Reform with normative Islam, but this last remained, in practical terms, undefined, general indications apart, open to whatever specific content the "public interest" and other broad normative categories might find opportune, of practical aptitude, all as defined by the reformist. The question of this content remained at the mercy of circumstances, as every undefined term can take on the meanings that specific actors attribute to it. Unsurprisingly, this undefined term of "Islam" became the object of struggle over its meaning and content. A ubiquitous indicator of this is the constant refrain that a certain action does not reflect real Islam, or that a certain tendency is only a travesty of Islam, and so forth. The first Islamic reformers of the nineteenth century sought to purge Islam of elements that hindered its operational interpretation conforming to the utilitarian orientation required by the present, according to the discretion of the Reformist.

However, the reformists, like Luther and other Protestants, sought deliberately to disencumber scripture from the weight of tradition, be it recent or in the distant past; this is what the reformist call to *ijtihād* entails, and is the original sense of *salafiyya*, understood as a return to the original texts or the conduct of the first epigones, much like the Protestant *ad fontes* and *sola scriptura* slogans of the Reformation. Scripture was thereby liberated from every context, while being made potentially adaptable to every context, given the political will. At the same time, this made possible that the term "Islam" be subject to a comprehensive ideological vision. When the normative was taken for objective reality – even if this reality were located in bygone times – it became possible to effect a convergence between the normative and the positive, and to reduce the former to the latter, or to attempt to force the positive to revert to the normative, even if this did not correspond to the possibilities of history or its direction. Hence the utopia on which political Islam was based, as Chapter 6 below shall argue.

2 Translation and Equivocation

Islamic modernist reformism based its intellectual enterprise and communicative motifs on the supposition that it was possible to establish a correspondence between contemporary secular reality as it understood them, and normative religion that, it was claimed – since it was a natural religion – had anticipated this reality and is now poised to re-appropriate it. Islamic modernism needed to constrain reality and religion, to cut both to a measure enabling them to become mutually translatable. Religion's register is able thereby to accommodate secular material by its transmutation into religious goods and vocabularies, and vice versa. This rhetorical manipulation is structurally constitutive of Muslim modernist discourse in all its enunciative locations, an instance of the "objective Machiavellianism", which characterises the broad sweep of reformist thought in its different fields.[79]

The earlier Muslim reformers did not disclaim their actual sources, especially those of a liberal character. Not all intellectual orientations associated with European ideas arrived by intercultural transfer. But objective conditions certainly existed conducive to thinking in terms of utilitarianism and receptive utilitarianism's European formulation.[80] Rifa'a al-Tahtawi was a pioneering reader of Rousseau, Voltaire, Montesquieu, and Condillac (1780), the cleric who had supplied Locke's sensualism into an elaborate psychology of knowledge.[81] Al-Tahtawi clearly grasped – without denial, or anxiety of influence – European concepts of constitutional government and absolute government.[82] The book *Takhlīṣ al-ibrīz fī talkhīṣ bārīz* (Cairo, 1834) was widely read in Turkey after its translation in 1839.[83]

Namik Kemal had also translated Rousseau, Montesquieu, Bacon, Volney (d. 1820: orientalist, historian, traveller in Syria and Egypt), and Condillac into Turkish.[84] Muhammad 'Abduh enjoined the learning of foreign languages in order to study the content of foreign works.[85] Rashid Rida, before adopting restrictive Salafism, underlined the debt owed by liberal Muslim reformism

79 The expression is that of 'Abd Allāh al-'Arwī, *Al-idiyūlūjiyya al-'arabiyya al-mu'āṣira*, trans. Muḥammad 'Ītānī (Beirut: Dār al-Ḥaqīqa, 1970), 73, who finds that it reflects an attempt to link two different temporalities and the social realities of two distinct historical moments.

80 See Laroui, *Islam et modernité*, 134–147.

81 Rifā'a Rāfi' al-Ṭahṭāwī, *Al-a'māl al-kāmila li Rifā'a Rāfi' al-Ṭahṭāwī*, vol. 2, 190–193.

82 Ibid., 94–95, 102, 201–203.

83 English translation as *An Imam in Paris. Accounts of a Stay in France by an Egyptian Cleric (1826–1831)*, translated by Daniel L. Newman (London: Saqi Books, 2004). See Berkes, *The Development of Secularism in Turkey*, 121, note 46.

84 Zaydān, *Tarājim mashāhīr al-sharq fī al-qarn al tāsi' 'ashar*, vol. 2, 120–121.

85 'Abduh, *Al-a'māl al-kāmila*, vol. 2, 174. Zaydan, *Tarājim mashāhīr al-sharq fī al-qarn al-tāsi' 'ashr*, vol. 2, 215.

to Western political thought, and avowed the borrowing of political ideas and forms of political organisation: this borrowing is not so much a function of prior intent but is rather "the natural outcome" of Western entry into Arab lands.[86] In 1906, he wrote: "O Muslim, do not claim that this form of government [constitutionalism] is a base of our religion, deriving from the Qur'an and the conduct of the Rightly-Guided Caliphs, rather than from association with Europeans and knowledge of the affairs of the West. If it were not for considering the situation of these people, you and your like would not have thought that this was part of Islam, and the first to call for the establishment [of constitutionalism] would have been the *ulama* in Constantinople, Cairo and Marrakesh."[87] He clearly pointed to the simple operational rhetoric of reformist interpretation: avowing the transmission of political culture from elsewhere, then immediately and in the same breath stating that government controlled by law was "clear and obvious in the Qur'an".[88] He thus took the same course pursued by European Protestantism, which adopted a similar transhistorical translation strategy: not to attempt to have religion appropriate the world entirely, but rather to indicate that the world was not free from divine direction.[89]

In this way, the Qur'an came to function as a lexicon of modern meanings. It thus became necessary to divest the Qur'anic text of the protection afforded by its specific historical meanings and indicators, and to adopt anachronism, in effect, as a prime interpretative strategy, to render it open to arbitrary interpretations. Thus also it was necessary to assign to it the limitless flexibility and a semantic generality that is, again in effect and strategically, boundlessly indeterminate. This enabled translation into the register of modernity, a modernity that was Islamic by virtue of its Muslim anticipation in a capacious Qur'an. The Reformist enjoins direct access to scripture that, bereft of history, is open to modernist interpretation. Thus, 'Abduh's injunction: "Persevere in reciting the Qur'an and understanding its commands and prohibitions, as it was recited before the believers and the unbelievers at the time of Revelation. And be wary of the various ways of interpretation, except in order to come

86 Muḥammad Rashīd Riḍā, "Manāfi' al-ūrūbbūyīn wa maḍārruhum fī al-sharq", *al-Manār* 10/3 (1907), 194.

87 Riḍā, *Mukhtārāt siyāsiyya min majallat al-manār*, 97.

88 Ibid, 99.

89 Simon Schama, *The Embarrassment of Riches: An Interpretation of Dutch Culture in the Golden Age* (New York: Alfred Knopf, 1987), 97.

to understand a word whose usage by Arabs had escaped you, or the obscure connection of one word to another."[90] This is of course a double-edged sword: allowing open-ended interpretation, but also authorising explicitly literal interpretations so important to more restrictive Salafism, and unavoidable if one wanted to take the Qur'an for the Qur'an, irrespective of the degree of tokenism involved. With the Qur'an thus made capable of rendering any desired meaning, it becomes possible to subvert reality, as described above by Rida, and to say with 'Abduh: "The longing of some people for consultative government does not result from the imitation of foreigners. It is because consultation is a duty of the *sharī'a* and despotism is forbidden by the *sharī'a. Sharī'a* orders that the ordinances of the Book be followed and that Sunna be adhered to. Tyranny is contrary to the *sharī'a*, because it is is unrestricted by law."[91]

Points of authoritative reference therefore fluctuate, according to context: it is secular and irreligious, political, constitutional, and utilitarian, and is also shar'ist, rendering constitutionalism and restricted government as prescriptions of the shari'a. This authoritativeness of reference to religion was constituted, according to al-Afghani and 'Abduh, by the need to generate political unity, with Islam operating as a utilitarian element in a political struggle.[92] It is also constituted Qur'anically, as in the text of 'Abduh quoted, in turn constitutive of shari'a, in very much the same way as had been done by Khayr ad-Din al-Tunisi, who, as indicated, was regarded as a conservative. Ideas of rule-bound constitutional government therefore appear to have accompanied the *Tanzimat* almost by default, without a deliberate intellectual grounding, except for that which might be provided by religion and its intellectual equipment rhetorically: notions of scripture, of capacity to rule by divine dispensation, and so on. The result was a mutual identification of worldly and shar'ist arguments, in the framework of a universality attributed to those of the shari'a, absorbing the world in its self-referentiality. This occurred without regard to the violent displacement of sense attendant upon a shift from one cognitive, temporal and political domain to another in terms of which the notion of constitutionalism was expressed.[93]

---

90 'Abduh, *Al-a'māl al-kāmila*, vol. 1, 589.

91 Ibid., vol. 1, 355, 351, and Riḍā, *Fatāwā*, 295.

92 See, for example, al-Afghānī and 'Abduh, *Al-'urwa al-wuthqā*, 479 and Khūrī, *Al-fikr al-arabī al-ḥadīth*, 101.

93 'Abd al-Laṭīf, *Al-ta'wīl wa al-mufāraqa: Naḥwa ta'ṣīl falsafī li'l-naẓar al-siyāsi al-'arabī*, 11–12, 15, 18–19, 68–69.

This constitutionalism was in no sense republicanist,[94] but rather a call for a political order, at once monarchical, dynastic, and caliphal, in which rights are guaranteed by a constitution that refers to consultation among those in authority.[95] This was in line with Young Ottoman thinking, in which constitutionalism – *meşrutiyet* – was taken for protection against the arbitrariness of rulers and high officials. The Young Ottomans compared this to government restricted by shariʿa, which came to figure as a metaphor for abidance by law, which became impersonal, severed from patrimonial reliance on the person of the ruler and his will. The Young Ottomans, led by Namik Kemal, had participated in the discussions concerning the preparation of the 1876 Constitution.[96] The positions of Arab Islamic reformers with regard to constitutionalism varied in practice according to their diverse and wide-ranging political positions. In all cases, however, the idea of government restricted by law was conceptualised by referring it to imagined bases in the governments of Muhammad, his immediate successors, and the Qur'an.

Al-Kawakibi, quoting throughout his work the book on tyranny by the Italian dramatist Vittorio Alfieri (1749–1803),[97] agreed with "those who examined the natural history of religions", that political tyranny derived from religious tyranny, and indicated that rulers and deities shared many characteristics, referring to Fatimid caliphs and the "Persian sultans" and others throughout Islamic history.[98] Al-Kawakibi nevertheless excluded from historical enquiry that part of the history of Islam that he and like-minded Islamic reformers saw as a binding authoritative model. This part of history – the Qur'an and the early period of Islam – acquired currency for practical purposes as a golden age of perfection, with the presumption that it was clearly defined and that it could be represented synoptically by a few stereotypical motifs ceaselessly repeated. This age was hallowed, protected from historical enquiry, or even from the recollection of very well-known

94 See al-Afghānī, *Al-aʿmāl al-kāmila li Jamāl al-Dīn al-Afghānī*, 473, 477.

95 Al-Afghānī and ʿAbduh, *Al-ʿurwa al-wuthqā*, 117, and ʿAbd al-Raḥmān al-Kawākibī, *Al-aʿmāl al-kāmila*, ed. Muḥammad ʿAmāra (Beirut: al-Mu'assasa al-ʿArabiyya li'l-Dirāsāt wa al-Nashr, 1975), 147, and Riḍā, *Mukhtārāt siyāsiyya min majallat al-Manār*, 134.

96 Berkes, *The Development of Secularism in Turkey*, 223 and Mardin, *The Genesis of Young Ottoman Thought*, 105, 202.

97 English translation: *On Tyranny*, trans Julius A. Molinaro and Beatrice Corrigan (Toronto: Toronto University Press, 1961).

98 al-Kawākibī, *Al-aʿmāl al-kāmila*, 141–142.

facts: that Muhammad's successors ruled by the sword and warred against one another, that they constituted an oligarchy, and that three of the four immediate caliphs of Muhammad met violent deaths, and that Qur'anic proof-texts can be used to support both despotic and consultative government. The only validating means of a particular modernist interpretation or translation – such as mutually translating *shūrā* into constitutionalism (later, democracy) – is the cultural and political authority of the interpreter who transmits and accredits this interpretation, and who renders it binding, even causes it to appear self-evident, by access to social and other means of enforcement, or eventually by hegemony and persuasion creating a public habitus of acceptance.

In this way history was ensnared, parried away by its construction according to a paradigm rooted in the present day. In its turn, the present day is itself dodged as it is assumed to correspond to this supposed past. Past and present are conjoined as both are taken to betoken the ideological soundness of Islam. Modernist Islamic Reformism undertook the secularisation of Islam, that is, applying the name of Islam to that which is, historically, not remotely Islamic in any respect. Reformism incorporated a world that was politically desired and intellectually hegemonic into the context attributed to Islamic authority. This authority, while remaining nominal, that is, symbolic, continued to be effective as an ideological and historical token capable of interpretations ranging from the modernist to the primitivist, all this pointing to the transitional nature of Islamic Reformist thought between religious and secular culture. This was doubtless clear intellectual progress over what came before it, in, for example, the writings of al-Tahtawi, where vocabularies from liberal political thought are given traditional Islamic content, in accordance with what was current in Ottoman society. An excellent instance was *ḥurrīya*, "freedom", which al-Tahtawi took in the traditional frame of Muslim jurisprudence to mean a legal attribute of free disposition in contrast to the impediments of slavery, and also to imply the licit nature of choice among the mutually certifying and acknowledging schools of Muslim jurisprudence or between doctrinal options within the the Ash'ari or Maturidi schools of theology.[99]

99 al-Ṭahṭāwī, *Al-a'māl al-kāmila li Rifā'a Rāfi' al-Ṭahṭāwī*, vol. 2, 473–474 and compare Ūmlīl, *Al-islāḥiyya al-'arabiyya wa al-dawla al-waṭaniyya*, 116; 'Abd al-Laṭīf, *Al-ta'wīl wa al-mufāraqa*, 37; 'Awaḍ, *Al-mu'āththirāt al-ajnabiyya fī al-adab al-'arabī al-ḥadīth*, al-mabḥath al-thānī, 133–134, 125–126.

Reformist discourse on the reform of Muslim jurisprudence, on its nature, and its relation to the new and changing circumstances was most accommodating of Reformist efforts to derive desired worldly consequences from religious discourse, while formulating this discourse in terms of secular terms of reference. 'Abduh did not consider this matter at all elaborately. His contribution consisted of practical legislative innovation, some of which has been discussed previously, and of broad general observations and maxims, such as his statement that "in the days when Islam was really Islam, *shari'a* was flexible enough for the whole world, but now, it is too narrow even for its own adherents, to the extent that they need to look elsewhere and seek to protect their rights with what is inferior to *shari'a*".[100] There is no doubt, however, that 'Abduh inspired the contributions made by his pupil Rashid Riḏā, before his loyalties shifted to Wahhabism, with major consequences.[101]

It would not have occurred to 'Abduh to link his statement quoted above with the presumption that pure Islam was an exact historical description of bygone societies preceding the secular cognitive changes of the modern age, including reflections on law. He sought to preserve shar'ist points of reference and anchorage for matters that had by then overtaken the shari'a and placed its pertinence in serious question. He was still enough of the classical *'alim* to resist any ideas that the golden age might be revived in any consequential way. He sought to preserve an Islamic character for society while keeping pace with the changes that had overtaken Muslim jurisprudence. The motif of reforming shari'a by eliciting its internal possibilities became a matter of high importance, protecting its symbolic value and normative status from ruin in principle as its anachronism and practical irrelevance to the conditions of modernity were becoming evident.

In this discussion the issue of the laws of nature was decidedly relevant, for it was a crucial acquisition of the modern age that the natural world was self-sufficient, with its particular laws and ways, even though sometimes by various rhetorical contrivances linked to divine providence, proximate or remote. The social world fared likewise. Al-Tahtawi sought to translate the natural workings of legislation into the Mu'tazilite notion of rational approbation

100 'Abduh, *Al-a'māl al-kāmila*, vol. 3, 323.

101 On the rigourist salafication of Reformist Islam after Riḍā and until the present, see Henri Lauzière, *The Making of Salafism. Islamic Reform in the Twentieth Century* (New York: Columbia University Press, 2016).

and disapprobation (*taḥsīn, taqbīḥ*). He applied this notion to the enactment of laws in Europe according to the notion of natural rights that he described as the "universal laws of nature", which al-Tahtawi, at the meta-level, conceived in terms of the Ash'arite proposition that God was the only real actor. While these natural laws in the domain of human society (Muslim jurisprudence would have used the notion of *fiṭra* already encountered) preceded the norms of Muslim jurisprudence, the greater part of the latter did not depart from the natural laws governing human society anyway.[102] Namik Kemal proposed a comparable theory, with a similar attempt to translate in between registers and times and to find equivalences.[103] This approach – congruence between general principles of Muslim jurisprudence and the natural laws governing human society through its variations – became a standard feature of Modernist Islamic Reformism, alongside another, represented first by the Algerian Islamic reformist Ibn Badis in the 1930s. He considered that Muhammad had put in place a law that was "religious, social and natural", foreclosing the necessity for translation across conceptual registers, a viewpoint that has endured until the present day and that, if anything, has been strengthened in recent decades.[104]

Translation across registers required two closely connected operations: first, the sacrifice in principle of the legacy of Muslim jurisprudence, and, second, the claim that this sacrifice was in keeping with the principles of the shari'a. Positive juristic rulings are displaced by the invocation of general principles. These general principles were ascribed to the Principles of Jurisprudence. The first volley of this operation involved severely restricting the scope of binding legal rulings. The stable and enduring part of Muslim positive legislation consisted of devotions and basic dogmatics, excluding, in the words of the younger, still latitudinarian Rida, "worldly rulings entrusted by shari'a to those in authority, so they might be related by analogy to general juristic principles laid down by shari'a. Particulars are unlimited in number and therefore unspecifiable by shari'a, but differ according to custom, time and place."[105] Detailed rulings do not, according to this interpretation, go beyond a small number of fixed sanctions for particular crimes. Beyond this, one

102 Al-Ṭahṭāwi, *Al-a'māl al-kāmila*, vol. 2, 191, 479–481.
103 Berkes, *The Development of Secularism in Turkey*, 210–212.
104 Ibn Bādīs, *Kitāb āthār Ibn Bādīs*, vol. 4, 20.
105 Riḍā, *Fatāwā*, 36.

finds general considerations for the preservation of life, property, and virtues, such as justice, the refinement of character and morals and the interdiction of fraud.[106] The Reformists do not say in what respect these generalities might be termed Islamic, and how they differ from the general rules prevalent in most societies, with their moral and legal bases. It is, however, evident that there was an attempt to link these general principles of right with certain elements from the Principles of Jurisprudence taken for general slogans rather than, as they were in reality, parts of a coherent system of regulations existing in the framework of an Islamic judicial system and Muslim institutions of justice.

The most important of these principles is a general proposition, intended, among other things, to underline elasticity and adaptability, but incompatible with the principle of change. This is that Islamic shari'a will persist until the end of time, and that its persistence and continuing relevance is correlated to the five general categories, at once of law and of human interest, discussed in the discussion of al-Shatibi in Chapter 1 above: the safeguarding and preservation of life, religion, wealth, sanity, and progeny. Rida added other procedural rules that he ascribed to his mentor Muhammad 'Abduh: primary attention to meaning rather than words, necessity overrides prohibition, expediency can be equivalent to necessity, rulings change with time, and specifying laws (in terms of range of applicability) by custom is akin to specifying them by a canonical text.[107]

It will be noted that specific appeal to the five general categories is not methodically connected to specific rulings or to proof-texts, with the exception of the safeguarding of religion. Appearing as the foundation of any legal system, these generalities seem to relate to a vague general concept of natural right. The appropriation of al-Shatibi by Rashid Rida was in this vein. Perhaps more significant still was Rida's appropriation of Najm ad-Din al-Tufi (d. 1276), one of whose important texts he published in his journal *al-Manār* in 1906. This Egyptian Hanbalite legal scholar held that, in legislation, requirements of public interest outweighed the prescriptions of scripture and of consensus in cases of conflict. This gave greater clarity and cogency to what Rida wished to have from al-Shatibi, who saw that all legal rulings needed to conform to "what is customary in such matters", and to

106 Riḍā, *Muḥāwarāt al-muṣliḥ wa al-muqallid*, 35, 57, 59.

107 Riḍā, *Tarīkh al-ustādh al-imām al-shaykh Muḥammad 'Abduh*, vol. 1, 614.

suspend legal obligation if this created unusual difficulties. Every textual source of legislation (Qur'an, Sunna, consensus, and analogy) that is not in concord with custom, he held, cannot be adopted as a legal principle of consequence. On the contrary, legal usage and custom form the basis of the notion of open public interest.[108] This suspension of text and, in practical terms of the shari'a, in favour of non-religious considerations did not only secure the approbation of Rida, but also the approbation of other Islamic Reformists such as al-Qasimi in Damascus and the educationist Abd al-Aziz Jawish (1876–1929) in Egypt, among others.[109]

This broadening of the domain of the world and narrowing of the domain of religion was the substance of the *ijtihād* that the modernist reformists advocated. The call for *ijtihād* was linked to the rejection of tradition, including legal precedent, that is, in shar'ist terms, the imitation of the established schools of Muslim jurisprudence. This was the rejection of Islamic tradition in favour of the foundational texts that were seen as the repository of natural law. This was combined with the call for *talfiq* or syncretic adoption of elements from various legal schools, even defunct ones such as the Zahiriyya literalists, founded in the ninth century CE (both Ibn Hazm and Ibn 'Arabi were Zahiris). This call had been supported by al-Tahtawi and (unsuccessfully, given local conditions) by Khayr ad-Din, as well as by al-Afghani and 'Abduh, Ibn Badis, and Rashid Rida.[110]

It is difficult to establish the relative weight in practice of general statements concerning public interest and its legal justification: legal purposes or the five generalities. Despite the repeated confirmation of the priority of public interest, implying the secular consideration of legal transactions, Rida nevertheless completely recoiled before abrogating or suspending canonical texts, as noted earlier in the case of slavery; he affirmed continually the importance of applying canonical punishments (*ḥudūd*), while none of his writing deals with the question of the respective jurisdictions of religious and positive

108 al-Shāṭibī, *Al-muwāfaqāt fī uṣūl al-aḥkām*, vol. 1, 63–64.

109 al-Qāsimī, *Jamāl al-Dīn al-Qāsimī wa 'aṣruhu*, 233 and Ḥusayn, *Al-ittijāhāt al-waṭaniyya fī al-adab al-mu'āṣir*, vol. 1, 361.

110 al-Ṭahṭāwī, *Al-a'māl al-kāmila li Rifā'a Rāfi' al-Ṭahṭāwī*, vol. 1, 544–555; al-Afghānī, *Al-a'māl al-kāmila*, 199–201, 329-330; Riḍā, *Muḥāwarāt al-muṣliḥ wa al-muqallid*, 135–136; and Merad, *Le Réformisme musulman en Algérie de 1925 à 1940*, 222–228; Berkes, *The Development of Secularism*, 381; and Green, *The Tunisian Ulama, 1873–1915*, 116–117.

law. He held that shari'a is based on the four traditional sources of jurisprudence while positive law is based on deliberative opinion. He further held that positive law had clear limits of applicability, the most important of which is "non-violation of the *ḥudūd* of God, for the ruler may not permit what is prohibited, or prohibit what is permissible". One must act according to the precepts of the shari'a except if thwarted by public interest; yet, he considered, this does not entail rejection or replacement of the shari'a by discretionary judgment or discretionary legal preference *istiḥsān*. Thus, it would be impermissible, for example, to increase the share of inheritors, for instance, those of women, to serve a particular interest or for any other reason.[111]

Thus, Rashid Rida confirmed the modernity of shari'a in the possibility of it being, in principle, suspended due to considerations of public interest, but rejected this in practice. He prevaricated: he saw in the principles of shari'a only confirmation of the requirements of natural law, the norms of society and change, emphasising the role of necessity in the formulation of public interest and the incorporation of such necessities in the framework of the aims of shari'a.[112] At the same time Rida stated that Muslim jurisprudence and its particular rulings could not be outweighed by public interest. He in effect secularised shari'a, but refused to see in this anything but a validation of shari'a, understood in terms of its general purposes. As noted previously, these purposes of legislation are not specific to Muslim jurisprudence, but apply to almost all legal systems. Thus, according to Rida, the world came to enclose religion reconceived according to worldly norms, and religion came to enclose the world that must of necessity run according to religious law. This was the path towards the rejection of modernism within Muslim reform: both the modern world and shari'a, but in terms of the shari'a. Sayyid Qutb was later to reverse the terms of reference and claim that it is contemporary circumstances that need to be brought into conformity to shari'a as constituted textually.

On this basis, the reformist interpretative was channelled into political fundamentalism. Religion is religion and it encompasses the world. Secularism is entirely evaded as it complicates the relation between religion and world and indicates their distinction. The circle was thus squared, the square

111 Riḍā, *Muḥāwarāt al-muṣliḥ wa al-muqallid*, 136–137.

112 Compare the cogent observations of Malcolm H. Kerr, *Islamic Reform: The Political and Legal Theories of Muḥammad 'Abduh and Rashīd Riḍā* (Berkeley and Los Angeles: University of California Press, 1966), 201–207 and Muhammad Zaki Badawi, *The Reformers of Egypt: A Critique of Al-Afghani, Abduh and Ridha* (London: Croon Helm, 1978), 109–111.

became a circle; the Reformist translation was based on the evasion of contradiction, suppression of difference, and the eradication of distinction. A bluff certainly, but a bluff called as political religion hardened. An imaginary connection was made between distinct matters related in complex ways, nevertheless identified with one another only by the words of the reformist interpreter. Such a rhetoric, with its body of incoherent assertions, is assured only by a political institution or a politico-cultural alliance that bars the access of reason to historical reality.

This dodging of history necessary for the Reformist interpretation applies equally to what was transmitted from the past. In exactly the same way that the present is arbitrarily and selectively construed and naturalised into religion, arbitrariness is also exercised from the pragmatic requirements of today in the application of historical judgements, resulting in a type of historical criticism that is pragmatically and tactically driven. Widening the scope of the secular world, as mentioned earlier, by restricting the domain of religion, with or without bluffing, is also related to hadith criticism.

The relentless criticism of hadith by Rida was of this kind. For Rida, action according to a certifiable hadith is obligatory as long as there was no contradiction to public interest. In squaring the circle, he also held that if a hadith were to be in contradiction to public interest, it can only be in contradiction to general legal purpose as sustained by the canon, and it can therefore only be a type of hadith that is only probable rather than certain.[113] Thus hadith are in effect rejected only on grounds of utility, without serious consideration of their historical deficiencies, allowing an open-ended opportunity for mutual polemicising: thus as Rida could accuse his contemporary Jawish of rejecting "true, consensual hadith" if their meaning was disagreeable to him – Rida, who himself recognised that not all hadiths in the authentic (*ṣaḥīḥ*) collection of al-Bukhari were authentic, that criticism to which it was subjected was generally sound.[114]

Among the hadith that Rida disputed on legal grounds – he affirmed others were invalid on rational grounds – was the hadith of *al-gharāniq*, known today as the Satanic Verses (when the Prophet is reported to have mistaken words of satanic suggestion for divine revelation).[115] 'Abduh had previously challenged

113 Riḍā, *Muḥāwarāt al-muṣliḥ wa al-muqallid*, 126.
114 Ibid., 737.
115 Muḥammad, Rashīd Riḍā, "Bab al-intiqād 'alā al-manār", *al-Manār* 28 (1927), 474.

these on the doctrinal ground that they denied the impeccability of the Prophet and his communication from God, without saying that they were contrary to sound reason. Critical scholars, Tabari (839–923) and Ibn Hajar (1371–1449) among them, had accepted this hadith on technical grounds of verification common in hadith.[116] In the same utilitarian spirit, Rida corroborated the view of Ibn Khaldun that eschatological material in hadith was "weak", seeing that it gave rise to the "Babi heresy" of the 1840s (later, Bahaism) and diverted Muslims from military and religious preparation.[117]

A similar approach was adopted in commenting on Qur'anic verses. Protestant proselytising propaganda censured Muhammad, and one text declared that "the Qur'an is full of Muhammad's personal affairs . . . even had the Qur'an been the word of God, as they [Muslims] claim, it would be incongruous for the Creator of the Cosmos and the Maker of Creation to reveal matters which concern none of His creation except Muhammad and his wives." These texts asserted that the Qur'an went into exhaustive detail about the supposed adultery of 'A'isha, the Copt Mariya, and Muhammad's marriage to Zeinab ibn Jahsh after her divorce from Zaid ibn Haritha.[118] 'Abduh made a major effort to counter this polemic,[119] and even sought to include some elements of new critical approaches of biblical scholarship on the Old Testament in order to raise doubts about this text.[120] He was followed by his pupil Rida, who did not refrain from pointing out that the Torah had a history, and that many of its narratives derived from the mythology of the Chaldeans, Assyrians, and other peoples. He did not, however, indicate that he concurred in this with a Protestant polemical text of wide circulation that not only attacked Islam, but also indicated that Chaldean and Egyptian myths were at the origin of the Jewish myth of Ishmael: a figure through whom the Jews supposedly ingratiated themselves with the Arabs, "using them as a means to drive the Byzantines from Jerusalem, or

---

116 'Abduh, *Al-a'māl al-kāmila*, vol. 5, 283–289. On traditions relating to this matter, see Mohammed Shahab Ahmed, *Before Orthodoxy: The Satanic Verses in Early Islam* (Cambridge, MA: Harvard University Press, 2017).

117 Riḍā, *Fatāwā*, 44.

118 Jirjis Sīl [George Sale], "Tadhyīl" [Appendix] in idem, *Maqāla fī al-islām*, trans. Hāshim al-'Arabī (Cairo: al-Maṭba'a al-Inkilīziyya al-Amīrikiyya, 1909), 364–375.

119 Muḥammad 'Abduh and Rashīd Riḍā, *Tafsīr al-fātiḥa* (Cairo: Maṭba'at al-Mawsū'āt, 1319/1901), 100–123.

120 'Abduh, *Al-a'māl al-kāmila*, vol. 5, 22–23 and elsewhere.

to found a kingdom for themselves in Arab lands where they might take refuge".[121] Faris al-Shidyaq (1805–1872) had preceded Rida and 'Abduh by nearly half a century in his work *Mumāḥakāt al-ta'wīl fī munāqaḍāt al-injīl* ("Disputes of interpretation of the contradictions of the Gospel"), basing himself less on nineteenth-century European criticism of sacred texts than on works in Muslim traditions.[122]

In these matters, Islamic Reformists continued to practise a selective zeal, thus imitating their Evangelical critics who, while deploying historical and rational criticism against the Qur'an, exempted the Bible from such criticism. Similarly, Islamic Reformists had exempted Qur'an and Sunna from the rigorous historical criticism they considered it permissible to apply to the Bible and Torah.[123] Muslims and Christians for long continued to consider the content of scripture to be history, even freethinkers such as Salim 'Anhuri (1856–1933), who relied on the Torah for his assertion that Solomon constructed Palmyra.[124]

Not all dealings of Islamic Reformism with fundamental texts were marked by this kind of artifice. There were indications of an incipient, serious historical-critical consideration, directed selectively to certain historical texts to the exclusion of others. One such was the *Kitāb al-Maghāzī* of the historian al-Waqidi (747–822)[125] – an easy target due to the author's reputation among traditionalists and Ibn Khaldun as well, but in historiographic terms an inappropriate target – although the methodological premises of a historical approach, truncated as it was, were only applied with any consistency in the work of the Indian modernist Reformist Sir Sayyid Ahmad Khan (1817–1898).[126] Islamic Reformists had to confront new scientific, natural, and historical knowledge, based completely on secular cognitive authority, and its unequivocal contradiction with Qur'anic statements. They relied on

121 Riḍā, *Shubuhāt al-naṣāra*, 2–14, 15, 33–36 and Sīl, "Tadhyīl", 364–375.

122 al-Ṣulḥ, *Aḥmad Fāris al-Shidyāq*, 76–78, 246, note 87. See al-Bagdadi, "The cultural function of fiction". An uncritical edition of this manuscript was published by Muḥammad Aḥmad 'Amāyirah as *Mumāḥakāt al-ta'wīl fī munāqaḍāt al-injīl*, ed. Muḥammad Aḥmad 'Amāyirah (Amman: Dār Wā'il, 2001).

123 Sīl, "Tadhyīl", passim.

124 'Anḥūrī, *Siḥr hārūt*, 71.

125 'Abduh, *Al-a'māl al-kāmila*, vol. 2, 424–425.

126 Christian Troll, *Sayyid Ahmad Khan: A Reinterpretation of Muslim Theology* (New Delhi: Vikas Publishing House, 1978), ch. 4.

the same strategy employed in interpretation of shari'a, beginning by restricting the domain of what was binding on religious grounds and narrowing the religious sphere, in the face of a modern world in which an independent secular cognitive authority was unrelated to Islam or any other religion. Thus, some of the Prophet's statements, as presented by Rida, became matters of guidance and not of command, expressing a salutary opinion rather than transmitting a divine message directly. Examples of such utterances included Prophetic statements on medicine, agriculture, and other worldly matters.[127] The second step concerned matters that could not be disregarded or tampered with, such as the literal text of the Qur'an, and here a cognitive agnosticism as the safest recourse. According to 'Abduh, following a long tradition, if reason and tradition be at variance, tradition must either be relegated to fideism (*tafwīḍ*), claiming that God only knew, or it must be subject to interpretation, which must adhere to the rules of the Arabic language. In the same breath, 'Abduh would claim that the results of such a disciplined interpretation would necessarily conform to what was established by reason.[128]

In other words, Reformist discourse posited an a priori correspondence between text and scientific truth. The validity of both was to be affirmed in parallel, each in its own sphere and by its own appropriate means, then juxtaposed and declared equivalent. It is this presumption of congruence that squares the circle. An example will help here: the Qur'an asserts the existence of a world of jinn parallel to the human world, creatures fashioned "from smokeless fire". This does not indicate a literal truth, according to Rida, without informing his readers why it should not, saying only that the creation of Adam from dust and foetid mud itself does not, for its part, indicate a literal truth – proferring a judgement of reason without offering a criticism of texts that are manifestly mythological in character. One should refrain from surmising about the supernatural, and Qur'anic verses are to be believed without interpretation, consigning them, according to the venerable fideist position often associated with the Hanbalites, to the knowledge of God alone.[129]

It will be clear to readers that the generalisation of such a procedure of interpretation to the Qur'anic text as a whole will have momentous consequences,

---

127 Riḍā, *Fatāwā*, nos 209, 731–733.

128 'Abduh, *Al-a'māl al-kāmila*, vol. 3, 282.

129 Riḍā, *Fatāwā*, no. 111.

rendering the text a collection of enunciations without ascertainable semantic articulation. Reformist interpretation therefore depends for its cogency and power of persuasion entirely on its ability to exercise cultural and social control over this operation of *tafwīḍ*. Such power to control and choose verses that can and cannot be subject to *tafwīḍ* can only be that of a social and institutional authority over the text, an authority in which are vested the powers of exegesis and interpretation, the production of articulate meaning. The precondition for the exercise of this control is an authority with the power of decision in matters of religious truth and untruth, that is to say the religious ulamaic institution or Muslim Church, or some other emergent authority, whenever it has the means of self-assertion and of determining truth in a socio-politically – rather than cognitively – binding way.

What applies to verses pointing to the existence of intangible preternatural beings is also true of matters on which certainty might be obtained. In matters pertaining to history and nature, clear contradiction became manifest, between the Qur'an and what educated persons of that period had learned in government schools and in foreign-run private schools. Some missionary activity highlighted these contradictions on a wider scale. One such case was the myth of Noah and the Flood, with the examination of this narrative representing a transitional stage between *tafwīḍ* and interpretation, it being open to the possibility of doubt, contestation, and, if necessary, *tafwīḍ*. 'Abduh considered that the claim that flooding covered the entire world lacked a Qur'anic basis. It was based on individual hadiths that did not provide for certainty. He then cited the objections of some churchmen and scientists to the effect that the existence of shells and fossilised fish on mountain-tops was proof enough that the water had risen to such levels and "that would not have happened unless the flood had covered the earth". 'Abduh went on to quote the opinion of modern commentators to the effect that "the flood was not universal, for reasons that would take too long to explain". Reticent to proffer long explanations, he then came to the following conclusion: "No Muslim may deny that the Flood was universal, merely because of the possible interpretation of the Qur'an. On the contrary, no one who firmly believes in religion should reject something indicated by the literal meaning of verses and of hadith whose *isnāds* are trustworthy and in favour of this interpretation, except by rational evidence which positively shows that the literal meaning is not the one intended by the text. Arriving at this conclusion is a matter that requires lengthy research, great application, and extensive knowledge of stratigraphy and geology. This depends in turn on various rational and traditional sciences. Whoever babbles without certain knowledge is reckless, should not be heeded and should not be permitted to propagate their ignorance. God in His majesty knows best."[130]

The fundamental point that this semantic and conceptual flailing, and the evident lack of argumentative control, affirm is that, with resort to interpretation, one may affirm that the literal meaning is "not the one intended". The "intended meaning" – a mysterious and extremely interesting and telling term deserving of close analysis – in the age of modernity becomes identified with the "intended meaning" of the time when the Qur'anic text emerged. Affirmation of the decisive authority of the text attributes to it meaning conforming to modern knowledge that is incompatible with any original "intended meaning" it may have had in the seventh century. Arbitrariness, the socio-political and cultural will driving interpretation, is not a technical flaw but a constitutive feature of this procedure of interpreting a text outside the text. Cognitive certainty and the text are posited as correlative, despite the escape clause of fideism (that God knows best), which is activated at the moment when semantic compatibility with modern knowledge is impossible to assert while interpretation is seen to be inappropriate. In such cases, when the literal meaning does not concur with natural or human history, it is said that the meaning of the text is in fact a general one or that it is not intended to inform but rather to guide by example or allegory. "Human history as related in the Qur'an is similar to what the Qur'an relates in the way of natural history: animals, plants, inanimate objects, and Qur'anic statements about the stars. The intention of all this is to demonstrate by inference the omnipotence of the Creator and His wisdom, rather than to give a detailed exposition of questions which God has enabled humans to understand through study, contemplation and experience. God has guided man by intuition and revelation together. We therefore assert that, if we presume that historical and natural matters mentioned in the Qur'an conform only to what all or some of the Prophet's contemporaries held or believed, this does not discredit the Qur'an. These matters are not intended for themselves but to provide guidance."[131]

---

130 'Abduh, *Al-a'māl al-kāmila*, vol. 5, 512–513.
131 Riḍā, *Fatāwā*, no. 45.

The Qur'an and related canonical texts were therefore shielded from the kind of history that might indicate the texts' historicity and their temporal frames of reference, despite the allusion made earlier to the historicity of some elements of the Qur'an. The Qur'anic text was thereby saved from historical scrutiny and the desiderata and consequences of such scrutiny, and from its meaningful exposure to the register of secular knowledge bearing a compelling intellectual and cultural weight that religious reason could no longer reject or resist.

Reformist religious reason therefore resorted to interpretation, imposing on the text meanings that it could not possibly have if regarded from the perspective of the time in which it emerged. The Qur'anic text, especially verses referring to cosmic matters, came to be understood and delivered in code, whose key was modern scientific knowledge, connected to the words of the Qur'an by wilful association. Then-modern means, such as wireless and telegraph, became keys for understanding Qur'anic reference to communication between Solomon and the Queen Sheba.[132] Similarly, Qur'anic statements about the heavens, the splitting of the moon, and the subversion of cosmic order when God so wills are interpreted in terms of cosmic events such as interstellar collision.[133] The parting of Red Sea waters and the drowning of Pharoah's army are explained in terms of Moses' crossing of the sea at a shallow point, and the inundation of Pharoah and his army by the incoming tide.[134] As for the defeat before Mecca of the Abyssinian king Abraha through the intervention of "birds in flight/ hurling against them stones of baked clay" (Qur'an, 55:4–5), 'Abduh viewed the matter in these terms: "It is possible to conceive that this bird was a variety of mosquito or fly which carries the germs of some diseases, and these stones were of poisonous dry mud which the winds had blown and which had got stuck to the legs of some of these insects. If these insects came into contact with a body they would enter its pores and cause sores that eventually lead to the decay and decomposition of that body. A multitude of these weak birds can be considered the mightiest of God's soldiers in His destruction of whatever people He wills. This small animal, nowadays called the microbe, is of the same type. The groups and communities of these microbes are so numerous that only their Creator can

132 al-Afghānī, *Al-a'māl al-kāmila*, 267–269.
133 'Abduh, *Al-a'māl al-kāmila*, vol. 5, 365–366.
134 Riḍā, *Shubuhāt al-naṣārā wa ḥujaj al-islām*, 5.

count them. But God's manifest ability to defeat tyrants does not depend on birds being of the dimension of the summits of vast mountains, nor on their being a kind of griffin, nor that they be of special colour . . . for God has soldiers of everything."[135] Here we find a typical combination of incoherent elements: pious reserve (sententious reference to limitless capacity), a desire for rationalisation while preserving a sense of wonder and of the miraculous (reference to the griffin, God's soldiers, the size of mountains, and recourse to *mirabilia* genre), and the evocation of modern epidemiology.

Scientific interpretations of miracles were not uncommon. Husayn al-Jisr (1845–1909) interpreted the splitting of the moon (Qur'an, 54:1) in terms of earthquakes. He interpreted the Prophet's miracle of giving his followers water to drink from his fingers while travelling in the desert in terms of what he saw as the chemical possibility of condensing air into water.[136] In the same way, Rida explained the evil eye in terms of hypnotism, practised at his time (and by Freud as well), which he interpreted in the medieval terms of spirits acting upon other spirits at a distance.[137] He had a strong belief in spiritual influences, including the summoning of spirits (spiritualism was all the rage, even among Muslim reformists), the efficacy of amulets, and his own personal power to perform wonders.[138] An instructive illustration of the mechanism of reformist interpretation involving anachronism, denial, and arbitrariness is Rida's on the virgins of Paradise (*houris*) promised to the Blessed by the Qur'an – a point often raised by contemporary Christian polemicists. He repudiated the entire Islamic tradition, and insisted, in a spirit of Victorian prudery consonant with prevailing concepts of sexual morality in nineteenth-century Europe, that the *houris* were the earthly wives who accompanied their husbands in paradise.[139]

Offering natural scientific interpretation of Qur'anic statements, on the assumption that the text cannot produce anything that is inadmissible

135 'Abduh, *Al-a'māl al-kāmila*, vol. 5, 529.

136 al-Jisr, *Al-risāla al-ḥamīdiyya*, 64–65.

137 Riḍā, *Fatāwā*, no. 209.

138 Text by Rashīd Riḍā in Arslān, *Al-Sayyid Rashīd Riḍā*, 85–86.

139 Riḍā, *Fatāwā*, 193, 196. On the Victorianisation of sexuality among modern Arabs, see Nadia al-Bagdadi, "Eros und Etikette – Reflexionen zum Bann eines zentralen Themas im arabischen 19. Jahrhundert", in *Verschleierter Orient – Entschleierter Okzident?* eds Bettina Dennerlein, Elke Frietsch, and Therese Steffen (Munich: Wilhelm Fink, 2012), 117–135. On Riḍā and Christian polemics, see Umar Riyad, *Islamic Reformism and Christianity* (Leiden: Brill, 2009), ch. 3. Riḍā's systematic anti-Christian apology is available in English translation: Rida, *Christian Criticisms*.

rationally,[140] became a widespread genre, starting with al-Jisr, a genre also used by Muhammad Shukri al-Alusi (1856–1924) in Iraq, despite his opposition to interpretation in general, al-Qasimi in Syria, and students of 'Abduh, most copiously and comprehensively Shaykh Tantawi Jawhari (1870–1940). Jawhari shared al-Jisr's philosophical naivete, and produced a twenty-six volume exegesis of the Qur'an based on the contents of contemporary science textbooks.[141] Many others had previously written on this subject, such as Muhammad b. Ahmad, an Alexandrian physician resident in Damascus who, in 1300/1882, had published a book entitled *Tibyān al-asrār al-rabbāniya fī al-nabāt wa al-ma'ādin wa al-mawāshī al-ḥayawāniyya* ("Revealing the Divine Secrets of Plants, Minerals and Quadruped Animals") and another entitled *Kashf al-asrār al-nūrāniyya bi al-Qur'ān* ("Revealing the Luminous Secrets by the Qur'an").[142]

Undoubtedly the Aleppan intellectual and physician Francis Marrash (*c.*1836–1873) was the pioneer in this field of scientific interpretation. Husein al-Jisr's *Al-risāla al-ḥamīdiyya*, the source of much subsequent writing, was linked to Marrash's *Shahādat al-ṭabī'a fī wujūd allāh wa al-sharī'a* (The Witness of Nature to the Existence of God and Shari'a – Shari'a here given a broad, non-shar'ist sense), initially serialised in Ottoman state journals, approximately two decades before al-Jisr's book.[143] There was a close connection between Jisr's book and that of Marrash in the arrangement of chapters, types of argumentation and demonstration, and the view of science and religion. This link could be subjected to scrutiny in order to determine its nature in detail, and it is to be hoped that further research will do so with greater precision than the present volume allows.

The Marrash-al-Jisr intellectual lineage appropriated an extensive body of apologetic arguments produced by European religious thought in the face of science and positivism, arguments that had become universal and were used by religions to defend and justify elements within them that were clearly contrary to reason. Muslim reformers followed their predecessors in viewing nature as a sign of perfection manifesting of God and His acts. From this one was able to reach conclusions about the systematic arrangement of nature

140 'Abduh, *Al-a'māl al-kāmila*, vol. 3, 357.

141 Jad'ān, *Usus al-taqaddum*, 231–238 and Ḥusayn, *Al-ittijāhāt al-waṭaniyya fī al-adab al-mu'āṣir*, vol. 2, 334–343.

142 Sarkīs, *Mu'jam al-maṭbū'āt*, 438.

143 al-Jisr, *Al-risāla al-ḥamīdiyya*, 180–206.

and the interdependence of its parts. For Islamic Reformists, recollection of Islamic philosophy was conjoined to contemporary European Christian apologetics in demonstrating the existence and active intervention of God in nature, as studied particularly by Catholics[144] – and to a lesser degree in Protestant natural theology – when countering the criticism of religion in the eighteenth century.[145]

Catholics, notably in France under the Restoration and thereafter, produced the most extensive apologetic legacy in the nineteenth century, armed with the long heritage of anti-rationalist scepticism. The works of the celebrated preacher of Notre Dame and highly influential religious thinker de Lammenais (1782–1854), the philosopher and politician de Bonald (1754–1840), and other nineteenth-century writers were adopted as part of the philosophical and sceptical heritage of modern religious thought.[146] Thus, it was claimed that the principles and laws of natural science rested on mere assumption, that knowledge derived from the senses was unreliable, and that beyond human knowledge were matters that reason could not comprehend.

Francis Marrash was the connecting link between Catholic apologetics and modern Islamic thought in confronting science with Hussein al-Jisr's *Al-risāla al-ḥamīdiyya* as a seminal text. Marrash had acquired these concepts while a medical student in Paris in the early 1860s. At that time a Catholic philosophical movement led by, among others, the philosopher and physiologist Félix Frédault (1822–1897) was active in the Paris faculty of medicine.[147] This movement had continued the thought of de Lamennais and others, and defended religion by affirming its conformity with science and its superiority over it, based on cognitive scepticism. Natural theology characterised the whole heritage of Arab, Islamic, and Christian thought in the face of science, although among early modernist Islamic reformists, it was scientism rather than scepticism that was highlighted.[148] This has continued until the present

144 Palmer, *Catholics and Unbelievers in Eighteenth-Century France*, 106–107, 108–112.

145 Rāndāl, *Takwīn al-ʿaql al-hadīth*, vol. 2, 222.

146 Louis Foucher, *La philosophie catholique en France au XIXᵉ siècle avant la renaissance thomiste et dans son rapport avec elle 1800–1880* (Paris: Vrin, 1955), 23–25, 36–38, 258.

147 Ibid., 257–261.

148 Marrāsh, *Shahādat al-ṭabīʿa fī wujūd Allāh wa al-sharīʿa*; al-Jisr, *Al-risāla al-ḥamīdiyya*; Fr. Louis Cheikho S. J., "Tanāquḍ al-dīn wa al-ʿilm", *al-Mashriq* 3 (1900), 304–305, 308–309.

day under the celebrated slogan of Anwar Sadat, "Science and Faith". Sceptical apologetism and relativism came to the Arab world only with the emergence of postmodernism.

3 Explicit Secularism and Accord with Reality

Previous sections of this chapter have shown that Islamic Reformism was a political and intellectual response to the educational, socio-political, and cultural conditions created by the *Tanzimat* state. At its base, Muslim Reformism was utilitarian in character, manoeuvring around what it took for its bases in history by stripping these of temporality, fossilised in their supposed moment of origin in Qur'anic and Prophetic beginnings, and in the same breath insinuating modern meaning into that moment of supposed origin, thus making present the past and declaring past and present equivalent. Islamic Reformism, as concept and discourse, inhabited two worlds, one based on a supernatural and supra-human source, the other in reach of human reason and without reference to the supernatural, except for 'Abduh's second order statement that all this is after all knowledge inspired and made possible by God. The secular nature of present reality was enwrapped into the register of the supernatural or put under the authority of texts emanating from the religious past. Reformism was based on cultivating the illusion that matters of the world – the utilitarian and rational dimensions of human experience – were inherent in religion as expressed canonically. It thereby conflated the distinct points of reference that were actually rational, socio-political, and symbolic. This tendency sponsored the muddled incongruities and imperviousness to concrete and rational demonstration that continued to mark sectors of Arab intellectual life until the present day.

Islamic Reformism, therefore, was grounded in an objective opportunism in which incoherence was a constitutive feature, combining heterogenous material according to the advantages of the moment. It evokes simultaneously the religious and the secular according to utilitarian, conservative, and apologetic considerations, situated in every particular moment without looking further, thereby dissipating long-term cumulative effect. Reformism sought ceaselessly to conserve its religious symbolic point of reference, and the social authority of its carriers, forward-looking members of the religious establishment, and subaltern state intellectuals. It arose from secular concerns in a secular reality, packaged in religious language and sustained by religious sentiment.

As for secularism, this was the world founded by the *Tanzimat* state, although it did not announce secularism, nor were its agents necessarily conscious that theirs was a secularising historical dynamic. The *Tanzimat* reforms sustained two simultaneous ideological moments. One was ceremonial, at times ritually festive, announcing the patronage and protection of religion through respect shown to the religious institution, opening proclamations and inaugurating institutions and laws in the name of God with use of religious formulae, and the unabated general dissemination of a religious culture. The second was as implicit as it was constitutive of its new institutions and the cognitive and normative equipment it necessitated, its intervention in the shaping of society, and the thought and lifestyle of senior state functionaries.

The first moment persisted under the sultan Abdülhamid II. Islamic Reformism corresponded to this regime in terms of its socio-intellectual project directed towards what was taken to be autochtonous and indigenous, with deep roots in the past, alongside the state's economic orientation that entailed freeing the legal order from the burdens of the past in conformity with the global capitalist system. In all this, Reformist discourse as well as traditionalist religious discourse built themselves on the denial of changes taking place, and of construing them in terms that were inapposite and, in the final analysis, fantasmatic.

Not so secularism; at a time that secularisation governed the implicit outcomes of structural developments under the *Tanzimat*, it proceeded objectively, often imperceptibly, and not necessarily intentionally. Explicit secularism was a militant sentiment and discourse that corresponded to this implicit dynamic. It added to it a note of clarity and an ideological moment that had been absent or had been obscured deliberately, through the agency of intellectuals effective in a proportion greater than would be allowed for by their marginal profiles.

Before broaching the theme of secularist thought, it is useful to mention vestiges of medieval rationality that may have fed secular inspiration. Among these was the metaphorical secular use of religious topoi in literature, which could provoke resentment in religious circles, as it did in classical times. An example is the line of love poetry by Butrus Karama (1774–1851) of Hims, in which he said: "The all-Compassionate One wrote on her mouth: We have given you abundance." The reference was to "we have given thee abundance" (*al-kawthar*) in the Qur'an (58:2), implying here the sensual abundance of the beloved's lips. As a result, the "riff-raff of Hims" rose up against him and the hapless lover was driven to take flight and become court poet to Amir Bashir Shihab (1767–1850), ruler of Mount Lebanon, before going on to spend his final years in Istanbul.[149]

Another vestige of long traditions was the suspicious, hostile, and scornful scrutiny of religious functionaries, a vein of virulent and scurrilous anti-clericalism at which the "Jahiz of the nineteenth century", Ahmad Faris al-Shidyaq (1805–1887), was very adept. The Maronite Patriarch Youssef Hubaish had detained his brother As'ad, a convert to Protestantism, in a monastery, where he was kept chained as a lunatic for several years until his death in 1832. Shidyaq became an outstanding scourge of the clergy and religious functionaries.[150] After his flight from Lebanon in 1825 this subject became an obsession for him, while the tragedy of As'ad remained an inspiration for many Lebanese Christian authors. Shidyaq's personality and voice still echoed through the writing of Jubran Khalil Jubran (1883–1931),[151] and still echo today.

Such medieval continuities were not limited to Christians. One can include under the same heading sceptical positions towards religion and divinity that recall the irreverence and blasphemy of the Middle Ages, with figures such as Bashshar b. Burd (714–783), Ibn al-Rawandi (*c.*827–*c.*911), and Abu al-'Ala' al-Ma'arri (973–1057). These positions simply parodied incongruities and absurdities in dogmatic and ritual matters without scientific elaboration, arriving at highly sceptical conclusions. Scepticism was a sentiment and not an indication of modernity.[152]

The Iraqi intellectual Jamil Sidqi al-Zahawi (1863–1936) held strange views on physics and astronomy, while his metaphysics were clearly materialist. He seems to have held ideas of cosmic cycles and conceptions akin to those of monistic deism, affirming the identity of God and the aether in a

149 'Anḥūri, *Siḥr hārūt*, 151.

150 al-Shidyāq, *Al-sāq 'alā al-sāq*, 138–139, 187–188, and al-Ṣulḥ, *Aḥmad Fāris al-Shidyāq*, 27–30, 176–177.

151 Khalil S. Hawi, *Khalil Gibran: His Background, Character and Works*, foreword by Nabih Amin Faris, American University of Beirut, Publications of the Faculty of Arts and Sciences, Oriental Series, no.41 (Beirut: Arab Institute for Research and Publishing, 1972), 43, 136, 169.

152 See Aziz al-Azmeh, "Freidenkertum und Humanismus. Stimmungen, Motive und Themen im Zeitalter der Abbasiden", in *Humanismus, Reformation, Aufklärung*, ed. Hubert Cancik and Hubert Schöpner (Berlin: Humanistische Akademie, 2017).

monistic conception.[153] Nevertheless, he also held a providential conception of divinity and a belief – tinged with scepticism – in angels, and a Darwinism accompanied by an affirmation of cosmic cyclism.[154] Al-Zahawi's sceptical poetry was therefore restless and ambivalent, somewhat akin to al-Ma'arri. It was also moody and cannot be regarded in itself as secular culture although it does feed into this. This may explain his composition of verses of this kind:[155]

> I paused unknowing before facts [wondering]/Was it I who created [. . .] or He who created me?
>
> . . .
>
> How can I believe in one who wished me/harm and rewarded me with the reward of one resentful
>
> . . .
>
> They said that [. . .] was alive/on His throne he is fast
> I said [. . .] is only illusion/amplified by description and epithets
> If knowledge were to be alive among the people/[. . .] will die of himself
>
> . . .
>
> [. . .] Satan approached our Lord/[. . .] , on His throne sulking
> I did not think that [. . .] is [. . .]/while the entire field is the devil's.

As noted earlier, al-Afghani had had recourse amply to terms originating in medieval natural philosophy. He defended medieval alchemy in its search to transmute base metals into gold against the criticism from Ibn Khaldun, although al-Afghani claimed he was not personally a practitioner of the art.[156] He was also interested in the relation of philosophy and prophecy and by the relative merits of philosophy and religion – he declared preference for the former in his Persian writings written in India.[157] For all his activism and glimmerings of open-mindedness in matters of knowledge and dogma, al-Afghani continued to be preoccupied with a conceptual world that had passed.

---

153 Nājī, *Al-Zahāwī wa dīwānuhu al-mafqūd*, 59–61, 94–102, 104–107, 125–127.

154 Ibid., 87–93, 121–187, 128–129.

155 Ibid., 321, 323–324, 333. Without access to the manuscript, I have followed the editor of the text in replacing excised words with brackets, although what was excised by the editor would seem clear from the context.

156 al-Afghānī, *Al-a'māl al-kāmila*, 213–218.

157 Keddie, *Sayid Jamāl al-Dīn "al-Afghānī"*, 156ff.

In rational terms, al-Afghani inhabited two worlds, or rather, two worlds inhabited his mind, leavened by utilitarianism. It was previously noted that during his first sojourn in Istanbul he was counted as something of a free-thinker, and had been expelled at the initiative of the Ottoman *şeyhülislam* after a public lecture in which he considered prophecy to be a psycho-spiritual habitus similar to philosophy, superior only in some respects.[158] This was perhaps evidence of the man's restlessness: he was judged in Istanbul to be progressive in terms of a theme arising in medieval philosophy, not on account of modern themes. Thus, the departure from central Muslim Sunni traditions was interpreted as contumacy, and the *şeyhülislam*'s vexation might well have parsed this medieval dissent in terms of the modern.

There is, however, no uncertainty about al-Afghani's reply to Ernest Renan's famous lecture at the Sorbonne in March 1883, in which he stated his well-known thesis that the Arabs, being Semites, were congenitally incapable in the field of philosophy. Al-Afghani's reply was published in the Parisian daily *Journal des Débats* of 17 May 1883, and included a defence of the role of the Semites in science and philosophy, concluding by saying that all religions have narrow-minded attitudes to science. Hence there is nothing to prevent Muslims from advancing, just as Christian Europe had progressed despite Christianity, regardless of the fact that believers were like oxen harnessed to a plough: ploughing a single path and believing that they possess the whole truth. Islam was responsible for the decline of Arab civilisation and was the strongest ally of tyranny.

The members of al-Afghani's party sought to mitigate his statement or claimed that the French text had corrupted the original (it is unknown whether this was in Arabic or Persian). They also sought to interpret his article away in various ways, so as to shield its author from the burden of actual history. Excerpts were published in the newspaper *al-Siyāsa* in 1923 by Mustafa 'Abd al-Raziq (1885–1947), who was to become Shaykh al-Azhar.[159] Rashid Rida was indignant.[160] The published text was included in al-Afghani's complete works, taken from a redaction by Jurji Zaydan but

158 Ibid., 67–71. Rashīd Riḍā refused this claim when advanced by Salīm 'Anḥūrī, and sought to conceal al-Afghani's position. See Riḍā, *Tarīkh al-ustādh al-imām al-shaykh Muḥammad 'Abduh*, vol. 1, 30–31, 44.

159 *al-Siyāsa*, 22 March 1923, 21.

160 Riḍā, *Tarīkh al-ustādh al-imām al-shaykh Muḥammad 'Abduh*, and Arslān, *Al-Sayyid Rashīd Riḍā*, 369–370.

with numerous errors and lacunae.[161] A complete translation was published much later, with a scholarly commentary on the history of the text and the controversy although, in the end, it does not engage directly with the question and leans towards the apologetic in the manner of Rida and others.[162] None of the interpretations drew the necessary conclusions from remarks by Muhammad 'Abduh in a letter sent from Beirut to al-Afghani on 8 Sha'aban 1300/2 June 1883:

> We received, before the arrival of your honourable letter, word of what was published in the *Journal des Débats* about your defense of the Islamic religion (and what a defense it is!) in reply to Monsieur Renan. We thought it to be the sort of banter which the faithful might appreciate, and urged some religious person to translate it but – God be praised – before the arrival of your text copies of the *Journal des Débats* were not available to the translator. When we came to peruse the actual texts in the two issues of the *Journal*, translated for us by Fadil Hussain Effendi Bayhum, we diverted our first friend's mind from translating these two issues of the *Journal*, telling him the texts had not been received and were still to come . . . and that there was no immediate need for a translation. And so, damage was averted. Thank God, we are following your sound path: decapitate religion only by the sword of religion. Were you to see us now, you would see faithful persons, kneeling and bowing, never disobeying what God commands, doing what we are commanded. How narrow life would be without the perspective of hope![163]

An interpretation of 'Abduh's comments is not a central aim of this discussion, which has been concerned with highlighting a duality in his life and thought and those of his mentor, reflecting incoherently the disparate worlds, simultaneous but belonging to different temporal schemes, unevenly combined, in which they lived and acted. Second, 'Abduh's comments highlight in a most poignant manner the acute nature of the divergence and explicit distinction

161 al-Afghānī, *Al-a'māl al-kāmila*, 210.

162 'Alī Shalash, "Jamāl al-Dīn al-Afghānī fī raddihi 'alā Ernest Renan", *al-Azmina* 1 (1987): 50–66.

163 'Alī Shalash (ed.), *Muḥammad 'Abduh, silsilat al-a'māl al-majhūla* (London: Riyad al-Rayyis li'l-kutub wa al-nashr, 1987), 53.

between the common mass of the populace and intellectual elites,[164] between commoners as oxen harnessed to a plough and leaders, between common popular religiosity and those who aspired to lead the Muslims.

Al-Afghani's Parisian statement of 1883 was based on an evolutionary theory of religion whose basic features were set out in the first part of this chapter. He seems to have taken this theory, or at least to have considered it, in its extended sense and with its secular implication, that the idea of divinity abstracted from quality and quantity is but a more developed form of primitive illusions arising from the fear of death compensated by the delusionary idea of eternity.[165] His bivalent positions stemmed from his different worlds, and from the pronounced political pragmatism of his views. He did write a critique of irreligious materialism, what was commonly called Dahrism, refuting materialism's dismissal of religions as illusion: Dahrists "built upon this idea the view that no community has the right to proclaim itself superior to others on the basis of the tenets of its religion. In the opinion of the materialists it was more fitting that such a community believe that it is not distinguished by virtue or merit. It is clear what the consequences of this corrupt opinion are in terms of diminishing energy and stagnation of the will in the quest for noble things,"[166] given that religion is "the ordering principle of social organisation".[167]

The text of al-Afghani was a response to what, at the time of the Ottoman sultan Abdülhamid II as in medieval times, was termed *al-dahriyya*, or materialism,[168] whose pioneers were Beshir Fuat (1852?–1887), a bitter critic of Namik Kemal, along with Shibli Shumayyil, who circulated the thought of the French materialist and atheist Baron d'Holbach and translated work by Ludwig Büchner and the novels of Émile Zola.[169] *Dahriyya* at that time corresponded to what atheism would represent in the Arab world in the 1960s and

164 See, for example, the content of the letter from Rashīd Riḍā to Shakīb Arslān in Arslān, *Al-Sayyid Rashīd Riḍā*, 334–335.

165 'Anḥūrī, *Siḥr hārūt*, 177–178. 'Anḥūrī corrected himself in the press after 'Abduh met with him and persuaded him not to damage al-Afghani's public reputation: Riḍā, *Tārīkh al-ustādh al-imām al-shaykh Muḥammad 'Abduh*, vol. 1, 49–50.

166 al-Afghānī, *Al-a'māl al-kāmila*, 149.

167 Ibid., 130.

168 Berkes, *The Development of Secularism*, 237, 260, 264, 294, 297.

169 In English, see Susan Laila Ziadeh, "A radical in his time: The thought of Shibli Shumayyil" (PhD dissertation, University of Michigan, 1991).

secularism in more recent times: a repository of cognitive iniquities because of its use of historical and natural concepts as well as opposition to the insinuation of religion in politics. It was associated with a spectrum of ideas stretching from vague ideas of reform and emancipation all the way to atheism, and resisted calls for retreat into historical introversion or to regarding Europe as a supra-historical satanic force. *Dahriyya* was clearly inclined towards secularism or adopted it completely. Polemics against *dahriyya* grounded themselves in the claim that they represented authentic concepts unconnected to global circulation of culture. In this way and in these terms, secularism was later created as a mythical antithesis to the myth of origins and continuity, and emerged in a context of controversy, not as a free-standing idea. Al-Afghani's text was therefore confused and contradictory, poorly informed and heavily sophistical, identifying Darwinism with Epicureanism, the polemical topos countered to freethinking in Europe since the seventeenth century, and criticised Darwinism in a way that shows that he had only a fleeting and a most superficial acquaintance with it. He then went on to say that his quibble with it was concerned, not with evolution, but with the first breath of life that must have been divine, thus adopting an eighteenth-century solution for the contradiction between Darwinism and religion, adopted by certain European Christians, by differentiating creation on the one hand and natural causation on the other.[170]

Darwinism or the "theory of emergence and evolution" as it was known at the time was one of the basic loci for the polemics against secular thought that, it was noted earlier, was latent in the *Tanzimat* state policies. The extent of effective opposition to Darwinism is difficult to estimate. At the end of the nineteenth century, Darwinism was one type and one specific redaction of evolutionary theory overall and in all domains, which constituted the sinew of nineteenth-century thought, accepted by Westerners and Easterners alike. It does not seem that a majority of intellectuals considered it with the enmity and the fearfulness that characterised the position of the religious lobby, intellectually and politically. Salim 'Anhuri (1862–1940),

170 Ismā'īl Maẓhar, *Multaqā al-sabīl fī madhab al-nushū' wa al-irtiqā' wa āthāruhu fī al-inqilāb al-fikrī al-ḥadīth* (Cairo: al-Maṭba'a al-'Aṣriyya, 1926), chs 5 and 6 and Abdullah O. A. Al-Omar, "The reception of Darwinism in the Arab world" (unpublished PhD dissertation, Harvard University, 1982), 117–118, 150, ch. 2, and passim. See too Palmer, *Catholics and Unbelievers in Eighteenth-Century France*, 165. On the critique of materialism, see now Elshakry, *Reading Darwin in Arabic*, ch. 3.

for example, one of the disciples of al-Afghani mentioned above, used Darwinism ironically as a literary trope in a love poem that deployed a classical Arabic poetic topos to insist that his beloved's eyes were those of an oryx, the very emblem of beauty according to the tropes of the classical Arabic poetical canon: "they claimed that one emerged from a monkey / They lied! for this one evolved from an oryx."[171]

It does seem that this everyday use of the theory was considered routine, given that it was a prevailing thought of the period, a matter that suggests a degree of general assimilation of universal ideas, at least in certain circles. 'Anhuri and others drew on images and motifs that came from numerous sources: Arab, Muslim, Christian, ancient Greek, and contemporary European. Opposition to Darwinism was not a general phenomenon, and developed in the Arab lands first in controversies in the early 1880s in the Syrian Protestant College (later to become the American University of Beirut), reflecting contemporary American Evangelical moods rather than local conditions as reflected in the medical students of the College who were partial to Darwinism. After this controversy, the two founders of the journal *al-Muqtaṭaf*, Ya'qub Sarruf and Faris Nimr, left the College in 1884 and moved to Egypt, where they continued to spread modern universalist culture with Darwinism as one of its essential elements.[172]

Opposition to Darwinism was limited to the reactions against Shibli Shumayyil published by the Jesuit publishing houses and others, using natural and religious pretexts, such as the riposte of obscure Maronite clerics Jurjis Faraj (or Jurjis Saghir), Ibrahim al-Haurani, and others, using both religious and natural arguments. In Baghdad, Abu al Majd al-Isfahani followed a similar course,[173] inspired, it appears, by ideas spread by Shaykh Hussain al-Jisr. Islamic reformism in general did not, as we noted, display enmity to Darwinism, except through the political sophistry of al-Afghani. We have already examined 'Abduh's Qur'anic sanction for Darwinism. Indeed, Shaykh Tantawi Jawhari affirmed that there was agreement between Darwinism and Islam on the grounds that both were essentially true.[174]

---

171 'Anḥūrī, *Siḥr hārūt*, 18.

172 Al-Omar, "The reception of Darwinism in the Arab world", ch. 1.

173 Ibid., 219–222, 336–337. Sarkīs, *Mu'jam al-maṭbū'āt*, 1,214.

174 Ḥusayn, *Al-ittijāhāt al-waṭaniyya fī al-adab al-mu'āṣir*, vol. 1, 358–359.

Syrian Christian circles were agitated by more intense intellectual conflicts than those that took place among Muslims, conflicts that were accompanied by a social and political conservatism to which reference was made in the previous chapter. Foreign schools were the setting for a multi-faceted education of contradictory character: intellectually progressive on the one hand, politically confessional on the other. A few Christians were perhaps to some extent exposed to Renan's historical reading of the Bible. Some commentators satirised parts of the Bible and particularly focused on the miracle of Joshua's suspension of the sun's movement (Joshua, 10:13).[175] Some, like the Lebanese historian, physician, and musicologist Mikhail Mashaqa (1800–1888), a Greek Catholic convert to Protestantism, followed in the footsteps of Voltaire in criticising the Church and religion, but subsequently changed course and wrote to attack the "ingratitude" of Voltaire.[176] Jibra'il Dallal (1836–1892) acted in a similar fashion, but with greater verve, and was persecuted because of a poem in the style of Voltaire called "The Throne and the Temple" in which he criticised religion and arbitrary authority. He was imprisoned on the instigation of the religious authorities in his native Aleppo where he worked as a primary school teacher, and died in prison.[177] He had been a member of the celebrated Aleppo literary salon of Maryana Marrash (1848–1919), sister of Francis Marrash who has already come up at many points in this book. Deistic ideas were not confined to Christians: Ruhi al-Khalidi, while rejecting the atheist (*al-jahud*, or the ingrate, used for atheists at the time) Voltaire, possibly as a sop to conservative circles, attested to the truth of some positions of Victor Hugo, assimilated in native terms as being "perhaps a *Ḥanīf* . . . the *Ḥanīf* is someone who believes in God without this belief taking a specific form of worship. Among the *Ḥunafā'* were people in the Arabian Peninsula such as Waraqa ibn Nawfal."[178]

Self-conscious secularism, cognizant of materialist foundations and social consequences, remained a minor current, no greater than its European counterpart, with Shibli Shumayyil and Salama Musa (1887–1958)

175 Hazīm, "Shawāghil al-fikr al-masīḥī mundhu 1866", 354–355.

176 Zaydān, *Tarājim mashāhīr al-sharq*, vol. 2, 215; al-Shidyāq, *Al-sāq 'alā al-sāq*, 188; Khūrī, *Al-fikr al-'arabī al-ḥadīth*, 230 (note).

177 Sarkīs, *Mu'jam al-maṭbū'āt*, 878.

178 Al-Khālidī, quoted in Khūrī, *Al-fikr al-'arabī al-ḥadīth*, 230. On the dubious historical reality of Hanifism, see al-Azmeh, *The Emergence of Islam in Late Antiquity*, 363–364.

as its best-known representatives. They had jointly founded the journal *al-Mustaqbal* in Cairo in 1914. It was alleged that Musa wrote an article "full of immorality and atheism" while Shumayyil propagated materialism and evolutionism in a "vulgar futuristic way".[179] The journal was suspended by the authorities after a great controversy. Some 600 copies of the journal were distributed weekly. Secularism completed by materialism remained the object of criticism by many secular thinkers who thought it necessary to resist "brutish materialism".[180]

Shumayyil embraced more general aspects of Darwinism as adopted by positivist materialism, linked to the names of Karl Dühring (1833–1921), Ludwig Büchner (1824–1899), and Jacob Moleschott (1822–1893). Animals, like humans, were composed of eternal matter, which harbour no transcendent causalities. Humankind is

> natural and every element within him is derived from nature. Today there is no way to doubt this reality, although some may persist in denying it, still influenced by old teachings, rooted in their minds like an inscription in stone. Humans are connected to the visible and perceptible world and nothing in their constitution shows a connection with a spiritual and supernatural world. All the elements which comprise humans are present in nature and human energies work according to natural forces. Humans, in physiological terms, resemble animals and in chemical terms, they resemble inanimate minerals. The difference between them is one of quality and not of quantity, form rather than matter, accident rather than essence.[181]

Thus, the human psyche resembled that of animals and this rigorous materialism precludes any notion of resurrection. As a consequence, a fundamental contradiction was revealed, one glossed over by Christian apologetics[182] and Islamic Reformism, that of religion and science, that is to say the impossibility

---

179 Mūsā, *Tarbiyat Salāma Mūsā*, 157 and Vernon Egger, *A Fabian in Egypt, Salāma Musa and the Rise of the Professional Classes in Egypt 1909–1939* (London: University Press of America, 1986), 28.

180 "Tamhīd" [Preface] by Faraḥ Anṭūn to As'ad Bāsīlī al-Ṭarābulsī, "Al-dīn wa al-'ilm wa ra'y al-faylasūf Spencer fīhā", *al-Jāmi'a* 3 (1902): 554–555.

181 al-Shumayyil, *Ta'rīb li sharḥ Büchner 'alā madhab Darwin*, ل ج ب.

182 On Christian apologetics as a phenomenon concomitant with Islamic Reformism, see Cheikho, "Tanāquḍ al-dīn wa al-'ilm", 304–305, 308–309.

of agreement between religious concepts of resurrection, spirit, and miracles and the results of science.[183] Humans therefore do not have any revealed laws save the legends and illusions revealing their ignorance. Human laws are made by humans and are subject to human conditions of decline and progress.[184]

Shumayyil thus adopted the most avant-garde and advanced ideas of his time, in somewhat simplified form, and linked them to the Enlightenment concepts of which he chose to highlight those of the materialist and atheist Baron d'Holbach (1723–1789).[185] Shumayyil derived these ideas directly from their context in wider evolutionary theory. Not unnaturally, he followed the path trodden by 'Abduh already, reflecting the wider historical context of ideas receptive to evolutionary theory, now deployed in the field of religion. Shumayyil saw religion as a feeling that evolved as society itself evolved, adding in a Humean spirit that religion developed from fear of natural forces that humans saw as exercising influence or power over them, and before which they grovelled. Humans subsequently made these forces into a spirit, which in turn was made into a god: "man then imagined his god as himself, provoked to anger by what angered him . . . He offered his god sacrifices and approached him with rituals and liturgies, conjured the licit and the illicit. Thereafter this inclination was, through natural heredity, ingrained within him and this belief was transferred through the line of descent by virtue of tradition." Religion developed from its idolatrous origins among uncivilised societies, origins that are are still alive today as shown by the visits to the tombs of holy men.[186] Religion came to encompass social systems intended to curb the powerful until it became the opposite of this – an instrument of repression – and a dead weight on the intellect.[187] This applied despite the superiority of monotheistic religions over other religions, as it had developed in successive stages with the "three great figures of Moses, Jesus and Muḥammad".[188] Thus, Shumayyil added, in the manner of other secularists, a materialist historical view of religion, a natural history

183 Shiblī Shumayyil, *Ārā' al-duktūr Shiblī Shumayyil* (Paris: Manshūrāt al-nuqṭa, 9, 1983) after the edition of Cairo: Dār al-ma'ārif, 1912, 10–12.

184 al-Shumayyil, *Majmū'at al-duktūr Shiblī Shumayyil*, 119.

185 Ibid., 119–120. Shumayyil, *Ta'rīb li sharḥ Büchner 'alā madhhab Darwin*, ق.

186 Ibid., ح-ط.

187 al-Shumayyil, *Ārā' al-duktūr Shiblī Shumayyil*, 14–18.

188 al-Shumayyil, *Majmū'at al-duktūr Shiblī Shumayyil*, 77.

of religion in the manner of Hume, and made Darwinism a general model for an evolutionary law that encompassed the development and progress of humanity, language, and laws, and declared as a consequence that the historicity of society is like that of nature and that morals and concepts of good and evil were relative.[189]

All the while many commentators were inclined to separate distant origins (divine creation) and proximate origins in the form of observable causalities and visible natural operations, thereby superadding to natural causality a prior, transcendent causality. They thereby crafted a sort of tribal reconciliation between science and religion in which each was confirmed in its particular field, even if by that time the field of religion in this arrangement was becoming increasingly remote from daily workings of the world, a religious field that was restricted and controlled effectively by the world, even as it was claimed that the world was in principle subject to a transcendent precedence. Not so Shumayyil, who consistently pursued ideas consonant with the transformations actually occurring. Religion was for him not a significant element in the intellectual context and structure of his thought. Not that he held that the concept of divinity in modern life had been exhausted, but he held it to be a negative impulse both cognitively and socially.

From this political and social standpoint, Shumayyil's thought converged with the implicit secularism of his contemporaries and, as noted earlier, Islamic Reformers found religion to be a natural element in society, and others agreed with them. Jurji Zaydan, for instance, held religion to be an instinctive impulse.[190] Secularists, however, diverged from Muslim modernists in their evaluation of this natural impulse and the role that it represented in the modern world. Following a very old trope, used in the ancient world no less than in classical Arabic writings and persisting until today, Zaydan saw religion as an irrational solidarity used by elites to manipulate and dominate the commoners in the service of their own goals. This made the history of religions (including Islam) a very violent history.[191] Shumayyil, for his part, held that the history of Christianity was a shameful one, and he linked, as did Farah Antun, religion and simple-mindedness.[192] He will have shared

189 al-Shumayyil, *Taʿrīb li sharḥ Büchner ʿalā madhab Darwin*, ن ٥.

190 Zaydān, *Mukhtārāt Jurjī Zaydān*, vol. 2, 23.

191 Ibid., 24–25.

192 al-Shumayyil, *Taʿrīb li sharḥ Büchner ʿalā madhab Darwin*, س.

the view of Adib Ishaq that fanaticism was born of corruption of authority among simple peoples, "until the bonds of illusion were strengthened and the ties of kinship were undone, so that it became a virtue for a human to kill their brother if he disagreed with him in matters of opinion".[193] This continued until knowledge advanced and spread and banished religion from public life.[194]

Shumayyil, like many others, linked intellectual enlightenment, clarity of interests, and the decline of religious enthusiasm. Thus, "the state of the nation will only be harmonious when the power of religion is weakened and religion is strong only when the nation is in decline . . . if religion only consisted of limiting the freedom of thought it would be sufficient to be the cause of human misfortune. If we consider humans as they struggle in a sea of illusion we would find them fearful, agitated, taking refuge in amulets . . . humans saw themselves surrounded by spirits which observed them, beyond human perception, manipulating humans from where humans could not reach them, holding the key to their livelihood, life and happiness. How can humans have confidence when preoccupied with approaching these spirits, confused about how to placate them when they do not know what angers them?"[195] The secularism of Shumayyil and his generation thus blended intellectual enlightenment with a clear perception of history and society based upon reason, without religion that led to an enfeebled intellect and communal conflict in history and society. This secularism presupposed universalist rationality based on the generalisation of ethics based in reason. With this in view, Shumayyil regarded the then popular idea of a league of Eastern nations to be a call "for a single common factor, which is the decline of order, corruption of laws, degeneration of the rational faculties and the corruption of ethical principles".[196] The religious state in its turn could be nothing but "a state of the weak, the cowardly, the lazy members of the nation".[197]

Farah Antun emphasised the close connection between the affirmation of the Islamic character of the Hamidian state – the immediate context of

193 Anṭūn, "Ṣawt min baʿīd", 190.

194 Adīb Isḥāq, *Al-kitābāt al-siyāsiyya wa al-ijtimāʿiyya*, ed. Nājī ʿAllūsh (Beirut: Dar al-Ṭalīʿa, 1982), 380–381.

195 al-Shumayyil, *Taʿrīb li sharḥ Büchner ʿalā madhab Darwin*, ن, n.

196 al-Shumayyil, *Majmūʿat al-duktūr Shiblī Shumayyil*, 194.

197 Anṭūn, "Ṣawt min baʿīd", 188.

his activity – and confessional conflicts. This awareness represented a wider current of thought that linked confessionalism and tyranny, and condemned religion for its link with both. This tendency, particularly after the Ottoman Constitutional Revolution in 1908, was represented by an abundant poetic production. Secularists strengthened this position through a direct attack on one of the basic principles of Islamic modernism, namely that Islam had a specific link and close connections to science and tolerance. In a pseudonymous article published in the newspaper *al-Mu'ayyad* on 30 March 1908, a Muslim defender of Shumayyil wondered how one should understand Moses's perception of the Burning Bush, the rivers of milk and honey, and the reality of God's breathing into the Virgin Mary's genitals (*farj* – the reference being to Qur'an, 21:91, 66:12),[198] if we were to accept the statement that Islam alone is the religion of reason and that reason be omniscient.[199] At the same time Shumayyil wrote in parodistic imitation of Qur'anic diction and rhyme about religion being "clear signs . . . and dazzling truths", an error to which people clung as though it were the firmest bond (*al-'urwa al-wuthqā*) uniting them all, with every party to it satisfied.[200]

Further, secularists considered that civilisation had priority over religion. Shumayyil characterised Islam as a religion of action but that Muslims had declined nevertheless. Christianity he characterised as a religion of instruction and investigation but that Christians took the path of practical life. For this reason, the claim that Islam is itself an obstacle to the development of Muslims cannot be sustained. Human society determines all and runs according to merciless and unforgiving laws. The only reason for the backwardness of Muslims is the existence of clerics and those who claim that they have authority over it. God forbid that the Qur'an, aspiring for the highest social aims, should seek its contents to be "a burden on the neck of society".[201] Farah Antun, in his controversy with 'Abduh, went further. This controversy led to the "amputation" of his life and the ruin of his journal *al-Jami'a* despite his great influence in the field of free thought and his complete integration into the Egyptian national movement.[202] Antun affirmed

198 Anīs al-Khūrī al-Maqdisī, *Al-'awāmil al-fa''āla*, 43–45.

199 See al-Shumayyil, *Majmū'at al-duktūr Shiblī al-Shumayyil*, 81–82.

200 Ibid., 85.

201 Ibid., 57–58, 60–62.

202 Mūsā, *Tarbiyat Salāma Mūsā*, 44, 46.

that the link between civil power and religious authority in the history of Islam made religious tolerance more difficult than in Christianity, which ultimately separated civil and religious authorities, a "remarkable separation which prepared the way for true civilisation and true civility".[203]

Thus, one basic demand of the secularists was the separation of religion from state, and rendering it a personal matter. Religion, for enlightened thinkers with a religious bent, was the link between believers and their deity, while for the non-religious, religion was a topic for social research and, seen in this light, it ceased to be a matter of social conflict – so Shumayyil.[204] From considering the individual conscience as the touchstone for the profession of a religion, it follows that force has no place in calls for the rejection of religion. Freedom of thought makes neither belief nor unbelief obligatory, and does not war with contrary views. Science is not itself an emblem of atheism but is merely a means of ascertaining the truth.[205] Truth, as made manifest by free reason, strengthens human resolve to subdue nature and guides humans, through reason, to their rights and their duties, and indicates how laws change with changing times.[206]

Shidyaq had earlier developed the position of the Young Ottomans who maintained that it was the state's adoption of a religion that restrained and checked tyranny. He held that what applied to the state should not apply to individuals. The state should not interfere in the beliefs of its citizens but should preserve religiosity as an assembly of virtues, rather than as an element of social division as it was in his day.[207] He seems to have accepted the grounds for the separation of religion from public life, except for the question of state adoption of religion as a sort of ethos. These grounds for separation were summarised by Farah Antun as the consequences of mixing religion and public life: fetters imposed on human thought, inequality between members of the same nation, use of religion in the world rather than directing it towards the other world, demagogy. At a political level, the result of this was the demand for patriotism and citizenship, instead of the community of religion as the basis for public life.[208]

203 Anṭūn, *Ibn Rushd wa falsafatuhu*, 216.
204 al-Shumayyil, *Majmū'at al-duktūr Shiblī al-Shumayyil*, 77.
205 Ibid., 285–286.
206 al-Shumayyil, *Ta'rīb li sharḥ Büchner 'alā maḏhab Darwin*, ق ص.
207 al-Ṣulḥ, *Aḥmad Fāris al-Shidyāq*, 207, 223, 228.
208 Anṭūn, *Ibn Rushd wa falsafatuhu*, 144–149.

Thus, one can see the link between the secularist claims and the logic of the *Tanzimat* developments. These claims had been the ideological and theoretical voice of the implicit secularism that the age had made possible in Ottoman territories, even if its ideological possibilities had been checked under the reign of the sultan Abdülhamid that nevertheless saw the first flowering of secular thought in Arab lands where Hamidian censorship could be evaded. Arab materialism as represented by Shumayyil accompanied another, parallel political and intellectual orientation emphasising history and emancipation from the dead weight of tradition. This parallel movement was what the Young Turks were to develop leading to the Kemalist Revolution. The Young Turk movement, and, later the Committee for Union and Progress, conjoined social and intellectual questions with the national question, which led to the movement's success.

As for the *Tanzimat* in its official guise, it was timid, allowing itself to be fettered by the religious institutions, and then by Islamic Reformism of the less modernist inclination. In their first phase, which was institutionally and implicitly revolutionary, the *Tanzimat* unfolded without considering the weight of international politics, in an unjustified atmosphere of optimism, filled with the utopian views of the nineteenth century with belief in evolution and reformist social engineering. It was shown earlier how foreign intervention and the correlative erection of sectarian cleavages worked to rein in these social and educational prospects that had implied, and indeed necessitated, the dismantling of intermediate patrimonial and ascriptive instances, including those of confession, and creating Ottoman citizens: foreign intervention stirred up and encouraged confessionalism and gave it the necessary support in intellectual and economic terms. The territory of the sultanate was maintained as a constellation of contiguous but disparate units caught in a cycle of global economic subservience. The *Tanzimat* dynamic did not take into account the way that colonial relations contributed to foiling progress and its possibility even if some *Tanzimat* statesmen and secular intellectuals were aware of this, but unable to resist. Farah Antun was not the only voice calling for unity on the basis of citizenship and not religion, in order to move with the tide of modern European civilisation "so that we may compete with Europe and not be swept away and be made subject to the rule of others".[209] This position underpinned the establishment

209 Ibid., 21.

of secular schools and parallel intellectual currents, and included initiatives such as the National School of Butros al-Bustani set up in Shoueifat outside Beirut in 1863, and the journal he founded in 1860, *Nafir Suriyya*. Such viewpoints remained without a philosophical basis other than the selective imitation of the bases of European progress, although Shumayyil naturally constituted an exception.[210]

Secular thought therefore corresponded to the dynamics made available by the *Tanzimat*, sharing some of its optimistic and simplistic views, with a measure of confidence in the coherence of European actions and its global character despite the colonial relationship with Europe. On the basis of the progressive globally oriented principle, secular thought was one of the basic underpinnings that led to the Kemalist revolution in what remained of the Ottoman domains, while effective political action in the Arab East was emasculated when the region became the arena of British and French geo-strategic policies and rivalries.

Therefore, the Lebanese Christian leaven that produced the majority of early explicit Arab proponents of secularism is an argument in favour of secularism, not against it, as many voices today continue to assert as they continue arguing in terms of fantasmatic inside/outside contrasts. It is held implicitly that the Christianity of these intellectuals led them to call for citizenship. In actual fact, the Christian affiliation of many early secularists leads to a contrary conclusion to that emerging from today's anti-secular discourse, with its sophistical finger-pointing. Lebanese Christians acting as Christians, and especially the Maronites, were decidedly sectarian in orientation, protected in this stance by European powers and buttressed by the privileges derived from links to Europe.

Secularists followed the Ottomanist course that was in accord with the historical orientation of the *Tanzimat* state, ideologically in correspondence to its dynamic; their secularism was a clear perception of reality and the record of a process. Secularists figured as intellectuals unaffiliated to a particular community. Their position was one opposed to confessionalism whether Islamic in character or not. In other words, these thinkers, like their counterparts in the Young Turks, the Committee of Union and Progress, and the Turkish materialists, were avant-garde intellectuals. They surveyed

210 ʿAbd al-Laṭīf, *Al-ta'wīl wa al-mufāraqa*, 92–93.

their modern history from a cultural position that enabled them to do this and from a social position whose relative marginality constituted an excellent vantage point from which the general interest could be differentiated from private interests. Al-Afghani was not reproached for his marginality, and Adib Ishaq, Salim 'Anhuri, and the satirist, journalist, dramatist, and Jewish Egyptian nationalist Ya'qub Sannu' (1839–1912)[211] – all disciples of al-Afghani and, like him, Freemasons[212] – were not arraigned for their confessional affiliations, as they adopted progressive thought, including the opposition to confessionalism.

211 Al-Bagdadi, *Vorgestellte Öffentlichkeit*, ch. 5.

212 Al-Afghani in his typical fashion tried to use Freemasonry to his own political purposes, a move that was not welcomed, prompting him to try to set up his own lodge: Albert Kudsi-Zadeh, "Afghani and freemasonry in Egypt", *Journal of the American Oriental Society* 92 (1972): 25–35.

4
Sites of Secularism in the Twentieth Century

The two previous chapters described and analysed sites of historical breaks in modern Arab history that accompanied its entry into a new universal era. The state assumed a presence of a novel nature, seeking to expand beyond taxation, military control, and overall administration (including the administration of law and cult), attempting in effect to penetrate society and remodel it. This presence brought with it features whose potential was not realised integrally in the ways that had been intended or that had been implicit. This was due to global political factors complemented with social conservatism in Arab societies favourable to a patrimonialist view of the state, social organisation, and culture. State and institutions, with their universalising dimensions, worked to restructure official culture, a culture that was connected to the state, to the future orientation of society and to universalist modules of political and social thought based on a secular compound of utilitarianism, scientism, and evolutionism. Analysis in the previous chapter of the link between sources of authority – both Islamic and the secular sources associated with modern global thought – showed that the fundamental positions for modernist Islamic reformist thought consisted of different strains of Western evolutionism apologetically redacted. Islamic reformist thought presented the range of its concerns as though they were based on Islamic authority. This authority was nominal, founded on illusion and on the interpretation of a supposed past in the light of the present, removing pastness from the Islamic past. In the same breath, it removed the actuality of actual Western ideas that became global as the West went global, both as exemplary and as colonial, soft as well as hard: positive, harmful, progressive, reactionary. This Western universalism contained elements of Enlightenment and of the counter-Enlightenment, as well as elements promoting subordination and backwardness. As a result, the world – including Ottoman and post-Ottoman lands – was making entry into the universalism of Europe from a subordinate position, by choice or by necessity. Entry was also being made to a new temporality that was the vehicle of historical breaks, a recent past with a high degree of internal articulation subverted by emergent conditions making for the modern reforming state, a state with an emergent reconfiguration.

Secularism, implicit, functional, and operational, or explicit, came to reshape the organisational apparatus of the state and its culture, and became a practical basis for social and intellectual life in the Ottoman and larger cities, particularly among senior officialdom and higher socio-economic layers, notably Muslims in Turkey and the Syrian provinces as well as educated Christians. Religious institutions continued to provide a significant part of basic education, continuing to impart its cognitive, pedagogical, and moral goods. Arab societies and cultures changed accordingly in relation to rhythms that were variable, uneven yet combined. Thus, there coexisted in independent, semi-independent, and colonised Arab countries political, social, cultural, and intellectual islands integrated in terms of their legal definition as countries by the agency of the state whose implicit tendency veered towards the creation of more homogeneous societies by acculturation through systems of education that were ultimately, in the course of the twentieth century, supplemented by state communication and information apparatuses. The independent or quasi-independent states – with significant democratic-liberal periods in Syria, Egypt, Iraq, and Lebanon, which are often forgotten – carried further the state of the *Tanzimat* as a centralising state emitting a homogenising culture seeking to install minimum degrees of homogeneity. Varied, balkanised temporalities existed, temporalities that the resources of the state and uncontrolled global forces of an economic and cultural type directed into a universal movement, assimilated with varying degrees of integration and coherence.

The independent or quasi-independent states, as well as colonial ones (such as Tunisia), and later, the nationalist revolutionary states, pursued the course inaugurated by the *Tanzimat* in their attempt to penetrate and reshape society in a variety of respects: first by the transmission, however uneven, of modern culture and cultural institutions, and subsequently by highly centralised political organisation, however uneven in turn. These states also sought to assume a moral – in the objective sense, often with preacherly turns – and intellectual role, tendentially of ideological hegemony and with pressure exercised upon forms of socio-cultural balkanisation. These processes moved in different and complex directions in the twentieth century. Earlier chapters scrutinised these processes in a synoptic fashion emphasising structures and systemic trends that proceeded unevenly but in the context of a discernible integrative historical movement. The unfolding of processes set in place in the nineteenth century will be pursued further here. This chapter will attend to some manifestations of signature secular values, cognitive as well as public, and secular institutions as they were implanted by reforming states. Such manifestations were rooted in both general and specific social practices carried forward by social and political actors whose culture was formed by the motifs of the *Tanzimat* state with its *dirigiste* approach to engagement with society.

Before concentrating on sectors and contexts of secularism in Arab societies in the first half of the twentieth century, it would be appropriate rapidly to survey regions of the Maghreb that can be seen as a laboratory in which can be observed in summary form the recapitulation of crucial moments in the recent history of the Mashreq. The general development of society in Tunisia and in Algeria had been frozen by French colonialism, while in Morocco a situation of defensive immobility prevailed, beginning with an attitude of despondent resignation after the proclamation of the French Protectorate in 1912 and Hubert Lyautey's assumption of authority as French Resident-General. At this time rapid changes effected restricted social groups and milieux, trickling down uncertainly at uneven rates. This was not necessarily a process of imitation of the Mashreq or making up for perceived deficits as might be implied by the determinism of Arab nationalist historiography. These changes were part of a global historical process with corresponding developments in India and elsewhere. This applies equally to the twin crises of Islamic reformism and secular politics.

Algerian Islamic reformism certainly developed under the direct influence of the East, notably Rashid Rida's journal *al-Manār*. The visit to Algeria of Muhammad 'Abduh in 1903 sowed decided seeds of reform, and many members of the Association of Muslim Ulama (officially founded in 1931) had studied and lived in the East. The Algerian Islamic scholar Bashir al-Ibrahimi, co-founder, with Ibn Badis, of the Association of Muslim Ulama, had studied in Damascus and was in close contact with nationalists there. He had also lived in the Hijaz as a child, as did Tayyib al-Uqbi (1888–1960) who, like al-Ibrahimi, was a member of the Association, whose primary slogan was, famously, "Islam is my religion, Arabic is my language, Algeria is my homeland". Islamic reformism in Algeria played principally an educational role alongside its para-nationalist activity, and created a space between French education and that of the Sufi lodges. In the eastern Algerian city of Constantine, the mosque of Sidi al-Akhdar where Ibn Badis taught was an institution that played an intermediary role in intercultural transmission between traditional education at a local level and the opening onto universalism – in Islamic reformist terms – provided by the Zeitouna mosque in Tunis.[1] Similarly, with regard to Morocco, there is no doubt about the important influence of the journal *al-Manār* on the emergence of the Salafiyya movement with Abu Shuʿayb al-Dukkali (1878–1937). The influence of Mashreq-based reformism was direct and manifest on Tunisians such as Abd al-Aziz al-Tha'alibi, Taher Haddad, Abu'l-Qasim al-Shabbi, and other figures associated with the Zeytouna in the period after the First World War.

In comparison with patrician ulama conservative allies of the French such as the Ben ʿAshur, Bayram, An-Naifar, and Ju'ayt families, the group of innovative Zeytouna thinkers of modest social origins exercised a decisive influence on the emergence of the Tunisian national movement. This movement had itself been influenced by an education system that included a variety of modern subjects as well as the French language, nurtured in the Sadiqiya College in Tunis (founded in 1876) and other institutions. Tunisian Islamic reformism had a nationalist orientation overall.[2] In its initial period, it blended the reactionary defensiveness perceptible in the origins of the Islamic reformism at the period of Abdülhamid with the constitutionalism that reconfigured shariʿa as indicating representative government, as we saw.

These currents of thoughts, and the Young Tunisians, together flowed into the Destour Party, founded in 1920 under the leadership of Thaʿalibi. Later, Habib Bourguiba (1903–2000) joined the party after finishing his study of law in France, and, considering it too conservative and reticent, went on to found the neo-Destour in 1934 and to lead Tunisia towards independence and the formation of the republic in 1957. It had become the practice for

1 Ali Merad, *Le Réformisme musulman en Algérie de 1925 à 1940*, 17–19, 88–90, 137, 208, 326 and Saʿad Allāh, *Al-ḥaraka al-waṭaniyya fī al-jazāʾir*, vol. 2, 437–438.

2 Mahmoud Abdel Moula, *L'Université Zaytounienne et la société tunisienne* (Tunis: Centre National de la Recherche Scientifique, 1971), 136–139.

upper-class Tunisians to send their children to study in French schools. The culture acquired by these students had a determining influence on the course of the development of Tunisian nationalism as well as a decisive effect on the growth and development of secularism that subsequently played a major role in the development of official culture in the Tunisian republic. While the *Tanzimat* and their architects had, as noted earlier, reached a political impasse, it does not seem that a similar situation prevailed in Tunisia after the first reforms had been initiated by the Young Tunisians in the early twentieth century. Reactions to French policy were a decisive factor, driving the *évolués* to adopt increasingly combative nationalist positions with secularising developments increasingly as one of their pillars, which were then allowed to come into their own after independence. This approach was in direct political and cultural opposition to the alliance of the Bays (hereditary rulers of Tunisia since the early eighteenth century) and the patrician ulama.

In Algeria, the reclamation of developments that had already been in place elsewhere came later than in Tunisia and in a more complex form. Algeria saw in the 1930s Francophone politico-cultural groups thoroughly acculturated into metropolitan culture decidedly secular in orientation. Most nevertheless saw in Islam a sign of separation between indigenous Algerians and the Franco-Algerian colonial settlers. The Fédération d'élus musulmans, founded in 1927, was liberal in orientation, enthusiastically supported general adoption of the revolutionary values of 1789, and called for the modernisation of Algerian society. The Étoile Nord-Africaine, led by Messali Hadj (1898–1974) and the forerunner of the National Liberation Front, had the same starting point and used Islamic symbols such as the Qur'anic verse 3:103 – "And hold firmly to the rope of God all together and do not become divided" – as a sign of separation from the French settlers, while downplaying the Islamic internationalism ceaselessly propagated from Geneva by the Lebanese (Druze) Shakib Arslan (1869–1946) and relayed locally by the Association of Muslim Ulama. The Étoile Nord-Africaine aligned itself with the French Popular Front in the 1930s, and its position on the link to France remained somewhat uncertain and multivalent. It did not perceive clearly and consequentially that there was a duality within French politics and culture: one enlightened, liberal, and potentially liberating, the other obscurantist and colonialist, deploying Jesuits across the empire. The makers of the *Tanzimat* in Ottoman Istanbul had been marked by a similar uncertainty. The Étoile Nord-Africaine was, however, distinct from other *évolué* tendencies that denied the existence of an Algerian national entity separate from

France, an approach principally articulated by Ferhat Abbas in his initial phase in the 1930s, before he came to adopt nationalist positions.[3]

In the Mashriq, after the First World War, two tendencies evolved that detached themselves from the secularising movement of Turkish history that had linked socio-cultural change and national liberation. In Egypt after the 1919 Revolution, a class of politicians came to power who were the product of modern education and the modernisation of tastes and manners that had affected the upper classes. In its internal party rivalries and in its struggles with the Royal Palace, which supported al-Azhar, this emerging class was inclined to use religion in its institutional dimension as well as popular sentiment as an element to gain tactical advantages and allies, especially during election campaigns. Tension developed in Egypt between the culture of politicians and the logic of government on the one hand and, on the other, the attempts of these same politicians to cede positions to religious forces in return for political returns, real or perceived. Few took account of the long-term abrasions of the body politic consequent upon this. With regard to the use of confessional loyalties by politicians, the national loyalty and confessional harmony characteristic of Egyptian Christians is due more to the wisdom and patriotism of the Copts themselves than to the good sense of Muslim politicians. It is no secret that the Free Constitutionalist Party, which had supported secular thought by its support for Taha Hussein (1889–1973), perhaps the most prominent literary and cultural figure in the Arab World in the twentieth century, and 'Ali 'Abd al-Raziq (1888–1966) in face of religious criticism to be discussed below, provoked communal sentiments when it used the claim that the Copts controlled the Wafd Party, when in political contestation with the latter. The Free Constitutionalists also called for proportional confessional representation in Parliament and in government positions. For its part, the monarchy sought political advantage through an alliance with al-Azhar and by imposing restrictions upon the Copts, reducing their access to government employment, and denying them parity with Egyptian nationals. A ministerial directive of 1940 barred Copts from teaching Arabic in schools, even if they were graduates of the Department of Arabic in the Faculty of Arts.[4]

---

3 Saʿad Allāh, *Al-ḥaraka al-waṭaniyya fī al-jazāʾir*, vol. 2, 389–390, 393, 399, 417, 421–427, vol. 3, 76–78, 115–116, 128, 132–135, 145–157.

4 Yūsuf, *Al-aqbāṭ wa al-qawmiyya al-ʿarabiyya*, 127–128 and al-Bishrī, *Al-muslimūn wa al-aqbāṭ fī iṭār al-jamāʿa al-waṭaniyya*, 201–207.

In Syria and the surrounding region, the situation was quite different. Syria had been the theatre for a strident policy of political confessionalisation followed by the French Mandate authorities from 1920 to 1943. According to the principles of the "Eastern Question" inherited from the previous century, Syria was divided into the states of Aleppo, Damascus, the Alawite state (including Latakia), and Jebel Druze, while the State of Greater Lebanon (1920) was created on a confessional (Maronite) majority basis; the Syrian east and north-east and the Golan Heights were given a special status, while Alexandretta was later ceded to Turkey. Except for Lebanon, the division of the rest of Syria lasted only until 1925. Given this situation it is not surprising that confessionalism and national counter-loyalties were among the most important factors that led nationalist movements to take a clearly secularising political course and to avoid mention of religion. Repudiating, indeed tabooing, the political uses of religion in politics also had clear parallels in Iraq. The proponents of the views of the Islamic League had little influence in Syria and the region. When in 1936 Shakib Arslan gave a speech in Damascus restricting Arab nationalism to Muslims, Syrian nationalist politicians such as the Aleppans Sa'adallah and Ihsan al-Jabiri (1893–1947) delivered public rebuttals and rebukes.[5]

1 Secular Legislation and Social Dynamics

We have seen that the course of modern universal history incubated secularising and secular outcomes, and modern Arab social and cultural history is governed by this complex and serpentine itinerary that bore, equally, conflicts and resistances, as conservatives adopted religion as the war-cry against change. After the Second World War, state education continued to spread even if this was in varying proportions, notably in Syria where primary education in state schools had become free from 1933 and Qur'anic *kuttāb* schools were on the point of disappearing. Meanwhile in Egypt, the situation was more complicated and more conflictual, and these issues highly politicised. Primary and secondary education provided by al-Azhar expanded. In

---

5 Firdīnānd Tawtal, *Wathā'iq tārīkhiyya 'an halab: Akhbār al-Lātīn wa al-Rūm wa mā ilayhim 1855–1963* (Beirut: al-maṭba'a al-Kāthūlīkiyya, 1964), 141–143. See William L. Cleveland, *Islam Against the West: Shakib Arslān and the Campaign for Islamic Nationalism* (Austin: University of Texas Press, 2011).

Tunis, from 1947 to 1949, *kuttāb* schools accounted for nearly 40 per cent of pupils in primary education.[6] Taha Hussein, former Azharite, was right when, in his celeberated book *The Future of Culture in Egypt* (1938), he called for reform of the teaching of al-Azhar so as to conform with the development of what he called the "national personality" and to state curricula. Al-Azhar should cease to be a state within the state; its provision of specialised training in religious sciences needs to be "within the law".[7] For his part, Ahmad Amin, also a former Azharite and initially an *ʿalim*, called on al-Azhar to give up primary and secondary education and to limit itself to tertiary religious teaching.[8]

What applied to al-Azhar applied to other forms of confessional education, and Taha Hussein called for Christian schools to be treated in the same way as al-Azhar.[9] Perhaps Hussein had in mind the institution of Dar al-ʿUlum, an institution intended to reform traditional education but that managed only to avoid meaningful study of religious sciences without rigorous study of modern subjects.[10] While the system of government schools in Syria expanded, the majority of schools remained foreign (notably but not exclusively French) and either secular in character or belonging to various Catholic organisations (Jesuits, Lazarists, and others) and some belonging to other denominations, until independence. These schools transmitted at least a general modern culture in addition to a religious or denominational instruction to some of their Christian pupils. State public institutions, in addition to the Civil Preparatory School (Maktab ʿAnbar) in Damascus, which was to play an interesting part in political mobilisation among students, were the pathway to a higher education with a secular character, the common character of university education overall. It does not at all appear that secular versus denominational schools were an issue to secularists and other modernisers. Either would have been considered proper, as routes to higher education and to higher government positions, and connected to the cultural resources of the state and of advanced Europe

6 Abdel Moula, *L'Université Zaytounienne et la société tunisienne*, 114, 119.

7 Ṭaḥa Ḥusayn, *Al-majmūʿa al-kāmila li muʾallafāt al-duktūr Ṭaḥa Ḥusayn*, 16 vols (Beirut: Dār al-Kitāb al-Lubnānī, 1984), vol. 9, 93–95, 99.

8 Aḥmad Amīn, *Fayḍ al-khāṭir* (Cairo: Maktabat al-Nahḍa al-ʿArabiyya, 1956–1961), 130.

9 Ḥusayn, *Al-majmūʿa al-kāmila*, 447–448.

10 Ibid., 350–354. See too Muḥammad ʿAbduh, *Al-aʿmāl al-kāmila*, vol. 3, 119–120. Muḥammad ʿAbduh had already addressed similar criticisms to Dār al-ʿUlūm.

Education in secular schools became an issue only when it became the target of attack by Christian religious figures, wary of secular education that, some held, urged us to allow ourselves to be moulded by the "morals of others" and brought up the issue of contradiction between science and religion.[11] Muslims such as Rashid Rida joined in the attack. In 1929 he gave a responsum, fatwa, intended to prevent Muslims from enrolling in foreign institutions until they had a firm mastery of the tenets of Islam.[12] Shaykhs of al-Azhar demanded government positions for graduates of al-Azhar who faced competition from graduates of Cairo University, Dar al-'Ulum, and other tertiary institutions. The controversy surrounding Taha Hussein's view of the apocryphal character of pre-Islamic poetry became the occasion for a fierce attack by al-Azhar on the Egyptian University, and on the state that, it was alleged, did not regulate the university in a way that served the interests of religious culture.[13] The pressure of al-Azhar on the university was severe and relentless, and in the 1930s al-Azhar was allowed to intervene in its affairs – George Bernard Shaw's play *Saint Joan* was removed from the curriculum because it purportedly contained material harmful to religion.[14] During the same period the Catholic Université Saint Joseph in Beirut was obliged to suspend the poet Marun 'Abbud (1886–1962) from his teaching post three months after commencing, as he was purportedly a danger to the Maronite Church and the Catholic faith.[15]

In this way, normal social and cultural changes were transfigured into specifically secular ones, and defined as such, when the religious parties of all denominations saw these changes as signs of opposition to religion. Among these changes was so-called Westernisation, so that objective transformations of social life were denominated as external, intrusive, immoral, alienating, leading to an abundant polemical literature in the 1920s and 1930s.[16] The

11 See Yūsuf al-'Amshītī, "Al-īmān wa al-'ilm akhawān lā yakhtalifān", *al-Mashriq* 21 (1923): 81–93.

12 Riḍā, *Fatāwā*, 780.

13 Muḥammad Aḥmad 'Arafa, *Naqd maṭā'in fī al-qur'ān al-karīm yataḍamman tafnīd mā alqāhu al-duktūr Ṭaha Ḥusayn 'alā ṭalabat kulliyat al-ādāb fī al-jāmi'a al-miṣriyya* (Cairo: Maṭba'at al-Manār, 1932), 112–130; Muṣṭafā Ṣādiq al-Rāfi'i, *Taḥta rāyat al-Qur'ān: Al-ma'araka bayn al-qadīm wa al-jadīd* (Cairo: Maṭba'at al-Istiqāma, 1946), 157, 171, 175–180.

14 Tawfīq al-Ḥakīm, *Naẓarāt fī al-dīn wa al-thaqāfa wa al-mujtama'* (Cairo: al-Maktab al-Miṣrī al-Ḥadīth, 1979), 168.

15 Mārūn 'Abbūd, *Ruwwād al-nahḍa al-ḥadītha* (Beirut: Dār al-'Ilm lil-Malāyīn, 1952), 225.

16 Ḥusayn, *Al-ittijāhāt al-waṭaniyya fī al-adab al-mu'āṣir*, vol. 2, 191–201.

religious lobby claimed that social justice should be codified in a way that they saw as conforming to what they took to be shari'a. They made Islam without specification the gauge for moral behaviour after they had made the move to redact customs and morals in terms of religion, in a way contrary to actual practice past and present. This entailed the removal of the authority of society and its ways and proposed instead religious norms and practices as an a priori criterion for rectitude, thereby expanding the social remit of religion. This conformed to the tendency of those speaking in the name of modern Islam to take religion as the world's double. Instead of being a diffuse and highly complex historical entity, Islam was thus made into a collection of all-embracing principles, effectively an alternative world or a counter-world whose features began to solidify in an operation that paralleled the development of modern social organisation on bases in the modern world. It was the religious institution that caused secular developments to break out of their implicitness and to become consciously secular, acknowledged by some, fudged by many. Religion was set up as the counterpoint, and counterweight, an abstract contrary to actual change in general, in an increasingly self-enclosed package.

The religious institution was not devoid of links to the wider society and could rely on hidden resources of conservatism in circles that were neither especially pious nor particularly religious or concerned with religion. One important liberal figure, Muhammad Hussein Haykal (1888–1956),[17] criticised modern trends in Arabic poetry composed by émigré poets in the Americas, although he recognised their artistic distinction. Nevertheless, he affirmed the need to resist such poetry as it was a danger for Islamic culture.[18] This position belonged to a general anxiety of ambivalence to which Egyptian figures seemed to have been especially prone. Haykal, like other major figures of Egyptian letters such as Taha Hussein and Abbas Mahmud al-'Aqqad (1889–1964), accepted modern aesthetic criteria without being able to appreciate and understand innovative poetry.[19] These positions can only be interpreted in terms of a visceral resistance to innovation in various

17 On whom: Baber Johansen, *Muhammad Husain Haikal: Europa und der Orient im Weltbild eines ägyptischen Liberalen* (Beirut: Orient-Institut der Deutschen Morgenländischen Gesellschaft, 1967).

18 Salma al-Khadra al-Jayyusi, *Trends and Movements in Modern Arabic Poetry*, Studies in Arabic Literature, 2 vols (Leiden: Brill, 1977), vol. 1, 98.

19 Ibid., 394.

domains, often, as with Hussein, against his better judgement. Specific areas – such as poetry – were specially favoured by traditionalists as sites of resistance to the advance of change. This temper indicated a profound seam of social conservatism at a time when such conservatism was not as generally prevalent or articulate as one might imagine. This is likely to be interpretable in terms of the uncertainty of certain social positions amidst profound transformation that renders many groups prone to fascination with moralism of the draconian variety, and with disciplinary, para-fascist political, and other authoritarian and disciplinarian formations. Rigourist moralism had been Sayyid Qutb's passage to the safety of exorbitant Islamism (*ghuluw*, in classical Muslim traditions). That moralism did not accord with social practice remained unrecorded. The religious lobby was nonetheless pioneeringly active in its attacks on new literary styles, attacking the novel as foreign and destructive of morals, and considering drama as leading to the ruin of the language of the Qur'an and a Trojan horse for writing Arabic in Latin script.[20] Whatever cogency there may have been in these positions, they belonged to the perspective of a counter-culture, a religious project harnessed by its architects to claim guardianship over society, and to maintain inherited institutional privileges and political influence. Modern poetry and personal freedoms were and still remain a strategic reserve for politico-religious claims to entitlement, domains that many progressives shied away from as they evaded psychological and social issues raised by poetry.

The politically liberal period in the Arab world coincided with the Kemalist transformations in Turkey, and it is not surprising that the Kemalist revolution from above was widely considered to be an example to follow. The echoes of Kemalism in the writing of Ibn Badis in Algeria have already been mentioned. Even Rashid Rida esteemed Mustafa Kemal before the abolition of the caliphate in 1924.[21] Atatürk was held in high regard[22] by the Syrian nationalists who gave the Ankara government substantial assistance in the campaign against French forces in Cilicia in 1920, although the Turks refrained from establishing permanent relations with them.[23] In Egypt Mustafa Kemal was

20 Ḥusayn, *Al-ittijāhāt al-waṭaniyya*, vol. 2, 254–259, 259–365.

21 Rashīd Rida in a letter to Shakīb Arslān, dated 30 January 1923 in Arslān, *Al-Sayyid Rashīd Riḍā*, 316–317; private family information of the present author.

22 'Abd al-Raḥmān al-Shāhbandar, "Hal yutāḥ li'l-sharq an yasta'īd majdahu?" *al-Hilāl* 42/1 (1933): 26–27.

23 Arslān, *Al-Sayyid Rashīd Riḍā aw ikhā' arba'īn sana*, 327–328.

highly estimated and the poet Ahmad Shawqi compared him with Khalid b. al-Walid, the seventh-century premier military commander of the Arab conquest, although Shawqi's enthusiasm also cooled after the abolition of the caliphate.[24] One Islamist commentator saw Egyptians of a different mind to his as copycats of the Turks: when Kemalists adopted the white wolf, a symbol derived from the pagan ancestors of the Turks, as a symbol to be depicted on postage stamps, Egyptians followed their example and placed an image of the Sphinx on Egyptian bank notes and postage stamps.[25] When the Kemalists specified a minimum age for the marriage of boys and girls, the Egyptians followed suit. Following the abolition of shariʿa courts in Turkey in 1924, some Egyptians began to discuss their abolition in Egypt. When Mustafa Kemal compelled Turkish women to unveil and to socialise and dance with men, this provoked controversies in many Egyptian circles and in the press. The obligation for Turkish men to wear hats instead of the fez led some Egyptian writers to reflect on what they termed the "problem of dress", some calling for the adoption of a uniform, while others expressed partiality to hats. When Turkey replaced Arabic script with Latin script, many writers and journalists in Egypt began debating what they termed "the problems of writing and Arabic script". Yet the Egyptian situation involved more than imitation of the pioneering Turkish conditions: global tendencies were at work (not least with the adoption of Latin script in many countries), exemplified in the region by the rapidity and success of Kemalist transformations. The labelling of local Egyptian changes as foreign, reprehensible, and anomic is one of the effects of the Islamic campaign against Kemalism led by Mustafa Sabri (1869–1954), the last Ottoman *şeyhülislam* from 1919 to 1922. Intellectually accomplished and capable, he had taken refuge in Egypt where he spent the rest of his life. His controversial campaigns, of broad remit, were joined by Rashid Rida and the conservative nationalist lawyer, historian, and political figure ʿAbd al-Rahman al-Rafiʿi (1889–1966), and by many others, despite widespread suspicions about Sabri's motives.[26]

The matter of replacing the tarboosh with the hat is not a matter of great importance, but it stood metonymically for wider issues in Egypt if not elsewhere. There was a short-lived movement that called for adopting the

24 Ḥusayn, *Al-ittijāhāt al-waṭaniyya fī al-adab al-muʿāṣir*, vol. 2, 26–29, 33–36.
25 Ibid., 97.
26 Ibid., 31.

Turkish example. At one point, the Ministry of Education forbade pupils in its schools to wear hats at a time when some ulama decreed that wearing hats was an illicit imitation of Europeans.[27] The journal *al-Hilāl* commented sarcastically in 1926 that "some turban-wearers succeeded in replacing the fez with the turban but the wearers of the fez were not able to adopt the hat".[28] Some progressive thinkers such as Salama Musa said quite clearly that discussion about the subject in utilitarian terms such as protection from sun and rain evaded the essential matter, which was that hats "inspire in us a European mentality".[29] And he was right, as the terms of the discussion rarely addressed the underlying motifs and resorted to arguments from utility. The matter quickly lost relevance in the course of the 1920s when men gradually shed the fez and started to go bare-headed instead. This also became the prevailing custom in Turkey, with the exception of the flat cap still worn in rural areas. Outside Egypt vestimentary transformations occurred almost naturally without leading to the eruption of any significant public acrimony.

The question of women had always been the pivotal question in matters of personal freedoms,[30] knotting together in complex fashion a variety of issues of motifs, the unravelling of which, as suggested, facilitates the undoing of numerous social impasses. The issue arose in the folds of the tension generated between the realities of social change on the one hand and, on the other, the religious formulation of social conservatism and backward-looking practices, armoured by conservative mysogyny. This made the feminine question at once one of public morality, and one of the contrast between secularising developments resisted by a conservatism and a patriarchy that resorted to expressing itself in religious terms when it sensed itself to be especially under siege. The position consonant with the development and advancement of society became a secular opposition to a religious offensive. This resulted in a defensive, apologetic, or equivocating position by many secularists, often erring on the side of caution, and believing the mass of their compatriots to be irredeemably irrational and puerile. Many of these postures and attitudes of compromise were not always as appreciated by religious adversaries as

27 See Ḥusayn, *Al-ittijāhāt al-waṭaniyya fī al-adab al-mu'āṣir*, vol. 2, 263–266.

28 Anonymous, "Al-Sharqiyyūn wa'l-qubba'a", *Al-Hilāl* (1926): 171.

29 Salāma Mūsā, *Al-yawm wa al-ghadd*, 126.

30 See the interesting synoptic overview of Leyla Dakhli, "Du point de vue des femmes", in *Le Moyen-Orient, fin XIXe–XXe siècle*, ed. Leyla Dakhli (Paris: Seuil, 2016), 31–57.

might have been hoped, and tended rather to embolden religious critics, who sought traction from the misogyny that permeated wide sectors of patriarchal societies, with women – not only in religious circles – seen in fundamentally negative terms as deficient, or indeed as objects of fear, scorn, and contempt. This attitude was not limited to popular circles but can be identified in the writing of the confirmed bachelor al-'Aqqad, for instance, in a particularly bitter form. It was displayed with an air of superiority by the playwright Tawfiq al-Hakim, who considered educated women to be a source of intellectual pleasure, making the home more attractive than it would otherwise be, as upscale domestic ornaments – he had kept his own marriage clandestine, and regarded it as a practical convenience. Taha Hussein adopted a characteristically balanced position, mocking, for instance, Ahmad Amin's suggestion for founding a school for wives, retorting that it was rather husbands who needed instruction, they being in greater need of correction and more corrupt than women.[31]

The beleaguered position imposed on women in intellectual and social terms was one instrument of defence open to sets of social and family relations subjected to wrenching and rapid change. To this can be added a psychological dimension in which older social arrangements guard themselves by manipulating categories of female impurity, contagion, and sexuality. It makes women, as bearers and rearers of children – albeit deficient intellectually, morally, and legally, so according to a traditionalist Muslim refrain – guardians of social rectitude, hinges of honour and shame, and of social turpitudes and virtues.[32] This did not escape the notice of those calling for the liberation of women. The Lebanese early feminist Nazira Zayn al-Din (1908–1976) berated her critics in 1929: "You did not evolve with the times, so time furled your standard and put it away. You have lost the heritage of your ancestors . . . or do you now want to unfurl your standards over the faces of your women, substituting them for your lost dominion?"[33] Attitudes towards women's freedom and rights evolved in conformity with the newer imperatives of social practice, and attitudes were not ideologised overall. This

31 Ṭaḥa Ḥusayn, "Madrasat-al azwāj" in *Fī qaḍāya al-mar'a*, ed. Faysal Darrāj (Beirut: Mu'assasat Nāṣir li'l-thaqāfa, 1980), 163–169.

32 Bouhdiba, *Sexuality in Islam*, 220–221, 232.

33 Zayn al-Dīn, *Al-fatāt wa al-shuyūkh*, 40.

was typified by Ahmad Lutfi al-Sayyid's calm and serene statements,[34] and by the negative position of Ahmad Amin towards the imperatives of woman's obedience that obtain in Muslim practice, called *bayt al-ṭāʿa* or restitution of conjugal rights, despite being obliged to issue judgments on this basis when he was a judge in a shariʿa court dealing with personal status.[35] The implicit attitudes of the wider public were natural corollaries to the increasing number of unveiled women, interaction between the sexes, and the education of girls and women.

Ideologisation and the transmutation of this issue into a zone of contention between secularists and the religious lobby was spurred principally by religious claims to moral entitlement. Rashid Rida's comment in 1929 on the relative emancipation of women (which he called, *tahattuk*, depravity, or licentiousness) is exemplary:

> women, mothers and housewives alike, educated maidens, all walk about the streets by night and day, holding men by the waist, attending clubs and parks, clothed and unclothed, swaying suggestively as they walk, while some swim in the sea where men swim or together with men. Others go to mixed dance halls and dance with men, with more shamelessness and undress than foreign women, with greater abandon, profligacy and debauchery. Yet others go to hairdressers' parlours where male hairdressers cut their hair, shave their behinds and beautify their necks and bosoms. There they meet with their friends. Ask not about their loud conversations and their secret assignations.[36]

Such statements speak for the distance between unfamiliar worlds, and emanate from a world remote from the movement of society, arising from people presuming total social authority grounded in what they claim for religion. Their opposition was all-encompassing, despite an unknowingness born of social distance and relative marginality. It was especially acute in view of the Victorianised sexual prudishness of some Muslim reformists that came, partly in reaction to proselytising Christian polemics, towards the end

34 al-Sayyid, *Al-muntakhabāt*, 33, 241, and passim.
35 Amīn, *Ḥayātī*, 206–207.
36 Muḥammad Rashīd Riḍā, "Fātiḥa" [Editorial] to vol. 30 of the journal *Al-Manār*, 30/1 (1929): 12–13.

of the nineteenth century, as mentioned before, and that contrasted to a far more latitudinarian set of social practices that had prevailed before.[37]

This is a strident social location whose social maladroitness easily drifted into a violence of deed that matched the violence of language. Vigilante proponents of veiling attacked unveiled women in Damascus streets in the 1920s, some sprayed with acid or assaulted. The government was petitioned to bar women from leaving their homes, and to close girls' schools, while at the same time some night clubs and bars were attacked.[38] The strong attack on Nazira Zayn al-Din's[39] 1927 book *Unveiling and Veiling: Lectures and Views on the Liberation of Women and Social Renewal in the Arab World* sometimes proceeded similarly, some booksellers menaced, anathema pronounced in some mosques, and an attempt was made to intervene with the government to prevent the book's distribution.[40] A similar situation prevailed in Egypt, albeit with a more negative tone (before the turn to the worse became a standard feature of public life under Sadat) with the coming to fruition of Hassan al-Banna's establishment of the Society of Muslim Brothers. In 1926, Rashid Rida issued a fatwa to the effect that a woman who had evoked the prejudicial effect of shari'a on women's rights was an unbeliever and an apostate. Consequently, it was unlawful for her to marry a Muslim or for her property to pass on to her heirs.[41] Unusually for someone of his milieu, Prince Umar Tusun (1872–1944), great-grandson of Muhammad 'Ali Pasha and erudite philanthropist, tried to intervene at an official level to quell discussion of modifying the Islamic laws of marriage, divorce, and inheritance, as well as calls for unveiling and socialising between the sexes.[42] Mention must be made in this context of what was termed the "social homicide" of Taher Haddad by Zeitouna scholars in Tunisia after the publication of *Our Woman in Shari'a*

37 For studies based on historical realities and avoiding standard clichés, see Judith E. Tucker, *In the House of Law: Gender and Islam in Ottoman Syria and Palestine* (Berkeley: University of California Press, 2000) and Elyse Semerdjian, *Off the Straight Path. Illicit Sex, Law and Community in Late Ottoman Aleppo* (Syracuse: Syracuse University Press, 2008).

38 Zayn al-Dīn, *Al-fatāt wa al-shuyūkh*, vol. 3, 69; Tawtal, *Wathā'iq tārīkhiyya 'an ḥalab*, 138–139; Philip S. Khoury, *Syria and the French Mandate: The Politics of Arab Nationalism, 1920–1945*, Princeton Studies on the Near East (Princeton: Princeton University Press, 1987), 609–611.

39 Miriam Cooke, *Nazira Zeineddine: A Pioneer of Islamic Feminism* (Oxford: OneWorld, 2010).

40 Zayn al-Dīn, *Al-fatāt wa al-shuyūkh*, vol. 1, 60–61.

41 Riḍā, *Fatāwā*, no. 672.

42 Salāma Mūsā, "Al-raj'iyya al-fikriyya wa kayfa tunaẓẓam al-da'wa li iḥyā'ihā", *al-'Uṣūr* 6/32 (1930): 360–363.

and Society in 1930. This controversy spread to Algeria and provoked similar discussion of the question of women. Ibn Badis sided with the Zeitouna scholars and echoed the views of Rashid Rida.[43]

Authoritarian and sensual urges provided many Arab Muslim males with the "last remnants of . . . superiority", as Jacques Berque put it, and identified the sense of superiority over women with national sovereignty.[44] Arab women, in their officially subordinate position, were made into a symbol of national sovereignty and the integrity of the national personality – again, this to be treated with the caveat that observation of social practices yields more complex pictures, and that novels and cinematic productions convey a closer appreciation, including of what women may have thought of claims made. It was considerations of notions of collective honour that induced Habib Bourguiba, of all people, to resist calls for unveiling in 1929, on the pretext that such matters should be postponed until the "Tunisian personality" had been rescued from colonialism.[45] Similarly, some secularists who were strong allies of the women's cause in the Mashreq suspended their activity in support of women. One such was the exceedingly broad-minded Muhammad Jamil Bayhum, despite being the husband of Nazik al-'Abid (1898–1959),[46] a prominent Syrian nationalist and champion of women's rights.[47] The pretext was the unity of nationalist ranks that the Islamists threatened if this point was not conceded – an early manifestation of the habit among many secular groups of one-sidedly conceding strategic advantages to their adversaries, which has plagued the Arab world and still does. Shaykh Abd al-Qadir al-Maghribi, the prominent Islamic reformist in Syria and disciple of al-Afghani, was the most perceptive observer in terms of political and national sensibility, but warned against mixing registers demagogically. He was also aware of the

43 Merad, *Le Réformisme musulman en Algérie de 1925 à 1940*, 317–328; Ibn Bādīs, *Kitāb āthār Ibn Bādīs*, vol. 2, 44, 199.

44 Jacques Berque, *The Arabs: Their History and Future*, trans. Jean Stewart (London: Faber and Faber, 1964), 253.

45 Aḥmad Khālid, "Aḍwā' 'alā al-khalfiyya al-tārīkhiyya li majallat al-aḥwāl al-shakhṣiyya al-ṣādira 1956", *Fikr* 19/6 (1974): 57–73.

46 See now Fruma Zachs, "Muhammad Jamil Bayhum and the Woman Question", *Die Welt des Islams*, 53 (2010): 50–75.

47 Muḥammad Jamīl Bayhum, *Fatāt al-sharq fī ḥaḍārat al-gharb: Taṭawwur al-fikr al-'arabī fī mawḍū' al-mar'a fī al-qarn al-'ishrīn* (Beirut: n.p., 1952), 6, 8–9; Zayn al-Dīn, *Al-fatāt wa al-shuyūkh*, vol. 1, 3–4, vol. 2, 37–38.

course of natural change in society. He supported Nazira Zayn al-Din on the grounds that removing the veil in Turkey had been, overall, carried out by Turkish Muslims but he feared that its removal in Syria by the French mandate might be done by "undesirable hands".[48]

In this atmosphere where the threat of violence in various forms was present, it is not surprising that many writers, ingenuously or warily, sought mileage from religious arguments in support of women's rights. This was the case of Nazira Zayn al-Din herself who filled her *Unveiling and Veiling: Lectures and Views on the Liberation of the Women and Social Renewal in the Arab World* with Qur'anic verses and Sunni and Shi'i hadith, following the practice of Islamic reformist discourse – a drift that rebounded on her ultimately and mightily.[49] It has already been shown how bluffs of this kind can be called in practical ways. The authenticity of historical reports wounding to and disparaging women was denied, and called for socialising between the sexes and unveiling as defined by shari'a only, a type of argument that persists today among Muslim feminists, with a certain optimism – in the case of Zayn al-Din, with the generational leap suggested by the title of her book. The book promoted the idea that women's instincts were sounder than those of men, and maintained that the primacy accorded to men in inheritance, legal witness, and divorce and marriage was an argument against men, not for them, as they indicated the hardness of men's hearts, their corrupt character, and the ingrained nature of pre-Islamic practices that Islam had sought gradually to overcome.[50] 'Ali 'Abd al-Raziq gently criticised the book's use of religious arguments, which also provoked the gentle mockery of the progressivist Ismail Mazhar, as he praised the author patronisingly.[51] Taher Haddad followed a similar course with regard to the use of religious arguments. The first part of his famous book contained a defence of the rights of women in Islam using the reformist claim that there is a world of difference between the essence and aims of Islam on the one hand and its historical situation and changing

48 Zayn al-Dīn, *Al-fatāt wa al-shuyūkh*, vol. 2, 12.

49 Elizabeth Thompson, *Colonial Citizens: Republican Rights, Paternal Privilege, and Gender in French Syria and Lebanon* (New York: Columbia University Press, 2000), 135.

50 Zayn al-Dīn, *Al-fatāt wa al-shuyūkh*, 67–70, 91–93.

51 Ibid., vol. 2, 15, 60–63; book review by "'Ayn 'Ayn" of Naẓīra Zayn al-Dīn, *al-Sufūr wa'l-Ḥijāb*, in *al-'Uṣūr* 3/13 (1928): 101–106.

material conditions on the other.[52] It is necessary to note that unveiling at that time often referred to the removal of face veils, not necessarily or always to the removal of head covering, although this complete unveiling proceeded apace from the 1920s.

In this way the supporters of the freedom of women and their education buttressed the Islamist position and helped substantively in shifting the debate from the terrain of society and progress to that of religious authority, despite their persistent criticism of the instrumental uses of religion and the conservatism of their critics. They proposed to prove that shari'a admitted unveiling, an argument that could not get beyond a call for unveiling as defined by shari'a, a definition that was out of their hands. Tahar Haddad left the door open to custom – traditional women's dress, be it in Tunisia or in Syria, is not veiling as such and as defined by the guardians of religion; it is not impelled by religion, and as such becomes hijab only when so classified by religious actors seeking to appropriate social practices to their account. The basic argument for veiling was the obviation of discord and strife, and this position seemed highly incoherent in the light of the texts.[53] Veiling was also criticised on social and moral grounds by some who used religious arguments in support of women's causes. Taher Haddad wrote: "there is a strong similarity between veils women place over their faces to prevent immorality, and the muzzle that is placed on the snouts of dogs to prevent them from biting passers-by. We inspire ugly feelings in the hearts and consciences of girls, since we proclaim that they have been arraigned and that we only trust them when we impose physical barriers upon them. We compel them to be persuaded of what we have adjudged to be their extreme weakness, and to be certain that this weakness is perpetual, deriving from their natural constitution." Haddad affirmed clearly that unveiling was not a cause of immorality but that it was a social question with its origin in male immorality: fornication, pederasty, polygamy, forced marriage, untrammelled divorce, in addition to poverty, which is the primary factor in moral corruption.[54] These

---

52 Ṭāhir Ḥaddād, *Imrā'atunā fi al-sharī'a wa al-mujtama'* (Tunis: al-Dār al-Tūnisiyya li'l-Nashr, 1977), 22–23.

53 Zayn al-Dīn, *Al-fatāt wa al-shuyūkh*, vol. 1, 11, 27, vol. 3, 3.

54 Ḥaddād, *Imrā'atunā fi al-sharī'a wa al-mujtama'*, 183–184, 190. Compare Naẓīra Zayn al-Dīn, *Al-sufūr wa al-hijāb: Muḥāḍarāt wa naẓarāt fi taḥrīr al-mar'a wa al-tajaddud al-ijtimā'i fi al-'ālam al-islāmi* (Beirut: Maṭābi' Qūzma, 1928), 93.

views were not limited to Taher Haddad or Nazira Zayn al-Din, but were also held by balanced Islamists of robust intellect and moral fibre such as Allal al-Fasi.[55]

It does not seem that the evolution of society was affected by these debates to any great extent, although Islamist criticism may have had occasional concrete consequence, such as incidents of rioting and vigilantism mentioned above. Perhaps one of the most honest comments on this prevailing situation marked with much equivocation and passion was that of a major figure, Muhammad Kurd Ali, founder of the Academy of the Arabic Language in Damascus and Minister of Education under the French mandate. He held that Qur'anic statements on veiling were specific to the women of the Prophet's family, with very restricted remit, and that unveiling was more beneficial to society, and, in historical terms, was the usage that was about to prevail. There was no need to impose the removal of the veil but rather it was necessary to proceed gradually.[56] Although there was no direct intervention in the debate by many periodicals and personalities in Egypt, Lebanon, Syria, and Iraq and among Arab expatriates, Nazira Zayn al-Din did receive support from many quarters. These included *al-Kulliya*, *al-Muqtaṭaf*, *al-Muqaṭṭam*, *al-Ahram*, and *al-Ḥadīth* along with a number of personalities, including the mufti of Beirut, Huda Sha'rawi, 'Ali Abd al-Raziq, the Lebanese-American *littérateur* and traveller Amin al-Rihani (1876–1940), the poets Khalil Mutran, Jamil Sidki al-Zahawi, and Ma'ruf al-Rusafi (in Iraq), as well as Syrian ministers, among them Muhammad Kurd Ali, and the French High Commisisoner of the Levant Henri Ponsot.[57]

There is no doubt that the effective participation of the women's movement in the national struggle in Syria and the wider region as well as in Egypt gave the progressive trend a degree of protection. It also allowed it to turn to specific concerns of women that accompanied social progress, such as unveiling and education, despite the reticence of some men whose alibi was unity of the body national. The women's movement in Egypt – as in Syria, in this period, primarily an upper-class phenomenon[58] – under the patrician Huda

55 'Allāl al-Fāsī, *Al-naqd al-dhātī*, 2nd edn (Tetouan: dār al-fikr al-Maghribī, n.d.), 305.

56 Muḥammad Kurd 'Alī, *Al-mudhakkirāt*, 4 vols (Damascus: Maṭba'at al-Taraqqī, 1948–1951), vol. 3, 1,048–1,049.

57 Zayn al-Dīn, *Al-fatāt wa al-shuyūkh*, vol. 2.

58 For women of more humble condition, see Judith Tucker, *Women in Nineteenth-Century Egypt* (Cambridge: Cambridge University Press, 2002).

Sha'rawi (1879–1947)[59] advanced rapidly towards the removal of the veil after the revolution of 1919, when the first women's demonstration took place, led by the nationalist and feminist activist Safiya Zaghloul (1876–1946), wife of the national leader Sa'ad Zaghloul and "Mother to the Egyptians", and Huda Sha'rawi. Women's committees were founded within the Wafd Party, whose leadership was asumed by Safiyya Zaghloul after her husband's exile by the British to the Seychelles in 1919.[60] With regard to Syria, mention has been made of the activity of Nazik al-Abed and others and the first women's nationalist marches were held in Damascus in 1922.[61] A delegation of women had congratulated Amir Faisal on his return from the Paris Peace Conference in 1919.[62] Conferences of Syrian, Lebanese, and Iraqi women were held in 1928 and 1930 and culminated in the women's conference to support the Palestinian cause that was held in Cairo in 1938 on the initiative of Huda Sha'rawi and Bahira al-Azmah, both of whom donned slight head covering. The veil, and especially the face veil, had begun to disappear from the 1920s amid difficult circumstances, in Cairo, Beirut, and Aleppo, and then in Damascus.[63] It seems that the first public speech given by an unveiled woman in Tunis was in 1929.[64] The matter involved an exceedingly complex and rapidly shifting interplay of class, gender, education, nationalism, conservatism, religion, and Kemalist exemplarity.[65] One conservative observer in Damascus described this evolution, saying critically that women had begun to cover their faces with a diaphanous veil instead of a black one, and some had moved on to removing these light veils entirely and went about "unveiled with embellished clothes", their heads covered with silk scarves "that bared the forehead with hair showing

59 See Sania Sharawi Lanfranchi, *Casting Off the Veil: The Life of Huda Shaarawi* (London: I. B. Tauris, 2015); Shaarawi, *Harem Years*.

60 Ḥusayn, *Al-ittijāhāt al-waṭaniyya fi al-adab al-mu'āṣir*, vol. 2, 251; Mūsā, *Tarbiyat Salāma Mūsā*, 128–129.

61 Reference needs now to be made to Thompson, *Colonial Citizens*, for an account of the complex issues and interconnections pertaining to women and a broader gendered account of the Mandate period, with valuable and enriching analyses of a number of issues arising in the present discussion.

62 Ẓāfir al-Qāsimī, *Maktab 'anbar: Ṣuwar wa dhikrayāt min ḥayātinā al-thaqāfiyya wa al-siyāsiyya wa al-ijtimā'iyya* (Beirut: al-Maṭba'a al-Kāthūlīkiyya, 1964), 117 and 'Anbara Salām al-Khālidī, *Jawla fi al-dhikrayāt bayna Lubnān wa Filasṭīn* (Beirut: Dār al-Nahār li'l-Nashr, 1978), 126.

63 Khālidī, *Jawla fi al-dhikrayāt bayna Lubnān wa Filasṭīn*, 129–150.

64 Khālid, "Aḍwā' 'alā al-khalfiyya al-tārīkhiyya li majallat al-aḥwāl al-shakhṣiyya al-ṣādira 1956", 60–63.

65 See Thompson, *Colonial Citizens*, parts III and IV, and Beth Baron, *Egypt as a Woman* (Berkeley and Los Angeles: University of California Press, 2005).

to the front".[66] This evolution led, as is known, to more or less complete unveiling in the large cities by the 1950s, except for the more traditional and humble elements of the middle classes. The conduct of the state and the social groups higher up the educational and socio-economic ladder were the driving forces behind this change. The same is true of mixing between the sexes, in work places and government departments and educational establishments, occasionally disturbed for political or temperamental reasons. Taha Hussein gave one example of this when, in the late 1930s, he told of a minister of education who considered that mixing between young girls and young men could endanger morals, setting up a teacher training college for women, but forgetting that these young women and men had already studied together co-educationally at university before entering the college.[67]

Overall, Syrian feminism, gaining traction from the patrician location of its main protagonists, was not to succeed spectacularly in political terms, but it did acquire a cumulative effect with the transformations of society. Syrian women were the first to be enfranchised in the Arab world, in 1949, fifteen years after Turkey, and ahead of Greece and Switzerland. Much the same would apply to Egypt, where women's suffrage was introduced by Nasser in 1956. The movement for women's emancipation, first social, including the removal of vestimentary restrictions, and then professional, did not necessarily bring an effective improvement in their position in all fields of action of patriarchal society.

A status of inferiority was presumed in the laws of personal status that are important structural components in the system of social organisation. The laws of inheritance were an integral part of society's circulation of wealth, in addition to figuring as a symbol of historical continuity cherished by the confluence of patriarchy, including rapacious male siblings and collaterals, and religious conservatism. Moreover, the principal economic changes that affected the Arab lands were yet to result in new and re-articulated social structures. Internal cycles of production were not integrated at the national level, a situation governed by the confluence of new economic activities and a global division of labour, yielding a global social and socio-economic hierarchy, whereby social structures were not re-integrated when their old structural

66 al-ʿAẓma, *Mirʾāt al-Shām*, 75.

67 Ṭaha Ḥusayn, *Mustaqbal al-thaqāfa fi Miṣr*, vol. 9 of *Al-majmūʿa al-kāmila li muʾallafāt al-duktūr Ṭaha Ḥusayn* (Beirut: Dār al-Kitāb al-Lubnānī, 1984), 323.

conditions had passed. Social conservatism has been an obstacle to healthy normative developments corresponding to emergent social needs norms. Normative conservatism, redacted in the name of religion, itself served to signal an illusory stability conveyed by images of historical continuity with tradition, while the religious monopoly of the formal regulation of family relations (inheritance, marriage, divorce) had become a form of insurance against further change. More egalitarian views of gender were thereby kept energetically at a distance from changes to the legal regulation of society, with the complicity of secularists. Social transformations resulting from the education of women, their participation in the workforce, and their greater liberties outside domestic confines were also kept distant from the field of law. This screening of the law from the effects of social change was seen as an apotropaic defence against attacks by the capaciously covetous religious lobby, for whom nothing ever seemed to be good enough.

The laws of confessional personal status, with many modifications and sometimes considerable improvements, generally remained in force, and still remain one site of strategic social and cultural contestation. Patriarchy and social conservatism combined to ensure continuation of an Islamic discourse about women and marriage, unrestricted by and invulnerable to reason, public interest, or good taste, and came often to acquire the credibility of common sense and immutable practice. Throughout, appeal is made to a heavily edited and restrictive notion of shar'ist provisions for gender, marriage, and divorce.[68] This unthinking credulity concealed the incoherence and retrogressive character of the usual arguments, of which Rida was an excellent exponent. Thus, there were arguments about the innate difference of disposition and capacity between men and women, their respective capacities and incapacities for certain types of employment, and arguments for guardianship of men over women, of the inequality in inheritance as arising from the greater responsibilities of men, the supporters of families, and for the restriction of the right of divorce by women on the grounds that men were more patient than women and do not divorce hastily, a claim that contradicts even the most superficial acquaintance of social interaction.[69] Note

68 See above all Judith E. Tucker, *Women, Family and Gender in Islamic Law* (Cambridge: Cambridge University Press, 2008).

69 Muḥammad Rashīd Riḍā, *Nidā' ilā al-jins al-laṭīf yaum al-mawlid al-nabawī al-sharīf sanata 1351 fī ḥuqūq al-nisā' fī al-Islām wa ḥaẓẓuhunna min al-iṣlāḥ al-muḥammadī al-'āmm* (Cairo: Maṭba'at al-Manār, 1932), 11–12, 17–27, 98.

that these arguments are common and pretty much universal, not restricted to religious discourse in whose name they are made, thereby being appropriated by it, extending the remit of religion. It was also possible shamelessly to persist in defending the (Qur'anic) licence of men to punish their wives physically, despite acknowledging the obnoxious character of this practice, and to argue that Muslim traditions of informal marriage and concubinage (also Qur'anic) existed to preserve the reputation of captives, although it was permissible to forbid the practice[70] – a reference to conditions of war and the enslavement of captives that belong to a different world, one that someone like Rida still inhabited in many ways, excepting its re-enactment by Daesh in recent years.

One result of the persistence of Islamic discourse among the defenders of women's rights was that Nazira Zayn al-Din felt constrained to accept the status of men as guardians of women, but restricted this to husbands over wives, excluding sons and brothers.[71] In such a situation it is not odd that Salama Musa's call to reform Islamic inheritance law did not secure the support of Huda Sha'rawi, who said, with evasive irrelevance and specious sophistry characteristic of Muslim reformist argumentation, that Muslim women were more fortunate than Western women in this regard.[72] There was a self-perpetuating dynamic relating to discussions of these matters by the religious lobby, members of the ulama institution, and some of the prevaricating secular voices, all of which cumulatively allowed for the unblushing use of medieval language and values. Thus, when Ibn Badis was asked about the licitness of the use of contraceptives by women in poor health, he stated: "the ground rule is that of withdrawal, meaning that a man would not ejaculate sperm into the vagina. This practice was considered reprehensible by some. The general opinion in the Maliki school is that this practice is licit with the permission of a free woman, as she has a right to intercourse and ejaculation that complete her pleasure [female ejaculation is a medieval Arab and ultimately Aristotelian medical notion associated with orgasm]. Withdrawal involves the prevention of childbirth. Withdrawal is therefore analogous to ingesting a contraceptive drug, which is allowed as long as it does not harm the body and if the husband agreed, as he has the right to a

70 Ibid., 31–32, 93–95.
71 Zayn al-Dīn, *Al-fatāt wa al-shuyūkh*, vol. 3, 88–98.
72 Mūsā, "Al-raj'iyya al-fikriyya wa kayfa tunaẓẓam al-da'wa li iḥyā'ihā", 362.

child. If she is too weak to bear children the question does not depend on the husband's consent."[73]

Calls for legal reform in the family domain, not all of which were secular in character, had only limited perceptible effect on the religious monopoly of words and action regarding judgments of personal status, despite institutional changes in the legal system, some of them of serious consequence for this monopoly that, however, remained the public face of this matter. As mentioned earlier, Muhammad 'Abduh had held that polygamy could be banned because of the impossibility of observing a chief legal condition that renders it valid, and many agreed with him, including Haddad,[74] hoping to add 'Abduh's prestige to their roundabout ambitions for legal reform. Rashid Rida thought that marriage with one wife was "the aim of human advancement" although there were general and particular necessities that made polygamy "a licence, neither a duty nor advisable for itself, restrained by the conditions stated in the holy verse".[75] Allal al-Fasi supported the principle of banning polygamy that, he considered, was socially detrimental. Polygamy was and remains quite uncommon, and was not a prevailing social custom, at least in Syria and Egypt until the coming of Islamism to positions it has come to hold in recent years. It was generally considered unconscionable and indecent in educated circles and in the middle and upper middle classes, where it could, if practised, disturb broader social relations between families and family networks. It was generally confined to certain parts of the countryside and the smaller provincial towns. Nevertheless, Fouad I of Egypt refused a proposal to ban polygamy in 1929.[76]

Polygamy was not the only subject of criticism by those who sought to reform personal status laws. In 1910 the ability for men alone to decide on divorce had already been criticised in the pages of *al-Mu'ayyad* – so also inequality in inheritance and capacity for legal witness. Inequity in the Muslim paradise had been criticised by al-Zahawi, who questioned why men could enjoy the company of large numbers of *houris* while women had to content themselves with their earthly husbands.[77] Tahir Haddad also criticised men's

73 Ibn Bādīs, *Kitāb āthār Ibn Bādīs*, vol. 3, 413.

74 Ḥaddād, *Imrā'atunā fī al-sharī'a wa al-mujtama'*, 65.

75 Riḍā, *Nidā' ilā al-jins al-laṭīf*, 38–41; al-Fāsī, *Al-Naqd al-dhātī*, 219–220.

76 Anderson, *Law Reform in the Muslim World*, 62.

77 Jamīl Ṣidqī al-Zahāwī, "Al-mar'a wa al-difā' 'anhā", *al-Mu'ayyad* 21/6138 (1910), text reprinted in Hilāl Nājī, *Al-zahāwī wa dīwānuhu al-mafqūd* (Cairo: Dār al-'Arab, 1964), 355–360.

conduct in divorce proceedings and asked for it to be restricted as it degraded the lives of women and made them insecure.[78] Muhammad Jamil Bayhum wished for Islam to be the preferable religion, one disposed to latitudinarianism, so that it could consider in a rational and deliberate way whatever persisted today from its past, such as patriarchy in the legal domain.[79] Ismail Mazhar was one of few to take this view to its concrete conclusions, believing that Islam, although distinctive from previous religions, made women only half of men whereas today we live in an age of "the complete and unique person indivisible", using for the person the epithetic locution *lā sharīka lahu*, used in the Qur'an for God. Islam gave to women what was possible fifteen centuries ago, and they need to be given today what is appropriate for the present: complete civil and political rights, equality in inheritance, and undiminished capacity for witness, intellectual and economic freedom, and the ability to obtain a divorce in court on an equal footing with men.[80] Mazhar was not the only commentator who believed that Islam's attitude to women was incapable of improvement. Taher Haddad considered that the Islamic law on inheritance was tied to the historical circumstances in which it had originated, and saw no obstacle to women's equality in inheritance, but took a step back with caveats, once the conditions of equality existed in the labour market and when infant schools became widespread.[81]

Codifications of personal civil status came therefore in the form of administrative codification, and streamlining and relative rationalisation of inherited legal material, with little modification in their fundamental principles. In Syria, Iraq, and Trans-Jordan, the Ottoman Family Law of 1917 was in use – and is still in force today in Lebanon – although it was abolished in Turkey in 1919. This 1917 law codified Hanafi jurisprudence and made a timid gesture towards contemporary conditions. It provided for formal measures to be taken regarding marriage, restricted early marriage and permitted divorce initiated by women under special circumstances. It also provided for women to stipulate in the marriage contract that, should the husband contract a second marriage, she or the second wife shall be

78 Ḥaddād, *Imrā'atunā fī al-sharī'a wa al-mujtama'*, 78–81.

79 Bayhum, *Al-mar'a fi'l Islām*, 53–55, 63–69.

80 Ismā'īl Maẓhar, *Al-mar'a fī 'aṣr al-dimūqarāṭiyya: Baḥth ḥurr fī ta'yīd maṭālib al-mar'a* (Cairo: maṭba'at miṣr, 1949), 135–138, 188.

81 Ḥaddād, *Imrā'atunā fī al-sharī'a wa al-mujtama'*, 38–43.

considered divorced. In Egypt, legislation in 1920 and 1929 codified some elements of Hanafi jurisprudence and regulated aspects of divorce by giving women the right to initiate divorce in case of harm or damage, and restricted the husband's discretion in this matter. It also codified the issue of adequate support of the wife. Subsequent laws on personal status regulations were passed in Jordan (1951), Syria (1953), Iraq (1959), and Egypt (1955), and again since the 1970s. For the first time, Muslim inheritance rulings were codified as laws. In Iraq, this included judgments from both Sunni and Shi'i legal schools, the latter seen in 1959 to have been more equitable to women (later repealed with the advent of the Baath party, and subjected to further retrogressive changes after the American invasion of 2003). The 1959 law in Iraq used Ja'fari legal provisions in ways that implicitly took the nuclear family as the basic unit for inheritance, to the exclusion of collateral male cousins and other relatives. If a man died and had only one daughter, she inherited all his property, on the principle that descent excluded brothers of the deceased and their descendants from inheritance. The other codifications of inheritance inclined towards encouraging the nuclear family to be seen as the basic unit for inheritance even if this was within the framework of what was possible within Sunni jurisprudence. Syrian personal status law was the most innovative in this respect.[82]

Much the same reticence applies to Moroccan codifications in general. Despite audacious and forward-looking positions adopted by Allal al-Fasi, in relation to polygamy, divorce, secularisation, and other matters, the Moroccan personal status laws of 1958 did not show much progress, but proceeded with codification in a very traditionalist spirit, although al-Fasi was one of the legislators[83] – this code, or *Mudawwana*, was subject to superficial adjustment in 1993, and major reform in 2004. The Maliki position granting a father the power to marry off his daughter without her consent was confirmed, and while the number of wives was limited by certain conditions, no restrictions were placed on discretionary divorce by the husband. Divorce was also regulated in Algeria although its legislators did not intervene in the question of the number of wives. In 1956, Tunisia promulgated what remained the most progressive codification of personal status law in Arab lands until the Arab

82 Anderson, *Law Reform in the Muslim World*, 70–71, 149–153.

83 al-Fāsī, *Al-Naqd al-dhātī*, 211–212, 219–220, 224–225, 227–229.

Spring, after which its modern content was very considerably enhanced, even more progressive than a similar subsequent codification in the Popular and Democratic Republic of Yemen (1974 – revoked in 1978), since the Tunisian code of 1956 disallowed polygamy and stipulated a minimum age for marriage (twenty for men and seventeen for women), and gave women the right to contract marriage independently of a male guardian, and the right to sue for divorce and to maintain guardianship of children.

Although Tunisian legislators continued to move Tunisian society in a direction consonant with the development of society and changing social mores, the Code of 1956 still maintained some core elements of social backwardness in its description of the relation (in section 23) between spouses as one defined by the husband as head of the family, requiring conjugal obedience – this provision was recently removed. Permission had to be sought from the husband if a wife sought work with the aim of financial participation in the household. The origin of this condition, which corresponds to a clause in Lebanese civil law forbidding women from engaging in commercial activity except with the permission of their husbands, lies in a French law abolished in 1938, but it is one that reinforced proclivities for control. Laws in Arab countries went quite a way to fostering and maintaining inequality between the sexes in keeping with the least desirable of social practices: the penalties for adultery were generally harsher for women than for men in Arab criminal law, and men benefited from a legal discharge or a mitigated penalty if they murdered their spouse or sister caught *in flagrante delicto*. Egyptian law did not punish male adultery except when committed in the conjugal home, while the law stipulated that wives who committed adultery anywhere were to be sanctioned. What are known as "honour crimes" were still subject to extra-judicial considerations that confine the operation of the law and degrade it to what might be considered customary among the more archaic parts of society, while it is undeniable that provisions and operations of the law incline to what is somewhat in advance of what otherwise might be tolerated. It is as if there were many social worlds coexisting, with parallel normative and legal workings. There were undoubtedly polygamous practices in parts of Iraq with no basis in law, but it was not considered unlawful despite being tolerated.[84]

84 Anderson, *Law Reform in the Muslim World*, 64.

In Algeria, similarly, not all courts have taken account of the restrictions placed upon divorce.[85]

Ambiguity and a considerable degree of denial characterised the way that personal status laws were framed, contributing little to a social dynamic that occurred alongside it. On the one hand, these laws drew on traditionalist religious grounds of ultimately supernatural command for specific rulings. On the other, they departed from traditional Muslim jurisprudence in the very act of codification, restricting the range of possibilities in a manner more amenable to modern bureaucratic norms of administration. By making the administration of this law the prerogative of the secular legal system of courts, the state extended its control over the legal provisions based on a supernatural authority. Shari'a justice, which covered personal status, was integrated into the system of civil justice in Syria in 1953 and in Egypt in 1955, whereby civil judges adjudicated in matters of divorce sitting in civil courts (in Syria). Collaterally, *awqāf* were abolished in Syria in 1949 and in Egypt in 1952, and what remained in place, and these were considerable properties, passed from ulama control to state administration. The outcome of these changes was a considerable reduction in the areas of competence and authority of religious officials in favour of the institutions of the secular state. This contraction occurred at a time when the state was making progress in supervising and regulating religious authorities and institutions administratively, authorities that had an important input in framing laws of personal status. It thus created for itself a need for religious officials to help decide on matters that belonged to its remit and the remit of its secular institution.

Civil law was in a situation unlike that of personal status, with lower ideological density overall until the rise to prominence of political Islamism. The law of personal status was concerned with primary social relations, the detailed scrutiny and social engineering of which the state considered might wait; many officials thought one needed to await the maturation of society. Civil laws, with their long and complicated history from the early nineteenth century, concerned matters that needed practical attention of direct consequence. Changes needed to conform to the global capitalist economy, to serve the convenience of state administration as it developed. As noted

85 Ḥafīda Shuqayr, "Dirāsa muqārana li'l-qawānīn al-khāṣṣa bi'l-mar'a wa al-usra fī al-Maghrib al-'arabī: Tūnis wa al-Maghrib wa al-jazā'ir", in *Al-mar'a wa dawruhā fī ḥarakāt al-waḥda al-'arabiyya*, ed. Markaz Dirāsāt al-Waḥda al-'Arabiyya (Beirut: Markaz Dirāsāt al-Waḥda al-'Arabiyya, 1982), 102.

above, the primary level of social relations was one of the bastions of social conservatism claimed by the religious lobby as its own, but was still liable to regulation in some respects complementing the conservative changes to the laws of personal status. Articles 34–39 of the Egyptian Civil Code of 1949 determined the meaning of family and kinship even if it made shariʿa the basic source for inheritance law (article 915). The same is true of Syrian Civil Law of 1949 (article 876). The major Arab jurist of the twentieth century, Abd al-Razzaq al-Sanhuri (1895–1971), held that personal status laws needed to be based on "our religious beliefs and the ways of our social life".[86]

In line with the general direction of legal reforms from the nineteenth century onwards, civil and criminal legislation continued the trend of increasing marginalisation and abrogation of the Muslim jurisprudential dimension of law. By 1973, in the Egyptian code of criminal law all reference to bloodwit or indemnity for bodily injury was omitted, preceeded in this by the Syrian Penal Law of 1949, which also removed all mention of physical chastisement and flogging, in its turn inspired by Lebanese law. As for the requirement for the oral delivery of witness, and verification by professional witnesses, both of which were fundamental to the workings of shariʿa courts, this was dropped from all law codes.[87] French North Africa lived a duality in the legal systems, between what was applied to foreigners and those local people who had obtained French nationality, and the indigenous inhabitants whose special "indigenous" legal systems, as previously noted, were framed on a presumption of local archaism.

Civil legislation was among the most significant signs of secularism in Arab life, although it was not framed as such, and there has been no equivalent to the abolition of the shariʿa as occurred in Turkey. Al-Sanhuri was the major juristic driving force in drafting the Egyptian Civil Code of 1948, together with committees whose members included other major jurists such as Shafiq Shihata. Syria adopted the Civil Code drawn up by Sanhuri in 1949, with modifications relating to local conditions, and it served as the

86 al-Sanhūrī, "Ḍarūrat tanqīh al-qānūn al-madanī al-miṣrī", 59–60, 94; Abd Al-Razzak Al-Sanhūri, *Le Califat: Son évolution vers une société des nations orientales*, Travaux du séminaire oriental d'études juridiques et sociales, tome 4 (Paris: Geuthner, 1926), 583.

87 See in particular Bernard Botiveau, *Loi islamique et droit dans les sociétés arabes* (Aix-en-Provence and Paris, IREMAM-Karthala, 1993), esp. chs 4, 7–9; the position of laws of personal status is taken up in ch. 6.

base for the Iraqi Civil Code of 1953. This law also laid the foundation of civil laws in Kuwait and the United Arab Emirates.[88] The basic characteristic of the legislative orientation underlying the formation of these legal codes was the implicit principle of all thinking on human sociality, namely, that of historicity and mutability of cultures and values.[89] This was a fundamental cognitive principle of any secular order. In consequence, a basic distinction was made by Arab civil legislators as they considered what might have remained relevant from the rulings of Muslim jurisprudence: between alleged sources, and technical legal provisions, which were the only ones relevant for civil legislation. Technical provisions were then considered elements in comparative law. Although the religious fundamentals "retain a moral strength that conscience imposes on the Muslim", it is the technical legal dimension alone that enters into the ambit of law as such and applies to all citizens, be they Muslims or not.[90]

Thus, the utilisation of provisions from Muslim law rested on two considerations, practical and theoretical.[91] The first was that many provisions of Muslim law formed part of living legal practice, and needed to be adopted or adapted without necessarily taking account of more general jurisprudential and meta-legal issues it may raise, particularly in a society undergoing rapid change, and whose legal conditions have not yet definitively stabilised. In such a rapidly changig society the legal system needed to be flexible and accommodating to the discretion of judges.[92] This practical consideration had as consequence the development of civil law systems that were integrated into the legislative heritage of Arab countries since the setting up of mixed and, later, a national network of courts, which facilitated the transition from old to new conditions.[93]

88 See in general Nabil Saleh, "Civil codes of Arab countries: The Sanhuri codes", *Arab Law Quarterly* 8/2 (1993): 161–167.

89 'Abd al-Razzāq Aḥmad al-Sanhūrī, *Maṣādir al-ḥaqq fi al-fiqh al-islāmī: Dirāsa muqārana bi al-fiqh al-gharbī*, 3 vols (Cairo: Jami'at al-Duwal al-'Arabiyya, Ma'had al-Buḥūth wa al-Dirāsāt al-'Arabiyya al-'Āliya 1967–1968), vol. 3, 81–82.

90 Ibid.

91 al-Sanhūrī, "Ḍarūrat tanqīh al-qānūn al-madanī al-miṣrī", 61–63, and al-Sanhūri, *Le Califat*, 580–581. A translation exists in Arabic of this text although it does not cover the full version of the original French text. See 'Abd al-Razzāq Aḥmad al-Sanhūri, *Fiqh al-khilāfa wa taṭawwuruhā* (Cairo: al-Hay'a al-Miṣriyya al-'Āmma li'l-Kitāb, 1989).

92 al-Sanhūrī, "Ḍarūrat tanqīh al-qānūn al-madanī al-miṣri", 70–71, 77–93.

93 See Egypt, Ministry of Justice, *Al-qānūn al-madanī: Majmū'at al-a'māl al-taḥḍīriyya*, 2 vols (Cairo: Maṭba'at Dār al-Kitāb al-'Arabi, n.d.), vol. 1, 120.

As for the technical aspect, it related to al-Sanhuri's consideration of the nature of Muslim law in the context of comparative jurisprudence, and in relation the concrete sources of Egyptian civil law – the argument applies to all the civil codes arising. Muslim legal provisions formed part of practical legal practices, in addition to French legislation that had become a living part of existing Egyptian – and indeed overall, late Ottoman and post-Ottoman – legal practice. To this legislation legal practice based upon custom needed to be added when a systematic code was being drawn up. Egyptian law and its living traditions were thus not restricted to legal provisions arising from Muslim jurisprudence. This made the automatic adoption of Muslim legal rulings into the civil code "without due consideration" a matter that would cause confusion, as al-Sanhuri stated in a debate in the Egyptian Senate on the bill introducing the Civil Code in 1949.[94]

Al-Sanhuri was conservative by instinct, a practical legislator but not a revolutionary, but his conservatism was tempered by a highly conscientious and deliberate legal professionalism, and he sought from shari'a those elements that conformed with Egyptian legal practices so the Code would be coherent.[95] Comparative law – and, in its context, Muslim jurisprudence and the traditions of Egyptian legal practice – became the primary source for civil law, since this was considered the most developed form of legislative progress. Thus, the 1949 draft Code was based on an examination of each of its articles as they occurred in twenty civil codes, including the French, Swiss, and German codes. The Memorandum accompanying the draft could legitimately claim that "one can say that, considered from the point of view of the international trend of codification, this bill presents an international example which serves as the basis for the unification of many civil law codes". In its sources and scope, the Code went beyond both Muslim jurisprudence and French law, considered by al-Sanhuri and his colleagues as falling behind the cutting edge of international legal standards represented then by Switzerland and Germany.

Positive legal provisions were thereby disassociated from their sources and taken to correspond to the requirements of the present time and were on their own associated with the concrete circumstances of their provision.[96]

---

94 Ibid., 77.
95 Ibid., 83.
96 "Al-mudhakkara al-īḍāḥiyya", in ibid., 13–18.

Muslim jurisprudence was mentioned in the text of the code's first article, which provided that, in the absence of a statute, the judge must reach legal decisions on the basis of custom and, in the absence of a relevant custom, on the basis of the general principles of shari'a. If these were not to be appropriate, the judge must refer to the principles of natural justice and the general foundations of justice. It was al-Sanhuri who was responsible for placing the shari'a in the place it came to occupy in the Code. In an earlier draft, it came as default position after natural law and the general principles of justice in the draft law. He considered that shari'a – that is, the provisions of *fiqh* – was more precise than natural law, whose meaning was vague. He also considered that it was more precise than appeal to natural justice, which was ultimately susceptible to subjective evaluation.[97] The primary consideration was technical, legalistic, and realistic, not religious or moral. Nevertheless, this matter attracted criticism from one of al-Sanhuri's major associates, his former student Shafiq Shihata, who considered that this approach was defective and confusing. Concrete legal provisions of Muslim jurisprudence, it was argued, were contradictory and incoherent, while the Principles of Muslim Jurisprudence were not conducive to formulating a general theory of contract or obligation, being a legal hermeneutics that might arguably serve a prefatory function to natural law based in reason and to considerations of social interest.[98] Al-Sanhuri, for his part, considered Muslim jurisprudence from the perspective of comparative law to be a body of advanced legal material that bore a material and objective orientation. Like English and unlike French law, the objective and material orientation of Muslim jurisprudence rested on the extraction of meaning from concrete terms rather than from intangible intent lodged in the minds of individuals, assuring legal predictability and stability.[99]

With regard to detailed articles, Egyptian Civil Code took from Muslim law elements that included a prohibition on the advance sale of future harvests, and considering a sale concluded by a terminally ill seller to be equivalent to a bequest. The Code provided that shari'a be the point of reference in matters of inheritance, and resorted to considerations of "necessity" with

97 Ibid., 93, 183, 190.

98 Chafik Chehata, "Les survivances musulmanes dans la codification du droit civil égyptien", *Revue internationale du droit comparé* 17/4 (1965): 839–853, 852–853.

99 Egypt, Ministry of Justice, *Al-qānūn al-madanī*, vol. 1, 20–21.

regard to unexpected circumstances, and to detailed provisions deriving from Muslim law on the subject of contracts, the rental of *awqāf* properties as well as a number of agricultural matters, with regard to which the Syrian Civil Law code of 1949 had similar dispositions.[100] In addition, Syrian Civil Law abolished *shuf'a* (the right of pre-emption or first refusal) that had been a recognised right in Muslim jurisprudence for centuries, although in Egypt pressure was successfully brought to ensure its retention.[101] One would need to seek explanations in the way certain types of market transactions operated on the ground.

Civil transactions in Syria under the French Mandate were incoherently managed, as the French restored the Mixed Courts in accordance with their colonial policy, and the Ottoman *Mecelle* of 1877 remained in force despite the promulgation of many new civil laws, especially in the domains of property and contracts. The result was incoherence in the judicial system, especially since the *Mecelle* had become steadily more distant from practice. The Syrian government promulgated the new Civil Law code in 1949 on the basis of Egyptian law given, as was claimed, the shared traditions and similar social conditions of Syria and Egypt, and as a contribution to Arab legislative unity.[102] The Syrian Civil Code deleted all the Egyptian provisions relating to land ownership and replaced them with the Syro-Lebanese law of land ownership of 1932, in the light of prevailing conditions in Syria and the imbrication of land ownership across the border between Syria and Lebanon. In addition, the Syrian cadastre of material property ownership was far in advance of the Egyptian register of personally owned property.[103] With regard to shari'a, it was clear that the Syrian government – following the coup of Colonel Husni al-Za'im (1897–1949), who promulgated the code by decree – had made a gesture to Islamists since the Civil Code stipulated that "if there is no legal provision applicable, the judge shall judge according to the principles of Muslim jurisprudence, failing which he shall resort to

100 See Egyptian Law Code of 1948 (https://searchworks.stanford.edu/view/1760807), articles 45–47, 110–116, 118–119, 601–602, Syrian Civil Code of 1949 (http://www.wipo.int/wipolex/en/text.jsp?file_id=243234), articles 47–49, 111–117, 119–120, 590–601. See Shiḥāta, *Al-ittijāhāt al-tashrī'iyya*, 62–63.

101 Ibid., 139.

102 Syrian Civil Code of 17 May 1949 (Damascus: Ministry of Justice, n.d.), 8–9.

103 Muṣṭafā al-Zarqā, *Muḥāḍarāt fī al-qānūn al-madanī al-sūrī* (Cairo: Jāmi'at al-Duwal al-'Arabiyya, ma'had al-Dirāsāt al-'Arabiyya al-Aliya, 1954), 7–8.

custom, failing which, judgment shall be reached according to the principles of natural justice and the principles of justice". For its part, the Iraqi Civil Code included a greater presence of Hanafi material, as the Ottoman *Mecelle* was still the effective basic source for civil transactions in the land when the Iraqi Civil Code was promulgated in 1951.

Thus, for the first time in Arab lands, the legislative salience of history was recognised, and religious encrustation was cleared away, law being thereby restored to its proper place in the world as studied in the first chapter of this book. Muslim jurisprudence was perceived, not as summation of society's legal structure, but as emerging from history and answerable to it, acquiring relevance and irrelevance with reference to changing conditions. Al-Sanhuri had even composed an academic study aimed at codifying and restating categories of personal capacity and rights contained in Muslim jurisprudence in terms of comparative law and modern laws, and to formulate these in terms of the latter's categories, particularly with reference to legal capacity and to what constitutes a legal event.[104] It is unclear to what extent he was successful, as it is not clear what validity the terms of Muslim jurisprudence have for this type of categorisation.[105] It is, however, as clear to observers today as it was to al-Sanhuri that codification must cover all fields of legal life on uniform bases. What is also clear is that, irrespective of the great jurist's own leanings, public law in a modern state needs to be integrated indivisibly in the same terms that applied to civil law, including constitutional, administrative, and criminal law, and provisions relating to the judicial system.[106] Superstitions regarding its points of origin and reference were technically irrelevant.

Al-Sanhuri was reproached for this by his Islamist critics. One charged him, quite rightly, with an understanding of law "restricted" to pure jurisprudence, without connection to the sources of religion in the Qur'an and Sunna. It thus became positive legislation whose link to its origin had been severed.[107] It was argued above that this had little to do with severance but

104 Al-Sanhūrī, *Maṣādir al-ḥaqq fī al-fiqh al-islāmī*, vol. 1, 5–7, 66–69.

105 See the comment of Ḥusayn Aḥmad Amīn, "Ta'qīb", on Ṭāriq al-Bishrī, "Al-mas'ala al-qānūniyya bayn al-sharī'a al-islāmiyya wa al-qānūn al-waḍ'ī", in *Al-Turāth Wa Taḥaddiyāt al-'Asr fī al-Waṭan al-'Arabī*, ed. Markaz Dirāsāt al-Waḥda al-'Arabiyya (Beirut: Markaz Dirāsāt al-Waḥda al-'Arabiyya, 1985), 649.

106 Al-Sanhūrī, *Maṣādir al-ḥaqq fī al-fiqh al-islāmī: Dirāsa muqārana bi al-fiqh al-gharbī*, vol. 1, 5–7.

107 al-Bishrī, "Al-mas'ala al-qānūniyya", 629, 633.

rather a reconnection with the practical, historical, and socio-economic sources and undoing the mythical links claimed for it by the Islamist ideological imagination. Opposition to the Civil Code was bitter, however, even though it had not undergone any significant development in argumentation from its inception until shar'ist claims today. Hasan al-Hudaibi (1891–1973), successor to the assassinated Hassan al-Banna as General Guide of the Society of Muslim Brothers, expressed this opposition during the debate of the Civil Code bill in the Egyptian Senate (30 October 1948), proposing a move in exactly the opposite direction to that proposed by Sanhuri. He declared that it mattered little to him whether the bill was right or wrong, as legislation in Egypt must be based on the provisions of the Qur'an and the Sunna, and that whatever provisions might be adopted from Western legislation must be traceable to these two sources.[108] Opposition was and remained expressed in the formulaic repetition of general slogans, and it was evident in the debates that al-Sanhuri enjoyed a very clear and distinct intellectual advantage over his opponents, be they from the Muslim Brothers or from the Wafd Party,[109] members of which voiced small-minded opposition to Sanhuri because he had broken away from the party in 1937, together with the prominent politicians Ahmad Maher (1888–1945) and Mahmoud Fahmy al-Nuqrashi (1888–1948), to establish the Saadist Institutional Party in 1938. Al-Azhar had tacitly announced their opposition. The fundamental opposition on the part of the Islamists continued after the Egyptian Senate approved the Civil Code on 10 October 1949. Five months earlier the promulgation of the Syrian Civil Code had been announced, enacted by a decision of the cabinet and by legislative decree issued by Husni al-Za'im, Prime Minister and commander of the army and the armed forces, following a proposal from the Minister of Justice. The Islamist opposition to the Civil Code and the alternative offered in the shape of attempts to codify classical Muslim jurisprudence comprehensively reveal the limitations of Islamic reformism and its inability to take a turn from ideological slogans and political passions to addressing issues of modern life.

Modernist Islamic reformism, it was noted earlier, insisted on the adaptability of shari'a and the comprehensiveness of its scope. As the twentieth century advanced and Arab legal systems tried to keep up with the requirements of universalism and secularism, Islamic reformism was compelled to

108 Egypt, Ministry of Justice, *Majmū'at al-a'māl al-taḥḍīriyya*, vol. 1, 48–49.
109 Minutes of the Senate discussions: ibid., 34–118.

make attempts to move from general slogans and sentimentalist declamations to attempt to offer specific and practical solutions. There was little opportunity for general Islamic legal codification such as that to which Allal al-Fasi aspired after the adoption of the *Mudawanna* of personal status in Morocco in 1958.[110] Public life as it developed was generally averse to this attempted sacralisation of law. Islamic reformism continued to repeat the general formulae enabling its constitutive duality, moving between the general principles of the shari'a generally stated (as in the preambles to civil codes cited) as hallowed by time, without much specification, and the present time. There was continuous reference to the perpetual pertinence of the shari'a, claiming it to have invariant bases, "whereas evolution and improvement occur to the human understanding of the shari'a, its deductions from it, its application to new particulars".[111]

To this approach belongs the refusal by Islamic reformists to admit that the stipulations of the shari'a were subject to change, while maintaining that these are renewed while the text remains unchanged, so that innovation becomes "the means of maintaining the continuing pertinence of the text as realities change".[112] This is a characteristic instance of squaring circles, performing translations that were rationally and concretely impossible but desirable to the sentimental and ideological impulse to bring together disparate elements that can stand together only rhetorically, as a speech act rather than as a proposition. Some Islamic modernists incline to the view that emphasis on shar'ist general principles, including public interest, justified disregarding foundational texts altogether. In line with structures of reformist discourse discussed above, there is the presumption of "an intended meaning" behind the revelation that may not accord with the sense of the text. This would justify going beyond the letter of text, another justification being the uncertainties obtained from the considerable degree of disagreement among jurists. "The established opinion of many of our scholars that there is no possibility of independent judgment in the presence of the text has to be placed in its proper context." Further, the presence of Qur'anic or hadith text, understood as an indicator of a judgment in detail, does not necessarily disallow reason and independent judgment. For if the "intent of

110 'Allāl al-Fāsī, *Difā' 'an al-sharī'a*, 2nd edn (Beirut: Manshūrāt al-'aṣr al-Ḥadīth, 1972), 17.

111 Ibid., 125.

112 al-Bishrī, "Al-mas'ala al-qānūniyya", 641–642.

the lawmaker", who is God, was ascertained, and the precise meanings of the words were established; and if the most probable interpretation is made from different relevant texts that may seem to be contradictory, "no proof-text can then debar independent judgment".[113] According to this enthusiastic and somewhat loose discourse, shari'a was so lissome that it could accommodate everything and nothing. Such discourses of legalistic, nomocratic Islamism carefully and with casuistical locutions averted reference to the historical conditions of Muslim legal stipulations. A few found this circumlocution unsatisfactory. Hussein Ahmad Amin, for one, in a discussion of calls for the "implementation of the shari'a", traced back the punishment of amputation and polygamy to historical circumstances that no longer obtained. He criticised the oblivion of Muslims to the historical dimension of their religion.[114] Indeed he charged "so-called Islamic movements" with going against the will of God, neglecting the determining influence of history that would show that the punishment of amputation arose in a desert society where moveable property was the basic form of ownership.[115] Amin rightly saw that the position of Islam in modern times was one marked by deviousness and artifice, based on the presumption that the Qur'an does not mean what it says, and says what it does not mean.[116]

Yet Islamic reformists persisted in maintaining that the shari'a was valid in all times and places. The most that could be concretely done in this context was a reformist translation into an Islamic idiom of the law in actual use, giving it the normative and ideological denomination of Islam, or to say that the law was in conformity with Islam and to trace its Islamic origins in a vague manner requiring casuistical *legerdemain*. Allal al-Fasi conceived the idea of a general Moroccan law based on shari'a, Moroccan customary practice, and French law and other sources, but only after ulama certified that its constituents could be

---

113 Abū al-Majd, *Ḥiwār la muwājaha*, 13. See Abū al-Majd, "Al-mas'ala al-siyāsiyya: Waṣl al-turāth bi al-'aṣr wa al-niẓām al-siyāsī li'l-dawla", paper presented at a conference organised by Markaz Dirāsāt al-Waḥda al-'Arabiyya. See *Al-turāth wa taḥadiyyāt al-'aṣr fī al-waṭan al-'arabī: Al-aṣāla wa al-mu'āṣara*, 2 vols (Beirut: Markaz al-Dirāsāt al-Waḥda al-'Arabiyya, 1987), 573.

114 Amīn, *Ḥawl al-da'wa ilā taṭbīq al-sharī'a al-islāmiyya*, 45–46 and ch. 4.

115 Ḥusayn Aḥmad Amīn, *Dalīl al-Muslim al-ḥazīn ilā muqtaḍā al-sulūk fī al-qarn al-'ishrīn*, 2nd edn (Beirut and Cairo: Dār al-Shurūq, 1983), 130–132, published in English translation as Hussein Ahmad Amin, *The Sorrowful Muslim's Guide*, trans. Y. Amin and N. Amin (Edinburgh: Edinburgh University Press in association with the Aga Khan University Institute for the Study of Muslim Civilisations, 2018).

116 Amīn, *Ḥawl al-da'wa ilā taṭbīq al-sharī'a al-islāmiyya*, 45.

integrated into the general foundations of Islamic jurisprudence.[117] This conception was equally the significance of other proposals for the codification of a civil code presumed to be contained in Muslim law.[118]

Such, at any rate, was the view of the Syrian author of the project, the noted legal scholar (and pioneer of "Islamic banking") Mustafa al-Zarqa (1907–1995). This project began with a broad erudite survey, emphasising the five general principles of Muslim jurisprudence, the application of discretion and considerations of public interest in legislation. It then turned towards the detailed provisions of law and formulated them in the context of a general theory of liability in modern law. A modern law code was thus formulated under the signature of shari'a, which assimilated the classical provisions of Muslim law bereft of the contexts of emergence and formulation in the framework of modern law. Thus was formulated a system of reformist Muslim law that was nominally possible, but in practice incoherent, in that what was fundamentally involved was renaming: labelling religious heritage actual reality, and packaging actual reality as religious heritage. What was intended in this reformist translation was the erection of existing positive law upon religious ideas of licit and illicit, seen by reformism as a basis for the translation of the generalities of the foundations of jurisprudence to detailed legislation.[119] However, legal arguments, despite the general form in which they are presented, need to produce particular sense in the form of specific statutes. If conceived only nominally, as was the case here, with assumptions of a priori accord with natural justice or the concept of justice, then it would constitute "a diversion of shari'a towards formulations and methods which are foreign to it. The shari'a is clear and it cannot admit the vagueness of natural justice or the principles of justice."[120] The Muslim legist must move from the general to the specific as identified by Muslim legal traditions and on the basis of certain scriptural support, rather than pronouncing preferences among contradictory judgments on vague grounds.

For, in fact, all this effort was not so much adapted to the prevailing situation as steeped in romantic anachronism, assiduous in emphasising

117 al-Fāsī, *Al-naqd al-dhātī*, 127.

118 Muṣṭafā al-Zarqā, *Al-madkhal al-fiqhī al-'āmm*, 6 vols (Damascus: Maṭba'at Jām'iat Dimashq, 1959).

119 Ibid., 28.

120 al-Fāsī, *Difā' 'an al-sharī'a*, 137.

dissimilitude from modern life. If shari'a were to be codified, this would entail the codification of detail, not of general principles. It was therefore a natural and simple move from incoherence to coherence, from vague general declarations with a tolerant stamp to concrete legal rulings, and, one might say, from utopia to dystopia, when the slogan that shari'a is valid everywhere and at all times is taken seriously rather than rhetorically, and without equivocation. This concretisation also turns away from the magical procedure subtending reformist evasion: presuming that the circle can be squared because the squaring is willed by the reformist. This straightforwardness was expressed in a massive book on penal law considered by many Islamists as their pride and joy. For its author, the Egyptian Abd al-Qadir 'Awda (b. 1906, condemned for his part in the Muslim Brother conspiracy to assassinate Gamal Abdel Nasser, and executed in 1954), contrary to laws that evolved with the evolution of societies, "the Shari'a was not composed of a small number of rulings which then multiplied, or scattered principles which were then collected, or initial theories which were then refined. Shari'a was not born as a child with the infant Islamic community which then followed this community's evolution and grew alongside it. It was born fully developed, and was revealed by God, complete, comprehensive and exclusive, without defect . . . shari'a came into existence . . . covering every case, and allowing no case to escape its remit."[121]

According to this concept, therefore, crimes are not worldly matters but "things forbidden in shari'a, God's disapproval expressing itself in punishment".[122] Moral values can only be such if commanded by shari'a.[123] Nevertheless public interest is always in view, and punishment is exacted for this purpose.[124] Legislation finds its origin in divine command, and not the general interest. The desire for moral purity converged with the utopia of a perfect society, all the while disregarding the corpus of jurisprudence inherited from al-Sarakhsi or even Rashid Rida as previously discussed on the question of apostasy's anachronism. 'Awda affirms, for example, that the sanction for adultery was "commonly known", although stoning has in fact

121 'Abd al-Qādir 'Awda, *Al-tashrī' al-jinā'i al-islāmī muqāranan bi al-qānūn al-waḍ'i*, 3 vols (Cairo: Maktabat Dār al-'Urūba, 1959–1960), vol. 1, 15–16.

122 Ibid., 66.

123 Ibid., 70–71

124 Ibid., 68.

no Qur'anic foundation.[125] There was also a tendency to assign sanctions for matters that were inexistent, such as "revolt against the Imam", be the imam's authority established by consent or by coercion, among other matters that were discussed in classical works of Muslim law.[126] Punishments for fornication were the most ostentatious, underlined also by Sarakhsi and Riad, although in modern legislation well known to 'Awda, fornication was regarded as a misdemeanor, not a crime. It is unsurprising that punishments were a subject of special attention, as they are savagely particularistic, very graphically distant from modern law, and make for impressive political theatre as witnessed in past decades from Khomeinist Iran to Mosul under Daesh. Stoning was the "accepted and uncontested" punishment for fornication, divinely imposed.[127] Awda does not inform us of the legal reasons for the statute or for the absence of any Qur'anic proof-text relating to it. He then proceeds to provide almost obsessively voyeuristic detail as he describes stoning procedures in elaborate, almost loving particulars.[128] He luxuriates in archaism as he informs us which of the imams (Shafi'i and Ahmad ibn Hanbal) considered introducing the penis of a dead male into the pudendum of an unrelated woman to be fornication, and which (Abu Hanifa and the Zaidis) did not. He also explains why male and female masturbation (he calls both *istimna'*, onanism, self-induced ejaculation, as in medieval medical and erotic texts) must be regarded as veritable and therefore punishable fornication.[129]

During Awda's lifetime, there was no longer justification for considering necrophilia as an act requiring punishment rather than a condition requiring treatment. At best, this and the obsession with primitive regimes of punishments sustain the argument that Islamist codification of law was conceived by definition and quite consciously as the contrary of civil law codes, lifeless stipulations of demented imaginings. Claims for the validity of shari'a for every place and time, is, in the end, only a slogan. When taken seriously with practical consequences sought, be it by 'Awda, in Iran, in Saudi Arabia, by Daesh, it becomes a politically theatrical departure from

125 Ibid., vol. 2, 706 ff.
126 Ibid, 675–677 ff.
127 Ibid., 376–377, 675.
128 Ibid., 445–447.
129 Ibid., 352–370.

the historical present. Indeed, such claims seek to manipulate reality violently, as they seek to oblige reality, out of keeping with these para-legal ordinances, to display submission to them. That is the only trace remaining of the coherence of the shari'a, and Awda was extraordinarily coherent, to the point of inhumanity, with a rigour the like of which was practised only by Daesh. Claims for the validity of shari'a across time and space remove shari'a from contemporary reality and take it back to a past that produced a shari'a relevant to it and to the level of civilisation it had reached, put forward today as an alternative reality.

2 Intellectual Secularism and Reformist Retrogression

Previous chapters discussed how the end of the nineteenth century saw the early stages of the emergence of a new class of intellectuals.[130] These possessed new cognitive resources while secular culture, especially its historical and scientific varieties that sought to perceive the present in the context of its contemporaneity and in the context of a changing history, had penetrated into the vanguard of Islamic reformist thinkers who were not beholden to official religious institutions such as al-Azhar, and compelled into revisions they were not able to pursue consequentially. Modern reflection on social, political, and cultural matters, including matters of religion and shari'a, was integrated into frames of Western thought that had become universal for modern times. Evolutionist theory in its generality and its varied forms was the point of convergence. It continued in its Comtean positivist form among many secular or quasi-secular thinkers. Isma'il Mazhar (1891–1962), Darwin's translator, believed that the intellectual life of humans had three capacities: a capacity for belief linked to religion, followed by one for contemplation connected to philosophy, rising to a capacity for demonstration – that is to say positivism connected to science. Mazhar considered that the West had won for itself vitality while the East rested content with imaginings of the hereafter, somnolently reliant upon "the rule of *fuqahā'* and princes exercising absolute authority as representatives of

130 For overall context and emergences over a number of decades, see Keith David Watenpaugh, *Being Modern in the Middle East. Revolution, Nationalism, Colonialism and the Arab Middle Class* (Princeton: Princeton University Press, 2006). For further precisions, see also Edhem Eldem, "La bourgeoisie ottomane fin de siècle", in *Le Moyen-Orient fin XIXe–XXe siècle*, ed. Leyla Dakhli (Paris: Seuil, 2016), 135–144.

God on earth".[131] Muhammad Husayn Haykal found that Auguste Comte's law of three stages explained the cognitive evolution of humanity that, in its last stage, separated science from religion, each with its own field of competence and relevance.[132] The Syrian intellectual Zaki al-Arsuzi (1899–1968), a figure of almost oracular inspiration for the early Baath party, considered that the theological stage was one that ended before the entry of the world into modern times.[133] Even Hassan al-Banna adapted the tripartite evolutionary model to place Islam, as Muhammad 'Abduh did, at the top end of the evolutionary scale possible for humanity.[134] The sober-minded Moroccan Islamist Allal al-Fasi was disposed to reflect freely, without confusing what is contemporary with what is modern, and accepted that contemporary Arab societies contained much that was obsolete that ought not necessarily be conserved.[135]

In the same way that reflection on religion at the time of the *Tanzimat* followed the evolutionist template, this same orientation was maintained during the liberal period. Historical-critical considerations of religion on the model of Western sociological and anthropological studies moved towards a detailed study of the origins of the religious phenomenon in society without this necessarily entailing declarations of atheism. Some of those, like the Syrian nationalist politician Abd al-Rahman al-Shahbandar (1880–1940), emphasised that scientific research on the origins of religious consciousness was not concerned with matters of revelation, but rather with the social and mental origins of religion only.[136] This evasive position was common. Ismail Mazhar criticised Shibli Shumayyil for his attachment to materialist metaphysics and his rejection of divinity, given that the theory of

131 Ismā'īl Maẓhar, "Bayn al-dīn wa al-'ilm", *al-'Uṣūr* 37 (1929), 18 and Ismā'īl Maẓhar, *Wathbat al-Sharq: baḥth fī anna al-'aqliyya al-turkiyya al-ḥaditha hiyā mithāl al-'aqliyya al-salīma allatī yajib an yantaḥiluhā al-sharq li yujāriya sayr al-haḍāra al-'ālamīya* (Cairo: Dār al-'Uṣūr li'l-ṭab' wa al-Nashr, 1929), 6–7.

132 Muḥammad Ḥusayn Haykal, "Al-dīn wa al-'ilm" (1926), reprinted in Muḥammad Ḥusayn Haykal, *Al-īmān wa al-ma'rifa wa al-falsafa* (Cairo: Maktabat al-Nahḍa al-Miṣriyya, 1964), 28–29.

133 Zakī al-Arsūzī, *Mashākilunā al-qawmiyya wa mawqif al-aḥzāb minhā* (Damascus: Dār al-Yaqaẓa al-'Arabiyya, 1956), 22–23.

134 Ḥasan al-Bannā, *majmū'at rasā'il al-imām al-shahīd Ḥasan al-Bannā* (Beirut: Dār al-Andalus, 1965), 65–67.

135 al-Fāsī, *Al-Naqd al-dhātī*, 67–68.

136 al-Shāhbandar, *Al-qaḍāya al-ijtima'iyya al-kubrā fī al-'ālam al-'arabī*, 145, 155, 160.

evolution, he considered with Spencer, did not investigate religious beliefs and their origins, but only religion's impact on human society, driving society to "a special form of elevation".[137] Religion was to Mazhar natural to society, in a way he was not quite able to define clearly, in a book that dealt with the myth of the Flood from Babylonia to the Qur'an.[138] It entailed neither a confirmation of the existence of God nor its denial. It arose from an instinct to belief based on fear and ignorance that anthropomorphised observable phenomena, such that the idea of divinity rested on an analogy with humanity and human characteristics projected onto non-human entities.[139] For Salama Musa, religion was the belief in a force transcending the laws of nature, which evolved from simple forms among primitive peoples who blended divinity and the spirits of the dead.[140]

For some who rested upon Islamic reformism as a guarantee for belief and the defensibility of belief, the history of religions included a view of society and history similar to that discussed above. Abbas Mahmud al-'Aqqad had recourse to a similar evolutionism in two delightful books displaying much reading in contemporary anthropology and history of religion dealing with Allah and with Satan, in the spirit of Islamic reformism where monotheism is the apogee of evolution. But he refrained from applying to Islam the kind of social and historical analysis applied to other religions. For al-'Aqqad, the history of the concept of divinity exhibited progress from illusion to sure knowledge, which was, he believed, expressed in a neo-Ash'arite concept of divinity.[141] For all their eccentric eclecticism, al-'Aqqad's studies were certainly no less developed in terms of its readings and arguments than other studies written at the time in any language, and were often better developed and argued than work by other Arab authors of the time. Ismail Mazhar's positivist philosophical culture was proficient and accurate, and it was fairly precise. In contrast, Salama Musa's was superficial, crudely imitative of ideas

137 Maẓhar, *Multaqā al-sabīl*, 87–88.

138 Ismā'īl Maẓhar, *Qiṣṣat al-ṭūfān wa taṭawurruhā fī thalāth madaniyyāt qadīma hiya al-āshūriyya al-bābiliyya wa al-'ibraniyya wa al-masīḥiyya wa intiqāluhā bi al-luqāḥ ilā al-madaniyya al-islāmiyya* (Cairo: Dār al-'Uṣūr, 1929), 21–22.

139 Maẓhar, "Bayn al-dīn wa al-'ilm", 6–9. 10–18.

140 Mūsā, *Al-yawm wa al-ghadd*, 66–67.

141 'Abbās Maḥmūd al-'Aqqād, *Allāh: Kitāb fī nash'at al-'aqīda al-ilāhiyya*, 3rd edn (Cairo: Dār al-Ma'ārif, 1960) and 'Abbās Maḥmūd al-'Aqqād, *Iblīs* (Cairo: Dār al-Hilāl, n.d.).

that circulated among British intellectuals of the second rank such as H. G. Wells and George Bernard Shaw.[142]

Nevertheless, Musa's attitudes to religion were among the most radical, with an inclination to atheism bereft of agnostic or deist indirection.[143] The only openly atheist thinker with a clearly articulated approach was the Alexandrian author Ismail Adham (1911–1940),[144] a very peculiar man by any account. He tried to prove, on the basis of the concept of probability that had clearly been acquired autodidactically, that "the world is subject to the comprehensive law of chance not a comprehensive first cause", and that the cause of creation is not outside the world but immanent in it. Nothing lurks beyond the world, and belief in divinity is no more than a primitive concept emerging from illusion, fear, and ignorance of the nature of things.[145]

Few thinkers proclaimed themselves, as Adham did, a "first-class atheist".[146] Salama Musa sought to apologise, uninvited, on behalf of al-Zahawi quoted previously, claiming that his vexation with the East "caused him to feel that he should become a supporter of Satan. Much like a commoner, who gets into a quarrel and becomes so angry and enraged that he speaks deliriously and says foolish things arising from vexation."[147] Other authors assented to claims for the infallible truthfulness of prophets, perhaps with cautious intent, and adopted old Stoic-Deistic ideas of the equivalence of God and the order of nature, as Ismail Mazhar did: "the system of the universe in which humans consider themselves one of its links does not allow us to believe that God cares for each human on the earth in a manner exceeding the influence on the laws of nature which the Creator infused into matter."[148] In the same way, the Iraqi

142 Compare Kamāl ʿAbd al-Laṭīf, *Salama Mūsā wa ishkāliyyāt al-nahḍa* (Beirut: Dār al-Fārābī and Casablanca: al-Markaz al-Thaqāfī al-ʿArabī, 1982), 103–108, 234–235.

143 Ibid., 181.

144 On whom see G. H. A. Juynboll, "Ismail Ahmad Adham (1911–1940), the Atheist", *Journal of Arabic Literature* 3 (1972): 54–71.

145 Ismāʿīl Adham, *Limādhā anā mulḥid? (Paris: Manshūrāt al-Nuqṭa,* no. 9, n.d.) reprint of the original, which appeared in *al-Amām* (Alexandria), August 1937. The pages are not numbered in the Paris edition consulted for the present study.

146 Maḥmūd Ḥusayn, "Al-mu'minūn", *al-ʿUsūr* 20 (1929): 436.

147 Salāma Mūsā, "Jamīl Ṣidqī al-Zahāwī", *al-Majalla al-Jadīda* (1932): 46. It was reprinted in *al-Ṭalīʿa* 8 (1965): 144–145. Jamīl Ṣiqdī al-Zahāwī, *Al-zahāwī wa dīwānuhu al-mafqūd*, ed. Hilāl Nājī (Cairo: Dār al-ʿArab, 1964), 226–228, 232.

148 Ismāʿīl Maẓhar, "ʿIlāqat al-insān bi Allāh laysat mubāsharatan bal bil-wāsāṭa", *al-ʿUṣūr* 2/9 (1928): 922.

poet Ma'ruf al-Rusafi considered that it was obvious from the Qur'an that "the name of majesty, God, is a term synonymous with instinct and nature. There is no doubt that all elements of creation, animate and inanimate, are subjected to the rule of nature and natural disposition for which these elements have a propensity." The Egyptian Romantic poet – but also physician, bacteriologist, and apiculturalist – Ahmad Zaki Abu Shadi (1892–1955) also affirmed a natural religion: the eternal nature of matter and the instinctive character of Sufi sentiments, which he attributed to participation with the rest of the cosmos in a united electric impulse,[149] a kind of electrical protoplasm. It is unclear if the Tunisian littérateur, folklorist, and broadcaster Taher Khemiri (1899–1973) sought to affirm an atheistic position when, in 1929, he proposed cruder concepts of Freudian psychoanalysis as a key to studying religion – a form of consideration not uncommon in Arab culture from the 1960s. Khemiri thought that the sexual instinct might well be seen to have established the foundation of religion, providing imaginary pleasure with a masochistic foundation, where actual sexual pleasure was lacking to the poor and middling elements of society.[150]

Generally speaking, then, the criticism of religion by considering its origins in nature evaded criticism of the tenets of religious faith, especially the doctrine of divinity, but stood instead on two other foundations: positivistic scientism and social and intellectual secularism. The consequences were the removal of cognitive claims for religion, accompanied by rational, historical, and social research into religion's sources in the world, without this being seen as necessarily vitiating religion's assertion of divinity's existence. Some authors with clear secularist affiliations attacked atheism despite their open opposition to the religious lobby and their clear scepticism of matters proposed by religion and its practice. The avant-garde poet Ahmed Zaki Abu Shadi was one such, criticising Ismail Adham's justification for atheism that he saw to be an argument against atheism, not for it. He saw probability as a natural law that composed the complexity of things with the needs of regularity and order, not of chaos.[151] Secularists, despite their suspension

149 Ma'rūf al-Ruṣāfi, *Al-a'māl al-majhūla*, ed. Najdat Fatḥī Ṣafwat (London: Riyad al-Rayyis li'l-Kutub wa al-Nashr, 1988), 64 and Aḥmad Zākī Abū Shādī, *Limādhā anā mu'min?* (Alexandria: Maṭba't al-Ta'āwun, 1937), 8–9.

150 Ṭahir Khamīrī, "Al-dīn wa 'ilm al-nafs al-jadīd", *al-'Uṣūr* 21 (1929): 524–526, and *al-'Uṣūr* 22 (1929): 780.

151 Abū Shādī, *Limādhā anā mu'min?*, 15–16.

of or lack of interest in any clear and explicit scrutiny of theism, continued to perceive religion in the light of reason, and studied various religious phenomena through the lens of history. Salama Musa found that religions adapted to their environment and deduced, in a characteristically hasty and impressionistic manner that was not uncommon in Europe also, that monotheism was a religion of nomadic peoples such as the Jews, Arabs, and the Hyksos, unskilled in sculpting statues and idols in the classical style. Such peoples believed in one opmnipresent God accessible everywhere without the onerous effort of carrying idols.[152] Musa then considered the origins of certain Christian doctrines in Semitic religions, tracing back the Trinity and the Cross to ancient Egyptian religions, and considering Christ to be a particular version of the seasonal divine sacrificial victim figure among the Semites, such as Adonis.[153] Likewise, Muhammad Husayn Haykal, in an article published in 1925, traced some monotheistic doctrines to Pharaonic beliefs.[154] Ismail Mazhar made a detailed comparison of some monotheist doctrines such as the myth of the Flood to Babylonian, Egyptian and Greek myths, among others, in studies that, he said, were not linked in any way to religion or dogma, being based on "pure search for the truth which religious people might interpret as they will and from which freethinkers may deduce what they wish. The issue is not one of affirmation or denial, but one of relating different versions . . . and comparing them with one another, allusively rather than by explication."[155]

A historical and intellectual approach to religion requires the relativisation and contextualisation of their historical manifestation, and the denial of the infallibility and completeness attributed to them. To the religious lobby, this meant the denigration of religion, its humanisation and subjection to moral, aesthetic, and objective judgements. An example of this was the Tunisian poet al-Shabbi's opinion of Islamic Arab poetry. His views provoked uproar in Tunis. Shabbi, a Zeitouna-trained writer with a keen aesthetic sensitivity and deep appreciation for Greek myths, compared these to Arab myths and their poetic imagery, and not in favour of the latter. Shabbi reproached

152 Mūsā, *Mukhtārāt Salāma Mūsā*, 59, 62–63.

153 Salāma Mūsā, *Al-yawm wa al-ghadd*, 88–90.

154 Muḥammad Muḥammad Ḥusayn, *Al-ittijāhāt al-waṭaniyya fi al-adab al-mu'āṣir*, vol. 2, 295.

155 Maẓhar, *Qiṣṣat al-ṭūfān wa taṭawurruhā fi thalāth madaniyyāt qadīma*, 66; Maẓhar, "Muṭāla'āt fī sifr al-takwīn", *al-'Uṣūr* 5/23 (1929): 2–15 and Maẓhar, "Muṭāla'āt fī sifr al-khurūj", *al-'Uṣūr* 5/2 (1929): 161–174.

Muslims for their lack of understanding of poetry, their suspicion of it, and its use only as a means of interpreting obscure passages of the Qur'an. He also praised the 'Abbasid-era libertine poet Abu Nuwas (d. 814) for his mockery of this practice.[156] For his part, Zaki al-Arsuzi compared the morals of the pre-Islamic Arabs favourably with those of Islam. The former rested, he held, on a natural disposition that allowed for mastery of the world, as opposed to Islam that proved deficient in proportion to its distance from Jahiliyya. The Jahiliyya enjoyed an almost absolute superiority in its communal and artistic sensibilities. Idols of that period were "symbols in which form prevailed over meaning to the extent that these symbols were independent of their *raison d'être*, being thus analogous to the Beatific Names of God".[157] Ismail Mazhar scrutinised the concept of *I'jāz al-Qur'ān* – the inimitability of the Qur'an – in his review of the book *I'jāz al-qur'ān* by the neo-classical poet and conservative author Mustafa Sadiq al-Rafi'i, and he considered the inimitability ascribed to it to be relative: it was inimitable in the same sense that *The Illiad* or *The Divine Comedy* were considered inimitable by Greeks and Italians. The Qur'an was inimitable in terms of Arab conventions, and implies no qualities added to this.[158]

Antoun Saadeh (1904–1949), founder of the Syrian Social Nationalist Party, considered the development of Islam and its particular features in the context of a great historical movement. He mentioned first the parallels between Qur'anic enunciations "which Muhammad attributed to God"[159] and regulations in the Old Testament about marriage, diet, usury, theft, and the religious state. He then related these to the level of social organisation made possible by the environment from which these emerged. With keen historical sense, Saadeh asserted that Islam, like Judaism, appeared in a poor and rudimentary environment, spreading in more developed regions in Syria, Persia, and Andalusia. It began with material concerns necessary for organising and unifying the Arabs, imposing a rigid religious law to discipline primitive nomadic peoples, and developed in spiritual terms only

156 Abū-l-Qāsim al-Shābbī, *Al-khayāl al-shi'rī 'ind al-'Arab* (Tunis: al-sharika al-qawmiyya li'l-nashr wa al-tawzī', 1961), 31–45, 135–137.

157 Zakī al-Arsūzī, *Al-mu'allafāt al-kāmila*, 5 vols (Damascus: Maṭābī' al-Idāra al-Siyāsiyya li'l Jaysh wa al-Quwwāt al-Musallaḥa, 1975), 56, 59–73, 110.

158 Maẓhar, "'Ilāqat al-insān bi Allāh laysat mubāsharatan bal bil-wāsāṭa", 966–967.

159 Anṭūn Sa'āda, *Al-islām fī risālatayhi, al-masīḥiyya wa al-muḥammadiya* (Beirut, n.p.: 1958), 112.

when it moved out of the Arabian Peninsula and was integrated into cultural contexts that enabled it to develop in this way.[160] Islam, as known to history, emerged thus as the result of an evolution and a historical movement, and was not born in complete form as religious people are wont to claim.

Of all these historical contributions to the understanding of early Islam from various points of view, the efforts of Taha Hussein and 'Ali 'Abd al-Raziq were to have the greatest impact, without being necessarily the most radical or the most accomplished. They represented two methodical attempts to study in detail sensitive issues relating to the history of Muslims. Ismail Mazhar had raised a matter of great precision and importance when he expressed the view that the collection of the Qur'an in the form of a book with a specific sequence of textual components "was neither beneficial nor useful. Nothing in the old chronicles indicates that the Prophet ordered such a collection with such an arrangement. The efforts of 'Uthman, Commander of the Believers, in this regard, were not meritorious in any case. There are in the Qur'an a few commands and prohibitions. These were independent orders, as required by the nature of central authority at that period. There was no idea of compiling a coherent book. The Prophet did not command this and did not attempt to do it himself. Those who collected the Qur'an ignored this fact. Every command contained in the Qur'an was related to a specific circumstance of the time. As for the *ḥadīth* narratives, nobody can prove their validity, except for a small number which does not exceed ten or fifteen. If we referred to the regulations and rules which the *fuqahā'* put in place after the time of the Prophet, no weight can be attached to any of them. The decisions and rulings which they issued had, through imitation and practice, become themselves the principles of Islam, but in their own time they had only a relative and momentary importance."[161] Ismail Mazhar introduced the dimension of history and time into the Qur'anic text and gave it a real history instead of the traditional faith-history, although he did not conduct a precise or detailed study.

Taha Hussein subjected the Qur'anic text to historical and, within limits, rational scrutiny. One of his critics reported that, following the controversy surrounding his 1926 book *Fī al-shi'r al-jāhilī* (On pre-Islamic

160 Ibid., 18–21, 23–27, 31–35, 40–46.

161 Maẓhar, *Wathbat al-Sharq*, 51–52.

poetry), he dictated to his students a critical study of the Qur'anic text in which he said that researchers should not differentiate between the Qur'an and any other text as texts under scrutiny. Such an approach allows the distinction between two styles, Meccan and Medinan. The first underlines the characteristics of underdeveloped and simple environments: violence, severity, the evasion of reasonable argument, and an absence of logic, while the second period is marked by a tenor at once serene, sober and law-making. This, Hussein is supposed to have maintained, reflected the influence of the more refined urban milieu of Medina, influenced by Judaism. Hussein went on to consider the so-called mysterious letters that figure at the beginning of twenty-nine out of 144 chapters of the Qur'an. He suggested that these elements had been placed in the text in order to mystify, or as notation to distinguish different redactions of the text, and that "subsequently the passage of time attached them to the Qur'an so they became Qur'an".[162] This purely secular, historical approach to the text of the Qur'an was what enabled Hussein to present the critical approach he introduced through *Fī al-shi'r al-jāhilī* when he announced his programme in the following terms: "Let us strive to study Arabic literature unconcerned by glorification of the Arabs or their denigration, by defending Islam or criticising it, unconcerned with the reconciliation between Arabic literature and the results of modern scientific and literary research, unafraid about where this research will lead us in terms of what nationalism might refuse or political passions might spurn or religious sentiment might detest. We have managed to free ourselves to this extent so we shall no doubt attain through our research results which the Ancients did not reach."[163]

Hussein – with Azharite formation, a former student of Émile Durkheim's at the Sorbonne, where he wrote a doctoral thesis on Ibn Khaldun – relied on a neat separation between the spheres of science and religion, which enabled the former to scrutinise the latter on its own conditions. Scholars should therefore study religion "as they study language or law . . . inasmuch as all these are social phenomena produced by collective existence. We thus come to the conclusion that religion for the scholar did not descend from heaven nor was it brought by revelation. It emerged from the world as human

162 'Arafa, *Naqd maṭā'in fī al-Qur'ān al-karīm*, 4–8.
163 Ṭaḥa Ḥusayn, *Fī al-shi'r al-jāhilī* (Cairo: Matba't Dār al-Kutub al-Miṣriyya, 1926), 14.

communities do themselves."[164] Hussein thus placed the historical dimension of the emergence of Islam within the realm of the possible. He wrote that "the Torah may tell us about Abraham and Ishmael, and the Qur'an may do likewise. But the occurrence of these two names in the Qur'an and the Torah does not suffice to prove their historical existence, let alone the tale of Ishmael son of Abraham's migration to Mecca and the emergence there of a community which assimilated Arab culture."[165] Hussein situated Islamic tales in the history of myth, and he concluded that the account of Ishmael as father of the Arabs was a political tale sought to establish a link between Jews and Arabs on the one hand and between Islam, Judaism, Qur'an, and Torah on the other, in an attempt by Quraysh to unite the Arabs against the Byzantines and the Persians. Quraysh adopted the myth of the founding of the Kaaba as the Romans adopted a myth, compiled for them by the Greeks, of Aeneas son of the Trojan king Priam, asserting kinship between Romans and Greeks.[166] Such were historical analyses evident to minds unencumbered by the burden of tradition; the Iraqi poet al-Rusafi held the view that this Ishmaelism aimed to justify Qussay's seizure of authority over the Kaaba from Khuza'a.[167] Some Christian critics of Islam also adopted Hussein's approach, although he went further than most in doubting the historicity of Abraham and Ishmael completely, a point stressed by one of his Islamist critics.[168] Hussein's scepticism did not, however, reach its full extent of possibility, and did not cast doubt explicitly on the existence of transcendant entities, on the history of the Qur'an (despite comment of a historical character), its collection and canonisation.[169] Taha Hussein had been a keen student of that other blind erudite, Abu 'Ala' al-Ma'arri, who often denied prophecy as traditionally received, and has often been perceived as an atheist or at least an egregious heretic. In his study of Abu al-'Ala, he announced: "I do not have the power to pronounce anyone a Muslim, nor expel anyone from the Islamic fold." His was a consideration of Islam that was open-minded, broad, and that involved a fully historical perspective.[170]

---

164 'Arafa, *Naqd maṭā'in fī al-Qur'ān al-karīm*, 113.

165 Ḥusayn, *Fī al-shi'r al-jāhilī*, 26.

166 Ibid., 26–27.

167 al-Ruṣāfī, *Al-a'māl al-majhūla*, 76.

168 Sīl, "Tadhyil", 323, 325 and 'Arafa, *Naqd maṭā'in fī al-Qur'ān al-karīm*, 100–108.

169 Louis 'Awaḍ, *Thaqāfatunā fī muftaraq al-ṭuruq* (Beirut: Dār al-Ādāb, 1974), 125.

170 Ḥusayn, *Al-majmū'a al-kāmila li mu'allafāt al-duktūr Ṭaḥa Ḥusayn*, vol. 1, 16.

The Azharite patrician 'Ali 'Abd al-Raziq (1888–1966),[171] for his part, used the facts of history to elaborate the issue of the caliphate in terms of Muslim jurisprudence. His legalistic starting point was no obstacle to his discernment. He did not transmute historical events into jurisprudential material, as a contemporary Islamist critic claimed.[172] On the contrary, 'Abd al-Raziq used history with a sensitivity and a sure touch that went beyond the average secular understanding of history as found in his time, with a sensibility to historical realities that was unmatched by his critics. Political conditions prevailing when this work was conceived have not diminished its continuing value.[173] Two factors make up the significance of 'Abd al-Raziq's work: he denied, first, the consummateness, perfection, and infallibility of the beginnings of Islam, seeing in it a changing worldly history from which he removed the utopian characteristic beyond the capacities of the human condition. Second, this work precluded the common modernist reformist indeterminacy that allowed the possibility that the sound understanding might be able to use early Islam to demonstrate contradictory positions. This would have been possible only if texts and histories were interpreted anachronistically and stripped of connections to context, as previously discussed. 'Abd al-Raziq presented the polity founded by Muhammad as rudimentary, simple, and unrefined, unlettered, close to nature, lacking an integrated system of government and institutions such as that imagined by modern Islamists who project developed state institutions onto the past.[174] The caliphate, as understood by 'Abd al-Raziq, was a political entity linked to highly specific circumstances, the *Ridda* or "Wars of Apostasy", which he saw as a response to the withdrawal of allegiance to Abu Bakr that had once been given to Muhammad, a war by nature related to politics and tribalism, among other factors.[175]

---

171 'Abd al-Raziq's famous book appeared in English translation as Ali Abdel Razek, *Islam and the Foundations of Political Power*, trans. M. Loutfi, ed. A. Filali-Ansary (Edinburgh: Edinburgh University Press in association with the Aga Khan University Institute for the Study of Muslim Civilisations, 2012). See S. T. Ali, *A Religion not a State: Ali 'Abd al-Raziq's Islamic Justification for Political Secularism* (Salt Lake City: University of Utah Press, 2009).

172 al-Bishrī, *Al-Muslimūn wa al-Aqbāṭ fī iṭār al-jamā'a al-waṭaniyya*, 293.

173 One can compare Kamāl 'Abd al-Laṭīf, *Al-ta'wīl wa al-mufāraqa: Naḥwa ta'wīl falsafī li'l-naẓar al-siyāsī al-'arabī* (Casablanca: al-Markaz al-Thaqāfī al-'Arabī, 1987), 88–89.

174 'Alī 'Abd al-Raziq, *Al-islām wa uṣūl al-ḥukm, baḥth fī al-khilāfa wa al-ḥukūma fī al-islām*, 2nd edn (Cairo: Maṭba'at Miṣr, 1965), 44–47, 60–62.

175 Ibid., 93–94, 96–101.

In this way, the study of historical themes began to buttress cognitive secular orientations, by extending their remit of validity pertinence to objects of study and reflection that religious thinking had rendered out of bounds. These studies generalised cognitive activity with a secular authority, in tandem with a culture connected to the state. The generalisation of a secular perception in studies of Islam had far-reaching repercussions, potential as well as erratically actual. It was linked to a struggle for authority between two camps. On the one hand there was fideist religious and supernaturalist reasoning, still prevalent in important sectors of education as noted earlier, supported by the religious institution headed by al-Azhar and backed by King Fouad of Egypt and later by King Farouk (r. 1936–1952). On the other hand, there were new cultural actors active in associations, the press, journals, and some political parties, notably the Liberal Nationalist Party with which members of the ʿAbd al-Raziq family were affiliated, along with figures such as Taha Hussein, Muhammad Hussein Haykal, and Ahmad Lutfi Sayyid. This party represented orientations that were politically liberal, socially paternalistic, and intellectually progressive, in contrast to the somewhat demagogic pandering to a supposedly religious public by the Wafd party. It was the Wafd government that intervened in 1936, at the behest of al-Azhar, to suppress Ismail Adham's book on early Islam, a work clearly marked by the critical scholarship then available in European languages – Ahmad Amin was one among those who protested[176] – which supported the attacks against ʿAbd al-Raziq and Hussein, and rarely refrained from instrumentalising religious issues for immediate political benefit, treating religion as political theatre in which one pandered to the gallery. This struggle – discussed later in this chapter – was fundamentally articulated around al-Azhar's resistance to new ideas and its cultural consequences, seeking to ensure the pre-eminence of religious forms of knowledge, making al-Azhar itself the custodian of knowledge and thought, pushing its graduates competing with secular personnel for teaching and administrative posts.

Modernist Islamic reformism declined, due to inability to move intellectually beyond the transitional phase represented by Muhammad ʿAbduh, and retreated in the face of the pressure of religious institutions. Its forever embryonic form of rhetorical argumentation, described in detail above, was ossified and rendered vulnerable to forms of retrogression, the calling of a

176 Sāmī al-Kayyālī, *Al-rāḥilūn* (Cairo: Dār al-Fikr, n.d.), 97–100.

bluff, as it became a standard apologetic element in Arab liberal culture, most particularly in Egypt. It also became the standard form of official religion, such that satirical secular critics were led to say that religious culture disseminated through official organs of state and its institutions, was that a believer "according to the modern definition is he who possesses a pilfered thought, a borrowed thought, a quoted thought or sacred thought. He allows this thought to occupy every part of his mind, and unsurprisingly, as this part of him is not extensive, he holds to his opinions whatever distortion or stupidity may occur in them, and if contrary ideas are displeasing to him he considers their authors to be atheists."[177] Thus the field of thought saw developments parallel to those previously noted in the social arena. The religious institution diverted the course of scientific thought from being a force that marginalised the religious institution in the public sphere, to one cast as directly opposing religion, facilitating the reframing of religion as not only a contrary, but as a free-standing alternative. It was as though the religious institution in the Arab world followed a course charted by currents of European religion in the nineteenth century. Thus that which had lost all links with religion was construed as non-religion, conveying an impression of enmity to religion, with a complete readiness on the part of believers to pronounce on infidelity, apostasy, atheism.[178] For that reason Taha Hussein praised Athenian paganism because he held that it was a simple religion with little tendency to fanaticism because of its absence of theology and of priests, with, he claimed, no accusations of infidelity and no priests claiming a monopoly of knowledge.[179]

Among the results of religious opposition to secular modern thought was that secular criticism of religious learning remained generally confined to precautionary limits intended to ward off the malevolence of the religious lobby, although forthright criticism was not absent. Emphasis was placed on the distinction between scientific and religious knowledge, while calling for the primacy of science. Some held that the materialist atheist brought greater benefit to humanity than a citizen for whom religious belief meant nothing but zealotry, and who was enslaved by his dogma that he holds as the obsessive compulsion of the mentally disturbed, an allusion to what clinical

177 Maḥmūd, "Al-mu'minūn", 433.

178 Sāṭi' al-Ḥuṣrī', *Al-a'māl al-qawmiyya li Sāṭi' al-Huṣrī': Silsilat al-turāth al-qawmī*, 3 vols (Beirut: Markaz Dirāsāt al-Waḥda al-'Arabiyya, 1985), 1,390–1,392.

179 Ḥusayn, *Al-majmū'a al-kāmila li mu'allafāt al-duktūr Ṭaḥa Ḥusayn*, vol. 12, 154–155.

psychology of that time called monomania.[180] For this reason, freedom of thought was held by many to be incompatible with the spirit of religion, and education was to be freed from the chains of religion. It became possible to compare Descartes with al-Ghazali and to prefer Descartes because in the end he aspired to control nature rather than to cultivate attitudes of awed fascination.[181] Progress and secularism were assimilated to one another while religion was associated with decadence.[182] Secularism and progress led to the knowledge of realities of high civilisation preceding religious laws, while believers maintained erroneously that religious laws are the cause of civilization. As one religious scholar explained, writing under the pseudonym "Free-thinking Azharite": "the opposite is true from every point of view. They [the religious] do not say that laws proscribed theft because it was harmful to society, but that it was the menace of theft that caused the existence of [legally organised] society. Thus they sought to prove that the natural order of society is dependent on the maintenance of their laws as they stand and that, were these laws to change, the foundations of society would be demolished."[183]

Taken together, the logical conclusion from and the basic starting point for contending with the intervention by the religious lobby in intellectual and cultural matters, and their attempt to acquire in effect a right to veto certain turns of thought, was the call to uphold the distinction between religion and science, to distinguish them, and restrict each to a particular domain: one centred on cognition, objective, rational, and historical, the other concerned with faith, belief, and the otherworld. Taha Hussein held that religion was older than science and that, in the past, it had dealt with matters such as cosmology that were to become the preserve of science today. This recollection of older vintage rendered religion refractory to change, attributing to itself stability and fastness. Science, on the other hand, is premised on change and the affirmation of change and advancement over time.[184] Muhammad Hussein Haykal held a similar view, considering religion and science to have been initially contiguous, as inspiration explained what the senses could not

180 Ismāʿīl Maẓhar, "Ḥawl al-ilḥād wa al-īmān", *al-ʿUṣūr* 22 (1929): 661.

181 Al-Arsūzī, *Al-muʾallafāt al-kāmila*, vol. 5, 122–124, compare 267–268 and 289.

182 Salāma Mūsā, *Mā hiya al-nahḍa?* (Cairo: Salāma Mūsā li'l-Nashr wa al-Tawzīʿ, n.d.). 18–19.

183 Azharī ḥurr al-fikr, "Al-jāmiʿa al-azhariyya", *al-ʿUṣūr* 2/11 (1928): 1,237.

184 Ḥusayn, *Al-majmūʿa al-kāmila li muʾallafāt al-duktūr Ṭaḥa Ḥusayn*, vol. 12, 169.

explain. Thereafter the two diverged, with sense and observation going to science, belief and the spirit to religion.[185] Awareness of the impossibility of agreement between them[186] led to an emphasis on the necessity of their separation, especially as every episode of mutual interference between religion and science led to struggles between their respective supporters for power with the aim of securing exclusive control.[187] Less diplomatic was the journal *al-'Uṣūr*, which allocated responsibility for this violent struggle to the religious lobby, with their dogmatism and refusal to confine themselves to matters pertinent to salvation, and keeping well away from the explanation of cosmic matters and the management of evolving social relations in this world.[188]

The basic orientation of the type of view exemplified in *al-'Uṣūr* was to remove from religion any specific social competence as a condition of the coexistence of religion and science, leaving social affairs to positive law and custom, and politics to national interest.[189] Religion is a matter of belief and a support for ethical behaviour in its promotion of moral excellence, as the Syrian nationalist al-Shahbandar held.[190] So also Muhammad Kurd 'Ali, who said of himself that, having adopted reason as his arbiter, and found no convincing solution to matters concerning the otherworld, he conceded what had been received and, in practical terms, retained from religion only moral teachings and laudable values, such as truthfulness and honesty.[191] The jurist al-Sanhuri was perhaps expressing the view of most practical de facto secularists when he said that the disappearance of religion as a social bond in Europe did not mean that "religion has disappeared from hearts, for humanity, whatever the degree of progress it has reached, cannot do without religion. The throne of religion rests in hearts and consciences."[192] This intellectual endeavour resulted in reinforcing the common motif, at once cognitive and politically defensive, of the generic and functional distinction between religion and politics running parallel to that

185 Haykal, "Al-dīn wa al-'ilm", 17–19 and passim.
186 Ḥusayn, *Al-majmū'a al-kāmila li mu'allafāt al-duktūr Ṭaḥa Ḥusayn*, vol. 12, 151.
187 Ibid., vol. 10, 297 and Haykal, "Al-dīn wa al-'ilm", 9–16.
188 Anonymous, "Al-adyān wa hal tuṣbiḥu shārā'i' 'ibādiyya?" *al-'Uṣūr* 2/7 (1928): 657–659, at 658–659.
189 Ḥusayn, *Al-majmū'a al-kāmila li mu'allafāt al-duktūr Ṭaḥa Ḥusayn*, vol. 12, 170–171 and Maẓhar, "Ḥawl al-ilḥād wa al-īmān", 664.
190 'Abd al-Raḥmān al-Shāhbandar, *Al-qaḍāya al-ijtimā'iyya al-kubrā fī al-'ālam al-'arabī*, 169–170.
191 Kurd 'Alī, *Al-mudhakkirāt*, 490–491.
192 'Abd al-Razzāq Aḥmad al-Sanhūrī, "Al-nahḍāt al-qawmiyya al-'āmma fī ūrūbbā wa fī al-sharq", *al-Risāla* 4/148 (1936), 727.

between religion and cognitive endeavour, both of which together figured as a scaffolding for social and intellectual secularism. A primary consequence was the reconfiguration of the field of religious authority, henceforth reconceived as restricted to issues of morals rather vacuously and evasively understood, thereby signalling the hope that religion and the religious institution would refrain from interference in politics and culture, which was a major preoccupation in Egypt. In Syria, such a reconfiguration would be deployed against communalism. As the Lebanese Communist essayist Ra'if Khouri (1913–1967) held, national politics cannot be realised if the "degraded attitude to religion persisted, an attitude which is a toxic fruit of ignorance and degrading human slavery, one which perceives in religion not its essence, which is to promote good and forbid evil, to call people to mutual sympathy and cooperation, and sees in it only its communialist husks, associated with hateful and rotten memories that arouse mutual disgust and hostility between people."[193]

The rather hollow, rhetorical import of statements such as those just cited is clear: there was much reticence to attack the religious lobby frontally, and criticism was directed against what was rather hopefully regarded as the mere externals of religion, or the abuse and politicisation of religion on the part of politicians and religious institutions, without engaging directly with the elements of belief and practice of actually existing religion as propagated by its public custodians, or indeed questioning in any serious way either the reality of the right of the prerogatives that they arrogate to themselves. If any collateral benefit accrued from such positions, it will have been the circulation of an elementary notion of the historicity of religions, and how they are moulded by the contemporary world and by those who have the charge of religion. The religious lobby, for their part, pretended to be the arbiters of intellectual life, and their encounter with secularists, implicitly or openly, was violently confrontational, again in Egypt especially. Egypt of the 1920s, it is true, did have a government generally organised along modern lines, but nevertheless preserved "oriental organs" such as the Ministry of Awqaf, the shari'a courts, and the College of al-Azhar, which "disseminated the culture of the Middle Ages among us".[194] In religious circles, hordes of atheists relentlessly assaulting the territories of the believers were invented. Rashid

193 Ra'īf Khūrī, "Al-qawmiyya", *al-Ṭalī'a*, 2/9 (1936), 772.
194 Salāma Mūsā, "Al-qadīm wa al-jadīd", in *Mukhtārāt Salāma Mūsā* (Beirut: Maktabat al-Mā'arīf, 1962), 230–231.

Rida spoke of the secularists as "Westernised atheists", affirming that their "party" was poorly organised in Egypt and weak in Syria.[195] He was soon thereafter to add that anyone who described Kemalism as "reformism" was ipso facto an atheist, and that atheists came in different shapes and forms. Some, Rida claimed, proclaimed atheism openly, turning away from religion and repudiating it. One such was the proprietor of a journal and a printing press in Egypt (an allusion to Ismail Mazhar); another a journal published in Aleppo (an allusion to *al-Ḥadīth*), and yet another was an atheist Iraqi poet (an allusion to al-Zahawi). To this class also belonged all those who were averse to the constitution indicating Islam as the religion of the state, those who advocated a civil law of personal status, such as the editor of the newspaper *al-Siyāsa al-Usbū'iyya* (organ of the Liberal Constitutionalist Party – the allusion is to the jurist Dr Mahmud Azmi, 1889–1954). Rida added a motif that was later to become standard in these polemics, namely that Dr Azmi was linked to certain Jewish societies.[196] To this gallery Rida added a second class of atheist, to whom he applied the medieval epithet *zanādiqa* or freethinkers. He said (in an allusion to the Azharite 'Ali 'Abd al-Raziq) that these were people, allied to foreigners and Christians, who only appeared to profess Islam although they cast doubt on its fundamentals and denied that which "is known by necessity" from it.[197] Al-Azhar took the initiative of publishing a monthly journal under the title *Nūr al-islām* ("The Light of Islam") with the conservative Muhammad Farid Wajdi (1875–1954) as editor, to confront publications appearing "in the name of science".[198]

It is noteworthy that this religious offensive was more or less limited to Egypt, and that Syria witnessed no clerical offensive against secularism of comparable amplitude, consistency, and persistence. Syrian sensitivity to sectarianism may have gone some way in forestalling the use of religion for political purposes, in addition to an important institutional factor: the absence in Syria of an analogue to the sprawling fortress of al-Azhar and its cultural, educational, and social extensions. France deliberately fostered sectarianism by adopting a "mosaic" model of colonial society, enabling the transformation of sects into

195 Muḥammad Rashīd Riḍā, *Al-khilāfa aw al-imāma al-'uẓmā* (Cairo: Maṭba'at al-Manār, 1341/1922), 63.

196 Muḥammad Rashīd Riḍā, Editorial, *al-Manār* 30/1 (1929): 3–4.

197 Ibid., 4–7.

198 Ḥusayn, *Al-ittijāhāt al-waṭaniyya fī al-adab al-mu'āṣir*, vol. 2, 324, 326.

administrative categories, an act that inevitably led to the formation of groups around vested interests. Local sectarian clashes rarely had a cultural dimension, with secular culture remaining central. Secularists in general escaped accusations of unbelief and atheism, with the exception of the nationalist al-Shahbandar, who had an extraordinary number of political enemies.[199] In addition, scale needs to be considered. The volume of secular – and other – cultural products and its rhythm in Egypt was much greater than in any other Arab region, commensurate with the size of the country. Secular novels of a didactic character, *Bildungsromane*, fiercely attacked religious figures and defended Taha Hussein, the theatre, and the social mixing of genders. Examples include the now forgotten novel *Su'ād* (1927) by 'Abd al-Halim al-'Askari (1927), and veteran secular journals such as *al-Muqtaṭaf* (founded in Beirut in 1876, transferred to Cairo in 1888, closed in 1952, edited by Ismail Mazhar in the period 1945–1947) and *al-Hilāl*, founded by Jurji Zaydan in 1892 and still running. This trend gathered pace with the *al-Majalla al-jadīda* (1929–1942) by Salama Musa and Ismail Mazhar's *al-'Uṣūr* (1927–1931). In 1930, Fouad Sarrouf (editor of *al-Muqtaṭaf* from 1927 until his death in 1944) and Salama Musa founded the Egyptian Academy for Scientific Culture. Ismail Mazhar joined them, although the Academy's work was handicapped for political reasons and operated only until 1940.[200] In Syria the journal *al-Ḥadīth* was founded in Aleppo in 1926 by three prominent intellectuals, the philosophers Sami al-Kayyali (1898–1972)[201] and Muhammad Kamil 'Ayyad (1901–1986), and the jurist Edmond Rabbath (1902–1991). It is interesting to note that it would not have occurred to anyone's mind at the time to think that the title hadith was received and understood in anything but its modern lexical sense of "the modern", as the Muslim religious sense was not familiar outside clerical circles, and was not to be until recently. The journal *al-Ṭalī'a* was published in Damascus from 1935, the first Arabic journal with a Socialist and Marxist orientation. Among its supporters and contributors were the nationalist politician and intellectual Ihsan al-Jabiri (1879–1980), the philosopher Jamil Saliba

199 'Abd Allāh Ḥannā, *Al-ittijāhāt al-fikriyya fī sūriyyā wa lubnān 1920–1945* (Damascus: Dār al-Taqaddum al-'Arabī, 1973), 226–228.

200 Mūsā, *Tarbiyat Salāma Mūsā*, 109–110.

201 Manfred Sing, "Illiberal metamorphoses of a liberal discourse: The case of the Syrian intellectual Sami al-Kayyali", in *Liberal Thought in the Eastern Mediterranean*, ed. Christoph Schumann (Leiden: Brill, 2008), 293–322.

(1902–1976), the prominent historian, prime Arab nationalist thinker, professor at the American University of Beirut, and one-time President of Damascus University, Constantine Zureik (1909–2000), the *littérateur* and traveller Amin al-Rihani, and Jibra'il Jabbur (1900–1991), a professor of Arabic and Semitic Studies at the American University of Beirut. Ra'if Khoury was one of its editors.[202]

Syrian secular journals generally avoided religious subjects (except sectarianism) and spread a secular culture without regard to religion, implicitly adopting the motif of functional and cognitive distinction discussed above. *Al-Muqtaṭaf* likewise did not deal with religious matters in detail and announced that it did not desire to do so. It even refrained from voicing an opinion on the question of unveiling and veiling, and only congratulated 'Abd al-Raziq on his book in so far as it "strengthened initiative", clearly contrasted to traditionalist lethargy, and "encouraged research".[203] Other journals did not neglect this matter, however, as they all disseminated a rational, scientific culture marked by scientism and confronted religion indirectly by widening the scope of secular culture extending scientific research to specifically religious subjects. These latter journals saw in myths spread by the religious party a fundamental barrier against societal and cognitive development. They especially mocked religious superstitions and the conduct of members of the ulama, and published highly critical reviews of certain books, criticised the Church, and eagerly published writings of free-thinkers, including writings of atheist character, such as the translations in its fourth volume of the writings of Charles Lee Smith (1887–1964), the founder in 1925 of the American Association for the Advancement of Atheism. It is unclear whether this association was connected to the attempt by Ismail Adham to found Egyptian and Lebanese associations to spread atheism along the lines of the Turkish Association for the Propagation of Atheism founded by a mathematics professor, Ahmed Zakariyya. Adham himself claimed to have been a mathematician. The Turkish Association for the Propagation of Atheism joined the World Union, which Charles Smith founded. Adham estimated that *al-'Uṣūr* was a "moderate movement for the spread of freedom of thought, reflection and the propagation of atheism".[204]

---

202 See the list in *al-Ṭalī'a* 3/10 (1937).

203 Anonymous, book review in *Al-Muqtaṭaf* 67/3 (1925): 332–333.

204 Adham, *Limādhā anā mulḥid?*

In their attempt to reinforce the position of religious culture that had lost its centrality in the structure of official culture, and to regain lost ground, the religious lobby accused the poet Ahmad Zaki Abu Shadi and others of atheism.[205] Rashid Rida declared the infidelity of the ideas of Taha Hussein, on the pretext that he cast doubt on the truthfulness of the Qur'an by considering Ishmael and Abraham mythical figures.[206] He accused Hussein of spreading the "poison of atheism" and the "narcotic of freethinking and incitement to sensual desires".[207] Rida urged al-Azhar to prosecute 'Abd al-Raziq, in whose book Rida perceived licence to disobey God, the ascription of ignorance to Muhammad's companions and Muslim traditions. He falsely ascribed to al-Azhar the position that 'Abd al-Raziq was an apostate, and claimed without foundation that al-Azhar's position was a fatwa declaring such.[208] Rida made himself an exponent of a scabrous mode of disparagement when he wrote about 'Abd al-Raziq's exchange of his Azharite turban for the fez.[209] For the first time, he surpassed al-Azhar in petulant vehemence, and charted a way ahead towards adopting even more acute positions against 'Abd al-Raziq, urging al-Azhar to expel him, one of their own, from the college of ulama.

This indicated Rida's location in the two historical registers of reformist Islam in the twentieth century: the open modernist moment associated with the name of Muhammad 'Abduh, and then the aggressively introverted moment increasingly conjoined to Wahhabi Salafism, of which Rida became the chief propagandist. The only one to match Rida's strident tones of calumniation was the sentimentalist Islamist, poet, and literary critic Mustafa Sadiq al-Rafi'i (1880–1937), who treated Taha Husein's work on pre-Islamic poetry with scorn, defamation, insults, and ignominy, without proper argumentation.[210] This was clearly a dialogue of the deaf. Other critics of Hussein used texts whose authenticity he had put in doubt against him, accusing him of impertinence and slander. They used traditional

205 Abū Shādī, *Limādhā anā mu'min?*, 4.

206 Riḍā, *Fatāwā*, 719.

207 Introduction by Muḥammad Rashīd Riḍā to 'Arafa, *Naqḍ maṭā'in fī al-Qur'ān al-karīm*, 4.

208 *Al-Manār* 26/1 (1925), 104, 392. For the declaration of the Azhar and the judgement of the council of senior scholars and other Azhar documents, see ibid., 214–382.

209 *Al-Manār* 27/9 (1926): 716.

210 Al-Rāfi'i, *Taḥta rāyat al-Qur'ān*, 106, 159–161, and passim.

methods whose rejection had formed the basis for his work.[211] The only critical attack on Taha Hussein that approached any measure of sobriety was that made by Muhammad Farid al-Wajdi before he took up official duties at al-Azhar, although the argumentation was unconvincing and based on the repetition of traditional narratives in even-tempered tones. Wajdi limited his disparagement of Hussein to repeating the motif of wilful secession from the community, that is, of independence of tradition,[212] to which Hussein would have agreed gladly.

The controversies around Taha Hussein and 'Ali 'Abd al-Raziq were two significant milestones in the religious attack on the generalisation of secular rationality and of incipient historical scrutiny to domains hitherto seen by the religious figures as their exclusive territory. These controversies resulted in success for the religious lobby, assisted by state authorities and political parties, as will be shown, in claiming and reiterating the claim that a rational historical approach to Islamic religious texts and traditions needs to be proscribed. Another result was first to reclaim, and then to reiterate and reinforce the related claim, that Islam was both religion and the world, a claim subsequently to be repeated so incessantly as to have come to be imagined to be self-evident. For al-Azhar, the Qur'an criticism of Taha Hussein was as impugning as the authenticity of the Qur'anic text.[213] The Egyptian state gave legal backing to the position of al-Azhar. The report of the Egyptian chief prosecutor on 30 March 1928 in the case of Taha Hussein was reasoned, balanced, and objective, with most precise commentary on *Fī al-shi'r al-jāhilī*, although the report concluded that there was, in the book's discussion of Ishmael and the lineage of Quraysh, an attack on religion. Yet the chief prosecutor refrained from calling for prosecution as he had no evidence of criminal intent on the part of the author.[214] However, this interference by the Prosecutor confirmed implicitly the religious

211 See, for example, Muḥammad al-Khidr Ḥusayn, *Naqḍ kitab "Fī al-shi'r al-jāhilī"* (Cairo: al-Maṭba'a al-Salafiyya, 1926), 88–89, 106–107, and passim.

212 Muḥammad Farīd Wajdī, *Naqd kitāb al-shi'r al-jāhilī* (Cairo: Maṭba'at Dā'irat Ma'ārif al-Qarn al-'Ishrīn, 1926), 11.

213 Text of the declaration of the committee of Azhar scholars in al-Rāfi'i, *Taḥta rāyat al-Qur'ān al-ma'araka bayn al-qadīm wa al-jadīd*, 175–180.

214 Khayrī Shalabī (ed.), *Muḥākamat Ṭaha Ḥusayn: Naṣṣ qarār al-ittihām ḍidd Ṭaha Ḥusayn sanat 1927 ḥawl kitābihi "fī al-shi'r al-jāhilī"* (Beirut: al-Mu'assasa al-'Arabiyya li'l-Dirāsāt wa al-Nashr, 1972), 51–53, 66, 70.

lobby's claim that a departure from religious traditions as defined by them was a matter falling under the definitions and provisions of criminal law, handing them thereby a new instrument with which to intervene in society and culture. The 'Ali 'Abd al-Raziq controversy gave the religious lobby another cause célèbre, a precedent used to anathemise the consequent historisation of Muslim political history and, in turn, to claim that the guardians of religion possessed rightfully the exclusive voice in this domain. It will be recalled that Muhammad 'Abduh had maintained that political authority, the caliphate, and the judiciary were civil offices that disallow their holders from claiming "the right to control anyone's conviction or their worship of God or to contest their views".[215] Although the newspaper *al-Siyāsa* published on 6 July 1925 texts of 'Abduh connected with the caliphate and with the civil nature of power in Islam, 'Abduh's view, according to Rida in a text of earlier vintage,[216] presumed that this power stood on the pillars of religion, or that it was a religious authority seeking to conserve and protect shari'a, with all calls for the distinction between religious and political authorities being therefore non-religious – *lā dīniyya*, a negative used polemically by Rida when wishing to keep the words then used for secularism (*'ilmāniyya*, *madaniyya*) out of circulation. The Council of Senior Ulama in al-Azhar went so far as to hold that 'Abd al-Raziq's views that the shari'a was a spiritual matter, and that the seventh-century Prophetic State was an incomplete project still in process, constituted with other points made a clear departure from the bounds of what is conscionable. The religious lobby did not merely silence 'Ali 'Abd al-Raziq. The controversy has become a basic symbolic turning point and a sign of religious opposition to those who call for the separation of religion from politics, until the present day – at every stage when this matter is brought up, it is considered to be still alive and contemporary. Some commentators – such as Islamists of a later generation like the ranking Muslim Brother Muhammad al-Ghazali (1917–1996) or the Islamist former Marxist Muhammad 'Amara (1931–) – have repeatedly made the unfounded claim that 'Abd al-Raziq had abjured his earlier positions. These claims were all made after he died in 1966 and was no longer able to speak for himself.[217]

215 'Abduh, *Al-a'māl al-kāmila*, vol. 3, 287, 289.
216 Riḍā, *Shubuhāt al-naṣārā wa ḥujaj al-islām*, 77–78.
217 See *Al-Hayāt*, 16/5/1990, 13.

This assault on secularism generally and on Hussein and 'Abd al-Raziq in particular had many consequences, of which two were particularly important in relation to the theme of this book: the slackening and diminishment of Islamic reformism, the gradual – but by no means complete – dissipation of its modernism, and its enclosure upon stagnant, sclerotic beginnings on the one hand, and, on the other, the corrosion of many secularist positions, especially in Egypt. Both were linked to the rising incidence of irrationalism taking root in Arab thought, in line with global trends in the 1920s and 1930s, with effects still present in the cant made famous to the widest possible public by former President Anwar Sadat (1918–1981), "science and faith". This irrationalism began in belle-lettrist articles about the importance of spirituality for humans, their instinctive inclination to religion, sentiment, and sensibility, and the aridity of life without a measure of spirituality.[218] It was accompanied by an unhistorical view of history and civilisation, not unfamiliar elsewhere as well, in east Asia, India, Germany, and Russia, by figures such as Ahmad Amin, Muhammad Hussein Haykal, and 'Abbas al-'Aqqad, who assured their readers that there was a qualitative difference between "Easterners" and "Westerners". To Easterners were attributed elevated spiritual, aesthetic, and moral sensibilities and a creative blend of feeling and reason. To Westerners was ascribed a dry, even decadent materialism in the eyes of some observers.[219] Needless to say that this discourse deals with an imaginary, stable "West" and "East", both homogenous, homeostatic, incommensurable, complete, and historically closed around putative stable, essential characteristics elevated above history and in clear contradiction to observed reality. The Arabs, after all, are not "Eastern" in a determinate sense, and "Easterners" are not entirely innocent of materialism, of covetousness and avarice, and moral and intellectual bestiality. Similarly, "Westerners" are not far removed from concepts of justice and law and public responsibility, nor are they strangers to spirituality. The clear difference between this imaginary,

218 For example, Amīn, *Fayḍ al-khāṭir*, 45-46, 156–157, 171–172, and passim.

219 Ibid., vol. 3, 26–27; Muḥammad Ḥusayn Haykal, *Ḥayāt Muḥammad*, 5th edn (Cairo: Maktabat al-Nahḍa al-Miṣriyya, 1952), 516–519; Muḥammad Ḥusayn Haykal, "Al-sharq wa al-gharb" (1933) in Muḥammad Ḥusayn Haykal, *al-sharq al-jadīd* (Cairo: Maktabat al-Nahḍa al-Miṣriyya, n.d.), 133–137; and al-'Aqqād, *Iblis*, 222–226. For commentary on al-'Aqqād see Ibrāhīm Badrān and Salwā al-Khammāsh, *Dirasāt fi al-'aqliyya al-'arabiyya: al-khurāfa*, 2nd edn (Beirut: Dār al-Ḥaqīqa, 1979), 103–105. For a moral reproach directed at the West, see, for example, Rashīd Riḍā, *Al-khilāfa aw al-imāma al-'uẓmā*, 6, and al-Fāsī, *Al-naqd al-dhātī*, 79–82.

desired separation between East and West and their reality shows that the discourses in question have the quality of a daydream.

The auxiliary notion that the West was declining and decadent was current in Europe from the end of the nineteenth century, and became a chic and fashionable mood of disenchantment in the 1920s and 1930s and in the circles, not all on the Right of the political spectrum, which were the seedbed of Nazi and Fascist criticism of decadence and degeneration. The Preface to this book has already commented on this. This irrationalist criticism of civilisation was an all-encompassing criticism, many participants in which sought a new beginning as comprehensive as the purported extent of decline itself, and decline was in this sense understood to indicate the complete collapse of order and a sign of the systemic collapse that the proponents of the decline theory sought to replace with a corrective rival system – an idea that was fundamental to fascism, and was to be equally fundamental to Islamist political ideology. Although some saner voices warned against the drift inherent in such ideas, with, for example, Ahmad Amin careful to qualify "decline" and clearly perceiving in the West much that is positive and indeed salutary in the domains of public and private life,[220] this realism did not diminish the energy stored in the idea of separation between East and West, materialism and spirit, secularism and religion and other unhistorical contradictions that conceal basic realities. Taha Hussein mocked the folly and untruth of the caricature of separation between the spiritual East and moral West.[221] He was not alone in this and others such as Muhammad Kurd 'Ali and other earlier commentators mentioned in the preceding chapter recalled that the Arabs had taken from the West ideas of nation, nationalism, the foundations of the press and education, and the regulated organisation of social and political life through parliamentary assemblies and constitutional governments.[222] Many evaluated very positively the contribution of Orientalists in acquainting Arabs with their own heritage.[223] The question of Orientalism was one of

220 Ibid., vol. 2, 54–55. See too Ḥusayn Aḥmad Amīn, *Fī bayt Aḥmad Amīn* (Cairo: Dār al-Hilāl, 1985), 106–107.

221 Ṭaha Ḥusayn, *Mustaqbal al-thaqāfa fī miṣr*, 75–80 and compare Qāsim Amīn, *Al-a'māl al-kāmila*, ed. Muḥammad 'Amāra, 2 vols (Beirut: al-Mu'assasa al-'Arabiyya li'l-Dirasāt wa al-Nashr, 1976), vol. 2, 209–221.

222 Kurd 'Alī, *Al-Mudhakkirāt*, 1,080–1,081.

223 See, for example, Amīn, *Ḥayātī*, 149–150; Kurd 'Alī, *Al-Mudhakkirāt*, 194–200.

the themes around which Islamist ambitions for cultural domination against "foreign knowledge" were articulated, and precipitated many controversies,[224] as it still does.

Clear-sightedness did not preclude the need for irrationalist mystification, even self-mystification, probably of bad faith as well. Muhammad Hussein Haykal found that Christianity, although certainly predominant in Europe, was ill-suited to this continent, with its calls for abstention and clemency.[225] Writing on culture and civilisation often degenerated to low cant, all the way to composing ledgers of civilisational debts. Al-'Aqqad concluded a generally balanced and sensible work on the Arabs and Europe with the following words: "the present era will reach its full extent after a short period, the stellar orbits will complete their revolution in which the end closes the beginning. It is not to be excluded that a cry will be heard again in a corner of the globe soon afterwards, and that this will come from the East this time around, and in a novel way. The world of the spirit will be broad enough for her, if the two other worlds, of science and thought, and of government and power, are not sufficient to accommodate its amplitude."[226]

Irrationalist sentimentalism of this kind was not limited to calls to various forms of personal dervishism or at least to use spiritual sensibilities and theosophical leanings as a hallmark of authenticity, nor was this spirituality limited to Muslims. The Lebanese poet and meditative visionary Mikha'il Nu'ayma (1889–1988) and others also took part, adopting the style of the time and supporting this Arab tendency.[227] Irrationalism had other more profound effects on Arab thought, notably the taste for the irrational in history and society, including the heroic and the transhistorical, as found, for example, in the reception of Gustave Le Bon (1841–1931), the conservative French aristocratic student of crowd psychology, an author frequently praised by Arab authors, still estimated for a history of the Arabs he wrote in which he extolled their heroic ethos and contributions to civilisation. Taha Hussein translated into Arabic his book on education. Sati' al-Husri

224 Kurd 'Alī, *Al-Mudhakkirāt*, 1,241–1,242, on a controversy in Cairo in 1926.

225 Haykal, *Ḥayāt Muḥammad*, 12.

226 'Abbās Maḥmūd al-'Aqqād, *Athar al-'arab fī al-ḥaḍāra al-ūrūbbiyya* (Cairo: Dār al-Ma'ārif, 1963), 134.

227 Muḥammad Jābir al-Anṣārī, *Taḥawwulāt al-fikr wa al-siyāsa fī al-sharq al-'arabī 1930–1970*. Silsilat 'ālam al-ma'rifa 35 (Kuwait: al-Majlis al-Waṭanī li'l-Thaqāfa wa al-Funūn wa al-Adāb, 1980), 48–52.

(1880–1968), the positivist, educationist, and modernist theorist of Arab nationalism, criticised the book severely, and compared Le Bon's work to the vague, theosophical, and Sufi elements of nationalist thought articulated by Michel 'Aflaq (1910–1989), the main ideologist of the Baath party. This recalls al-Husri's related criticism of Ismail Mazhar's reliance on the theory of race in the interpretation of literature,[228] which was by no means uncommon at the time.

Departure from the orderliness of nineteenth-century positivist thinking generally came to imply an anti-modernist criticism of scientism and indeed of science, not by an analysis of the history and historicity of science, but by censuring of science in favour of the positive evaluation of religion, quite a common apologetic strategy in modern times, as the previous chapter showed with reference to Husayn al-Jisr, Francis Marrash, and French Catholic physicians in the mid-nineteenth century. According to this view, the results of science were conjectural, not certain, what might today be called a premise of constructivism, and it was proposed that science is unable to explain natural phenomena such as gravity, whatever the claim might mean. Thus, these phenomena and their laws amounted, in effect, to miracles and, as a consequence, breaches in natural regularity becomes possible, and are not in themselves any more marvellous than regularities that follow natural laws. The preternatural does not contradict reason as it surpasses reason's capacities.[229] According to al-'Aqqad, reason leads us to prove a quasi-material reality of abstract entities as exemplified by anti-matter in elementary particle physics.[230] Inspiration is thereby sought from science and from positivist consideration of material reality in order to demonstrate the opposite of science. Scientific materialism is used to prove the validity of spiritualism, occultism, and theosophy, very common at the time everywhere,[231] as in the case of Muhammad Farid Wajdi when he discussed in detail theosophy,

---

228 Al-Ḥuṣrī, *Al-a'māl al-qawmiyya li Sāṭi' al-Ḥuṣrī*, 353–357, 1043–1048, 2403, 2405. On this trend in the global perspective of political irrationalism, see al-Azmeh, *Islams and Modernities*, "Prologue" and chs 1 and 2.

229 'Abbās Maḥmūd al-'Aqqād, *Al-tafkīr farīḍa islāmiyya* (Cairo: dār al-qalam, n.d.), 118–127.

230 al-'Aqqād, *Allāh*, 9–11.

231 See in general, Ruth Brandon, *The Spiritualists: The Passion for the Occult in the Nineteenth and Twentieth Centuries* (New York: Knopf, 1982). The spirituality often ascribed to the East, as mentioned above, seems in fact to have originated in Victorian drawing rooms. On the crucial Victorian theosophical element in Gandhi, for instance, see Kathryn Tidrick, *Gandhi: The Political and Spiritual Life* (London, Verso, 2013), chs 1–4.

spiritual séances, and hypnotism – then called "magnetic sleep induction", *tanwīm maghnaṭīsī* – to prove through the senses that a spiritual word did in fact exist, one perceived by the Sufis centuries previously when the spirits appeared to them.[232] Wajdi, almost in the manner of an exorcist, even ascribed madness to the control of spirits over the body.[233]

A generally sober intellect such as that of Ahmad Amin was not immune to the eclectic indiscipline of the time, averring that "natural laws are part of what are called 'angels', which are the executive principles in this world and the executive authority through which the causative will is realised". Nature is but a transient event subject to divine Will.[234] The traditionalist cleric Mustafa Sabri was in his turn a most eloquent exponent of anti-rationalism in the name of the Ash'arim, using European philosophers including David Hume (1711–1776) and Nicolas Malebranche (1638–1715). Sabri was the best equipped in knowledge and rigorous argumentation, and most zealous in the defence of miracles and in the affirmation of the lack of certainty in science. He found that Wajdi, Haykal, and Rida had sought to remove from religion all reference to the supernatural on which religion stands. Sabri thus expressed an extreme form of irrationalism nurtured by these and other writers.[235] Al-'Aqqad's own mystificatory cant was not far distant from this when he claimed that the Qur'an had no imperfections, that it encompassed everything, contrary to the theories of natural scientists that are liable to improvement and modification. This is why he cautioned against excessive scientific interpretation of the Qur'an, as what the mind can devise can never encompass or comprehend the words and meanings of the Qur'an.[236] Sabri, like authors before him, insisted on the teleology of nature and its link to what was beyond it. This is not far in purpose, if not in content, from what Ahmad Amin said about natural teleology, without revealing exactly what it might be.

The nexus of such discourses was therefore confirmation of providence, a retreat from earlier traces of deism: nature is neither independent nor

232 Muḥammad Farīd Wajdī, *Al-islām fī 'aṣr al-'ilm*, 2 vols, 2nd edn (Cairo: al-Maktaba al-Tijāriyya wa Maṭba'at al-Mu'āṣir, 1932), vol. 1, 340–365, 382–438.

233 Ibid., 438–439.

234 Aḥmad Amīn, *Yawm al-islām* (Cairo: Mu'assasat al-Khānjī, 1958), 18.

235 Muṣṭafā Ṣabrī, *Al-qawl al-faṣl bayn alladhīna yu'uminūn bi al-ghayb wa alladhīna lā yu'minūn* (Cairo: Matba'at 'Īsā al-Bābī al-Ḥalabī, 1361/1942), 30–44.

236 al-'Aqqād, *Al-tafkīr farīḍa islāmiyya*, 89–100.

self-sufficient,[237] but wavers between the natural and supernatural, between superstitious rhetoric and naturalism, from the pens of intellectuals with a generally secular vocation, inhabiting two epochs at once, striving for the one and shying away from abandoning the other, its new structures still emergent and, albeit institutionalised, relentlessly chipped away by the religious lobby, the Palace, and demagogic politicians. Views that appear to be bizarre, erratic, and outlandish are not peculiar to one or other of these Egyptian intellectuals of the period, but appear to be the result of a broader phenomenon of disorientation, manifested by alternation between hypercriticism and uncritical reading, aggravated by autodidacticism, addiction to summaries and simplified abridgments, deficient technical capacity mirroring a technologically challenged society, and half-baked procedures of thought, with a leaven of personal eccentricity and conceptual idiosyncracy – and many of these individuals were eccentric indeed. This impressionistic drift, alongside weak technical proficiency, often careless and perfunctory habits of scholarhip, and an extraordinary degree of tolerance to that which is patently absurd, yielded the lack of cumulative cognitive traditions resulting from weak criteria of validation or invalidation apart from the requirements of partisanship, courtesy, and polemic, which make for impressionistic statements where better ones might indeed have been reached. Overall, not a salutary example to younger generations. Even Taha Hussein's exquisite, mellifluous style, and the boldness of his ideas, were not matched by technical scholarly proficiency.

While al-ʿAqqad grounded his faith in the unseen and the supernatural on the newest popular science of his time, Muhammad Husayn Haykal sought out science that had in his time become obsolete, in order to salvage the traditional heritage of the Prophetic biography, *sīra*, from the scrutiny of historical-critical reason, with its secular sources and points of reference. Haykal relied, in one part of his work, on the hypothesis of the aether, which physicists had postulated as the medium for the transmission of light. The Michelson–Morley experiment in 1887 had proved that luminiferous aether was an imaginary concept and that there was no scientific necessity to assume its existence. This, incidentally, opened the way for Albert Einstein to create his theory of special relativity in 1905, relying on

237 Amīn, *Fayḍ al-khāṭir*, 63–65.

a series of experiments whose fame spread worldwide four decades before the publication in Cairo of Haykal's biography of Muhammad (*Ḥayāt Muḥammad*) (1933).[238] The author insisted, however, on considering the transmission of images and sounds "on waves of aether" – a metaphorical expression not uncommonly used in Arabic for radio transmission, and still used infrequently – as a scientific model accounting for the myth of Muhammad's overnight journey to Jerusalem and on to the seven heavens. It was, he proposed, the aether that made possible the movement of a spirit as strong as Muhammad's. The report of this journey was to be verified not only by traditionalist arguments from textual authenticity of transmission, but by scientific means. Haykal gave no preference to either of the two traditional interpretations of this journey, the one claiming it was entirely spiritual, the other that it was bodily, with yet another position that proposed both at the same time. "There is no harm", he suggested, "in holding to the one rather than the other," since the essential matter was the spiritual and mystical character of Muhammad in this translation to Jerusalem and to the heavens, "since the whole universe was gathered into his spirit, Muhammad perceiving it in its eternal nature".[239]

It cannot be asserted with certainty that Haykal was ignorant of the scientific status of the aether in his time, and it would be futile to pursue the argument seriously as it appears to be a counterfeit argument. As with other positions just sketched, Haykal's concern was not with the cogency and cognitive integrity of the argument, but rather with its instrumental, token value in bringing together rhetorically religion and science into a common discursive space in the most accessible way and with the least cost in intellectual effort. The most economical way was to use an expression that had become and was to remain a kind of scientific shorthand for the carrier of electromagnetic waves, used as an image to convey a scientistic analogy for Muhammad's means of spatial translation in accessible terms. There is no doubt that this irrational and meaningless interpretation of Muhammad's nocturnal journey represents a retreat from the better possibilities of relative demythologisation afforded by the allegotical rhetoric of modernist Islamic reformism that Haykal doubtless sought to reconfirm. In 1916 already, Rida

---

238 English translation as Muhammad Muhammad Husayn, *The Life of Muhammad*, trans. Isma'il Ragi al-Faruki (Plainfield: American Trust Publications, 2005).

239 Haykal, *Hayāt Muḥammad*, 193–195. Compare Wajdī, *Al-islām fī ʿaṣr al-ʿilm*, vol. 1, 373–382.

argued facilely that the Prophet's vision of Jerusalem from Mecca did not mean that he was actually present there, but that Jerusalem appeared to him in a way that recalls Plato's myth of the cave.[240] Instead of considering the positions of 'Abduh and the early Rida as transitional points from a traditional, faith-centred mythical view of religious texts to a historical interpretation of them, points from which one strove for improvement, they seem to have set them up as a ceiling beyond which one could not venture.

This was the approach that Haykal thought would attract younger people and invite them again to reflect upon religion: an appeal to science and the publication of a book on the biography of the Prophet "according to the modern Western method, faithful to the truth alone".[241] Clearly with an eye to lines of least resistance, Haykal sought to obviate attacks from traditionalists that had undermined 'Abduh's position.[242] There is also no doubt that he wanted to protect hallowed traditions, and, by extension, traditionalists in the religious lobby, from the rationalism of Taha Hussein and the historical sensibility of 'Ali 'Abd al-Raziq, without openly declaring this. This was an agenda for reformist Islam of the more conservative variety in which *Ḥayāt Muḥammad* reaffirmed certain myths and superstition concerning early Islam, while not being entirely captive to all. Haykal did reject many manifestly legendary accounts of the miracles attributed to Muhammad, and this exposed him to attacks from both Sufi brotherhoods and the Azhar.[243] His criteria of deciding what was and was not credible remained unclear and, in my estimation, largely sentimental and a matter of personal taste. Mustafa Sabri, among others, reproached Haykal for his comments on the Prophet's nocturnal journey and his acceptance of 'Abduh's interpretation of the avian host that devastated Abraha's army, mentioned above. He was also attacked by some who favoured the more credulous approach of al-'Aqqad, which was not, according to them, counter-intuitive, and steered away from wanting to demystify the miraculous that Sabri considered the pivot of prophecy.[244]

Yet overall, Haykal's premises remained highly conservative, traditionalist with a twist. In the reformist mode, he decided that the Qur'an is the central

240 Riḍā, *Fatāwā*, 518.

241 Haykal, *Ḥayāt Muḥammad*, 18.

242 Ibid., 15.

243 Ibid., 53.

244 Ṣabrī, *Al-qawl al-faṣl bayn alladhīna yu'uminūn bi al-ghayb wa alladhīna lā yu'minūn*, 12–14, 100–102, 189.

source, from which, without further ado, he decided it was the major source for the biography of Muhammad. Correlatively, he accepted the traditionalist accounts of the Qur'an's history of composition and redaction, accepted that hadith in agreement with the Qur'an – in itself a difficult connection to establish – must be true, and affirmed that, until the assassination of 'Uthman, Muslims were in complete accord with one another, that the accounts of their history at that period were accurate and are the certain gauge of the authenticity of later material, and, finally, that Muhammad had "completed" the religion of the Muslims and put in place a plan for its propagation.[245] Thus, with a few strokes of his pen, in this influential and widely read book Haykal provided an example of how historical reflection on early Islamic history might be emasculated, and recentred attention on the authority of tradition: the inherited understanding of the text of the Qur'an and its history, the vision of Islam as a perfect and coherent religion born complete, all of which supported the Salafist position and attracted the support of Rashid Rida and the rector of al-Azhar, Shaykh Mustafa al-Maraghi (1881–1945), and other religious activists who combatted the spread of secular authority in the historical scrutiny of Muslim traditional learning. Haykal is often presented as a modernist, but he had put forward, in the name of modern science, a vision of the fundamentals of Islam that dealt with hadith in a Salafist spirit grounded in an understanding of infallibility – explicit infallibility for Muhammad, implicit infallibility of the major part of the Muslim traditionalist consensus. The so-called Satanic Verses were subjected to a traditionalist critique, supplemented by the assertion that the most important argument against their historical authenticity was their lack of concordance with Muhammad's infallibility, an argument in which historical analysis and considerations of historical verisimilitude are absent entirely.[246]

Haykal was in this respect emblematic of a generation of Egyptian liberals. After *Ḥayāt Muḥammad*, where scientistic pretence is bandied as science, it became difficult to engage with questions of early Muslim history with an open mind. Through this book the religious lobby oriented their engagement with scientific research in an erratic and instrumentalist direction

245 Haykal, *Ḥayāt Muḥammad*, 1, 18–38, 47–52, 61–63.

246 Ibid., 161–167. On this position of retreat in general, see Johansen, *Muhammad Husain Haikal*, esp. chs 8 and 10. For a serious historical study of traditions concerning the Satanic verses, see Ahmed, *Before Orthodoxy*.

that buttressed the inviolability of Islamic prohibitions on research that went beyond the implicit red lines thereby set. The initial resistance against attempts from within institutional Islam to engage with early Islam and its texts in a secular approach with an open historical rationality, following 'Abduh and 'Abd al-Raziq, despite the limitations of their approach, were reinforced by the reformist recoil represented by Haykal. Thus, for instance, Shaykh 'Abd al-Mit'al al-Sa'idi (1894–1966), an Azharite of extraordinarily progressive and consistently reformist views, who is inexplicably forgotten today. He was the author in 1937 of *al-Siyāsa al-Islāmiyya fi 'ahd al-nubuwwa*[247] (*Islamic Politics in the Period of Prophecy*) which is in many ways comparable to 'Abd al-Raziq's book, and was punished by administrative transfer from al-Azhar to the department of public education. He considered, for instance, that the Islamic legal punishments were not intended as obligations, and that they were the product of historical circumstances and did not require repetition.[248] More famous was Khalid Muhammad Khalid (1920–1996), an al-Azhar graduate and author in 1950 of *Min hunā nabdā'* (*From Here We Start*), arguing for the separation of religion and state and, in a very anti-clerical spirit, encountered resistance.[249] The police, the Muslim Brothers, al-Azhar, and the courts successively prevented the circulation of the book, and the fatwa committee of al-Azhar decided that the book had been compiled with a spirit hostile to religion: "it seeks to demolish religion and wrest from it its most specific role, hegemony over matters of life and their organisation and management" – in all social, financial, criminal, and personal aspects, and in matters of international politics.[250]

This was ambitious indeed. Al-Azhar broadened the scope of its competence in its riposte against an author – Khalid Muhammad Khalid – who considered that the Qur'an was subject to interpretation, that religion was

247 'Abd al-Mit'āl al-Ṣa'īdī, *Al-siyāsa al-islāmiyya fi 'ahd al-nubuwwa* (Cairo: Dar al-Fikr al-'Arabi, n.d.).

248 Muḥammad al-Ghazālī, *Min hunā na'lam*, 4th edn (Cairo: Dār al-Kitāb al-'Arabī, 1954), 13.

249 English translation as Khaled Muhammad Khaled, *From Here We Start*, trans. Isma'il Tagi al-Faruqi (Washington, DC, American Council of Learned Societies, 1953). The main lengthy response came from the Muslim Brother Muhammad al-Ghazali, translated into English as *Our Beginning is Wisdom*, trans. Isma'il Tagi al-Faruqi (Washington, DC, American Council of Learned Societies, 1951).

250 Khālid Muḥammad Khālid, *Min hunā nabda'*, 7th edn (Cairo: Matba'at Aḥmad ibn Mukhaymir, 1954), 11–15, 203.

a guide to souls and to communicating the word of God, that the function of men of religion should not exceed preaching and admonition. Khalid warned against every religious government because they are anti-rational, with tyrannical and despotic instincts. He criticised the ulama, describing them as a priesthood,[251] a description still today guaranteed to release acutely allergic reactions on their part. The rancour of al-Azhar was all the greater as thoughts similar to those of 'Abd al-Raziq seemed to keep appearing, and to be put forward by Azharites or former Azharites. Muhammad Ahmad Khalfallah (1916–1991) bore the brunt of al-Azhar's acrimony and was persecuted by it for adopting a reformist approach to Qur'anic interpretation, very much in the tradition of 'Abduh, a figure towards whom, for all the veneration, al-Azhar had never had a favourable disposition, and never quite forgave. Khalafallah studied the narrative styles in the Qur'anic methodically, considering that it was not a book of history but a book of morals and religion that used rhetorical and discursive turns and styles, including analogies and metaphors. Part of this comprised the stories about, among others, prophets, snakes, and the jinn. The aim of these narratives was to exhort and chide, and to reflect by example. The stories of the prophets do not constitute prophetic history but stories and myths that were compiled with aims at social and moral guidance. This, Khalafallah suggested, explained the different versions and contradictions between the Qur'anic naratives, the attribution of the same events to different persons in different parts of the text, and the variant narrations of the same story. Khalafallah's book was full of quotations from 'Abduh and Rida's Exegesis, and his approach was circumspect,[252] his intention clearly being to preserve the inviolable integrity of the Qur'an and its authenticity. None of this protected him against the assertiveness that had energised al-Azhar after it had, by means of politics and polemics, successfully seen off the rational openness of 'Abduh, however limited and naïve.

The matters described reflected a situation that saw a double movement. Islamic reformism, with notable exceptions, expressed itself in a diminished form, while virtually all but the most explicit of secularists had come to adopt such positions by default, and assured a politico-cultural position they thought

251 Ibid., 134–138, 150–155, 159–165, 167–170; al-Ghazālī, *Min hunā na'lam*, 101, 150.

252 Muḥammad Aḥmad Khalafallāh, *Al-fann al-qaṣaṣī fi al-qur'ān al-karīm*, 2nd edn (Cairo: Maktabat al-Nahḍa al-Miṣriyya, 1975), 4–7, 28–38, 119–127, 170–178, 181–184, 227–233, and passim.

was less vulnerable to the vituperations of the religious lobby. The repetition of a number of generalities concerning faith with little specific detail became a central habitus, and a bundle of topoi and clichés were repeated formulaically and without end, constituting a kind of common sense, much more compellingly and consistently so in Egypt than in the Mashreq, where many intellectuals did not, as they did in Egypt, feel compelled to deal with issues of religion, and to do so apologetically. The formulaic refrains concerned the broad theses of Islamic reformism: that Islam is valid for all times and all places, the Islamic anticipation of modernity, the rational character of the Muslim religion.

These general formulae came to be established as discursive refrains, without for the most part going into detail, the rhetorical purpose of which resulted in a reluctance to engage with domains that might challenge these authors to produce cogent meanings or interpretations. Such were, for instance, the traditional narrative of early Islamic history or the history of Muslim scriptures. In the writings of Ahmad Amin, for example, an implicit secularist like most Arab intellectuals in the modern period, one finds these general theses translated in the standard reformist fashion described, not very compellingly: thus the Mu'tazila are compared to Descartes and Bacon, legal secularism acquires the Muslim jurisprudential term *ijtihād muṭlaq* (fully discretionary legislation), the Qur'anic "*sunna* of God among nations" become the general features of human society and polity, and Islam becomes rational in a general and loose sense.[253] Taha Hussein, ever sober, nevertheless Protestantised Islam in confirming that it did not confront human reason with mysteries it would surely reject, and that it was free from the violent conflict between reason and religion because of the absence of clergy in Islam – this despite his own experiences and those of those around him with this sodality.[254] Islam is made innocent of the sins of Muslims and of their failings, and a distinction is posited, still very common today, between Islam and Muslims, whereby Abu Shadi and others were able to claim that Islam can be construed in a reformist, rationalist, progressive, and democratic way[255] – the fit between a desirable religion and deplorable religionists is not addressed.

253 Amīn, *Fayḍ al-khāṭir*, 32–40, 116–117, 124–125, 172–175, 177, 199–200.

254 Ḥusayn, *Mustaqbal al-thaqāfa fī Miṣr*, 65, and Ḥusayn, *Al-majmūʿa al-kāmila li muʾallafāt al-duktūr Ṭaḥa Ḥusayn*, vol. 12, 163–164.

255 Abū Shādī, *Limādhā anā muʾmin?*, 2–3; Amīn, *Fayḍ al-khāṭir*, vol. 8, 265–267, vol. 9, 1.

This sort of accommodation between intangible and imprecise entities exacted a heavy intellectual price.[256] First, it encourages an intellectual sleight of hand, many examples of which have been cited, that characterises vast swathes of Islamic thought up until the present day, affirming in the same breath, for example, that shari'a prescribed unconditional equality with no exceptions, and that it distinguished between men and women and placed men "one degree" above women in the context of a single text. Take also the affirmation that human rights in Islam were analogous to the International Declaration of Human Rights as Islam stresses the right to freedom (without mentioning slavery), to equality before the law (with no mention of legal disabilities of women, slaves, *dhimmīs*), to life (with no mention of statutory capital punishments).[257] Premises, summarily stated, are thereby severed from consequences in this interplay of symbolic, conceptual, and concrete registers. Criteria for the assessment of cogency and credibility appear to evanesce before they are approached, and seem little relevant to the discursive purposes at play. As a consequence, cumulative development became irrelevant to the reformist enterprise, and the preoccupation with adaptation to the pressures of the moment and the evasion of real or imagined menace, rendered reformism molluscar in texture. Thus, the distinctive promise of a Kemalist moment was dissipated, to be replaced by a collective *apologia pro vita sua*, at worst dissolving into paeans of self-commendation. Religious pressures paralysed independent thought in Egypt and this tendency spread in various measures to the rest of the Arab world.

Muhammad Hussein Haykal was not alone in undergoing an upheaval in sensibility and cognitive tastes that led, in his case, to a taste for the supernatural and to the new-fangled and ostentatious declaration of preference for the use of the Hijra calendar over the Gregorian.[258] Neither was Salama Musa alone when he became "domesticated prematurely", as he put it, because of circumstances prevailing in Egypt, and averring towards

256 The accommodationist secularism of some of the best of the authors discussed has been described overall as close to the position of Kant, wishing to see religion as a matter of personal conviction and as a support for ethics: Bishāra, *Al-dīn wa'l-'almanīya*, 1:150–151, n. 115. See also the characterisation of the Kantian position at 260–262.

257 'Awda, *Al-tashrī' al-jinā'ī al-islāmī*, vol. 1, 26, 28; and 'Aẓmī Islām, "Min ḥuqūq al-insān fī al-islām", *al-Fikr al-Mu'āṣir* 47 (1968): 84–93. See Jacques Waardenburg, *Islam: Historical, Social and Political Perspectives* (Berlin: Walter de Gruyter, 2008), ch. 8.

258 Ḥusayn, *Al-ittijāhāt al-waṭaniyya fī al-adab al-mu'āṣir*, vol. 2, 172, note 1.

the end of his life that all national sensibility contained a religious sentiment.[259] Intimidation and threats to livelihood and limb (threat to life was a later phenomenon) had a notable effect. Ahmad Amin and Taha Hussein spoke of this openly. The latter said that after harm had been done to him and to a group of critical minds who had injected dynamism into intellectual life, "criticism has become patronage and deference, while literature became flattery and imitation". His supporters, he averred, offered him only Platonic support. "They hummed and hawed and preferred safety, going with the crowd where it wanted to go." Ahmad Amin, Hussein said, looked on from the "safety of shore" as others were battling the waves.[260] Hussein felt compelled to write to the President of the Egyptian University, where he taught, about his book *On Jāhilī Poetry* (1926), saying: "Much controversy has been generated around the book I published some time ago under the name *On Jāhilī Poetry*. It was said that I deliberately insulted religion and repudiated it, and that I taught atheism in the university. I assure your Excellency that I did not wish to insult religion or to abandon it. It was not for me to do this as a Muslim believing in God and his angels, his Scriptures, his prophets, and the Last Day. I am a person who strove as much as he could to strengthen religious education in the Ministry of Education when I worked in the Committee of Religious Education. The Minister and his assistants who participated with me in this work are witness to this. I affirm to you that my university teaching was without any affront on religion, as I know that the University was not established for this purpose. I hope you will be so kind as to send this announcement to whoever you wish and publish it wherever you choose."[261]

The controversy involved personal humiliation as well as restraint upon rational thought. Hussein went on to modify his book and publish it in truncated form under the title *On Jāhilī Literature*, and this is the text that is in general circulation today rather than the original, which is available on the market nonetheless. Hussein, along with Haykal, Tawfiq al-Hakim, Ahmad Amin, al-'Aqqad, and others together went on to publish studies of the Prophetic *Sīra* and the early history of Islam in a way that al-Azhar

259 Mūsā, *Tarbiyat Salāma Mūsā*, 157, 313.

260 Ṭaḥa Ḥusayn, "Ilā ṣadīqī Aḥmad Amīn", *al-Risāla* 4/152 (1936): 922; Aḥmad Amīn, "Al-naqd ayḍan", *al-Risāla* 4/152 (1936): 882–883.

261 The text is in al-Rāfi'i, *Taḥta rāyat al-Qur'ān*, 180–181.

found laudable.[262] Hussein, outwardly chastened, became the "Azharite of whom Al-Azhar is proud".[263] He praised al-Azhar for its reception and dissemination of European culture, "neglecting no field and excelling in all". It was, he affirmed, "the dawn of day in a new age".[264] Even Ismail Mazhar was vulnerable to this trajectory. In the 1940s and 1950s he blended the spirit of Arabism and the spirit of Islam, criticised the separation of religion and state, and called for an Islamic community on the basis of Arab identity and an Islamic spirit.[265] In later life he made detailed declarations on Islam as the religion of natural disposition, freedom, evolution, justice, and democracy with a reformist spirit going back to Muhammad 'Abduh.[266]

There can be little doubt that this situation involved somewhat more than etiquette of old age and the unease it may bring, and more than the "disposition to belief" mentioned by Mahmud al-'Aqqad with reference to what he acquired from his environment.[267] This is not a matter of return to some form of cultural normalcy prior to thought, to an alleged social nature prior to social reality and social dynamics, an alleged nature defined by Islam, an idea manifestly attractive to hasty or indifferent commentators as shall be discussed in the last chapter. There was no repentance, nor retreat from practical secular positions, not least in the case of Taha Hussein. What we have is the contiguity and coexistence of various positions inconsistent with one another, with perhaps al-'Aqqad exemplifying this with intense turbulence. Nor were these various positions – intellectual, normative, symbolic – just reflections of individual eccentricities, but were rather arising from and made possible by general cultural, political, and intellectual dynamics alive in this period. Mention has already been made of the rise of irrationalism as a central conceptual sensibility of the age. The Islamic writings of Taha Hussein stood, as he said, on the assumption that reason was not all that mattered.

262 Al-shaykh Muḥammad Muḥammad al-Faḥḥām, "Muqaddima [Introduction]", in Sāmiḥ Kurayyim, *Islāmiyyāt: Ṭaḥa Ḥusayn, al-'Aqqād, Ḥusayn Haykal, Aḥmad Amīn, Tawfiq al-Hakīm*, 2nd edn (Beirut: Dār al-Qalam, 1977), 10–12.

263 Muḥammad Kāmil al-Fiqī, *Al-azhar wa atharuhu fi al-nahḍa al-'arabiyya al-ḥadītha*, 2nd edn (Cairo: Maktabat Nahḍat Miṣr, 1965), 145.

264 Ṭaḥa Ḥusayn, "Introduction", in ibid., 4–6.

265 Ismā'īl Maẓhar, "Bilād al-'arab li'l 'arab", *al-Muqtaṭaf* 4 (1945), 309–312.

266 Ismā'īl Maẓhar, *Al-islām, lā al-shuyū'iyya* (Cairo: Dār al-Nahḍa al-'Arabiyya, 1961), 12–13, 19–21, 28–37, 69–70.

267 'Abbas Maḥmūd al-'Aqqād, *Anā* (Cairo: Dār al-Hilāl, n.d.), 152.

They contained what might cause unease among some modernisers such as hadith, material traditionally received, uncritically, hagiographically, almost devotionally. He argued that this responded to the need in people's hearts for simplicity, eliciting worthy sentiments, inhibiting inclinations to evil.[268] These writings, very widely read, presented an unhistorical, reformist, and Salafist reading of the Muslim past, counterposing unity and internal dissension rather than any other terms for the consideration of history. 'Uthman, for instance, was taken as the turning point to disunity and worse without actual historical justification,[269] except for the dramatic effect of particular types of narration. Clearly, we have here a case of addressing different audiences according to their capacities, but that also involved silence on matters that might perhaps have mattered more to the author.

The writings of al-'Aqqad also drifted more decisively to the prevailing atmosphere of religious reaction. Mustafa Sabri praised the book on Muhammad's genius (and others on Muslim patristic figures) despite his objection to the use of the term "genius" instead of prophecy[270] – heroic biographies of genius were part of the irrationalist tendencies of the 1930s. Muhammad al-Siba'i translated Thomas Carlyle's *On Heroes, Hero Worship and the Heroic in History* (1841), written in the register of high romanticism, in 1930, followed in 1934 by publishing Carlyle's essay on Muhammad separately, under the title "Prophet of Guidance and Clemency". We have here the beginning of a genre of historical writing that reclaimed symbolic figures from early Islam for the wider public and in a medium quite separate from that through which religious culture was transmitted, figures beginning with the Prophet and considered not only as impeccably heroic, somewhat like Aeneas, but as models and salutary examples for behaviour in the twentieth century – a smooth development from Islamic Reformism's pursuit of origins. This type of literary activity precipitated a definite trend that received strong state encouragement, and narrativised the mediated positions on religion that have been described in previous paragraphs.[271] These positions acquired

268 Ṭaḥa Ḥusayn, *'Alā hāmish al-sīra* (Cairo: Dār al-Ma'ārif, n.d.).

269 'Alī Umlīl, *Al-iṣlāḥiyya al-'arabiyya wa al-dawla al-waṭaniyya* (Beirut: Dār al-Tanwīr and Casablanca: al-Markaz al-Thaqāfī al-'Arabi, 1985), 141–147.

270 Ṣabrī, *Al-qawl al-faṣl bayn alladhīna yu'uminūn bi al-ghayb wa alladhīna lā yu'minūn*, 12–14.

271 Kurayyim, *Islāmiyyāt: Ṭaḥa Ḥusayn, al-'Aqqād, Ḥusayn Haykal, Aḥmad Amīn, Tawfīq al-Hakīm*, 27–29.

media outlets: the journal *al-Risāla* (1933–1953) founded by the educationist and publisher Hassan al-Zayyat (1885–1964) and the new turn taken by *al-Siyāsiyya al-usbūʿiyya* under Haykal's editorship after 1933.[272] This trend held fast to the pull of the receding frontiers of Islamic Reformism, reinforced by the self-censorship of a Taha Hussein or an ʿAli ʿAbd al-Raziq. One radical critic, Ismail Mazhar, had already reproached these two authors for their subterfuge and reticence, and their lack of clarity about what they really wanted to say or were capable of saying: in Hussein's case, that Muhammad had authored the Qur'an and, in ʿAbd al-Raziq's case, that democracy was a more valid basis for government than Islam.[273]

To the mind of Egyptian liberals, these drifts were connected to an emphasis on the irrational and, as noted earlier, to the psychology of the crowd, opposition to materialism, and the purported superiority of Eastern spirituality and Islam. Analogous ideas were all the rage world-wide at that time. The anti-materialism of some liberals, such as Mazhar and al-ʿAqqad, were more often than not animated by anti-Communism, as was also the case with the European Right. Marxism was seen by many as a second wave of foreign conquest following colonialism,[274] an important motif in the rise and persistence of political Islamism from its very beginning. Opposition to Communism developed among wealthy or comfortable notables in large and medium-sized cities alongside the development of radical social and political movements. This was not limited to Muslims but led in Christian circles to the emergence of confessional Coptic parties, such as the Democratic Party.[275] Quasi-Fascist movements developed at the same time under the banner of Islam and regrouped under the umbrella of the Muslim Brothers, under global and ideological conditions comparable to other such movements like the Rashtriya Swayamsevak Sangh (RSS) in India under Golwalkar and Hedgewar. Opposition to Communism was linked to Islamic opposition to Orientalism and Westernisation.[276]

These elements give credibility to the claim of one socialist critic that the Egyptian liberal reconciliation with religion was primarily a political act, aimed

---

272 Al-Anṣārī, *Taḥawwulat al-fikr wa al-siyāsa fī al-sharq al-ʿarabī 1930–1970*, 65–67.

273 Fīlībūnus, "Ta'ammulāt fī al-adab wa al-ḥayāt", *al-ʿUṣūr* 2/8 (1928): 860–866.

274 Maẓhar, *Al-islām, lā al-Shuyūʿiyya*, 37.

275 Yūsuf, *Al-aqbāṭ wa al-qawmiyya al-ʿarabiyya*, 145.

276 Kurayyim, *Islāmiyyāt: Ṭaḥa Ḥusayn, al-ʿAqqād, Ḥusayn Haykal, Aḥmad Amīn, Tawfīq al-Hakīm*, 31–34.

at currying favour with al-Azhar, but above all contagion by the example of mounting Fascism in Europe,[277] accompanied by opposition to Communism and materialism and the glorification of the irrational in Fascist and other states. These attitudes were accompanied by the corrosion of educational and political efforts among Egyptian liberals, at the level of thought if not of practice: Taha Hussein certainly counts as the model liberal and educationist in the Arab world of the twentieth century, but he moved from addressing the intellect to stirring the emotions of the masses, irrational by nature as was generally understood at the time.[278] Here he was in line with the key irrationalist concepts of the French polymath Gustave Le Bon, already mentioned, namely his theory of the crowd (*la foule*) as a band of depersonalised individuals driven by suggestion and imitation. The Egyptian literary and academic figure Louis 'Awad (1915–1990) was correct when he mentioned that Taha Hussein's translation of Xenophon and Ahmad Lutfi al-Sayyid's translation of Aristotle's *Politics* were attempts to warn against the perils of democracy.[279] The Islamic culture disseminated by Egyptian liberals was therefore more generally directed towards a broad base of readers and listeners (radio was much involved) than to their own milieu; many were very prolific, Taha Hussein prodigiously so. If Islam were a constituent of the national personality, as Hussein came to believe – a position corresponding to claims made by the religious lobby – it would be vain to seek and improve this personality by elevation to secular culture; safer and surer for it to be maintained in its present condition until it is possible to foresee and control its future direction.[280] He and others, living in a society with several superimposed and exacting senses of hierarchy, alternated between holding that the masses were incapable of advancing cognitively and morally beyond religion, and attempting improvement by the introduction of a secular progressive culture, in marked contrast to views prevalent in Syria. This ambivalence, such fluctuations in position, with an extreme attitude of prudence, and a tendency to give the masses what suited them while keeping truth to the initiated, came to spread in the post-socialist era in Arab countries, and has become a fundamental feature in contemporary Arab thought.

---

277 Yūsuf Mattā, "Al-muyūl al-raj'iyya 'inda ba'ḍ udabā' al-'arab al-mu'āṣirin", *al-Ṭalī'a* 2/8 (1936): 717–718.

278 See al-'Aqqād's comments in Aḥmad 'Abbās Ṣāliḥ, "Dhikrayāt 'an al-'aqqād", *al-Thawra* (Baghdad), 17 November 1989.

279 'Awaḍ, *Thaqāfatunā fī muftaraq al-ṭuruq*, 93.

280 Ḥusayn, *Mustaqbal al-thaqāfa fī Miṣr*, 93.

Islamo-reformist intellectuals, especially in Egypt, increasingly drew inspiration from this condition, which bears some analogy with ancient priestly practices based on a mystified monopoly of literacy, with quasi-magical attributes. The broad consequence, as the last chapter will show, was to disfigure Arab thought and the politics related to it. Without doubt this Islamo-reformist approach is based on the ahistorical nature of modernising discourses, its removal from the context of history, and, by extension, from politics in a broad sense, and its location in the realm of pure contemplation with doubtful social relevance. There it was vulnerable to corrosion by the political instrumentalisation of religion, without it being checked by a concerted political culture of secularism. This retreat by Egyptian liberals into a diminished, inconsequential, and immediately instrumental understanding of politics and the role of culture therein corresponded to the approach of the political parties with which some of these liberals were linked, especially, in Egypt, the Wafd. Such an understanding of politics considered commoners to be an inchoate mass to be converted into an electoral constituency and, when necessary, a troublesome crowd, by pandering demagogy. Thus, it became possible to evoke the need to meet the spiritual needs of the masses at a time when material needs were very, very far from being met.

The recourse to notions of stable, natural temperament of the crowd to which the people are thereby reduced, changeless for all practical purposes, not especially permeable to improvement, was parallel in its turn to the idea of separation between East and West, based not on an examination of history but on a presumption of stable, generic differences. Taha Hussein, in this domain as in others, was soberer and more precise than others, not given readily to facile statements and generalisations, and was less moved by a craving for definitiveness. Histories could in this regard be relativised, beyond identitarian conceits. Thus, the history of Egypt could be connected substantively to the history of Europe in a common cultural ancestry going back to the Greeks, an idea shared by Taha Hussein, Salama Musa, and others. Yet such identity came to Hussein, at the price of, again, denying history as complex process, with progress defined as the East, a category he used, becoming West,[281] in an exercise of attempted politico-cultural control over time,

281 Sharāra, *Ḥawl baʿḍ mushkilāt al-dawla*, 109–110. The basic text of Husayn pertinent to this discussion is available in English: Taha Hussein [Ṭaḥa Ḥusayn], *The Future of Culture in Egypt*, trans. Sidney Glazer (Washington, DC: American Council of Learned Societies, 1954).

denial of the specific in favour of the universal.[282] In the writing of Hussein this lineage had a decidedly rational character, but one available only to a small elite, based on considerations of absolute historical gain whose rationality was so consummate as to be "shorn of all symbolic elements in which it is enwrapped".[283] If the East represented the past uniquely and the West represented future and progress uniquely, that was also translated into a hierarchy within each, which could be overcome and levelled out only by education – an enterprise that, as we have seen, had been approached with reticence and with a certain scepticism by some, and abandoned in favour of what were presumed to be the natural dispositions – and congenital indispositions and deficiencies – of the rabble. The view that progress and improvement had education as a primary instrument corresponded, it will be recalled, to what was implicit in the impulse of the *Tanzimat* state.

One can reproach Egyptian liberalism not only for its shallowness, but more importantly for its neglect of the specifity of Arab incorporation into the global, and the way in which this transformed whatever is identified as specifically local, or some might prefer, authentic. This is perhaps unsurprising in the light of an abstract theory of the stable national characters. The claim, common enough but commoner still in post-colonialist declamations, that Taha Hussein and others surrendered to Western values because they were defeated and pusillanimous, is hollow.[284] Unhistorical is such a claim, as it neglects the crucial fact that Western universalism has long been an internal constituent of the condition of Arabs, that it is authentic, if authenticity were to be evoked, with older tradition still alive or vestigially present, or indeed folklorised. It rides roughshod over the cultural preferences and paradigms of these liberal Arab intellectuals seeking the advancement and improvement of their societies,[285] and over the fact that repudiation of European culture was not an option because it was not possible – except as the ideological slogan of conservatives, especially of Islamists. Western paradigms were in place whether or not they were specifically identified as such; duly made local, as elsewhere.

---

282 'Abd Allāh al-'Arwī, *Al-idiyūlūjīya al-'arabiyya al-mu'āṣira*, trans. Muḥammad 'Ītānī, intro. Maxime Rodinson (Beirut: Dār al-Ḥaqīqa, 1970), 156.

283 Sharāra, *Ḥawl ba'ḍ mushkilāt al-dawla*, 114.

284 Jad'ān, *Usus al-taqaddum*, 324–325.

285 One such case would be that of Salāma Mūsā. See 'Abd al-Laṭīf, *Salāma Mūsā wa ishkāliyyāt al-nahḍa*, 165–166.

Arab secularism in general, represented in this discussion by Egyptian liberalism with its possibilities and interesting ambivalences and twists, adopted the West as a model and a standard. As foregoing discussions have shown, this lacked a critical theoretical base and a proper consideration of history and context, or the impress of a social history. It was rather a festive and commemorative history of Reason and Reason's heroes, who defended it from the obscurantist web woven over centuries by the Church and its ideology. This history of universal reason was imagined as continuous and even, beginning in Greece, passing into Arabo-Islamic civilisation and attaining a final station in contemporary Europe – North America was still at that time in the ante-chamber of history. This view of history was current in Europe itself, and came in these narrations to incorporate all that was non-West and still of any historical significance, such as the ancient Near East. Memory of the present – with Taha Hussein for instance – comes to organise historical time in a way that involves "moving from the present, controlled by the West with its military prowess, institutions and economy, towards one common past".[286] This one common historical time ingests other pasts and assimilates them. Thus, the global present, pioneered by Europe, is projected onto every past, making it easy for opponents to accuse Arab liberals of disregarding the specificities of their societies. Liberals made hardly any conceptual or historical estimation of distinctions, beyond repeating general clichés about particularity, and of the imbrication of societal distinctions and unevennesses with the present universalising character of Europe in the age of European hegemony. They were therefore unable to grasp concretely the extent and nature of their structural connections with their own Arab societies, reproducing the model of relations between an advanced secular Europe and a backward religious Orient in their own conception of their link to society. Thus, an internal segment, liberal secular intellectuals, is translated by the imagination into the presence of an external element, in a manner that accorded with the polemical motifs that Islamists and other conservatives deployed against liberals. With the lack of political mediation and a cultural politics between themselves and what they saw as the commoner, liberal enlighteners exemplified by Taha Hussein remained enlightened individuals, genuine and distinctive. But they were unable to craft a political culture concordant

286 Sharāra, *Ḥawl ba'ḍ mushkilāt al-dawla*, 116.

with this personal enlightenment or parallel to it, corresponding to its ambitions while retaining social and cultural differences. They looked on from the lectern.

3 Secularism and Politics

We have examined the characteristic features of the *Tanzimat* state, as a historical dynamic that continued its modernist momentum, later bequeathed to the successor independent, colonial, or Mandate-regime post-Ottoman Arab states. Education and related sectors were, as noted, fundamental vehicles for the objective secularisation of life, under the auspices of a form of state impelled by the internal logic characterising interventionist modern states: the tendency towards cultural homogenisation, powered by a specialised class of new intellectuals – the Saudi instance was an exception confirming the rule, energised by its own distinctive body of ulamaic intellectual sodality in alliance with the ruling house. Objective secularisation, implicit and often explicit, scandalously evident to the religious lobby. The text of some constitutions – such as the Egyptian constitution of 1923 that stated that Islam was the religion of state – had little more than symbolic significance and sectoral impact in regions of society and polity that involved religious institutional actors; al-Azhar with support from the Palace saw to the artificial political elevation of religion in public life, aided further by the instrumentalisation of religion in electoral politics. The history of secularism in the independent Egyptian state was the history of the spread of secularism as we have discussed it, with its limitations, and, simultaneously, the history of the diminishing capacities and possibilities available to secularists. In this regard, the history of the Egyptian state charted a very particular history apart from other Mashriqi states (Saudi Arabia is not here considered), these paths recomposing themselves together after the defeat of June 1967.

Al-Azhar was resistant to change, despite compulsion to piecemeal reform in order to continue its educational activity in an evolving administrative and social situation. This activity was crucial to constructing points of direct socio-political and cultural impact. The establishment in 1907, at the initiative of Sa'd Zaghloul, of a college of shari'a justice was an attempt to break the monopoly of the al-Azhar and its backers in the royal palace for the control of shar'ist legal training, by training judges exposed to measures of modern education. Following plans inspired by Muhammad 'Abduh, al-Azhar itself, under the rectorates of Shaykh Abd al-Rahman al-Sharbini (1900–1905) and Shaykh Salim al-Bishri (1909–1917), implemented some dilatory and minor reforms. Later, impelled by further plans by Shaykh Muhammad Mustafa al-Maraghi (1927–1929), 'Abduh's former pupil, Muhammad al-Zawahiri (1929–1935) implemented a curricular reform, removing obsolete material, as judged by Azharites. A comparative religion element was also introduced, as well as the teaching of the Principles of Jurisprudence and legal innovation, and instruction in Muslim jurisprudence eliminated partisanship for particular schools of Muslim jurisprudence. Al-Azhar was reorganised into faculties, along university lines: of shari'a, theology and Arabic, with professionalisation in mind, aiming to train muezzins, judges, preachers, and teachers of the Arabic language for schools.[287] In Tunis the Zeitouna had taken similar steps a short time before.[288]

In the meantime, in 1930, Shaykh al-Zawahiri, who enjoyed strong support from King Fouad I, succeeded in closing down Zaghloul's School of Shari'a Justice after it had been linked administratively to al-Azhar in 1923 by a royal decree, to be reversed in 1925 by a parliamentary vote. Thus, al-Azhar's complete control over the reproduction of the religious and shari'a legal institution was reconfirmed. It became an independent authority, a "state within the state", and, as such, criticised by Taha Hussein, who called for its integration into the state education system, to be given independence only within the limits of the law, and to be disallowed from establishing institutions parallel to state educational institutions, with graduates thereby entering state service irregularly.[289] But Hussein refrained from calling openly for the abolition of al-Azhar's activities in tertiary education, or for the confinement of such to the Egyptian University, although others, among them Salama Musa, did make such a call.[290] In 1925 a second call

287 Riḍā, *Tarīkh al-ustādh al-imām al-shaykh Muḥammad 'Abduh*, vol. 1, 428–465; Fakhr al-Dīn al-Aḥmadī al-Ẓawāhirī, *Al-siyāsa wa al-Azhar: Min mudhakkirāt Shaykh al-islām al-Ẓawāhirī* (Cairo: Maṭba'at al-I'timād, 1945), 137–139, 153–162; Fakhr al-Dīn al-Aḥmadī al-Ẓawāhirī, *Al-Azhar: Tarīkhuhu wa taṭawwuruhu* (Cairo: al-Ittiḥād al-Ishtirākī al-'Arabī, 1964), 260–269; 'Abd al-Mit'āl al-Ṣa'īdī, *Tārīkh al-iṣlāḥ fī al-Azhar wa ṣafaḥāt min al-jihād fī al-iṣlāḥ* (Cairo: Maṭba'at al-I'timād , 1952), vol. 1, 112–138.

288 Abdel Moula, *L'Université Zaytounienne et la société tunisienne*, 124–127.

289 Ḥusayn, *Mustaqbal al-thaqāfa fī Miṣr*, 93–95, 440–441.

290 Mūsā, *Al-qadīm wa al-jadīd*, 233–234; Ḥusayn, *Al-ittijāhāt al-waṭaniyya fī al-adab al-mu'āṣir*, vol. 2, 237.

was made to integrate al-Azhar into the Ministry of Education system. Al-Azhar protested, claiming this was out of the question at a time when there was discussion of the independence of the university from the Ministry.[291] Thus, al-Azhar, the School of Shari'a Justice and the Dar al-'Ulum (founded in 1872 to teach secular subjects) became fields of rivalry between the King, political parties, and parliament for ultimate control, including control of finance and administration. The employment of al-Azhar graduates and the conditions of this employment constituted a basic aspect of the relations between al-Azhar and secular institutions in Egypt.[292] It was not only a matter of teaching and administration; there was also the question of the power to appoint the Shaykh of al-Azhar. This led the King, the Wafd Party, and the Liberal Constitutionalists to form shifting alliances, leading sometimes to the supremacy of the Ministry of Education and Parliament, although the 1930 Constitution provided that the appointment of the Sheikh be the privilege of the King.[293]

State and politicians were thus the primary support empowering the intervention of the religious lobby in public life. In addition, state religion stipulated religious ceremonies for enthronement at the expense of the civil character of the head of state. The same provision was used to identify Islam and the demands of the Shaykh of al-Azhar.[294] All the while, people were occupied with their working lives, as Taha Hussein said, "fully prepared to engage with their particular times and places . . . knowing full well that Islam was well, and that prayers will be held, fasting will take place in Ramadan and the pilgrimage will take place, carrying out their religious duties like other reasonable people, neither inordinately religious nor excessively rebellious and depraved." Nevertheless, the ulama interpreted the text of the Constitution on state religion in such a way as to allocate the state new religious duties unconnected to devotions or to whatever desiderata might have been entailed by the provision that Islam be the religion of the head of state. The religious lobby assigned to the state responsibility for chastising atheists and preventing them from expressing their opinions. "This means

291 al-Ẓawāhirī, *Al-siyāsa wa al-Azhar*, 218–220.

292 Ḥusayn, *Al-ittijāhāt al-waṭaniyya fī al-adab al-mu'āṣir*, vol. 2, 269–270; Azharī ḥurr al-fikr, "Al-jāmi'a al-azhariyya", 1,241–1,243; al-Bishrī, *Al-Muslimūn wa al-Aqbāṭ*, 222–224, 323–337.

293 al-Bishri, *Al-Muslimūn wa-l-Aqbāt*, 365, 346–352, 357–361; al-Ẓawāhirī, *Al-siyāsa wa al-Azhar*, 61.

294 Abū Shādī, *Limādhā anā mu'min?*, 4–6.

that the state has the duty to eliminate freedom of expression in all that concerns Islam from far or near . . . that the state has the constitutional duty to heed the voice of the sheikhs in this regard." The High Council of Ulama – whose very existence was not constitutional but purely administrative and self-appointed – exploited the unstable political circumstances of the mid-1920s until the "feathers became increasingly abundant in the wings of the sheikhs". They exercised a quasi-monopoly over primary education, obliged students of Dar al-'Ulum to don clerical garb, and intervened – in the matter of *On Jāhili Poetry* – in the affairs of the Egyptian University, an independent institution.[295]

Al-Azhar continued to blur the boundaries between Islam and al-Azhar's own interests at the expense of the secular constitution and the law, and to follow this practice in the case of 'Abd al-Raziq. A controversy was provoked when an internal al-Azhar commission dismissed 'Ali 'Abd al-Raziq from the College of Ulama because his views did not correspond to the judgment of al-Azhar about what conformed and did not conform to religion, without taking account of the freedom of belief guaranteed by civil law.[296] 'Abd al-Raziq considered the college's decision unconstitutional, as it was an educational and not a religious entity, established by civil legislation for administrative purposes that did not include dogma.[297] Al-Azhar, however, decided to expel 'Abd al-Raziq from his position as shari'a judge, dismissing him in effect from state employment – he rebounded, the Azhar's decision was revoked in 1945, and he was twice named Minister of Awqaf after 1947. The jurist and ex-Wafdist, Minister of Justice, 'Abd al-Aziz Fahmi (1870–1951), then leader of the Liberal Constitutionalists, refused to implement the Azhar decision as it contravened the constitution. This gave the King the opportunity to dismiss Fahmi in his turn, and to put pressure on the Prime Minister to resign and implement the royal will. This pattern of behaviour contrary to the law, based on a claim to transcend the law, continued with al-Azhar despite an attempt to defend it by claiming that its attitude to 'Abd al-Raziq had been uncharacteristic.[298] The judge of the Court

295 Ḥusayn, *Al-majmū'a al-kāmila li mu'allafāt al-duktūr Ṭaḥa Ḥusayn*, vol. 9, 173–179.

296 See the highly vindictive report on the 'Abd al-Rāziq case, presumably by Riḍā, "Tanfīdh al-ḥukm" in *Al-Manār*, 62/1 (1925): 384–391; al-Bishrī, *Al-Muslimūn wa al-Aqbāṭ*, 297.

297 'Alī 'Abd al-Raziq, *Al-islām wa uṣūl al-ḥukm*, ed. Muḥammad 'Amāra (Beirut: al-Mu'assasa al-'Arabiyya li'l-Dirāsāt wa al-Nashr, 1972), 93–94.

298 Ibid., 17–22.

of First Instance found in the case of the campaign in 1950 against Khalid Muhammad Khalid (1920–1996) that the author, critical of the religious claims of the government and the religious institution, did not, through his action, criticise religion itself. This contradicted the view of the al-Azhar ulama. The same judge lifted the ban on Khalid's book *Min hunā nabda'*.[299]

One might be surprised at the capacity for al-Azhar to act given its distance from the exercise of direct political influence through the normal instruments of politics or parliamentary activity, or mechanisms of information and communication, at a time when the public ear was attuned rather to political parties, particularly the Wafd. Al-Azhar's fundamental means of expression were limited to rather introverted defence of its privileges disseminated through its publications and mosques. The fundamental explanation would lie in the Egyptian state, represented by the King, made vulnerable to al-Azhar in a political situation that saw al-Azhar manipulate the tensions and balances between political parties. King Fouad I's encouragement and sponsorship of conservative religion was not limited to al-Azhar but also included the Coptic Church, seeking to win over religious Copts at a time when the Wafd had succeeded in winning over the majority of the Copts in a situation that saw acute conflicts between the Coptic clergy and the laity.[300] King Fouad I was not the only one to pervert al-Azhar from its religious missions and encouraged its appetite for political ambitions and its aim to broaden the remit of religion at the expense of the normal development of society and culture. As we saw, the Wafd used demagogic, Islamic propaganda while its policies were fundamentally secular, and the Liberal Constitutionalsts attacked it, demagogically, for favouring Copts. The Wafd's position in the 'Abd al-Raziq affair was incoherent, and it sought to exploit this against the Liberal Constitutional Party.[301] The signal position of Abbas Mahmud al-'Aqqad, then a Wafdist member of Parliament, in defending the freedom of expression of Taha Hussein and his position in the university was at variance with his party's political exploitation of this matter.[302]

299 Khālid, *Min hunā nabda'*, 294–295.

300 al-Bishrī, *Al-Muslimūn wa al-Aqbāṭ*, 388–425.

301 Ibid., 295–297.

302 'Āmir al-'Aqqād, *Ma'ārik al-'aqqād al-adabiyya* (Beirut/Sidon: al-Maktaba al-'Aṣriyya, 1971), 81–82.

The most important source for al-Azhar's self-confidence was King Fouad himself. The apparently consuming desire of King Fouad to become caliph after the First World War was a golden opportunity; it empowered al-Azhar and allowed it to move from a defensive position centred on the preservation of its own privileges into a broader public vocation. It is unsurprising that the leading critics of 'Ali 'Abd al-Raziq were the al-Azhar scholars who were partisans of an autocratic understanding of the caliphate.[303] A proclamation was made that the caliphate was an obligatory office and that it was endowed with complete executive powers, in contradiction to the Egyptian Constitution of 1923. At the same time, a call was made for a caliphal convocation to be held, and Fouad I was nominated candidate for the post. Al-Azhar then issued a fatwa invalidating the pledge of allegiance to the last caliph Abdelmedjid II (elected caliph in November 1922 by the Turkish National Assembly) on the grounds that the pledge had been defective, and al-Azhar also criticised the candidacy of al-Hussein b. 'Ali, Sharif of Mecca, on the grounds that he was being manipulated by the British. Azharites were active in setting up an Egyptian political organisation in provincial towns and the countryside, sponsored and supported financially by the royal palace, and directed this organisation against the Wafd. It was also supported by the Council of Senior Ulama of al-Azhar headed by a certain Shaykh Muhammad Faraj al-Minyawi, along with the Shaykh of al-Azhar, Abu'l Fadl al-Jizawi. Muhammad al-Zawahiri, later to become Shaykh of al-Azhar from 1929 to 1935, was active in setting up the rural network of this organisation. He was involved as a legal adviser in the trial of 'Abd al-Raziq, even though he was not a member of the Council of Senior Ulama.[304] The Wafd, after hesitation, opposed the idea of the caliphal convocation and the Ministry of the Interior banned civil servants – including shari'a judges – from involvement in the committees of the caliphate. The Wafd Party supported an opposing Islamic opinion put forward by gentleman-scholar and archaeologist Prince Umar Tusun (1872–1944) and others, who considered that Egypt was disaqualified from holding the caliphate because it was under British domination. The Wafd Party and the Liberal Constitutional Party insisted that

303 al-Bishrī, *Al-Muslimūn wa al-Aqbāṭ*, 294–295.

304 Ibid., 287; Ḥusayn, *Al-ittijāhāt al-waṭaniyya fī al-adab al-mu'āṣir*, vol. 2, 47–50; al-Ẓawāhirī, *Al-siyāsa wa al-Azhar*, 210; 'Abd al-Raziq, *Al-islām wa uṣūl al-ḥukm*, 56 and Kramer, *Islam Assembled*, 87–89.

these were political matters and should be dealt with by the Parliament, and not by extra-constitutional bodies.[305] As is well-known, the 1926 convocation was held, with few participants, and failed to reach any practical aims.[306]

It will come as no surprise that the King gave al-Azhar this extra-constitutional leave to attack ʿAbd al-Raziq. His book had reached conclusions concordant with those that had appeared in the Turkish text prepared at the time of the abolition of the caliphate, *The Caliphate and Authority in the Islamic community*, mentioned already. This book held that Muhammad was not the founder of a polity in the normal sense, that the imamate/caliphate had no justification in the Qur'an and hadith, and that "Islam is innocent of that Caliphate with which Muslims are familiar, innocent of inducement and fear of glory and strength surrounding it. The Caliphate forms no part of the institutes of religion, nor does the judiciary or other functions of government and state. These are merely political institutions, unconnected to religion which neither knows nor denies them, neither prescribes nor proscribes them. These institutes were left to us to consider by reason, the experience of nations and the rues of politics . . . nothing in the experience of nations shows [the Caliphate] to be the best base of government."[307]

ʿAbd al-Raziq gave expression to political realities of his time, to a tendential orientation conforming to the implicit logic of the modern state, recording the reality of a secular order as the reality of his time (without theorising it), noting the caliphate's obsolescence and that of every kind of political piety and religious politics. He proposed in a different language what the likes of Ismail Mazhar had raised previously, that the caliphate was a deleterious mix of religious and civil power united in one overbearing hand, arising from an uncertain heritage that had become "a crucible from which is spread the corruption of the religious scholars".[308] For these commentators, as for Jurji Zaydan before them, it was clear that the notion of an Islamic league was an idea with a literary, material, or charitable merit, "unless extremists were to incite the masses and excite their impulses to the point where they display what a civilised person would call religious zealotry, whereby any benefit hoped for would become

305 Ḥusayn, *Al-ittijāhāt al-waṭaniyya fī al-adab al-muʿāṣir*, 52–53; Kramer, *Islam Assembled*, 89–90.
306 Kramer, *Islam Assembled*, 96–101.
307 ʿAbd al-Raziq, *Al-islām wa uṣūl al-ḥukm*, 103.
308 Maẓhar, *Wathbat al-Sharq*, 15–16.

harmful to them, and God is the most knowledgeable".[309] Irresponsibility in this case originated not only that of zealots, but of the royal palace, which whetted the appetite of al-Azhar for repeated interference in politics that made religion an element of political conflict.

This move towards a state Church was an important element driving Egyptian society towards confessional conflicts, which grew in intensity as Islamist political movements emerged. This is especially true of the Muslim Brethren, with their Boy Scouts, Black Shirts paramilitary wing (Shabāb Muḥammad: Muhammad's Young Men), all movements independent of al-Azhar that drove the venerable institution towards more extreme and militant positions in order to protect its flanks. As for Coptic intellectuals, they gravitated towards engagement with questions of national politics, education, and culture in the context of the Egyptian national movement. The majority of Coptic spokesmen refused the inclusion in the 1923 Constitution of a text protecting the minority and making it an object of exceptional legislation. The proportion of Coptic members of Parliament exceeded their percentage in the Egyptian population in the elections of 1924, 1925, 1929, 1932, and 1943, bearing in mind that these parliamentarians were elected on a political party rather than personal or confessional ticket.[310] A new, emerging social constituency, almost a social estate in certain important ways comparable to the German Bildungbürgertum, grounded in culture and education, which participated in politics, veered towards the radicalism on the Right – represented by the Muslim Brotherhood and Young Egypt that eventiually coalesced, and the Association of the Coptic Nation – as well on the Left, as the political class restricted access to social ascension. The growth of the Muslim Brotherhood led to confessional conflict and the growth of paramilitary organisations opposed to Leftists and liberals. This was an example for a middle class weakly formed and socially confined – with limited prospects – tending to use violence against perceived opponents, be they Leftists, the Wafd, or the Copts. This terrorised liberals driving them to paralysing circumspection, and encouraged the Copts to adopt sectarian positions.[311]

309 Zaydān, *Mukhtārāt Jurjī Zaydān*, vol. 3, 51.

310 Yūsuf, *Al-Aqbāṭ wa al-qawmiyya al-ʿarabiyya*, 118, 122, 125–126.

311 Ibid., 133–134, 142. Al-Bishri's treatment of the Islamists is more clement than seems to be deserved, in contradiction with historical data; he makes no mention of *Shabāb Muḥammad.* al-Bishrī, *Al-Muslimūn wa al-Aqbāṭ fī iṭār al-jamāʿa al-waṭaniyya*, 485–489.

The politicisation of religion in Egypt was not intrinsically linked to nationalism; neither was a confessional conflict. But it is possible to assert that the politicisation of religion was correlated to antithetical trends in the particular context of the 1920s, if nationalism were to be defined contextually as adhesion to a line of national liberation and support of the national political parliamentary system that emerged from the 1919 Revolution and the 1923 constitution. The national question in Egypt was not straightforward in many of its contours, with nationalist governments developing even as the country was under British rule, with the issue of sovereignty simultaneously resolved and unresolved, and with the Anglo-Egyptian Treaty of 1936 granting only partial independence. Political religion was linked, basically, to the position of the Egyptian monarchy. Unsurprisngly, the national liberal bourgeois current was antagonistic to the religious-political tendency. Rashid Rida, Shakib Arslan, Mustafa Sadiq al-Rafi'i, all Syrians/Lebanese, and other Islamists of non-Egyptian origin were the targets of chauvinistic criticism by Salama Musa and others.[312] Rida needed to defend himself against accusations that he had enriched himself with his Islamic wares and his connections with Abd al-Aziz Ibn Saud.[313] The Islamist political position associated itself with the call for the caliphate, in turn associated with Britain and her policies. At the level of government and parties, the nationalist position was opposed to the caliphate, as parliament and the monarchy struggled for control.

Parallel to this was the tendency for secular liberals, and others in their moments of greater sobriety, to seek out another line of historical heritage, and to link contemporary Egypt to its Pharaonic past. This was reflected in architecture, literature, and other fields of artistic expression[314] – Sa'd Zaghloul's splendid mausoleum in Cairo (1927) is an Egyptianate monument protected by a winged sun. There were occasional calls from this quarter for an Egyptian

---

312 Salāma Mūsā, "Awkar al-raj'iyya fī Miṣr", *al-Majalla al-Jadīda* 4 (1930): 433–435.

313 Rashīd Riḍā, "Amwāl Ibn Sa'ūd allatī ittuhima bihā ṣāḥib al-manār", *Al-Manār* 28/2 (1928): 465–473. For archival resources on this question see Kramer, *Islam Assembled*, 10.

314 Anīs Ṣāyigh, *Al-fikra al-'arabiyya fī Miṣr* (Beirut: Haykal al-Gharīb, 1959), 225–228. Ḥusayn, *Al-ittijāhāt al-waṭaniyya fī al-adab al-mu'āṣir*, vol. 2, 146–154. For antecedents and cultural conditions, see Donald Malcolm Reid, *Whose Pharaohs? Archaeology, Museums and Egyptian National Identity from Napoleon to World War I* (Berkeley and Los Angeles: University of California Press, 2003).

national literature and even for using dialectal Egyptian Arabic as a literary language, and the use of the Latin alphabet. This Pharaonist tendency was short-lived and remained episodic; more central was a cultural Arabism without a political or pan-Arab dimension, as in the cases of Tawfiq al-Hakim, Taha Hussein and Muhammad Hussein Haykal in his new position, as well as al-Sanhuri and many others.[315] Rashid Rida characterised the idea of a national – that is a secular and non-Islamist – culture as a new invention by atheists, propagated by the newspaper *al-Siyāsa*, the organ of the Liberal Constitutionalists, and he counterposed it to the political Islam of al-Afghani.[316] This was the first time that patriotism was parsed in favour of religion, a matter that still had no purchase outside Islamist circles. For Ismail Mazhar, al-Afghani and his Pan-Islamic policy seemed "a reduced or magnified image of a defunct period in human thought. In his political inclinations he is close to a fossil whose vestiges survive among us bodily, even if its history goes back to the deepest recesses of time . . . He inherited from the Arabs a mentality limited to the supernatural."[317] Ismail Mazhar's use of the term "Arab" to designate the Islamic tendency is not unusual in the circumstances of his time.

The concept of Pan-Arabism in Egypt of the 1920s was closely associated with that of Pan-Islamism, and most of its proponents had been proponents of Ottomanism in the pre-First World War period, and many championed the idea of the caliphate. The sentiment was diffuse and not exclusive to Egypt, where it had a stronger constitution. Perhaps a fatwa by Rashid Rida might illustrate this. When the Lebanese Arab nationalist Fawzi al-Qawuqji (1899–1977), once an Ottoman officer, requested in 1924 that he pronounce on candidates to elevate the condition of Muslims, national concerns or concern for progress seemed remote from his mind. His candidates – and he was given to much flourish and hyperbole – were the Wahhabi king, the Zaidi imam, and the King of the Afghans.[318] For Rida, Egyptian liberals were merely sectarian proponents of "superstitions which spread among the

315 Ḥusayn, *Mustaqbal al-thaqāfa fī Miṣr,* 297–298; Ḥusayn, *Al-ittijāhāt al-waṭaniyya fī al-adab al-mu'āṣir*, vol. 2, 172–175.

316 Anonymous [Rashīd Riḍā,], "Di'āyat al-ilḥad fī Miṣr", *Al-Manār* 27/2 (1926): 119–127 at 119–121.

317 Ismā'īl Maẓhar, *Tārīkh al-fikr al-'arabī* (Cairo: Dār al-'Uṣūr li'l-ṭibā'a wa al-Nashr, 1928), 109, 113.

318 Riḍā, *Fatāwā*, no. 656.

Egyptian commoners in the name of nationalism, impugning Wahhabism which criticises these superstitions and eliminates their abominations".[319] This prevailing confusion in Egypt, in addition to the factors already mentioned, are among the factors that led to an incoherence of Arabism and nationalism. Arab nationalist thought in the period after the First World War in general excluded Egypt from its perspectives; Amin al-Rihani and Najib 'Azuri made no reference to the country. Egypt was not a subject of the negotiations between Sharif Hussein and Great Britain, although there was a considerable degree of support in Egypt for other Arab concerns such as the Great Syrian Revolt of 1925 against French mandatory rule.[320] The idea of an Arab political league was in Egypt only erratically differentiated from the Islamic and wider Eastern contexts. That it needed to be clearly explained shows that the notion was not in wide circulation.[321] An Arab political league only entered wider currency at a later period, by a group of political actors distinct from the groups who circulated the term in the 1920s in connection with Islam. Its link with Islam was raised again and from an early stage, but it was subject to discussions and distinctions only in the later context of Nasserism, under very different circumstances.

Circumstances in Syria and Iraq were very appreciably different. Syria in particular was in closer and wider contact with Istanbul, and King Faysal of Syria (March–July 1920) and his entourage were more intensively and extensively connected to the currents of political thought in Turkey. Nevertheless, communalist antagonisms and ambitions, as previously noted, had been an important factor in the weakness of Ottoman reforms in the region and staggered or impeded the creation of citizens. Syria had had some bitter experiences in the nineteenth century, and the Syrian Arab Kingdom sought to provide the widest possible leeway for the political participation of Christians. The Fundamental Law of the Kingdom, its primary constitutional document, stipulated that "the government of the Syrian Arab Kingdom is a civic government . . . the religion of its king is Islam". It was a state with a secular system, a state that, apart from the religion of the sovereign, was not allocated

319 Ibid., no. 682.

320 Ḥusayn, *Al-ittijāhāt al-waṭaniyya fī al-adab al-mu'āṣir*, vol. 2, 130–135.

321 Maḥmūd 'Azmī, "Al-rābiṭa al-sharqiyya amm al-islāmiyya amm al-'arabiyya?", *al-Hilāl* 42/1 (1933): 53–58.

a religion, and did not make the promotion of this religion one of its constitutional tasks. Up until the present day the Syrian state has remained without an official religion although most Syrian constitutions have stipulated that the religion of the head of state is Islam. This conferred on the post of leader a socio-political communalist character denuded of religious doctrine.

As noted earlier, the notion of an Islamic league had little impact in Syria. Abd al-Hamid al-Zahrawi, for instance, had derided the notion of Pan-Islamism for its lack of a historical or political basis as well as its lack of substance in contemporary Arab life, and he was not alone in this opinion.[322] Political life in Syria and Iraq since the 1920s based itself on nationalist grounds, as duly transmuted to pan-Arab nationalism, to which the educational and other initiatives of Sati' al-Husri made signal contributions. The professional religious class used the concept of a transnational Islamic league as a counterpoint to nationalism and its bases in secular political ideas.[323] The idea that a wider, transnational religious community might have political or para-national relevance remained over time unusual and was generally viewed with suspicion in political circles. Unsurprisingly, ideas proposed by certain European powers that gave priority to an imaginary Islamic communal bond over the national community, such as the idea of making Faisal, son of Ibn Sa'ud and later king of Saudi Arabia (1906–1975), king of Syria in 1928, found little success. But equally unsurprisingly, Rashid Rida was enthusiastic. He attributed the refusal to accept this idea to "atheists and irreligious Syrians" unwilling to set up an Islamic state.[324] The caliphate remained a matter that provoked little real interest and Sati' al-Husri unhesitatingly recommended 'Abd al-Raziq's *Al-islām wa uṣūl al-ḥukm*, describing it as the best that was written on the caliphate, drawing out in theoretical and historical terms what politics had demonstrated after the abolition of the caliphate: that politics was one thing, and religion quite another.[325]

In its central formulations, the political theory of Arab nationalism considered the national community to be the one commensurate with contemporary conditions, transcending religious denominations as a basis for

322 Ḥusayn, *Al-ittijāhāt al-waṭaniyya fī al-adab al-mu'āṣir*, vol. 1, 102–104.

323 Sāṭi' al-Ḥuṣri', *Mā hiya al-qawmiyya: Abḥāth wa dirāsāt 'alā ḍaw' al-aḥdāth wa al-naẓariyāt*, 2nd edn (Beirut: Dār al-'Ilm lil-Malāyīn, 1963), 207–208.

324 Riḍā, *Mukhtārāt siyāsiyya min majallat al-Manār*, 270–271.

325 Sāṭi' al-Ḥuṣrī', *Al-a'mal al-qawmiyya*, 1,962–1,964.

state-building. The present age was an age of nationalism.[326] Religion had been an important factor of unity preceding modern nationalism in its developed form, best represented by Turkey.[327] One of the requirements of this view, with its two correlates, secular thought and anti-communalist politics, was to construct for itself a national lineage distinct if not entirely divided from the history of Islam, a lineage supported by historical study to distinguish between national and Islamic histories.[328] Al-Husri quoted the speech of King Faysal of Syria in Aleppo in June 1919 in the following text, destined to become proverbial: "There is among us no majority and no minority, nothing divides us . . . we were Arabs before Moses, Muhammad, Jesus and Abraham."[329] The Arab nationalists in Syria and Iraq produced secular history for Arabism similar to the Pharaonic history of Egypt that contained the secular crafting of Egyptian history. One Iraqi Arab nationalist, the physician Sami Shawkat (1893–1987), once Minister of Education, linked the Semites to the Arabs of the Arabian Peninsula, and attributed to them the construction of states, the promulgation of laws, and the invention of the alphabet, arithmetic, and the bases of medicine and engineering. The Chaldeans, he believed, like the Assyrians and the Himyarites, and even the ancient Egyptians, were Arabs whom Muhammad later joined together.[330] The Syrian jurist and historian Edmond Rabbath reached comparable historical conclusions, in a less rhetorical and more cogent and detailed manner, with better knowledge of history. He considered that calling the Arab Conquests "Islamic" was an error. Early Islam, he held, was essentially a national Arab religion.[331] Islam, for the theory of Arab nationalism, was merely an element of great historical importance in the history of the Arabs, but Islam was not the receptacle for Arabism. The contrary he considered more congruent with actual history, Arabism being the receptable of Islam, and Arabism takes ideological priority in this relationship.

326 Shawkat, *Hādhihi ahdāfunā*, 59.
327 al-Shāhbandar, *Al-qaḍāya al-ijtimāʿiyya al-kubrā fī al-ʿālam al-ʿarabī*, 112–113.
328 Sāṭiʿ al-Ḥuṣrī', *Al-aʿmal al-qawmiyya*, 2, 902–908.
329 Sāṭiʿ al-Ḥuṣrī', *Yawm maysalūn: Ṣafḥa min tārīkh al-ʿarab al-ḥadīth* (Beirut: Maktabat al-Kashshāf, 1947), 215.
330 Shawkat, *Hādhihi ahdāfunā*, 63.
331 Edmond Rabbath, *Unité syrienne et devenir arabe* (Paris: Marcel Rivière, 1937), 46–53.

Arabism and Islam were for al-Husri historically distinct, even if the latter boosted the former. There is no common culture uniting Muslims, as Islam is really Islams, with elements of division prevailing over elements of unity.[332] As Islam was imagined in its historical boundaries within this secular conception of history, it was also understood against its historical situation within the sober and realistic understanding of politics supported by this secular conception. Thus, the celebration of Muhammad as, above all, a culture and national hero. The poet Khalil Mutran (1872–1949) may have been the first Christian Arab to celebrate the prophet, and Constantine Zurayq (1909–2000),[333] a professional historian and philosopher of history, followed his example with a spectacular celebration of the Prophet's birthday. Islam was in its middle centuries a historical unity that prevailed over the national community, a matter fully comprehensible in the Middle Ages. Today, according to figures such as Zurayq, priority is for the Arabness of Muhammad, which does not contradict the religion of Islam, as Islam is a historical and spiritual reality, a spirituality similar to the national spirit, and its heritage is an element of Arab life. Muhammad was an Arab hero. As a religion, Islam is neither opposed to nor contradicts Arab nationalism. Islamic spirituality counters destructive sectarianism that elevates the religious bond above the national bond.[334] Thus, secular and historical imagination was incorporated into the rhetorical flourish of nationalism and its politics. To this, a measure of mysticism was added to the concept of nationalism that has no proper place in historical secularism, with negative consequences for the evolution of Arab nationalism that will be examined later. Constantine Zurayq's formulation of Arabism remained in general balanced and clear despite the rhetoric and tone required by the occasion of a celebration and a commemoration.

---

332 Tikhonova, *Sāṭi' al-Ḥuṣrī'*, 51–56.

333 On this most interesting nationalist and cultural figure, see 'Azīz al-'Aẓma, *Qusṭanṭīn Zurayq. 'Arabī li'l-qarn al-'ishrīn* (Beirut: Institute of Palestine Studies, 2001). In English: Aziz al-Azmeh, "History, Arab nationalism and secularism: Constantine Zurayk in counterpoint", in *Configuring Identity in the Modern Arab East*, ed. Samir Seikaly (Beirut: American University of Beirut Press: 2009), 121–137.

334 Ḥusayn, *Al-ittijāhāt al-waṭaniyya fī al-adab al-mu'āṣir* and Qusṭanṭīn Zurayq, *Al-wa'ī al-qawmī: Naẓarāt fī al-ḥayāt al-qawmiyya al-mutafattiḥa fī al-sharq al-'arabī* (Beirut: Dār al-Makshūf, 1925/1940), 109–118.

In the work of Syrian thinker Michel 'Aflaq (1910–1991), a founder of the Baath party and its chief ideologue, this rhetorical tonality took greater freedom, and incorporated major motifs of European irrationalism, brewed by Bergson and Nietzsche and seasoned by Fichte. For 'Aflaq, the life of the Prophet, which is perceived not by the intellect but by direct experience, is linked to the "absolute life" of the Arabs. Islam is a permanent readiness among the Arabs for the supremacy of spirit over matter, Arabism being renewed and revived by Islam, which in its turn was a manifestation of Arabhood. Islam was an Arab movement that renewed Arabism and consummated it; the link between the two was organic and Islam was the basic personality of Christian Arabs also.[335] 'Aflaq criticised traditional Islam and set out an open, highly modern form of Islam, using the reformist interpretation without caveats or constraints. Yet the discourse of concupiscent nationalism produced only vague sentimentalist concepts with no clear parameters, interchangeable one for another, bounded only by the will of the orator and the style of heroic discourse. It was the obscure, even obscurantist references and meanings that conferred credibility to the criticism of Arab nationalist discourses. These criticisms emanated initially from Christian confessionalist intellectuals, especially in Lebanon, and also from the thoroughly secularist Syrian Social Nationalist Party (SSNP), who opposed Arabism on the presumption that it was in some way Islamic in essence. The founder, chief ideologist and Leader of the SSNP Antun Saadeh (1904–1949) thought that Arabism was merely the dream of an Islamic state narrow in geographical extent, resulting necessarily from fusing the religious and the secular domains.[336]

Such an identifiation was not a habit of mind or of deed in Syria. As noted earlier, the Syrian Arab nationalist Zaki al-Arsuzi gave the pre-Muhammadan period in the history of the Arabs preference over Islam because of its broader Arab amplitude. Syria did not see, outside Islamist circles, the production of heroic chronicles of the Prophet and the early period of Islam current among liberals and others in Egypt. The one nationalist to take a serious interest in Islam and the example of Muhammad was the Palestinian Muhammad Izzat Darwaza (1888–1983), who spent the second half of his life in Damascus, and wrote on the Prophet and his age, and on the composition of the Qur'an. He

335 Michel 'Aflaq, *Fī sabīl al-ba'th* (Beirut: Dār al-Ṭalī'a, 1959), 52–58.

336 Sa'āda, *Al-islām fī risālatayhi, al-masīḥiyya wa al-Muḥammadiyya*, 204–206.

did not, however, accept Muslim traditions uncritically, and did not seek to defend myths or interpret them in a scientific manner, but considered them in an Islamic reformist perspective of firmly modernist character. The religious formulation and spiritualisation of nationalist doctrine remained an attitude marked by European irrationalism whose effect on the writings of Egyptian liberals was noted above. 'Aflaq was deeply impressed by Bergson – while al-Arsuzi instructed his adepts in the ideas of Nietzsche, Spengler, Fichte, Bergson, and others.[337] All were especially enthused by the romantic heroic figure of Garibaldi; Hitler and Mussolini exerted the same fascination on Arab nationalists and other intellectuals in the 1930s and 1940s as on other nationalists in India and elsewhere, as Ho Ci Minh did in the 1960s. Irrationalist political and social doctrines had always been part of a larger current arising in reaction to revolutionary situations – in 1789, 1871, 1917. Anti-Communism was globally a constitutive element, in pronounced form with Baath, competing for the same social and intellectual constituency.

In addition to these specific aspects of political, constitutional, and nationalist life, there was not in Syria an institution similar to al-Azhar. Religion did not take on a political role specific to it and as an independent actor. It did not possess the instruments for political action, although action in the name of religion was often witnessed, if not in a concerted or coherent way, rather in localised, short-term, and situation-specific ways, with no cumulative strategic capital as was the case in Egypt. It was in sectarian conflicts that were quickly brought under control, and especially in Aleppo, with local conflicts conducted by local mechanisms. Religious sentiment was supportive of the national movement and aligned itself with liberal politicians of whom many were Christian. Syria was the one Arab country that had a Christian prime minister (Faris al-Khuri, 1877–1962, PM in 1944–1945 and 1954–1955). The state generally dealt with the violence that accompanied the demands of some Islamists, such as the al-Gharra' group, for banning parties and dancing, as it did other disturbances of public order, with little special consideration.[338] There was popular resistance to such disturbances, especially by nationalist students, with parallels in Syria to the clashes between the Islamists and supporters of the Wafd in Egypt. 'Aflaq's use of reference to Muhammad, at

337 Ḥannā, *Al-ittijāhāt al-fikriyya fī Sūriyyā wa Lubnān*, 51.
338 Khoury, *Syria and the French Mandate*, 610–612.

once symbolic and hyperbolic, might have been designed to attract religiously inclined youth in Syria.

The Islamist tendency was marginal in the social and cultural life of Syria with, unlike in Egypt, few literary or intellectual expressions in the central areas of cultural life. Syrian liberals did not display sympathy for the idea of integrating religion into culture in ways that went beyond ritual references and lip service, or of making shari'a a metonym of proper social order. Perhaps the difference between the Egyptian Ahmad Amin and the Syrian Muhammad Kurd 'Ali in relation to the Muslim Brothers is an eloquent expression of this contrast. The Egyptian regarded doctrines of the Muslim Brothers favourably, while opposing their use of violence and assassination,[339] wishing to advise them not to be over-hasty in achieving their salutary aims. The Damascene, comparable as a type in many ways, was more realistic. He regarded the Muslim Brothers as a group who sought to instrumentalise religion for worldly purposes, and to occupy exclusively the terrains of religion, patriotism, and nationalism.[340] Syrian nationalists and the Syrian government both debarred Islamists from claiming to represent patriotic and nationalist sentiment as they had been able to do in Egypt.

The Maghreb saw in its turn other forms of the link between religion, politics, and secularism. A specific feature of Morocco that distinguished it completely – although some recent authors have sought to generalise this retrospectively across the Arab world – was the close connection between Salafism and the national movement. Moroccan nationalism, in a way similar to some recent movements in the East, contained constitutive Islamist elements that divided Moroccans from Christian France. Salafism attended Makhzen centralism first, and then buttressed bourgeois reformism ideologically, and finally was a mainstay for the clerical class in general. It was associated with the founding of the private schools that the bourgeoisie in Fès basically sponsored in order to counter the Francophone schools set up especially for the Berbers. From this milieu emerged the National Action Bloc in 1932, which was banned in 1937 and reconstituted itself under the name of the The National Party for the Achievement of Reform, finally to

339 Amīn, *Yawm al-islām*, 155–157.

340 Kurd 'Alī, *Al-Mudhakkirāt*, 531–532, 852–853, and passim.

assume the name Independence Party in 1943.[341] At the end of the 1920s Muhammad V, the sultan of Morocco, leant towards this political current, which was associated with the state aspiring to rapid modernisation and modern institutions similar to those of the *Tanzimat*, alongside sultanic and aristocratic systems centred on the sultan, which had control over religious and administrative structures with religious roots. This inherited system was based on the figure of the sultan as Prince of the Faithful, *amīr al-mu'minin*, whose profile might well bear comparison with the Hamidian view of state and caliphate.

The other trend concurrent and intersecting with these was a popular movement led by the traditional bourgeoisie that ultimately introduced liberal concepts. National and secular liberalism in Morocco, as 'Abdallah Laroui showed, was not, as in Egypt, India, or Syria, a liberalism of the upper classes, and it did not have, in Morocco, the institutional means to defend its political and social positions. It thus remained for long unable to create a sustainable social and political base for itself.[342] These different tendencies converged in the person of Allal al-Fasi, whose political vocabulary was redolent with terms derived from Rousseau and others, such as the "general spirit" and "general will". Al-Fasi considered Voltaire a person "who spoke much truth although he lost his way".[343] Partly because it was theoretical without practical demands being made of it, liberalism in the case of al-Fasi was better developed and more coherent than other Arab varieties, and was accompanied by a consolidated, national, democratic, and cultural programme of Salafi character without parallel in modern Arab history.[344] His political and social programme of reform, however, seems to have been far greater than the sum of movements

341 Abdallah Laroui, *Les origines sociales et culturelles du nationalisme marocain 1830–1912* (Paris: Maspéro, 1977), 424, 429 and Jamil-Abun Nasr, *A History of the Maghreb* (Cambridge: Cambridge University Press, 1971), 367–368.

342 Laroui, *Les origines sociales et culturelles*, 423.

343 Al-Fāsī, *Al-naqd al-dhātī*, 55; See 'Abd al-Ḥamīd Abū al-Kabīr, "Al-shurūṭ al-tārīkhiyya li'l-nahḍa fī al-Maghrib al-'arabī", in *Durūs fī al-ḥaraka al-salafiyya*, eds 'Allāl al-Fāsī, et al. (Casablanca: Manshūrāt 'Uyūn, 1986), 124–143 and Muḥammad 'Ābid al-Jābirī, "Al-ḥaraka al-salafiyya wa al-jamā'āt al-dīnīya al-mu'āṣira fī al-Maghrib", paper presented at the conference "Al-ḥarakāt al-islamiyya al-mu'āṣira fī al-waṭan al-'arabī", in *Maktabat al-mustaqbalāt al-'arabiyya al-badīla: Al-ittijāhāt al-ijtimā'iyya wa al-siyāsiyya wa al-thaqāfiyya* (Beirut: Markaz Dirāsāt al-Waḥda al-'Arabiyya, 1987), 204–209.

344 Al-Fāsī, *Difā' 'an al-sharī'a*, 49–50.

he led. After independence, the various elements to which this programme was attractive were dispersed among different political, social, and cultural currents, especially after the cultural temper of the upper classes changed, moving from the service of the Makhzen to Francophone secular culture in thought and action, in a process closely similar to the change in the administration of the *Tanzimat* Ottoman state.

The colonial context was the point of connection between nationalism and Islamist cultural and identitarian advocacy in a situation where France sought to divide Arabs from Berbers, limiting the shari'a to the Arabs while constructing a customary law to apply to Berber populations in the context of a legal system independent of the Makhzen. The Berber decree, the *ẓahīr* of 1930, "put the Moroccan national model to the test".[345] Defence of the shari'a became readily transposable as defence of the authority of the central national institution, the royal Makhzen, and therefore of Moroccan central authority menaced by fragmentation. Just as in Egypt Islamism was conjured by Islamist polemicists as they constructed a phantom secular enemy in a situation of objective secularisation, so also in Morocco Islamism was constructed in counterpoint to what was here in actual fact an objective colonial assault on a body national that was to emerge from the joint action of the royal state and the national movement.

As for Tunisia and Algeria, such a strongly rooted central local authority did not exist in the same measure, and in Algeria hardly at all. But society within colonial borders was vulnerable to colonising fragmentation. The economic interests of the local population and their education and cultural conditions were neglected, abandoned to backwardness and obsolescence. The Salafism of Ibn Badis was based on the creation of an Arabophone cultural class, without neglecting French, adopting Arab culture as a marker of Algerian nationalism and Salafism as a model for the translation of modernity. This activity was restricted to the educational and cultural fields, a strategic site of resistance as France did not look favourably upon the educational activities of Ibn Badis and his associates. They sought to regain control of Algeria's mosques from the French authorities, invoking the French constitutional provision of 1904 separating religion and state, which the French authorities did not observe in Algeria. The Association des oulémas musulmans algériens

345 Merad, *Le Réformisme musulman en Algérie de 1925 à 1940*, 311–315, 339–340, 343–38, 366–371.

(Association of Algerian Muslim Ulama), founded in 1931, was a religious, social, and cultural actor that in the socio-cultural domain pursued a policy at once of introversion and renewal. Politically, the association combatted Berberist sentiments encouraged by France only culturally, with appeal to the Arabic language as a means of resistance, with Islam taken simply as the indigenous religion and marker of separation from the coloniser of all Algerians. The association was not nationalist in the political sense of the word and had to tread a careful path; it was buffeted and consequently incoherent in its approach. "It resented the French administration in Algeria and believed in the democracy of France in Europe, called for freedom and independence for Algeria through France. It protested against conservative Muslim clerics loyal to France and called for clerical unity. The Association of Ulama nevertheless remained socially conservative and loyal to France politically. It warned deputies in the Algerian Assembly and the elite against integration into French ways and against demanding equality in rights, at the same calling on their help against the colonial administration's ban of the Association's press and restrictions on the activities of its ulama and of mosques controlled by the Association."[346]

The association did not take part in the 1936 Algerian Islamic Conference, which presented general demands without calling for Algerian independence, being preoccupied with freeing Islam from the authority of the administration and with spreading private Islamic education in Arabic. All the while, the Algerian nationalist movement and its political activities were in the hands of secularists. The association represented only a minority non-political movement that was based on a mission of moral uplift and the teaching of Arabic. The leadership of the Algerian national movement, including the leadership of the National Liberation Front (formed in October 1954 mainly from members of the Organisation spéciale) was established and led by bilingual or trilingual *évolués*, many of them Berbers of modest social origins, some of whom had experience of the Movement for the Triumph of Democratic Liberties presided over by Messali Hadj.

Belonging to Islam was a sign of the division between indigenous Algerians and settlers and was a sociological rather than a doctrinal marker, except in the case of the association that kept alive and propagated concepts, ideas

346 Ibn Bādīs, *Kitāb āthār Ibn Bādīs*, vol. 3, 226.

that were on the margins of modern education and its cognitive and ideological goods, originating in France. It was in the context of the latter that the leadership of the national movement and of the National Liberation Front was educated into concepts of nationalism and national political liberation rather than cultural separatism, and into ideas of secularising progress.

Comparable conditions prevailed in the environment of the Tunisian national movement, ultimately led by Habib Bourguiba in the struggle for independence. As previously indicated in some detail, the Tunisian ulama were in general not especially well-disposed towards the national movement and collaborated with the French administration and the Bays of the palace of Bardo. Issues with a religious dimension, such as the veil or the burial in Muslim cemeteries of Tunisians who had taken French nationality, were in the first instance questions of a sociological nature. Nevertheless, the Islamic idiom was occasionally used to describe the sanctity of Muslim cemeteries as rendering inammissible the corpses of Tuniasians who, with French nationality, had removed themselves from the authority of the shari'a. The sociological and administrative criteria were here blurred; properly religious terms were circulated in the world of traditional religious scholars.

5
The Nationalist Era and the Future Besieged

We have seen how the first century of Arab secularisation, extending from the mid-nineteenth century to the mid-twentieth century, reflected the historical and evolutive process and potential of *Tanzimat* state culture over the prevalent cultures of Arab societies, and its greater organisational efficacy. This state's insertion into a combined and uneven direction of global development tended to subordinate the localism of Arab societies and, gradually and unevenly, to attune their changing intellectual and practical resources, in various measures, to the implicit secularising direction of modern history. A second point to emerge has been that of the incipient separation of the once dominant official cultural register emerging from the immediate past or asserting continuity with it, and the new culture's ineluctable integration, unevenly and by degrees, into a global culture based on modern cognitive and ideological goods, with secular content and points of reference. This culture became the constituent feature of a new class of intellectuals – educators, lawmakers, and literary figures – with the basic elements of what might arguably be compared with bourgeois culture based on education, the Bildungsbürgertum, one that came to be dominant and was implicitly and explicitly nurtured by the state, its institutions, and new means of communication, especially the press and education. It must be said with reference to the sometimes violent instability of this social group, especially in Egypt, that it did not succeed in crystallising itself as an estate, status class, and in differentiating itself sufficiently in terms of the functional differentiations of modernity, as this was undermined at once by individual identification with state patronage and by exposure to social, political, and religious pressure. Unlike the situation in nineteenth-century Germany, for instance, the state itself did not make sure it guaranteed the autonomy of the cognitive field.

The induction of Arab societies into the basic cognitive, ideological, and normative culture of universalist modernity through the instruments of the state and its intellectuals was, as shown already, met with resistance under a variety of circumstances. This resistance was not random, spontaneous, or somehow "natural" in character, but had decided measures of coherence and organisation, in political, cultural, and social terms, led by the Islamic and Christian religious and legal institutions, which had been losing ground with the advent of modern culture and institutions, although, as noted earlier, they retained, particularly in Egypt, important educational and other instruments. Such resistance was not mounted by "authentic", "heritage-historical", or local means of cultural action, as often asserted, but required the formation of a new type of culture called Islamic and the expansion of its social and cognitive remit, through which the religious lobby could confront the comprehensive spread of modern culture and institutions with an equally comprehensive form of Islam organised and reconfigured in a modern mould.

Egypt apart, where the strength of al-Azhar was reinforced by royal patronage and alliance, and by the pandering of political parties instrumentalising religion at the expense of normal political evolution, such resistance did not lead to the recovery of strong political positions for religious institutions and their cultures. By the middle of the twentieth century, the Arab world had been nourishing the minds of its rising generation, its politicians and intellectuals, with a secular culture that did not announce or articulate itself as such, or forge for itself a theory and an explicit ideology that was central or dominant or in any way comparable to that of Turkey. This culture was in principle established on modern cognitive premises and points of reference, with an outlook implicitly secular and given to exhortations of reason both theoretical and organisational, ideologically grounded in basic secular principles drawn, according to time and place and milieu, from paternalistic authoritarianism, liberalism, and nationalism, and somewhat later very substantially from Marxism in the early stages of its broad spread in the Arab World. This culture also assumed a state rooted in implicitly secular principles of law and public life more generally, while declaring normative sponsorship and protection of religion. And while the beginnings of the nationalist or national independence and post-colonial periods in modern Arab history brought in its train a national culture that was implicitly and sometimes openly secular, the end of the twentieth century saw the emergence and growth of a massive, historically regressive social and religious drift, a rancorous reconfiguration of religious cultures moving to the centre from marginal social, political, cultural, and regional locations it had come to occupy in the preceding century. Another crucial element that intervened, especially during the last decades of the twentieth century, was the recession, with few exceptions, of state cultural and social direction, and its historical retreat before the advances of religious actors capitalising on the recession of state capacities arising from both local inadequacies and impasses and international neo-liberal conditions crowned in 1989.

Manifestations of this recession and atrophy of state were, in some cases, the reinvention and instrumentalisation of communal and tribal structures in politics and the resuscitation of normative debris left by older conditions, and the assertion of an archaic understanding of state paternalism as a system of patrimonial subordination (Syria, Iraq). One element in this inertial drift was the sponsorship of religious movements by Arab regimes. Another was the decision of the parliament in a major Arab country to abolish legal sanctions against persons committing "honour crimes" – a decision that the head of state of that country refused to recognise. Yet another was the claim, made posthumously, that Michel 'Aflaq had converted to Islam, and the growing tendency to accentuate the religious element of national and nationalist discourse. In sum, the period between the middle and the end of the twentieth century saw the flowering of Arab secularism, the retreat of the state to a certain extent from the cultural leadership of society following hyper-authoritarian and tyrannical practices, the bonding between intellectuals and the state and their subordination to its political and cultural vicissitudes, and a connection between Arab culture and petro-Islam and its associated means of communication.

1 The Flowering of Secularism and its Social Dynamic

It is generally recognised that Arab cultural and political life from the mid-twentieth century onwards flourished uninterruptedly, albeit with regional variations, in a manner largely unconcerned with religion, religious issues, or religious figures, spreading letters and national cultures in various forms, especially periodicals, and a cinematic culture as well, of generally forward-looking social and intellectual perspectives. It is noticeable how Azharites, for instance, appeared generally as clumsy, out of touch, and almost farcical stock characters in the Egyptian cinema in its golden age *c.* 1940–1970.[1] This was in cumulative continuity with previous decades. Among indicators of the dominance of the new over the old in Arab life was the record kept by the prominent Egyptian literary figure Mahmud Taymur (1894–1973) in his *Mu'jam al-ḥaḍāra* (1961), the *Dictionary of Civilisation*: entries relating to household effects, dress, food, places, economic activities, markets, cultural issues, personal grooming, arts, all of which were elements adopted and domesticated by Arabs and that became the features of modern Arab life, distinct, sometimes ostentatiously, from older styles inasmuch as they required the crafting of a new vocabulary.[2] The marginalisation of religion in social, cultural, and intellectual terms was manifested in reduced concern with it in public and literary life. Religious matters were the business of niche religious publications, confirming separation of religion from other social and cultural activities and relegation to their margins. Scrutiny of periodicals with a wide circulation, or cultural journals addressed to a narrower, better educated reading public, shows little interest in or engagement with religious issues arising from social and intellectual matters, except in infrequent cases, where modernist Islamic reformism of an intellectually open variety came to interpret religious concepts in a socialist perspective, such as that of the leftist Egyptian journal *al-Ṭalī'a* (1965–1977). Secular criticism of religion was not especially widespread, and in fact infrequent. Journals such as *Dirāsāt 'Arabiyya* (1965–2000) and *Mawāqif* (1965–1993), both published in Beirut, did print critical articles about religion and Muslim traditions and practices, while secularism was implicit and assumed axiomatically in contributions to this body of periodical publication, predominantly scientific and modernist in outlook (exemplified by the journal *al-Fikr al-Mu'āṣir*) and the absence of religion from the area of research and intellectual interest. Often enough, religion was discussed in the context of indices of the folk backwardness and constraints upon progress of social structures and norms.

One of the most eloquent indicators of this effective secularisation was the secularisation and humanisation of religious symbols as used in literature. The

1 See in general Viola Shafik, *Popular Egyptian Cinema: Gender, Class and Nation* (Cairo: American University of Cairo Press, 2007). More broadly: Viola Shafik, *Arab Cinema: History, Culture and Identity*, rev. edn (Cairo: American University of Cairo Press, 2016).

2 Maḥmūd Taymūr, *Mu'jam al-ḥaḍāra* (Cairo: Maṭba'at al-Ādāb, 1961).

poets of al-Rābiṭa al-Qalamiyya (League of the Pen) (1920–1931) in North America, and especially Khalil Gibran, had a considerable influence on the evolution of modern Arabic poetry, especially in the use by Gibran of images and style drawn from the Gospels and Torah that were given a secular character, albeit with connections and evocations of spiritual and symbolic nature that did, however, remove such images from their Christian setting.[3] The same can be said of the Lebanese poet Said ʿAql (1912–2014) in his Romantic period. Gibran greatly admired the Sufi poet of inebriated and sensuous divine love Ibn al-Farid (1181–1234), and preferred al-Ghazali to Saint Augustine.[4] The figure of Christ for Gibran became a tragic personality taking on a universal dimension, expressing renewal and rebellion.[5] So it also was in modern Arabic poetry in general.[6] The Iraqi Badr Shakir al-Sayyab (1926–1964), a very major poet, was able to integrate and adapt Christian symbols that would not have been possible had he not considered them universal and disengaged from Christianity as a religion, deployed alongside Muslim and pagan images associated with the Mesopotamian deity Tammuz (the name used in the Mashriq for the month of July, graecified in the ancient world as Adonis – Assyrian Dumuzi), of great importance in modern Mashriqi poetry.[7] Al-Sayyab, it seems, completely assimilated religious symbolism and used it in the act of poetic creation. The features of Christ are blended with those of Muhammad, as al-Sayyab returned to his natal village, Jaykur, declaiming:

> This is my Ḥirā' [where Muhammad is reported by Traditions to have had his first alleged encounter with Gabriel]/
> The spider has woven his web to the door.

He continues his dire, almost prophetic vision:

> Death is in the streets, sterility in the fields . . .
> Muhammad the orphan they burnt and the evening/

3 Al-Jayyusi, *Trends and Movements in Modern Arabic Poetry*, vol. 1, 93, 98, 493.

4 Ibid., 546, 565.

5 Ibid., 378–379, passim.

6 See Peggy Rosenthal, *The Poets' Jesus* (Oxford: Oxford University Press, 2000), ch. 6 passim, and David Pinault, "Images of Christ in Arabic literature", *Die Welt des Islams* 27 (1987): 103–125.

7 See Rosenthal, *The Poets' Jesus*, 100–105, and Gert Borg, "The humanized God in the poetry of Badr Shakir al-Sayyab", in *Representations of the Divine in Arabic Poetry*, eds Gert Borg and Ed de Moor (Amsterdam: Editions Rodopi, 2001).

is still illuminated by his fire/
Blood flowed out/
from his feet, hands and eyes/
the god in his eyelids was burned/
Muhammad the Prophet was in Ḥirā' fettered/
the day he was nailed where he was nailed/
tomorrow the messiah will be crucified in Iraq/
dogs will eat of the blood of al-Buraq [the mythical beast which carried Muhammad to the heavens on his nocturnal journey].[8]

Accomplished cognitive and aesthetic secularisation is the first condition for this complete control over religious symbols. These symbols were used as part of a tragic vision, one of present decadence, symbolised by defunct divinity, often with a perspective open to the future, linking the individual and the collective in a critical poetic discourse, emancipatory in an absolute sense, often associated with a scepticism of positive intent. In his poem *Marthiyat al-āliha* (Elegy for the gods) was a poetico-philosphical text in the manner of al-Zahawi:[9]

How many gods we raised up and how many there fell/
A god becoming a third as he was fourth/
All that was venerated was what we feared and hoped for, or what nature caused to be imagined.

The Syro-Palestinian Tawfiq Sayigh (1923–1971), son of a pastor, proceeded with many points of comparison of sensibility to al-Sayyab. In his collection *Thirty Poems*, published in 1954, infused with a Christian spirit and a secular culture, blending love and a falling god, he wrote:

I am an old god/
the nations seek his inspiration/
I opened the small window to spy out/

8 Badr Shākir al-Sayyāb, *Dīwān Badr Shākir al-Sayyāb* (Beirut: Dār al-'awda, 1971), 425, 467–468. Partial English translation, "Return to Jaykur", published in the online review *Banipal*, available at www.banipal.co.uk/selections/19/138/badr-shakir-al-sayyab

9 Ibid., 351.

I found myself crippled muted
And I quietened
A ruser I had concocted and believed
One in which I had faith as I gained certainty
The fog receded
revealing four eyes/
. . . . /
It was I who raised the statue/
Upon which it was I who was made to collapse/
And if today I have been destroyed/
I had previously crafted what I imagined were miracles.[10]

There was also recourse to pagan gods and other cultural symbols: Oedipus and Jocasta in the case of al-Sayyab, Ulysses, Prometheus, and Sisyphus, and especially the most potent symbolism of Tammuz and Baʿal, associated with rebirth. To al-Sayyab the drought of the parched earth, standing for historical stagnation, appeared like the "earth . . . in it Ishtar without Baʿal".[11] Tammuzate poetry, a term applied to a poetical trend, expressed the clash of the modernist personality with recalcitrant surroundings, praised difference, and satirised the sterility of social and cultural traditions, represented as disfigured gods and degraded patriarchal models.[12] The motif of renaissance and renewal was adopted and was figured in terms of the annual resurrection of Tammuz, transcending sterility, futility, and debris of history.[13] Christian and pagan symbols came together for the Lebanese poet Khalil Hawi (1919–1982) to craft the lineaments of national – in his case, Syrian – resurrection:

O God of fertility, O Baʿal who deflowers
barren soil, O sun of the harvest
O god clearing the tomb/
and O glorious Easter/

10 Tawfīq Ṣāyigh, *Al-muʿallafāt al-kāmila* (London: Riyad al-Rayyis li'l-Kutub wa al-Nashr, 1990), 101–102. See Roger Allen, "The Christ figure in Sayigh's poetry", in *Representations of the Divine in Arabic Poetry*, eds Gert Borg and Ed de Moor (Amsterdam: Editions Rodopoi, 2001), 227–241.

11 Al-Sayyāb, *Dīwān badr Shākir al-Sayyāb*, 326.

12 Khālida Saʿīd, "Al-ḥadātha aw ʿuqdat Jiljāmesh", *Mawāqif* 51/52 (1984): 17 and passim.

13 Asʿad Razzūq, *Al-usṭūra fī al-shiʿr al-muʿāṣir: Al-shuʿarāʾ al-tammūziyyūn* (Beirut: Manshūrāt Majallat Āfāq, 1959), 9, 61, 106–107, and passim.

You, Tammuz, sun of the harvest/
bless the earth which yields men/
men of solid grit and an imperishable progeny/
so they inherit the earth forever.[14]

National resurrection, represented by a Syrian or Arab nationalist party, became a token of renaissance and a counterpart to the ancient Semitic mythical figures, while its faltering political instruments were signs of the failure of the revival. Such was Lazarus, addressed thus by Khalil Hawi: "You were the echo of collapse at the beginning of the struggle, you have become the clamour of myriad crashes as they endured and staggered." He added in a fit of disenchantment: "You Lazarus do not belong to one group only. I was a witness and I saw you in the ranks of all."[15]

To the use of Christian, pagan, and Sunni symbols can be added esoteric mystical symbolism used by the Syrian poet Adonis (1930–), in a poetical output that continued after the flagging of political creativity, in a world of changes, with the universe absorbed into a primal, visceral universalism that renders the poet's interiority an exterior texture for the world, and renders engagement with life the continuation of an absolute, knowing subject:

I choose neither God nor the Devil/
Both a wall/
Both close my eye/
Shall I exchange a wall for a wall/
and my confusion for that of one who illuminates/
. . .
I burn my inheritance, I declare my land virgin land/
. . .
I cross above God and Devil/
. . . . .
I call out: no paradise, no fall after me/
I efface the language of sin.

14 Khalīl Hāwī, *Dīwān Khalīl Hāwī* (Beirut: Dār al-ʿAwda, 1972), 89, 97.
15 Ibid., 309, 312.

The poet becomes the "language of a god to come", linking resurrection – standing for a political and national future – with creativity in the same way as Portal (*bāb*) and Veil (*ḥijāb*) are used in esoteric Shi'ite belief, expressing the aridity of his world in comparison with his aspirations: "My map is a land without creator/ Refusal is my Gospel." Then Adonis uses the universal dimension of esotericist symbolism

> I create an earth which rebels with me and betrays/
> I create an earth I sensed with my veins/
> I drew its skies with my thunder/
> I adorned it with my lightning[16]

with resonances of thunder as voice and lightning as the eyes of a mythological figure of 'Ali, with demiurgical capacities associated, grafted upon the person of the poet. Modern Arabic poetry therefore was a distinctive and distinguished domain for the expression of secular modernity represented in the use of religious symbols, duly domesticated but removed from their contexts of religious deployment, then deployed with profuse associations with themes of decadence and revival with a unique power of evocation. Religious references, and the control of such references, are premised here on the exclusion of religious authorities.

The novel and short story were also important fields for setting out the social, critical, and cultural approach to literature, represented by restless personalities who departed decidedly from the paths of tradition, in the work of the Egyptians such as Yusuf Idris (1927–1991), and Ihsan 'Abd al-Quddus (1919–1990), the Lebanese Laila Ba'albaki (b. 1936) and Suhayl Idriss (1925–2008), who apart from writing also founded a premier publishing house for literary texts, the Syrians Ghada al-Samman (b. 1942), a very prominent feminist, and Hanna Mina (1924–2018), among very many others. They were eagerly read in literate circles from the 1950s into the 1990s. Novels by such authors took for granted issues of personal freedom, social progress, rebellion, and the free conduct of women, with stress on backgrounds of social stagnation and the rigidity of traditions, with religious

16 Adūnīs ('Alī Aḥmad Sa'īd), *Aghānī Mihyār al-Dimashqī*, 2nd edn (Beirut: Manshūrāt Majallat Mawāqif, 1970), 51–52, 61, 99, 106.

figures, when they occur at all, often satirised. Themes of breaking taboos, social hypocricy and conformism, social liberation and women's empowerment initiated by Samman and Baalbaki were to thrive and develop further almost into a genre of its own, involving from the 1980s free celebrations of eroticism to a significant degree, and of feminist libertine literature such as that of the Syrian Salwa al-Nu'aimi, without the use of a pseudonym, in 2007.[17] Women and sexuality were topoi in the context of the progress/backwardness problematic supervening over the face of Arab culture for more than a century.

With greater indirection, the novel, in the case of Egyptians like Naguib Mahfouz (1911–2006) and Jamal al-Ghitani (1945–2015), was deployed and infused with allegorical means to represent Islamic symbols; borrowed traditional styles of medieval Arabic story-telling, used as literary devices, including rhyming prose; and embedded nested stories as in *One Thousand and One Nights*, and stories of visions and Sufis within the conditions of modern narrative styles. In the work of the Nobel laureate Naguib Mahfouz, despite his circumspect words and the various dimensions of his writing, was a child of the 1930s, and his mind was attuned to a clear orientation towards positivism, evolutionism, and scientism in which science was made the inheritor of religion in the modern world.[18] Religious culture and its authority were concealed in pockets of society and secular culture prevailed publicly. The use of religious symbols began to extend from the field of literature to more direct engagement in political critique and more precise historical knowledge that had faded from view after the campaign of intimidation against Taha Hussein before the Second World War, to return in the 1960s and thereafter, in a more consequent and less hesitant fashion.

---

17 Al-Nu'aimi is well translated into many European languages: see one English translation as Salwa al-Neimi, *The Proof of the Honey*, trans. Carol Perkins (London: Europa Editions, 2009). On this theme more generally, see among others Wen-Chin Ouyang, *Poetics of Love in the Arabic Novel. Nation, State, Modernity and Tradition* (Edinburgh: Edinburgh University Press, 2012). A review of the field can be found in Radwa Ashour, Ferial Ghazoul, and Hasna Reda-Mekdashi (eds), *Arab Women Writers, 1873–1999* (Cairo: American University of Cairo Press, 2008). See especially Jūrj Ṭarābīshī, *Ramziyyat al-mar'a fī al-riwāya al-'arabiyya* (Beirut: Dār al-Ṭalī'a, 1981).

18 Rashīd al-'Inānī, "Al-dīn fī riwāyāt Najīb Maḥfūẓ", *al-Nāqid* 19 (1990): 25–29, and Rashīd al-'Inānī, "Najīb Maḥfūẓ yushakhkhiṣ al-dā'", *Al-Ahrām*, 2 April 1990. In English: Rashid El-Enany, "Religion in the novels of Naguib Mahfouz", *Bulletin of the British Society for Middle East Studies* 15 (1988): 21–27.

Heritage – *turāth*, the leitmotiv of conservatism in all its forms, and the title it reserves almost as a technical term for the patterned narratives and motifemic clichés of what more recently came to be referred to as "cultural memory" – came in this setting to be perceived as the remains of a remote past, with hardly any but a token place in cognitive culture of the present. It was to become a huge industry from the 1980s. A comparable attitude extended to elements of Muslim belief such as divinity, spiritual worlds, jinn, and demons, as well as stories of past times, generally taken for myths appropriate for moribund social and normative arrangements, or at least with a grain of salt.[19] It became possible to reclaim classical Muslim motifs and see the story of the banishment from God's company and from the heavens of Iblis, Satan, for example, as a tragic tale, like stories in Greek tragedy, indicating the wrong done to Satan. He had been obliged to choose between divine will (*irāda*) and divine command (*mashī'a*), caught between what was due to the divine and what the divine had commanded should be due to a mere creature of the divine, Adam. His tribulations could only be ascribed to the amoral arbitrariness of divine conduct as described in the Qur'an.[20] The narratives of Abraham, the Arabian prophets of legend Salih and Hud, and other figures were attributed to legends and myths of Israelite, Sumerian, or Babylonian origin, mobilised as part of the political project of Muhammad.[21] As with Taha Hussein, the tracing of Arab ancestry back to Ishmael was interpreted as a political act.[22] The origin of the ninety-nine Muslim names of God was also scrutinised and conjectures made about the connection between the worship of Allah and the Canaanite supreme god El.[23] Observations were made on the link between the moon god in Semitic

19 See Khalīl Aḥmad Khalīl, "Maḍmūn al-usṭūra fī al-fikr al-'arabī", *Dirāsāt 'Arabiyya* 7 (1972): 19–71.

20 Ṣādiq Jalāl al-'Aẓm, "Ma'sāt Iblīs", in Ṣādiq Jalāl al-'Aẓm, *Naqd al-fikr al-dīnī*, 2nd edn, 5th impression (Beirut: Dār al-Ṭalī'a, 1982), 55–87. English translation: Sadiq Jalal al-Azm, "The tragedy of Satan", in *Secularism, Fundamentalism and the Struggle for the Meaning of Islam* (Berlin: Gerlach Press, 2013), vol. 2, ch. 5. On this theme in Arabic letters more broadly: Whitney S. Bodman, *The Poetics of Iblis* (Cambridge, MA: Harvard University Press, 2011).

21 Thurayyā Manqūsh, *Al-Tawḥīd fī taṭawwurihi al-tarīkhī: al-tawḥīd al-Yamānī* (Beirut: Dār al-Ṭalī'a, 1977), 26, 32–39, and passim.

22 Sayyid Maḥmūd al-Qimnī, "Madkhal ilā fahm al-mithūlūjiya al-tawrātiyya", *al-Karmil* 30 (1988): 45–48 and Maḥmūd al-Qimnī, "Al-ḥizb al-hāshimī wa ta'sīs al-dawla: Al-wāqi' al-ijtima'ī li 'arab al-jāhiliyya", *al-Karmil* 31 (1989): 43–45, 47, 51–56.

23 Bū 'Alī Yāsīn, *Al-thālūth al-muḥarram, dirāsa fī al-dīn wa al-jins wa al-ṣirā' al-ṭabaqī*, 2nd edn (Beirut: Dār al-Ṭalī'a, 1985), 81.

religion and the deity El, as well as the link between the supposed cult of Venus and the divine names al-'Aziz and al-Mun'im, and the origins of the cult in the rituals of goat sacrifice. Stories of Solomon and Bilqis, the Queen of Sheba, were traced back to a female sun goddess and a male moon god who had been a pretext for liturgies of a sexual nature that, in the pre-Islamic period, had parallels with sexual rites carried out by women in the proximity of the Ka'aba. The crescent moon and star in its interior were linked to the transformation of El to Allah, with the continued presence of Venus in the divine entourage.[24]

Much of this was autodidactic and impressionistic,[25] but it does point to an interpretative trend and attitude, and its cognitive agenda was clear. Although Jawad Ali's monumental history of the Arabs before Islam, published in Baghdad in the 1950s, opened the door to historical criticism, his scholarship was more one of collection than of historical criticism. Criticism was by no means absent but it was on occasion timorous, leading him to attribute to Orientalists critical points that he considered controversial or risqué. This included the surmise that the name of Hud could be an allusion to a Jewish group although the name was used to designate a single person.[26] Ali's criticism remained patchy, and he continued to use the pseudo-historical narratives of the Qur'an and the Torah as though they were historical, conveying his doubts and scepticism with frequent use of the expression "they claimed".[27]

Historical scrutiny was not limited to the pre-Islamic period and its continuation in Islamic concepts and doctrines, but extended to the question of sources for the early period of Islam, sources still used uncritically, in a manner no better advanced methodologically and historiographically than in religious discourse.[28] It is known that the texts of Qur'an, hadith, and

---

24 Sayyid Maḥmūd al-Qimnī, "Al-qamar al-abb aw al-ḍil' al-akbar fī al-thālūth", *al-Karmil* 62 (1987): 43–47, 50–52.

25 For recent scholarship on these themes, see al-Azmeh, *The Emergence of Islam in Late Antiquity*, chs 4 and 5.

26 Jawād 'Alī, *Al-mufaṣṣal fī tārīkh al-'arab qabl al-islām*, 9 vols (Baghdad: Maktabat al-Nahḍa and Beirut: Dār al-'Ilm li'l-Malāyīn, 1968–1981), vol. 6, 31–32, 34 ff., 347 ff., vol. 1, 310–311.

27 Ibid., vol. 1, 53–55, 433 ff., vol. 5, 5 ff.

28 Ḥusayn Ṣaffūrī, "Muṭāla'a li kitāb Muḥammad: Naẓra 'aṣriyya jadīda", *Mawāqif* 28 (1974): 98–109. See 'Āṭif Aḥmad, *Naqd al-fahm al-'aṣrī li'l-qur'ān*, 2nd edn (Beirut: Dār al-Ṭalī'a, 1977).

the early chronicles have very complex histories, and require certain skills in order for them to be properly used as sources – scholarship in this field has grown exponentially in the past quarter-century.[29] Not least of these is our limited understanding of the history of the collection of the Qur'an, and the weight of traditions of interpretation, many highly anachronistic, over the original senses in the text, which render these meanings difficult to attain. Again, scholarship on this topic has seen exponential growth recently.[30] The Qur'an has a mythical dimension that requires study with the techniques of anthropology and the history of religions. In his Preface to the Arabic translation of Maxime Rodinson's *Muhammad* – the translation itself was not printed, only the introductory pamphlet – the translator wrote: "If believers in it [the Qur'an] do not acknowledge the mythical character of its myths, that is only an essential part of the very definition of myth itself." The concordance of traditional narratives could be no more than an "image handed down repeatedly, which corresponded to what was expected among the audience which received the narratives".[31] It was proposed that the early narratives switched register from history to myth starting from the *Ṭabaqāt* of Ibn Sa'ad (784–845). Perhaps one of the best examples of this was the narrative known as *Sha'an al-shāh* (the affair of the lamb), relating to the alleged poisoning of Muhammad, in which the narrative was transposed from history to religion.[32]

Building on historical hyper-criticism of early Arabic sources – ones that since 2011 are again attracting great interest and credulity with renewed sensibilities of disenchantment with religion – it was proposed that knowledge of the Prophet's biography steadily diminishes, with little plausibility, but with much enthusiasm, as our knowledge of the sources increases. According to Suliman Bashear (1947–1991), one of the most trenchant critics of Islamic narratives, researchers need "to isolate the lacunae and digressions

29 For an overall view see Richard C. Martin, "Understanding the Koran in text and context", *History and Religions* 21 (1985): 361–384. For recent scholarship, see al-Azmeh, *The Arabs and Islam in Late Antiquity*.

30 Muḥammad Aḥmad Maḥmūd, "Ḥawl ba'ḍ ishkāliyyāt al-naṣṣ al-qur'āni", *Mawāqif* 60 (1989): 53–73. See now Aziz Al-Azmeh, "Canonisation of the Qur'an," in *Encyclopedia of Islam*, 3rd edn, eds Fleet, Krämer, Matringe, Nawas and Rowson, online.

31 Ḥasan Qubaysī, *Rodinson wa nabī al-islām: muqadimma ḥawl al-tafsīr al-māddī al-tārīkhī li nash'at al-islām* (Beirut: Dār al-Ṭalī'a, 1981), 30–33, 41.

32 Ibid., 37–39.

which the Islamic narrative leaves in the historical biography of the Prophet as well as the passages of repetition and parallel narratives recalling other narratives which the Prophetic narrative brings to us through its events and symbols".[33] Bashear articulated this sceptical viewpoint in his *Introduction to Another History*, an ambitious work that, however, promised more than it was able to deliver. It held that there was confusion between disparate narrative elements emanating from different sources (Medinan, Syrian, Iraqi) and confusion between elements attributed to Muhammad ibn 'Abd Allah and the pretty shadowy Muhammad b. al Hanafiyya (d. 700), a son of 'Ali, others between 'Umar ibn al-Khattab and 'Abd al-Malik b. Marwan – in a play of fact, interpretation, and alternative fact to which this hyper-criticism is given. Bashear found that the attempt to efface the legitimacy of the Umayyads in historical sources could be linked to the existence of the caliphate of Medina as a sovereign entity at the period of the Umayyads and that it was the Umayyad dynasty that opposed the Banu Hanifa tribe in eastern Arabia. The Umayyads also unified the Arabian Penisula, Arabised Islam, and founded Islam in history. Bashear also suspected that the Prophet and the Banu 'Abd al-Muttalib clan were not at all of Qurayshi origin.[34]

Despite the impossibility of making definitive pronouncements in these matters on the basis of existing research, such studies as those mentioned, many impressionistic and auto-didactic, others better instructed and formed, betoken an atmosphere that is the prime concern in this discussion. They opened the way to a certain liberation from uncritical captivity to traditional narratives that facilitates the attainment of historical knowledge on a scientific understanding of sources as distinct from them being endowed religious, doctrinal, or symbolic authority, or indeed with the compelling dead weight of habit. Demystifying studies of the Muhammadan period and immediately post-Muhammadan period were many. Al-Qimni has been mentioned, and one might also mention the pious Khalil 'Abd al-Karim (1930–2002), popularly known as The Red Shaykh – previously a Muslim Brother, later a left-wing political figure. The reclamation of unorthodox trends, such as the Qarmatians and the Zanj, as forerunners of popular revolution in much the

33 Sulaymān Bashīr, *Muqaddima fi al-tārīkh al-ākhar: Naḥwa qirā'a jadīda li'l-riwāya al-islāmiyya* (Jerusalem: n.p., 1984), 7–103, 158.

34 Ibid., 104–157, 160–163, 331–369, 394, ff.

same way as Thomas Müntzer was considered a forerunner of modern revolution in Germany, were favoured historical pastimes for left-wing cadres.

The rejection of uncritical approaches, as some intellectuals familiar with historical research have done, has sometimes been officiated summarily and defensively, by repeating slogans of political import rather than practising critical engagement with history on the basis of critical historiography. One argued that attention should not be given to modern Qur'anic studies because the Qur'an is the "foundational text of the Umma and the Sunna is the field of application of this text in history . . . the distraction of consciousness in this way distracts from our awareness of our existence, our reality and our continuity in history".[35] Equally inadequate to the cognitive task, and rendering pathos rather than sense, is the sort of historical criticism admissible to Islamic reformism, which uses a simple understanding of bias in historical sources without any further probing, when a historical report is manifestly at variance with normal criteria of credibility.[36] In the final analysis, the reformist critical approach was procedurally guileless and ultimately amounted to the protection of original texts from effective critical study, as in the case of Muhammad Hussein Haykal. It is now clear that the conditions of scrutiny of the factual history of early Islam were established through the seeds sown by some of the studies evoked in these pages. The same can be said of research on the historical and narrative formulation of Islamic heritage,[37] including the mythical character of some of its elements, and of research on certain Islamic texts.[38] Textual criticism of Christian texts had begun by penetrating the Church institution, but very patchily in churches that have known no theological reform. This led the former Orthodox Bishop of Mount Lebanon, celebrated for his liberalism and broad-mindedness, Georges Khodr (b. 1923), to say quite rightly and legitimately that "when Christians speak critically about the Gospel in scientific or historical terms, one cannot ask them not to adopt the same approach in discussion of the Qur'an".[39] But the fact of the

35 Book review by Raḍwān al-Sayyid in *al-Ijtihād* 2 (1989): 230.

36 See Amīn, *Dalīl al-muslim al-ḥazīn*, 60, passim.

37 'Azīz al-'Aẓma, *Al-kitāba al-tārīkhiyya wa al-ma'arifa al-tārīkhiyya: Muqadimma fī uṣūl ṣinā'at al-tārīkh al-'arabī* (Beirut: Dār at-Talī'a, 1983), chps 1–3.

38 Waḍḍāḥ Sharāra, *Isti'nāf al-bad': Muḥāwalāt fī al-'ilāqa bayn al-falsafa wa al-tārīkh* (Beirut: Dār al-Ḥadātha, 1981).

39 Georges Khuḍr, "Al-Masīhiyya al-'arabiyya wa-l-gharb", in *Al-masiḥiyyūn al-'arab*, ed. Ilyās Khūrī (Beirut: Mu'assasat al-Abḥāth al-'Arabiyya, 1981), 98–99.

matter is that attention to Gospel critique among local Christians was just as much evaded.

It was natural that avant-garde thought in matters of heritage – a word that became ubiquitous at the time when anti-secular polemics were growing – was correlated to a general attitude to religion, although in fact systematic reflection upon religion was not widespread, as suggested. The teleological evolutionary view of religion discussed in Chapter 3 prevailed generally in the folds of general culture, subtending an evolutionist metaphysics that implied for many that the disappearance of religion was only a matter of time. This was one of the features of secular thought on religion, especially among left-wing commentators, and explains to some extent the reticence in approaching and in tackling religion directly, a matter regarded as potentially troublesome, perhaps not worth the effort, as it was inevitably to wane. What direct consideration of religion existed was better developed than the schematic evolutionism that characterised the founding positivistic period of modern Arab thought. The simplistic psychological theory that ascribed the origins of religion to a fear of death, for instance, was criticised on the grounds that fear is a psychological phenomenon that does not necessarily give rise to a need to suppose the existence of another world.[40] Nevertheless, the psychologistic and cognitivist (cognitivist in a general and vague way, not in light of cognitive science of the last three decades) views religion still prevailed. It is facile and easily repeatable, explaining the phenomenon of religion by hypothetical origins, such as fear or the desire to explain natural phenomena.[41] The Marxist view of religion, drawing on Ludwig Feuerbach (1804–1872, translations of whose work were to appear in Arabic only in 2007), was widely circulated at second hand, seeing religion as alienation and dispossession of the human self and its projection onto an illusory supernatural world. Marxism saw in this alienation and projection of human consciousness one of the mechanisms of class domination and ideological anaesthesia.[42] This situation would

40 Nāṣīf Naṣṣār, "'Awda ilā al-qurūn al-wusṭā: Mulaḥaẓāt ḥawl ārā' Kamāl Yūsuf al-Ḥājj fī al-ṭā'ifiyya", *Mawāqif* 1/1(1967): 94–96.

41 al-Qimnī, "Al-qamar al-abb aw al-ḍil' al-akbar fī al-thālūth", 39.

42 Manqūsh, *Al-tawḥīd fī taṭawwurihi al-tārīkhī*, 15–18 and Hādī al-'Alawī, "Ashyā' min fuṣūl al-masraḥ al-dīnī fī al-waṭan al-'arabī", *Mawāqif* 21 (1972): 67.

continue until "the natural evolution of humanity" had been consummated, leading to the undoing of this "knot of human weakness".[43] Marxist evolutionism nevertheless had the advantage of encouraging – beyond Marxism and Marxists – consideration of the history of religion that involved general social, cultural, and natural conditions.[44] This was not limited, as in positivist evolutionism, to the cognitive advancement of one historical stage and another.

The two orientations, evolutionist and sociological, combined to produce the beginnings of a sociology of religion in Arab lands, insofar as an awareness developed of the significant and important link between the concept of divinity and the patriarchal social structure, a link that became clearer when the deity was related to certain tangible patriarchal moorings in the popular cult of saints.[45] Sociological awareness of religion is nevertheless still at an early stage and detailed sociological studies by Arab researchers publishing in Arabic are still few,[46] despite the abundant anthropological literature in other languages, especially on Egypt and Morocco. One might mention the anthropological study of letters of supplication deposited in a Cairo mausoleum.[47] This growing general clarity in intellectual circles of the sociological and historical accounts betokened increasing awareness of the global dimension of religious practice and the application of the general characteristics of religion in general to Islam in particular. This accounts for the importance of certain books presented to Arab readers in translation, not least Spinoza's *Tractatus Theologico-Politicus* (1677). The translator, the Egyptian philosopher and champion of the "Islamic Left" and of the Iranian Ali Shariati, Hassan Hanafi, said of the book that it explained there was "one common structure to scriptural texts of whatever kind, accessible to all". He then gingerly opened the possibility that for Spinoza's material, the stories of the Torah, might be substituted other material, "which might be the heritage of Islam",[48] to which Spinoza's critical analysis could be applied.

43 Manqūsh, *Al-tawḥid fi taṭawwurihi al-tārikhī*, 612.

44 Ibid., 94–160.

45 Ḥalīm Barakāt, *Al-mujtama' al-'arabī al-mu'āṣir*, 232–237.

46 See the proceedings of the *Al-dīn fi al-mujtama' al-'arabi*, Colloquium organised by Markaz Dirāsāt al-Waḥda al-'Arabiyya, Beirut, 1990.

47 Sayyid 'Uways, *Rasā'il ilā al-Imām al-Shāfi'ī*, 2nd edn (Kuwait: Dār al-Shāyi', 1978).

48 Baruch Spinoza, *Risāla fi al-lāhūt wa al-siyāsa*, trans. Ḥasan Ḥanafī, introduced by Fu'ād Zakariyyā, 2nd edn (Beirut: Dār al-Ṭalī'a, 1981), 7.

The question of Islam and science, and of religion and science in general, was a ubiquitous theme. The Syrian philosopher and culture critic Sadiq al-Azm (1934–2016) indicated their cognitive dissonance and their utter distinction from one another. Each has its own way and method, dealing with regions of reality and the imagination. Religion is just an imaginary alternative to science, according to this scientistic and rationalist view untouched by anthropological considerations of religion, in the tradition of eighteenth- and nineteenth-century materialism.[49] In this Enlightenment view, religion was just a breeding ground for myths and legends, and an attempt to interpret the universe in a pre-scientific way by recourse to demons, the Devil, and similar beings. The "nesting" of these notions in Arab mentality is one of the reasons for its backwardness and its lack of awareness of cognitive modernity.[50] Supernaturalist thinking and the culture that sustains it were one of the bases of Arab backwardness. The contradiction between dogmatic reason and historical and scientific reason was irreducible, and needs to be resolved decisively by clear partiality to the latter.[51]

Islam emerged as a religion devoid of an internal moral sense, based on commands and prohibitions without other elements, ready to be overtaken by universalist thought of European origin.[52] "The scope of Arabo-Islamic civilisation was too narrow to accommodate the character of Prometheus, robber of the divine fire and of the secret of creation. It is too narrow for the myth of Christ, the divine human, who sacrifices his body for the salvation of human souls. Without rebellion and sacrifice there is no alternative for the self-aware Arabs . . . than to enter with God and with His sword into a hypocritical game of conscious, self-seeking submission."[53] Thus religion, represented by Islam, was associated with social and intellectual repression, an objective recognition of the role that religious authorities claimed for themselves throughout the twentieth century.

49 Ṣādiq Jalāl al-ʿAẓm, *Naqd al-fikr al-dīnī*, 5th edn (Beirut: Dār al-Ṭalīʿa, 1982), 15–20, passim.

50 Ibrāhīm Badrān and Salwā al-Khammāsh, *Dirāsāt fī al-ʿaqliyya al-ʿarabiyya: Al-khurāfa*, 2nd edn (Beirut: Dār al-Ḥaqīqa, 1979), 7, 15, 26, 77–78.

51 For an excellent and coherent clarification of the difference between the two see Fayṣal Darrāj, "Al-shaykh al-taqlīdī wa al-muthaqqaf al-ḥadīth", in *Ṭaha Ḥusayn: Al-ʿaqlāniyya, al-dimūqrāṭiya al-ḥadātha*, ed. Fayṣal Darrāj, Qaḍāya wa Shahādāt, 1 (Nicosia: Mu'assasat ʿĪbāl li'l-Dirāsāt wa al-Nashr, 1990), 65–66.

52 Munṣif Shallī, "Al-tafkīr al-ʿarabī wa al-tafkīr al-gharbī", *Mawāqif* 13, 14 (1971): 40–61.

53 Bashīr, *Muqaddima fī al-tārīkh al-ākhar*, 27.

The articulation of religion and ideology, faith and politics, was always noted in circles where such ideas were common, as religious practice was associated with the desire to arrest rationality, and characterise all that was not religion as enmity and unbelief. In radical circles, the emancipation of reason and of the will became one with the critique of religion,[54] as in Germany in the mid-nineteenth century, and with Marx quite explicitly at one point in his life. These radical elements in the Arab world came to the realisation that religion had become the central node of intellectual stagnation and retrogression, alongside sexual mores produced by social structures based on the inferiority of women and the politicisation of intellectual output. The Syrian Bu Ali Yassin (1942–2000), a veteran of Frankfurt communes in 1968 who, recalling Rosa Luxemburg, named his daughter Rosa (now a well-known novelist), authored a celebrated work *The Forbidden Trinity: Religion, Sex, Class Struggle*, linking political positions that blended forms of Trotskyism and anarchism under the name of *al-mujālisiyya*.[55] In a same direction were artists and poets with surrealist leanings associated with the journal *al-Raghba al-Ibāḥiyya* (Libertine Desire). In manifestos recalling a favourite Surrealist and Dadaist genre, there was a call for the destruction of the superstructure – a Marxist term – of Arab society, seen as a pillar of the "counter-revolution". That group – mainly Iraqis, with some Syrians and Lebanese – declared war on religion, family, and morals in an appeal that embraced "the interior desires of the working classes" and "addressed themselves to all Arab atheists".[56] They regarded religion as the mainstay of repression and violence against life, and perceived the same negative potential and practice in the state and nationalist ideology, whose counterpart was seen as Surrealism, constantly changing and refractory, ever resistant, as they asserted.[57] Arab Surrealism in the 1970s was not an entirely new phenomenon. The Egyptian Ramses Younan (1913–1966) had previously criticised Taha Hussein in 1940 for his gradualist reformism, which did not advance to an atheist revolution, while defending him against reactionary attacks.[58]

54 Adūnīs ('Alī Aḥmad Sa'īd), "Al-'aql al-mu'taqal", *Mawāqif* 43 (1981): 3–5.

55 Yāsīn, *Al-thālūth al-muḥarram.*

56 *Al-raghba al-ibāḥiyya* 1 (1973): 1–3.

57 Abū Ṭāhir al-Qarmaṭī, *Rubba dunyā ḍidd al-dīn wa ḍidd kull ba'ath* (Paris: Manshurat al-Nuqṭa, n.d.), 3, 6–7, and 'Abd al-Qādir al-Janābī, *Al-ḍāli'ūn fī ma'ārik min ajl al-raghba al-ibāḥiyya* (Cologne: Manshūrāt al-Jamal, 1990), 13, 17–18.

58 'Iṣām Maḥfūẓ, *Al-suryāliyya wa tafā'ulātuhā al-'arabiyya* (Beirut: n.p., 1987), 62.

Surrealism continued to call for liberation through internal human liberation from social and intellectual fetters whose prime example was religious constraints. Surrealism was an all-embracing libertarian manifesto, including social liberation and placing the secret of this liberation in poetic expression. Poetry, this group believed, is the "unrighteous path" par excellence.[59]

While surrealism was and remained marginal and, to many, especially as a social milieu, an acquired taste, Marxism in all its shades and varieties, Baathified, Nasserised, or straightforwardly Communist with shades to the left of Communist parties, was hugely important in Arab intellectual, cultural, and political life from the 1950s through to the 1980s and beyond. Until their bloody suppression, Communist parties were particularly strong in Iraq, Sudan, somewhat less so, but strong enough in Syria, and influential in Lebanon, until the 1970s; their intellectual influence was broader and lasted longer.[60] Marxist influence on Arab political vocabulary was dominant, until the advent of the global *koine* of neo-liberalism. At the radical edge of the spectrum of Arab Marxism was the call for the creation of the free individual emancipated from the collective compulsion of religion and tribalistic nationalism; this was formulated as a Marxist and atheist manifesto that found in the criticism of religion the essence of its criticism of exploitation and mystification, since it saw in religion the wrapping of class exploitation in political status quo. This Marxist current also saw itself as representing proletarian criticism, moving, to paraphrase Marx, from criticism of heaven to criticism of earth, from the exploitation and spoliation operated by religion to economic exploitation.[61] To the socio-political criticism of religion was added a critique of its economic ill-effects from a Marxist position, or one influenced by Marxism even if not in itself connected to Marxism. It was a position analogous to that held by Habib Bourguiba in the years following Tunisian independence, when he criticised the loss of

59 ʿAbd al-Qādir al-Janābī, "Al-ḥawāmil", in *Thawb al-māʾ* (Cologne: Manshūrāt al-Jamal, 1990), 1–7.

60 See Maxime Rodinson, *Marxism and the Muslim World* (London: Zed Books, 1972) (reprinted with Introduction by Gilbert Achkar, 2015); Alexander Flores, *The Communist Movement in the Arab World* (London: Routledge, 2005); Johan Franzen, "Communism in the Arab world and Iran", in *The Cambridge History of Communism*, eds Norman Naimark, Silvio Pons, and Sophie Quinn-Judge (Cambridge: Cambridge University Press, 2017), 518–543.

61 See the introduction by al-ʿAfīf al-Akhḍar to "Min naqd al-samāʾ ila naqd al-arḍ", in *Vladimir Lenin: Nuṣūṣ ḥawl al-mawqif min al-dīn, mukhtārāt jadīda*, trans. Muḥammad al-Kubba (Beirut: Dār al-Ṭalīʿa, 1972), 9–13.

output resulting from Ramadan fasting. One intellectual gathered and published statistical evidence indicating that the working day of Syrian officials in Ramadan was down to three hours.[62] Others calculated in detail the devastation of family budgets in Ramadan, Egypt's loss of approximately 100 million hours of work during the holy month, and the waste of millions of animals every year during the Hajj and the following feast of sacrifice, all in poor societies.[63]

Criticism of religion, whether cautious or radical, was closely linked to politics in a broader sense, especially if one remembers that politics was rarely understood technocratically, and pursued with considerable ideological animation with nationalist, socialist, and developmentalist commitments. This criticism was directed at religion's position in opposition to progress associated with rationality, historism, science, social liberation, and secularism, all seen as preconditions for national empowerment. After the Second World War such criticism was linked to the political Left, although this criticism did not often go beyond criticisms made by earlier positivistic critics, even in the nihilistic Jacobin phase evoked above. These left-wing tendencies were part of a more general popular and nationalist context in which criticism was directed against the clannishness and parochialism of governing elements and the religious support given to them. Emphasis was placed on setting up a new national culture based on the primacy of national belonging, or regional, in the case of Tunisia, over any other sense of belonging, particularly religious identity. This was seen as the critical crux of the link between politics and religion, linking religion to authoritarianism tinged, in the case of Lebanon, with political sectarianism. Calls for the separation of religion from politics and vice versa were routine.[64]

The close connection between politics and religion in Lebanon explains the turbulent and overt nature of Lebanese secularism and Lebanon's avant-garde position in this field in comparison to other parts of the Arab world. This was correlative with a basic fact, that Lebanon received many political

62 Yāsīn, *Al-thālūth al-muḥarram*, 142–144. Cf. Ṣādiq Jalāl al-'Aẓm, *Al-naqd al-dhātī ba'd al-hazīma*, 2nd edn (Beirut: Dār al-Ṭalī'a, 1969), 52.

63 al-Akhḍar, *Vladimir Lenin: Nuṣūṣ ḥawl al-mawqif min al-dīn*, 32–33.

64 Joseph Mughayzil, "Al-islām wa al-masīḥiyya al-'arabiyya wa al-qawmiyya al-'arabiyya wa al-'ilmāniyya", in *Al-qawmiyya al-'arabiyya wa al-islam: Buḥūth wa munāqashāt*, 3rd edn (Beirut: Markaz Dirāsāt al-Waḥda al-'Arabiyya, 1988), 382–384.

and intellectual exiles from a variety of Arab countries; it was a playground also for intelligence services of all descriptions, and had a lively press and a very considerable publishing sector. It is crucially important to emphasise that this criticism gathered tremendous force following the Arab defeat by Israel in 1967 – much soul-searching was involved, Islamists blaming the Arabs for the abandonment of religion, some Islamists thanking God for the defeat, and others blaming backwardness that inhibits the organisational capacity of a modern power. Constantine Zureik (Qusṭanṭīn Zurayq), who coined the term *nakba* – catastrophe – in a celebrated book after the loss of Palestine in 1948, emphasised backwardness as a cause, and came to back this theme again in a 1967 book entitled *Ma'nā al-nakba mujaddadan* (The Meaning of the Nakba Anew). This particular fire was stolen by the somewhat more radical and daring critique that said much the same in a more Marxist and revolutionary language, Sadiq al-Azm's *Al-naqd al-dhātī ba'd al-hazīma* (Self-criticism after the Defeat), which confronted religion more frontally, and appealed to a younger and more radical public, and took up the complicity of the Egyptian state in the making of superstitions, apparitions, and related issues.[65] Unsurprisingly, the same author's essays collected under the title *Critique of Religious Thought* appeared only two years later, in 1969, precipitating a furious controversy.[66] It provided a rationalistic Enlightenment-critique of religious superstition, and commentary on the political uses of religion.

This hostility to religion had also been evident in an earlier period. The relentless assault of religious forces against the nationalist movements and the workings of the modern political systems from the middle of the 1950s mined a seam of atavism and fostered and aggravated sectarian sentiments, first in Egypt. Inevitably, emphasis was placed on King Faysal I's famous slogan of 1919, "religion belongs to God, the nation to all", in the face of tendencies that would work against national integration. Secularism was in general utilitarian in outlook and untheorised, without an effective framework in philosophical and conceptual terms outside radical circles, but

65 English translation: *Self-Criticism After the Defeat* (London: Saqi Books, 2011). See, comparatively, Wolfgang Schivelbusch, *The Culture of Defeat: On National Trauma, Mourning and Recovery*, 2nd edn (London: Picador, 2004).

66 English translation under this title, Berlin, Gerlach Books, 2014. For analysis in a language other than Arabic, see Stefan Wild, "Gott und Mensch im Libanon: Die Affäre Ṣādiq al-'Aẓm", *Der Islam* 48 (1971): 206–253.

some held that such a basis could be found in the proposition to dialectical materialism, although this did not constitute an effective philosophical basis for secularism.[67] Secularism, generally, as has been argued throughout, was implicit in character, practice, and the building of habitus rather than theory, let alone an ideology, arising objectively from the secularisation of life and the marginal status still occupied by religion – apart from the persistence of public ceremonial – and from the modernist orientation in politics, thought, and culture. Secularism was one of the practical complements of modernity. There were no broad social or cultural movements with an exclusively secularist title, but explicit secularism was well represented in the left-wing components of the Lebanese National Movement (an alliance of Pan-Arab and leftist parties) just before, during, and after the Lebanese Civil War, and progressive Christian individuals and tendencies, Orthodox, Maronite, or Catholic, in the 1960s, 1970s, and 1980s. These groups included both clerical and secular activists under Leftist or liberal influence, and were critical of the political, social, and confessional role of churches in Lebanon. The Melkite bishop Grégoire Haddad (1924–2015) and his journal *Afāq* were the voice of these clerical progressive movements in Lebanon – there had been a significant Syrian Nationalist tendency among both the Orthodox and Maronite clergy in Lebanon as well. Haddad criticised the Church and suggested, on the grounds that Canon Law was temporal, the abolition of confessional marriages, a cornerstone of the confessional system and in a country where civil marriages across confessions were indeed contracted, usually in Cyprus, a thirty-minute flight from Beirut. What was eternal in Christianity was limited to belief in Christ as human and divine; "all the rest could be discarded like an old garment." Haddad welcomed the lessons drawn from secularism on the separation between the absolute and the relative, between the essence of Christianity and its historical manifestations. He made secularism a requirement of Christianity, following concepts close to radical liberal forms of Protestantism and modernist Islamic reformism.[68] The works of the Lebanese philosopher Nassif Nassar (b. 1940) on secularism

67 There were a few exceptions. For philosophical argumentation and criticism of religious positions see 'Ādil Ḍāhir, "Naqd al-ṣaḥwa al-islāmiyya", *Mawāqif* 58 (1989): 49–74.

68 Grégoire Ḥaddād, "Hall al-baḥth al-dīnī al-jadhrī kufr wa shirk aw hall huwa fī manṭiq al-injīl", *Afāq* 1 (1974): 32–54 and Grégoire Ḥaddād, "Al-masīḥiyya wa al-'ilmāniyya", *Mawāqif* 39 (1980): 88–89.

were among the most outstanding and closely argued works to emerge from this atmosphere in Lebanon and from the Arab World as a whole in the 1960s, 1970s, and beyond.

These previous positions, the conditions for articulating them, and the modernist national revivalist approach in its global sense are linked by a project of social and cultural transformation in which progress might be realised through the implantation of progressive modernist culture catching up with global civilisation, whose quintessence for leftists would have been a socialist system. This orientation with widely different tonalities and pitches dominated most areas of culture except for the Islamist margins. The social targets of criticism were quite constant over a long period of time, expanding and contracting in constituency and reach according to changing circumstances and geographical and cultural locations: clannishness, a thoughtless culture of collective narcissism represented as pride and dignity, social conformism and hypocrisy, and in many respects and with many authors, generalised social and political patriarchy – the last a major highlight of the Palestinian-Lebanese Hisham Sharabi's (1927–2005) reputation.[69] The necessity was affirmed of implanting what are recognisably global bourgeois cultural and cognitive values based on the freedom of reason as a basis for a modern society, one focused on the affirmation of the objectivity of nature and the rejection or at least the suspension of the supernatural world and its associated elements. For a figure such as the Syrian Yassin al-Hafez (1930–1978), founder of the Arab Revolutionary Workers' Party (a Baathist-Marxist splinter group) in 1966, and one of the most accomplished and nuanced thinkers of this tendency, modernity had the future as its axis and was based on a historical orientation rather than on some political theory.[70] His thinking was much exercised by analysis of Vietnam, especially in relation to social transformation and national liberation, development that he compared, favourably and in some detail, with the Arab World, emblematised by a nation defeated totally in 1967, and another victorious over the might of a superpower. The vestiges of the past, including religion and sectarianism, were only "residues" despite their intense resistance to modernity, and that he analysed with unusual sensitivity.[71]

---

69 Hisham Sharabi, *Neopatriarchy* (Oxford: Oxford University Press, 1988).

70 Yāsīn al-Ḥāfiẓ, *Al-tajriba al-tārīkhiyya al-fitnāmiyya: Taqyīm naqdī muqāran ma'a al-tajriba al-'arabiyya*, 2nd edn (Beirut: Dār al-Ṭalī'a, 1979), 20–25.

71 Ibid. 17, 22.

Yassin al-Hafez depended in many of his analyses on previous studies by the Moroccan historian ʿAbdallah Laroui (b. 1933), author of remarkable and extraordinarily learned and conceptually developed works on Arab intellectual history, the history of the Maghreb, and concepts such as reason, history, and the state and freedom. Laroui interpreted Arab backwardness – and the reasons for Arab desire for progress and elevation – with highly developed and nuanced argumentation, but on the basis of an elementary simple historicist axiom, asserting retardation with respect to progress made elsewhere in a world profoundly connected.[72] Progress became a reordering of society and culture in such a way as to restore it to the regularity and orientation of modern history. Global modern history is analogous to a natural history that encompasses and organises all histories and corrects their unevenness with respect to one another, including historical retardation. This attitude of universalist finality does not perceive that retardation, missing stages of development, and persistence of backwardness can itself be the mode of contemporaneity for the developing world in the age of imperialism, aggravated later by post-colonialist discourses of identity.[73] Backwardness is a distinctive quality describing a socio-cultural morphology and is not in absolute terms equivalent to a missing stage in development. It is important in this particular discussion to differentiate between different horizontal and vertical sections of society and its social, economic, and geographical sectors, and also to distinguish between "balkanised" elements at a level of culture, society, thought, art, and so on. One needs to gain a composite picture before evoking globalism, which is never entirely external to any given unit of analysis in the modern world. It is clear that in Arab societies certain sectors have developed normally according to Laroui's criteria, principally literature, art, consumption patterns, and financial operations for certain classes in society. It appears insufficient and far too summary to consider the present as a complete, integrated period of retardation. The way forward is to envisage globalisation by affirming unevenness within a global unity with a European orientation, and eschew the assumption of homogeneity in the Arab world or in the West. Such assumptions, although historicist, are not historical. The same applies

72 See ʿAzīz al-ʿAẓma, "Bayn al-marksiyya al-mawḍūʿiyya wa saqf al-taʾrīkh: Munāqasha li fikr ʿAbd Allāh al-ʿArwī", in *Al-turāth bayn al-sulṭān wa al-taʾrīkh*, 2nd edn (Beirut: Dār al-Talīʿa, 1990), 105–127.

73 See al-Azmeh, *Islams and Modernities*, ch. 2.

equally and separately to the two currents of thought – liberal and Marxist – which converge in the work of Laroui.

Nationalism in abstract form, without complication by Marxist elements, inclined towards a greater abstraction in its view of history, seeing an almost natural ecumenical convergence of histories of people sharing one single human nature, entailing the rhetorical imperative of integration and coordination between different experiences of civilisation.[74] The action of history in this process is attributed to good sense and proper engagement with the claims of reason unaffected by politics or passion. Reason in this discourse appears to be self-sufficient, arising from a nature that always reasserts itself despite being hampered by external circumstances.[75] This discourse leads to a valorisation of an abstractly technical and organisational understanding of reason and its future, as a necessary condition of progress. In the work of Constantine Zurayq and in liberal thought more generally, this discourse remains outside the context of historical analysis of the conditions of the historical appropriation of rationality. It is precisely such conditions that are analysed by Laroui historically, and with signal sensitivity to politics and the role of the state – a consequent awareness of a sociology of knowledge, in short.

Marxism did not differ greatly in its commitment to universality except in the configuration of the West in universal history: this was a waystation on a grander historical continuum. If, for liberals, historical finality was a hope with no hard metaphysical base, Marxists held that the West contained "the matter of preceding history without any surplus" and the local included the West as an implicit finality, such that teleology was perceived both in general and in detail.[76] The West was thus no longer Western, nor the Orient Oriental, both partaking of a predetermined finality. Most Marxists, particularly those in the Communist parties, inclined towards a rigorous adherence to this teleology with all its conceptual wherewithall, proletariat included. If shorn of teleology, and inclined to look at process, factoring in combined global developments with considerable unevennesses and rhythms, this would approximate historical reality more closely than both the deterministic and the voluntarist views reviewed, both predominant in modern Arabic thought until the rising

74 Qusṭanṭīn Zurayq, *Fī ma'arakat al-ḥaḍāra: Dirāsa fī māhiyyat al-ḥaḍāra wa aḥwālihā fī al-wāqi' al-ḥaḍārī* (Beirut: Dār al-'Ilm li'l-Malāyīn, 1964), 69–73.

75 Ibid., 204–205.

76 Sharāra, *Ḥawl ba'ḍ mushkilāt al-dawla*, 124, 118–127.

hegemony of identitarian Islamism. With this last, and even before the advent of postmodern and post-colonialist conceits, "global culture" became merely an ideological mask for colonial plunder based on a denial of cultural specificity to all eternity.[77]

The conception of secularism in both its implicit and overt forms arose from the universalist and revivalist tendency associated with revivalist culture: the orientation of "reason, as a disciplined organising and creative" faculty instead of "narrating, imitative, repetitive memory".[78] Secularism was connected in its overt form, as noted earlier, to a tendency generally critical of the condition of Arab societies and especially a diagnosis of the defeat of June 1967, for which the religious turn of mind was seen as a primary cause, in addition to clannishness, patriarchal upbringing, a social upbringing productive of frivolous, pretentious, hypocritical, manipulative, exhibitionistic, and violent personalities, and an absence of modern concepts of science, time, organisation, discipline, and secularism. The contribution of al-Azm to this critical tendency has already been signalled, but he was not the only one, and a whole literature on the social and psychopathologies of Arab societies and individual personality types ensued. One might cite the psycho-social studies of the Lebanese psychoanalyst Ali Zai'ur published in eleven volumes under the title *Psychological and Anthropological Studies of the Arab Self* by Dar al-Ṭalī'a in Beirut from 1977, a premier left-wing and Arab nationalist publishing house with its own influential cultural journal *Dirāsāt 'Arabiyya*, already mentioned.[79] Studies of women in these contexts and terms became legion, one of the best known outside the Arab World being those of the ferociously anti-clerical Egyptian Nawal al-Sa'dawi (b. 1931), who benefited greatly in the collection of her material from her medical practice.[80] Masculinity in the context of the above was not very extensively discussed, but Georges Tarabishi (1939–2016) did make a significant contribution,[81] as did Zai'ur on issues of narcissisim and heroism.

77 Darrāj, "Al-shaykh al-taqlīdī wa al-muthaqqaf al-ḥadīth", 190–191.

78 Qusṭanṭīn Zurayq, *Naḥnu wa al-tārīkh: Maṭālib wa tasā'ulāt fī ṣinā'at al-tārīkh wa ṣun' al-tārīkh* (Beirut: Dār al-'Ilm l'il-Malāyīn, 1963), 100.

79 al-'Azm, *Al-naqd al-dhātī ba'd al-hazīma* is the most complete expression of this tendency.

80 See, for instance, Nawal El Saadawi, *Memoirs of a Woman Doctor* (London: Saqi Books, 1987) and Nawal El Saadawi, *The Hidden Face of Eve: Women in the Arab World*, new edn (London: Zed Books, 2007).

81 Jurj Ṭarābīshī, *Al-rujūla wa idiyūlūjiyyat al-rujūla fī al-riwāya al-'arabiyya* (Beirut: Dar al-Ṭalī'a, 1983).

The secular orientation, especially in its radical form, corresponded well with the realities of social practice among certain sectors of society, the intelligentsia in major urban centres and the educated modernist bourgeoisie. The greater personal freedom for women, and feminism, were the clearest token. These matters were connected to explicit secularism by natural links, namely the indivisibility of freedom on the one hand, and the polemical identification in the mind of the religious lobby and its ample polemical output between irreligion, freedom, and depravity on the other. In the face of apologetic claims about Islam having liberated women from the supposedly abject condition of pre-Islamic society, it was retorted that the physical infanticide of new-born girls practised by ancient Arabs had been simply replaced by the social infanticide of females.[82] A link was made between religion, authoritarian family structures, gender inequalities and inequities, sexual frustration and irrationality in matters of personal and public morals.[83]

A feminist discourse spread, linking women's liberation, socialism, and secularism.[84] Secularists were not the only defenders of women's rights. Some found in Khalid Muhammad Khalid (1920–1996) an Islamic modernist defender of women's political, social, and human rights.[85] Secularists embarked on a defence of social liberation and women were a key element in this liberation and constituted its Gordian knot. The fettering of women occurred at every level. A Tunisian female commentator highlighted the need to free women from types of amusement considered appropriate for girls and forms of dress that restrain their capacity to play in a normal healthy way, preventing them from attaining their full capacity.[86] Secularists found in the treatment of women a point at which the patriarchal ideology and practice were reproduced, and the hinge of social backwardness. Women's recovery of their capacity to act freely in moral and physical terms, and especially in terms of control over their own bodies, was a departure from the system of general repression, an intimation of its collapse, and provided a perspective

82 Salwā al-Khammāsh, *Al-mar'a al-'arabiyya wa al-mujtama' al-taqlīdī al-mutakhallif*, with an introduction by Ibrāhīm Badrān (Beirut: Dār al-Ḥaqīqa, 1973), 100.

83 Yāsīn, *Al-thālūth al-muḥarram*, 59–71.

84 See Nawāl al-Sa'adāwī, *Al-mar'a wa al-jins, awwal naẓra 'ilmiyya ṣarīḥa ilā mashākil al-mar'a wa-l-jins fī al-mujtama' al-miṣrī*, 5th edn (Cairo: Maktabat Madbūlī, 1983), and Khalīl Aḥmad Khalīl, *Al-mar'a al-'arabiyya wa qaḍāyā al-taghyīr: Baḥth ijtimā'ī fī tārīkh al-qahr al-nisā'ī*, 2nd edn (Beirut: Dār al-Ṭalī'a, 1982).

85 Khālid, *Min hunā nabda'*.

86 Fatḥiyya Mzālī, "Shakhṣiyyat al-mar'a al-tūnisiyya", *Fikr* 1 (1955): 3.

freeing women from the mythical, religious, social, and institutional burdens placed upon them.[87] The women's movement was linked with secularism in every part of the Arab world, from Lebanon to Egypt and Algeria. This was especially true as Islamists saw in the women's movement and secularism two facets of the one enemy; demanding the rights of women was a colonialist innovation, as the Tunisian Islamist Rashid Ghannouchi (b. 1941 – now leader of Annahda party in Tunisia) thought, aimed at distorting the conscience of the nation, not least as women's vulnerability and credulity is all the more so as they are more lustful than men.[88]

Clearly calls associated with secularism for women's emancipation emanated from a sector of society in advance of the rest. Islamic discourse was aware of this and used it against its proponents to support retrogressive social positions held by the religious lobby. With regard to women, for example, an implicit attitude of scorn coincided with fear of their supposedly greater sexual potency.[89] Supposedly of deficient reason and discernment, women were made into tokens of social rectitude, and, paradoxically given their supposed deficiencies, the repositories and emblems of family and clan honour.[90] A field survey carried out among educated Tunisians in 1960 showed that those in favour of free association and mixing between the sexes without restriction amounted to no more than 20 per cent of the sample. Half of the sample were highly reticent about unrestricted mixing, although the grounds for this were often associated with a certain awareness of social change, holding, for example, that the time was not yet ripe, rather than a fundamental conservatism that stood in principle against such change, although this could of course be camouflaged in survey responses that might be thought pleasing to the surveyor or socially expected.[91] With regard to women's work, statistics tend to be insufficiently attentive, reflecting a tendency to diminish the value

87 Janīn Rubayz, "Ḥawl ahammiyyat al-taḥarrur al-jinsī fī 'amaliyyat taḥarrur al-mar'a", *Mawāqif* 28 (1974): 110–112; Ilhām Kallāb al-Bisāṭ, "Fī ma'nā al-taḥarrur al-jinsī", *Mawāqif* 28 (1974): 113–116; Bouhdiba, *Sexuality in Islam*, 237–239.

88 Rāshid al-Ghannūshī, *Al-mar'a bayn al-qur'ān al-karīm wa wāqi' al-muslimīn* (Damascus: Markaz al-Rāya li'l-Tanmiya al-Fikriyya, 2005), 89–90, 111, 168–174. See Shukrī Laṭīf, *Al-islāmiyyūn wa al-mar'a*, 2nd edn (Tunis: Dār Bayram li'l-Nashr, 1988), 18.

89 For specific studies see 'Abd al-Ṣamad al-Dayālamī, *Al-mar'a wa al-jins fī al-Maghrib* (Casablanca: Dār al-Nashr al-Maghribiyya, 1985), 31–40, 35–82. See Laṭīf, *Al-islāmiyyūn wa al-mar'a*, 72–74.

90 al-Khammāsh, *Al-mar'a al-'arabiyya wa al-mujtama' al-taqlīdī al-mutakhallif*, 60–67.

91 C. Camilleri, "Les jeunes Tunisiens cultivés face au probléme de la mixité", *Confluent* 20 (1961): 264–265, 268.

of women's work under patriarchal conditions characterised and sustained by inequitable and anachronistic laws of marriage and inheritance.[92] Encouragement of women's work in Tunisia and Algeria is linked with these countries' promotion of a low-skilled workforce in the context of a liberalised economy dependent on foreign investment.[93] In Syria – a relatively progressive country in this regard – government plans to train rural women for work emphasised supposedly traditional occupations such as embroidery, sewing, nursing, and secretarial work.[94] Discourse about the biological differences between men and women still prevails, entailing the assertion of differences in social capacity. Such commentary takes little account of masculinity and femininity as roles socially defined and variable.[95] It is still quite possible, without incurring any disapproval or embarrassment, to put forward viewpoints that reveal pronounced vicious, misogynistic fantasies. These include the fatwa issued by a shaykh of al-Azhar that, although the practice of female genital mutilation had no justification in terms of shari'a, medicine, or morals, it but can be, nevertheless, honourable and creditable (*makrama*) to men.[96] Some Islamic reformists deployed in their own way not dissimilarly violent ideas contemptuous of women. One widely read author, Mustafa Mahmoud (1921–2009), also Egyptian, whose name was associated with the "science and faith" trope, thought it appropriate to use his authority as a physician to assert authoritatively and unblushingly that the Qur'anic authorisation for the physical chastisement of wives is beneficial to them, in agreement with the discoveries of psychology, affording the wife masochistic pleasure that enhances her submission to her husband,[97] by a kind of addiction, one would presume.

---

92 Fāṭima Marnīsī, *Nisā' al-gharb: Dirāsa maydāniyya,* trans. Fāṭima Zahrā' Arzawīl (Casablanca: al-Sharika al-Maghribiyya li'l-Nāshirīn al-Muttaḥidīn, 1985), 22–23, 101–104.

93 Durra Maḥfūẓ, "Al-mar'a al-'arabiyya fī al-Maghrib al-'arabī bayn al-istighlāl wa al-taḥarrur", in *Al-mar'a wa dawruhā fī ḥarakat al-waḥda al-'arabiyya,* ed. Markaz Dirāsāt al-Waḥda al-'Arabiyya (Beirut: Markaz Dirasat al-Waḥda al-'Arabiyya, 1982), 319–340.

94 Kasturi Sen, "Women, employment and development: Two case studies", *Journal of Social Sciences* (Kuwait) 1 (1982): 120–138, 133.

95 al-Khammāsh, *Al-mar'a al-'arabiyya wa al-mujtama' al-taqlīdī al-mutakhallif,* 33–34. For a refutation of the Islamic rejection of this discourse see Laṭīf, *Al-islāmiyyūn wa al-mar'a,* 28–37 and for the historical and anthropological considerations to reject this discourse and the various definitions of masculinity and femininity, see Carol MacCormack and Marilyn Strathern (eds), *Nature, Culture and Gender* (Cambridge: Cambridge University Press, 1980).

96 Maḥmūd Shaltūt, *Al-fatāwā: Dirāsa li mushkilāt al-muslim al-mu'āṣir fī ḥayatihi al-yawmiyya wa al-'āmma* (Cairo: Dār al-Qalam, 1965), 333–334.

97 Muṣṭafā Maḥmūd, *Ḥiwār ma'a ṣadīqī al-mulḥid* (Cairo: Maṭba'at Rūz al-Yūsuf, 1974), 47–48.

The religious polemic against tokens of social progress was, as suggested, continuous, but outside Egypt, rather patchy, and often really a matter of pot luck – much radical material goes past without much fuss; some gets caught up in peculiar conjunctures. A storm of protests was raised against avant-garde literature. One such protest was directed against Leila Baʿalbaki's collection of short stories, *Safīnat Ḥanān ilā al-qamar*, first in Egypt (the book had been published in Beirut, not in Cairo). The vice squad in Lebanon was provoked into confiscating the novel on its publication in 1963 – her title to fame, the novel *Anā aḥyā* (I Live) had been published in 1958.[98] Such events have continued up to the present with religious attacks on avant-garde literature and secular thought.[99] New critical studies on heritage, such as those by the autodidactic Egyptian writer Sayyid al-Qimni (b. 1947), mentioned earlier, provoked anger in religious circles that threatened author and publisher with dire consequences. The Egyptian censor confiscated *Fī fiqh al-lugha al-ʿarabiyya* (On Arabic Philology) by Louis ʿAwad (1915–1990) at the request of al-Azhar because ʿAwad inclined – most likely a form of indirection and circumspection rather than conviction – to the position of the Muʿtazilites that God's word was not co-eternal with His essence and that His word was therefore created in time and that the inimitability of the Qur'an – as maintained by the great Muʿtazilite theologian al-Qadi ʿAbd al-Jabbar (932–1025) – meant only that it was the most perfect in terms of its place in its language, without this meaning that it is the most eloquent book in any language, as such a statement would be meaningless.[100] ʿAwad aimed at studying and classifying the phonetic changes in Arabic in comparison with similar changes in Indo-European languages according to methods of modern historical philology. He was, however, largely unsuccessful in his attempted project, as he had relied on what had by his time become obsolete scholarship, and on the theory of the singular Caucasian origin and the single linguistic source for Indian and European languages, no longer justified by modern archaeological and linguistic discoveries.[101] Nasser had him awarded the State Prize for culture.

---

98 Anonymous, "Difāʿan ʿan al-ḥurriya: Layla Baʿalbakī", *Ḥiwār* 11, 12 (1964): 176–182.

99 See ʿAwāḍ ibn Maḥmūd al-Qurnī, *Al-ḥadātha fī mizān al-Islām* (Gīza: Hājir li'l-Ṭibāʿa wa al-Nashr wa al-Tawzīʿ wa al-Iʿlān, 1988).

100 Louis ʿAwaḍ, *Muqaddima fī fiqh al-lugha al-ʿarabiyya* (Cairo: al-Hay'a al-Miṣriyya al-ʿAmma li'l-Kitāb, 1980), 69, 75–77.

101 Ibid., 30–49 and passim. For the present state of research see Colin Renfrew, *Archaeology and Language: The Puzzle of Indo-European Origins* (Harmondsworth: Penguin Books, 1987).

Undoubtedly the major controversy of this period concerned *The Critique of Religious Thought* by Sadiq al-Azm, on which a little has already been said. It raised a series of questions about the intellectual and social defects of Arab societies that rendered Israeli supremacy so overwhelming: Israeli military supremacy was based on a scientific, cultural, cognitive, and organizational supremacy, constituting superiority in absolute terms in a wider historical perspective. Among the Arab collective defects were a cognitive authority that veered towards appeal to the supernatural and based in religion, and social reaction with clannish connections, based on patrimonial, authoritarian structures of subordination. There was also a general lack of a sense of public responsibility, and a skewed method of upbringing. *The Critique of Religious Thought* criticised some aspects of culture inherited from medieval times, such as the figures of Satan (which has been discussed previously), and the fostering by state organisms of myths, such as Egyptian officialdom's promotion of the tale that the Virgin Mary appeared in the Zeitoun district of Cairo in 1968, thereby appealing to the supernatural as a solution to the defeat of 1967 instead of acting politically. The book also dwelt on the hollowness of what in Lebanon was known as the Islamo-Christian dialogue, carried out by means of what is locally known as "kissing beards" – burying the hatchet, the exchange of compliments and courtesies rather than effective debate, intended ritually to maintain the confessional status quo and existing leaderships.

Al-Azm's contributions were, in terms of political orientation, nationalist, Marxist, and progressive in origin, while the criticism of religion took a rationalist direction in the elementary manner of eighteenth-century materialism. The author held that religion was a theoretical weapon for political reactionaries and a demagogical instrument for covering up the 1967 defeat. The book provoked vituperative comment and a noisy controversy in which various elements were connected. Their convergence foreshadowed the forces that would coalesce in the decades after the book and led to the present condition in the Arab World. Guardians of Lebanese sectarianism, Christian Muslim, opposed *The Critique of Religious Thought* and its author in a way revelatory of deep-rooted communal alliances, and al-Azm felt sufficiently menaced to go into hiding for a short while. The book was also confronted by a discourse in which Islamism blended, as suggested earlier, with animosity to Arab nationalism and Socialism, part of the context of the Cold War and the global anti-Communist movement led by the United States with ideology as one of its dimensions – the cultural plank of the Truman Doctrine.[102] Intellectual opposition to *The Critique of Religious Thought* came from Islamic Reformism, which saw in the Qur'an the anticipation of modern science, and was in many ways sceptical towards science, as previous paragraphs have shown,[103] especially as al-Azm refuted the equivalence posited between science and religion, and insisted on questioning the existence of the mysterious Qur'anic Harut and Marut, the existence of demons, and similar matters. These criticisms of *The Critique of Religious Thought* were to feed intellectually into the retrograde direction adopted by nationalist political regimes following 1967, which sought succour from the religious lobby and their supporters in the world of petro-Islam who were to become the effective saviours of these nationalist regimes in Egypt and Syria.

The specious religious arguments against *The Critique of Religious Thought*, the vitriolic discourse and imprecations, with charges of infidelity and betrayal freely flying about, need not be repeated here; they have become familiar in the meantime. In content and methods attacks on this book did not differ from the anti-secular discourse that will be discussed in Chapter 6 and from that brought up from the foregoing analysis of the controversies in the 1920s surrounding Taha Hussein and 'Ali 'Abd al-Raziq. Such discourse has stable plot structures, and argumentative and rhetorical modules and motifs that, as in folk tales and detective stories, do not change from one subject to another. Two fundamental aspects of *The Critique of Religious Thought* controversy are worthy of note. Al-Azm and his Lebanese publisher Bashir al-Daʿuq (1931–2007), founder and proprietor of Dar al-Ṭalīʿa already mentioned, were tried in Beirut following the charge brought by the official Sunni Muslim organism in Beirut (The Fatwa Authority). In the absence of laws that criminalised unbelief or apostasy, it was charged that the book intended to provoke inter-confessional conflict. No fewer than thirty-five lawyers volunteered to defend the author and his publisher, and their defence team was a star chamber of lawyers: Joseph Mughayzel (1924–1995), Edmond Rabbat

102 The role of propaganda and culture in the Cold War has been the topic of increasing interest and research in the past two decades. See, for instance, Frances S. Saunders, *The Cultural Cold War: The CIA and the World of Arts and Letters* (New York: The New Press, 1999).

103 Muḥammad 'Izzat Naṣr Allāh, *Al-radd 'alā Sādiq al-'Aẓm: Munaqashāt 'āmma li kitāb "naqd al-fikr al-dīnī"* (Beirut: Mu'assasat Dār Filasṭīn li'l-Ta'līf wa al-Tarjama, 1970).

and Basim al-Jisr (b. 1931 – son of a former Mufti of Tripoli). Their legal argument was that al-Azm's criticism was directed to all religions without provoking one against another. Both author and publisher were acquitted. This signalled the fact that secularism in the Arab world had an established intellectual and social position, many of its elements established in law and by law, being an integral component of contemporary Arab legal heritage, as shown in previous discussions. This goes some way towards explaining the strength and breadth of support received by al-Daouk and al-Azm. Not all supporters shared al-Azm's views. One of his defenders was a religious figure, Shaykh Uthman Safi, who wrote a book entitled *'Alā hāmish al-fikr al-dīnī* (On the Margins of Religious Thought) published in 1970 by the same Dar al-Tali'a. By the same token, the breadth of the critical camp was significant as a summary prefiguration of the direction of intellectual and social regression that was to accelerate subsequently, manifested in the orientation of the national state trading in its cultural and educational hegemony and its elevating institutional role for intangible benefits following the 1967 war.

The above controversy is one of many manifestations of an ebullient chapter in the modern intellectual history of the Arabs, one that saw much activity and a lively publication scene, not least in cultural reviews, many published in Beirut, which had become the hub from the 1950s, for publication, debate, and political exiles from many Arab countries.[104] It witnessed both the best, and glimmerings of downward slopes that were to be pursued. The coming pages will study this in detail.

2 State, Religion and the Beleaguered Future

Arab states of the independent period and the nationalist period inherited from the *Tanzimat,* the colonial and the Mandate states, the foundations of an educational and cultural system whose features have been previously examined in this book. In general, state Islamic discourse or state discourse

104 See Georges Corm, *Pensée et politique dans le monde arabe. Contextes historiques et problématiques, XXe–XXIe siècle* (Paris: La Découverte, 2015). Published in English as Georges Corm, *Arab Political Thought: Past and Present,* trans P. Phillips-Batoma and A. T. Batoma (London: Hurst in association with the Aga Khan University Institute for the Study of Muslim Civilisations, 2019); Abdou Filali-Ansary, *Réformer l'Islam? Une introduction aux débats contemporains* (Paris: La Découverte, 2005); Elizabeth Suzanne Kassab, *Contemporary Arab Thought. Cultural Critique in Comparative Perspective* (New York: Columbia University Press, 2009).

on Islam tended towards modernism, but was variable, confused, and unbalanced, subject to social and political considerations of the moment, sometimes in accordance with and at other times dissonant from discourse diffused by religious and cultural institutions, both private and political. The general cultural climate was perturbed, its contours unclear, and of variable conceptual geometry alongside the Islamism/secularism range. Clarity was to be had at the extremities only, the Islamist and the secularist.

Syria and Tunisia were the two states that worked to firmly establish these foundations most consistently. After independence in 1946 the first mission of the post-independence regime in Syria was to abolish proportional representation for religious communities in the National Assembly, which had been a French wish. Under Adib al-Shishakli (1949–1954), jurisdiction of personal status for different Muslim sects was integrated into a single legal system supervised by civil courts. The Shishakli regime also banned all organisations and associations based on confessional, ethnic, or geographical origins, all of which was an attempt at socio-political engineering fostering national integration. The regime followed a pan-Arab policy that was to remain a standard feature of subsequent Syrian regimes. This broad cultural orientation was deepened after the neo-Baath coup of February 1965, at which time all confessional schools were placed under direct state control, provoking indignation in certain, notably Catholic, circles. Successive Syrian constitutions (1950, 1954, 1964, 1966, and 1973) did not stipulate a state religion, although some did specify Islam as the religion of the head of state. Syria was the only Arab state without an official religion, in addition to Lebanon and Tunisia, whose constitution asserted the adherence of the Tunisian people to the teachings of Islam. The temporary constitution of the United Arab Republic, drawn up in 1958, did not mention religion, while Syrian constitutions noted the place of shari'a as a principal source of legislation, stated in vague, tokenist terms. The neo-Baath reinforced secularism when, from 1966, the presidential oath of office was made by the incumbent's honour rather than by the name of God – the latter was restored after Hafez al-Assad (1930–2000) took power in 1970. Assad was the instigator of the proposal in 1973 to stipulate the religion of the head of state, which had earlier been removed, in a concession to certain sectors of the population after Islamist-provoked disturbances about this issue.[105] Constitutional

105 Yāsīn, *Al-thālūth al-muḥarram*, 119–120.

provisions came with secular tonalities, with oscillating gestures towards religious constituencies in response to direct and immediate pressures. Assad's state went so far as to set up a faculty of shari'a at Damascus University, where previously Muslim jurisprudence had been studied as a course among others in the faculty of law, approached in such a way as to give shari'a a place in the history of law and in comparative law. The Syrian state may have sought in this way to produce religious cadres associated with the state and under its influence.

In Tunis after independence in 1956, educational policy was based on attaching the Zeitouna colleges to the Ministry of National Education until these were abolished in 1960 with the establishment of the Tunisian University as the sole tertiary institution. A series of other relevant reforms also took place, such as the abolition of *ḥubūs* (*awqāf* in the *Mashriq*), a measure previously enacted in other Arab countries.[106] Those with a traditional Islamic education in Tunisia were doubly marginalised through their lack of competence in French, as were their counterparts in Morocco where the al-Qarawiyyin mosque was made into a university in 1963. Following the example of Atatürk's Turkey, a special school for the training of religious cadres was established (Dār al-Ḥadīth al-Ḥasaniyya), which, in 2015, was amalgamated as a faculty within the Qarawiyyin University.

Nasser's Egypt saw the state continue its implicitly secular course, although Nasser considered it politic to grant al-Azhar powers and responsibilities that were much greater than those it previously possessed, as yet another instrument for projecting Egyptian influence internationally. The clash between the regime and the Muslim Brothers was clearly a prime factor. A law of 1961 allocated to al-Azhar responsibilities of a nationalist, Islamic, and socio-educational character. It became a modern university, to which was attached a wide network of religious schools. The Shaykh of al-Azhar was given almost absolute doctrinal authority by a law of 1965 and its 1975 amendment. The Ministry of Awqaf became an unrestrained institutional octopus, a state within the state, almost; after 1953 ministers of Awqaf tended to be active Azharites, whereas in the period from 1878 to 1952 only four of the fifty-four ministers of Awqaf were graduates of al-Azhar.[107] Al-Azhar continued to interfere in the

106 See Abdel Moula, *L'Université Zaytounienne et la société tunisienne*, 176–183, 208–211.
107 al-Bishrī, *Al-muslimūn wa al-aqbāṭ fi iṭār al-jamāʿa al-waṭaniyya*, 282–283.

cultural field, and was responsible for the banning in 1956 of *Awlād ḥāritnā* (boys of our district) by Naguib Mahfuz (translated into English as *Children of Gebelawi*) among other books. Shaykh Abd al-Hamid Bakhit and other al-Azhar scholars were persecuted for independent opinions in various matters including unusual views of fasting during Ramadan, supported in 1954 by Taha Hussein,[108] given that the revolutionary regime in Egypt consistently appointed conservatives to the post of Shaykh of al-Azhar.[109]

It is clear that the Egyptian state position with regard to al-Azhar was merely political, with little sense of possible social or cultural consequences, and was linked to the Nasser regime's campaign against the Muslim Brothers. Public interest in the institution of al-Azhar went little beyond the fields left to shari'a by Egyptian law. One indicator of this lies in the types of fatwa solicited from al-Azhar in 1963. Of 2,147 requests for fatwas, 70 per cent concerned personal status questions and the remainder were spread out over questions of liturgy and a few matters of transactions.[110] There were no innovations in al-Azhar's fatwas and there was a repetition of the fatwas of Muhammad 'Abduh and Rashid Rida that legitimated interest on Post Office bank accounts and the use of alcoholic substances in pharmaceuticals. There were innovations with regard to permitting artificial insemination on condition that a husband provided the sperm.[111] When the principles of the shari'a were indicated in the 1971 Egyptian Constitution and, in the 1981 Constitution, as the main source for legislation, this did not have the nominal or the merely conventional and pro-forma character of similar dispositions earlier, especially in Syria. In Egypt wider access was given to public life for the religious institution that had been sponsored by the monarchy before the 1952 Revolution, and that thereafter was increasingly supported by Nasser, later by Sadat and strengthened by Sadat's ostentatious support for Islamist activism. It had become of considerably greater practical consequence.

There did not exist in Syria a similar institution whose strength and influence extended into politics. The mission of the Syrian religious institution was limited to religious matters and its degree of independence in opinion

108 'Abd al-Mit'āl al-Ṣa'īdī, *tārīkh al-iṣlāḥ fī al-Azhar wa ṣafḥāt min al-jihād fī al-iṣlāḥ*, 2 vols (Cairo: Maṭba'at al-I'timād, 1952), vol. 2, 17–18.

109 Ibid., 9–10, 12–17.

110 al-'Arabī, *al-Azhar, tārīkhuhu wa taṭawwuruhu*, 356.

111 Shaltūt, *Al-fatāwā*, 351, 327–328, 381–382.

from the state was small, while the Ministry of Awqaf was not entrusted to religious figures.[112] The religious sector remained limited and the number of students in shari'a *madrasas* (shari'a schools) was 12,009 in 1978, a number that decreased constantly and rapidly until the exponential increases of the last decade of the twentieth century. The Syrian state was criticised for its sponsorship of a "class of Don Quixotes which would have dwindled away had the state not undertaken to sponsor them".[113] In Tunis, however, the religious institution remained under the almost complete control of the state, until a short period of relief following 2011. The same is true of Morocco, where the king is still, after all, Commander of the Faithful with Sharifian charisma in his blood.

The Nasserite state in Egypt strengthened the religious institution in the manner described, but also pursued a cultural policy that in no way diminished the vigour of secular cultural production. Quite the contrary, Nasser himself often surprised some of his officials and timid members of the intelligentsia by quite deliberately promoting persons and works of a resolutely secular character.[114] Not so the Sadat-era state, which saw an orientation away from the cultural character of the *Tanzimat* and nationalist states. It saw wider official dissemination of a supernatural culture in the media and education, and the injection of religious content into the cognitive components of secular culture. The Egyptian state, and others to a lesser degree, became agents of the dissemination of a central religious culture that had taken a decided conservative turn that included a large religious element bereft of the once dominant reformist sensitivity – often an allergy – towards matters that defy belief. Radio, television, and print media produced programmes about jinn and devils and raised the profile of religious personalities, generally of Wahhabi leanings or political loyalties, who were made into points of reference in general matters of morals, society, science, and history, as well as religion.[115] The curricula of religious education

112 Dieter Sturm, "Zur Funktion der Grossmufti in der Syrischen arabischen Republik", *Hallesche Beitrage zur Orientwissenschaft* 4 (1982): 59–67.

113 Yāsīn, *Al-thālūth al-muḥarram*, 116, 122–123.

114 A balanced account has recently been well prepared by Ṣaqr Abū Fakhr, "'Abd al-Nāṣir wa shaghaf al-kalimāt", *Al-'Arabī al-Jadīd*, 27 May 2018.

115 al-'Alawī, "Ashyā' min fuṣūl al-masraḥ al-dīnī fī al-waṭan al-'arabī", 57–60, and Yāsīn, *Al-thālūth al-muḥarram*, 147 where the author determines the percentage of religious programmes on Syrian television to be 5 per cent.

in schools came increasingly to include Islamic discourse from a Wahhabi viewpoint, sometimes ornamented with specious reformist phraseology about the unity of the Islamic *umma*, the role of Islam in social progress, and the promotion of women in society, among other topical subjects. During the Nasserist period in Egypt and in Baathist Syria and Iraq, emphasis had been placed on a purported link between Islam and Socialism.[116]

But there were differences. Syrian school curricula distinguished between Arabism and Islam, a distinction that was weak in Iraqi or Egyptian textbooks; so also was encouragement of women's employment overall and beyond what had been recognised as professions appropriate for women, such as nursing or clerical assistance. Syrian books alone looked into traditional proofs for the existence of God, a scrutiny lacking from other national curricula.[117] School books in Morocco and Tunisia inclined towards a moral conception of religion with little reference to doctrine, with the Tunisian approach keeping itself at a distance from Salafism. Algerian books followed the Egyptian approach.[118] Tunis in this period seems to have been a laboratory for unconventional educational policies and outcomes, with the Tunisian approach to religious education and the study of history giving rise to a new context of cultural reference, and the relativisation of traditional sources of symbolic authority.[119] Surveys showed that Tunisian students of both sexes regarded figures such as Hitler, Atatürk, and Napoleon as compelling historical figures, while Saladin and Muhammad were relegated to an intermediate position of authority and exemplarity.[120] It was regrettably impossible to obtain similar data – assuming they even existed – for other Arab regions and the likely conclusion to be drawn is that the general pedagogical approach to the teaching of Islam remained fideist in character, even in a country such as Syria.[121]

The Egyptian state was thus active in spreading an al-Azhar-sponsored religious culture. Different types of Islamic discourse, or discourse on Islam,

116 Olivier Carré, *La légitimation islamique des socialismes arabes: Analyse conceptuelle combinatoire des manuels scolaires égyptiens, syriens, et iraqiens* (Paris: Presses de la Fondation nationale des sciences politiques, 1979), 110 ff., 161 ff., chs 9 and 10, passim.

117 Ibid., 27.

118 Ibid., 25–26.

119 Herman Obdeijn, *L'Enseignement de l'histoire dans la Tunisie moderne, 1881–1970* (Tunis : n.p., 1975), 67–71.

120 Ibid., 58.

121 Yāsīn, *Al-thālūth al-muḥarram*, 123.

emanated from Arab regions through various instruments for promoting their ideology. Although the notion of an overarching transnational Islamic *umma* dear to fundamentalist groups was absent from Nasserist discourse, and despite the differentiation in this discourse between the Arab and Muslim fields, in line with pan-Arab political discourse in general, al-Azhar's relative independence and its freedom of manoeuvre enabled it to vandalise this central secular direction of Arab nationalist thought in important ways. This trend, under circumstances that followed the 1967 war with the nationalist states weakened, started becoming tangible outside Egypt in the 1980s and 1990s. Michel 'Aflaq came to emphasise the "organic link" between Arabism and Islam as Saddam Hussein was becoming visibly pious, and inducing Iraqis to be likewise.[122] The Baathist regime in Iraq adopted parallel discourses and affirmed Arabism and Islam separately, blending the two on some occasions, notably during the Iran–Iraq War (1980–1988) and the period after the occupation of Kuwait in 1990–1991.[123] Among the factors facilitating this was the possible relation of metonymy between Arabism and Islam in political discourse as they seemed appropriate to immediate events.[124]

Following independence from France in 1962, Algeria witnessed somewhat similar developments. As we saw earlier, during the colonial period, being a local Algerian and being a Muslim became almost synonymous for most in the confrontation with the coloniser. The leadership of the nationalist Front de Libération Nationale (National Liberation Front) (FLN) had a secular ideology in which Islam served symbolically as a token of cohesion and external differentiation. This had far-reaching results. In the long term, it prepared at least some ground to the strengthening of the Islamists at the expense of the more secularist elements within the FLN, the idea of identification of religion and nationality in the face of colonialists of a different religion having long been familiar. Yet the realisation of these initially latent and symbolic notions, and their transformation into programmatic political and social material, at variance with the basic ideological principles of the Front, took place only in the 1980s, by which time the wholesale importation

122 Mārlīn Naṣr, *Al-taṣṣawur al-qawmī al-ʿarabī fī fikr Jamāl ʿAbd al-Nāṣir (1952–1970): Dirāsa fī ʿilm al-mufradāt wa al-dalāla*, Silsilat Uṭrūḥāt al-Dukturāh 2 (Beirut: Markaz Dirāsāt al-Waḥda al-ʿArabiyya, 1981), 344–347, 360–362.

123 al-Anṣārī, *Taḥawwulāt al-fikr wa al-siyāsa fī al-sharq al-ʿarabī 1930–1970*, 122–129.

124 Aziz al-Azmeh, "Islamism and Arab nationalism", *Review of Middle Eastern Studies* 4 (1988): 41–42.

of teachers of Arabic had begun to result in consequences, especially as many of these teachers came from Egypt, among whom very many were Muslim Brothers. The economy of symbolic capital changed with the rearrangement of its constituent elements, secularism and Francophone culture becoming linked and even identified, at a time when Islamisation was associated with cultural Arabisation through social agency carrying a band of possible locations between Reformism and fundamentalism. After the social and economic crises over which the FLN presided, especially after the death of Houari Boumedienne in 1978, conflict within state hierarchies between Francophones linked to cultural secularism and the material possibility of a "Western" lifestyle, and Arabophones linked to conservatism and a narrowing of social horizons and possibilities ensued, the latter deploying a programme formulated in Islamic moralising language. This conflict in many cases was connected with ethnic associations, paralleling the Arab/Berber distinction that arose under these circumstances, following a period during which the leadership of the FLN was largely in the hands of *évolué* secular intellectuals of Berber extraction, such as Hocine Ait Ahmed (1926–2015), who had constructed a basis for action by crafting the concept of national liberation in the manner described above.

Many elements arising from the evolution of the situation in Algeria can with some contextual adaptation be applied to Morocco, although the ethnic dimension was present in less acute form. But in Morocco, Arabism as a current of cultural commitment was closer to the liberal wing of Islamic Reformism than to fundamentalism. It also introduced into the secular culture prevailing among the cultural elite elements of *rapprochement* between secularism and religion, with the one paying compliments to the other, and the claim that they were mutually supportive in the project of nation building almost to the point where distinctions were blurred. This blurring was accentuated with the passage of time into the twenty-first century, a process, if one were to refer to earlier discussions, of "Egyptianisation". This trend might well be symbolised by the Moroccan philosopher and latter-day Averroist Muhammad 'Abid al-Jabiri (1935–2010). He has had a huge pan-Arab audience, helped by considerable institutional support, catering to an insatiable political taste for rhetorical Arab-Islamic irenicism in the Arab World arising in the conditions following 1967. In this atmosphere, the work of another Moroccan, Abdallah Laroui, far more in control of conceptual rigour, was relegated to ritual references of appreciation, but in effect submerged under the fog of Jabiri's pleasing senses of certainty.

This wriggles between reclamations of authenticity and of modernity, Islam and the West, squaring circles in a compromise so elusive in these general terms as to have the quality of suppressing both exploration and controversy.[125] The context was the ideological capitulation of the main bodies of secular nationalists to Islamist concepts of history and society as arose at the close of the Cold War, with the appeal to democracy and to notions of a "historical block" as the mainstays of a "civilisational project". This entailed to these nationalists giving ideological concessions to Islamism – chiefly, as regards secularism – with no quid pro quo, enabling Islamist projects of cultural hegemony.

The position of the Tunisian state with regard to Islam was the clearest despite being composed in part of elements with imprecise meanings open to multiple and sometimes contradictory referents, such as "the spirit of Islam" or the "true reality of Islam", which could indeed be susceptible to interpretations opposed in sense to the political or cultural intent behind official Tunisian discourse. Scrutiny of the journal *al-Fikr* founded in 1955 by Muhammad Mzali (1925–2010), a prominent intellectual and politician, shows that there was, as in other Arab journals, little interest in religion. Articles that did engage with religion equivocated in the reformist manner, here pushed to the limits of possibility. Scripture is held rather like a relic or a museum exhibit, beyond history, and not probed. Yet interpretation when this did occur tended to be audacious, implicitly allowing these texts' contents to be invalidated, in the name of the text. There was an emphasis on respecting social evolution and the necessities of history and going beyond the exterior form in order to attain "spirit and meaning". Articles called for a consideration of the reality of history, drawing consequences from such as the fact that three of the four Rightly-Guided Caliphs died violently, disallowing folk romanticisation of that period. There were ritual calls for Islam to be saved from stagnation.[126] At the same time articles were published critical of pan-Islamism and in praise of Turkish secularism.[127]

125 In English: Mohammed Abed al-Jabri, *The Formation of Arab Reason* (London: I. B. Tauris, 2010). His large output, academic in appearance but an ideological fantasy to the core, has been the subject of a thorough, precise, and devastating analysis by Jūrj Ṭarābīshī, in a four-volume study of the overall themes of medieval Arab intellectual history: *Naẓariyyat al-ʿaql al-ʿarabī*; *Ishkāliyyāt al-ʿaql al-ʿarabī*; *Waḥdat al-ʿaql al-ʿarabī*; *Al-ʿaql al-mustaqīl fī'l-islām* (Beirut: Dār al-Sāqī, 2002–2004).

126 See, for example, ʿĀmir Ghadīra, "Limādhā anā muslim wa kayfa anā muslim?" *al-Fikr* 9 (1960): 9–28, and Farḥāt al-Dashrāwī, "Alā anqidhū al-islām", *Fikr* 1 (1963): 40–42.

127 Muḥammad al-ʿItrī, "Al-thawra al-turkiyya wa al-thawra al-yābāniyya", *Fikr* 5 (1956): 5–14.

Perhaps one of the most coherent texts to express the official situation in Bourguiba's Tunisia was the lecture delivered in 1965 by the Tunisian sociologist Abdelwahab Bouhdiba (b. 1932) on the occasion of the Muslim *laylat al-qadr*, Night of Destiny in Ramadan AH 1385, in the presence of President Bourguiba and the Mufti of the Tunisian Republic, the determinedly modernist al-Fadl Ben Achour (1909–1970). The Mufti opened the session with a statement encouraging believers to take an interest in modern life.[128] The starting point of Bouhdiba's lecture was that Islam was one constituent element of the Tunisian nation, but this Islam had to open its horizons, avow that it did not monopolise the truth, and should not take a narrow Talmudic understanding of things. The Muslim religion needed to transcend the formalism of Qur'anic institutions and reach for the interior, for what is original and essential in religion, that is to say the human conscience, the source of values. The mission of religion was to revive the religious conscience as a source of virtues, disregarding traditional religious disciplines.[129] Thus, the social and cognitive attributes of religion were pronounced obsolete, and religion is integrated into the context of secular life as a personal and individual disposition, addressing conscience and urging restraint from turpitude and encouragement to virtue, without intervening in public life and without any need for institutionalisation. The text contains an Islamic Reformist modernism taken to its furthest extent insofar as it contains no criticism of Islam or religions as such, but highly critical of a type of religious practice characterised by immobility and resistance to progress. The Tunisian state did not tamper with the symbolic authority of religion; untouched and untouchable as such, it retained the possibility of contrasting and contrary interpretations. This preserved an area that might become an ideological battleground, as it did indeed become after Bourguiba's removal from office in 1987, and by the adoption by his successor, Zayn al-'Abidin Ben Ali (b. 1936) of an Islamic visual profile, appearing on huge posters around the country wearing the ritual garments of Meccan pilgrims, and announcing himself as the protector of religion as well as of the fatherland in the campaign for the 1989 presidential elections.

128 'Abd al-Wahhāb Būḥdība, *Al-ḍamīr al-dīnī fī al-mujtama' al-ḥadīth* (Tunis: al-Dār al-Tūnisiyya li'l-Nashr, 1968), 10–11.

129 Ibid., 16–20, 23–24, 34, 39.

This change in practice came as though it were a delayed announcement of developments in Arab cultural and political life that had started earlier in other countries. As indicated above, the period following the Second World War, under the overall auspices of the Truman Doctrine, a global anti-Communist ideological movement of various forms under European or US sponsorship or through local initiatives was put in place, with huge logistical machinery and capacities. This movement had a clear form in Islamic lands, and encouraged Islamic religious practice and associated political movements as a rampart against Communist "infiltration". These developments were swept along in the new currents of thought on the importance of Islam sponsored by the United States in the 1950s and the 1960s, based on opposition to Communism, the Soviet Union, and nationalist movements.[130] It came frequently to be claimed that a special bond connected the Arabs to Pakistan rather than to Greece, for instance, despite the frequency with which numerous Arab voices saw in the creation of Pakistan from the outset a development similar to the founding of Israel: a state created and sponsored by colonialism on the basis of an ethno-religious concept, and a way of fragmenting the Indian anti-colonial nationalist effort.[131] This is also clear enough from American political science literature of the 1950s. This had a direct effect on the religious "opening" in Turkey and the return of religious teaching (on a voluntary basis) to schools in 1949, and indeed the expansion of the religious education sector overall.[132] In 1950 an institution for training imams and preachers was established, and a faculty of theology opened in the University of Ankara in 1949. The purchase of foreign currency for pilgrims was authorised and the ban on the use of Arabic for the call to prayer was lifted. The seeds were sown in Turkey of the beginning of politico-religious movements, with as a consequence state-induced social changes, including facilitating the rise of a provincial bourgeoisie in areas that the state, with its ideological apparatus, was unable to penetrate sufficiently. Underemployment and blocked horizons among the educated

---

130 This topic is now being actively researched. See Robert Dreyfuss, *Devil's Game. How the United States Helped Unleash Fundamentalist Islam* (New York: Owl Books – Henry Hilt and Company, 2005).

131 Kurd ʿAlī, *Al-mudhakkirāt*, 1,242–1,243 and ʿAbd al-Raḥmān al-Bazzāz, *Hādhihi qawmīyyatunā* (Cairo: Dār al-Qalam, 1963), 207–212.

132 For instance, Walter Laqueur, *Communism and Nationalism in the Middle East* (London: Routledge, 1956); Rustow, "Politics and Islam in Turkey, 1920–1955", 93.

of humbler origins, similar to what exists in the Arab world and across the developing world, and towards the end of the nineteenth century as well, all precipitated the sorts of changes that have been witnessed in Turkey since the turn of the millennium.[133]

In the Arab world the social changes due to the effects of oil revenues were accompanied by an Islamic ideological offensive from countries on the eastern shores of the Red Sea and adjoining regions, to which the last chapter will return. This Islamist current of thought and personal conduct, inflected by Wahhabism as the standard model of fundamentalist Salafism, grew after the defeat of June 1967 and notably in the 1970s when educational, media, and cultural infrastructures of oil-producing countries began rapid and comprehensive expansion. The Islamist current also grew through its nurture of large numbers of intellectuals residing in the Gulf and elsewhere, along with Arab cultural institutes and, as in Saudi Arabia, by disseminating a wholly fundamentalist culture, novel to the larger sections of Arab populations. Kuwait and Bahrain enjoyed large margins of secular freedoms. The spread of Wahhabisation also came from the repatriation to various Arab countries of a large number of residents and former residents influenced by a highly conservative religiosity induced by the official culture and education of Saudi Arabia and her neighbours. And indeed, religion and the spread of particular types of Islamic discourse became a very lucrative occupation. The Islamic formulation of cultural and social affairs thus came to acquire a practical legitimacy that had been absent in the 1950s and 1960s, and sought parity with that of the practical and historical culture disseminated by Arab states for a century in broad and central areas of the Arab world. Particularly in Egypt, a deep-rooted opposition to Communism at the heart of the governing regime accompanied this Islamic resurgence as well as broad, expansive powers for al-Azhar, in addition to the encouragement given by Anwar al-Sadat in the 1970s to radical fundamentalist movements in the hope of eliminating Communist and other left-wing influence in working-class and student circles.

133 Şerif Mardin, "Religion in modern Turkey", *International Social Science Journal* 19/2 (1977): 279–297, 288–289, 292–293. For these subsequent developments, see Joshua D. Hendrick, *Gülen: The Ambiguous Politics of Market Islam in Turkey and the World* (New York: New York University Press, 2014); Necati Polat, *Regime Change in Contemporary Turkey* (Edinburgh: Edinburgh University Press, 2016); Caroline Tee, *The Gülen Movement. The Politics of Islam and Modernity* (London: I. B. Tauris, 2016).

Television also gave increasing prominence to Shaykhs whose deeply reactionary views and the extensive Saudi connections of many of whom led to the imposition of a siege on secularism, word as well as concept, which the next chapter will study in detail. The modernist Islamic Reformist tendency after the model of Muhammad 'Abduh lost ground and only a few Islamic thinkers would be bold enough to defend the value of 'Abd al-Raziq or Taha Hussein.[134] The advocates of free interpretation and for historical contextualisation in the religious domain tended to become fewer in number.[135] So also were affirmations that Islam was not a political system and that its governments had been worldly throughout history;[136] the view that religion and politics were separate domains came to strike an increasingly odd tone.[137] Indeed the atmosphere had become such, and the rush to conform to ostentatious shows of religiosity so oppressive, that some of those who affirmed the civil character of political power were obliged to make amends by uncalled for, ritual disavowals of 'Abd al-Raziq.[138] Manners of dress started to change, women's attire being the most significantly visible. The public sphere was occupied increasingly centrally by supernatural discourse, stultifying and highly reactionary, of Solomon subduing the jinn, riding the winds, his dialogues with birds (as recounted in the Qur'an), Moses cleaving the waters of the Red Sea, the physical nature of suffering in hell: all this became, unapologetically, common sense and objective truth.[139] Scorn for science and objectivity knew no bounds and dense volumes were published, deriving modern knowledge from the Qur'an.[140] This engendered widespread intellectual quackery, at best intellectual derangement, as when computers were used to unlock the secrets of wisdom behind the distribution of the so-called Mysterious Letters in the text of the Qur'an.[141] Comparisons with US Evangelicanism are very suggestive.

---

134 Amīn, *Dalīl al-muslim al-ḥazīn*, 113–127.

135 al-Majd, *Ḥiwār la muwājaha*, 42; Amīn, *Ḥawl al-da'wa ilā taṭbīq al-sharī'a al-islāmiyya*, 61.

136 al-Majd, *Ḥiwār lā muwājaha*, 82–83, 115–119. Muḥammad Aḥmad Khalafallāh, "Al-ṣaḥwa al-islāmiyya fī Miṣr", in *Al-ḥarakāt al-islāmiyya al-mu'āṣira fī al-waṭan al-'arabī*, ed. Markaz Dirāsāt al-Waḥda al-'Arabiyya (Beirut: Markaz Dirāsāt al-Waḥda al-'Arabiyya, 1987), 83–84.

137 Khalafallāh, "Al-ṣaḥwa al-islāmiyya fī Miṣr", 93–95.

138 Abū al-Majd, *Ḥiwār la muwājaha*, 77.

139 Maḥmūd, *Ḥiwār ma'a ṣadīqī al-mulḥid* 17, 32.

140 Ḥanafi Aḥmad, *Al-tafsīr al-'ilmī li al-āyāt al-kawniyya fī al-Qur'ān*, 2nd edn (Cairo: Dār al-Ma'ārif, 1980).

141 Mahmūd, *Ḥiwār ma'a ṣadīqī al-mulḥid*, 108–113.

Egypt was not the only instance of encouragement of Wahhabified religious movements by a nationalist state, although the results elsewhere did not have the same effect on the nature of official culture as rapidly or as thoroughly. There was a tendency towards a degree, albeit modest, of giving the state a shaykhly character, as well as distributing religious literature seen as being in the state's interest, as in Syria in the early 1970s and after the elimination of the Islamic movements in the early 1980s. In these circumstances it is not surprising that Egyptian secular discourse fell behind that of other countries, given that this discourse was produced in a period where the Egyptian state promoted the figure of the shaykh, in parallel with sectarian outbreaks in Egypt in the 1970s and 1980s. This in itself was productive of Egyptian secular discourse by authors such as Faraj Fuda (b. 1946, assassinated by an Islamist in 1992) and the philosopher Fouad Zakaria (1927–2010), and other audacious authors, for by the 1980s, one needed to be especially audacious in Egypt to propound views that would have appeared normal half a century previously.

Participation of the nationalist state in the sabotage of cultural and intellectual foundations on which it had been based for a century or more went beyond disfiguring the content of public culture. The concept of the progressive Arab state, nationalist and in a variety of ways socialist in orientation, and that of left-wing forces generally, had grounded their self-conceptions in a classification of friends and enemies. The latter implied a consequent disavowal of the *status quo ante*, prior to the coups that brought these once progressive forces to power. The nationalist state in effect effaced the achievements of the liberal state that had preceded it, and denounced it. This was a short step towards reprobating liberal progress altogether, and associating this reprobation with even more radical forms of authoritarianism, which was the political desire of Islamism. Thus, the premier Syrian playwright Sa'd Allah Wannus (1941–1997): "We were forced once again into historical vacillation in the face of issues which we could have overcome with the resources at hand, except that we had repudiated the accumulation of [local] Enlightenment, preferring coups d'etat, and the propagation of rhetorical bluster in which critical judgements and security criteria converged."[142] The celebration of Socialism was at a

142 Sa'd Allāh Wannūs, "Bi mathābat taqdīm", in *Ṭaḥa Ḥusayn: Al-'aqlāniyya, al-dimūqrāṭiya al-ḥadātha*, ed. Fayṣal Darrāj, Qaḍāya wa Shahādāt, 1 (Nicosia: Mu'assasat 'Ībāl li'l-Dirāsāt wa al-Nashr, 1990), 11.

time when the previous liberal heritage was rejected. Socialism was an evolved political and economic programme that retreated in the face of the Arab progressive movement's refusal of Socialism's bases – liberal, cultural, intellectual, and cognitive advances, often inimical to authoritarianism.

Socialism came to be a practice of authoritarianism rather than of enlightenment, its vocabularies replete with terms of polemic that betokened intellectual policing – a particular inflection of the language of vituperation against what came to be called "cultural colonialism", in terms that became habitual after the examples of Rashid Rida and Abbas Mahmud al-'Aqqad. Thus, for instance, policing "cultural colonisation", a threat to the cultural security of the nation of which many very distinguished intellectual personalities were accused. Constantine Zurayq was one such accused, associating the American University of Beirut and hostility to Arabism:[143] the university that numbered among its graduates Dr Georges Habash, and where Zurayq himself incubated the extraordinarily potent clandestine Arab nationalism in the al-'Urwa al-Wuthqā Society, a university that spread a culture of progress and anti-sectarianism to the degree that the Lebanese Phalange party considered that it produced "apostate" graduates,[144] through its departure from the system of confessional education in Lebanon.[145] Nationalist culture became rhetorical, ascribing infallibility to itself, given to imprecation, thereby acquiring many of the characteristics of religious polemic. It denied itself the principal element of resistance that it had gained from the heritage of liberalism: rationality, historicism, and breadth of perspective. This nationalist culture was disseminated in an impoverished and formulaic fashion, in an educational system in which curricula were poorly delivered and given insufficient resources. As a result of this overall tendency, along with the prevailing cultural orientation of the oil-rich states, the class of state intellectuals was linked to the state by technocratic service or patronage, later patronage of security services as in Syria. In parallel with this situation, state control was strengthened over the institutions of higher education, with the exception of al-Azhar, and the institutional structures of Islam. Intellectuals,

---

143 For example Ghālī Shukrī, "Istrātījiyyāt al-isti'mār al-jadīd fī ma'rakat al-thaqāfa al-'arabiyya", *al-Ṭalī'a* 7 (1967): 15–16.

144 Fāris, *Al-naza'āt al-ṭa'ifiyya fī tārīkh lubnān al-ḥadīth*, 137, n. 152.

145 See the observations on Constantin Zurayq and the American University in Beirut in Mārūn 'Abbūd, *Mu'allafāt Mārūn 'Abbūd, al-majmū'a al-kāmila* (Beirut: Dār Mārūn 'Abbūd, Dār al-Thaqāfa, 1966–1967), 671–683.

once the mainstay of revolutionary regimes, became a corps of pliant and often supine technocrats and functionaries.

In these circumstances combined, it was difficult for secularism to hold its intellectual and socio-cultural grain against attrition by countervailing forces, including the force of social inertia. We have already seen that secularism had been implicit in social relations and modes of cognition, and that a conciliatory relationship to religion was above all a matter of course, as religion had few points of intersection with social and political practice, and as some secular political forces sought to instrumentalise religion. The trucial condition prevailed generally, especially the mainstream Leftist tendencies with a populist inflection when liberals tended to greater consistency in their secularism, although some inclined towards adopting positions akin to those of Islamic Reformism as a default position in situations of defence. In time, some went the whole hog and came to forestall further controversy by concessions that tended to weaken their position mortally. Indeed, some deployed a pseudo-historical argument common among Islamist polemicists as they announced that the issue of secularism did not arise, it being unnecessary because of the absence of a priesthood in Islam. The avant-garde literary review *Ḥiwār* (1961–1967), for example, published articles to this effect by the philosopher Syed Hossein Nasr (b. 1933), then the Shah of Iran's and the Shahbanu's philosopher, and by the historian Hassan Saʿab (b. 1922), the then non-clerical, presentable intellectual face of Lebanese Sunni communalism. The journal, edited by Tawfiq Sayigh, which also published Sadiq al-Azm and avant-garde poetry, closed promptly once it was revealed, and when the editor learned that its backers, the Berlin-based Congress for Cultural Freedom, was a Central Intelligence Agency (CIA) organism – no connection is made here between its editorial decisions and CIA preferences.

There is little doubt that this amiable tolerance of ambitious historical adversaries was connected to dispositions by Arab left-wing movements that generally abstained from taking stock in practical ways of societal archaism. The only exceptions were movements on the left that took seriously the obstruction of emancipation and advancement by patriarchal and religious structures. This matter did not escape the attention of critics of the mainstream left in its heyday. It was reproached for shying away from intervention in social matters such as personal status[146] and for reticence in confronting

146 Ghāda al-Sammān, "Al-thawra al-jinsiyya wa al-thawra al-shāmila", *Mawāqif* 12 (1970): 68.

mythical public pronouncements.[147] It was commonly affirmed that the negative attitude of Arab revolutionaries towards social revolution constituted a consecration of revolution's enemies. Arab Communists and those influenced by them or who adopted socialism directly or indirectly were among those primarily responsible for this situation;[148] they were also generally responsible for the ideological training given to important sectors of those involved in cultural activities in socialist national states – it needs to be recalled in fairness that the People's Democratic Republic of Yemen (1967–1990) had been far ahead of the others in this domain. Political considerations apart, a determinist historical materialist metaphysics seems to have justified the ease with which ideological concessions were made. This was a metaphysics according to which the consequences of alliances, including ideological concessions made to serve temporary purposes, were waystations on the path of an inevitable realisation of Communism. This goes some considerable way towards explaining the egregious opportunism of these Communist parties in Arab countries, similar in many respects to that of the Islamic parties – equally confident of victory.

It was unusual to find openly hostile attitudes to religion; this was anyway more common among radical Baathists than among Communists. One instance from the time of the neo-Baath in Syria was a notorious 1967 article written by an officer, editor of the weekly magazine of the Syrian armed forces: "The Arab nation sought help from divinity, it sought out old values in Islam and Christianity, it called on the help from feudalism and capitalism and some of the regimes of government known in the Middle Ages, and none of this was any help . . . the only way to construct the civilisation of the Arabs and to build Arab society is to create the new Arab Socialist who believes that God, religions, feudalism, capitalism, bloated exploiters and all prevailing values in society to be merely embalmed figures in the museums of history."[149] This article became the pretext for Islamist disturbances with their origins in the opposition of bazaar merchants to the regime weighing down on business and nationalising large sections of the private sector. The author of the article was arrested, and the symbolic price was accepted quickly.

More common was self-defence against accusations of atheism, together the ritual affirmation of the progressive role, as belief in spiritual values,

147 Khalīl, "Maḍmūn al-usṭūra fī al-fikr al-ʿarabī", 62–70.
148 Cf. al-Akhḍar, "Min naqd al-samāʾ ila naqd al-arḍ", 26–29, 39.
149 Ibrāhīm Khalāṣ, "Istanjadat al-umma bi'l-ilāh", *Jaysh al-Shaʿab*, 24 April 1967.

ascribed to religion on occasion, more typically in Egypt, allied to what was presented as a scientific analysis of the purported role of religious heritage in social progress.[150] The invention of Islamic socialism was a component in the ideological output of Nasserism, and intellectuals who adopted this course did not only defend themselves against accusations of atheism but adopted methods that were conciliatory to Islamic Reformism, squaring many circles as previously argued. Standards for evaluation from very distinct points of reference, religious and secular, were grafted upon one another, the one interpreted through the lens of the other. Religious symbols were deployed in socialist interpretation that gave these symbols a boundless capacity for extension. Thus, the Muhammadan virtues and deeds became socialist virtues and deeds, as in the very well-known hagiographic *Bildungsroman* by the popular novelist 'Abd al-Rahman al-Sharqawi (1920–1987), *Muhammad the Apostle of Freedom* (1962).[151]

Socialist discourse inclined towards a panegyric discourse in the heroic mode, apparently unaware of or indifferent to consequences of the continuous use of religious symbols beyond their appropriate areas of deployment, not least that such symbols, duly spread, are better and more consistently and consequently used by Islamists than by others, Islamists who use them with a greater sense of ease and a surer and more sincere hand. Historical rationality is in effect suspended from considerations of religious heritage when the last was used instrumentally. Thus, for one Lebanese Communist, the Qur'an was the forerunner of historical materialism. The Book stressed "the importance of calculation, and even more: the Qur'an says 'we have calculated the measure of each thing.' This is very similar to the modern idea that all manifestations of nature and thought, in addition to their being subject to specific and known dialectic principles, are closely linked to the exact sciences and especially mathematics, biology and physics . . . Recently the sweeping technical and scientific revolution of the past twenty years has confirmed the validity of the Qur'an's intuitions in a surprising fashion, with its cybernetic models."[152]

---

150 For example, Luṭfī al-Khūlī, "Mulāḥaẓāt ḥawl al-ṣirā' al-fikri fī mujtama'inā", *al-Ṭalī'a* 16 (1966): 23–24.

151 'Abd al-Raḥmān al-Sharqāwī, *Muḥammad rasūl al-ḥurrīya* (Cairo: 'Ālam al-Kutub, 1962), 52–53, 72–73, and passim.

152 Muḥammad ' Ītānī, *Al-qur'ān fī ḍaw' al-fikr al-māddī al-jadalī* (Beirut: Dār al-'Awda, 1972), 97.

Heritage was divided into the valid for purposes of the present, and the defective, not on grounds of historical assessment but on a basis of wishful thinking, a heritage deprived of its temporality and independence from the present, heritage "as a guide to the future and an anticipation of what is to come, based on an overwhelming teleology, moulding the past after the image of a future already past".[153] The Lebanese Communist Hussein Muruwwa (b. 1910, assassinated in 1987) and the Syrian Marxist Tayyib Tizini (b. 1934) both wrote multi-volume studies of classical Arabic and Muslim thought; this was quite a genre in the 1970s and 1980s, from which we have multi-volume studies of classical Arab and Muslim intellectual history also by, among others, the poet Adonis (a doctoral thesis at the Université Saint Joseph, Beirut) and the philosophy professor Muhammad 'Abid al-Jabiri. From the perspective of Muruwwa and Tizini considered to be historical materialist, Arab and Muslim heritage had no effective dimension of historicity, and no historical self-sufficiency. In the framework of a scholastic form of Marxism, this intellectual history of the medieval period was characterised by them in terms of the contrast between progressive forces and retrograde forces, in the perspective of a Marxism whose utter artlessness was matched only by the enormity of the effort deployed by these authors.[154] As this Marxist revaluation of Arab and Muslim bookish heritage was figured after the patterns of Islamic Reformism on the one hand and teleology on the other, these intellectuals were not content to leave the past in its independence of us, and to turn towards a hoped-for future from a precise moment in the present, but went on to link the future directly to the past, in a perspective from which the concrete historical present was absent. Consideration of the present moment was absent at a determinate and fully fledged, sui generis historical moment; it was conceived, as was the future, primarily under the aspect of a seamless continuity with the past that, itself, was normatively divided between desirable progressive (such as Mu'tazilism, forms of philosophical thinking described as materialist) and undesirable retrograde elements (idealism). Marxist historiography therefore adopted a conception of historical continuity that was located within Islamic Reformist apologetics and nationalist romanticism, to the exclusion of history as an

153 al-'Aẓma, *Al-turāth bayn al-sulṭān wa al-ta'rīkh*, 17.

154 For a critique of such work see the contributions of Nāyif Ballūz, 'Alī Ḥarb, and Bū 'Alī Yāsīn in *Al-mārksiyya wa al-turāth al-'arabī* (Beirut: Dār al-Hadātha, 1980).

autonomous domain conceptually as well as ontologically, one that can do without us.

It was as though the authors of this approach were in a position sufficiently transcendent and sovereign as to be able to manipulate elements deriving from continuity with the past at will, retaining the desirable and agreeable and casting off what they find distasteful or reactionary or unsuitable into a world of forgetfulness. Radical left-wing critics of the communism represented by Communist parties used a similar approach but with different historical *dramatis personae* of preference, and with a different accent, one placed upon normative and sentimental exemplarity rather than assertions of historical continuity. Thus, an affection for Abu Dharr al-Ghifari (d. 652) as a proto-socialist, for instance, and appreciation of the Qarmatians (ninth–tenth centuries) for the communism ascribed to them polemically by their critics, and for their supposed rationalism and atheism, evidently with scant knowledge of their history or of the severe authoritarian conceptions of the history of the imamate.[155] This very imamate, together with Sufism, were seen as the root of modernity: such is the reading of Adonis, who considered that these trends exemplified one of the two modes of history that he discerned – change and constancy, transformation and stagnation – his preference being for the dynamism and promise of the former that, he believed, implied a constant modernity, to be continually evoked for creativity in the future. Creativity is here taken as an abstract form of activity without determination or specification, perhaps a poet's fetish conceit. This, in Adonis's view, was in contrast to the Sunni heritage that betokened rigidity and tyranny, being thereby a mainstay of backwardness.[156] For his part, Jabiri did not diverge from this historiographic framework of continuities permitting voluntarist reconnection; his positive figures of choice were Ibn Rushd and Ibn Khaldun, whence he sought rationality and enlightenment; his pet enemies were Ibn Sina, mystics, imamites.[157] It needs hardly be emphasised that the secular notion of history as the domain of change and of historical mutations, of historical practice as implying anachronism as a

155 al-Akhḍar, "Min naqd al-samā' ilā naqd al-arḍ", 41, 53–54, and passim.

156 'Azīz al-'Aẓma, "Istishrāq al-aṣāla: Adūnīs wa al-turāth", in al-'Aẓma, *Al-turāth bayn al-sulṭān wa al-ta'rīkh*, 146–160. Cf. Mahdī 'Āmil, *Azmat al-ḥaḍāra al-'arabiyya am azmat al-burjwazīyāt al-'arabiyya?* (Beirut: Dār al-Fārābi, 1979), 84 ff. 100 ff.

157 'Azīz al-'Aẓma, "Fī tārīkhiyyat al-'aql wa naqd al-'aql", in al-'Aẓma, *Al-turāth bayn al-sulṭān wa al-ta'rīkh*, 129–145.

major concept, is subjected to corrosive attrition the wider such historiographies of nostalgia and exemplarity are spread, not least in a domain like that of Arab culture in the period under discussion, in which Islamists had actually succeeded in making "heritage" into a prime preoccupation and into a favoured domain in which the anti-secular and anti-modernist culture war was waged. By destroying the idea of breaks in history and founding the idea of continuity, historism enters the game of historical essentialism by which Islamist historiography is structured, as previously shown, and makes their favoured historiographic modules habitual to the degree that they come to appear as common sense.

The historist notion of continuity, here, as we saw, modified by a voluntarist perspective, did not only impair the developing and expanding conceptual possibilities of secularisation. The same conception lies at the heart of a type of corporate state that agglutinates around itself entire social units of birth and descent – ethnic, religious, spatial. Such a state, which in political science literature goes by the name of consociational, is one of socio-political annexation in which the state forms a vertical hinge of self-enclosed units and, as in the case of the Lebanese state – and in the past fifteen years, extending to Iraq and Syria – forming a membrane for socio-political relations, without there being a stable network for such relations. In this arrangement, private institutions, often known as civil, share sovereignty with the state: these include local leaderships based on family and religious confession, and financial conglomerates with potentially armed complements sharing, with the state, the deployment for organised violence, and sharing with one another the oligarchic and patrimonial arrangement of public affairs.[158] Within the subordinating state, confessionalism is based on the ideological and historiographic trope of continuity, presented by its adepts as an adequate explanation of a situation of great socio-historical complexity.[159] This arrangement emerged in Lebanon from various historical contexts that divested capitalism of its capacities for abstraction, and

158 Waḍḍāḥ Sharāra, *Ḥurūb al-istitbā' aw Lubnān al-ḥarb al-ahliyya al-dā'ima* (Beirut: Dar al-Ṭalī'a, 1979), 651 and Edmond Rabbath, "Quel Liban demain?", *L'Orient-Le Jour*, 3 April 1977 and 4 April 1977.

159 Fu'ād Shāhīn, *Al-ṭā'ifiyya fī Lubnan: Ḥādiruhā wa judhūruhā al-tārīkhiyya wa al-ijtimā'iyya* (Beirut: Dār al-Ḥadātha, 1980), 19–28, 129; Ussama Makdisi, *The Culture of Sectarianism: Community, History and Violence in Nineteenth-Century Lebanon* (Berkeley: University of California Press, 2000).

also limited its possibilities of even a properly statist policy pursued under the strong presidency of Fouad Chehab (1902–1973) from 1958 to 1964, which succeeded only in suspending temporarily the patrimonial segmentation of political authority.[160] The Lebanese state followed the template of the nineteenth-century European fantasy, the idea of a mosaic society, transposed to policy, coming to acquire reality in recent years.

The erosion of citizenship attendant upon this was starting to spread across the Arab World in the eighties, in a variety of forms. The 1989 Jordanian election law made parliamentary representation include ethnic and confessional quotas. The Egyptian situation was the most dangerous – before things got worse there and elsewhere in subsequent decades – amid a rising political and social Islamisation, with serious discussions of issues of apostasy that would have been considered fantastical in previous decades, and clamorous insistence upon "the application of shari'a". The communitarian strife of the 1980s resulted from political, economic, and social conditions, some of which have been discussed and that will come up again in the next chapter. "Christian families" were formed as public organisations to confront "Muslim families" in the universities, while in Upper Egypt clashes – usually over land, water, and other matters of crucial importance – took on the character of internecine confessional conflict. This reflected the state's inability to control and regulate the apparatus of government amid a situation of systemic crisis.[161] Suggestions were made using archaising Islamist language, without raising eyebrows any more, for working out a "covenant" embodying the spirit of Muhammadan, Medinan intergroup conventions (the *Ṣaḥīfa*) on the basis of the primacy ascribed to an Islamic political identity, and the subordinate, consociational satellitisation of Christians.[162] Such suggestions were only possible on the understanding that citizens are not so much individual free persons but as members of groups defined by birth rather than by volition or formation. It implies the negation of secularism that guarantees the state the character of transcendence with respect to civic and private groups, and as the locus of a national

160 Sharāra, *Ḥurūb al-istitbā'*, 241–255; Fawaz Traboulsi, *A History of Modern Lebanon*, 2nd edn (London: Pluto Press, 2012), ch. 9.

161 Yūsuf, *Al-Aqbāṭ wa al-qawmiyya al-'arabiyya*, 163–187.

162 Fahmī Huwaydī, "Bayān min ajl al-waḥda", *al-Ahrām*, 9 May 1989.

political culture transcending collectivities of birth. Prevailing discourse of this type counterposes the fact of secularisation to the purported continuity that predetermines the classes of citizens communally. This discourse was and still is an invitation to regression: from a society of politically defined autonomous individuals to one of individuals politicised from birth in confessional or ethnic terms. This discourse asserts the savagely identitarian definition of an individual that throws back what might be defined and wished as "political animal" to the realm of biology.

6
Secularism at the Turn of the Millennium in the Context of its Adversaries

Over a not inconsiderable period, the Arab world has witnessed two interconnected phenomena. The first is the rapid growth of religious propaganda and preaching, calling for the re-organisation of state and society around a decidedly rigid, literalist, and exclusivist template, claiming to be a salutary return to the textual and mythic authorities invoked by this propaganda. This call is emblematised visually by symbols of commitment, such as ostentatious displays of devotion and piety. The second, correlative phenomenon is assiduous attempts to compel others to comply with what Islamic propagandists consider to be the necessary desiderata for remodelling society on bases pleasing to God and to themselves. These include the veil, called for on every possible occasion, however inappropriate, and the deployment of violence to impose the declamations of a single, clamorous voice in these matters: violence against individuals – particularly women – in Algeria, for example, against a whole society on which Islamic legislation was imposed, as in Sudan, violence against state, intellectuals, and Christians in Egypt in the 1980s, and against the Syrian state in the late 1970s. It is clear that these developments were only possible because of the increased organisational, political, and logistical capacities of the Islamic groups and the growth of their cultural and political influence. These developments would not have occurred had it not been for the increased attention given to religious discourse in general, and the expansion of the field of social, political, and cultural action labelled religious. The resulting self-confidence, and the attrition, by repetition, of any sense of embarrassment were manifest, for example, in the announcement by a professor in the University of Abhā in south-western Saudi Arabia that it is polygamy that is the fundamental form of marriage, monogamy being the resort of necessity only. Similarly, the Egyptian Muslim Brother clerical grandee Muhammad al-Ghazali expressed surprise that any embarrassment should be felt about polygamy, which was, as he said, a salutary Muhammadan practice.[1]

These developments taking place from the 1970s and 1980s are connected to the reluctance of Arab national states – secular in character as previously shown – to assume their responsibilities towards their citizens as private actors to set up parallel sources of authority, and the tendency of the state to display various degrees of shaykhification and only timidly warding off Islamist propaganda. In Egypt, the Ministry of Justice did not react against a provincial appeals court judge, Justice Mahmud Abd al-Hamid Ghurab (1935–1993), who persisted in passing judgments in a civil court over which he presided on the basis of what he considered to be the prescriptions of shari'a, desisting from applying the law of the land, despite the procedural impossibility of implementation for his judgments – such as, in 1987, imposing the sentence of flogging (unavailable in Egyptian penal law) for drinking (on which there is no ban in Egypt). This judge's indifference to the harm caused by his actions to the interests of citizens involved in lawsuits speaks volumes, as does his violation of law and of his oath, taken by all judges and stipulating that the law and the Constitution should be respected.[2] He was not disciplined, and the president of the republic, Hosni Mubarak, sent a representative to his funeral.

The complex interactions between private initiatives, many connected with polemics initiated by the Islamist media connected to the Muslim Brothers and other groups, is perhaps displayed most consequently in the notorious tribulations of Nasr Abu Zayd (1943–2010) during the period 1992 to 1994, which well illustrates the ambiguities of the relationship between Islamist political expansion in the public sphere, agitators and demagogues, greed, a complaisant and indifferent state, a vulnerable and enfeebled legal institution, and brittle cultural production, together yielding further attrition of the constitution and integrity of both state and legal institutions. Abu Zayd

---

1 Darwīsh Junainah in *Al-Muslimūn*, 19–25 January 1990.

2 See Sa'd al-'Utaibī, "Namūdhajān min al-raqāba al-shar'īya 'alā al-anẓima wa'l-qawānīn", http://www.saaid.net/Doat/otibi/119.htm (5 March 2018). Compare the observations of Yūsuf, *Al-Aqbāṭ wa al-qawmiyya al-'arabiyya*, 180.

was a faculty member of the Department of Arabic at Cairo University who had applied for promotion to full professorial status. Among the material submitted was work on the Qur'an of a philological and linguistic character, which pursued a moderately modernist hermeneutical reading, very much in the spirit of al-Khuli and Khalafallah, both of whom have been encountered above.[3]

Of the evaluation reports solicited by the university, two were laudatory. Not so was the third, by the firebrand 'Abd al-Sabur Shahin (1929–2010), a professor of shari'a at al-Azhar-Dar al-'Ulum, and a popular preacher at 'Amr b. al-'As mosque in Cairo, who accused Abu Zayd of godlessness, and cited essays by Abu Zayd in which he questioned the continuing validity of Qur'anic provisions for *jizya* and for slavery. The jittery promotion committee voted to deny promotion by seven votes to six, a decision contested by the department and the faculty. All appeals were overruled by higher instances, and Shahin then took the matter to his mosque, denouncing Abu Zayd as an apostate. It did not help that Abu Zayd had commented on the Rayyan Investment Company, a fraudulent scheme on a massive scale whose collapse ruined thousands of small investors who entrusted their life savings to a company that supposedly operated according to the principles of the shari'a, with Shahin as their expert legal advisor.

Finally, the matter was submitted to a court of personal status in private litigation. *Ḥisba* was invoked. This is a category of prosecution in classical Muslim jurisprudence under "enjoining good and forbidding turpitude", which takes individuals to account because of infractions against matters that have religious significance. The procedure is extra-legal in Egypt, but still on the books of personal status legislation. Abu Zayd was charged with apostasy, which when established leads to the dissolution of marriage. The case against him was won by Shahin and other plaintiffs, on appeal in a court whose presiding judge had worked in Saudi Arabia for many years.[4] Abu Zayd went into exile and spent his final years in The Netherlands. He was a victim of the social, cultural, and political expansion of Islamist

3 See Nasr Abū Zayd, *Rethinking the Qur'an: Towards a Humanistic Hermeneutics* (Utrecht: Humanistics University Press, 2004).

4 See, with very different approaches, H. A. Agrama, *Questioning Secularism: Islam, Sovereignty and the Rule of Law in Egypt* (Chicago: University of Chicago Press, 2012), ch. 1 and passim and B. Johansen, "Apostasy as objective depersonalized fact", *Social Research* 70 (2003): 687–710.

organisations, their infiltration of the state apparatus, and the undermining of this apparatus from within, as the state looked on or was complicit through the involvement of members of the then ruling party. In the same time period Islamists assassinated Faraj Fuda, who published scathing and mocking writings on Islamism, in 1992, and attempted to assassinate Naguib Mahfouz in 1994.

This situation, and the continual pressures it produces, have as a direct consequence a greater inclination towards closure, control, and narrow-mindedness on the part of official religious institutions. The University of al-Azhar intervened enthusiastically in investigating and disciplining one of its professors of Spanish literature, who had produced a competent translation of a novel of Mario Vargas Llosa that the al-Azhar authorities, instigated by the newspaper *al-Sha'b* (the organ of the Islamic alliance) considered to have the effect of corrupting morals. This led the translator to comment, rightly and bravely under the circumstances, that this practice of seizure and confiscation could also be applied to many classical works of Arabic literature.[5] And while official Islamic institutions successfully rebuffed pressure to ban and confiscate a recording of a song by the musical star and national icon Muhammad Abd al-Wahhab (1902–1991),[6] they turned from the sublime to the ridiculous and made no objection to the decision of the Egyptian People's Assembly to order the confiscation of Ibn 'Arabi's (d. 1240) major mystical treatise *Al-futūḥāt al-makkiyya* in 1979, displeasing to the Wahhabi-minded. The Directorate of Publication and Research in al-Azhar was the entity that decided to impound Louis 'Awaḍ's *Muqadimma fi fiqh al-lugha al-'arabiyya* (Introduction to Arabic Philology),[7] on the grounds that he adopted some Mu'tazilite positions concerned with the origin of languages and creation of the Qur'an.[8] Other scholars had voiced such ideas in recent years without this leading to confiscation. With few exceptions, intellectuals and senior figures not directly concerned with the accusations of al-Azhar and the Islamic groups protected themselves by silence in the face of the dangers of accusations of unbelief, of the use or the threat of violence, keeping their opinions to private fora.

5 *Al-Quds al-'arabī*, 17 January 1990.
6 *Al-Ḥayāt*, 16–17 December 1989.
7 Nabīl Faraj, "Louis 'Awaḍ amām maḥākim al-taftīsh", *al-Nāqid* 1 (1989): 38.
8 'Awaḍ, *Muqadimma fi fiqḥ al-lugha al-'arabiyya*, 69, 85–86.

This was clear in the case of the controversy surrounding a novel that satirised the Qur'anic paradise and legends of prophets. The author was one 'Ala' Hamid, an employee of the state taxation authority, known to the subsequent controversy as the "Egyptian Salman Rushdie", with al-Azhar alleging that the author had mocked the heavenly religions – the author was dismissed from his employment, and received a jail sentence.[9] The position of al-Azhar with regard to the authorising, banning, or proscription of cultural goods, and its policy of seeking the punishment of those it considered sinners, wrongdoers, and miscreants, was one that was chronically unstable and inconsistent for which al-Azhar was criticised for nearly four decades.[10] It appears that al-Azhar's judgements depended on political contingencies of every moment, while later moving towards a greater measure of inquisitorial activity. In all, and not least because of a history of reformist manoeuvering inscribed in institutional memory, al-Azhar has been less consequently inquisitorial than private litigation and other initiatives connected to Islamist political parties – including internal pressure brought to bear from Azharites with Muslim Brother inclinations.

These and comparable events occurred in an overall situation in which states – such as Iran or Sudan – pronounced themselves Islamic, when visible indices of religious zealotry became ubiquitous, when growing numbers of individuals became habituated to ostentatious displays of piety hitherto unfamiliar in form or extent. Televisual dissemination produced an Arab-wide multiplier effect, intensifying the images and sending feedback to countries of origin such as Egypt and Saudi Arabia, feeding an impression directed inside the Arab World as well as outside of an extraordinary politico-religious stamp marking Arab societies primarily and as a whole, one of the order of nature and without a recent history. In these circumstances it is perhaps unsurprising that many intellectuals and others have been captive impressionistically and superficially to these images. These images have the advantages of facility, repeatability, and predictability, and the ease of clichés. They feed into a populist politics that rests on stereotyping a national ethos easily communicated by visual tokens, of which veiled women are particularly evocative.

9 *Al-Quds al-'arabī*, 14–15 May 1990.

10 Muḥammad al-Ghazālī, *Min hunā na'lam*, 4th edn (Cairo: Dār al-Kitab al-'Arabī, 1954), 14.

Many have thereby been inclined to believe, with varying degrees of conviction, a fundamental thesis of the Islamist polemic against modernity and secularism, and coming to internalise this thought as their own: that there is an effective link between an imagined pattern of Arab society defined and constituted by the Islamist designation for this society as an Islamic society, with the name itself being taken for an adequate definition. This correspondence is also posited in relation to the seamless link between the present and the past preceding the immediate past: between a present that reveals a stable, homogeneous essence attributed to Arab societies, whose primary definition in this context is Islamic, and a past whose features disappeared in the fall from grace precipitated by colonialism, as the Arabs slumbered until jolted back into wakefulness today by a supposed Islamic revival, restoring the present to its true nature and origin, and recovering history by reclaiming its metahistorical essence. The eager reception of this view, its transformation into a kind of national intellectual and political doxa in the closing decade of the twentieth century, was facilitated by the rise of Islamist forces, and by the rather brittle consistency of Arab secularist thinking deprived of a hegemonic secularist ideology, and the potential of its earlier corporate constitution as a status group with a corporate ethos compromised and very much dissipated except at the radical edges – as we have seen, by state service of a bureaucratic character and, among the left, by party-political commitment that targeted mercilessly and thoughtlessly the specifically bourgeois character of the culture they carried. It was aided and abetted by the generally low level of technical competence in scholarship, by the defective and facile techniques of argumentation overall, sometimes quite shabby, reflecting vulnerability to pressures of the moment and the underdevelopment of technical competences across society. A later part of this chapter will take up the implicit metaphysics of supra-historical essences beyond the normal workings of societies. What is pertinent to the present discussion is not so much the structure of the ahistorical discourse and its origins in Islamic Reformist discourse, as its diffusion into intellectual, cultural, and social domains much wider than had been the original constituency of Islamism.

This second phenomenon consists of the integration by many currents of non-religious Arab thought – especially Arab nationalism and liberalism – of key affirmations of modern Islamic tendencies. One major actor here was the so-called Nationalist-Religious Dialogue mentioned already, which started in the late 1980s under the auspices of Beirut's Centre for Arab Unity Studies, the then premier research institution and think-tank in the Arab World, which resulted in ideological concessions by nationalists to the claims of Islamism. Assimilation of or concessions to the underpinnings of Islamist claims on history and society by contrary opinions is not unknown in modern Arab history. The success of Islamism in imposing on its adversaries, including liberals, the anti-modernist tropes of polemic and of analysis, and the concessions by many secularists to Islamist views of secularism, is a feature of the late twentieth century that shall be encountered repeatedly in the pages to come. The discussion does not concern the intentions of those who feel impelled to make such concessions, but the cultural and political cost of the admission of the fundamental Islamist historical, social, and, consequently, a political claim to full and exclusive representative capacity:[11] the supposedly Islamic character, indeed, nature, attributed to the Arabs and their history. These results can only be evaluated by considering the balance of forces active at the time of such irenicism.

It is true that some of the egregiously mythical Islamist statements about secularism have not been accepted by secularist currents, such as it being the result of a Masonic–Jewish–Communist conspiracy for world domination detailed in the Protocols of the Elders of Zion[12] – part and parcel of a broader tendency to attribute historical causality to clandestine personal volition, thinking in terms of conspiracy theories, demotically as well as among the most educated, and certainly not in the Arab World alone.[13] Yet many – most – of secularist nationalists and others were inclined to think of ideological concessions as mere courtesies, but they were nevertheless led to adopt some crucial conceptual and argumentative rhetorics of the Islamic Reformists, and to take apologetic discourses for descriptions of actually existing historical realities transcending ideology and political or identitarian passions. One idea of especial consequence for a variety of arguments was that Islam did not have a specific clerical class of religious professionals, an idea adopted even by the once-Azharite Taha Hussein before he fell victim of this class.[14]

11 See al-Azmeh, "Populism contra democracy", 112–129.

12 See, for example: Anwār al-Jundī, *Suqūṭ al-ʿilmāniyya* (Beirut: Dār al-Kitāb al-Lubnānī, 1973), passim; Muḥammad Zayn al-Hādī al-ʿArmābi, *Nash'at al-ʿilmāniyya wa dukhūluhā ilā al-mujtamaʿ al-islāmī* (Riyadh: Dār al-ʿĀṣima, 1987), 27–32, passim.

13 Matthew Gray, *Conspiracy Theories in the Arab World, Sources and Politics* (London: Routledge, 2010). There is a large literature, but the reader may start – or rest content with – Emma A. Jane and Chris Fleming, *Modern Conspiracy: The Importance of Being Paranoid* (London: Bloomsbury, 2014).

14 Ṭaḥa Ḥusayn, *Al-majmūʿa al-kāmila li-muʾallafāt al-duktūr Ṭaḥa Ḥusayn*, 16 vols (Beirut: Dār al-Kitāb al-Lubnānī, 1984), vol. 12, 164.

The assertion that Islam does not have a professional class of religious specialists, ulama, with priestly devotional, dogmatic, and magical functions as defined sociologically, acting as intermediaries between humans and their God, is not the only characteristic of Islam from which the conclusion is generally drawn that secularism is not necessary or relevant to Muslims because of the lack of a clerisy that drove secularism in Europe. But this assertion is a basic support for denying the relevance for the Arab World of the issue of the relationship of religion to state as a matter of broad global relevance and in global perspective. This issue, according to a defective understanding of European history, is seen as a European-Christian problem involving religion and state: a religious understanding of the world within Christianity on the one hand and European state understanding of religion on the other.[15] This issue was discussed in Chapter 1 above (and in the Preface), but it is nevertheless appropriate here to recall it as the basic characteristics of anti-secular discourse are examined. It structures its fundamental elements and arguments by an a priori separation between the interior – what is seen as indigenous, autochtonous, homeopathic, authentic, Islamic, Arabo-Islamic, originating from local homogeneity and historical continuity, and its contrary – the exterior, exogenous, contrived, inauthentic, alienating, originating outside, Christian or European. Secularism according to this interpretative schema is something the Arabs have no need of because it manifests a foreign, intrusive essence, Christian and European, deriving from the alien doctrine of giving to Caesar what is Caesar's, and to God what is God's – a characteristic argument reducing history to inferences from textual fragments. Secularism in this perspective stands refuted because it derived from the essence of a religious doctrine contrary to what is authentic to Arabs, to Islam. Thus, a Gospel narrative about Christ is made to be the entire description and conception of a religion with 2,000 years of history and a universal geographical and historical extension. A comparable metaphysical understanding of stability and the supra-historical transcendence of essence are attributed to the religion of Islam, which is also a global religion with very diverse historical experiences.

15 See, for example, Muḥammad ʿĀbid al-Jābirī, "Al-ʿilmāniyya wa al-islām", *al-Yawm al-Sābiʿ*, 3 April 1989, and "Al-dīn wa al-siyāsa wa al-ḥarb al-ahliyya", *al-Yawm al-Sābiʿ*, 19 March 1990. The detailed discussion of secularism in European history presented by ʿIṣmat Saif al-Dawla, *ʿAn al-ʿurūba wa al-islām*, Silsilat al-Thaqāfa al-Qawmiyya 2 (Beirut: Markaz Dirāsat al-Waḥda al-ʿArabiyya, 1986), 196–233, relies on uncommonly detailed knowledge, but is highly selective and summary in its conclusions.

The critics of secularism then add to this separation between the incommensurable metaphysical essences of separate histories, and their concrete instantiations. This gives substance to a discourse of exceptionalism, carried by the rhetoric of pathos rather than by argument, and carried forward by tonalities of adamant and insistent assertion, which are taken for cogency. It is sometimes said, in dark inquisitorial tones, that secularism is a cover for propaganda seeking to distance Islam from everyday life.[16] Or, to demonstrate the essentially alien nature of secularism in Arab history, it is affirmed that the proponents of secular ideas were Christians who did not belong to the religion and civilisation of Islam, or were persons who had been educated in foreign schools, and that they launched their secularism in the nineteenth century as a slogan for Arab nationalism seeking to break away from the Ottoman union that was based on Islam.[17] It appears as though Arab Christians in this discourse are not and cannot be Arabs in essence. It has been shown how this perception is at variance with historical reality, to say nothing of the damage that such opinions inevitably cause to Arab national unity at a period when the forces of fragmentation are so much alive.

As a matter of historical and anthropological fact, cultural differences between Muslim and Christian Arabs in the domain of daily practice and popular ritual are much exaggerated, although there are very many micro-sociological tokens of communal distinction that are flagged and noted, expressed in certain words used in conversation no less than in certain forms of behaviour, quite apart from forms of worship. In Egypt, basic homogeneity is clear to observers of Muslims and Copts in Upper Egypt with respect to family structures, style of daily worship, and veiling of women. Secular Christians in Ottoman Syria at the end of the nineteenth century were not calling for separation from the Ottoman state but were Ottoman in terms of nationality and political loyalty; Shibli Shumayyil and Butrus al-Bustani are good cases in point. The proponents of Arabism in the Ottoman period were not secularists as detailed examination showed in Chapter 2. Advocates

16 Saif al-Dawla, *'An al-'urūba wa al-islām*, 235–267.

17 Ḥanafī, "Al-'ilmāniyya wa al-islām"; al-Jābirī, "Al-'ilmāniyya wa al-islām". Not dissimilar in its assumptions is the view of a secularist author, whose academic trade is sociology, which holds that Arab modernists and those who admired Western civilisation were in a position of "refusal of the self", or self-haters, as some would have it: Burhān Ghalyūn, *Ightiyāl al-'aql: Miḥnat al-thaqāfa al-'arabiyya bayn al-salafiyya wa al-taba'iyya* (Beirut: Dār al-Tanwīr, 1985), 35.

of secession were advocates of communal Balkanisation, not of secularism. But it is unclear whether historical realities are matters of relevance in an anti-secular pseudo-historical discourse premised upon metaphysical incommensurabilities. Realities or quasi-realities play only an emblematising role.

There was in the late twentieth century a drift to consider patterns ascribed to the history of the Maghreb as a model that can be applied to the Mashreq, implicitly considering the lack of confessional uniformity in the Mashreq and Egypt as anomalous in a history patterned after the normative Maghreb. This came in the context of the internalisation of Islamist claims upon history and society. It is claimed that Islam in the Maghreb was apolitical, and that the links between religion and politics were ever harmonious because of the evenness and homogeneity of Morocco's religious domain. By this account, Morocco's pagan beliefs had been completely eliminated following the establishment of Islam there. According to this account, the Maghreb has and had known only the Maliki school in jurisprudence, and only the Sunnite creeds of the Salafis and the Ash'arites.[18] This perception of the religious landscape is merely a retrojection on an ideological Neo-Makhzenian, and specifically Sherifian Moroccan view of the history, but with a load of denial that excludes a rich, varied, and highly conflictual religious history, and much paganism, the clearest manifestation of which is the Sherifian and mystical *baraka*, or that of the *Aghwārim* in the Middle Atlas of Morocco. Emphasis on the Maliki school excludes the violent struggles within Malikism and between Malikis and Zahiris in the Almohad and the Almoravid periods. The Neo-Makhzenian view also juxtaposes Ash'arism and Salafism without commentary or definition, and conceals the doctrinal disputes between the above-mentioned periods.[19] Thus, in this context, modern Makhzen and Reformist Islam and their combat against the Islam of the Sufi fraternities throughout the Maghreb goes unmentioned even though the Neo-Makhzenian view of history might find support in Abdallah

18 Muḥammad 'Ābid al-Jābirī, "Al-ḥaraka al-salafiyya wa al-jamā'āt al-dīnīya al-mu'āṣira fī al-Maghrib", paper presented at the conference "Al-ḥarakāt al-islamiyya al-mu'āṣira fī al waṭan al-'arabī", in *Maktabat al-mustaqbalāt al-'arabiyya al-badīla: Al-ittijāhāt al-ijtimā'iyya wa al-siyāsiyya wa al-thaqāfiyya* (Beirut: Markaz Dirāsāt al-Waḥda al-'Arabiyya, 1987), 190–191.

19 In this context an overview suffices of the original versions of Māliki histories of the Maghreb such as 'Abd al-Wāhid al-Marrākishī, *Al-mu'jib fī talkhīṣ akhbār al-Maghrib, al-kitāb al-thālith*, ed. Muḥammad Sa'īd al-'Aryān (Cairo: Lajnat iḥyā' al-Turāth al-Islāmi, 1963), 235–237, 254–256, and passim; Ibn Farḥūn, *Al-dībāj al-mudhahhab fī ma'arifat a'yān 'ulamā' al-madhhab*, 286.

Laroui's analysis, according to which Makhzen Salafism is a defensive position for a group whose contours are incompletely defined and can be seen as a model on which the characteristics of local nationalisms could be based more generally.[20] This construction gives inconsiderable weight to the difference between today's Salafism and that of earlier periods in Morocco. That Morocco-centrism evades the region's specificity in relation to other Arab regions is to be expected, as the setting up of Morocco, in this type of discourse, as the norm, is intended to present an image of seamless normative homogeneity in the context of which modernism and secularism are unthinkable.

Clearly, this photoshopping of historical reality bespeaks only a purely instrumental link to reality. Its cogency is related less to its merits than to its decisionist character. In turn, such decisionism, carried by political will, assertion, and declamation, irrespective of connection to fact, is a feature of direct ideological and political discourse, which is performative and illocutionary rather than informative. What this photoshopped historical discourse in fact enunciates is the Islamist claim that Islamists alone can represent a society whose character is uniform and homogeneous, in space as well as in time, and has a specific religious character, and that, as a corollary and by direct implication, any different characterisation of society involving mutability, inner differentiation and secularism, be illicit. Thus, it would seem ingenuously self-evident that Islam – presumed to be even and uniform and changeless – is an essential constituent of Arab existence, and that secularism is thus an "ambiguous slogan".[21]

The reality is that such a statement is not without strong implication. By rejecting secularism and parsing it as a slogan, and by accepting some of its possible correlates such as democracy as indicative of its sense, this statement allocates to claims made in the name of Islam the capacity for defining such content more concretely. As Islam is, according to the claim in circulation, the foundational component of Arab existence, construing concepts and arrangements such as democracy as a common ground between Islam and secularism will amount, in the Islamist or Islamicised register, ultimately to the position that Islam comes to contain. In some instances, this is claimed

20 Laroui, *Les Origines sociales et culturelles du nationalisme marocain 1830–1912*, 437. See 'Azīz al-'Aẓma, *Al-turāth bayn al-ṣultān wa al-ta'rīkh*, 2nd edn (Beirut: Dar al-Ṭalī'a, 1990), 115–116.

21 al-Jābirī, "Al-'ilmāniyya wa al-islām".

on the assumption – rhetorical and decisionist at once – that Islam contains secularism because in its essence it is secular,[22] or that it resembles secularism in the beneficial effects it brings to the common good.[23] In other words, there is between secularism and anti-secularism no middle ground in which democracy and rationality might be situated and be partaken equally. These are not separable from assumptions underlying secularism, as was affirmed by a voluble critic: liberation from religious control of knowledge, the assumption that the world was to be explained by its own laws, the idea of constant change of nature and society, the idea of continuous evolution entailing that moral and spiritual values were not constant, and that the objective of religion lay in the next world and not the present one.[24]

However, when secularism and secular political arrangements, including democracy, are severed from their foundational secular moorings, and made peripheral to another, religious point of reference to which ultimate authority is allocated, the rhetorically dual system becomes unitary in its submission to an Islamist point of reference. And the determinate content with which secular political arrangements, including democracy, are here filled will be virtual, acquiring substance from that interpretation that is able to impose itself politically and socially, rather than from theoretical debate. The "ambiguous slogan" thus turns out to be the rejection of secularism and not secularism itself that is not, as noted earlier, a slogan but a historical reality identifiable as modernity and secularisation and their consequences. The confusion arises from the ideological docility of liberals that links the democratist current, as a subaltern player, politically, to the Islamist current. For once it is admitted that Islam is the source, infrastructure, and protoplasm of society. The idea that "Islam is the solution", the mainstay of Islamist politics and election campaigns, wherever they might take place, appears as a natural corollary, leaving aside personal intentions, meanings, capacity for comprehension and self-reflexivity, and motivations.

This apologetic concession to Islamist descriptions of past and present has not been rare in modern Arab history, although its pace intensified and its extent widened with the closing of the twentieth century, following the

22 Ibid.

23 ʿAmāra, *Al-dawla al-islāmiyya bayn al-ʿilmāniyya wa al-sulṭa al-dīniyya*, 170.

24 al-Jundī, *Suqūṭ al-ʿilmāniyya*, 82, 95–96.

growing resonance of political Islam. Such willing ideological self-subjection is not always an ingenuous gesture of courtesy unaware of political consequences attendant upon it.[25] But it is always allied to the abdication of historical reason, which is the primary constituent of all progress. The spectral invocation of historical continuities, and of destiny, essential for this exercise in public self-effacement was made possible by two conditions. First, was the translation of Islamist theses from being distinct ideological and conceptual contraries to be engaged or accommodated in an increasingly gingerly manner, to being admitted into liberal and other non-Islamic discourses as component and indeed constituent elements. It thus became possible for anti-secular discourse to impose its premises and render them unquestionable, such as the pseudo-historical idea that secularism and nationalism were the handiwork of Arab Christians. This Islamist takeover of the historiographic premises underlying secular ideologies and discourses is also to be found among many Arab intellectuals who moved towards Islamism from other ideologies or who sought a political appeasement by ideological concession, and who transferred their criteria of historical reference and historical description for continuities with the past from Arabism to Islamism. Arab heritage thus becomes Islamic, having been previously characterised as Arab with Islamic elements within it; a shift of emphasis is perceptible from occupation with Arab traditions in literature, philosophy, and profane knowledge, to strikingly inexpert burrowing into works of Muslim exegesis, theology, and jurisprudence. More than verbal flattery is involved, for naming is not innocent, but is rather a classificatory act entailing associations and consequences intimately related to politics and ideology. Names can run away with concepts.

Appeasing discourse of this kind, seen by some, of late, implicitly or explicitly to be the only effective and coherent modernist position given circumstances they imagine,[26] is strongly associated with the belief that its proponents occupy a unique, rather Olympian position in society and, potentially, the state,

25 For a discussion of this phenomenon with regard to the case of Salman Rushdie one can consult ʿAzīz al-ʿAẓma, "Baʿīdan ʿan saṭwat al-qawl al-dīnī", *al-Nāqid* 16 (1989): 78–80 and ʿAzīz al-ʿAẓma, "Ṣādiq al-ʿAẓm wa istibṭān al-fawāt", *Qalamūn* 1 (2017): 141–152; Ṣādiq Jalal al-ʿAẓm, *Secularism, Fundamentalism and the Struggle for the Meaning of Islam* (Berlin: Gerlach Press, 2013), vol. 2.

26 For instance, Ghalyūn, *Ightiyāl al-ʿaql*, 322.

standing above political and social forces and passions, and destined to lead by sageliness. Yet an observer of sane mind would also note that these same intellectuals seem to believe that they also give expression to society, speaking from inside it, according to a populist understanding that shall be discussed presently. Reality shows, however, that the effectiveness of the irenical approach is limited to the intentions of those who adopt it as a default position, and that it remains without practical effect on the structure and premises of appeasing discourses, be they Arab nationalist or liberal in orientation. A crucial element of this discourse, that of historicity, is voided as it becomes hitched to a crucial premise of Islamist discourse, that Islam is the essence of society and history and, as destiny, its one possible authentic outcome. Notions such as democracy and rationalism are extruded from the context of their formation and are subordinated to the exigencies of a discourse of rhetorical reconciliation, based in the denial of historicity for these and other concepts, as would be required by revivalist motifs. Such motifs require time as a series of moments re-enacting origins and beginnings. Democracy and rationalism are grafted onto the register of a Muslim past. Actual history is extruded, and then appropriated virtually in the name of purported origins, with the Islamic description of things ingesting the past and re-describing histories as Islamic: thus, for instance, Islamic medicine, Islamic economics, Islamic socialism.

The second element in the subordination of liberal and Arab nationalist discourses to Islamic discourse was one that explains the ease of transition from Arabism to Islam, and the oscillation between them, as points of historical reference and primary parameters of historical categorisation. This element is the structural conceptual homology in the theory of history on which claims of historical continuity, both Islamic and Pan-Arab, are based. It is such that homologous discourses might be produced by switching between the terms "Arab" and "Islamic" as categorical descriptors, each of which yields a different world of connotation. This second element also bespeaks the assimilation by Arab nationalist historico-ideological discourses of Islamic heritage in the course of the twentieth century, and particularly after the end of the Nasser era when important elements from Islamist ideology pierced through to some political and ideological nodes of Arabism, and developed within its ideological ferment – for instance, within the institutional structures of the Nationalist–Religious Dialogue mentioned above, of some left-wing political parties in Morocco, and of the vast body of liberal, democracy-oriented organisations and non-governmental organisations (NGOs).

The use by both Islamism and Arabism of the term *umma* – the modern Arabic word for nation – was perhaps a regrettable accident of language that facilitated confusion between the registers and associations of two distinct currents of thought and ideologies.[27] There was a discernible shift by important currents of Arabism away from its historical and realist phase that had disallowed, often quite methodically, any confusion between Arabism and Islam, and that maintained their distinction (represented by Sati' al-Husri and the Iraqi 'Abd al-Rahman al-Bazzaz [1913–1973], for instance).[28] The conflation of the two took many forms, such as a move to derive Arab nationalism from Qur'anic texts,[29] or the claim, albeit in highly particular political circumstances, that Michel 'Aflaq had secretly converted to Islam before his death in 1989, as if to symbolise the lack of distinction between Arabism and Islam and the necessity of their identity.[30] This shift did not only signal a historism shared by Islamists and Arab nationalists, but also showed that many Arab nationalist currents had conceded politically the ideological primacy of Islamism and its symbolic requirements, even before this concession was perceived as a pressing political necessity under the signature of democracy. This will now be discussed in greater detail.

Both conflation and subordination shared a habitual invocation of historical exceptionalism, affirmed by Islamists in the name of Islam, an affirmation conceded by many Arab nationalists and liberals. It therefore became possible to claim, as a matter of self-evidence, that secularism was directly proportional to a sense of estrangement,[31] that is, deracination from the *umma*. But which *umma*? Is this to be taken for a homogenous whole? Does the Islamist critic of society not feel estranged from the society that she seeks to correct? The claim to exceptionalism and the characterisation of anyone who does not share a specific understanding of this claim as somehow uprooted and foreign is a basic element in the discourse of invective, malediction, and castigation

27 On these resemblances see al-Azmeh, "Islamism and Arab nationalism", 43 and passim.

28 al-Ḥuṣrī', *Al-a'māl al-qawmiyya*, 2,902–2,907, passim; al-Bazzāz, *Hādhihi qawmīyyatunā*, 178–192.

29 Saif al-Dawla, *'An al-'urūba wa al-islām.*

30 See the commentary of Ghālī Shukrī, "Al-masiḥīyūn wa al-'urūba: Man yadfa' al-thaman?" *al-Nāqid* 2 (1989): 12–14.

31 Ṭāriq al-Bishrī, "Al-khulf bayn al-nukhba wa al-jamāhīr izā' al-'ilāqa bayn al-qawmiyya al-'arabiyya wa al-islām", in *Al-qawmiyya al-'arabiyya wa al-islam,* ed. Markaz Dirāsāt al-Waḥda al-'Arabīya, 1st edn (Beirut: Markaz Dirāsāt al-Waḥda al-'Arabiyya, 1981), 292.

used to criticise secularism, and that was also used by Islamists to denounce and censure those who disagree with them, from Taha Hussein and 'Ali 'Abd al-Raziq to Sadiq al-Azm and Salman Rushdie.[32] Indeed, the book in defence of Salman Rushdie written by al-Azm was attacked by intellectuals of Marxist extraction for precisely this, that it abjured what the nation held dear, in terms little different from what one would find in pamphlets issued by the Muslim Brothers.[33]

1 The Discourse of Exceptionalism and its Auxiliaries

Islamist discourse was brought in to occupy moulds of ideological reception and transmission associated with Arabism as mentioned earlier, in a way comparable to the way in which Islamism merged with xenophobic hyper-nationalism in Iran after 1979. This was not common to all currents of Arabism that, as argued earlier, had taken two distinct views of the issue of historical continuity. One was linked to the names of al-Husri and Zurayq, historical positivists both, and saw nations as historical entities subject to the logic of the movement of history, and particularly the evolutionary theory that al-Husri adopted in its universal form. This current of thought considered the formation of nations as a historical process that proceeded according to a logic of improvement and progress in which nations were the most developed political form of human sociality, a form that succeeds temporally as well as surpassing culturally, politically, and in terms of civilisation forms of social organisation based upon race, religion, and geneaology, even if these factors did undoubtedly have an effect on the process of national formation. In this current of Arabism, national political form was a global, universal reality. Conflict is between national entities that are distinct in language and culture, but not in terms of the social and political constitution of a national formation, which is the product of a particular historical moment common to all national formations and therefore constitutive of them. There is doubtless a basic assumption here, variously implicit or clear, of the combined

32 On the structure of the vituperative and castigating discourse see Jābir 'Aṣfūr, "Islām al-nafṭ wa al-ḥadātha", in *Al-islām wa al-ḥadātha: Nadwat mawāqif* (London: Maktabat al-Sāqī, 1990), 191–206.

33 al-'Aẓma, "Ṣādiq al-'Aẓm wa istibṭān al-fawāt", 145–146.

social and political change at a world level, change driven by European capitalism from the seventeenth century onwards. This bespeaks the historical realism of this type of Arab nationalist historical thinking,[34] which enquired into history and sought to register transformation without seeing the past as the necessary support of the present in any but a symbolic sense, unlike the essentialism of the other current, to which we shall now come. History for nationalist positivists was something more than a spur to action: although the motivating spur is shared by positivists and romanticists, the former tended to see historical continuities and the appeal to past glories as rather a burden upon the present, one from whose effects one needed to emancipate oneself – the past here is a substantive burden, and a symbolic incentive.[35]

The second current within Pan-Arab discourse and thought was constituted by Romantic concepts, approximating mysticism in its view of the nation, with strong emphasis on the uniqueness of the Arab *umma* and its qualitative difference to other nations. It needs to be borne in mind that these two currents are not utterly distinct and mutually exclusive, and that there is inevitably a certain romantic element that enters the positivistic redaction, especially when applying itself to aims and to mechanisms of mobilisation.[36] The Syrian Social Nationalist Party bears comparison with this current, with stress on identity, like comparable regional – Lebanese and Egyptian – nationalisms emerging at the same time, between the First and Second World Wars. The nation itself comes here to assume a strongly anthropomorphic aspect. Khalil Gibran, a literary pioneer of Arab Romanticism, characterised this well when he described the nation as a collective self whose essence resembles the nature of an individual. The Arab *umma* is independent of the Arab people, that is, of a concrete social and political entity, and possesses a particular will of its own that does not fade away, but, regarded as history, grows and falls into light interrupted sleep. It may rise again to reveal what remained hidden within its spirit, after it bore the Arab prophet and "rose up like a giant and erupted like a storm".[37]

34 Readers might wish to consult Tikhonova, *Sāṭi' al-Ḥuṣrī'*.

35 Zurayq, *Naḥnu wa al-tārīkh*, 54, 184.

36 See the detailed discussion in al-'Aẓma, *Qusṭanṭīn Zurayq*, chs 2 and 3.

37 Jubrān Khalīl Jubrān, "Al-'awāṣif", in *Al-majmū'a al-kāmila li-mu'allafāt Jubrān Khalīl Jubrān*, 3 vols (Beirut: Dār Ṣādir, Dār Bayrūt, 1964), 431–432.

This is a revivalist discourse, constituted around an image of a vitalist and biological metaphor of the organism.[38] History and the past go far beyond the symbolic appeal of Zurayq's "incentive history", which affirms the actual and consequential historicity of the *umma*[39] whose supra-historical continuity is affirmed only symbolically, and not substantively. The revivalist and romantic conception, in contrast, classifies historical events into two metahistorical categories, one being a record of glory and dominion, and the other of abjection and effacement. Thus, the contrast and the differential between past and present is not something that emerges from objective historical forces, but from estimations of the abstract, decisionist capacity to act.[40] The identification of the national self is not, in this view, possible by recourse to theories of history or of the nation, but by the self-affirmation of the living self, as Arabism is not, in this register, a theory but "source of the theories" and the "wet nurse of thought", in 'Aflaq's words, inasmuch as the nationalist action is an act of resurrection quite literally (*ba'th* is Arabic for resurrection), and nationalism is "living remembrance". Arabism does not characterise a place nor does it indicate the passage of time, for Baathist politics is an "eternal mission".[41] An outstanding Arab nationalist thinker like al-Arsuzi flew high on this irrationalism, invoking Bergson and Spengler, and saw the mission of the Arab *umma* as the aspiration of the "values around which its life was woven" to manifest themselves "like the intonation of rhythm within the system of the name bearing the mission".[42] Piling one mystification upon another, al-Arsuzi made nationalist action one based on what he called Rahmanism, *Raḥmānīya*, metaphorical and metonymic play on associations of the root r-h-m with God (al-Rahman) and the womb (*raḥm* in Arabic).[43] Notions of "destiny" and "mission" are mystificatory intangibles that, as one scholar of German vitalist philosophy observed, is a negation of the notion of causality.[44] Thus, the

38 On which see al-Azmeh, *The Times of History*, ch. 1

39 Zurayq, *Naḥnu wa al-tārīkh*, 184, 208 ff.

40 'Aflaq, *Fī sabīl al-ba'th*, 50–51.

41 Ibid., 41–43, 60, 73, 158, and passim. A recent attempt has been made to compare Baathist and Islamist ideologies in certain crucial areas, including those under discussion: Ḥammūd Ḥammūd, *Baḥth 'an al-muqaddas: Al-ba'th wa al-uṣūliyya* (Beirut: Dār Jadāwil, 2014).

42 al-Arsūzī, *Mashākilunā al-qawmiyya wa mawqif al-aḥzāb minhā*, 50–51; Ḥannā, *Al-ittijāhāt al-fikriyya fī sūriyyā wa lubnān*, 50–51.

43 Ḥannā, *Al-ittijāhāt al-fikriyya fī sūriyyā wa lubnān.*

44 Stepan Odouev, *Par les sentiers de Zarathoustra,* trans. Catherine Emery (Moscow: Éditions du Progrès, 1980), 177.

nation and the nationalist mission are in the Romantic vitalist mode defined as a continuous organic self, connected to other absolute and irreducible subjects by separation, positing a self-enclosed and irreducible subject. Such is also a relatively new ideological invention on the Arab scene: the "Lebanese Man" of the Lebanese civil war period, distinguished by being "like his homeland, Lebanon: whole, complete, self-sufficient, in need of nothing to complete him, or of an attribute to differentiate him from another".[45]

Arab nationalist revivalist discourse was linked to Islamist revivalism by structure and recollection. The earliest revivalist – as distinct from modernist – discourse in the Arab world grew out of Young Ottoman discourse, a local patriotic, Ottomanist, Easternist, Islamic, indeterminate in its direct political point of reference, although its Islamic point of reference was clear enough. It developed as al-Afghani and 'Abduh worked together and edited the journal *al-'Urwa al-Wuthqā* discussed in Chapter 3. This recalls German discourses of national revival, structurally homologous, which appeared in its early form in the writings of Johann Gottfried Herder (1744–1803) in an organismic, vitalist discourse of national individuality. In other periods it took a historical as well as historist turn, some of intense irrationality in periods following military defeat and under National Socialism. Not dissimilarly, Arabism took a historical and positivist turn at the period of the ascension and historical optimism associated in regimes led by what can be arguably described as nationalist bourgeoisies. Later, in periods of decline after the Arab defeat of 1967, it inclined towards revivalist irrationalism. The connection between Arab nationalist revivalism and Islamic revivalism is therefore contingent on a number of factors: an act of recollection, reclaiming the revivalist discourse at the end of the nineteenth century, rendering al-Afghani a contemporary hero of the Islamic vision of Arabism. Then there is influence, with the entry of Islamist ideas and motifs into the sinews of nationalist revivalism in an age of defeat translated into intellectual incapacity and porousness, and lastly, the factor uniting these two previous elements, namely the understandings of history and society on which ideas of revivalism are based overall.[46]

This historical imaginary presupposes a uniformity and homogeneity over time – a continuous and linear history – and space – the homogeneous space

45 Fu'ād Ifrām al-Bustānī, *Mawāqif lubnāniyya* (Beirut: Manshūrāt al-Dā'ira, 1982), 11.

46 For a detailed examination of these questions see al-Azmeh, *Islams and Modernities*, ch. 5.

of Arab society, incommensurable in essence, an essence persisting in history: essence in the strict ontological sense of quiddity, something tangible and kickable, understood literally and physically, not as a metaphor. This inherent continuity and homogeneity renders historical change, such as that of modern history, which caused substantive breaks and disruptions and a disassembly of previous structures, a matter entirely external and extrinsic, merely superficial elements with respect to the abiding essence postulated. Time is thereby cleft between what preceded modernity and what followed, an interregnum that cannot affect the original core of Arab society. Western influence flows accidentally over the surface of the original Arab essence whose existence continues as it had been before the impact of the West, with primal innocence and cultural chastity preserved, occasioning myriad narratives of victimhood in folk tale mode (Aarne–Thompson–Uther folktale type 333). Arabs and Others, specifically meaning Europe, are related by juxtaposition only, being two generically separate historico-ethnological units, which might, nevertheless, be disturbed in a way that produced an internal duality in the Arab body-social, although this occupies a marginal position within the crucible of ethnological individuality. The Arab relationship with Europe does not, in this view, take on the characteristics required by the reality of global modernity as an objective dynamic, combining elements unevenly, nor can Europe, from this perspective, be perceived objectively as a constituent structural component of that which goes for Arab interiority or subjectivity. Continuity of essence with the past is the prime token of national individuality, which identifies and indicates itself through refusal, and displays refusal ostentatiously. Revival becomes the realisation of an accomplished past, with the present in between figuring as an absolute negative, of desuetude, hollow, bereft of historical dynamic.[47] As this view of history is imaginary, the only means of passage between past and present becomes abstract will and abstract decisionism, unconcerned with reality that it presumes to appropriate and to connect to as it connects to its narcissistic self, much like the Terror according to Hegel's analysis of the French Revolution.[48] There is a vast literature on notions of pure action as an assertion

47 See al-ʿArwī, *Al-idiyūlūjiyya al-ʿarabiyya al-muʿāṣira*, 18–109 and passim. Sharāra, *Ḥawl baʿḍ mushkilāt al-dawla*, 100–113 and passim; ʿAzīz al-ʿAẓma, "Fī al-aṣāla wa akhawātihā", *Dirāsāt ʿArabiyya* 12 (1990): 31–52. See too al-ʿAẓma, *Al-turāth bayn al-ṣultān wa al-taʾrīkh*, 165–167 and passim.

48 Georg Wilhelm Friedrich Hegel, *Phenomenology of Spirit*, trans. A. V. Miller (Oxford: Clarendon Press, 1977), paras 593, 584, 590.

of will in the context of absolute decisionism in studies of National Socialist ideology and its sibling ideologies.

All such conceptions arise from historical Romanticism that, towards the end of the twentieth century, established homologies between Arab nationalist revivalism with political Islamism, seeing in action towards the future recovery rather than progress, in which perspective resistance for the sake of resistance becomes a practical consequence, retrogressive, almost autistic resistance frozen in the moment of pure resistance, unable to elicit, conceive, or forge a modern history – perhaps best expressed later in the nihilistic violence perhaps most fully emblematised by al-Qaeda and, more intensely, by Daesh.[49] The impression of absolute individuality is the complement of historical incapacity. Politics thus becomes direct violence and, at the limit, nihilistic terror whose only link to the reality of politics, society, and their possibilities is political desire. Ideas of revival are thus made to mutate from a humanist, open, future-oriented conception of progress, to an irrationalism, retrogressive imaginary of rolling back history and the phantasmagoric rejuvenation of a freshness and energy long vanished.

The term "authenticity" – and its contrary, alienation, which in Iran went by the fortunate coinage "Westtoxification", alternatively "Occidentosis"[50] – was and remains the privileged port of entry of Islamist ideology into the depths of Arab nationalism and into the folds of liberal and Marxist ideologies.[51] For this there have been many reasons, chief among them being that "authenticity" is generally considered to be a good and laudable term proclaimed by many Arab nationalists[52] without their having given thought to anything but its rhetorical resonance and suggestion of a historical tonic, and with no alertness to the associations it elicits, or that these might not be altogether benign. The notion underlines a sense of historical exclusivity and incommensurability of the self that many proponents of authenticity may not

49 See Sharāra, *Isti'nāf al-bad'*, 121; al-'Aẓma, *Al-turāth bayn al-ṣultān wa al-ta'rīkh*, 165–167, passim. See now al-Azmeh, *Islams and Modernities*, ch. 10.

50 See A. Mirsepassi, *Transnationalism in Iranian Political Thought. The Life and Times of Ahmad Fardid* (Cambridge: Cambridge University Press, 2017), ch. 5.

51 On this term and its critique see al-Azmeh, *Islams and Modernities*, ch. 5.

52 'Abd al-Laṭīf Sharāra, *Al-jānib al-thaqāfī fī al-qawmiyya al-'arabiyya* (Beirut: Dār al-'Ilm li'l-Malāyīn, 1961), 137–143; 'Abd Allāh 'Abd al-Dā'im, "Al-mas'ala al-thaqāfiyya bayn al-aṣāla wa al-mu'āṣara", in *Al-turāth wa taḥaddiyyāt al-'aṣr fī al-waṭan al-'arabī: Al-aṣāla wa al-mu'āṣara*, 2nd edn (Beirut: Markaz Dirāsāt al-Waḥda al-'Arabiyya, 1987), 687–714.

intend in any consequent way beyond the rhetoric of assertion. Clearly, we have here another instance of words running away with those who favour and promote them, leading to consequences as concrete as they are unintended. With few exceptions, the notion is received and deployed and accompanied, visibly or invisibly, by another without which it is inconceivable, namely "contemporaneity (*mu'asara*)", with the constant implication of conjoining an individual inner self, an incommensurable collective subject, and a general, global other, joining a continuous ethnological self and a universality that can be abbreviated to the acquisition of contemporary techniques in a way that does not sully the depths of the authentic self. In this tautological conception, authenticity and individuality are the two qualities of the self, indicating that it is not another, that it is essence as distinct from being an accident, that it is nature and not contrivance.

The discourse on authenticity came to sweep everything before it in the closing decades of the twentieth century. Collective individuality and specificity, in the generally accepted terms perhaps best expressed by the Egyptian philosopher Hassan Hanafi (b. 1935), champion of an "Islamic Left" whose head had been turned by the Iranian Revolution, is not that of a particular entity contrasted to something more general and universal, but rather a being asserted in contrast to loss of particularity and therefore of individuality and dissolution into another. Authenticity and particularity reside in heritage, which Hanafi takes to be bookish and religious, and not practice, signifying historical depth as against external borrowing, authentic plenitude as against dilution of essence, continuity and homogeneity over time. The consequence of this celebratory and elixiric rhetoric is a general conservative disposition irrespective of any particular description, and a readiness to defer to retrogressive ideological and social forces. Not long before, such a suggestion would have been associated with marginal, reactionary intellectual propaganda. This retrogressive desire is precisely the sense of the tiresomely repeated call for "complete historical independence for the Arab self",[53] associated institutionally with a large-scale research and publications programme using the considerable pan-Arab networks and resources of the Centre for Arab Unity Studies in Beirut, seeking with exquisite fanfare and pomposity, but using a technocratic mode of procedure,

53 Muḥammad 'Ābid al-Jābirī, "Min haymanat al-namūdhaj ilā al-istiqlāl", *al-Safir*, 10 April 1982.

programming, and tabulation, to develop a blueprint for no less than a comprehensive, political, geo-political, social, cognitive, and cultural Arab Renaissance. When the process of political and economic independence and empowerment stalled following military defeat and neo-liberal transformations, calls were made, as if in a world of fantasy, for "a civilisational Arabo-Islamic project which realises for this *umma* the revival by which it can proceed with carrying out its eternal mission for which God chose it since Islam appeared in and by this *umma*".[54]

While the call mentioned above for "independence of the self" is sometimes, in a gesture towards older intellectual traditions still very much alive, supplemented by suggesting that this independence needs also to be expressed in abjuring the dominance of Heritage and not merely that of the West,[55] this supplementation has no pragmatic effect on the economy of this type of identitarian discourse, fettered by the concept of self that almost naturally brings associations with the past, and thereby occupies a hegemonic location in the economy of this discourse. In terms of discursive pragmatics, all enunciations on a self-presumed setting individual to the extent of being entirely autonomous and sui generis are unable to engage with the present, for the present is by definition incomplete, and such discourse ultimately devolves to sheer evocations of historical continuity and generic individuality, for it is not in this way confronted with heteronomy, as it must if it were considered concretely. The key term is origins, not historical dynamics or the dynamics of the present, so it matters little if double origins are proposed, local and Western, the local considered only in terms of what is presumed to be original, abiding, authentic, and in continuity with the past.[56] In reality the Arab inheritance from the past, as well as what has been taken from the West, in addition to the results of two centuries of social change, are things whose authority is rooted in the present, not in their presumed points of origin. Referring these elements to the West, or to an illusory continuous self, yields to the ideological supremacy of a discourse of particularity and continuity and the primary Islamist carriers of this discourse. It requires a

54 ʿAmāra, *Al-dawla al-islāmiyya bayn al-ʿilmāniyya wa al-ṣulṭa al-dīniyya*, 6.

55 al-Jābirī, "Min haymanat al-namūdhaj ilā al-istiqlāl."

56 Muḥammad ʿĀbid al-Jābirī, "Ishkāliyyāt al-aṣāla wa al-muʿāṣara fī al-fikr al-ʿarabī al-ḥadīth wa al-muʿāṣir: Ṣirāʿ ṭabaqī am mushkil thaqāfī", in *Al-turāth wa taḥaddiyyat al-ʿaṣr fī al-waṭan al-ʿarabī: al-aṣāla wa al-muʿāṣara*, 2nd edn (Beirut: Markaz Dirāsāt al-Waḥda al-ʿArabiyya, 1987), 34.

denial of the present moment as the present, concretely regarded, denies the separation between original and foreign, and belies narcissistic delusions of absolute selfhood.

In cognitive terms, this perspective results in an extreme impoverishment and in the reduction of the activity of reason to that of classification, classifying matters into the authentic and the inauthentic and their many cognates. Classificatory operations are basic of human thought at its elementary, incipient state. The discourse of authenticity operates by allocating matters to two categories of historical objects, circumstances and events, the authentic and the foreign. The terms in which reality is purportedly described – Islam, or Islamised Arabism – becomes not so much the apprehension and analysis of something actual, as much as judging allocation to one of the two classificatory categories.[57] The preference, in other words, is for ontology over sociology. A common corollary of this stance is to hold that there are specific regimes of historical and social knowledge pertinent to every separate "civilisation", as knowledge is inseparable from the "the interior" of each of these units and its metaphysical bases. Islamic society can only be known by Muslims, because there is no universality in human knowledge: so the Muslim Brother Sayyid Qutb, expressing in the 1940s a view very common in European irrationalism no less than in postmodern and post-colonial studies.[58] This solipsistic epistemology is accepted by Islamist thinkers[59] as well as by liberal champions of ideological accommodation.[60] Let it again be underlined that this is by no means unique to currents in Arab culture, but has been a feature of German and more broadly European vitalist and conservative thought that proposed that life and thought belonged to the same ontological register, and that knowledge was a vital process that conveyed no meaning beyond direct action,[61] that it was, in other words, entirely illocutionary. This representation communicates no effective social or historical knowledge beyond a classification. Classificatory reason in this context is the activation of a particular name, Islam. Naming is not only a gesture: in ideological terms, naming is a node of singularity, separation, appropriation. Such is the ideological import

57 al-Azmeh, *Al-turāth bayn al-ṣulṭān wa al-tārīkh,* 151.

58 Sayyid Quṭb, *Ma'ālim fī al-ṭarīq* (Cairo and Beirut: Dār al-Shurūq, 1981), 141.

59 'Ādil Ḥusayn, *Naḥw fikr 'arabī jadīd: Al-nāṣiriyya wa al-tanmiya wa al-dīmūqraṭiyya* (Cairo: Dār al-Mustaqbal al-'Arabī, 1985), 30–31 and passim; Al-Jundī, *Suqūṭ al-'ilmāniyya,* 43, 49, 50, 63.

60 Zākī Najīb Maḥmūd, *Tajdīd al-fikr al-'arabī* (Beirut: Dār al-Shurūq, 1981), 274.

61 Odouev, *Par les sentiers de Zarathoustra,* 131–142.

and, consequently, political and social consequence of construing "Islam" as a primary category of perception and classification that ingests both history and society, political grist to the mill of political movements that described themselves in terms of the name.

2 Islam, Politics and Society

This transformation of a quasi-religious phenomenon, akin to that of ancestor worship, into a cognitive conceit, is an anthropological phenomenon that still awaits appropriate ethnological research. With regard to contemporary Arab politics and culture, the discourse of particularity leads to the evacuation of secularism from Arab life, on the assumption that it is extraneous to the presumed Arab self and does not arise from it organically. Thus for one author Islam is "the doctrine and the ideology of the *umma*".[62] The application of shari'a is merely the return of things to their proper order, and a resumption of the natural law of the *umma* so that "the application of shari'a" is declared to be, according to a former Marxist, "a national demand".[63] In the same vein, it is claimed, by another former Marxist, that Islam in Iran and elsewhere is the "natural" response to the West.[64] So much for Islamist authors: for liberal irenicists, "returnees" to Islam or to Islamic discourses, such as Taha Hussein or Muhammad Hussein Haykal, was simply the restoration of the condition appropriate to them in a location absolutely distinct from the "West".[65]

A contemporary representative of the Egyptian Left, with no alertness to political and cultural consequences of his statement, asserted that Islamic thought is "the popular doctrine of the Arab masses". Despite his distinction between religious practice that he attaches to "popular doctrine", and Islamist political movements,[66] this renowned Marxist, Lutfi al-Khuli (1928–1999), littérateur and editor of the widely read left-wing cultural journal *al-Tali'a*, did not bother to engage with the claim by Islamist parties he detested that it is they who might be able to lay a greater claim to representing and carrying this "popular doctrine" with greater credibility than he ever could. This

62 Muḥammad 'Amāra, in *Al-ḥiwār al-qawmī al-islāmī*, ed. Markaz Dirāsāt al-Waḥda al-'Arabiyya (Beirut: Markaz Dirāsāt al-Waḥda al-'Arabiyya, 1989), 121.

63 Ibid., 201.

64 Walīd Nuwayhaḍ, "'Aqdam al-aqallīyāt", *al-Safir*, 8 February 1981.

65 al-Anṣārī, *Taḥawwulāt al-fikr wa al-siyāsa fī al-sharq al-'arabī 1930–1970*, 129, 118.

66 Luṭfī al-Khūlī in *al-Qabas*, 12 February 1989.

is typical of the defensive stance that characterised the Egyptian Left especially, from the middle of the 1960s, surprising as there was not yet a need to adopt such a position at a time when Islamism had not yet started its social and ideological expansion. The only possible explanation would relate to the fragility of a secularism assumed and affirmed, sometimes very robustly, but not properly elaborated or theorised, and would also relate to an emergent populism when the left had been coopted into Nasser's structures of politics, culture, and ideology. Such leftists might have opted for positions articulated by modernist Muslims such as Khalafallah, who maintained that the religion of the Egyptian people is one of belief and devotion, with no correlation to politics, and that popular political instinct would place the majority on the side of the state rather than Islamist activists.[67] To reiterate: accepting the description of society or polity in terms of Islam is innocent politically only in a world different to the one in which we live. Names are resonant labels, and represent ideological phenomena par excellence, identifying name and the nature of the thing described, extruding what might be at variance with the connotations from the scope of that which is natural and right, so it becomes a fragment of circumstances. It thus becomes liable to – or requires – purgation by decisionist action of the party that can enforce its claim to represent the name.

For scholars, and for persons with a sound understanding overall, this image of "Islamic society" formed from an absolute interior against an absolute exterior is bewildering. One wonders how such a claim can be made in circumstances following capitalist expansion and imperialist penetration. One wonders how Islamists and their supporters, true believers and fellow travellers alike, can make such a claim while they continually reassert that imperialism subverted Arab life by penetrating its interstices. One seeks in vain to understand what is meant by claims that the Arabs live in Islamic societies, or that Arab societies are in fact Islamic societies. One comes across general references to such specifications as "the living element of our being" or "the pillars of our personality".[68] Then there are categorical affirmations,

67 Khalafallāh, "Al-ṣaḥwa al-islāmiyya fī Miṣr", 63.

68 Jalāl Amīn, "Al-turāth wa al-tanmiya al-'arabiyya", in *Al-Turāth wa taḥddiyāt al-'asr*, ed. Markaz Dirāsāt al-Waḥda al-'Arabiyya (Beirut: Centre for Arab Unity Studies, 1985), 766–767. The author later revised his positions, especially with regard to his claim that Islam was the basis of the Nahḍa and the anti-secular statements resulting from this. See his contribution in Jalāl Amīn, "Al-waḥda al-waṭaniyya fī muwājahat al-ṭā'ifiyya wa al-ta'aṣṣub", *al-Ahālī*, 18 April 1990.

without further precision or explanation, that colonialism failed to destroy local, national culture, its language, literature, religion, and thought. This culture purportedly puts itself forward as competitor to and participant in the culture of the present age, and joins together "our" intellectual fundamentals and interior sentiments.[69] Being, as suggested, concerned with ontology and not sociology, this identitarian discourse simply dwells upon continuity rhetorically, with continuous social-romantic motifs purporting to see in normal Arab sociability and propensity to chattiness an instance of "collective cognition", and "the pathways of living relationships" between people and, as such, a basis for effective democracy."[70] There is no object; the voice of the subject is realised by whoever enforces a claim for representation of the subject.

One often hears that the spread of the phenomenon of political Islam and manifestations of religious fanaticism are only a reaffirmation and renewal of Arab particularity in the confrontation with Westernisation and the estrangement of an authentic essence. Discriminating and balanced consideration of reality will reveal a different picture. Even the most fleeting consideration of empirical reality would reveal that there is nothing necessary or inevitable about the political ambitions of Islamism, nor are they some force of nature destined to triumph. The successful expansion of Islamist movements and their attraction of new members and supporters is linked to economic and social factors arising from social and economic disaggregation and from rapid, sometimes violent change in their wider environment, complemented by the erosion of state cultural hegemony. By way of example, this happened in the Syrian city of Hama, as research of outstanding quality has shown. This city had been the scene of the most violent attack against Syrian state authority in the 1970s and early 1980s.[71] In the city of Tunis a form of political organisation comparable to that in Hama is witnessed, whereas the city of Sfax was

69 al-Jābirī, "Ishkāliyyāt al-aṣāla wa al-mu'āṣara fī al-fikr al-'arabī al-ḥadīth wa al-mu'āṣir: ṣirā' ṭabaqī am mushkil thaqāfī", 46.

70 al-Bishrī, "Al-khulf bayn al-nukhba wa al-jamāhīr", 337.

71 F. Lawson, "Social bases for the Hamah Revolt", *MERIP Reports* 12 (1982): 24–28. After the start of the Syrian Civil War in 2011–2012, a huge amount of scholarship has emerged, with important contributions to the political economy of conflict. Suffice it here to cite Shamel Azmeh, *The Uprising of the Marginalised* (London: LSE Middle East Centre Paper Series, 2014). For research seeking to re-balance the common crude views that overdetermine the civil wars of Iraq and Syria in the opening decades of the twenty-first century, see www.strikingmargins.com.

solidly resistant to Islamist organisation as its socio-economic fabric preserved a high degree of consistency and constancy. The coastal region of the Tunisian Sahel also resisted the Islamists, for other reasons.[72] In Iraq, discernible reasons and conditions of a social and political nature can be brought to bear in the analysis of the reasons why certain social groups in Iraq tended to move away from Communism and towards Shi'ite Islamism in the last decades of Saddam Hussein, elements that trump interpretation in metaphysical terms of identity.[73] Finally one can mention the fact that the Islamist mass constituency in Syria, for example, was identical in socio-economic and regional makeup to those who had earlier rallied to Nasserism and Pan-Arabism, while the Communist Party and the movement of the Muslim Brothers competed for the loyalty of the same constituency in Homs and other Syrian cities.[74] In the Egyptian city of Shubra al-Khaima Communists and Muslim Brothers competed for members among textile workers with the Communists for long enjoying a greater degree of success.[75] Can one talk of a single Islamic nature among all Arabs? If Islam constituted the basic instinct of the Arabs, one may wonder why a considerable amount of violence has always accompanied necessarily all Islamist movements of expansion, with violence and terrorism carried out by Islamist groups against dissidents and society in Egypt, Algeria, and elsewhere, and acts of extreme violence in the founding of Islamic states such as Saudi Arabia, Iran, and Sudan. Clearly, Islamism was a product of socio-economic transformations and of Islamist infrastructures, and indeed of its encouragement by official state instances (President Sadat in Egypt, the security services, and the presidency in Syria), and did not spring from the recesses of the "self", but needed rather to remake this "self", by exemplary

---

72 Muḥammad 'Abd al-Bāqī al-Hirmāsī, "Al-islām al-iḥtijājī fī Tūnis", in *Al-ḥarakāt al-islāmiyya al-mu'āṣira fī al-waṭan al-'arabī*, ed. Markaz Dirāsāt al-Waḥda al-'Arabiyya (Beirut: Markaz Dirāsāt al-Waḥda al-'Arabiyya, 1987), 252–259, 263–264, 290–294.

73 Hana Batatu, "Shi'i Organization in Iraq: Al-Da'wah al-Islamiyah and al-Mujahidin", in *Shi'ism and Social Protest*, eds J. R. I. Cole and Nikki Keddie (New Haven and London: Yale University Press, 1986), 184, 194.

74 Johannes Reissner, *Ideologie und Politik der Muslimbrüder Syriens,* Islamkundliche Untersuchungen, Bd.55 (Freiburg: Klaus Schwartz Verlag, 1988), 198–199; Hanna Batatu, "Syria's Muslim brethren", *MERIP Reports* 12 (1982): 18; Raymond Hinnesbusch, "Islamic movements in Syria", in *Islamic Resurgences in the Arab World*, ed. Ali E. Hillal Dessouki (New York: Praeger, 1982), 154.

75 Joel Beinin, "Islamism, Marxism and Shubra al-Khayma textile workers", in *Islam, Politics and Social Movements*, eds Edward Burke III and Ira M. Lapidus (London: I. B. Tauris, 1988), pp. 207–227.

violence and its continuous use, and by acts of persuasion deploying various means, including extensive social engineering.

From this it is clear that political Islam has no link to any purported social nature to which there is a return after it has been estranged and its proprietors alienated. Religion is a political language for very particular socio-economic circumstances. In the same way it was not "heritage" that caused the Islamic political movement in Iran.[76] It emerges clearly that Islam constitutes an ideological and normative charge, one that is determined and defined by a variety of actors rather than itself exercising a determining influence before a self-sustaining Islamist momentum had been built. Where is the Islam of authenticity and continuity, in the light of the resistance of the city of Sfax and its religious practices to Islamist parties, more authentic, one must conclude, than political Islam, as it constitutes the lived religion of the city? The discourse of recovery of origins, their revival, and the location of Islam in these origins, has as its primary context a will to power in the name of Islam, building on the identitarian premise a claim for Islamist representation of identity. Among non-Islamists, such discourse constitutes an ahistorical trope of continuity that came to replace a Pan-Arab orientation that had been mortally wounded, or a liberalism either bereft of social confidence or captive to a sentimentalism of older social models. The final outcome is merely ideological performance, illocution, hence the vapid sentimentalist rhetoric, and the preference of ontology over sociology. The outcome, as one prominent, pragmatic, and reflective Islamist thinker noted with a mixture of apprehension and questioning, is the creation of a new and absolute partiality towards "a civilisational essence whose contours are unknown and the creation of enmity – psychological and cultural – with others whose contours are likewise unknown".[77] The recognition of the Islamic nature of Arabism therefore surrenders Arab nationalist ideology to Islamist requirements on sufferance, while it subordinates the politics of Arab nationalists to that of Islamist organisations.

---

76 J. R. I. Cole and Keddie, N. R., "Introduction", in *Shi'ism and Social Protest* and J. P. Digard, "Shi'isme et état en Iran", in *L'Islam et l'état dans le monde d'aujourd'hui*, ed. Olivier Carré (Paris: Presses Universitaires de France, 1982), 65–88. See Said Amir Arjomand, *The Turban and the Crown* (Oxford: Oxford University Press, 1988) and E. Abrahamian, *Khomeinism* (Berkeley and Los Angeles: University of California Press, 1993).

77 al-Majd, "Al-mas'ala al-siyāsiyya: waṣl al-turāth bi al-'aṣr wa al-niẓām al-siyāsī li'l-dawla", 574.

One purpose of the present study has been to highlight the incoherence of this way of imagining Islam's relation with Arab societies, and it will be right to recapitulate a few points that have been arrived at. Islam does not define the particularity of anything apart from that of the Muslim religion.[78] There are, however, societies and histories with specificities that have been marked by the complex interplay and imbrications between their social and cultural structures and the religion of Islam and its symbolic sources of authority, no less than its normative claims and institutional structures. Within these multiple convergences, Islam occupied particular cultural, legal, ideological, and political positions, which varied with time and location, inasmuch as the secular world was linked to religion in ways that were not specifically Islamic, as indicated in Chapter 1. It also emerged that Islam, leaving aside claims made for it in ideological slogans, is not recognisable as a single entity, but has consisted and still consists of variant and sometimes contrasting ways of defining a link between believers, individuals, and specific collectivities defined as such, with a number of texts, and with ways of understanding and interpreting these texts in terms of dogmas, rituals, and norms. Islam is in regard to the present discussion an ideological signal distributed by political actors, allocating authenticity to that which falls within the purview of the actor, and thereby able to define determinate content for this Islam and, if lucky, enforce its understanding of what can be included and excluded from it.

Who is the Muslim, without further specification? And what is the Arab-Muslim when removed from the dynamics of modern history? What, indeed, is this strange entity, free of all contamination by otherness, of the realities of social transformation under the influence of imperialism and its global effects? One result of this transformation was the effective elimination of boundless particularity; yet there is a desire to rescue this Arabo-Islamic entity by abolishing its universal dimension – or rather, its insertion in global conditions – in an illusory manner but with little imagination. Is the West, with its political concepts such as democracy, parliamentary government, and the centralised state, not a fundamental constituent of the life of Arabs today? Is not the West with its eagerly anticipated technical culture, system of state administration, and educational structure of schools and universities, cultural tendencies and legal principles, a basic and original part of Arab societies? In such circumstances, are not calls for a "return" to a purported

78 al-ʿAẓma, *Al-turāth bayn al-sulṭān wa al-taʾrīkh*, 50–52.

pre-lapsarian condition any more than the quest for hegemony, the deployment of an ideological sign with undefined but definite resonance, Islam, a name taken for reality, all the while this nominal indicator of authenticity is taken for the source and origin of present and past, society and history? In the best of cases, this is a reduction of complex historical entities to one presumed cultural essence, reduced in its turn to a religion named "Islam", and this in turn reductively parsed according to ideological taste. Islam is merely an imaginary concept that indicates itself, or rather the indication by Islamists of what they wish it to be, with a programme of comprehensive re-socialisation into norms that are either dead or never existed in practice.

Such egregious reductionism, substituting moralised religion for politics, society, and economy, moving today towards a yesterday crafted, in its turn, of lifeless models bereft of historical reality: such is by no means unknown or unusual. Myths are common in attempts to make history by retrograde practices and the invention of traditions and of "heritage", the spread of false memories, duly substituted for history. All populist and nationalist revivalism without historical horizons open to the future incline to these imaginary histories with extraordinary determination. In this respect, proponents of romantic Arabism and Arabo-Islamism trod a global path already well-worn in Fascist Italy, National Socialist Germany, Falangist Spain, by the Action Française and among Slavophile Eastern European movements.[79]

The tendency of some Arab intellectuals to associate Arabism with Islam is not, basically, so far removed in its mythological bases and its primary

79 The bibliography on nationalism in the variety of its forms in recent decades is vast and the following is just a sampler: H. Kohn, *The Idea of Nationalism: A Study in Its Origins and Background* (London: Transaction Publishers, 1944/2005); Paul James, *Nation Formation: Towards a Theory of Abstract Community* (London: Sage, 1996); A. Smith, *Nationalism*, 2nd edn (Cambridge: Polity Press, 2010); Benedict Anderson, *Imagined Communities: Reflections on the Origin and Spread of Nationalism* (London: Verso, 1977); Gellner, *Nations and Nationalism*; Partha Chatterjee, *Nationalist Thought and the Colonial World* (London: Zed Books and Delhi: Oxford University Press, 1986); Hobsbawm, *Nations and Nationalism since 1780*; Tom Nairn, "Nationalism: The modern Janus", in *The Break Up of Britain* (London: New Left Books, 1977), 329–363. For the artistic construal of Arab nationalism as memory, depicted in works of art and in museum exhibitions, see the material in Peter Wien, *Arab Nationalism. The Politics of History and Culture in the Modern Middle East* (London: Routledge, 2017) – the author's analyses are Islamised, in a way somewhat routine in the twenty-first century, to an extent far beyond what is admissible by his material. The phenomenon of nationalism has occasioned in recent years some outstanding research. Studies of identitarian hyper-nationalism are growing, but suffice here to refer to Sternhell, *The Anti-Enlightenment Tradition.*

cultural and psychological mechanisms from Catholic Irish nationalism, for example.[80] The imagined homogeneous and continuous self confronts the similarly construed external other in the imagination, but it also collides with reality. The *umma*, however defined and in whichever terms, is not a smooth surface but is a complex and dynamic being, a structure, assembly, and network with many hierarchies within it, of women and men, classes and regions, and kinsfolk and cities, cohorts and generations, norms and behaviours, cultures and confessions. None of these elements are characterised by permanence or autochtony, of their relationships with the other elements: the body-politic they compose, the state to which they belong, the global system. Most of these individual elements – economic activities, cultural practices, social norms – are connected separately to the global system that determines the mode and extent of integration into the global division of labour, as well as its degree and mode of underdevelopment. Underdevelopment is a form of contemporaneity; rates and rhythms of change within every historical and societal unit vary, sometimes very widely, to an extent of what might be described as temporal Balkanisation, with non-contemporaneous elements living and indeed thriving contemporaneously in regional and social contiguity, such as the coexistence of information technology practices, the hygienic habits of another age, and belief in supernatural causality, within the same body-politic.

Consequently, an effective and constructive political programme cannot be built on a supposition of the generic unity and homogeneity of these constituent elements of a social and political formation, or on the supposition that it might have a single collective will, as one often hears from Islamist ideologues. It is rather individual citizenship as a political concept of the individual that is the more effective means suitable to an age like ours. The intellectual and cultural involution of some social groups rendered marginal over past decades, their retrograde self-constitution, results from the possibilities of their evolution having been confiscated. The apparent energy of such groups in recent years as they have come to reconstitute themselves in Syria and Iraq as political actors under tribal, sectarian, and local signatures is an outcome of social and economic blockages and of structures of internal segmentation and exclusion that became systematic and self-perpetuating

80 Richard Kearny, *Transitions: Narratives in Modern Irish Culture* (Dublin: Wolfhound Press, 1988), 242, 248.

at the close of the twentieth century. The extraordinarily dynamic internal variability and strain in times of uncontrolled change with its primary dynamics outside national borders produces a situation without a discernible historical direction, overlaid by a sense of crisis. Hence the hyperbolised and distended import of the ideological moment in the public sphere.[81] Hence also, with the lack of relatively stable, self-sustaining structuration, the particular importance of decisionism and voluntarism. Arab societies are no different in this respect from the majority of other developing societies.

The obsession with unity and uniformity coercively asserted (and attempted by Islamist politics, on the model of older nationalist practices), might comfortably accommodate a pop-psychological explanation in terms of compensation or over-compensation in situations of disaggregation. The obsession itself is not, in the light of previous considerations, one foreign to Arab polities with, as noted, a decided despotic drift. It can legitimately be claimed that that unity was a Form – in the Kantian sense – in the modern Arab political imaginary, and in modern Arab political thought.[82] This is further represented in postulating spatial and temporal homogeneity, as suggested, correlated with the supposed harmonious surface of the national fabric, relating to alterity by negation. This applies to anti-secular polemic fully. Thus, secularism appears to one populist nationalist as a cultural alternative to what he calls "the religious subjectivity". This is by way of affirmation that religion be the essence of national sentiment, the corollary of which is that secularism, in as much as it is independent of religious sentiment, must, according to this sociologist, be "merely a denial of the national self".[83] Reality is thus cleft between an essential interior with an ontological truth and a false exterior that undermines origins and essences. Democratic political activity is genuine only if it proceeds in the name of this essence, which is the Islamic origin and nature attributed to the people taken for a political constituency. In Arab society since the early 1980s, democracy as a political project, according to a widespread concept, had become construed as an inclination to "correct" the link between the state and people by identifying the one with the other as the legitimate template, and by assuming that the

81 'Abd Allāh al-'Arwī, *Al-'arab wa al-fikr al-tārīkhi* (Beirut: Dar al-Ḥaqīqa, 1973), 125.

82 Sharāra, *Ḥawl ba'ḍ mushkilāt al-dawla*, 70.

83 Burhān Ghalyūn, *Al-mas'ala al-ṭā'ifiyya wa mushkilat al-aqallīyāt* (Beirut: Dār al-Ṭalī'a, 1979), 12–13, 22–23.

dislocation between them consists of a cultural and civilisational dualism, presumably unnatural, in which modernity and heteronomy are identified.[84] It is assumptions such as this that allow for the now very common statements of pathos to the effect, for instance, that the secular state in the Arab world is based on a surrender by all communities of their distinctive personalities, and on a shared sacrifice of identity – a situation clearly, in this manner of speech, in need of correction by restoration of various heritages. State and nation can recover their pre-lapsarian harmony, and be made once again to correspond to each other, once the condition of secularity and secularism, productive of estrangement and alienation, has been dismantled.

National and identitarian formations and issues are not, however, as simple as is ingenuously held in these discourses. Subaltern nationalisms, like Arabism and Islamism in its atavistic and para-nationalist mode, once they merged with hyper-nationalist and nativist currents, not unlike European nationalisms, came to owe their genesis to processes of nation-state state formation, a model that is equally imprinted on Pan-Islamism. It is commonly known, but commonly forgotten, that nations are not eternal social units or metaphysical essences, but political units with internal particularities and external delimitations of great complexity within which the state – or projects of state, such as the projected Islamic state – played a critical role. At the time of the creation of the Italian state only 2.5 per cent of Italians spoke what is known today as standard Italian, while in 1789 only 50 per cent of the French were French-speaking, and only 12 per cent spoke what is today normative French.[85] Italian and French only became national languages after the French and Italian nation states were engendered through national education and upbringing, and through central political communication and after a long period of time and centralised statist administration. This did not prevent Italian and French nationalisms, particularly the former, from speaking the language of revivalism, of the Italian *Risorgimento*, resurrection or revival, the exact equivalent of the Arabic Ba'th. The link between the state and statist elites with the people – with its numerous internal particularities – are highly complex and cannot be summarised in expressions about the emanation of state from society or their correspondence, ideas that found their theoretical

84 Al-Bishrī, "Al-khulf bayn al-nukhba wa al-jamāhīr izā' al-'ilāqa bayn al-qawmiyya al-'arabiyya wa al-Islām", 278–282.

85 Hobsbawm, *Nations and Nationalism since 1780*, 38, 60.

foundations in Rousseau's general will, a term often serviceable while crafting discourse in the name of an imagined people, "Islamic" in the context of the present discussion. The state cannot be a "reflection" of society, whatever this might mean, but is a separate instance. It is a mechanism for the control of social, economic, and cultural conflicts as well as the management and allocation of disparities amidst disparities in rhythms of change (Balkanisation of temporality) in such a way that maintains geographical, political, and, ideally, legal integrity and the monopoly of violence.

It was previously argued that Islamic discourse in some of its better developed forms occupies the ideological space previously occupied by Arabism in its populist, organismic, vitalist, and revivalist redactions, that of accentuated romanticism. At this confluence a state is conceived in which division is banished, correspondence achieved between people and state. The state comes ontologically to stand for the people, a "state with an intense presence, embodied in a new prophet who occupied the presidency of the republic".[86] The discovery by Arab intellectuals in the 1980s of "the spirit of the people" in which Islam is embedded essentially is only a facet of their fascination with the totalitarian state or at least the corporatist state, notwithstanding democratism. Democratist discourse that reclaimed Islam came as an auxiliary to Islamist politics, and insinuated Islamist ideology under the canopy of populist nationalism.

It is perhaps not altogether surprising that critical capacities and historical realism were shod, without this being the result of a serious political and social challenge or menace, by the main bulk of the Arab nationalist, liberal, and left-wing intelligentsia; this occurred before the move of Islamism to the centre. Broad swathes of nationalist thought were animated by populist desire or became ensnared by it, for love of the people. In the circumstances following 1967, canonised after 1989, with the notions of development and progress spurned and then scoffed at, the condition of society and culture that had hitherto been designated as backward or underdeveloped came to be portrayed as authentic, a historical ceiling for some who described themselves as realists, less enthusiastic than but fully complicit with the true believers in populism, much exercised by the example of the Iranian Revolution. Islamism assimilated Islamism and Arabism in terms of ideological modules of

86 ʻAbd Allāh al-Wazzān, "Michel ʻAflaq: Widāʻan", *Zawāyā* 2–3 (1989–1990), 62.

long standing, to which vitalist nationalism, in the form of Islamist nativism and hyper-nationalism was a later addition. Briefly to recapitulate and then continue: this current developed in the 1960s in the context of the struggle between Arab revolutionary forces and socially conservative forces opposed to socialism on economic grounds and politically aligned to the United States following sponsorship and patronage by Great Britain in alliance with Jordan. This clash was not limited to that of the Nasser and Baath regimes with Saudi Arabia and the United States. It was global (Indonesia, Angola, Latin America, Vietnam), and manifested itself clearly in Tunisia where criticism of the attempt to create agricultural cooperatives in the late 1960s was a key area for an offensive by religious and socially conservative forces against the technocratic and modernist cadres of the Neo-Destour party. These religious and conservative forces placed their campaign under the general heading of the "moral decline" they perceived in the emancipation of Tunisian women and in the ideas of university-educated intellectuals.[87] The fundamental campaign regionally was, however, directed against socialism – and by implication, Marxism – and Pan-Arabism, seen as the antithesis of Islam and destructive of society, a vision set out in works by authors such as the Damascene Muslim Brother erudite, publisher and gentleman-scholar, Salah al-Din al-Munajjid, author of *Al-taḍlīl al-ishtirākī* (The Socialist Deception, 1966), *Balshafat al-islām* (The Bolshevisation of Islam, 1967) and *Fayṣal ibn 'Abd al-'Azīz min khilāl aqwālihi wa af'ālihi* (Faysal b. 'Abd al-'Aziz in Word and Deed, 1972) and the Egytian Muhammad Jalal Kishk (1929–1993), author of *Al-sa'ūdiyyūn wa al-ḥall al-islāmī* (The Saudis and the Islamic Solution, 1980) and of a four-volume series on socialism and secularism whose first volume was entitled *Al-mārksīya wa al-ghazw al-fikrī* (Marxism and the Intellectual Invasion, 1966), and in newspapers such as *al-Ḥayāt*, published in Beirut. This attack gained intensity after the secession in Syria from the United Arab Republic, when the Muslim Brothers rebelled against the leadership of Mustafa al-Siba'i (1915–1964), leader of the Islamic Socialist Front from 1945 to 1964, who did not attack the Soviet Union. Siba'i – whose brother had been a leading Communist – and others from the Syrian Muslim Brothers had discussed socialism since the middle of the 1940s.[88] The

87 Abdelkader Zghal, "The reactivation of tradition in post-traditional society", *Daedalus* 101/1 (1973): 225–237, 232–233.

88 Ḥannā, *Al-ittijāhāt al-fikriyya fī sūriyyā wa lubnān*.

attack developed certainly under the influence of the enmity of certain groups of the Syrian Muslim Brothers connected to the bazaar. In addition, many Egyptian Muslim Brothers took refuge in Saudi Arabia from the 1960s, no longer the object of stern criticism by Islamists.[89]

This attack against socialism and Pan-Arabism contained the same terms used implicitly today by those seeking conciliation with Islamist discourse, some of whose ideas were discussed in previous pages. These included the claim that secularism and socialism were only alien elements, foisted on Arab society from outside, on the assumption that history does not move, that change is illusory, that socialism and secularism bear no relation to process or to social transformation. Socialism, Pan-Arabism, and secularism were responsible for the division of the *umma* whose salvation was to be had from reliance on Islam.[90] Soviet atheism was correlated to socialism. It was not only Islamic discourse that took this direction; certain anti-secular and anti-Communist Christian tendencies also followed suit, as they did in Poland, Italy, Latin America, and elsewhere.[91] After 1967 this tendency quickly gathered force, encouraged after the 1967 Arab League summit in Khartoum in which Nasserism signalled its ideological capitulation. In the gloating words of al-Munajjid: "after the Egyptian leader had called for beards to be plucked out, he came to seek help from the bearded."[92]

Aspects of this capitulation and the shaykhification of the state have already been discussed. A few further indices will be suggested here. One of the clearest signs of disorientation and weakness was the encouragement given by the Egyptian religious and media authorities to collective hallucination that seemed to Egyptians to be a response to the shock of defeat, as manifested in the purported apparitions in 1968 of the Virgin in Cairo.[93] Subsequently the supernatural and the marvellous, and the conspiratorial as well, came to sweep across the print and audio-visual media followed by Sadat's encouragement of some Islamism in his quest for overturning the

89 al-Ghazālī, *Min hunā na'lam*, 23–24, 95.

90 Ṣalāḥ al-Dīn al-Munajjid, *A'midat al-nakba: Baḥth 'ilmī fī asbāb hazīmat Ḥuzayrān*, 2nd edn (Beirut: Dār al-Kitāb al-Jadīd, 1967), 18, 57–59, 87–91.

91 René Ḥabashī, *Ḥaḍāratunā 'alā muftaraq* (Beirut: Manshūrāt al-Nadwa al-Lubnāniyya, 1960), 151–162.

92 al-Munajjid, *A'midat al-nakba*, 85.

93 Ṣādiq al-'Aẓm, "Mu'ijizat ẓuhūr al-'adhrā' wa taṣfiyat āthār al-'udwān", in *Naqd al-fikr al-dīnī*, 2nd edn, 5th impression (Beirut: Dār al-Ṭalī'a, 1982), 151–179.

previous, Nasserist regime from inside. This left serious political fallout. Newly founded political parties in Egypt, including the Wafd, distanced themselves from their own liberal and secular elements as they entered into electoral fronts and coalitions. As one disenchanted observer noted, these were sacrificed for alliances that, oddly and not too cleverly, were based on maximalist programmes, making wholesale ideological concessions to potential Islamist allies rather than making tactical accommodations with them.[94] This, in an atmosphere of growing moralisation, in religious terms, of various aspects of life, and of Islamisation, including the Islamisation of common locutions, and the Islamisation of dress. Both local Islamism and regional Petro-Islamic infrastructure swept Egypt. "Islamic finance" expanded,[95] with a multitude of scams, and penetration of the media, financial and economic institutions, and political parties.[96] The emphasis on unfettered neo-liberal values in the economy and in the operation of these institutions, and by such as the Egyptian ultra-reactionary Shaykh Muhammad Mutawalli al-Sha'rawi (1911–1998), a pioneer of televisual religion, was a continuation of the attack on socialism in the 1960s.[97]

What is termed "Islamic revival" is really less a response to the defeat of 1967 as the ascendancy of forces already in place, and their move from the margins to the centre. It is not so much a solution to problems revealed by military and political defeat as much as the expression of defeat accomplished.[98] The staging was a socio-dramatic, a scenario with ready-made roles[99] that came to play in the case of Sadiq al-Azm, mentioned already, and responses to it.[100] Al-Azm's concern with inner backwardness was transmuted into an obsession

---

94 Faraj Fūda, *Qabla al-suqūṭ: Ḥiwār hādi' ḥawl taṭbīq al-sharī'a al-islāmiyya* (Cairo: n.p., 1985), 186.

95 On which I. Warde, *Islamic Finance in the Global Economy*, 2nd edn (Edinburgh: Edinburgh University Press, 2010).

96 Maḥmūd 'Abd al-Faḍīl, *Al-khadī'a al-māliyya al-kubrā: Al-iqtiṣād al-siyāsī li sharikāt tawẓīf al-amwāl* (Cairo: Dār al-Mustaqbal al-'Arabi, 1989) and Fūda, *Qabla al-suqūṭ*, 161–165.

97 Fu'ād Zakariyyā, *Al-ḥaqīqa wa al-wahm fī al-ḥarakāt al-islāmiyya al-mu'āṣira*, 2nd edn (Cairo and Paris: Dār al-Fikr li'l-Dirāsāt wa al-Nashr wa al-Tawzī', 1986), 33–40.

98 Few were aware of this situation or openly voiced awareness. Two exceptions were Fahmī Jad'ān, "Al-ḥarakāt al-islāmiyya al-mu'āṣira fī al-waṭan al-'arabī", *Majallat al-'Ulūm al-Ijtimā'iyya* 17 (1989), 284–285 and Zakariyyā, *Al-ḥaqīqa wa al-wahm fī al-ḥarakāt al-islāmiyya al-mu'āṣira*, 134–135.

99 Zāhī Sharfān, "Qaḍiyyat naqd al-fikr al-dīnī aw al-maqāma al-lubnāniyya", *Dirāsāt 'Arabiyya* 6 (1970): 4.

100 See, for example, Naṣr Allāh, *Al-radd 'alā Ṣādiq al-'Aẓm* and especially 17, 24, 224, 225 and the introduction by Ṣalāḥ al-Dīn al-Munajjid.

with inner purgation, railing against "cultural imperialism" and "intellectual invasion", later against "Crusading", a trope that had hardly ever been used to describe Europe except among some of the most determinedly retrograde marginal forces. To recover authenticity, the term "Third World" disappeared, replaced by focus on an "Islamic world".

The Iranian Revolution of 1979 seemed to confer added credibility to the change from existing reality to its depiction in terms of Islamic continuity and harmony. Many Arab intellectuals were fascinated by the Revolution, and fascination of course impedes judgement. It seemed to confirm an orientation that seemed better to represent reality, reality of the people, and restore shape to the people's spirit. Many took this pathway and led themselves away from Marxism. Contemplating this revolution, the poet Adonis, never a Marxist, nor ever religious, but rather with libertarian views, saw in religion "the breath and sigh of exhausted Iran, in a positive not negative sense . . . it is a new wakefulness in sunlight . . . the guide for the emergence of Iran from its suffering, it is the path which gives people the fullness life and its complete flowering and its overall coherence." Not as elaborate or eloquent as Foucault in its breathless sentimentalism, but still further pursuit of the invalidity of Marxist social analysis, and the preference for ontology over sociology.[101] In an indication of a strategic shift in favour of Islamist discourse whose motifs and historist and folk-sociological premises were coming to occupy the centre and crowd out all else by cooptation or polemic, the older target, atheism, virtually disappeared and came to be replaced by secularism, which came to be set up as the major cultural turpitude and a major site of ideological and polemical contestation. Politically and culturally inert, many intellectuals adopted the conceit of Olympian height, and in coopting themselves into the Islamist ideological register spoke of "national unity", even in heightened tonalities of "a historical block", between liberals, leftists, nationalists, and Islamists, on the conditions of the last.

This was the situation in intellectual circles. At a popular level, increased Islamist political activity was not in general sign of an essence estranged and

101 Adūnīs ('Alī Aḥmad Sa'īd), "Bayn al-thabāt wa-l-taḥawwul: Khawāṭir ḥawl al-thawra al-islāmiyya fī Īrān", *Mawāqif* 34 (1979): 152 and "Al-'aql al-mu'taqal", *Mawāqif* 43 (1981), 7–8 where Adūnīs, replying to criticism, expressed his reservations about the Iranian Revolution. For Foucault, on which much has been written, see Mirsepassi, *Transnationalism*, ch. 6.

then corrected and recovered by Islamic consciousness. Islamist political language as a language of protest was associated with the exhaustion of socialist and nationalist languages in its consecration of authoritarianism in the national state.[102] The mood was emblematised by the extraordinary spread – and uniformisation – of head scarves and other forms of veiling, symbolically an important psychological crutch for solidarity between kinsfolk and the link between this solidarity and a pact of honour based control over women, symbol of this pact. In fact, women and their veils are used metaphorically as a sign for numerous purposes of which the most important are the purported stability of origins, claimed with increasing rigidity, the slogan of a social unity closed in upon itself, while the veil is also the final surviving proof of the authority of Arab men who find themselves isolated in the face of precarity and mass downward mobility, with little control over their destinies, in a variety of ways de-masculanised.[103] It was unsurprising that the incipient Bolshevik state considered unravelling the strategic knot of women's status and gender relations in Central Asia a cornerstone of its social engineering. The assumption was that control over women and confirmation of their inferiority were the mainstay of the status quo ante and of resistance to the new order.[104]

3 The Context of Secularism

Preceding pages have shown how central Arab societies at the close of the twentieth century, led by religious and non-religious intellectuals pandering to the former, had attempted to roll back the history of a century of progress and set upon a path of cognitive and cultural impoverishment consonant with social, political, and global conditions. This is a path conveying imaginary solutions to social and national crises. In intellectual terms the decisive factor in this process was the trope of revivalism that sought to recover the past and its glories, affirming continuity and perceived history in moral terms of disgrace and glorious deeds. Given its status as a new norm, the discourse of incommensurable particularity, origin,

102 Ilyās Khuri, "Rūh al-sharq wa thawrat al-sharq", *Mawāqif* 34 (1979), 124.

103 See Amīn, *Dalīl al-muslim al-ḥazīn*, 73; Berque, *The Arabs: Their History and Future*, 253; and Bouhdiba, *Sexuality in Islam*, 232.

104 Gregory J. Mansell, *The Surrogate Proletariat: Moslem Women and Revolutionary Strategies in Soviet Central Asia 1919–1929* (Princeton: Princeton University Press, 1974).

continuity, and revival is based on a leap across time and space. Time is unrelated to change, and consumed by origins and continuities, and both figure as rhetorical tropes for abeyance. Revival becomes an act of recognition and recovery, in which the present is a point of mere transit, with no qualities of its own, between a normative past that is entirely positive and a consequently normative future to which the positive charge of the past is to be conveyed.[105] How can the nineteenth and twentieth centuries measure against changeless abidance?

This representation has been put forward by irenicists who concede to the basic tenets of Islamism and regard their erstwhile modernist ideologies sceptically. Many want to believe that their concessions are purely cultural. Yet they are conceding to a body of motifs that disallows separating out culture on the assumption of correspondence between society, knowledge, history, politics, and Islam. One such intellectual hoped that a "recovered Islam" would enter politics as "a combatant for the democracy and equality which are absent from the secular state". He does recognise a tendency in all religions to exclusivism and coercion, but his only solution to this cognitive – and political – dissonance seems to be an inconsequent expression of regret.[106] When, in the course of a discussion between nationalists and Islamists, the suggestion was made that the way forward was for Islamists to drop calling for shari'a, and nationalists to drop secularism, an idea and a word that, it was claimed, was a cause for discord, this last assertion was made with an almost eschatological certainty: "if an Arab state were to be established in the national [as distinct from an Islamist] sense, [it needs to be considered] that nations have their practices and traditions and heritages, in culture and legislation and politics, and this in the case of the Arab nation is self-evidently Islam."[107] Islamist political discourse and its liberal, nationalist, and leftist auxiliaries repeatedly propose a maximalist programme in minimalist form.

An exclusivist and restrictive tendency of a society named by one singular and total descriptor has been a recurrent theme in this and the previous chapter. This is the tendency that led Islamist organisations such as the Muslim

105 al-'Azma, *Al-turāth bayn al-sulṭān wa al-ta'rīkh*, 146.

106 Ghalyūn, *Al-mas'ala al-ṭā'ifiyya wa mushkilat al-aqallīyyāt*, 12–13.

107 Riḍwān al-Sayyid, "Al-qawmiyyūn wa al-islāmiyyūn fī al-waṭan al-'arabī wa ḍarūrāt al-ḥiwār wa al-talāqi", in *Al-ḥiwār al-qawmī al-dīnī*, Markaz Dirāsāt al-Waḥda al-'Arabiyya (ed.) (Beirut: Markaz Dirāsāt al-Waḥda al-'Arabiyya, 1989), 80.

Brothers[108] to abjure the concept of political parties that, they considered, were divisive of the nation, the *umma*, and were not necessary, as the nature of society requires a particular type of rule. This bespeaks an irrepressible claim to the exclusive appropriation of power,[109] which would guarantee the implementation of what are considered to be imperative religious obligations such as particular types of punishment, jihad, and alms, considered "social devotions" according to an eloquent expression of Muhammad al-Ghazali, performed by individuals through the intermediary of the state.[110] The starting point is a purported self-evidence that indicates the Islamic essence of society, with the aim of reaching total domination in the name of Islam self-evidently intuited as belonging to the domain of anthropology and not subjected to the laws of history. The clash between this purported social instinct and existing reality was always violent, as manifested in every attempt in modern history to set up political systems on the basis of Islam: in Iran, in Pakistan, in Saudi Arabia as in Sudan. Yet the 1979 Iranian Revolution, for example, was not so much an Islamic as a popular revolution with broad social, economic, and political bases, which resulted in the success of the Islamic Republican Party in eliminating all the other political actors and appropriating power exclusively. Similarly, the Russian Revolution of 1917 was only Bolshevik retrospectively, in view of results. All religious politics, Islamic or otherwise, inclines in its revivalism towards a politics of purgation and purification, precipitating inquisitorial procedures of various kinds.

But Islamist regimes are, after all, regimes; their title to Islamism is one that produces, inquisitions apart, a thriving political theatre. A state becomes Islamic when, apart from its name, it displays tokens of Islamity, the more garish the more convincing: veiling, public punishments, and ostentatious devotions are only the most spectacular. For the rest, economy and society are left to the effective forces of history, principally capitalism. Thus, the speed, after the first amputation, with which Numeiri was congratulated by Muhammad al-Ghazali, the Mufti of the Arab Republic of Egypt, the Muslim Brothers' Guide 'Umar al-Talimsani (1904–1986), the Egyptian-Qatari international Islamist oracle Yusuf al-Qaradawi (b. 1926)

108 Compare with Umlīl, *Al-iṣlāḥiyya al-'arabiyya wa al-dawla al-waṭaniyya*, 161.
109 Khalafallāh, "Al-ṣaḥwa al-islāmiyya fī Miṣr", 38–39.
110 al-Ghazālī, *Min hunā na'lam*, 44.

and the renowned boxer Cassius Marcellus Clay Jr, alias Muhammad Ali (1942–2016). Ja'afar al Numeiri, president of Sudan from 1969 to 1985, introduced a constitution in 1983 whose only link to the heritage of Islam was accomplished by naming and nominal signs.[111] This constitution was selective and maximalist in its use of Islamic motifs, with an authoritarian claim to absolute *ijtihād* alongside a scorn for juristic traditions and the removal of authority from society – the handywork, incidentally, of a highly skilled and sophisticated politician, Dr Hasan al-Turabi (1932–2016), a Sorbonne-trained jurist. He knew well what he was doing: maximalism in details of spectacular punishment, and an arrogation of very wide discretion to himself and his associates. The whole approach was regarded critically by those few Islamists who maintained an attitude of sobriety.[112]

That such are very few is in itself indicative of the idle hope that Islamism might move away in political terms from maximalism, despite the intentions of some Islamists. An "absolute Islam", integralist and fundamentalist, refusing all forms of modernity, including the translation of *shūrā* by the term democracy, is latent in the pores of Islamist discourse, for it makes absolute claims to rectitude, able to see the world only as a mirror of itself.[113] It is natural that the more forward-looking Islamist viewpoints need consideration. These include theses erratically and occasionally put forward by Rashid Ghannouchi, long before 2011, in his apparent repudiation of the legacy of the Muslim Brothers, with the acceptance of complete integration into a democratic order and his acceptance to what Tunisian society had acquired already in terms of social progress – especially with regard to women – during the period of Habib Bourguiba.[114] There is an incongruity and even a dissonance between these positions and those normally held by Islamists.[115] Doubts arise because of the constant

111 Fūda, *Qabla al-suqūṭ*, 121–124, 16, 139, 145–150.

112 Abū al-Majd, *Ḥiwār lā muwājaha*, 35–56.

113 Umlīl, *Al-iṣlāḥiyya al-'arabiyya wa al-dawla al-waṭaniyya*, 163–164, 167–189.

114 Rāshid al-Ghannūshi, "Ta'qīb: Taḥlīl li'l-'anāṣir al-mukawwina li'l-ẓāhira al-islāmiyya bi Tūnis: Ḥarakāt al-ittijāh al-islāmī", in *Al-ḥarakāt al-islāmiyya al-mu'āṣira fī al-waṭan al-'arabī*, ed. Markaz Dirāsāt al-Waḥda al-'Arabiyya (Beirut: Markaz Dirāsāt al-Waḥda al-'Arabiyya, 1987), 300–302.

115 Al-Hirmāsī, "Al-islām al-iḥtijājī fī Tūnis", 273–274.

manoeuvring and changes of tack that observers of Islamism have become accustomed to.[116] Deviousness, and playing simultaneously a visible and an invisible hand, and dissimulation, may well be involved, but more important is that Islamism is by nature exclusivist and finalist. It is based, in its populist conception of democracy, on a belief in a total and all-encompassing representation of the *umma* and that Islamism is the *umma*'s right order. Total control is seen therefore as inevitable, and temporary manoeuvres become insignificant in the perspective on eternity and social ontology. Opportunism is accommodation to the transient, ephemeral world, in contrast with the certainty of the Islamist outcome.

The justification for the robust reaffirmation of an integrated secular perspective today arises from the context that the preceding pages and chapters have discussed. Undoubtedly in current Arab democratist and other liberal literature, there is a tacit consensus of silence with regard to secularism and secularisation.[117] The dissonance between secular development and the brittleness of deliberately secularist thinking, and the lack of a central secularist ideology, is one between reality and the perception of reality. Secularism has not been a slogan but a historical orientation and an assembly of recognition and social, ideological, and theoretical forces that draw history together and conform to ideas of progress and global social change.[118] The Islamist erotics of political power and yearning for exclusivism, and the implicit or explicit assent to this tendency by ideological and cultural forces of a secular or even secularist nature discussed in some detail in this chapter, together constitute the context for secularism's re-emergence today.

116 Musṭafā al-Tuwāti, "Al-ḥaraka al-islāmiyya fī Tūnis", *Qaḍāyā Fikriyya* (1989): 208–210. With regard to the positions of Tunisian Islamists towards the Personal Status Laws see Laṭīf, *Al-islāmiyyūn wa al-mar'a*, 15.

117 'Abd al-Laṭīf, *Al-ta'wīl wa al-mufāraqa*, 79.

118 See Abdelmajīd Charfi, "La sécularisation dans les sociétés arabo-musulmanes modernes", *Islamochristiana* 8 (1982): 57–59. See the following study for an excellent presentation of some questions of secularisation in Muslim societies and related social conflicts: Nur Yalman, "Some observations on secularism in Islam: Cultural revolution in Turkey", *Daedalus* 102 (1973): 139–168.

Bibliography

Anonymous, *Al-khilāfa wa sulṭat al-umma*, trans. 'Abd al-Ghanī Sanī Bek (Cairo: Maṭba'at al-Hilāl, 1924).

Anonymous, "Book review", *Al-Muqtaṭaf* 67/3 (1925): 332–333.

Anonymous, "Al-Sharqiyyūn wa'l-qubba'a", *Al-Hilāl* (1926): 171.

Anonymous [Rashīd Riḍā], "Di'āyat al-ilḥad fī Miṣr", *Al-Manār* 27/2 (1926): 119–127.

Anonymous, "Al-adyān wa hal tuṣbiḥu shārā'i 'adabiyya?", *al-'Uṣūr* 2/7 (1928): 657–659.

Anonymous, "Difā'an 'an al-ḥurriya: Layla Ba'albakī", *Ḥiwār* 11–12 (1964).

Anonymous [As'ad Dāghir], *Thawrat al-'Arab ḍidd al-Atrāk: muqaddimātuhā, asbābuhā, natā'ijuhā*, Biqalam aḥad a'ḍā' al-jama'iyyāt al-sirriya *al-'Arabiyya*, ed. 'Iṣām Shbārū (Beirut: Dār Miṣbaḥ al-Fikr, 1987).

'Abbūd, Mārūn, *Ruwwād al-nahḍa al-ḥadītha* (Beirut: Dār al-'Ilm lil-Malāyīn, 1952).

'Abbūd, Mārūn, *Mu'allafāt Mārūn 'Abbūd, al-majmū'a al-kāmila* (Beirut: Dār Mārūn 'Abbūd, Dār al-Thaqāfa, 1966–1967).

'Abd al-Dā'im, 'Abd Allāh, "Al-mas'ala al-thaqāfiyya bayn al-aṣāla wa al-mu'āṣara", in *Al-turāth wa taḥaddiyyāt al-'aṣr fī al-waṭan al-'arabī: Al-aṣāla wa al-mu'āṣara*, ed. Markaz Dirāsāt al-Waḥda al-'Arabiyya, 2nd edn (Beirut: Markaz Dirāsāt al-Waḥda al-'Arabiyya, 1987), pp. 687–714.

'Abd al-Faḍīl, Maḥmūd, *Al-khadī'a al-māliyya al-kubrā: Al-iqtiṣād al-siyasi li sharikāt tawẓīf al-amwāl* (Cairo: Dār al-Mustaqbal al-'Arabi, 1989).

'Abd al-Karīm, Aḥmad 'Izzat, *Tārīkh al-ta'līm fī Miṣr min nihāyat ḥukm Muḥammad 'Alī ilā awā'il ḥukm Tawfiq*, 1848–1882, 4 vols (Cairo: Wizārat al-Ma'ārif al-'Umūmiyya, 1945).

'Abd al-Laṭīf, Kamāl, *Salāma Mūsā wa ishkāliyyāt al-nahḍa* (Beirut: Dār al-Fārābī and Casablanca: al-Markaz al-Th aqāfī al-'Arabī, 1982).

'Abd al-Laṭīf, Kamāl, *Al-ta'wīl wa al-mufāraqa: Naḥwa ta'wīl falsafī li'l naẓar al-siyāsī al-'arabī* (Casablanca: al-Markaz al-Thaqāfī al-'Arabī, 1987).

'Abd al-Raziq, 'Ali, *Al-islām wa uṣūl al-ḥukm, baḥth fī al-khilāfa wa al-ḥukūma fī al-islām*, 2nd edn (Cairo: Maṭba'at Miṣr, 1965). Translated into English by M. Loutfi as Ali Abdel Razek, *Islam and the Foundations of Political Power*, ed. A. Filali-Ansary (Edinburgh: Edinburgh University Press in association with the Aga Khan University Institute for the Study of Muslim Civilisations, 2012).

ʻAbd al Raziq, ʻAli, *al-islām wa uṣūl al-ḥukm*, ed. Muḥammad ʻAmāra (Beirut: al-Mu'assasa al-ʻArabiyya li'l-Dirāsāt wa al-Nashr, 1972).

Abdel Moula, Mahmoud, *L'Université Zaytounienne et la société tunisienne* (Tunis: Centre National de la Recherche Scientifique, 1971).

Abdel Razek, Ali, *Islam and the Foundations of Political Power*, trans. M. Loutfi, ed. A. Filali-Ansary (Edinburgh: Edinburgh University Press in association with the Aga Khan University Institute for the Study of Muslim Civilisations, 2012).

ʻAbduh, Muḥammad, *Al-aʻmāl al-kāmila*, collected, edited, and introduced by Muḥammad ʻAmāra, 6 vols (Beirut: al-Mu'assasa al-ʻArabiyya li'l-Dirasāt wa al-Nashr, 1972–1974).

ʻAbduh, Muḥammad, *Al-aʻmāl al-majhūla*, ed. ʻAli Shalash (London: Riyad al-Rayyis li'l-Kutub wa al-Nashr, 1987).

ʻAbduh, Muḥammad and Rashīd Riḍā, *Tafsīr al-fātiḥa* (Cairo: Maṭbaʻat al-Mawsūʻāt, 1319/1901).

Abi-Mershed, Osama, *Apostles of Modernity: Saint Simonians and the Civilizing Mission in Algeria* (Stanford: Stanford University Press, 2010).

Abrahamian, Ervand, *Khomeinism* (Berkeley and Los Angeles: University of California Press, 1993).

Abū al-Kabīr, ʻAbd al-Ḥamīd, "Al-shurūṭ al-tārīkhiyya li'l-nahḍa fī al-Maghrib al-ʻarabī", in *Durūs fī al-ḥaraka al-salafiyya*, eds ʻAllāl al-Fāsī, et al. (Casablanca: Manshūrāt ʻUyūn, 1986), pp. 124–143.

Abū al-Majd, Aḥmad Kamāl, *Ḥiwār lā muwājaha: Dirāsāt ḥawl al-islām wa al-ʻaṣr* (Kuwait: Majallat al-ʻArabī, 1985).

Abū al-Majd, Aḥmad Kamāl, "Al-mas'ala al-siyāsiyya: Waṣl al-turāth bi al-ʻaṣr wa al-niẓām al-siyāsī li'l-dawla", in *Al-turāth wa taḥaddiyyāt al-ʻaṣr fī al-waṭan al-ʻarabī: Al-aṣāla wa al-muʻāṣara*, ed. Markaz Dirāsāt al-Waḥda al-ʻArabiyya, 2nd edn (Beirut: Markaz Dirāsāt al-Waḥda al-ʻArabiyya, 1987), pp. 571–593.

Abū Manneh, Butros, "Sultan Abdelhamid II and Shaikh Abdulhuda Al-Sayyadi", *Middle Eastern Studies* 15/2 (1979): 138–139.

Abun-Nasr, Jamil, *A History of the Maghreb* (Cambridge: Cambridge University Press, 1971).

Abū Shādī, Aḥmad Zākī, *Limādhā anā mu'min*? (Alexandria: Maṭba'at al-Ta'āwun, 1937).

Abū Ya'lā ibn al-Farrā', Muḥammad ibn al-Ḥusayn ibn Muḥammad ibn Khalaf, *Tabaqāt al-Ḥanābila*, ed. Muḥammad Ḥāmid al-Fīqī, 2 vols (Cairo: Maṭba'at al-Sunna al-Muḥammadiyya, al-Tafsīr al-'Ilmi, 1952).

Abū Ya'lā ibn al-Farrā', Muḥammad ibn al-Ḥusayn ibn Muḥammad ibn Khalaf, *Al-aḥkām al-sulṭāniyya*, ed. Muḥammad Ḥāmid al-Fīqī, 2nd edn (Cairo: Maktabat wa Maṭba'at Muṣṭafā al-Bābī al-Ḥalabī wa Awlāduhu, 1966).

Abū Zayd, Nasr, *Rethinking the Qur'an: Towards a Humanistic Hermeneutics* (Utrecht: Humanistics University Press, 2004).

Adham, Ismā'īl, "Limādhā anā mulḥid?", in *al-Amām*, August 1937 (reprinted in Paris: Manshūrāt al-Nuqṭa, no. 9, n.d.).

Adūnīs ('Alī Aḥmad Sa'īd), *Aghānī Mihyar al-Dimashqī*, 2nd edn (Beirut: Manshūrāt Majallat Mawāqif, 1970).

Adūnīs ('Alī Aḥmad Sa'īd), "Bayn al-thabāt wa-l-taḥawwul: Khawāṭir ḥawl al-thawra al-islāmiyya fī Īrān", *Mawāqif* 34 (1979): 149–160.

Adūnīs ('Alī Aḥmad Sa'īd), "Al-'aql al mu'taqal", *Mawāqif* 43 (1981): 3–10.

'Aflaq, Michel, *Fī sabīl al-ba'th* (Beirut: Dār al-Ṭalī'a, 1959).

al-Afghānī, Jamāl al-Dīn, *Al-a'māl al-kāmila li Jamāl al-Dīn al-Afghānī*, ed. Muḥammad 'Amāra (Cairo: al-Mu'assasa al-Miṣriyya al-'Āmma, n.d.).

al-Afghānī, Jamāl al-Dīn and Muḥammad 'Abduh, *Al-'urwa al-wuthqā wa al-thawra al-taḥrīriyya al-kubrā* (Cairo: Dār al-'Arab, 1958).

al-Afghānī, Jamāl al-Dīn, *Silsilat al-a'māl al-majhūla*, ed. 'Alī Shalash (London: Riyāḍ al-Rayyis li'l-Kutub wa al-Nashr, 1981).

Agrama, Hussein Ali, *Questioning Secularism: Islam, Sovereignty and the Rule of Law in Egypt* (Chicago: University of Chicago Press, 2012).

Ahmad, Aijaz, *In Theory* (London: Verso, 1992).

Ahmad, Aijaz, "Post-colonial theory and the 'post' condition", *The Socialist Register* 33 (1997): 353–382.

Aḥmad, 'Ātif, *Naqd al-fahm al-'aṣrī li'l-qur'ān*, 2nd edn (Beirut: Dār al-Ṭalī'a, 1977).

Aḥmad, Ḥanafi, *Al-tafsīr al-'ilmī li al-āyāt al-kawniyya fī al-Qur'ān*, 2nd edn (Cairo: Dār al-Ma'ārif, 1980).

Ahmed, Mohammed Shahab, *Before Orthodoxy: The Satanic Verses in Early Islam* (Cambridge, MA: Harvard University Press, 2017).

Akan, Murat, *The Politics of Secularism: Religion, Diversity, and Institutional Change in France and Turkey* (New York: Columbia University Press, 2017).

Akarli, Engin, *The Long Peace: Ottoman Lebanon, 1861–1920* (Berkeley: University of California Press, 1993).

al-Akhḍar, al-ʿAfīf, "Min naqd al-samāʾ ila naqd al-arḍ", in *Vladimir Lenin: Nuṣūṣ ḥawl al-mawqif min al-dīn, mukhtārāt jadīda*, trans. Muḥammad al-Kubba (Beirut: Dār al-Ṭalīʿa, 1972), pp. 5–82.

al-Akhḍar, al-ʿAfīf, *Vladimir Lenin: nuṣūṣ ḥawl al-mawqif min al-dīn, mukhtārāt jadīda*, trans. Muḥammad al-Kubba (Beirut: Dār al-Ṭalīʿa, 1972).

al-ʿAlawī, Hādī, "Ashyāʾ min fuṣūl al-masraḥ al-dīnī fī al-waṭan al-ʿarabī", *Mawāqif* 21 (1972): 57–67.

Alfieri, Vittorio, *On Tyranny*, trans Julius A. Molinaro and Beatrice Corrigan (Toronto: Toronto University Press, 1961).

ʿAlī, Jawād, *Al-mufaṣṣal fī tārīkh al-ʿarab qabl al-islām*, 9 vols (Baghdad: Maktabat al-Nahḍa and Beirut: Dār al-ʿIlm li'l-Malāyīn, 1968–1981).

al-ʿAllām, ʿIzz al-Dīn, "Mafhūm al-ḥāshiya fī al-adab al-siyāsī al-sulṭānī", *Abḥāth* (Rabat) 4/13 (1986): 97–118.

Allen, Roger, "The Christ figure in Sayigh's poetry", in *Representations of the Divine in Arabic Poetry*, eds Gert Borg and Ed de Moor (Amsterdam: Editions Rodopoi, 2001), pp. 227–241.

ʿAmāra, Muḥammad, *Al-dawla al-islāmiyya bayn al-ʿilmāniyya wa al-ṣulṭa al-dīniyya* (Beirut and Cairo: Dār al-Shurūq, 1988).

al-Āmidī, Saif al-dīn Abū al-Ḥasan ʿAlī, *Al-iḥkām fī uṣūl al-aḥkām*, 4 vols (Cairo: n.p., 1914). ʿĀmil, Mahdī, *Azmat al-ḥaḍāra al-ʿarabiyya am azmat al-burjwazīyāt al-ʿarabiyya?* (Beirut: Dār al-Fārābi, 1979).

Amīn, Aḥmad, "Al-naqd ayḍan", *al-Risala* 4/152 (1936): 1.

Amīn, Aḥmad, *Fayḍ al-khāṭir* (Cairo: Maktabat al-Nahḍa al-ʿArabiyya, 1956–1961).

Amīn, Aḥmad, *Yawm al-Islām* (Cairo: Mu'assasat al-Khānjī, 1958).

Amīn, Aḥmad, *Ḥayātī*, 3rd edn (Cairo: Maktabat al-Nahḍa al-ʿArabiyya, 1958).

Amīn, Ḥusayn Aḥmad, *Dalīl al-Muslim al-ḥazīn ilā muqataḍā al-sulūk fī al-qarn al-ʿishrīn*, 2nd edn (Beirut and Cairo: Dār-al-Shurūq, 1983), published in English translation as Hussein Ahmad Amin, *The Sorrowful Muslim's Guide*, trans Y. Amin and N. Amin (Edinburgh: Edinburgh

University Press in association with the Aga Khan University Institute for the Study of Muslim Civilisations, 2018).
Amīn, Ḥusayn Aḥmad, *Fī bayt Aḥmad Amīn* (Cairo: Dār al-Hilāl, 1985).
Amīn, Ḥusayn Aḥmad, *Ḥawl al-da'wa ilā taṭbīq al-sharī'a al-islāmiyya* (Beirut: Dār al-Nahḍa al-'Arabiyya, 1985).
Amīn, Ḥusayn Aḥmad, "Ta'qīb", on Ṭāriq al-Bishrī, "Al-mas'ala al-qānūniyya bayn al-sharī'a al-islāmiyya wa al-qānūn al-waḍ'ī", in *Al-turāth wa taḥadiyyāt al-'aṣr fī al-waṭan al-'arabī: al-aṣāla wa al mu'āṣara*, ed. Markaz Dirāsāt al-Waḥda al-'Arabiyya, 2nd edn (Beirut: Markaz Dirāsāt al-Waḥda al-'Arabiyya, 1987), pp. 645–650.
Amīn, Jallāl, "Al waḥda al-waṭaniyya fī muwājahat al-ṭā'ifiyya wa-l-ta'aṣṣub", *al-Ahāli* 18 April 1990.
al-Amīn, Muḥsin, *Al-ḥuṣūn al-manī'a fī radd mā awradahu ṣāhib al-manār fī ḥaqq al-shī'a,* 2nd edn, 2 vols (Cairo: Dār al-Zahrā', 1985).
Amīn, Qāsim, *Al-a'māl al kāmila*, ed. Muḥammad 'Amāra, 2 vols (Beirut: al-Mu'assasa al-'Arabiyya li'l-Dirāsāt wa al-Nashr, 1976).
Amīn, Qāsim, *The Liberation of Women and The New Woman*, trans. Samiha Sidhom Peterson (Cairo: American University of Cairo Press, 1992).
al-'Amshītī, Yūsuf, "Al-īmān wa al-'ilm akhawān lā yakhtalifān", *al-Mashriq* 21 (1923): 81–93.
Anderson, Benedict, *Imagined Communities: Reflections on the Origin and Spread of Nationalism* (London: Verso, 1977).
Anderson, Betty S., *The American University of Beirut: Arab Nationalism and Liberal Education* (Austin: University of Texas Press, 2012).
Anderson, Norman, *Law Reform in the Muslim World* (London: Athlone Press, 1976).
Anderson, Perry, *Lineages of the Absolutist State* (London: Verso, 1979).
Anderson, Perry, *The H-Word. The Peripeteia of Hegemony* (London: Verso, 2017).
'Anḥūri, Salīm, *Siḥr Hārūt* (Damascus: al-Maṭba'a al-Ḥanafiyya, 1302/1885).
al-Anṣārī, Muḥammad Jābir, *Taḥawwulāt al-fikr wa al-siyāsa fī al-sharq al-'arabī 1930–1970.* Silsilat 'ālam al-ma'rifa 35 (Kuwait: al-Majlis al-Waṭanī li'l-Thaqāfa wa al-Funūn wa al-Ādāb, 1980).
Anṭūn, Faraḥ, "Tamhīd" [Preface], to "Al-dīn wa al-'ilm wa ra'y al-faylasūf Spencer fīhā", by As'ad Bāsīlī al-Ṭarābulsī, *al-Jāmi'a* 3 (1902): 554–555.
Anṭūn, Faraḥ, "Ṣawt min ba'īd", *al-Jāmi'a* 5/5 (1906).
Anṭūn, Faraḥ, *Mukhtārāt* (Beirut: Dar Ṣādir, 1950).

Anṭūn, Faraḥ, *Ibn Rushd wa falsafatuhu ma'a nuṣūṣ al-munāẓara bayna Muḥammad 'Abduh wa Faraḥ Antūn*, with an Introduction by Adūnīs al-'Akrā (Beirut: Dār al-Ṭalī'a, 1981).

al-'Aqqād, 'Abbās Maḥmūd, *Muḥammad 'Abdūh*. Silsilat a'lām al-'arab 1 (Cairo: al-Mu'assasa al-Miṣriyya al-'Āmma li'l Ta'līf wa al-Tarjama wa al-Nashr, n.d.).

al-'Aqqād,'Abbās Maḥmūd, *Al-tafkīr farīḍa islāmiyya* (Cairo: Dār al-Qalam, n.d.).

al-'Aqqād, 'Abbās Maḥmūd, *Anā* (Cairo: Dār al-Hilāl, n.d.).

al-'Aqqād,'Abbās Maḥmūd, *Iblīs* (Cairo: Dār al-Hilāl, n.d.).

al-'Aqqād,'Abbās Maḥmūd, *Allāh: Kitāb fī nash'at al-'aqīda al-ilāhiyya*, 3rd edn (Cairo: Dār al-Ma'ārif, 1960).

al-'Aqqād, 'Abbās Maḥmūd, *Athar al-'Arab fī al-ḥaḍāra al- ūrūbbiyya* (Cairo: Dār al-Ma'ārif, 1963).

al-'Aqqād, 'Āmir, *Ma'ārik al-'Aqqād al-adabiyya* (Beirut and Sidon: al-Maktaba al-'Aṣriyya, 1971).

'Arafa, Muḥammad Aḥmad, *Naqd maṭā'in fī al-Qur'ān al-karīm yatḍamman tafnīd mā alqāhu al-duktūr Ṭaha Ḥusayn 'alā ṭalabat Kulliyat al-Ādāb fī al-Jāmi'a al-Miṣriyya* (Cairo: Maṭba'at al-Manār, 1932).

Arjomand, Said Amir, *The Turban and the Crown* (Oxford: Oxford University Press, 1988).

Arkoun, Mohammed, *Ouvertures sur l'Islam* (Paris: Jacques Graucher, 1989).

Arkoun, Muḥammad, *Al-fikr al-'arabī*, trans. 'Ādil al-'Awwā (Beirut: Manshūrāt 'Uwaydāt, 1982).

Arslān, Shakīb, *Al-Sayyid Rashīd Riḍā aw ikhā' arba'īn sana* (Damascus: Maṭba'at Ibn Zaydūn and Cairo: Maṭba'at Dār al-Kutub al-Miṣriyya, 1937).

al-Arsūzī, Zākī, *Mashākilunā al-qawmiyya wa mawqif al-aḥzāb minhā* (Damascus: Dār al-Yaqẓa al-'Arabiyya, 1956).

al-Arsūzī, Zakī, *Al-mu'allafāt al-kāmila*, 5 vols (Damascus: Maṭābī' al-Idāra al-Siyāsiyya li'l Jaysh wa al-Quwwāt al-Musallaḥa, 1975).

al-'Arwī, 'Abd Allah [Abdallah Laroui], *Al- idiyūlūjīya al-'arabiyya al-mu'āṣira*, trans. Muḥammad 'Ītānī (Beirut: Dār al-Ḥaqīqa, 1970).

al-'Arwī, 'Abd Allah, *Al-'Arab wa al-fikr al-tārīkhī* (Beirut: Dār al-Ḥaqīqa, 1973).

al-'Arwī, 'Abd Allah, *Mafhūm al-dawla* (Casablanca: al-Markaz al-Thaqāfī al-'Arabi, 1981).

al-'Arwī, 'Abdallāh, *Mafhūm al-ḥurrīya* (Casablanca: al-Markaz al-Thaqāfi al-'Arabī, 2008).

Asad, Talal, *The Idea of an Anthropology of Islam* (Washington, DC: Georgetown University Press, 1986).

Asad, Talal, *Genealogies of Religion* (Baltimore and London: Johns Hopkins University Press, 1993).

Asad, Talal, *Formations of the Secular: Christianity, Islam and Modernity* (Stanford: Stanford University Press, 2003).

Asad, Talal, "Appendix: The trouble of thinking. An interview with Talal Asad", by D. Scott, in *Powers of the Secular Modern. Talal Asad and His Interlocutors*, eds D. Scott and C. Hirschkind (Stanford: Stanford University Press, 2006), pp. 243–303.

Asad, Talal, "Responses", in *Powers of the Secular Modern. Talal Asad and His Interlocutors*, eds D. Scott and C. Hirschkind (Stanford: Stanford University Press, 2006), pp. 206–241.

'Aṣfūr, Jābir, "Islām al-nafṭ wa al-ḥadātha", in *Al-Islām wa al-ḥadātha: Nadwat Mawāqif* (London: Maktabat al-Sāqī, 1990), pp. 191–206.

al-Ash'arī, Abū al-Ḥasan Alī Ibn Ismā'īl, *Kitāb al-luma' fi al-radd 'alā ahl al-zīgh wa al-bida'*, ed. Ḥammūda Gharāba (Cairo: Maṭba't Miṣr, 1955).

Ashour, Radwa, Ferial Ghazoul, and Hasna Reda-Mekdashi (eds), *Arab Women Writers, 1973–1999*, translated from Arabic by Mandy McClure (Cairo: American University of Cairo, 2008).

'Aṭiyya, Na'īm, "Ma'ālim al-fikr al-tarbawī fī al-bilād al-'Arabiyya fī al-mi'at sana al-akhīra", in al-Jāmi'a al-Amīrikiyya fī Bayrūt, Hay'at al-Dirasāt al-'Arabiyya (ed.), *Al-fikr al-'arabi fi mi'at sana: Buḥūth mu'tamar Hay'at al-Dirāsāt al-'Arabiyya al-mun'aqida fi Tishrīn al-Thānī 1966 fi al-Jāmi'a al-Amīrikiyya fi Bayrūt*, eds Fu'ād Ṣarrūf and Nabīh Amīn Fāris (Beirut: al-Jāmi'a al-Amīrikiyya, 1967), p. 480.

Augé, Marc, *Le sens des autres. Actualité de l'antropologie* (Paris: Fayard, 1994).

'Awaḍ, Louis, *Al-mu'āththirāt al-ajnabiyya fi al-adab al-'arabī al-ḥadīth*, 2 vols (Cairo: Jāmi'at al-Duwal al-'Arabiyya, Ma'had al-Dirāsāt al-'Arabiyya al-'Aliya, 1962).

'Awaḍ, Louis, *Thaqāfatunā fi muftaraq al-ṭuruq* (Beirut: Dār al-Ādāb, 1974).

'Awaḍ, Louis, *Muqadimma fi fiqḥ al-lugha al-'arabiyya* (Cairo: al-Hay'a al-Miṣriyya al-'Amma li'l-Kitāb, 1980).

'Awda, 'Abd al-Qādir, *Al-tashrī' al-jinā'i al-islāmī, muqāranan bi al-qānūn al-waḍ'ī*, 3 vols (Cairo: Maktabat Dār al-'Urūba, 1959–1960).

'Ayn 'Ayn [ع ع], "Review of Naẓīra Zayn al-Dīn, al-Sufūr wa'l-Ḥijāb", *al-'Uṣūr* 3/13 (1928): 101–106.

Azharī ḥurr al-fikr, "Al-Jāmi'a al-azhariyya", *al-'Uṣūr* 7 (1928): 1237–1244.

al-'Aẓm, Ṣādiq Jalāl, *Al-naqd al-dhātī ba'd al-hazīma*, 2nd edn (Beirut: Dār al-Ṭalī'a, 1969).

al-'Aẓm, Ṣādiq Jalāl, "Ma'sāt Iblīs", in *Naqd al-fikr al-dīnī*, 2nd edn, 5th impression (Beirut: Dār al-Ṭalī'a, 1982), pp. 55–87.

al-'Aẓm, Ṣādiq Jalāl, "Mu'ijizat ẓuhūr al-'adhrā' wa taṣfiyat āthār al-'udwān", in *Naqd al-fikr al-dīnī*, 2nd edn, 5th impression (Beirut: Dār al-Ṭalī'a, 1982).

al-'Aẓm, Ṣādiq Jalāl, *Naqd al-fikr al-dīnī*, 2nd edn, 5th impression (Beirut: Dār al-Ṭalī'a, 1982).

al-Azm, Ṣādiq Jalāl, "The importance of being earnest about Salman Rushdie", *Die Welt des Islams* 31/1 (1991): 1–49.

al-Azm, Ṣādiq Jalāl, *Self-Criticism After the Defeat* (London: Saqi Books, 2011).

al-Azm, Ṣādiq Jalāl, *Secularism, Fundamentalism and the Struggle for the Meaning of Islam*, 3 vols (Berlin: Gerlach Press, 2013).

al-Azm, Ṣādiq Jalāl, "The tragedy of Satan", in *Secularism, Fundamentalism and the Struggle for the Meaning of Islam*, 3 vols (Berlin: Gerlach Press, 2013), vol. 2, pp. 131–178.

al-Azm, Ṣādiq Jalāl, *Critique of Religious Thought* (Berlin: Gerlach Press, 2014).

al-Azm, Ṣadiq Jalāl, *On Fundamentalisms* (Berlin: Gerlach Press, 2014).

al-'Aẓma, 'Azīz [Aziz Al-Azmeh], *Al-kitāba al-tārīkhiyya wa al-ma'rifa al-tārīkhiyya: Muqadimma fi uṣūl ṣinā'at al- tārīkh al-'arabī* (Beirut: Dār al-Ṭalī'a, 1983).

al-'Aẓma, 'Azīz, "Al-siyāsa wa al-lāsiyāsa fī al fikr al-'arabī al-islāmī", in *Al-turāth bayn al-ṣultān wa al-ta'rīkh* (Beirut: Dār al-Ṭalī'a, and Casablanca: Manshūrāt 'Uyūn, 1986/1990), pp. 41–50.

al-'Aẓma, 'Azīz, *Mir'āt al-shām: Tārīkh dimashq wa ahluhā* (London: Riyāḍ al-Rayyis li'l-Kutub wa al-Nashr, 1988).

al-'Aẓma, 'Azīz, "Ba'īdan 'an saṭwat al-qawl al-dīnī", *al-Nāqid* 16 (1989): 78–80.

al-'Aẓma, 'Azīz, "Al-dīn wa al-idiyūlūjiya", in 'Azīz al-'Aẓma, *Al-turāth bayn al-sulṭān wa al-tārīkh*, 2nd edn (Beirut: Dār al-Talī'a, Manshūrāt 'Uyūn, 1990), pp. 83–112.

al-ʻAẓma, ʻAzīz, *Al-turāth bayn al-sulṭān wa al-tārīkh*, 2nd edn (Beirut: Dār al-Talīʻa, 1990).

al-ʻAẓma, ʻAzīz, "Bayn al-Marksiyya al-mawḍūʻiyya wa saqf al-ta'rīkh: Munāqasha li fikr ʻAbd Allāh al-ʻArwī", in *Al-turāth bayn al-sulṭān wa al-tārīkh*, 2nd edn (Beirut: Dār al-Ṭalīʻa, 1990), pp. 105–127.

al-ʻAẓma, ʻAzīz, "Fī al-aṣāla wa akhawātihā", *Dirāsāt ʻArabiyya* 12 (1990): 31–52.

al-ʻAẓma, ʻAzīz, "Fī tārīkhiyyat al-ʻaql wa naqd al-ʻaql", in *Al-turāth bayn al-sulṭān wa al-tārīkh*, 2nd edn (Beirut: Dār al-Talīʻa, 1990), pp. 129–145.

al-ʻAẓma, ʻAzīz, "Istishrāq al-aṣāla: Adūnīs wa al-turāth", in *Al-turāth bayn al-sulṭān wa al-tārīkh*, 2nd edn (Beirut: Dār al-Ṭalīʻa, 1990), pp. 146–160.

al-ʻAẓma, ʻAzīz, *Al-ʻArab wa al-barābira* (London: Riyāḍ al-Rayyis li'l-Kutub wa al-Nashr, 1991).

al-ʻAẓma, ʻAzīz, *Qusṭanṭīn Zurayq. ʻArabī li'l-Qarn al-ʻIshrin* (Beirut: Institute of Palestine Studies, 2001).

al-ʻAẓma, ʻAzīz, *Dunyā ad-Dīn fī ḥāḍir al-ʻArab*, rev. edn (Beirut: Dār al-Ṭalīʻa, 2002).

al-ʻAẓma, ʻAzīz, *Sūrīya wa al-ṣuʻūd al-uṣūlī*, ed. Ḥammūd Ḥammūd (Beirut: Riyad al-Rayyes Books, 2015).

al-ʻAẓma, ʻAzīz "Bayn at-tārīkh wa'l-istikāna li'l-qadar", *Bidāyāt* 14 (2016): 104–111.

Al-ʻAẓma, ʻAzīz, "Ṣādiq al-ʻAẓm wa istibṭān al-fawāt", *Qalamūn* 1 (2017): 141–152.

al-ʻAẓma, ʻAzīz, "Al-iṣlāḥiyūn al-nahḍawīyūn wa fikrat al-iṣlāḥ fī al-majāl ad-dīnī", *Al-Mustaqbal al-ʻArabī* 455 (2017): 75–99.

al-Azmeh, Aziz [ʻAzīz al-ʻAẓma], *Arabic Thought and Islamic Societies*, Exeter Arabic and Islamic Series (London: Croon Helm, 1986).

al-Azmeh, Aziz, "Islamic Legal Theory and the Appropriation of Reality", in *Islamic Law: Social and Historical Contexts*, ed. Aziz al-Azmeh (London and New York: Routledge, 1988), pp. 250–265.

al-Azmeh, Aziz, "Islamism and Arab nationalism", *Review of Middle East Studies* 4 (1988): 41–50.

al-Azmeh, Aziz, "Orthodoxy and Hanbalite Fideism", *Arabica* 35 (1988): 253–266.

al-Azmeh, Aziz, "Utopia and the state in Islamic political thought", *History of Political Thought* 11 (1990): 9–20.

al-Azmeh, Aziz, "Islamic Revivalism and Western Ideologies", *History Workshop Journal* 30 (1991): 44–53.
al-Azmeh, Aziz, "Barbarians in Arab eyes", *Past and Present* 134 (1992): 3–18.
al-Azmeh, Aziz, "Populism contra democracy: Recent democratist discourse in the Arab world", in *Democracy without Democrats*, ed. Ghassan Salamé (London: I. B. Tauris, 1994), pp. 112–129.
al-Azmeh, Aziz, "Canonisation of the Qur'an", in *Encyclopedia of Islam*, 3rd edn, eds Kate Fleet, Gudrun Krämer, John Nawas, and Everett Rowsomn, https://referenceworks.brillonline.com/entries/encyclopaedia-of-islam-3/canon-and-canonisation-of-the-quran-COM_24606?s.num=0&s.f.s2_parent=s.f.book.encyclopaedia-of-islam-3&s.q=al-azmeh (2018).
al-Azmeh, Aziz, *Muslim Kingship: Power and the Sacred in Muslim, Christian and Pagan Polities* (London, I. B. Tauris, 1997).
al-Azmeh, Aziz, *Ibn Khaldun: An Essay in Reinterpretation* ([London, 1982] New York and Budapest: Central European University Press, 2003).
al-Azmeh, Aziz, "Identity in the Arab world", in *Keywords: Identity*, ed. NadiaTazi (New York: The Other Press, 2004), pp. 47–64.
al-Azmeh, Aziz, "Chronophagous discourse: A study of the clerico-legal appropriation of the world in an Islamic tradition", in *The Times of History* (New York and Budapest: Central European University Press, 2007), pp. 67–100.
al-Azmeh, Aziz, "Islamic political thought: Current historiography and the framework of history", in *The Times of History* (New York and Budapest: Central European University Press, 2007), pp. 185–266.
al-Azmeh, Aziz, *The Times of History: Universal Topics in Islamic Historiography* (New York and Budapest: Central European University Press, 2007).
al-Azmeh, Aziz, "Civilisation, culture and the new barbarians", in *Islams and Modernities*, 3rd edn (London: Verso, 2009), pp. 40–59.
al-Azmeh, Aziz, "Culturalism", in *Islams and Modernities*, 3rd edn (London: Verso, 2009), pp. 17–39.
al-Azmeh, Aziz, "History, Arab nationalism and secularism: Constantine Zurayk in counterpoint", in *Configuring Identity in the Modern Arab East*, ed. Samir Seikaly (Beirut: American University of Beirut Press, 2009), pp. 121–137.
al-Azmeh, Aziz, *Islams and Modernities*, 3rd edn (London: Verso, 2009).

al-Azmeh, Aziz, "Civilisation as a political disposition", *Economy and Society* 41 (2012): 501–512.

al-Azmeh, Aziz, "God's caravan: Topoi and schemata in the history of Muslim political thought", in *Mirror for the Muslim Prince. Islam and the Theory of Statecraft*, ed. Mehrzad Boroujerdi (Syracuse: Syracuse University Press, 2013), pp. 326–397.

al-Azmeh, Azīz, "Abbasid culture and the universal history of freethinking", *Critical Muslim* 12 (2014): 73–88.

al-Azmeh, Aziz, *The Arabs and Islam in Late Antiquity: A Critique of Approaches to Arabic Sources* (Berlin: Gerlach Press, 2014).

al-Azmeh, Aziz, *The Emergence of Islam in Late Antiquity: Allah and His People* (Cambridge: Cambridge University Press, 2014).

Al-Azmeh, Aziz, "Registers of genealogical purity in classical Islam", in *Discourses of Purity in Transnational Perspective*, eds M. Bely, N. Jaspert, and S. Köck (Leiden: Brill, 2015), pp. 387–405.

al-Azmeh, Aziz, "Freidenkertum und Humanismus. Universelle Stimmungen, Motiven und Themen im Zeitalter der Abbasiden", in *Humanismus, Reformation, Aufklärung*, eds Hubert Cancik and Hubert Schöpner (Berlin: Humanistische Akademie, 2017), pp. 15–31.

al-Azmeh, Aziz (ed.), *Islamic Law: Social and Historical Contexts* (London and New York: Routledge, 1988).

Azmeh, Shamel, *The Uprising of the Marginalised* (London: LSE Middle East Centre Paper Series, 2014).

'Azmī, Maḥmūd, "Al-rābiṭa al-sharqiyya amm al-islāmiyya amm al-'Arabiyya?", *al-Hilāl* 42/1 (1933): 53–58.

Badawi, Muhammad Zaki, *The Reformers of Egypt: A Critique of Al-Afghani, Abduh and Ridha* (London: Croon Helm, 1978).

Badrān, Ibrāhīm and Salwā al-Khammāsh, *Dirāsāt fī al-'aqliyya al-'arabiyya: al-khurāfa*, 2nd edn (Beirut: Dār al-Ḥaqīqa, 1979).

al-Bagdadi, Nadia, "The cultural function of fiction, from the Bible to libertine literature. Historical criticism and social critique in Aḥmad Fāris al-Šidyāq", *Arabica* 46 (1999): 375–401.

al-Bagdadi, Nadia, *Vorgestellte Öffentlichkeit: Zur Genese moderner Prosa in Ägypten* (Wiesbaden: Reichert Verlag, 2010).

al-Bagdadi, Nadia, "Eros und Etikette – Reflexionen zum Bann eines zentralen Themas im arabischen 19. Jahrhundert", in *Verschleierter Orient –*

Entschleierter Okzident?, eds Bettina Dennerlein, Elke Frietsch and Therese Steffen (Munich: Wilhelm Fink, 2012), pp. 117–135.
al-Bagdadi, Nadia, “Introduction”, to *Sacred Texts and Print Culture: The Case of the Qur’an and the Eastern Bible*, ed. Nadia Al-Bagdadi (New York and Budapest: Central European University Press, forthcoming).
Baldwin, James, *Islamic Law and Empire in Ottoman Cairo* (Edinburgh: Edinburgh University Press, 2017).
al-Bannā, Ḥasan, *Majmūʿat rasāʾil al-imām al-shahīd Ḥasan al-Bannā* (Beirut: Dār al-Andalus, 1965).
Barakāt, Halīm, *Al-mujtamaʿ al-ʿarabī al-muʿāṣir: Baḥth istiṭlāʾi wa ijtimāʿi* (Beirut: Markaz Dirāsāt al-Waḥda al-ʿArabīyya, 1984).
Baron, Beth, *Egypt as a Woman* (Berkeley and Los Angeles: University of California Press, 2005).
al-Bārūdī, Fakhrī, *Muḍakkarāt al-Bārūdī* (Beirut/Damascus: n.p., 1951).
Bārūt Muḥammad J., *Ḥamalāt Kisirwān fi al-tārīkh al-siyāsī li fatāwī Ibn Taymiyya* (Doha: Arab Center for Research and Policy Studies, 2017).
Bārūt, Muḥammad Jamāl, *Al-ṣirāʿ al-ʿUthmānī-al-Ṣafawī wa āthāruhu al-shīʿīya fi shamāl bilād al-Shām* (Doha: Arab Centre for Research and Policy Research, 2018).
Bashīr, Sulaymān, *Muqaddima fi al-tārīkh al-ākhar: Naḥwa qirāʾa jadīda liʾl-riwāya al-islāmiyya* (Jerusalem: n.p., 1984).
al-Baṣrī, Abū al-Ḥusayn Muḥammad ibn ʿAlī al-Ṭayyib, *Al-muʿtamad fi uṣūl al-fiqh*, eds Muḥammad Ḥamīd Allāh, et al. (Damascus: al-Maʿhad al-ʿIlmī al-Faransī liʾl-Dirasāt al-ʿArabiyya, 1964).
Batatu, Hanna, “Shiʿi organization in Iraq: al-Da’wah al-Islamiyah and al-Mujahidin”, in *Shiʿism and Social Protest*, eds J. R. I. Cole and Nikke Keddie (New Haven and London: Yale University Press, 1986), pp. 179–180.
Batatu, Hanna, “Syria’s Muslim Brethren”, *MERIP Reports* 12 (1982): 18.
Baubérot, Jean, *Histoire de la laïcité en France*, 4th edn (Paris: Presses Universitaires de France, 2007).
al-Bayḍāwī, ʿAbd Allāh ibn ʿAmr ibn Muḥammad ibn ʿAlī al-Shīrāzī Nāṣir al-Dīn. *Minhāj al-wuṣūl ilā ilm al-ʿuṣūl* (Cairo: n.p., 1326/1908).
Bayhum, Muḥammad Jamīl, *Fatāt al-sharq fi ḥaḍārat al-gharb: Taṭawwur al-fikr al-ʿarabī fi mawdūʿ al-mar ʾa fi al-qarn al-ʿishrīn* (Beirut: n.p., 1952).
Bayhum, Muḥammad Jamīl, *Al-marʾa fiʾl-islām wa fi al-ḥaḍāra al-gharbiyya*, introduced by Georges Ṭarābīshī (Beirut: Dār al-Talīʿa, 1980).

al-Bazdawī, *Kanz al-wuṣūl*, on the margins of ʿAbd al-Azīz al-Bukhārī, *Kashf al-asrār* (Constantinople: Maktabat al-Ṣanāyiʿ, 1889).

al-Bazzāz, ʿAbd al-Raḥmān, *Hādhihi qawmīyyatunā* (Cairo: Dār al-Qalam, 1963).

Beinin, Joel, "Islamism, Marxism and Shubra al-Khayma textile workers", in *Islam, Politics and Social Movements*, eds Edward Burke III and Ira M. Lapidus (London: I. B. Tauris, 1988), pp. 207–227.

Belting, Hans, *Florence and Baghdad: Renaissance Art and Arab Science*, trans. D. L. Schneider (Cambridge, MA: Harvard University Press, 2011).

Bely, M., Jaspert, N., and Köck, S. (eds), *Discourses of Purity in Transnational Perspective* (Leiden: Brill, 2015).

Benedict P., et al. (eds), *Turkey: Geographic and Social Perspectives* (Leiden: Brill, 1974).

Benveniste, Émile, "Euphémismes anciens et modernes", in *Problèmes de linguistique générale* (Paris: Vrin, 1966), pp. 308–314.

Benveniste, Émile, *Problèmes de linguistique générale* (Paris: Vrin, 1966).

Bergman, Gerald, "The history of the human female inferiority idea in evolutionary biology", *Rivista di Biologia* 96 (2002): 379–412.

Berkes, Niyazi, *The Development of Secularism in Turkey* (Montreal: McGill University Press, 1964).

Berque, Jacques, *Essai sur la méthode juridique maghrébine* (Rabat: M. Leforestier, 1944).

Berque, Jacques, *Structures sociales du Haut-Atlas*, Bibliothèque de sociologie contemporaine, série B: Travaux du centre d'Études sociologiques (Paris: Presses Universitaires de France, 1955).

Berque, Jacques, *The Arabs: Their History and Future*, trans. Jean Stewart (London: Faber and Faber, 1964).

Berque, Jacques, *Egypt and Revolution*, trans. Jean Stewart (London: Faber and Faber, 1972).

Bertrand, Romain, *L'Histoire à parts égales* (Paris: Seuil, 2011).

Beydoun, Ahmad, *Identité confessionnelle et temps social chez les historiens libanais contemporains* (Beirut: Université Libanaise, 1984).

Billig, Michael, "Towards a critique of the critical", *Discourse and Society* 11 (2000): 291–292.

Bilqazīz, ʿAbd al-Ilāh, "Muqaddimāt li taḥlīl al-khiṭāb al-siyāsī al-ʿarabī: Al-khiṭāb al-nahḍawī wa al-uṭur al-marjiʿiyya", *al-mustaqbal al-ʿarabī* 123 (1989): 4–26.

al-Bisāṭ, Ilhām Kallāb, "Fī ma'nā al-taḥarrur al-jinsī", *Mawāqif* 28 (1974): 113–116.

Bishāra, 'Azmī, *Al-mujtama' al-madanī* (Beirut: Markaz Dirāsāt al-Waḥda al-'Arabīya, 2000).

Bishāra, 'Azmī, *Al-dīn wa'l-'Almāniyya fī siyāq tārīkhī*, 2 vols in 3 parts (Doha: Arab Center for Research and Policy Studies, 2012–2015).

al-Bishrī, Ṭāriq, "Al-khulf bayn al-nukhba wa al-jamāhīr izā' al-'īlāqa bayn al-qawmiyya al-'arabiyya wa al-islām", in *Al-qawmiyya al-'arabiyya wa al-islam*, ed. Markaz Dirāsāt al-Waḥda al-'Arabiyya, 1st edn (Beirut: Markaz Dirāsāt al-Waḥda al-'Arabiyya, 1981), pp. 275–300.

al-Bishrī, Ṭāriq, *Al-muslimūn wa al-aqbāṭ fī iṭār al-jamā'a al-waṭaniyya* (Beirut: Dār al-Waḥda al-'Arabiyya, 1982).

al-Bishrī, Ṭāriq, "Al-mas'ala al-qānūniyya bayn al-sharī'a al-islāmiyya wa al-qānūn al-waḍ'ī", in *Al-turāth wa Taḥaddiyāt al-'Asr fī al-Waṭan al-'Arabī*, ed. Markaz Dirāsāt al-Waḥda al-'Arabiyya (Beirut: Markaz Dirāsāt al-Waḥda al-'Arabiyya, 1985), pp. 617–644.

Bloch, Marc, *Les Rois thaumaturges: Étude sur le caractère surnaturel attribué à la puissance royale particulièrement en France et en Angleterre* (Paris: Armand Colin, 1961).

Blumenberg, Hans, *The Legitimacy of the Modern Age*, trans. R. M. Wallace (Cambridge, MA: MIT Press, 1985).

Bodman, Whitney S., *Poetics of Iblis* (Cambridge, MA: Harvard University Press, 2011).

Borg, Gert, "The humanized God in the poetry of Badr Shakir al-Sayyab", in *Representations of the Divine in Arabic Poetry*, eds Gert Borg and Ed de Moor (Amsterdam: Editions Rodopoi, 2001), pp. 9–23.

Botiveau, Bernard, *Loi islamique et droit dans les sociétés arabes* (Aix-en-Provence and Paris: IREMAM-Karthala, 1993).

Bouhdiba, Abdelawahab, *Sexuality in Islam*, trans. Alan Sheridan (London and Boston: Routledge, 1985).

Bourdieu, Pierre, "Génèse et structure du champ religieux", *Revue française de sociologie* 12 (1971): 293–334.

Bourdieu, Pierre, "Une interprétation de la religion selon Max Weber", *Archives européennes de sociologie* 12/1 (1971): 3–21.

Bourdieu, Pierre, *Esquisse d'une théorie de la pratique, précédée de trois études d'ethnologie kabyle*. Collection "Travaux de sciences sociales", vol. 92 (Geneva: Droz, 1972).

Boyer, Pascal, *Tradition as Truth and Communication. A Cognitive Description of Traditional Discourse* (Cambridge: Cambridge University Press, 1990).

Brandon, Ruth, *The Spiritualists: The Passion for the Occult in the Nineteenth and Twentieth Centuries* (New York: Knopf, 1982).

Breik, Mīkhā'īl, *Tarīkh al-Shām* 1720–1782, ed. Qusṭanṭīn al-Bāsha (Harissa: n.p., 1930).

Brinner, William, "The Banu Ṣaṣrā: A study in the transmission of scholarly tradition", *Studia Islamica* 7 (1960): 167–195.

Browers, Michaelle L., *Political Ideology in the Arab World. Accommodation and Transformation* (Camrbidge: Cambridge University Press, 2009).

Brown, Callum G., *The Death of Christian Britain: Understanding Secularisation, 1800–2000* (London: Routledge, 2000).

Brown, Jonathan, *The Canonization of al-Bukhari and Muslim: The Formation and Function of the Sunni Hadith Canon* (Leiden and Boston: Brill, 2007).

Brunner, Otto, Werner Conze, and Reinhart Koselleck (eds), *Geschichtliche Grundbegriffe*, 8 vols (Stuttgart: Klett-Cotta, 2004).

Brunschwig, Robert, *La Berbérie orientale sous les Hafsides des origines à la fin du XVe siècle*, 2 vols (Paris: Adrien-Maisonneuve, 1940–1947).

Buckley J. M., et al., "Canon Law", in *New Catholic Encyclopaedia*, 15 vols (New York: McGraw Hill, 1967), vol. 3, pp. 29–53.

Būḥdība, 'Abd al-Wahhāb, *Al-ḍamīr al-dīnī fī al-mujtama' al-ḥadīth* (Tunis: al-Dār al-Tūnisiyya li'l Nashr, 1968).

Bulliett, Richard W., *The Patricians of Nishapur: A Study in Medieval Islamic Social History*, Harvard Middle East Studies 16 (Cambridge, MA: Harvard University Press, 1972).

Bulliett, Richard W., *Conversion to Islam in the Medieval Period* (Cambridge, MA: Harvard University Press, 1979).

Burchardt, Marian and Monika Wohlrab-Sahr, "Multiple secularities: Religion and modernity in the global age", *International Sociology* 28 (2013): 605–611.

Burke III, Edmund, "The Moroccan ulama, 1860–1912: An introduction", in *Scholars, Saints and Sufis: Muslim Religious Institutions in the Middle East since 1500*, ed. Nikki R. Keddie (Berkeley, CA: University of California Press, 1972), pp. 107–114.

Burke III, Edmund and Ira M. Lapidus (eds), *Islam, Politics and Social Movements* (London: I. B. Tauris, 1988).

Burtt, A. E., *The Metaphysical Foundations of Modern Physical Science* (London: Routledge, 1932).
al-Bustānī, Fu'ād Ifrām, *Mawāqif lubnāniyya* (Beirut: Manshūrāt al-Dā'ira, 1982).
al-Bustānī, Sulayman, *'Ibra wa dhikrā: Aw al-dawla al-'Uthmāniyya qabla al-dustūr wa ba'duhu* (Cairo: Maṭba'at al-Akhbār, 1908).
al-Būṭī, Muḥammad Sa'īd, *Ḍawābiṭ al-maṣlaḥa fī al-sharī'a al-islāmiyya*, 4th edn (Beirut: Mu'assasat al-Risāla, 1982).
Cahen, Claude, "Notes sur le début de la futuwwa d'Al Nāṣir", *Oriens* 6 (1953): 18–23.
Cahen, Claude, "Mouvements populaires et autonomisme urbain dans l'Asie musulmane du Moyen-Âge", *Arabica* 5 (1958): 225–250, 6 (1959): 25–56, 223–265.
Calhoun, Craig, "Review of Taylor, *A Secular Age*", *European Journal of Sociology* 49 (2008): 455–461.
Calhoun, Craig, M. Juergensmeyer, and J. van Antwerpen (eds), *Rethinking Secularism* (Oxford: Oxford University Press, 2011).
Cameron, Averil, *Byzantine Matters* (Princeton: Princeton University Press, 2014).
Camilleri, C., "Les jeunes Tunisiens cultivés face au probléme de la mixité", *Confluent* 20 (1961): 262–287.
Cancik, Hubert, Burkhart Gladigow, and Karl-Heinz Kohl (eds), *Handbuch religionswissenschaftlicher Grundbegriffe*, 5 vols (Stuttgart: Kohlhammer, 1988–2001).
Caro Baroja, Julio, *Estudios Mogrebies* (Madrid: Consejo Superior de Investigaciones Científicas, Instituto de Estudios Africanos, 1957).
Carré, Olivier (ed.), *La légitimation islamique des socialismes arabes: Analyse conceptuelle combinatoire des manuels scolaires égyptiens, syriens, et iraqiens* (Paris: Presses de la Fondation nationale des sciences politiques, 1979).
Carré, Olivier (ed.), *L'Islam et l'état dans le monde d'aujourd'hui* (Paris: PUF, 1982).
Casanova, José, *Public Religions in the Modern World* (Chicago: University of Chicago Press, 1994).
Casanova, José, "A reply to Talal Asad", in *Powers of the Secular Modern. Talal Asad and His Interlocutors*, eds D. Scott and C. Hirschkind (Stanford: Stanford University Press, 2006), pp. 12–30.

Casanova, José, "The secular, secularizations, secularism", in *Rethinking Secularism*, eds Craig Calhoun, M. Juergensmeyer, and J. van Antwerpen (Oxford: Oxford University Press, 2011), pp. 54–74.

Caton, Steve, "What is an 'authorizing discourse'?" in *Powers of the Secular Modern. Talal Asad and His Interlocutors*, eds D. Scott and C. Hirschkind (Stanford: Stanford University Press, 2006), pp. 31–56.

Chadwick, Owen, *The Secularization of the European Mind in the Nineteenth Century: The Gifford Lectures in the University of Edinburgh for 1973–74* (Cambridge: Cambridge University Press, 1975).

Chambers, Richard, "The Ottoman ulama and the Tanzimat", in *Scholars, Saints and Sufis: Muslim Religious Institutions in the Middle East since 1500*, ed. Nikki R. Keddie (Berkeley and Los Angeles: University of California Press, 1972), pp. 33–46.

Charfi, Abdelmajīd, "La sécularisation dans les sociétés arabo-musulmanes modernes", *Islamochristiana* 8 (1982): 57–59.

Charlton, Donald Geoffrey, *Secular Religions in France, 1815–1870* (London and New York: Oxford University Press, 1963).

Charnay, Jean-Paul, et al., *L'ambivalence dans la culture arabe* (Paris: Éditions Anthropos, 1967).

Chatterjee, Partha, *Nationalist Thought and the Colonial World* (London: Zed Books and Delhi: Oxford University Press, 1986).

Chehata, Chafik, "Les survivances musulmanes dans la codification du droit civil égyptien", *Revue internationale du droit comparé* 17/4 (1965): 839–853.

Chehata, Chafik, "Logique juridique et droit musulman", *Studia Islamica* 23 (1965): 5–25.

Chehata, Chafik, "L'*Ikhtilāf* et la conception musulmane du droit", in *L'Ambivalence dans la culture arabe*, ed. J.-P. Charnay (Paris: Éditions Anthropos, 1967), pp. 258–266.

Chehata, Chafik, "La religion et les fondements des droits en Islam", *Archives de philosophie de droit* 18 (1973): 17–25.

Cheikho, Fr Louis S. J., "Tanāquḍ al-dīn wa al-ʿilm", *al-Mashriq* 3 (1900): 303–309.

Cheikho, Fr Louis S. J., *Al-sirr al-maṣūn fī shīʿat al-Farmasūn*, 6 fascicles (Beirut: al-Maṭbaʿa al-Kāthūlīkiyya, 1910–1911).

Cleveland, William L., *Islam Against the West: Shakīb Arslān and the Campaign for Islamic Nationalism* (Austin: University of Texas Press, 2011).

Cole, J. R. I. and Keddie, N. R. (eds), *Shi'ism and Social Protest* (New Haven and London: Yale University Press, 1986).

Commins, David, "Religious reformers and Arabists in Damascus, 1885–1914", *International Journal of Middle East Studies* 18 (1986): 405–425.

Commins, David Dean, *Islamic Reform: Politics and Social Change in Late Ottoman Syria* (Oxford: Oxford University Press, 1990).

Compagnon, Antoine, *Les Antimodernes. De Joseph de Maistre à Roland Barthes* (Paris: Gallimard, 2006).

Comte, Auguste, *Système de politique positive* (Paris: Chez l'auteur, 1853).

Cooke, Miriam, *Nazira Zeineddine: A Pioneer of Islamic Feminism* (Oxford: Oneworld, 2010).

Corm, Georges [Jūrj Qurm], *Pensée et politique dans le monde arabe. Contextes historiques et problématiques, XXe–XXIe siècle* (Paris: La Découverte, 2015). Published in English as Georges Corm, *Arab Political Thought: Past and Present*, trans P. Phillips-Batoma and A. T. Batoma (London: Hurst in association with the Aga Khan University Institute for the Study of Mulslim Civilisations, 2019).

Corm, Georges, *Pour une lecture profane des conflits. Sur le «retour du religieux» dans les conflits du Moyen-Orient* (Paris: La Découverte, 2015).

Crecelius, Daniel, "Non-ideological responses in the Egyptian Ulama to Modernization", in *Scholars, Saints and Sufis: Muslim Religious Institutions in the Middle East since 1500*, ed. Nikki R. Keddie (Berkeley, CA: University of California Press, 1972), pp. 169–209.

Crombie, A. C., *Robert Grosseteste and the Origins of Experimental Science* (Oxford: Clarendon Press, 1953).

Crone, Patricia and Martin Hinds, *God's Caliph* (Cambridge: Cambridge University Press, 1986).

Dagron, Gilbert, *Empereur et prêtre. Étude sur le "césaropapisme" byzantin* (Paris: Gallimard, 1996).

Ḍāhir, 'Ādil, "Naqd al-ṣaḥwa al-islāmiyya", *Mawāqif* 57 (1989): 49–74.

Ḍāhir, 'Ādil, *Al-Usus al-Falsafiya li'l-'Ilmānīya* (Beirut: Dār al-Sāqī, 1993).

al-Dakhīl, Khālid, *Al-Wahhābīya bayn ash-shirk wa taṣaḍḍu' al-qabīla* (Beirut: al-Shabaka al-'Arabiyya li'l-Abḥāth wa'n-Nashr, 2013).

al-Dakhīl, Khālid, "Al-Wahhābīya: Murāja'a ukhrā", *Al-Ḥayāt*, 20 February 2016.

Dakhli, Leyla, "Du point de vue des femmes", in *Le Moyen-Orient, fin XIXe–XXe siècle*, ed. Leyla Dakhli (Paris: Seuil, 2016), pp. 31–57.

Darrāj, Fayṣal, "Al-shaykh al-taqlīdī wa al-muthaqqaf al-ḥadīth", in *Ṭaḥa Ḥusayn: Al-ʿaqlāniyya, al-dimūqrāṭiya, al-ḥadātha*, ed. Fayṣal Darrāj, Qaḍāya wa Shahādāt, 1 (Nicosia: Mu'assasat 'Ībāl li'l-Dirāsāt wa al-Nashr, 1990), pp. 25–95.

al-Dashrāwī, Farḥāt, "ʿAlā anqidhū al-Islām", *al-Fikr* 9:1 (1963): 40–42.

al-Dayālimī, 'Abd al-Ṣamad, *Al-mar'a wa al-jins fī al-Maghrib* (Casablanca: Dār al-Nashr al-Maghribiyya, 1985).

Debs, Richard A., *Islamic Law and Civil Code: The Law of Property in Egypt* (New York: Columbia University Press, 2010).

Deringil, Selim, *The Well-Protected Domains: Ideology and the Legitimation of Power in the Ottoman Empire, 1876–1909* (London: I. B. Tauris, 1998).

Dessouki, Ali E. Hillal (ed.), *Islamic Resurgences in the Arab World* (New York: Praeger, 1982).

Dictionnaire apologétique de la foi catholique (Paris: Gabriel Beauchesne, 1923).

Digard, J. P., "Shiʿisme et état en Iran", in *L'Islam et l'état dans le monde d'aujourd'hui*, ed. Olivier Carré (Paris: Presses Universitaires de France, 1982), pp. 65–88.

al-Dimashqī, Mīkhā'il, *Ta'arīkh ḥawādith al-Shām wa Lubnān (1197/1782–1275/1841)*, ed. Louis Maʿlūf (Beirut: n.p., 1912).

Dirlik, Arif, *The Postcolonial Aura* (Boulder: Westview Press, 1997).

Dixon, C. Scott, *Contesting the Reformation* (Oxford: Wiley-Blackwell, 2012).

Douwes, Dick and Norman N. Lewis, "The trial of the Syrian Ismaiʿilis in the first decade of the 20th century", *International Journal of Middle East Studies* 21 (1989): 215–232.

Dreher, J., "L'Imamat d'Ibn Qasi à Mertola (automne 1144–été 1145): Légitimité d'une domination soufie?", *Mélanges de l'Institut Dominicain d'Études Orientales* 18 (1988): 195–210.

Dreyfuss, Robert, *Devil's Game. How the United States Helped Unleash Fundamentalist Islam* (New York: Owl Books – Henry Holt and Company, 2005).

Duby, Georges, *The Knight, the Lady and the Priest: The Making of Modern Marriage*, trans. Barbara Bray (Harmondsworth: Penguin Books, 1985).

Duffy, Eamon, *Saints and Sinners: A History of the Popes* (New Haven and London: Yale University Press, 2006).

Dumont, Louis, *From Mandeville to Marx: The Genesis and Triumph of Economic Ideology* (Chicago: University of Chicago Press, 1977).

Dumont, Paul, "La Franc-maçonnerie ottomane et les 'idées françaises'", in *Les Arabes, les Turcs et la Révolution française*: special issue of *Revue du monde musulman et de la Méditerranée* 52–53 (1989): 150–159.

Dupret, Baudouin, *What is the Sharia?* (London: Hurst in association with the Aga Khan University Institute for the Study of Muslim Civilisations, 2018).

Edib, Halide, *Turkey Faces West. A Turkish View of Recent Changes and their Origin* (New Haven: Yale University Press, 1930).

Edwards, R., *La Syrie, 1840–1862* (Paris: n.p., 1862).

Egger, Vernon, *A Fabian in Egypt, Salāma Musa and the Rise of the Professional Classes in Egypt 1909–1939* (London: University Press of America, 1986).

Egypt, Ministry of Justice, *Al-qānūn al-madanī: Majmūʿat al-aʿmāl al-taḥḍīriyya*, 2 vols (Cairo: Maṭbaʿat Dār al-Kitāb al-ʿArabī, n.d.).

Egyptian Law Code of 1948, https://searchworks.stanford.edu/view/1760807

El Saadawi, Nawal, *Memoirs of a Woman Doctor* (London: Saqi Books, 1987).

El Saadawi, Nawal, *The Hidden Face of Eve: Women in the Arab World*, new edn (London: Zed Books, 2007).

El Shamsy, Ahmed, *The Canonization of Islamic Law* (Cambridge: Cambridge University Press, 2015).

Eldem, Edhem, "La bourgeoisie ottomane fin de siècle", in *Le Moyen-Orient, fin XIXe–XXe siècle*, ed. Leyla Dakhli (Paris: Seuil, 2016), pp. 135–144.

El-Enany, Rashid, "Religion in the novels of Naguib Mahfouz", *Bulletin of the British Society for Middle East Studies* 15 (1988): 21–27.

El-Nahal, Galal, *The Judicial Administration of Ottoman Egypt in the Seventeenth Century* (Minneapolis and Chicago: Bibliotheca Islamica, 1979).

El-Rouayheb, Khaled, "Was there a revival of logical studies in eighteenth-century Egypt?", *Die Welt des Islams* 45 (2005); 1–19.

Elshakry, Marwa, *Reading Darwin in Arabic 1860–1950* (Chicago: University of Chicago Press, 2013).

Emérit, Marcel, "La Crise syrienne et l'expansion économique française en 1860", *Revue historique* 20 (1952): 211–232.

Emon, Ahmed and Rumee Ahmed (eds), *The Oxford Handbook of Islamic Law* (Oxford: Oxford University Press, 2018).

Enayat, Hadi, *Islam and Secularism in Post-Colonial Thought. A Cartography of Asadian Geneaologies* (London: Palgrave Macmillan, 2017).

Encyclopædia of Religion and Ethics, ed. James Hastings, 12 vols (Edinburgh: T. and T. Clark, 1920).

Encyclopedia of Islam, 2nd edn, eds P. J. Bearman, T. Bianquis, C. E. Bosworth, E. van Donzel, and W. P. Heinrichs, et al., 12 vols (Leiden: Brill, 1954–2005).

Encyclopedia of Islam, 3rd edn, ed. K. Fleet, G. Krämer, D. Matringe, J. Nawas, and E. Rowson (Leiden: Brill, 1995 – in progress).

Ephrat, Daphna, *A Learned Society in a Period of Transition: The Sunni 'Ulama' of Eleventh-Century Baghdad* (Albany: SUNY Press, 2000).

Eymien, A., "Science et religion", in *Dictionnaire apologétique de la foi catholique*, eds A. d'Alès, et al., 4 vols (Paris: Gabriel Beauchesne, 1923), pp. 1,242–1,254.

al-Faḥḥām, al-Shaykh Muḥammad Muḥammad, "Muqaddima", in Sāmiḥ Kurayyim, *Islāmiyyāt: Ṭaha Ḥusayn, al-'Aqqād, Ḥusayn Haykal, Aḥmad Amīn, Tawfiq al-Hakīm*, 2nd edn (Beirut: Dār al-Qalam, 1977), pp. 9–12.

Fahmy, Khaled, *All the Pasha's Men* (Cambridge: Cambridge University Press, 1997).

Faraj, Nabīl, "Louis 'Awaḍ amām maḥākim al-taftīsh", *al-Nāqid* 1 (1989): 38–39.

Fāris, Hānī, *Al-naza'āt al-ṭa'ifiyya fī tārīkh Lubnān al-ḥadīth* (Beirut: al-Dār al-Ahliyya li'l-Nashr wa al-Tawzī', 1980).

Febvre, Lucien Paul Victor, *Martin Luther: A Destiny*, trans. Roberts Tapley (London and Toronto: J. M. Dent and Sons, 1930).

Febvre, Lucien Paul Victor, *The Problem of Unbelief in the Sixteenth Century: The Religion of Rabelais*, trans. Beatrice Gottlieb (Cambridge, MA: Harvard University Press, 1982).

Felski, Rita, "Suspicious minds", *Poetics Today* 32 (2011): 215–234.

Filali-Ansary, Abdou, *Réformer l'Islam? Une introduction aux débats contemporains* (Paris: La Découverte, 2005).

Fīlībūnus, "Ta'ammulāt fī al-adab wa al-ḥayāt", *al-'Uṣūr* 2/8 (1928): 860–866.

Fīlībūnus, "Ta'ammulāt fī al-adab wa al-ḥayāt", *al-'Uṣūr* 2/7 (1928): 715–720.

al-Fiqī, Muḥammad Kāmil, *Al-Azhar wa atharuhu fī al-nahḍa al-'arabiyya al-ḥadītha*, 2nd edn (Cairo: Maktabat Nahḍat Miṣr, 1965).

Flores, Alexander, *The Communist Movement in the Arab World* (London: Routledge, 2005).

Foucher, Louis, *La philosophie catholique en France au XIXe siècle avant la renaissance thomiste et dans son rapport avec elle 1800–1880* (Paris: Vrin, 1955).

Francastel, Pierre, *Peinture et société: Naissance et destruction d'un espace plastique de la Renaissance au Cubisme* (Lyon: Audin, 1951).

Franzen, Johan, "Communism in the Arab world and Iran", in *The Cambridge History of Communism*, eds Norman Naimark, Silvio Pons and Sophie Quinn-Judge (Cambridge: Cambridge University Press, 2017), pp. 518–543.

Freeman, Derek, *Margaret Mead and the Heretic. The Making and Unmaking of an Anthropological Myth* (Harmondsworth: Penguin Books, 1996).

Frei, Hans, *The Eclipse of Biblical Narrative* (New Haven: Yale University Press, 1980).

Frye, Richard Nelson (ed.), *Islam and the West* (Gravenhage: Mouton, 1957).

Fūda, Faraj, *Qabla al-suqūṭ: Ḥiwār hādi' ḥawl taṭbīq al-sharī'a al-islāmiyya* (Cairo: n.p., 1985).

Gadamer, Hans Georg, "Herder et ses théories sur l'Histoire", *Cahiers de l'Institut Allemand, II: Regards sur l'histoire*, ed. Karl Epting, Paris, 1941, pp. 9–36.

Geertz, Clifford, *Negara: The Theatre State in Nineteenth-Century Bali* (Princeton: Princeton University Press, 1980).

Geertz, Clifford, *After the Fact. Two Countries, Four Decades, One Anthropologist* (Cambridge, MA: Harvard University Press, 1995).

Gellner, David N., "Studying secularism, practising secularism. Anthropological perspectives", *Social Anthropology* 9 (2001): 337–340.

Gellner, Ernest and Vatin, Jean-Claude (eds), *Islam et Politique au Maghreb* (Paris: Éditions du Centre national de la recherche scientifique, 1981).

Gellner, Ernest, *Nations and Nationalism, New Perspectives on the Past* (Oxford: Basil Blackwell and Ithaca: Cornell University Press, 1983).

Georgon, François, *Abdulhamid II, le sultan caliphe* (Paris: Farard, 2003).

Gesinck, Indira Falk, *Islamic Reform and Conservatism: Al-Azhar and the Evolution of Modern Sunni Islam* (London: I. B. Tauris, 2014).

Ghadīra, 'Āmir, "Limādhā anā Muslim wa kayfa anā Muslim?", *al-Fikr* 9 (1960): 9–28.

Ghalyūn, Burhān, *Al-mas'ala al-ṭā'ifiyya wa mushkilat al-aqallīyyāt* (Beirut: Dār al-Ṭalī'a, 1979).

Ghalyūn, Burhān, *Ightiyāl al-'aql: Miḥnat al-thaqāfa al-'arabiyya bayn al-salafiyya wa al-taba'iyya* (Beirut: Dār al-Tanwīr, 1985).

al-Ghannūshī, Rāshid, "Ta'qīb: Taḥlīl li'l-'anāṣir al-mukawwina li'l-ẓāhira al-islāmiyya bi Tūnis: Ḥarakāt al-ittijāh al-islāmī", in *Al-ḥarakāt al-islāmiyya al-mu'āṣira fi al-waṭan al-'arabī*, ed. Markaz Dirāsāt al-Waḥda al-'Arabiyya (Beirut: Markaz Dirāsāt al-Waḥda al-'Arabiyya, 1987), pp. 300–308.

al-Ghannūshī, Rāshid, *Al-mar'a bayn al-Qur'ān al-karīm wa wāqi' al-muslimīn* (Damascus: Markaz al-Rāya li'l-Tanmiya al-Fikriyya, 2005).

al-Ghazālī, Abū Ḥāmid ibn Muḥammad, *Miḥakk al-naẓar fi al-manṭiq*, eds Badr al-Din al-Na'sāni al-Ḥalabī and Muṣtafā al-Qabbāni al-Dimashqī (Cairo: al-Maṭba'a al-Adabiyya, n.d.).

al-Ghazālī, Abū Ḥāmid ibn Muḥammad, *Al-muṣṭaṣfa min 'ilm al-uṣūl*, 2 vols (Cairo: n.p., 1356/1937).

al-Ghazālī, Muḥammad, *Our Beginning is Wisdom*, trans. Isma'il Tagi al-Faruqi (Washington, DC: American Council of Learned Societies, 1951).

al-Ghazālī, Muḥammad, *Min hunā na'lam*, 4th edn (Cairo: Dār al-kitāb al-'arabī, 1954)

al-Ghazālī, Abū Ḥāmid ibn Muḥammad, *Mīzān al-'amal*, edited and introduced by Sulaymān Duyā, *Dakhā'ir al-'Arab* 38 (Cairo: Dār al-Ma'ārif, 1964).

Gillespie, Michael Allen, *The Theological Origins of Modernity* (Chicago: University of Chicago Press, 2008).

Glass, Dagmar, *Der al-Muqtaṭaf und seine Öffentlichkeit. Aufklärung, Räsonnement und Meinungsstreit in der frühen arabischen Zeitschriftenkommunikation*, 2 vols (Würzburg: Ergon Verlag, 2004).

Gombrich, Richard, *Theravada Bhuddism. A Social History from Ancient Benares to Modern Colombo* (London: Routledge & Kegan Paul, 1988).

Goodrich, D. R., *A Sufi Revolt in Portugal* (unpublished PhD thesis, Columbia University, 1978).

Graham, Michael F., *The Blasphemies of Thomas Aikenhead* (Edinburgh: Edinburgh University Press, 2008).

Gray, Matthew, *Conspiracy Theories in the Arab World, Sources and Politics* (London: Routledge, 2010).

Green, Arnold Harrison, *The Tunisian Ulama, 1873–1915: Social Structure and Response to Ideological Currents* (Leiden: Brill, 1978).

Green, Richard F., *Elf Queens and Holy Friars: Fairy Beliefs and the Medieval Church* (Philadelphia: University of Pennsylvania Press, 2017).

Gregory, Frederick, *Scientific Materialism in Nineteenth Century Germany* (Dordrecht: D. Reidel, 1977).

Gribetz, Arthur, *Strange Bedfellows: Mutʿat al-nisāʾ and mutʿat al-ḥajj: A Study Based on Sunnī and Shīʿī sources of tafsīr, ḥadīth and fiqh* (Berlin: Klaus Schwarz Verlag, 1994).

Gurevich, Aron, *Medieval Popular Culture: Problems of Belief and Perception*, trans Janos Bak and Paul Hollingsworth, Cambridge Studies in Oral and Literate Culture 14 (Cambridge: Cambridge University Press and Paris: Éditions de la Maison des sciences de l'Homme, 1988).

Gusdorf, Georges, *Les principes de la pensée au siècle des lumières, Les sciences humaines et la pensée occidentale*, 14 vols, vol. 4 (Paris: Payot, 1971).

Ḥabashī, René, *Ḥaḍāratuna ʿalā muftaraq* (Beirut: Manshūrāt al-Nadwa al-Lubnāniyya, 1960).

Ḥaddād, Grégoire, "Hall al-baḥth al-dīnī al-jadhrī kufr wa shirk aw hall huwa fī manṭiq al-Injīl", *Afāq* 1 (1974): 32–45.

Ḥaddād, Grégoire, "Al-masīḥiyya wa al-ʿilmāniyya", *Mawāqif* 39 (1980): 139–148.

al-Ḥaddād, Muḥammad, *Ḥafriyyāt taʾwīliyya fī al-khiṭāb al-iṣlāḥī al-ʿarabī* (Beirut: Dār al-Ṭalīʿa, 2002).

al-Ḥaddād, Muḥammad, *Muḥammad ʿAbduh. Qirāʾa jadīda fī khiṭāb al-iṣlāḥ ad-dīnī* (Beirut: Dār al-Ṭalīʿa, 2002).Ḥaddād, Ṭāhir, *Imrāʾatunā fī al-sharīʿa wa al-mujtamaʿ* (Tunis: al-Dār al-Tūnisiyya li'l-Nashr, 1977).

Hadden, Jeffrey K., "Toward desacralizing secularization theory", *Social Forces* 65/3 (1987): 587–611.

Hadi-Sadok, M., "Ibn Marzuk", in *The Encyclopedia of Islam*, eds B. Lewis, V. L. Ménage, C. Pellat, and J. Schacht, with C. Dumont, E. van Donzel, and G. R. Hawting, 2nd edn, 12 vols (Leiden: Brill, 1954–2005), vol. 3 (1971), pp. 865–868.

al-Ḥāfiẓ, Yāsīn, *Al-tajriba al- tārīkhiyya al-fitnāmiyya: Taqyīm naqdī muqāran maʿa al-tajriba al-ʿarabiyya*, 2nd edn (Beirut: Dār al-Ṭalīʿa, 1979).

al-Ḥakīm, Tawfīq, *Naẓarāt fī al-dīn wa al-thaqāfa wa al-mujtamaʿ* (Cairo: al-Maktab al-Miṣri al-Ḥadīth, 1979).

Hallaq, Wael B., "Was the gate of Ijitihad closed?", *International Journal of Middle East Studies* 16 (1984): 3–41.

Halman, Loek and Veerle Draulans, "How secular is Europe", *British Journal of Sociology* 57 (2006): 263–288.

Ḥammūd, Ḥammūd, *Baḥth 'an al-muqaddas: Al-ba'th wa al-uṣūliyya* (Beirut, Dār Jadāwil, 2014).

Ḥanafī, Ḥasan, *Dirāsāt falsafiyya* (Cairo: Maktabat al-Anglo-Miṣriyya, 1988).

Ḥanafī, Ḥasan, "Al-'ilmāniyya wa al-islām", *al-Yawm al-Sābi'*, 3 April 1989.

Hanioğlu, Şükrü, *A Brief History of the Late Ottoman Empire* (Princeton: Princeton University Press, 2010).

Ḥannā, 'Abd Allāh, *Al-ittijāhāt al-fikriyya fī Sūriyyā wa Lubnān 1920–1945* (Damascus: Dār al-Taqaddum al-'Arabī, 1973).

Hanssen J. and M. Weiss (eds), *Arabic Thought beyond the Liberal Age* (Cambridge: Cambridge University Press, 2016).

Ḥarb, Ṭala'at, *Tarbiyat al-mar'a wa al-ḥijāb* (Cairo: Maṭba'at al-Taraqqī, 1899).

Haroun, Georges, *Šiblī Šumayyil. Une pensée évolutionniste arabe a l'époque d'An-Nahḍa* (Beirut: Publications de l'Université Libanaise, 1985).

Hartmann, Angelika, *An-Nasir li Din Allah, 1180–1225: Politik, Religion und Kultur in der späten Abbāsidenzeit*, Studien zur Geschichte und Kultur des Islamischen Orients, n.f., Bd; 8 (Berlin: Walter de Gruyter, 1975).

Havelock, Eric Alfred, *Preface to Plato* (Oxford: Basil Blackwell, 1963).

Ḥāwi, Khalīl, *Dīwān Khalīl Ḥāwī* (Beirut: Dār al-'Awda, 1972).

Hawi, Khalil S., *Khalil Gibran: His Background, Character and Works*, American University of Beirut, Publications of the Faculty of Arts and Sciences, Oriental Series, no. 41 (Beirut: Arab Institute for Research and Publishing, 1972).

Hawkins, M., *Social Darwinism in European and American Thought, 1860–1945* (Cambridge: Cambridge University Press, 1997).

Al-Ḥayāt, 16–17 December 1989.

Haykal, Muḥammad Ḥusayn, *Al-Sharq al-Jadīd* (Cairo: Maktabat al-Nahḍa al-Miṣriyya, 1962).

Haykal, Muḥammad Ḥusayn, "Al-dīn wa al-'ilm" (1926) in *Al-īmān wa al-ma'rifa wa al-falsafa* (Cairo: Maktabat al-Nahḍa al-Miṣriyya, 1964).

Haykal, Muḥammad Ḥusayn, "Al-sharq wa al-gharb" (1933) in Muḥammad Ḥusayn Haykal, *Al-Sharq al-Jadīd* (Cairo: Maktabat al-Nahḍa al-Miṣriyya, 1962), pp. 13–69.

Haykal, Muḥammad Ḥusayn, *Ḥayāt Muḥammad*, 5th edn (Cairo: Maktabat al-Nahḍa al-Miṣriyya, 1952). English translation as *The Life of*

Muhammad, trans. Isma'il Ragi al-Faruki (Plainfield: American Trust Publications, 2005).

Haykal, Muḥammad Ḥusayn, *Al-īmān wa al-ma'rifa wa-l-falsafa* (Cairo: Maktabat al-Nahḍa al-Miṣriyya, 1964).

Hazard, Paul, *The European Mind, 1680–1715* (Harmondsworth: Penguin Books, 1964).

Hazīm, Ignatius, "Shawāghil al-fikr al-masīḥī mundhu 1866", in Al-Jāmi'a al-Amīrikiyya fī Bayrūt (ed.), *Al-fikr al-'arabi fī mi'at sana: Buḥūth mu'tamar Hay'at al-Dirasāt al-'Arabiyya al-mun'aqida fī Tishrīn al-Thānī 1966 fī al-Jāmi'a al-Amīrikiyya fī Bayrūt*, eds Fu'ād Ṣarrūf and Nabīh Amīn Fāris (Beirut: al-Jāmi'a al-Amīrikiyya, 1967).

Hegel, Georg Wilhelm Friedrich, *Phenomenology of Spirit*, trans. A.V. Miller (Oxford: Clarendon Press, 1977).

Helali, Asma, *Étude sur la tradition prophétique: La question de l'authenticité du Ier/VIème au VIème/XIIème siècle* (unpublished doctoral thesis, École Pratique des Hautes Études [Vème Section: Sciences Réligieuses], Paris, 2004).

Hendrick, Joshua D., *Gülen. The Ambiguous Politics of Market Islam in Turkey and the World* (New York: New York University Press, 2014).

Herberg, William, *Protestant, Catholic, Jew* (New York: Doubleday, 1955).

Herrin, Judith, *The Formation of Christendom* (Oxford: Basil Blackwell and Princeton: Princeton University Press, 1987).

Hill, Christopher, *The Intellectual Origins of the English Revolution* (Oxford: Clarendon Press, 1965).

al-Ḥilū, Karam, *Al-fikr al-libirālī 'inda Fransīs al-Marrāsh* (Beirut: Centre for Arab Unity Studies, 2006).

Hinnesbusch Raymond, "Islamic movements in Syria", in *Islamic Resurgence in the Arab World*, ed. Ali E. Hillal Dessouki (New York: Praeger, 1982), pp. 138–169.

al-Hirmāsī, Muḥammad 'Abd al-Bāqī, "Al-islām al-iḥtijājī fī Tūnis", in *Al-ḥarakāt al-islāmiyya al-mu'āṣira fī al-waṭan al-'arabī*, ed. Markaz Dirāsāt al-Waḥda al-'Arabiyya (Beirut: Markaz Dirāsāt al-Waḥda al-'Arabīya, 1987), pp. 247–299.

Hobsbawm, Eric J., *Nations and Nationalism since 1780: Programme, Myth and Reality* (Cambridge: Cambridge University Press, 1990).

Honneth, Axel, "Anthropologische Berührungpunkte zwischen der lebensphilosophischen Kulturkritik und 'Der Dialektik der Aufklärung'", in *21.*

Deutscher Soziologentag 1982: Beiträge der Sektions- und ad hoc Gruppen, eds Friedrich Heckmann and Peter Winter (Wiesbaden: Westdeutscher Verlag, 1983), pp. 786–792.

Hourani, Albert H., "Ottoman reform and the politics of notables", in *The Beginnings of Modernisation in the Middle East: The Nineteenth Century*, eds William R. Polk and Richard Chambers, Publications of the Center for Middle Eastern Studies 1 (Chicago: University of Chicago Press, 1968), pp. 41–68.

Ḥusayn, ʿĀdil, *Naḥw fikr ʿarabī jadīd: Al-Nāṣiriyya wa al-tanmiya wa al-dīmūqraṭiyya* (Cairo: Dār al-Mustaqbal al-ʿArabi, 1985).

Ḥusayn, Muḥammad al-Khidr, *Naqḍ kitab "Fī al-shiʿr al-jāhilī"* (Cairo: al-Maṭbaʿa al-Salafiyya, 1926).

Ḥusayn, Muḥammad Muḥammad, *Al-ittijāhāt al-waṭaniyya fi al-adab al-muʿāṣir*, 2 vols (Beirut: Dār al-Irshād, 1970).

Ḥusayn, Ṭaḥa [Taha Hussein], *ʿAlā hāmish al-Sīra* (Cairo: Dār al-Maʿārif, n.d.).

Ḥusayn, Ṭaḥa, *Fī al-shiʿr al-jāhilī* (Cairo: Matbaʿt Dār al-Kutub al-Miṣriyya, 1926).

Ḥusayn, Ṭaḥa, "Ilā ṣadīqī Aḥmad Amin", *al-Risāla* 4/152 (1936): 921–922.

Ḥusayn, Ṭaḥa, "Introduction", in Muḥammad Kāmil al-Fiqī, *Al-Azhar wa atharuhu fi al-nahḍa al-ʿarabiyya al-ḥadītha*, 2nd edn (Cairo: Maktabat Nahḍat Miṣr, 1965).

Ḥusayn, Ṭaḥa, *Fī qaḍāya al-marʾa* (Beirut: Muʾassasat Nāṣir lil-Thaqāfa, 1980).

Ḥusayn, Ṭaḥa, "Madrasat-al azwāj", in *Fī qaḍāya al-marʾa*, ed. Faysal Darrāj (Beirut: Muʾassasat Nāṣir li'l-Thaqāfa, 1980), pp. 163–169.

Ḥusayn, Ṭaḥa, *Al-majmūʿa al-kāmila li muʾallafāt al-duktūr Ṭaha Ḥusayn*, 16 vols (Beirut: Dār al-Kitāb al-Lubnānī, 1984).

Ḥusayn, Ṭaḥa, *Mustaqbal al-thaqāfa fi miṣr*, vol. 9 of *Al-majmūʿa al-kāmila li muʾallafāt al-duktūr Ṭaha Ḥusayn* (Beirut: Dār al-kitāb al-Lubnānī, 1984).

al-Ḥuṣrī, [Abū Khaldūn] Sāṭiʿ, *Yawm maysalūn: Ṣafḥa min tārīkh al-ʿArab al-ḥadīth* (Beirut: Maktabat al-Kashshāf, 1947).

al-Ḥuṣrīʿ, Sāṭiʿ, *Al-bilād al-ʿArabiyya wa al-dawla al-ʿUthmāniyya: Muḥāḍarāt alqāhā ʿalā ṭullāb maʿhad al-dirāsāt al-ʿarabiyya al-ʿāliya* (Beirut: Dār al-ʿIlm l'il-Malāyīn, 1960).

al-Ḥuṣrīʿ, Sāṭiʿ, *Mā hiya al-qawmiyya: Abḥāth wa dirāsāt ʿalā ḍawʾ al-aḥdāth wa al-naẓariyāt*, 2nd edn (Beirut: Dār al-ʿIlm lil-Malāyīn, 1963).

al-Ḥuṣrī', Sāṭi', *Al-a'māl al-qawmiyya li Sāṭi' al-Ḥuṣrī: Silsilat al-turāth al-qawmī*, 3 vols (Beirut: Markaz Dirasāt al-Waḥda al-'Arabiyya, 1985).

Ḥussayn, Maḥmūd, "Al-mu'minūn", *al-'Uṣūr* 20 (1929): 436.

Hussein, Taha [Ṭaḥa Ḥusayn], *The Future of Culture in Egypt*, trans. Sidney Glazer (Washington, DC: American Council of Learned Societies, 1954).

Huwaydī, Fahmī, "Bayān min ajl al-waḥda", *al-Ahrām*, 9 May 1989.

Ibn 'Abd al-Barr, Abū 'Amr ibn Yūsuf ibn 'Abd Allāh, *Al-intiqā' fī faḍā'il al-thalātha al-a'imma al-fuqahā'* (Beirut: Dār al-Kitāb al-Jadīd, n.d.).

Ibn 'Ābidīn, Muḥammad Amīn, *Majmū'at rasā'il ibn 'Ābidīn*, 2 vols (Istanbul: Maṭba'at al-Sharika al-Suḥufiyya al-'Uthmāniyya wa Muḥammad Hāshim al-Kutubī, 1325/1907).

Ibn al-Jawzī, Abū al-Faraj 'Abd al-Rahman ibn 'Alī, *Kitāb al-quṣṣāṣ wa al-mudhakkirīn*, ed. M. S. Schwartz (Beirut: al-Maṭba'a al-Kāthūlīkiyya, n.d.).

Ibn al-Jawzī, Abū al-Faraj 'Abd al-Raḥmān ibn 'Alī, *Al-muntaẓam fī ta'rīkh al-mulūk wa al-umam*, ed. F. Krenkow, 10 vols (Hyderabad: Dā'irat al-Ma'ārif al-'Uthmāniyya, 1357–1358/1938–1939).

Ibn al-Jawzī, Abū al-Faraj 'Abd al-Rahman ibn 'Alī, *Manāqib al-Imām Aḥmad ibn Ḥanbal* (Beirut: Dār al-Afāq al-Jadīda, 1973).

Ibn al-Jawzī, Abū al-Faraj 'Abd al-Raḥman ibn 'Alī, *Al-miṣbāḥ al-muḍī' fī khilāfat al-Mustaḍī'*, ed. Nājia 'Abd Allah Ibrāhīm, Silsilat kutub al-turāth 19, 2 vols (Baghdad: Wizārat al-Awqāf, 1976).

Ibn al-Khūja, Muḥammad b. Muṣṭafā, *Al-iktirāth fī ḥuqūq al-ināth* (Algiers: n.p. 1895).

Ibn al-Khūja, Muḥammad b. Muṣṭafā, *Al-lubāb fī aḥkām al-zinā wa al-libās wa al-iḥtijāb* (Algiers: n.p., 1907).

Ibn al-Ṭiqṭaqā, Muḥammad ibn 'Alī ibn Ṭabātabā, *Al-fakhrī fī al-ādāb al-sulṭāniyya wa al-duwal al-islāmiyya* (Cairo: n.p., 1962).

Ibn al-Ukhūwwa, Ḍiyā' al-Dīn Muḥammad ibn Muḥammad, *Ma'ālim al-qurba fī aḥkām al-ḥisba*, ed. R. Leakey, revised and trans. Reuben Levy (Cambridge: Cambridge University Press, 1938).

Ibn 'Aqīl, Bahā' al-Dīn 'Abd Allāh ibn Abd al-Raḥmān, *Kitāb al-jadal 'ala ṭarīqat al-fuqahā'*, ed. Georges Makdisi, in *Revue d'Études Orientales* 20 (1967): 126–204.

Ibn 'Āshūr, Muḥammad al-Faḍl, *Al-ḥaraka al-adabiyya wa al-fikriyya fī Tūnis* (Cairo: Jāmi'at al-Duwal al-'Arabiyya, Ma'had al-Dirāsāt al-'Arabiyya al-'Āliya, 1956).

Ibn ʿĀshūr, Muḥammad al-Faḍl, "Dhikrā Ibn Khaldūn fī Tūnis", *al-Fikr* 6 (1961): 514–517.

Ibn Bādīs, ʿAbd al-Ḥamīd, *Kitāb āthār Ibn Bādīs*, ed. ʿImād al-Ṭālibī, 4 vols (Algiers: Dār Maktabat al-Sharika al-Jazā'iriyya li'l-Ta'līf wa al-Tarjama wa al-Ṭibāʿa wa al-Tawzīʿ wa al-Nashr, n.d.).

Ibn Farḥūn, Burhān al-dīn Ibrahīm, *Al-dībāj al-mudhahhab fī maʿrifat aʿyān ʿulamā' al-madhab* (Cairo: n.p.: 1351/1932).

Ibn Jamāʿa, Abū ʿAbd Allāh Muḥammad ibn Ibrāhīm, *Taḥrīr al-aḥkām fī tadbīr ahl al-islām*, ed. Hans Kofler, in *Islamica* 6 (1934): 349–414.

Ibn Jinnī, Abū al-Fatḥ ʿUthmān, *Al-khaṣā'iṣ fī falsafat al-lugha al-ʿarabiyya*, ed. Muḥammad ʿAlī al-Najjār, 2nd edn, 2 vols (Cairo: Dār al-Kutub al-Miṣriyya, 1952–1956).

Ibn Khaldūn, *Prologomènes d'Ebn Khaldoun*, texte arabe d'après les manuscrits de la bibliothèque impériale, ed. M. Quatremère, 3 vols (Paris: Institut impérial de France, 1858).

Ibn Khaldūn, *Al-taʿrīf bi Ibn Khaldūn wa riḥlatuhu gharban wa sharqan*, ed. and annotated by Muḥammad ibn al-Tāwīt al-Ṭanjī (Cairo: Lajnat al-Ta'līf wa al-Tarjama wa al-Nashr, 1951).

Ibn Khaldūn, *Tārīkh al-ʿallāma Ibn Khaldūn*, ed. Yūsuf Asʿad Dāghir, 15 vols (Beirut: n.p., 1956).

Ibn Khaldūn, *The Muqaddimah: An Introduction to History*, trans. Franz Rosenthal, 3 vols (New York: Pantheon Books, 1958).

Ibn Khallikān, Shams al-dīn Abū al-ʿAbbās Aḥmad, *Wafayāt al-aʿyān wa anbā' ahl al-zamān*, ed. Iḥsān Abbās, 8 vols (Beirut: Dār al-Thaqāfa, 1967).

Ibn Marzūq, ʿAbd Allāh, *Al-Musnad al-ṣaḥīḥ al-ḥasan fī ma'āthir mawlānā Abī al-Ḥasan*, ed. Évariste Levi-Provençal, *Hespéris* 5/4 (1925): 1–82.

Ibn Qayyim al-Jawziyya, Abū ʿAbd Allāh Muḥammad ibn Abū Bakr, *iʿlām al-muwaqqiʿīn ʿan rabb al-ʿālamīn*, revised by Ṭaḥa ʿAbd al-Ra'ūf Saʿd, 4 vols (Beirut: Dār al-Jīl, n.d.).

Ibn Qunfudh, Aḥmad Ibn Ḥusayn ibn ʿAlī ibn al-Khaṭīb, *Al-Fārisiyya fī mabādī' al-dawla al-Ḥafṣiyya*, eds Muḥammad al-Shādhlī Nayfar and ʿAbd al-Majīd al-Turkī, Nafā'is al-Makhṭuṭāt, al-Maktaba al-Ta'rīkhiyya 5 (Tunis: al-Dār al-Tūnisiyya lʿil-Nashr, 1968).

Ibn Rajab, *Al-dhayl ʿalā tabaqāt al-ḥanābila*, ed. Muḥammad Ḥāmid al-Fiqī, 2 vols (Cairo: Maṭbaʿa al-Sunna al-Muḥammadiya, 1952).

Ibn Rushd, *Al-muqaddimāt al-mumahiddāt li-bayān ma iqtaḍathu rusūm al-Mudawwana min al-aḥkām al-shar'iyyāt wa al-taḥṣīlāt al-muḥkamāt al-shar'iyyāt li ummahāt masā'il al-mushkilāt* (Cairo: n.p., n.d.).

Ibn Sallām, Abū 'Ubayd al-Qāsim al-Harawī, *Al-amwāl*, ed. Muḥammad Khalīl Harrās (Cairo: Maktabat al-Kulliyāt al-Azhariyya, 1968).

Ibn Taymiyya, Taqī al-Dīn Aḥmad ibn 'Abd al-Ḥalīm, *Al-siyāsa al-shar'iyya fī iṣlaḥ ar-rā'ī wa al-ra'iyya* (Cairo: al-Maṭba'a al-Khayriyya, 1322/1904).

Ibn Taymiyya, Taqī al-Dīn Aḥmad ibn 'Abd al-Ḥalīm, *Minhāj al-sunna al-nabawiyya fī naqḍ kalām al-shī'a wa al-qadāriyya*, 9 vols (Cairo: al-Maṭba'a al-Amīriyya, 1322/1904).

Ibn Taymiyya, Taqī Eddīn Aḥmad ibn 'Abd al-Ḥalīm, *Muwāfaqat ṣarīh al-ma'qūl li ṣaḥīḥ al-manqūl*, eds Muḥammad Muhyī al-Dīn 'Abd al-Ḥamīd and Muḥammad Ḥāmid al-Fiqī, 2 vols (Cairo: Maṭba'at al-Sunna al-Muḥammadiyya, 1950–1953).

Ibrahim, Ahmed Fekry, *Pragmatism in Islamic Law* (Syracuse: Syracuse University Press, 2017).

Iggers, Georg G., "Historicism: The history and meaning of the term", *Journal of the History of Ideas* 56 (1995): 129–152.

Iliffe, Rob, *Priest of Nature: The Religious Worlds of Isaac Newton* (Oxford: Oxford University Press, 2017).

al-'Ināni, Rashīd, "Al-dīn fī riwāyāt Najīb Maḥfūẓ", *al-Nāqid* 19 (1990): 25–29.

al-'Ināni, Rashīd, "Najīb Maḥfūẓ yushakhkhiṣ al-dā'", *Al-Ahrām*, 2 April 1990.

al-'Īrmābi, Muḥammad Zīn al-Hādi, *Nash'at al-'ilmāniyya wa dukhūluha ilā al-mujtama' al-islāmi* (Riyadh: Dār al-'Āṣima, 1987).

Isḥāq, Adīb, *Al-kitābāt al-siyāsiyya wa al-ijtimā'iyya*, ed. Nājī 'Allūsh (Beirut: Dār al-Ṭalī'a, 1982).

Islām, 'Aẓmī, "Min ḥuqūq al-insān fī al-Islām", *al-Fikr al-Mu'āṣir* 47 (1968): 84–93.

'Ītānī, Muḥammad, *Al-Qur'ān fī ḍaw' al-fikr al-māddī al-jadalī* (Beirut: Dār al-'Awda, 1972).

al-'Iṭrī, Muḥammad, "Al-thawra al-Turkiyya wa al-thawra al-Yābāniyya", *Fikr* 5 (1956): 5–14.

al-Ittiḥād al-Ishtirākī al-'Arabī, *Al-Azhar, tārīkhuhu wa taṭawwuruhu* (Cairo: al-Ittiḥād al-Ishtirākī al-'Arabī, 1964).

al-Jābirī, Muḥammad 'Ābid, "Min haymanat al-namūdhaj ilā al-istiqlāl", *al-Safīr*, 10 April 1982.
al-Jābirī, Muḥammad 'Ābid, "Al-ḥaraka al-salafiyya wa al-jamā'āt al-dīnīya al-mu'āṣira fī al-Maghrib", paper presented at the conference "Al-ḥarakāt al-islamiyya al-mu'āṣira fī al waṭan al-'arabī", in *Maktabat al-mustaqbalāt al-'arabiyya al-badīla: Al-ittijāhāt al-ijtimā'iyya wa al-siyāsiyya wa al-thaqāfiyya* (Beirut: Markaz Dirāsāt al-Waḥda al-'Arabiyya, 1987), pp. 187–235.
al-Jābirī, Muḥammad 'Ābid, "Ishkāliyyāt al-aṣāla wa al-mu'āṣara fī al-fikr al-'Arabī al-ḥadīth wa al-mu'āṣir: Ṣirā' ṭabaqī am mushkil thaqāfī", in *Al-turāth wa taḥaddiyyat al-'aṣr fī al-waṭan al-'arabī: Al-aṣāla wa al-mu'āṣara*, 2nd edn (Beirut: Markaz Dirāsāt al-Waḥda al-'Arabiyya, 1987), pp. 29–58.
al-Jābirī, Muḥammad 'Ābid, "Al-'ilmāniyya wa al-islām", *al-Yawm al-Sābi'*, 3 April 1989.
al-Jābirī, Muḥammad 'Ābid, "Al-din wa al-siyāsa wa al-ḥarb al-ahliyya", *al-Yawm al-Sābi'*, 19 March 1990.
al-Jabri, Mohammed Abed, *The Formation of Arab Reason* (London: I. B. Tauris, 2010).
Jad'ān, Fahmī, *Usus al-taqaddum 'inda mufakkirī al-islām fī al-'ālam al-'arabī al-ḥadīth* (Beirut: al-Mu'assasa al-'Arabiyya li'l-Dirāsāt wa al-Nashr, 1979).
Jad'ān, Fahmī, "Al-ḥarakāt al-islāmiyya al-mu'āṣira fī al-waṭan al-'arabi", *Majallat al-'Ulūm al-Ijtimā'iyya* 17 (1989): 263–288.
Jaish al-Sha'ab, 25 April 1967.
James, Paul, *Nation Formation: Towards a Theory of Abstract Community* (London: Sage, 1996).
al-Jāmi'a al-Amīrikiyya, *Al-fikr al-'arabi fī mi'at sanatin; buḥūth mu'tamar hai'at al-dirasāt al-'arabiyya al-mun'aqida fī Tishrīn al-Thāni 1966 fī al-Jāmi'a al-Amīrikiyya fī Bairūt*, eds Fu'ād Ṣarruf and Nabīh Amīn Fāris (Beirut: al-Jami'a al-Amīrikiyya, 1967).
al-Janābī, 'Abd al-Qādir, "Al-ḥawāmil", in *Thawb al-mā'* (Cologne: Manshūrāt al-Jamal, 1990), pp. 1–7.
al-Janābī, 'Abd al-Qādir, *Al-ḍāli'ūn fī ma'ārik min ajl al-raghba al-ibāḥiyya* (Cologne: Manshūrāt al-Jamal, 1990).
al-Janābī, 'Abd al-Qādir, *Thawb al-mā'* (Cologne: Manshūrāt al-Jamal, 1990).
Jane, Emma A. and Chris Fleming, *Modern Conspiracy: The Importance of Being Paranoid* (London: Bloomsbury, 2014).

Jayyusi, Salma al-Khadra, *Trends and Movements in Modern Arabic Poetry*, Studies in Arabic Literature, 2 vols (Leiden: Brill, 1977).

Jenkins, Richard, "Disenchantment, enchantment and re-enchantment: Max Weber at the millennium", *Max Weber Studies* 1 (2000): 11–32.

al-Jisr, Ḥusayn, *Al-risāla al-ḥamīdiyya fī ḥiqqīyat al-diyāna al-islāmīyya wa ḥaqīqat al-sharīʿa al-Muḥammadiyya*, ed. Khālid Ziyadā (Tripoli: Jarūs Press, al-Maktaba al-Ḥadītha, n.d.).

Johansen, Baber, *Muhammad Husain Haikal: Europa und der Orient im Weltbild eines ägyptischen Liberalen* (Beirut: Orient-Institut der Deutschen Morgenländischen Gesellschaft, 1967).

Johansen, Baber, "Secular and religious elements in Hanafi law: Function and limits of absolute character of government authority", in *Islam et politique au Maghreb*, eds Ernest Gellner and Jean-Claude Vatin (Paris: Éditions du CNRS, 1981), pp. 281–303.

Johansen, Baber, "Die sündige, gesunde Amme: Moral und gesetzliche Bestimmung (hukm) im Islamischen Recht ", *Die Welt des Islams* 28 (1988): 264–282.

Johansen, Baber, *The Islamic Law of Land Tax and Rent* (London: Croon Helm, 1988).

Johansen, Baber, "Apostasy as objective depersonalized fact", *Social Research* 70 (2003): 687–710.

Jokisch, Benjamin, *Islamic Imperial Law: Harun al-Rashid's Codification Project* (Berlin and New York: Walter de Gruyter, 2007).

Jomier, Jacques, "La place du Coran dans la vie quotidienne en Égypte", *Revue de l'Institut des belles-lettres arabes* 15 (1952): 131–165.

Josephson-Storm, Jason, *The Myth of Disenchantment: Magic, Modernity and the Birth of the Human Sciences* (Chicago: University of Chicago Press, 2017).

Joshi, V. C., *Rammohun Roy and the Process of Modernization of India* (Delhi: Vikas Publishing House, 1975).

Jubrān, Khalīl Jubrān, "Al-ʿawāṣif", in *Al-majmūʿa al-kāmila li-muʾallafāt Jubrān Khalīl Jubrān* (Beirut: Dār Sāder, Dār Beirut, 1964), pp. 365–492.

Jubrān, Khalīl Jubrān, *Al-majmūʿa al-kāmila li-muʾallafāt Jubrān Khalīl Jubrān*, 3 vols (Beirut: Dār Sāder, Dār Beirut, 1964).

Junainah, Darwīsh, *Al-Muslimūn*, 19–25 January 1990.

al-Jundī, Anwār, *Suqūṭ al-ʿilmāniyya*, 2 vols (Beirut: Dār al-Kitāb al-Lubnānī, 1973).

Juynboll, G. H. A., "Ismail Ahmad Adham (1911–1940), the Atheist", *Journal of Arabic Literature* 3 (1972): 54–71.

al-Ka"āk, 'Uthmān, *Al-taqālīd wa al-'ādāt al-sha'biyya aw al-fūlklūr al-tūnisī* (Tunis: al-Dār al-Qawmiyya li'l-Nashr wa-l-Tawzī', 1963).

Kant, Immanuel, *Religion Within the Limits of Reasons Alone*, trans. J. M. Green (Chicago, n.p.: 1934).

Kantorowicz, Ernst H., *The King's Two Bodies: A Study in Medieval Political Theology* (Princeton: Princeton University Press, 1957).

Karam, Anṭwān Ghaṭṭās, "Fī al-adab al-'arabī al-hadīth", in *Al-fikr al-'arabi fī mi'at sana; Buḥūth mu'tamar Hay'at al-Dirasāt al-'Arabiyya al-mun'aqida fī Tishrīn al-Thānī 1966 fī al-Jāmi'a al- Amīrikiyya fī Bayrūt*, eds al-Jāmi'a al-Amīrikiyya fī Bayrūt and Hay'at al-Dirasāt al-'Arabiyya (Beirut: al-Jāmi'a al-Amīrikiyya fī Bayrūt, 1967).

Kassab, Elizabeth Suzanne, *Contemporary Arab Thought. Cultural Critique in Comparative Perspective* (New York: Columbia University Press, 2009).

Katz, M. Holmes, *Body of Text: The Emergence of the Sunni Law of Ritual Purity* (Albany: State University of New York Press, 2002).

Kaviraj, Sudipta, "Outline of a revisionist theory of modernity", *European Journal of Sociology* 46 (2005): 497–526.

al-Kawākibī, 'Abd al-Raḥmān, *Al-a'māl al-kāmila*, ed. Muḥammad 'Amāra (Beirūt: al-Mu'assasa al-'Arabiyya li'l-Dirāsāt wa al-Nashr, 1975).

al-Kawākibī, 'Abd al-Raḥmān, "Tijārat al-raqīq wa aḥkāmuhā fī al-islām", in *Al-a'māl al-kāmila*, ed. Muḥammad 'Amāra (Beirūt: al-Mu'assasa al-'Arabiyya li'l-Dirāsāt wa al-Nashr, 1975), pp. 377–378.

Kawtharāni, Wajīh, *Al-sulṭa wa al-mujtama' wa al-'amal al-siyāsī: Min ta'rikh al-wilāya al-'uthmāniyya fī Bilād al-Shām*, Doctoral Thesis Series, 13 (Beirut: Markaz Dirasāt al-Waḥda al-'Arabiyya, 1988).

Kay, H. L., *The Social Meaning of Modern Biology: From Social Darwinism to Sociobiology* (New Haven: Yale University Press, 1986).

Kayali, Hasan, *Arabs and Young Turks. Ottomanism, Arabism and Islamism in the Ottoman Empire, 1908–1918* (Berkeley: University of California Press, 1998).

al-Kayyālī, Sāmī, *Al-rāḥilūn* (Cairo: Dār al-Fikr, n.d.).

al-Kayyālī, Sāmī, *Al-adab al-'arabi al-mu'āṣir fī Sūriyya* (Cairo: Dār al-Ma'ārif, 1968).

Kearny, Richard, *Transitions: Narratives in Modern Irish Culture* (Dublin: Wolfhound Press, 1988).

Keddie, Nikki R., *Sayyid Jamāl al-Dīn "al-Afghānī": A Political Biography* (Berkeley and Los Angeles: University of California Press, 1972).

Keddie, Nikki R. (ed.), *Scholars, Saints and Sufis: Muslim Religious Institutions in the Middle East since 1500* (Berkeley and Los Angeles: University of California Press, 1972).

Kee, Alistair, *Constantine versus Christ: The Triumph of Ideology* (London: SCM, 1982).

Kerr, Malcolm H., *Islamic Reform: The Political and Legal Theories of Muhammad 'Abduh and Rashīd Riḍā.* (Berkeley and Los Angeles: University of California Press, 1966).

al-Khālidī, 'Anbara Salām, *Jawla fī al-dhikrayāt bayna lubnān wa filasṭīn* (Beirut: Dār al-Nahār li'l-Nashr, 1978).

Khalāṣ, Ibrāhīm, "Istanjadat al-umma bi'l-ilāh", *Jaysh al-Sha'ab*, 24 April 1967.

Khalafallāh, Muḥammad Aḥmad, *Al-fann al-qaṣaṣī fī al-Qur'ān al-karīm*, 2nd edn (Cairo: Maktabat al-Nahḍa al-Miṣriyya, 1975).

Khalafallāh, Muḥammad Aḥmad, "Al-ṣaḥwa al-islāmiyya fī Miṣr", in *Al-ḥarakāt al-islāmiyya al-mu'āṣira fī al-waṭan al-'arabī*, ed. Markaz Dirāsāt al-Waḥda al-'Arabiyya (Beirut: Markaz Dirāsāt al-Waḥda al-'Arabiyya, 1987), pp. 35–98.

Khālid, Aḥmad, "Aḍwā' 'alā al-khalfiyya al-tārīkhiyya li majallat al-aḥwāl al-shakhṣiyya al-ṣādira 1956", *Fikr* 19/6 (1974): 57–73.

Khālid, Khālid Muḥammad, *Min hunā nabda'*, 7th edn (Cairo: Matba'at Aḥmad ibn Mukhaymir, 1954). English translation: Khaled, Khaled Muhammad, *From Here We Start*, trans. Isma'il Tagi al-Faruqi (Washington, DC: American Council of Learned Societies, 1953).

Khalīl, Khalīl Ahmad, *Maḍmūn al-usṭūra fī al-fikr al-'arabī* (Beirut: Dār al-Ṭalī'a, 1973).

Khalīl. Khalīl Aḥmad, *Al-mar'a al-'arabiyya wa qaḍāyā al-taghyīr: Baḥth ijtimā'i fī tārīkh al-qahr al-nisā'ī*, 2nd edn (Beirut: Dār al-Ṭalī'a, 1982).

Khamīrī, Ṭahir, "Al-dīn wa 'ilm al-nafs al-jadīd", *al-'Uṣūr* 21 (1929): 524–526.

Khamīrī, Ṭahir, "Al-dīn wa 'ilm al-nafs al-jadīd", *al-'Uṣūr* 22 (1929): 778–781.

al-Khammāsh, Salwā, *Al-mar'a al-'arabiyya wa al-mujtama' al-taqlīdī al-mutakhallif*, with an introduction by Ibrāhīm Badrān (Beirut: Dār al-Ḥaqīqa, 1973).

Khatib, Line, *Islamic Revivalism in Syria. The Rise and Fall of Ba'thist Secularism* (London: Routledge, 2011).

Khoury, Philip S., *Syria and the French Mandate: The Politics of Arab Nationalism, 1920–1945*, Princeton Studies on the Near East (Princeton: Princeton University Press, 1987).

Khuḍr, Georges, "Al-Masīhiyya al-'arabiyya wa al-gharb", in *Al-masiḥiyyūn al-'arab*, ed. Ilyās Khūrī (Beirut: Mu'assasat al-Abḥāth al-'Arabiyya, 1981), pp. 83–97.

al-Khūlī, Luṭfī, "Mulaḥaẓāt ḥawl al-ṣirā' al-fikri fī mujtama'inā", *al-Ṭalī'a* 16 (1966): 13–26.

al-Khūlī, Luṭfī, *al-Qabas*, 12 February 1989.

Khūrī, Ilyās, "Rūh al-sharq wa thawrat al-sharq", *Mawāqif* 34 (1979): 118–126.

Khūrī, Ilyās (ed.), *Al-Masiḥiyyūn al-'Arab* (Beirut: Mu'assasa al-Abḥāth al-'Arabiyya, 1981).

Khūrī, Ra'īf, "Al-qawmiyya al-'arabīya al-jāmi'a ṭarīq al-khalāṣ", *al-Ṭalī'a* 2/9 (1936): 768–782.

Khūrī, Ra'īf, "Al-qawmiyya al-'arabīya al-jāmi'a ṭarīq al-khalāṣ", *al-Ṭalī'a* 2/3 (1937): 99–109.

Khūrī, Ra'īf, *Al-fikr al-'arabī al-ḥadīth: Athar al-thawra al-faransiyya fī tawjjuhihi al-siyāsī wa al-ijtimā'ī* (Beirut: Dār al-Makshūf, 1943).

Kirkby, Dianne (ed.), *Religion and the Cold War* (Basingstoke: Palgrave, 2003).

Kohn, H., *The Idea of Nationalism: A Study in Its Origins and Background* (London: Transaction Publishers, 1944/2005).

Koyré, Alexandre, *From the Closed World to the Infinite University* (Baltimore: Johns Hopkins University Press, 1957).

Koyré, Alexandre, *Newtonian Studies* (London: Chapman and Hall, 1965).

Krämer, Gudrun, "Secularity contested: Religion, identity and the public order in the Arab Middle East", in *Multiple Secularities beyond the West: Religion and Modernity in the Global Age*, eds Marian Burchart, Monika Wohlrab-Sahr, and Matthias Middell (Berlin: De Gruyter, 2015), pp. 121–137.

Kramer, Martin S., *Islam Assembled: The Advent of the Muslim Congresses* (New York: Columbia University Press, 1986).

Küçük, Bekir Harun, *Early Enlightenment in Istanbul* (unpublished PhD dissertation, University of California, San Diego, 2012).

Kudsi-Zadeh, Albert, "Afghani and freemasonry in Egypt", *Journal of the American Oriental Society* 92 (1972): 25–35.

Kuper, Adam, *The Invention of Primitive Society* (London: Routledge, 1988).

Kuper, Adam, *Culture: The Anthropologist's Account* (Cambridge, MA: Harvard University Press, 1999).

Kurayyim, Sāmiḥ, *Islāmiyyāt: Ṭaha Ḥusayn, al-'Aqqād, Ḥusayn Haykal, Aḥmad Amīn, Tawfīq al-Hakīm*, 2nd edn (Beirut: Dār al-Qalam, 1977).

Kurd 'Ali, Muḥammad, *Al-mudhakkirāt*, 4 vols (Damascus: Maṭba'at al-Taraqqī, 1948–1951).

Lanfranchi, Sania Sharawi, *Casting Off the Veil: The Life of Huda Shaarawi* (London: I. B. Tauris, 2015).

Laoust, Henri, *Essai sur les doctrines morales et politiques de Taki-d-Din Aḥmad B. Taimiya* (Cairo: IFAO, 1939).

Laoust, Henri, "Le Hanbalisme sous les mamlouks Bahrides", *Revue d'études islamiques* 28 (1960): 1–71.

Laoust, Henri, "La pensée et l'action politiques d'al-Mawardi", in *Pluralismes dans l'Islam* (Paris: Geuthner, 1983), pp. 177–258.

Laoust, Henri, *Pluralismes dans l'Islam* (Paris: Geuthner, 1983).

Laqueur, Walter, *Communism and Nationalism in the Middle East* (London: Routledge, 1956).

Laroui, Abdallah ['Abd Allāh al-'Arwī], *Les Origines sociales et culturelles du nationalisme marocain 1830–1912* (Paris: Maspéro, 1977).

Laroui, Abdallah, *The History of the Maghreb: An Interpretative Essay*, trans. Ralph Manheim, Princeton Studies on the Near East (Princeton: Princeton University Press, 1977).

Laroui, Abdallah, *Islam et modernité* (Paris: La Découverte, 1986).

Lasker, Daniel J., "The Jewish critique of Christianity under Islam in the Middle Ages", *Proceedings of the American Academy for Jewish Research* 57 (1990–1991): 121–153.

Laṭīf, Shukrī, *Al-islāmiyyūn wa al-mar'a*, 2nd edn (Tunis: Bayram li'l-Nashr, 1988).

Latour, Bruno, "Ramsès II est-il mort de la tuberculose?", *La Recherche*, 307, March 1998, 84–85.

Laudan, Larry, "The pseudo-science of science", *Philosophy of Social Science* 11 (1981): 173–198.

Lauzière, Henri, *The Making of Salafism. Islamic Reform in the Twentieth Century* (New York: Columbia University Press, 2016).

Lawson, F., "Social bases for the Hamah Revolt", *MERIP Reports* 12 (1982): 24–28.

Lecerf, J., "La crise vestimentaire d'après-guerre en Syrie d'après la littérature populaire", *Renseignements coloniaux: Supplément au bulletin du Comité de l'Afrique Française* (1938): 45–47.

Le Cour Grandmaison, Olivier, *Coloniser, exterminer: Sur la guerre et l'état colonial* (Paris: Farard, 2005).

Le Goff, Jacques. *Time, Work and Culture in the Middle Ages*, trans. Arthur Goldhammer (London and Chicago: University of Chicago Press, 1982).

Lepenies, Wolf, *Between Literature and Science: The Rise of Sociology* (Cambridge: Cambridge University Press, 1988).

Līnīn, Falādīmīr [Lenin, V. I.], *Nuṣūṣ hawl al-mawqif min al-dīn, mukhtārāt jadīda*, trans. Muḥammad Kubba (Beirut: Dār al-Ṭalī'a, 1972).

Lombard, Maurice, *The Golden Age of Islam*, trans. Joan Spencer (Amsterdam: North Holland Publishing Company and New York: American Elsevier, 1975).

MacCormack, Carol and Marilyn Strathern (eds), *Nature, Culture and Gender* (Cambridge, MA: Cambridge University Press, 1980).

MacPherson, C. B., *The Political Theory of Possessive Individualism* (Oxford: Oxford University Press, 1964).

Madan, T. N., "Secularism and the intellectuals", *Economic and Political Weekly* 29/18 (1994): 1,095–1,096.

Maḥfūẓ, Durra, "Al-mar'a al-'arabiyya fī al-Maghrib al-'Arabī bayn al-istighlāl wa al-taḥarrur", in *Al-mar'a wa dawruhā fī ḥarakat al-waḥda al-'arabiyya*, ed. Markaz Dirāsāt al-Waḥda al-'Arabiyya (Beirut: Markaz Dirāsāt al-Waḥda al-'Arabiyya, 1982), pp. 319–340.

Maḥfūẓ, 'Iṣām, *al-Suryāliyya wa tafā'ulātuhā al-'arabiyya* (Beirut: n.p., 1987).

Mahmoud, Saba, "Rehearsed spontaneity and the conventionality of ritual: Disciplines of *ṣalāt*", *American Ethnologist* 28 (2001): 827–853.

Mahmoud, Saba, *Politics of Piety. The Islamic Revival and the Feminist Subject* (Princeton: Princeton University Press, 2004).

Mahmoud, Saba, "Secularism, hermeneutics, and empire: The politics of Islamic reformation", *Public Culture* 18 (2006); 323–347.

Maḥmūd, Muḥammad Aḥmad, "Ḥawl ba'ḍ ishkāliyyāt al-naṣṣ al-qur'āni", *Mawāqif* 60 (1989): 53–73.

Maḥmūd, Muṣtafā, *Ḥiwār ma'a ṣadīqī al-mulḥid* (Cairo: Maṭba'at Rūz al-Yūsuf, 1974).

Maḥmūd, Zākī Najīb, *Tajdīd al-fikr al-'arabī* (Beirut: Dār al-Shurūq, 1981).
Makāriyūs, Shāhīn, *Al-ādāb al-Māsūniyya* (Cairo: Maṭba'at al-Muqtaṭaf, 1895).
Makāriyūs, Shāhīn, *Faḍā'il al-Māsūniyya* (Cairo: Maṭba'at al-Muqtaṭaf, 1899).
Makdisi, Ussama, *The Culture of Sectarianism: Community, History and Violence in Nineteenth-Century Lebanon* (Berkeley: University of California Press, 2000).
Malamed, Yitzhak and Michael A. Rosenthal (eds), *Spinoza's Theological-Political Treatise: A Critical Guide* (Cambridge: Cambridge University Press, 2010).
Malone, G. K., "Apologetics", in *New Catholic Encyclopedia*, 15 vols, vol. 1, pp. 671, 669–677.
Mandaville, John E., "The Muslim judiciary in Damascus in the late Mamluk period" (unpublished PhD dissertation, Princeton University, 1969).
Mandrou, Robert, *From Humanism to Science, 1480–1700*, trans. Brian Pearce (Harmondsworth: Penguin Books, 1978).
Mann, Michael, *The Sources of Social Power*, vol. 1: *A History of Power from the Beginning to AD 1760* (Cambridge: Cambridge University Press, 1986).
Manqūsh, Thurayyā, *Al-tawḥīd fī taṭawwurihi al-tarīkhī: Al-tawḥīd al-yamāni* (Beirut: Dār al-Ṭalī'a, 1977).
Mansell, Gregory J., *The Surrogate Proletariat: Moslem Women and Revolutionary Strategies in Soviet Central Asia 1919–1929* (Princeton: Princeton University Press, 1974).
Mansell, Philip, *Sultans in Splendour* (London: André Deutsch, 1988).
Mansour, C., *L'Autorité dans la pensée musulmane. Le concept d'ijmâ' (consensus) et la problématique de l'autorité* (Paris: Vrin, 1975).
al-Maqdisī, Anīs al-Khūrī, *Al-'awāmil al-fa' 'āla fī al-adab al-'arabī al-ḥadīth*, fasc. 1, *Fī al-'awāmil al-siyāsiyya*, Silsilat al-'Ulūm al-Sharqiyya (Beirut: al-Jāmi'a al-Amīrikiyya, n.d.).
al-Maqqarī, Abū al-'Abbās Aḥmad ibn Muḥammad, *Nafḥ al-ṭīb min ghuṣn al-andalus al-raṭīb*, ed. Iḥsān 'Abbās, 8 vols (Beirut: n.p., 1968).
al-Maqrīzī, Taqī al-dīn Abū al-'Abbās Aḥmad ibn 'Alī, *Al-mawā'iẓ wa al-i'tibār bi dhikr al-khiṭaṭ wa al-āthār al-ma'rūf bi al-khiṭaṭ al-maqrīziya*, 2 vols (Cairo: Maṭba'at Bulāq, 1270/1853).

al-Maqrīzī, Taqī al-dīn Abū al-'Abbās Aḥmad ibn Alī, *Al-sulūk li ma'rifat duwal al-mulūk*, eds Muḥammad Muṣṭafā Ziyāda and Sa'īd 'Abd-el-Fattāḥ 'Āshūr, 3 vols (Cairo: Dār al-Kutub al-Miṣrīya, 1956–1971).
Mardin, Şerif, *The Genesis of Young Ottoman Thought: A Study in the Modernisation of Turkish Political Ideas*, Princeton Oriental Studies, vol. 21 (Princeton: Princeton University Press, 1962).
Mardin, Şerif, "Super Westernisation in urban life in the Ottoman Empire in the last quarter of the nineteenth century", in *Turkey: Geographic and Social Perspectives*, ed. P. Benedict, et al. (Leiden: Brill, 1974), pp. 403–446.
Mardin, Şerif, "Religion in modern Turkey", *International Social Science Journal* 19/2 (1977): 279–297.
Mardin, Şerif, *Religion and Social Change in Modern Turkey: The Case of Bediüzzaman Said Nursi* (Albany: State University of New York Press, 1989).
Markaz al-Dirāsāt al-Waḥda al-'Arabiyya (ed.), *Al-qawmiyya al-'arabiyya wa-l-islām*, 1st edn (Beirut: Markaz Dirāsāt al-Waḥda al-'Arabiyya, 1981).
Markaz al-Dirāsāt al-Waḥda al-'Arabiyya (ed.), *Al-mar'a wa dawruhā fī ḥarakat al-waḥda al-'arabīyya* (Beirut: Markaz al-Dirāsāt al-Waḥda al-'Arabiyya, 1982).
Markaz Dirāsāt al-Waḥda al-'Arabiyya (ed.), *Al-harakāt al-islamiyya al-mu'āsira fī al waṭan al-'arabi* (Beirut: Markaz Dirāsāt al-Waḥda al-'Arabiyya, 1987).
Markaz Dirāsāt al-Waḥda al-'Arabiyya (ed.), *Al-turāth wa taḥadiyyāt al-'aṣr fī al waṭan al-'arabī: Al-aṣāla wa al-mu'āsara. Buḥūth wa munāqashāt al-nadwā al-fikriyya allatī naẓẓamhā Markaz Dirasāt al-Waḥda al-'Arabiyya*, 2nd edn (Beirut: Markaz Dirāsāt al-Waḥda al-'Arabiyya, 1987).
Markaz Dirāsāt al-Waḥda al-'Arabiyya (ed.), *Al-ḥiwār al-qawmi al-islāmī* (Beirut: Markaz Dirāsāt al-Waḥda al-'Arabiyya, 1989).
Markaz Dirāsāt al-Waḥda al-'Arabiyya (ed.), *Al-dīn fī al-mujtama' al-'arabi* (Beirut: Markaz Dirāsāt al-Waḥda al-'Arabiyya 1990).
Marnīsī, Fāṭima, *Nisā' al-Gharb: Dirāsa maydāniyya*, trans. Fāṭima Zahrā' Arzawīl (Casablanca: al-Sharika al-Maghribiyya li'l-Nāshirīn al-Muttaḥidīn, 1985).
al-Marrākushī, 'Abd al-Wāḥīd, *Al-mu'jib fī talkhīṣ akhbār al-maghrib, al-kitāb al-thālith*, ed. Muḥammad Sa'īd al-'Aryān (Cairo: Lajnat iḥyā' al-Turāth al-Islāmi, 1963).

Marrāsh, Fransīs, *Shahādat al-ṭabī'a fi wujūd Allāh wa al-sharī'a* (Beirut: Maṭba'at al-Amīrkān, 1892).
Marshall, David, *God, Muhammad and the Unbelievers* (London: Curzon, 1999).
Martin, David, *A General Theory of Secularization* (Oxford: Basil Blackwell, 1978).
Martin, Richard C., "Understanding the Koran in text and context", *History and Religions* 21 (1985): 361–384.
Martines, Lauro, *Power and Imagination: City-States in Renaissance Italy* (Harmondsworth: Penguin Books, 1983).
Marx, Karl and Friedrich Engels, *Collected Works*, 50 vols (London: Lawrence and Wishart, 1975).
Masell, Gregory J., *The Surrogate Proletariat. Moslem Women and Revolutionary Strategies in Soviet Central Asia, 1919–1929* (Princeton: Princeton University Press, 1974).
al-Masīrī, 'Abdalwahhāb and 'Azīz Al-'Aẓma, *Al-'ilmānīya taḥt al-mijhar* (Beirut: Dar al-Fikr, 1990).
Masters, Bruce, *The Arabs of the Ottoman Empire* (New York: Cambridge University Press, 2013).
Mattā, Yūsuf, "Al-muyūl al-raj'iyya 'inda ba'ḍ udabā' al-'arab al-mu'āṣirin", *al-Ṭalī'a* 2/8 (1936): 717–718.Maẓhar, Ismā'īl, *Al-islām, lā al-Shuyū'iyya* (Cairo: Dār al-Nahḍa al-'Arabiyya, 1961).
al-Māturīdī, Muḥammad ibn Muḥammad ibn Maḥmūd Abū Manṣūr, *Kitāb al-tawḥīd*, ed. Fath Allāh Khulayf (Beirut: Dār al-Mashriq, 1970).
al-Māwardī, Abū al-Ḥasan 'Ali ibn Muḥammad, *Adab al-qāḍī*, eds Muḥyī Hilāl al-Sirhān, Iḥyā' al-turāth al-islāmī (Baghdad: Maṭba'at al-Irshād, 1971).
al-Māwardī, Abū al-Ḥasan 'Ali ibn Muḥammad, *Al-aḥkām as-sulṭāniyya wa al-wilāyāt al-dīniyya*, 3rd edn (Cairo: Maktabat wa Maṭba'at al-Bābī al-Ḥalabī, 1973).
Maẓhar, Ismā'īl, *Multaqā al-sabīl fi madhhab al-nushū' wa al-irtiqā' wa āthāruhu fi al-inqilāb al-fi krī al-ḥadīth* (Cairo: al-Maṭba'a al-'Aṣriyya, 1926).
Maẓhar, Ismā'īl, "'Ilāqat al-insān bi Allāh laysat mubāsharatan bal bil-wāsāṭa", *al-'Uṣūr* 2/9 (1928): 913–924.
Maẓhar, Ismā'īl, *Tārīkh al-fi kr al-'arabī* (Cairo: Dār al-'Uṣūr li'l-Ṭibā'a wa al-Nashr, 1928).

Maẓhar, Ismāʿīl, "Bayn al-dīn wa al-ʿilm", *al-ʿUṣūr* 37 (1929): 1–18.

Maẓhar, Ismāʿīl, "Ḥawl al-ilḥād wa al-īmān", *al-ʿUṣūr* 22 (1929): 657–664.

Maẓhar, Ismāʿīl, "Muṭālaʿāt fī sifr al khurūj", *al-ʿUṣūr* 5/2 (1929): 2–15.

Maẓhar, Ismāʿīl, "Muṭālaʿāt fī sifr al-takwīn", *al-ʿUṣūr* 5/23 (1929): 161–174.

Maẓhar, Ismāʿīl, *Qiṣṣat al-ṭūfān wa taṭawurruhā fī thalāth madaniyyāt qadīma hiya al-āshūriyya al-Bābiliyya wa al-ʿIbraniyya wa al-Masīḥiyya wa intiqāluhā bi al-luqāḥ ilā al-madaniyya al-Islāmiyya* (Cairo: Dār al-'Uṣūr, 1929).

Maẓhar, Ismail, *Wathbat al-Sharq: Baḥth fī anna al-ʿaqliyya al-turkiyya al-ḥadītha hiyā mithāl al-ʿaqliyya al-salīma allatī yajib an yantaḥiluhā al-Sharq li yujāriya sayr al-haḍāra al-ʿālamiya* (Cairo: Dār al-'Uṣūr li'l-ṭabʿwa al-Nashr, 1929).

Maẓhar, Ismāʿīl, "Bilād al-ʿarab li'l ʿarab", *al-Muqtaṭaf* 106 (1945): 309–312.

Maẓhar, Ismāʿīl, *al-mar'a fī ʿaṣr al-dimūqarātiyya: baḥth ḥurr fī ta'yīd maṭālib al-mar'a* (Cairo: Maṭbaʿat Miṣr, 1949).

Maẓhar, Ismāʿīl, *Al-Islām, lā al-shuyūʿiyya* (Cairo: Dār al-Nahḍa al-ʿArabiyya, 1961).

Mazower, Mark, *Salonika, City of Ghosts* (New York: Vintage, 2006).

McLeod, Hugh, *Secularisation in Western Europe, 1848–1914* (London: Palgrave Macmillan, 2000).

Merad, Ali, *Le Réformisme musulman en Algérie de 1925 à 1940: Essai d'histoire religieuse et sociale* (Paris and The Hague: Mouton, 1967).

Mestyan, Adam, *Arab Patriotism. The Ideology and Culture of Power in Late Ottoman Egypt* (Princeton: Princeton University Press, 2017).

Metczek, S. A., "Fideism", in *New Catholic Encyclopedia*, 15 vols, vol. 5, pp. 908–909.

Mirsepassi, Ali, *Transnationalism in Iranian Political Thought. The Life and Times of Ahmad Fardid* (Cambridge: Cambridge University Press, 2017).

Mission scientifique du Maroc, "Les musulmans français et la guerre", *Revue du monde musulman* 8/29 (1914): 343–557.

Mitchell, Timothy, *Colonising Egypt* (Cambridge and New York: Cambridge University Press, 1988).

Moore, James R., *The Post-Darwinian Controversies: A Study of the Protestant Struggle to Come to Terms with Darwin in Great Britain and America, 1870–1900* (Cambridge: Cambridge University Press, 1979).

Moosa, Ebrahim and Sher Ali Tareen, "Revival and reform", *The Princeton Enyclopedia of Islamic Political Thought*, ed. Gerhard Boewering (Princeton: Princeton University Press, 2013), pp. 462–470.

Morony, Michael, *Iraq after the Muslim Conquests* (Princeton: Princeton University Press, 1984).
Muehlenbeck, Philip (ed.), *Religion and the Cold War* (Nashville: Vanderbilt University Press, 2012).
Mughayzil, Joseph, "Al-Islām wa al-Masīḥiyya al-'arabiyya wa al-qawmiyya al-'arabiyya wa al-'ilmāniyya", in *Al-qawmiyya al-'arabiyya wa al-Islam: Buḥūth wa munāqashāt*, 3rd edn (Beirut: Markaz Dirāsāt al-Waḥda al-'Arabiyya, 1988), pp. 361–384.
al-Munajjid, Ṣalāḥ al-Dīn, *A'midat al-nakba: baḥth 'ilmī fi asbāb hazīmat Ḥuzayrān*, 2nd edn (Beirut: Dār al-Kitāb al-Jadīd, 1967).
Mundy, Martha, "The family, inheritance and Islam: A re-examination of the sociology of Farā'id law", in *Islamic Law: Social and Historical Contexts*, ed. Aziz al-Azmeh (London and New York: Routledge, 1988), pp. 1–123.
Mūsā, Salāma, *Mā hiya al-nahḍa?* (Cairo: Salāma Mūsā li'l-Nashr wa al-Tawzī', n.d.).
Mūsā, Salāma, *Al-yawm wa al-ghadd* (Cairo: Al-Matb'a al-Miṣriyya, 1927).
Mūsā, Salāma, "Al-raj 'iyya al-fikriyya wa kayfa tunaẓẓam al-da'wa li iḥyā'ihā", *al-'Uṣūr* 6/32 (1930): 360–363.
Mūsā, Salāma, "Awkar al-raj'iyya fī Miṣr", *al-Majalla al-Jadīda* 4 (1930): 432–435.
Mūsā, Salāma, *Tarbiyat Salāma Mūsā* (Cairo: Mu'assasat al-Khānjī, 1958).
Mūsā, Salāma, "Al-qadīm wa al-jadīd", in *Mukhtārāt Salāma Mūsā* (Beirut: Maktabat al-Mā'arīf, 1962), www.kadl.sa/pdfviewer.aspx?filename=ounxe6dtgzvois3enowoo8whuw9xnfhiwqmilsng7zpyuqounaysgqreo503iq1n&pub=%27%27.
Mūsā, Salāma, *Mukhtārāt Salāma Mūsā* (Beirut: Maktabat al-Ma'ārif, 1963).
Mūsā, Salāma, "Jamīl Ṣidqī al-Zahāwī", *al-Majalla al-Jadīda* (1932): reprinted in *al-Ṭalī'a* 8 (1965): 144–145.
Mzālī, Fatḥiyya, "Shakhṣiyyat al-mar'a al-tūnisiyya", *al-Fikr* 1:1 (1955): 2–9.
al-Nadīm, Abū Isḥāq Ibrāhīm al-Raqīq, *Quṭb al-surūr fī awṣāf al-khumūr*, ed. Aḥmad al-Jundī (Damascus: Majma' al-Lūgha al-'Arabiyya, 1966).
Nadler, Steven, *A Book Forged in Hell: Spinoza's Scandalous Treatise and the Birth of the Secular* (Princeton: Princeton University Press, 2011).
Nairn, Tom, "Nationalism: The modern Janus", in *The Break Up of Britain* (London: New Left Books, 1977), pp. 329–363.
Nairn, Tom, *The Break Up of Britain* (London: New Left Books, 1977).

Nājī, Hilāl, *Al-zahāwī wa dīwānuhu al-mafqūd* (Cairo: Dār al-'Arab, 1964).

Naṣr, Mārlīn, *Al-taṣṣawur al-qawmī al-'arabī fī fikr Jamāl 'Abd al-Nāṣir (1952–1970): Dirāsa fī 'ilm al-mufradāt wa al-dalāla*, Silsilat Uṭrūḥāt al-Dukturāh 2 (Beirut: Markaz Dirāsāt al-Waḥda al-'Arabiyya, 1981).

Naṣr Allāh, Muḥammad 'Izzat, *Al-radd 'alā Ṣādīq al-'Aẓm: Munāqashāt 'āmma li kitāb "naqd al-fikr al-dīnī"* (Beirut: Mu'asssasat Dār Filasṭīn li'l-Ta'līf wa al-Tarjama, 1970).

Naṣṣār, Nāṣīf, "'Awda ilā al-qurūn al-wusṭā: Mulaḥaẓāt ḥawl ārā' Kamāl Yūsuf al-Ḥājj fī al-ṭā'ifiyya", *Mawāqif* 1/1 (1967): 94–96.

New Catholic Encyclopedia (New York: McGraw Hill, 1967).

al-Nu'āymī, *Al-dāris fī tarīkh al-madāris*, 2 vols, ed. Ja'far al-Ḥusaynī (Damascus: al-Majma' al-'Ilmī al'Arabī, 1948).

al-Nubāhī, *Tarīkh quḍāt al-Andalus aw al-marqaba al 'ulyā fī man yastaḥiqq al-qaḍā' wa al-futyā* (Beirut: n.p., n.d.).

Nuwayhaḍ, Walīd, "'Aqdam al-aqallīyāt", *al-Safīr*, 8 February 1981.

Obdeijn, Herman, *L'Enseignement de l'histoire dans la Tunisie moderne, 1881–1970* (Tunis: n.p., 1975).

O'Connor, K. Malone, "Popular and talismanic uses of the Qur'an", in *Encyclopedia of the Qur'an*, ed. J. Dammen McAuliffe, 5 vols (Leiden: Brill, 2004), vol. IV, pp. 163–182.

Odouev, Stepan, *Par les sentiers de Zarathoustra*, trans. Catherine Emery (Moscow: Éditions du Progrès, 1980).

al-Omar, Abdullah O. A., "The reception of Darwinism in the Arab world" (unpublished PhD dissertation, Harvard University, 1982).

Ouyang, Wen-chin, *The Poetics of Love in the Arabic Novel. Nation, State, Modernity and Tradition* (Edinburgh: Edinburgh University Press, 2012).

Özdalga, Elizabeth (ed.), *Late Ottoman Society: The Intellectual Legacy* (London: Routledge Curzon, 2005).

Pagden, Anthony (ed.), *The Language of Political Theory in Early Modern Europe* (Cambridge: Cambridge University Press, 1987).

Palmer, Robert L., *Catholics and Unbelievers in Eighteenth-Century France* (Princeton: Princeton University Press, 1939/1971).

Parla, Taha, *The Social and Political Thought of Ziya Gökalp, 1876–1924* (Leiden: Brill, 1985).

Peters, Benjamin (ed.), *Digital Keywords. A Vocabulary of Information, Society and Culture* (Princeton: Princeton University Press, 2016).

Petry, C. F., *The Civilian Elite in Cairo in the Later Middle Ages* (Princeton: Princeton University Press, 1971).
Philipp, Thomas, *Jurji Zaidan and the Foundations of Arab Nationalism* (New York: Syracuse University Press, 2014).
Picard, Michel, "What's in a name? Agama Hindu Bali in the making", in *Hinduism in Modern Indonesia*, ed. Martin Ramstedt (London and New York: Routledge Curzon, 2004), pp. 56–75.
Pinault, David, "Images of Christ in Arabic literature", *Die Welt des Islams* 27 (1987): 103–125.
Polanyi, Karl, *The Great Transformation* (Boston: Beacon Press, 1957).
Polat, Necati, *Regime Change in Contemporary Turkey* (Edinburgh: Edinburgh University Press, 2016).
Polk, William R. and Richard Chambers (eds), *The Beginnings of Modernisation in the Middle East: The Nineteenth Century*, Publications of the Center for Middle Eastern Studies 1 (Chicago: University of Chicago Press, 1968).
Pollmann, Tessel, "Margaret Mead's Balinese: The fitting symbols of the American Dream", *Indonesia* 49 (1990): 1–35.
Popkin, Richard, *A History of Scepticism from Erasmus to Spinoza* (Berkeley and Los Angeles: University of California Press, 1979).
Porter, Ada (ed.), *Lead, Innovate, Serve: A Visual History of the American University of Beirut's First One Hundred and Fifty Years* (Beirut: American University of Beirut Press, 2016).
Powers, David S., *Studies in the Qur'an and Hadīth: The Formation of the Islamic Law of Inheritance* (Berkeley and Los Angeles: University of California Press, 1986).
Provence, Michael, *The Last Ottoman Generation and the Making of the Modern Middle East* (Cambridge: Cambridge University Press, 2017).
al-Qalqashandī, Abū al-'Abbās Aḥmad ibn Alī ibn Aḥmad, *Ṣubḥ al-a'shā fi ṣinā'at al-inshā*, 14 vols (Cairo: Dār al-Kutub al-Miṣriyya 1913–1919).
al-Qalqashandī, Abū al-'Abbās Aḥmad ibn Alī ibn Aḥmad, *Ma'āthir ināfa fi ma'ālim al-khilāfa*, ed. 'Abd al-Sattār Aḥmad Farrāj, 14 vols (Kuwait: al-Majlis al-Waṭanī li'l-Thaqāfa wa al-Funūn wa al-Ādāb, 1964).
al-Qarmaṭī, Abū Ṭāhir, *Rubba dunyā ḍidd al dīn wa ḍidd kull ba'th* (Paris: Manshūrāt al-Nuqṭa, n.d.).
al-Qasāṭli, Nu'mān, *Kitāb al-rawḍa al-ghannā' fi dimashq al-faiḥā'* (Beirut: n.p., 1879).

al-Qāsimī, Muḥammad Sa'īd and Jamal al-Dīn al-Qāsimī, *Qāmūs el-ṣinā 'āt al-dimashqiyya*, ed. Ẓāfir al-Qāsimī, 2 vols (Paris and The Hague: Mouton, 1960).

al-Qāsimī, Ẓāfir, *Maktab 'Anbar: Ṣuwar wa dhikrayāt min ḥayātinā al-thaqāfiyya wa al-siyāsiyya wa al-ijtimā'iyya* (Beirut: al-Maṭba'a al-Kāthūlīkiyya, 1964).

al-Qāsimī, Ẓāfir, *Jamāl al-dīn al-qāsimī wa 'aṣruhu* (Damascus: Maktabat Aṭlas, 1965).

al-Qimnī, Sayyid Maḥmūd, "Al-qamar al-abb aw al-ḍil' al-akbar fī al-thālūth", *al-Karmil* 26 (1987): 39–65.

al-Qimnī, Sayyid Maḥmūd, "Madkhal ilā fahm al-mithūlūjiyā al-tawrātiyya", *al-Karmil* 30 (1988): 29–64.

al-Qimnī, Sayyid Maḥmūd, "Al-ḥizb al-hāshimī wa ta'sīs li'l-dawla: Al-wāqi' al-ijtima'ī li 'Arab al-jāhiliyya", *al-Karmil* 31 (1989): 38–59.

Quataert, Donald. *Social Disintegration and Popular Resistance in the Ottoman Empire 1881–1908: Reactions to European Economic Penetration* (New York and London: New York University Press, 1983).

Qubaysī, Ḥasan, *Rodinson wa nabī al-islām: Muqadimma ḥawl al-tafsīr al-māddī al-tārīkhī li nash'at al-islām* (Beirut: Dār al-Ṭalī'a, 1981).

Al-Quds al-'arabi, 17 January 1990.

Al-Quds al-'arabi, 14–15 May 1990.

Qudsi, I., "Notice sur les corporations de Damas", in *Actes du VIème Congrès international des orientalistes*, 2 vols, vol. 2 (Leiden: n.p., 1885), pp. 29–30.

Al-Quds al-'arabi, 17 January 1990.

Al-Quds al-'arabi, 14–15 May 1990.

Qurm, Jūrj [Georges Corm], *Ta'addud al-adyān wa anẓimat al-ḥukm: Dirāsa sūsiyūlūjiyya wa qanūniyya muqārana* (Beirut: Dār al-Nahār li'l-Nashr, 1979).

Quṭb, Sayyid, *Ma'ālim fī al-ṭarīq* (Cairo and Beirut: Dār al-Shurūq, 1981).

Rabbath, Edmond, *Unité syrienne et devenir arabe* (Paris: Marcel Rivière, 1937).

Rabbath, Edmond, "Quel Liban demain?", *L'Orient-Le Jour*, 3 April 1977 and 4 April 1977.

Rabie, Hassanein, *The Financial System of Egypt, AH 564–741, 1169–1341 AD* (London and New York: Oxford University Press, 1972).

al-Rāfi'i, Muṣṭafā Ṣādiq, *Taḥta rāyat al-Qur'ān: Al-ma'araka bayn al-qadīm wa al-jadīd*, 2nd edn (Cairo: Maṭba'at al-Istiqāma, 1946).

Al-raghba al-ibāhiyya 1 (1973): 1–3.
Rāndāl, Jūn Hermān [John Herman Randall], *Takwīn al-'aql al-hadīth*, trans. of *The Making of the Modern Mind* (1926) by Georges Ṭu'ma, 2 vols (Beirut: Dār al-Thaqāfa/Mu'assasat Franklin, 1965–1966).
Rapaczynski, Andrejz, *Nature and Politics: Liberalism in the Philosophies of Hobbes, Locke and Rousseau* (Ithaca: Cornell University Press, 1979).
al-Rāzī, Fakhr al-Dīn Muḥammad ibn 'Umar, *Asās al-taqdīs* (Cairo: Maṭba'at al-Kulliyāt al-Azhariyya, 1967).
Raymond, André, *Artisans et commerçants au Caire au* XVIIIe *siècle*, 2 vols (Damascus: IFEA, 1973–1974).
Razzūq, As'ad, *Al-'Usṭūra fī al-shi'r al-mu'āṣir: Al-shu'arā' al-tammūziyyūn* (Beirut: Manshūrāt Majallat Āfāq, 1959).
Redondi, Pietro, *Galileo Heretic*, trans. Raymond Rosenthal (London: Allen Lane, The Penguin Press 1988).
Reid, Donald, *Cairo University and the Making of Modern Egypt* (Cambridge: Cambridge University Press, 1990).
Reid, Donald Malcolm, *Whose Pharaohs? Archaeology, Museums and Egyptian National Identity from Napoleon to World War I* (Berkeley and Los Angeles: University of California Press, 2003).
Reissner, Johannes, *Ideologie und Politik der Muslimbrüder Syriens*, Islamkundliche Untersuchengen, Bd.55 (Freiburg: Klaus Schwartz Verlag, 1988).
Renault, Henri, "Les survivances des cultes de Cybèle, Venus et Bacchus (Aissaoua, Ouled Nail, Kraabouz)", *Revue tunisienne* (1917); 150–158.
Renfrew, Colin, *Archaeology and Language: The Puzzle of Indo-European Origins* (Harmondsworth: Penguin Books, 1987).
Repp, Richard, "Qanūn and Shari'a in the Ottoman context", in *Islamic Law: Social and Historical Contexts*, ed. al-Azmeh (London and New York: Routledge, 1988), pp. 124–145.
Riḍā, Muḥammad Rashīd, *Muḥāwarāt al-muṣliḥ wa al-muqallid* (Cairo: Maṭba'at Majallat al-Manār, 1334/1916).
Riḍā, Muḥammad Rashīd, *Tarīkh al-ustādh al-imām al-shaykh Muḥammad 'Abduh*, 3 vols (Cairo: Maṭba'at al-Manār, 1350/1931).
Riḍā, Muḥammad Rashīd. *Shubuhāt al-Naṣārā wa ḥujaj al-Islām* (Cairo: Maṭba'at al-Manār, 1322/1904). English translation: *Christian Criticisms, Islamic Proofs*, trans. Simon A. Wood (Oxford: Oneworld, 2008).
Riḍā, Muḥammad Rashīd, "Manāfi' al-Ūrūbbūyīn wa maḍārruhum fī al-Sharq", *al-Manār* 10/3 (1907): 192–199.

Riḍā, Muḥammad Rashīd, *Al-khilāfa aw al-imāma al-'uẓmā* (Cairo: Maṭba'at al-Manār, 1341/1922).
Riḍā, Muḥammad Rashīd, *Al-wahhābiyūn wa-l-Ḥijāz aw Najd wa Ḥijāz* (Cairo: Matba'at al-Manār, 1925).
Riḍā, Muḥammad Rashid, "Tanfīdh al-ḥukm", *Al-Manār* 62/1 (1925): 384–391.
Riḍā, Muḥammad Rashīd, "Bāb al-intiqād 'alā al-Manār", *al-Manār* 28 (1927): 474–480.
Riḍā, Muḥammad Rashīd, "Amwāl Ibn Sa'ūd allatī ittuhima bihā Ṣāḥib al-Manār", *al-Manār* 28/2 (1928): 465–473.
Riḍā, Muḥammad Rashīd, "Editorial", *al-Manār* 30/1 (1929): 3–4.
Riḍā, Muḥammad Rashīd, "Fātiḥa" [Preface] to vol. 30 of the journal, *al-Manār* 30/1 (1929): 12–13.
Riḍā, Muḥammad Rashīd, "Introduction", in Muḥammad Aḥmad 'Arafa, *Naqḍ maṭā'in fī al-Qur'ān al-karīm* (Cairo: n.p., 1932), 3–32.
Riḍā, Muḥammad Rashīd, *Nidā' ilā al-jins al-latīf yaum al-mawlid al-nabawī al-sharīf sanata 1351 fī ḥuqūq al-nisā' fī al-Islām wa haẓẓuhunna min al-iṣlāḥ al-muḥammadī al-'āmm* (Cairo: Maṭba'at al-Manār, 1932).
Riḍā, Muḥammad Rashid, *Fatāwā*, 6 vols (Beirut: Dār al-Kitāb al-Jadīd, 1970).
Riḍā, Muḥammad Rashīd, *Riḥlāt al-Imām Muḥammad Rashid Riḍā*, ed. Yūsuf Ibish, 2 vols (Beirut: al-Mu'assasa al-'Arabiyya li'l Dirāsāt wa al-Nashr, 1971).
Riḍā, Muḥammad Rashīd, *Mukhtārāt siyāsiyya min majallat al-Manār*, ed. Wajīh Kawtharānī (Beirut: Dār al-Ṭalī'a, 1980).
Riyad, Umar, *Islamic Reformism and Christianity* (Leiden: Brill, 2009).
Rodinson, Maxime, *Islam and Capitalism* (London: Saqi Books, 2007).
Rodinson, Maxime, *Marxism and the Muslim World* (London: Zed Books, 1972) (reprinted with Introduction by Gilbert Achkar, 2015).
Roper, Geoffrey (ed.), *Historical Aspects of Printing and Publishing in Languages of the Middle East* (Leiden: Brill, 2014).
Rose, Matthew, "Tayloring Christianity", in www.firstthings.com/article/2014/12/tailoring-christianity (accessed on 27 April 2018).
Rosenthal, Peggy, *The Poets' Jesus* (Oxford: Oxford University Press, 2000).
Rubayz, Janīn, "Ḥawl ahamiyyat al-taḥarrur al-jinsī fī 'amaliyyat taḥarrur al-mar'a", *Mawāqif* 28 (1974): 110–112.
Rubin, Avi, *Ottoman Nizamiye Courts: Law and Modernity* (London: Palgrave Macmillan, 2011).

Rūdinsūn, Maksīm [Maxime Rodinson], *Al-Islām wa al-ra'smāliyya*, trans. Nazīh al-Ḥakīm (Beirut: Dār al-Ṭalī'a, 1968).

al-Ruṣāfi, Ma'rūf, *Al-a'māl al-majhūla*, ed. Najdat Fatḥī Ṣafwat (London: Riyāḍ al-Rayyis li'l-Kutub wa al-Nashr, 1988).

al-Ruṣāfī, Ma'rūf, *Al-shakhṣiyya al-muḥammadiyya* (Cologne: al-Kamel Verlag, 2002).

Rustow, Dankwart A., "Politics and Islam in Turkey 1920–1955", in *Islam and the West*, ed. Richard Nelson Frye (Gravenhage: Mouton, 1957), pp. 69–107.

Sa'ad Allāh, Abū al-Qāsim, *Al-ḥaraka al-waṭaniyya fī al-jazā'ir*, 3 vols (Cairo: al-Munaẓẓama al-'Arabiyya li'l-Thaqāfa wa al-'Ulūm, Ma'had al-Buḥūth wa al-Dirasāt al-'Arabiyya, 1977).

Sa'āda, Anṭūn, *Al-Islām fī risālatayhi, al-Masīḥiyya wa al-Muḥammadiya.* (Beirut: n.p., 1958).

al-Sa'adāwī, Nawāl, *Al-mar'a wa al-jins, awwal naẓra 'ilmiyya ṣarīḥa ilā mashākil al-mar'a wa-l-jins fī al-mujtama' al-miṣrī*, 5th edn (Cairo: Maktabat Madbūlī, 1983).

Sa'īd, Khālida. "Al-ḥadātha aw 'uqdat Jiljāmesh", *Mawāqif* 51/52 (1984): 11–51.

Ṣabrī, Muṣṭafā, *Mas'alat tarjamat al-Qurān* (Cairo: al-Matba'a al-Salafiyya, 1351/1932).

Ṣabrī, Muṣṭafā, *Al-qawl al-faṣl bayn alladhīna yu'uminūn bi al-ghayb wa alladhīna lā yu'minūn* (Cairo: Matba'at 'Īsā al-Bābī al-Ḥalabī, 1361/1942).

Ṣabrī, Muṣṭafā, *Qawlī fī al-mar'a wa muqāranatuhu bi aqwāl muqallidat al-gharb* (Cairo: al-Maṭba'a al-Salafiyya, 1354/1975).

Ṣaffūrī, Ḥusayn, "Muṭāla'a li-kitāb Muḥammad: Naẓra 'aṣriyya jadīda", *Mawāqif* 28 (1974): 98–109.

Ṣafwat, Najdat Fatḥī, "Muqadimma" to Ma'rūf al-Ruṣāfī, *Al-a'māl a- majhūla*, ed. Najdat Fatḥī Ṣafwat (London: Riyāḍ al-Rayyis lil-Kutub wa al-Nashr, 1988), pp. 7–55.

Sahlins, Marshall, *Culture and Practical Reason* (Chicago: University of Chicago Press, 1976).

al-Ṣa'īdī, 'Abd al-Mit'āl, *Al-siyāsa al-islāmiyya fī 'ahd al-nubuwwa* (Cairo: Dār al-Fikr al-'Arabi, n.d.).

al-Ṣa'īdī, 'Abd al-Mit'āl, *Tārīkh al-iṣlāḥ fī al-Azhar wa ṣafaḥāt min al-jihād fī al-iṣlāḥ*, 2 vols (Cairo: Maṭba'at al-I'timād, 1952).

Saif al-Dawla, 'Iṣmat, *'An al-'urūba wa al-islām*, Silsilat al-Thaqāfa al-Qawmiyya 2 (Beirut: Markaz Dirāsat al-Waḥda al-'Arabiyya, 1986).

al-Sakhāwī, Abū al-Khayr Muḥammad ibn 'Abd al-Raḥmān, *Al-i'lān bi al-tawbīkh li-man dhamma ahl al-tārīkh* (Damascus: Nashr al-Qudsī, 1349/1930).
Salamé, Ghassan (ed.), *Democracy without Democrats* (London: I. B. Tauris, 1994).
Salaymeh, Lena, *The Beginnings of Islamic Law: Late Antique Islamicate Legal Traditions* (Cambridge: Cambridge University Press, 2016).
Saleh, Nabil, "Civil codes of Arab countries: The Sanhuri codes", *Arab Law Quarterly* 8/2 (1993): 161–167.
Salibi, Kamal, "The Banu Jamā'a: A dynasty of Shāfi'i jurists in the Mamlūk period", *Studia Islamica* 9 (1958): 97–109.
Ṣāliḥ, Aḥmad 'Abbās, "Dhikrayāt 'an al-'aqqād", *al-Thawra* (Baghdad), 17 November 1989.
al-Sam'āni, Abū Sa'd 'Abd al-Karīm ibn Muḥammad, *Adab al-imlā' wa al-istimlā'*, ed. Max Weisweiler (Leiden: Brill, 1952).
al-Sammān, Ghāda, "Al-thawra al-jinsiyya wa al-thawra al-shāmila", *Mawāqif* 12 (1970): 68–73.
Sanhoury, Abdelrazzak, *Le Califat: Son évolution vers une société des nations orientales*, Travaux du séminaire oriental d'études juridiques et sociales, tome 4.
al-Sanhūri [see also Sanhoury], 'Abd al-Razzāq Aḥmad, *al-Siyāsa*, 22 March 1923.
al-Sanhūrī, 'Abd al-Razzāq Aḥmad, "Al-nahḍāt al-qawmiyya al-'āmma fī ūrūbbā wa fī al-sharq", *al-Risāla* 4/148 (1936): 725–727.
al-Sanhūrī, 'Abd al-Razzāq Aḥmad, "Ḍarūrat tanqīh al-qānūn al-madanī al-miṣrī wa 'alā ayy asās yakūn hadhā al-tanqīh?", *Majallat al-qānūn wa al-iqtiṣād* 6/1 (1936): 3–144.
al-Sanhūrī, 'Abd al-Razzāq Aḥmad, *Maṣādir al-ḥaqq fī al-fiqh al-islāmī: Dirāsa muqārana bi al-fiqh al-gharbī*, 3 vols (Cairo: Jami'at al-Duwal al-'Arabiyya, Ma'had al-Buḥūth wa al-Dirāsāt al-'Arabiyya al-'Āliya, 1967–1968).
al-Sarakhsī, Muḥammad b. Aḥmad, "*Min kitāb al-mabsūṭ*", annex to al-Shaybānī, *Al-makhārij fī al-ḥiyal*, ed. Joseph Schacht (Leipzig: Heinrichs, 1930), pp. 87–136.
al-Sanhūrī, 'Abd al-Razzāq Aḥmad, *Fiqh al-khilāfa wa taṭawwuruhu* (Cairo: al-Hay'a al-Miṣriyya al-'Āmma li'l-Kitāb, 1989).
Sarkar, Sumit, "The decline of the subaltern in Subaltern Studies", in *Mapping Subaltern Studies and the Postcolonial*, ed. Vinayak Chaturvedi (London: Verso, 2000), pp. 300–323.

Sarkīs, Yūsuf Ilyān, *Mu'jam al-maṭbū'āt al-'arabiyya wa al-mu'arraba*, 2 vols (Cairo: Maṭba'at Sarkīs, 1927–1931).

Saunders, Frances Stonor, *The Cultural Cold War: The CIA and the World of Arts and Letters* (New York: The New Press, 1999).

al-Ṣāwī, Aḥmad Ḥusayn, *Fajr al-ṣaḥāfa fī Miṣr: dirāsa fī i'lām al-ḥamla al-faransiyya* (Cairo: al-Hay'a al-Miṣriyya al-'Āmma li'l-Kitāb, 1975).

Ṣāyigh, Anīs, *Al-fikra al-'arabiyya fī Miṣr* (Beirut: Haykal al-Gharīb, 1959).

Ṣāyigh, Tawfīq, *Al-mu'allafāt al-kāmila* (London: Riyāḍ al-Rayyis li'l-Kutub wa al-Nashr, 1990).

al-Sayyāb, Badr Shākir, *Dīwān Badr Shākir al-Sayyāb* (Beirut: Dār al-'Awda. 1971). Partial English translation, "Return to Jaykur", published in the online review *Banipal*, available at www.banipal.co.uk/selections/19/138/badr-shakir-al-sayyab

al-Ṣayyādi, Abū al-Hudā, *Dā'ī al-rashād li-sabīl al-ittiḥād wa al-inqiyād* (Istanbul: al-Maṭba'a al-Sulṭāniyya, n.d.).

al-Sayyid, Aḥmad Luṭfī, *Al-muntakhabāt*, ed. Ismā'īl Maẓhar (Cairo: Maktabat al-Anglo-Miṣriyya, 1937).

al-Sayyid, Riḍwān, "Al-qawmiyyūn wa al-islāmiyyūn fī al-waṭan al-'arabī wa ḍarūrāt al-ḥiwār wa al-talāqi", in *Al-ḥiwār al-qawmī al-dīnī*, ed. Markaz Dirāsāt al-Waḥda al-'Arabiyya (Beirut: Markaz Dirāsāt al-Waḥda al-'Arabiyya, 1989), pp. 75–78.

al-Sayyid, Riḍwān, "Book review", *al-Ijtihād* 2 (1989): 230.

Schama, Simon, *The Embarrassment of Riches: An Interpretation of Dutch Culture in the Golden Age* (New York: Alfred Knopf, 1987).

Schaub, Nicolas, *Représenter l'Algérie. Images et conquête au XIXe siècle* (Paris: Comité des Travaux Historiques et Scientifiques, 2015).

Schivelbusch, Wolfgang, *The Culture of Defeat: On National Trauma, Mourning and Recovery*, 2nd edn (London: Picador, 2004).

Schlanger, Judith, *Les métaphores de l'organisme* (Paris: Vrin, 1971).

Schulze, Reinhard, "Islam und Judentum im Angesicht der Protestantisierung der Religionen im 19. Jahrhundert", in *Judaism, Christianity and Islam in the Course of History: Exchange and Conflicts*, eds Lothar Gall and Dietmar Willoweit (Munich: Oldenbourg, 2010), pp. 139–164.

Schumann, Cristoph, *Liberal Thought in the Eastern Mediterranean* (Leiden: Brill, 2008).

Scott, D. and C. Hirschkind (eds), *Powers of the Secular Modern. Talal Asad and His Interlocutors* (Stanford: Stanford University Press, 2006).

Sedgwick, Mark, *Muhammad Abduh* (Oxford: Oneworld, 2009).
Semerdjian, Elyse, *Off the Straight Path. Illicit Sex, Law and Community in Late Ottoman Aleppo* (Syracuse: Syracuse University Press, 2008).
Sen, Amartya, "Secularism and its discontents", in *Secularism and Its Critics*, ed. Rajeev Bhargava (Delhi: Oxford University Press, 1998), ch. 14.
Sen, Amartya, *Identity and Violence: The Illusion of Destiny* (London: Penguin Books, 2007).
Sen, Kasturi, "Women, employment and development: Two case studies", *Journal of Social Sciences* (Kuwait) 1 (1982): 120–138.
Seni, Nora, "Ville ottomane et représentation du corps féminin", *Les Temps Modernes* 456–457 (1984): 66–95.
Shaarawi, Huda, *Harem Years: The Memoirs of an Egyptian Feminist*, trans. Margot Badran (London: Virago Press, 1986).
Shafik, Viola, *Popular Egyptian Cinema: Gender, Class and Nation* (Cairo: American University of Cairo Press, 2007).
Shafik, Viola, *Arab Cinema: History, Culture and Identity*, rev. edn (Cairo: American University of Cairo Press, 2016).
Shāhīn, Fu'ād, *Al-ṭā'ifiyya fī Lubnan: Ḥādiruhā wa judhūruhā al-tārīkhiyya wa al-ijtimā'iyya* (Beirut: Dār al-Ḥadātha, 1980).
Shalabī, Khayrī (ed.), *Muḥākamat Ṭaha Ḥusayn: Naṣṣ qarār al-ittihām ḍidd Ṭaha Ḥusayn sanat* 1927 *ḥawl kitābihi "fī al-shi'r al-jāhilī"* (Beirut: al-Mu'assasa al-'Arabiyya li'l-Dirāsāt wa al-Nashr, 1972).
Shalash, 'Alī, "Jamāl al-Dīn al-Afghānī fī raddihi 'alā Ernest Renan", *al-Azmina* 1 (1987): 50–66.
Shallī, Munṣif, "Al-tafkīr al-'arabī wa al-tafkīr al-gharbī", *al-Mawāqif* 13 & 14 (1971): 40–61.
Shaltūt, Mahmūd, *Al-fatāwā: Dirāsa li mushkilāt al-muslim al-mu'āṣir fī ḥayatihi al-yawmiyya wa al-'āmma* (Cairo: Dār al-Qalam, 1965).
Sharabi, Hisham, *Neopatriarchy* (Oxford: Oxford University Press, 1988).
al-Sha'rānī, Abū al-Mawāhib 'Abd al-Wahhāb ibn Aḥmad, *Al-ṭabaqāt al-kubrā al-musammāt lawāḥiq al-anwār fī ṭabaqāt al-akhyār*, 2 vols (Cairo: Maṭba'at al-Bābī al-Ḥalabī, 1954).
al-Shābbī, Abū-l-Qāsim, *Al-khayāl al-shi'rī 'ind al-'Arab* (Tunis: al-Sharika al-Qawmiyya li'l Nashr wa al-Tawzī', 1961).
al-Shāhbandar, 'Abd al-Raḥmān, *Al-qaḍāya al-ijtimā'iyya al-kubrā fī al-'ālam al-'arabī* (Cairo: Maṭba'at Miṣr wa Matba'at al-Muqtaṭaf wa al-Muqaṭṭam, 1932).

al-Shāhbandar, ʿAbd al-Raḥmān, "Hal yutāḥ li'l-sharq an yastaʿīd majdahu?" *al-Hilāl* 42/1 (1933): 22–28.

Sharāra, ʿAbd al-Laṭīf, *Al-jānib al-thaqāfī fī al-qawmiyya al-ʿarabiyya* (Beirut: Dār al-ʿIlm li'l-Malāyīn, 1961).

Sharāra, Waḍḍāḥ, *Ḥurūb al-istitbāʿ aw Lubnān al-ḥarb al-ahliyya al-dā'ima* (Beirut: Dār al-Ṭalīʿa, 1979).

Sharāra, Waḍḍāḥ, "Al-malik, al-ʿāmma, al-ṭabīʿa, al-mawt", *Dirasāt ʿArabiyya* 16/12 (1980): 19–46.

Sharāra, Waḍḍāḥ, *Ḥawl baʿḍ mushkilāt al-dawla fī al-thaqāfa wa al-mujtamaʿ al-ʿarabiyyayn* (Beirut: Dār al-Ḥadātha, 1980).

Sharāra, Waḍḍāḥ, *Istiʾnāf al-bad': Muḥāwalāt fī al-ʿilāqa bayn al-falsafa wa al-tārīkh* (Beirut: Dār al-Ḥadātha, 1981).

Sharfān, Zāhī, "Qaḍiyyat naqd al-fikr al-dīnī aw al-maqāma al-lubnāniyya", *Dirāsāt ʿarabiyya* 6 (1970): 3–13.

al-Sharqāwi, ʿAbd al-Raḥmān, *Muḥammad rasūl al-ḥurrīya* (Cairo: ʿĀlam al-Kutub, 1962).

al-Shāṭibī, Abū Isḥāq Ibrāhīm ibn Mūsā, *Al-iʿtiṣām*, ed. Muḥammad Rashīd Riḍā, 2 vols (Cairo: n.p., 1332/1913).

al-Shāṭibī, Abū Isḥāq Ibrāhīm ibn Mūsā, *Al-muwāfaqāt fī uṣūl al-aḥkām*, ed. Muḥammad Munīr, 4 vols (Cairo: n.p., 1922).

Shatzmiller, Maya, "Les premiers Mérinides et le milieu religieux de Fès", *Studia Islamica* 43 (1976): 109–118.

Shaw, Stanford J., *Between Old and New: The Ottoman Empire under Selim III, 1789–1807* (Cambridge, MA: Harvard University Press, 1971).

Shawkat, Sāmi, *Hādhihi ahdāfunā: Majmūʿat muḥāḍarāt wa maqālāt wa aḥādīth qawmiyya* (Baghdād: Wizārat al-Maʿārif, 1939).

al-Shaybānī, Muḥammad ibn al Ḥasan, *Al-makhārij fī al-ḥiyal*, ed. Joseph Schacht (Leipzig: Heinrichs, 1930).

Sheehan, Jonathan, "Enlightenment, religion and the enigma of secularization: A review essay," *The American Historical Review* 108 (2003): 1,061–1,080.

Sheehan, Jonathan, "Thomas Hobbes, D.D.: Theology, orthodoxy, and history", *The Journal of Modern History* 88 (2016): 249–274.

al-Shidyāq, Aḥmad Fāris, *Al-sāq ʿalā al-sāq fī mā huwa al-Fāryāq aw ayyām wa shuhūr wa aʿwām fī ʿAjam al-ʿArab wa al-aʿJām* (Beirut: Dār Maktabat al-Ḥayāt, 1966).

al-Shidyāq, Aḥmad Fāris, *Mumāḥakāt al-ta'wīl fī munāqaḍāt al-injīl*, ed. Muḥammad Aḥmad ʿAmāyirah (Amman: Dār Wā'il, 2001).

al-Shidyāq, Aḥmad Fāris, *Leg Over Leg*, trans. Humphrey Davies, 4 vols (New York: New York University Press, 2014).

Shiḥāta, Shafīq, *Aḥkām al-aḥwāl al-shakhṣiyya li-ghayr al-muslimīn min al-Miṣriyīn*, 8 vols (Cairo: Jāmi'at al-Duwal al-'Arabiyya, Ma'had al-Dirasāt al-'Arabiyya al-'Āliya, 1958–1963).

Shiḥāta, Shafīq, *Al-ittijāhāt al-tashrī'iyya fī qawanīn al-bilād al-'arabiyya* (Cairo: Jāmi'at al-Duwal al-'Arabiyya, Ma'had al-Dirāsāt al-'Arabiyya al-'Āliya, 1960).

Shils, Edward, "Tradition", *Comparative Studies in Society and History* 13 (1971): 122–159.

Shklar, Judith, "The political theory of utopia: From melancholy to nostalgia", *Daedalus* 94 (1965); 367–381.

Shklar, Judith, *After Utopia: The Decline of Political Faith* (Princeton: Princeton University Press, 1957/2015).

Shorten, Richard, "The Enlightenment, communism and political religion: Reflections on a misleading trajectory", *Journal of Political Ideologies* 8 (2003): 13–37.

Shorten, Richard, "Reactionary rhetoric reconsidered", *Journal of Political Ideologies* 20 (2015): 179–200.

Shukrī, Ghālī, "Istrātījiyyāt al-isti'mār al-jadīd fī ma'rakat al-thaqāfa al-'arabiyya", *al-Ṭalī'a* 7 (1967): 15–17.

Shukrī, Ghālī, "Al-Masiḥīyūn wa al-'urūba: man yadfa' al-thaman?", *al-Nāqid* 2 (1989): 12–14.

al-Shumayyil, Shiblī, *Ta'rīb li sharḥ Buchner 'alā maḍhab Darwin fī intiqāl al-anwā'wa ẓuhūr al-'ālam al 'uḍwī wa iṭlāq dhālika 'alā al-insān* (Alexandria: Maṭba'at jarīdat al-Maḥrūsa, 1884).

al-Shumayyil, Shiblī, *Majmū'at al-duktūr Shiblī al-Shumayyil*, 2 vols, 2nd edn (Cairo: Maṭba'at al-ma'ārif, 1910).

al-Shumayyil, Shiblī, *Ārā' al-duktūr Shiblī Shumayyil* (Paris: Manshūrāt al-nuqṭa, vol. 9, 1983, after Cairo: Dār al-Ma'ārif, 1912).

Shuqayr, Ḥafīda, "Dirāsa muqārana li'l-qawānīn al-khāṣṣa bi'l-mar'a wa al-usra fī al Maghrib al-'arabī: Tūnis wa al-Maghrib wa al-Jazā'ir", in *Al-mar'a wa dawruhā fī ḥarakāt al-waḥda al-'arabiyya*, ed. Markaz Dirāsāt al-Waḥda al-'Arabiyya (Beirut: Markaz Dirāsāt al-Waḥda al-'Arabiyya, 1982), pp. 91–105.

Ṣidqī, Muḥammad Tawfīq, *Dīn allah fī kutub 'anbiyā'ihi* (Cairo: Matba'at al-Manār, 1916).

Sīl, Jirjis [George Sale], "Tadhyīl [Appendix]", in *Maqāla fī al-Islām*, trans. Hāshim al-'Arabī (Cairo: al-Maṭba'a al-Inkīlīziyya al-Amīrikiyya, 1909), pp. 364–375.

Sīl, Jirjis, *Maqāla fī al-Islām*, trans. Hāshim al-'Arabī (Cairo: al-Maṭba'a al-Inkīlīziyya al-Amīrikiyya, 1909).

Sing, Manfred, "Illiberal metamorphoses of a liberal discourse: The case of the Syrian intellectual Sami al-Kayyali", in *Liberal Thought in the Eastern Mediterranean*, ed. Christoph Schumann (Leiden: Brill, 2008), pp. 293–322.

Smith, Anthony D., *Nationalism*, 2nd edn (Cambridge: Polity Press, 2010).

Smith, Jonathan Z., *Imagining Religion* (Chicago: University of Chicago Press, 1982).

Soltau, Roger Henry, *French Political Thought in the 19th Century* (New York: Russell and Russell, 1959).

Somel, Selçuk Akşim, *The Modernization of Public Education in the Ottoman Empire, 1839–1908* (Leiden: Brill, 2001).

Sommer, Dorothé, *Freemasonry in the Ottoman Empire. A History of the Fraternity and its Influence in Syria and the Levant* (London: I. B. Tauris, 2015).

Sourdel, Dominique, "La politique religieuse du calife abbaside al-Ma'mūn", *Revue d'études islamiques* 30 (1962): 27–48.

Sparrow, W. J. S., *Religious Thought in France in the Nineteenth Century* (London: George Allen and Unwin, 1935).

Spencer, Philip, *The Politics of Belief in the 19th Century France* (London: Faber and Faber, 1954).

Sperber, Dan and Nicolas Claidière, "Defining and explaining culture (comments on Richerson and Boyd, *Not by genes alone*)", *Biology and Philosophy* 23 (2008): 283–292.

Spinoza, Baruch, *Risāla fī al-lāhūt wa al-siyāsa*, trans. Ḥasan Ḥanafī, introduced by Fu'ād Zakariyyā, 2nd edn (Beirut: Dār al-Ṭalī'a, 1981).

Spinoza, Baruch, *Theological-Political Treatise*, ed. Jonathan Israel (Cambridge: Cambridge University Press, 2007).

Stauth, Georg and Bryan S. Turner, "Ludwig Klages (1872–1956) and the origins of critical theory", *Theory, Culture and Society* 9 (1992): 45–63.

Sternhell, Zeev, *The Anti-Enlightenment Tradition* (New Haven: Yale University Press, 2010).

Sturm, Dieter, "Zur Funktion der Grossmufti in der Syrischen arabischen Republik", *Hallesche Beitrage zur Orientwissenschaft* 4 (1982): 59–67.

al-Subkī, Tāj al-Dīn Abū Naṣr 'Abd al-Wahhāb ibn 'Alī, *Mu'īd al-ni'am wa mubīd al-niqam*, ed. D. O. Myhrman (London: Luzac, 1908).

al-Subkī, Tāj al-Dīn Abū Naṣr 'Abd al-Wahhāb Ibn 'Alī, *Tabaqāt al-Shāfi'iyya al-kubrā*, eds Mahmūd Muḥammad al-Tanāḥī and 'Abd al-Fattāḥ Muḥammad al-Ḥilu, 6 vols (Cairo: n.p., 1964).

al-Subkī, Tāj al-Dīn Abū Naṣr 'Abd al-Wahhāb ibn 'Alī, *Herrn D. W. Myhrman's Ausgabe des Kitāb Mu'id An-Ni'am Wa-Mubid An-Niqam: Kritisch Beleuchtet*. ed. K. V. Zettersteen (London: Forgotten Books, 2018).

al-Ṣulḥ, 'Imād, *Aḥmad Fāris al-Shidyāq, āthāruhu wa 'aṣruhu* (Beirut: Dar al-Nahār li'l-Nashr, 1980).

Syrian Civil Code of 17 May 1949 (Damascus: Ministry of Justice, n.d.), http://www.wipo.int/wipolex/en/text.jsp?file_id=243234

Szombathy, Zoltán, *Mujun: Libertinism in Medieval Muslim Society and Literature* (London: Gibb Memorial Series, 2013).

al-Ṭahṭāwī, Rifā'a Rāfi', *Takhlīṣ al-ibrīz fī talkhīṣ Bārīz* (Cairo: n.p., 1834).

al-Ṭahṭāwī, Rifā'a Rāfi', *Al-a'māl al-kāmila li Rifā'a Rāfi' al-Ṭahṭāwī*, ed. Muḥammad 'Amāra, 5 vols (Beirut: al-Mu'assasa al-'Arabiyya li'l-Dirāsāt wa al-Nashr, 1973).

al-Ṭahṭāwī, Rifā'a Rāfi', *An Imam in Paris. Accounts of a Stay in France by an Egyptian Cleric (1826–1831)*, trans. Daniel L. Newman (London: Saqi Books, 2004).

Ṭarābīshī, Jūrj, *Ramziyyat al-mar'a fī al-riwāya al-'arabiyya* (Beirut: Dār al-Ṭalī'a, 1981).

Ṭarābīshī, Jūrj, *Al-rujūla wa idiyūlūjiyyat al-rujūla fī al-riwāya al-'arabiyya* (Beirut: Dār al-Ṭalī'a, 1983).

Ṭarābīshī, Jūrj, *Naẓariyyat al-'aql al-'arabī*; *Ishkāliyyāt al-'aql al-'arabī; Waḥdat al-'aql al-'arabī*; *Al-'aql al-mustaqīl fī'l-islām* (Beirut: Dār al-Sāqī, 2002–2004).

al-Ṭarābulsī, As'ad Bāsīlī, "Al-dīn wa al-'ilm wa ra'y al-faylasūf Spencer fīhā", *al-Jāmi'a* 3/7 (1902): 554–558.

Taşköprüzāde, *Miftāḥ al-sa'āda wa miṣbāḥ al-siyāda fī mawḍū'āt al-'ulūm*, eds Kāmil Bakrī and 'Abd al-Wahhāb Abū Nūr, 4 vols (Cairo: n.p., n.d.).

Tauber, Eliezer, *The Emergence of the Arab Movements* (London: Routledge, 1993).

Tawtal, Firdīnānd, *Wathā'iq tārīkhiyya 'an ḥalab: Akhbār al-Lātīn wa al-Rūm wa mā ilayhim 1855–1963* (Beirut: al-Maṭba'a al-Kāthūlīkiyya, 1964).

Taylor, Charles, *A Secular Age* (Cambridge, MA: Harvard University Press, 2007).

Taymūr, Maḥmūd, *Muʿjam al-ḥaḍāra* (Cairo: Maṭbaʿat al-Ādāb, 1961).

Tee, Caroline, *The Gülen Movement in Turkey. The Politics of Islam and Modernity* (London: I. B. Tauris, 2016).

Tezcan, Baki, *The Second Ottoman Empire. Political and Social Transformation in the Early Modern World* (Cambridge: Cambridge University Press, 2010).

The Economist, "The prince's time machine", 17 December 2016.

Thompson, Elizabeth, *Colonial Citizens. Republican Rights, Paternal Privilege, and Gender in French Syria and Lebanon* (New York: Columbia University Press, 2000).

Thoumin, R., "Deux quartiers de Damas: Le Quartier chrétien de Bab Musallâ et le quartier Kurde", *Bulletin d'études orientales* 1 (1931): 113.

Tidrick, Kathryn, *Gandhi: The Political and Spiritual Life* (London: Verso, 2013).

Tikhonova, Tatiana, *Sāʿṭi al-Huṣrī: Rāʾid al-manḥā al-ʿilmāni fi al-fikr al-qawmī al-ʿarabi*, trans. Tawfīq Sallūm (Moscow: Dār al-Taqaddum, 1987).

Todorov, Tzvetan, *Symbolism and Interpretation* (London: Routledge & Kegan Paul, 1983).

Toews, John Edward, *Hegelianism: The Path towards Dialectical Humanism 1805–1841* (Cambridge: Cambridge University Press, 1980).

Toscano, Alberto, *Fanaticism: On the Uses of an Idea* (London: Verso, 2010).

Traboulsi, Fawaz, *A History of Modern Lebanon*, 2nd edn (London: Pluto Press, 2012).

Tresse, R., "L'Evolution du costume syrien depuis un siècle", *Renseignements coloniaux: Supplément au bulletin du Comité de l'Afrique française* (1938), pp. 47–48, 63–64.

Troll, Christian, *Sayyid Ahmad Khan: A Reinterpretation of Muslim Theology* (New Delhi: Vikas Publishing House, 1978).

Tuck, Richard, *Natural Right Theories: Their Origin and Development* (Cambridge: Cambridge University Press, 1979).

Tucker, Judith, *Women in Nineteenth-Century Egypt* (Cambridge: Cambridge University Press, 2002).

Tucker, Judith E., *In the House of Law: Gender and Islam in Ottoman Syria and Palestine* (Berkeley: University of California Press, 2000).

Tucker, Judith E., *Women, Family and Gender in Islamic Law* (Cambridge: Cambridge University Press, 2008).

al-Tūnisī, Khayr al-Dīn, *Aqwam al-masālik fī ma'rifat aḥwāl al-mamālik*, ed. Muḥammad al-Munṣif al-Shanūfī, 2nd edn (Tunis: al-Dār al-Tūnisiyya li'l-Nashr, 1972).

Turki, Abdelmadjid, *Polémiques entre Ibn Ḥazm et Bājī sur les principes de la loi musulmane: Essai sur le littéralisme Zāhirite et la finalité Malékite* (Alger: Études et documents, n.d.).

Turner, Bryan S., *Religion and Modern Society. Citizenship, Secularisation and the State* (Cambridge: Cambridge University Press, 2011).

Turner, John P., *Inquisition in Early Islam* (London: I. B. Tauris, 2015).

al-Ṭurṭūshī, Abū Bakr Muḥammad ibn Walīd, *Sirāj al-mulūk* (Cairo: n.p., 1319/1901).

al-Tuwāti, Musṭafā, "Al-ḥaraka al-islāmiyya fī Tūnis", *Qaḍāyā Fikriyya* (1989): 200–211.

Udovitch, Abraham L., *Partnership and Profit in Medieval Islam* (Princeton: Princeton University Press, 1970).

al-'Umarī, Shihāb al-Dīn, *Waṣf 'Ifrīqiya wa al-Andalus*, ed. Ḥusayn Husnī 'Abd al-Wahhāb (Tunis: n.p., n.d.).

Umlīl, 'Alī, *Al-iṣlāḥiyya al-'arabiyya wa al-dawla al-waṭaniyya* (Beirut: Dār al-Tanwīr and Casablanca: al-Markaz al-Thaqāfi al-'Arabī, 1985).

Urvoy, Dominique, "La Pensée d'Ibn Tumart", *Bulletin des études orientales* 27 (1974): 38–39.

Al-'Uṣūr 3/13 (1928), 5/24 (1929).

al-'Utaibī, Sa'd, "Namūdhajān min al-raqāba al-shar'īya 'alā al-anẓima wa'l-qawānīn", http://www.saaid.net/Doat/otibi/119.htm (accessed 5 March 2018).

'Uways, Sayyid, *Rasā'il ilā al-Imām al-Shāfi'ī*, 2nd edn (Kuwait: Dār al-Shāyi', 1978).

Waardenburg, Jacques, *Islam: Historical, Social and Political Perspectives* (Berlin: Walter de Gruyter, 2008).

Wajdī, Muḥammad Farīd, *Naqd kitāb al-shi'ir al-jāhilī* (Cairo: Maṭba'at Dā'irat Ma'ārif al-Qarn al-'Ishrīn, 1926).

Wajdī, Muḥammad Farīd, *Al-Islām fī 'aṣr al-'ilm*, 2 vols, 2nd edn (Cairo: al-Maktaba al-Tijāriyya wa Maṭba'at al-Mu'āṣir, 1932).

Walker, Robert, "Saint-Simon and the passage from political to social science", in *The Language of Political Theory in Early Modern Europe*, ed. Anthony Pagden (Cambridge: Cambridge University Press, 1987), pp. 334–336.

Walter, Nicolas, *Blasphemy Ancient and Modern* (London: Rationalist Press Association, 1990).

Wannūs, Sa'd Allāh, "Bi-mathābat taqdīm", in *Ṭaha Ḥusayn: Al-'aqlāniyya, al-dimūqrāṭiya al-ḥadātha*, ed. Fayṣal Darrāj, Qaḍāya wa Shahādāt, 1 (Nicosia: Mu'assasat 'Ībāl li'l-Dirāsāt wa al-Nashr, 1990), pp. 5–23.

Warde, Ibrahim, *Islamic Finance in the Global Economy*, 2nd edn (Edinburgh: Edinburgh University Press, 2010).

Watenpaugh, Keith David, *Being Modern in the Middle East. Revolution, Nationalism, Colonialism and the Arab Middle Class* (Princeton: Princeton University Press, 2006).

Waterhouse, Eric, "Secularism", in *Encyclopedia of Religion and Ethics*, 13 vols (Edinburgh: T. and T. Clark, 1920), vol. 11, p. 348.

al-Wazzān, 'Abd Allāh, "Michel 'Aflaq: Widā'an", *Zawāyā* 2–3 (1989–1990): 56–63.

Weber, Max, *Economy and Society: An Outline of Interpretative Sociology*, trans C. Roth and C. Wittich (Berkeley and Los Angeles: University of California Press, 1968).

Wien, Peter, *Arab Nationalism. The Politics of History and Culture in the Modern Middle East* (London: Routledge, 2017).

Wild, Stefan, "Gott und Mensch im Libanon: Die Affäre Ṣādiq al-'Aẓm", *Der Islam* 48 (1971): 206–253.

Wilson, Brett, *Translating the Qur'an in an Age of Nationalism: Print Culture and Modern Islam in Turkey* (Oxford: Oxford University Press, 2014).

Wilson, Brian C., "From the lexical to the polythetic: A brief history of the definition of religion", in *What is Religion? Origins, Definitions, and Explanations*, eds Thomas A. Idinopoulos and Brian C. Wilson (Leiden: Brill, 1998), pp. 141–162.

Wissa, Karim, "Freemasonry in Egypt, 1798–1921: A study in cultural and political encounters", *Bulletin of the British Society of Middle East Studies* 16/2 (1989): 143–161.

Wohlrab-Sahr, Monika, Thomas Schmidt-Lux, and Uta Karstein, "Secularization as conflict", *Social Compass* 55 (2008): 127–139.

Wolf, Eric Robert, *Europe and the People without History* (Berkeley and Los Angeles: University of California Press, 1982).

Wolf, Eric Robert, *Europe and the People without History*, 2nd edn (Oakland: University of California Press, 2010).

Wolfson, Harry Austryn, *Repercussions of the Kalam in Jewish Philosophy* (Cambridge, MA: Harvard University Press, 1978).

Wolin, Richard, *The Seductions of Unreason. The Intellectual Romance with Fascism from Nietzsche to Postmodernism* (Princeton: Princeton University Press, 2004).

Wootton, David, *The Invention of Science. A New History of the Scientific Revolution* (London: Penguin Books, 2016).

Yalman, Nur, "Some observations on secularism in Islam: Cultural revolution in Turkey", *Daedalus* 102 (1973): 139–168.

Yamane, David, "Secularization on trial: In defence of a neosecularization paradigm", *Journal for the Scientific Study of Religion* 36 (1997): 109–122.

Yāsīn, Bū ʿAlī, *Al-thālūth al-muḥarram, dirāsa fī al-dīn wa al-jins wa al-ṣirāʿ al-ṭabaqī*, 2nd edn (Beirut: Dār al-Ṭalīʿa, 1985).

Yāsīn, Bū ʿAlī, et al., *Al-Mārksiyya wa al-turāth al-ʿarabī* (Beirut: Dār al-Hadātha, 1980).

Yates, Frances, *Giordiano Bruno and the Heremetic Tradition* (London: Routledge, 1964).

Yūsuf, Abū Sayf, *Al-aqbāṭ wa al-qawmiyya al-ʿarabiyya: Dirāsa istiṭlāʿīya* (Beirut: Markaz Dirāsāt al-Waḥda al-ʿArabiyya, 1987).

Zachs, Fruma, "Muhammad Jamil Bayhum and the woman question", *Die Welt des Islams* 53 (2010): 50–75.

al-Zahāwī, Jamīl Ṣidqī, "Al-mar'a wa al-difāʿ ʿanha", *al-Muʾayyad* 7/8 (1910): 4.

al-Zahāwī, Jamīl Ṣidqī, *Al-fajr al-ṣādiq fī al-radd ʿalā munkirī al-tawassul wa al-karāmāt wa al-khawāriq* (Cairo: Maṭbaʿat al-Wāʿiẓ, 1333/1914).

al-Zahāwī, Jamīl Ṣidqī, *Al-Zahāwī wa dīwānuhu al-mafqūd*, ed. Hilāl Nājī (Cairo: Dār al-ʿArab, 1964).

Zakariyyā, Fu'ād, *Al-ḥaqīqa wa al-wahm fī al-ḥarakāt al-islāmiyya al-muʿāṣira*, 2nd edn (Cairo and Paris: Dār al-Fikr li'l-Dirāsāt wa-l-Nashr wa-l-Tawzīʿ, 1986).

Zaman, Muhammad Qasim, *Religion and Politics under the Early Abbasids* (Leiden: Brill, 1997).

al-Zarnūjī, Burhān al-Islām, *Taʿlīm al-mutaʿallim ṭarīq al-taʿllum*, ed. Marwān Qabbāni (Beirut: al-Maktab al-Islāmi, 1981).

al-Ẓawāhirī, Fakhr al-Dīn al-Aḥmadī, *Al-siyāsa wa al-Azhar: Min mudhakkirāt Shaykh al-Islām al-Ẓawāhirī* (Cairo: Maṭbaʿat al-Iʿtimād, 1945).

al-Ẓawāhirī, Fakhr al-Dīn al-Aḥmadī, *Al-Azhar: Tarīkhuhu wa taṭawwuruhu* (Cairo: al-Ittiḥād al-Ishtirākī al-ʿArabī, 1964).

Zaydān, Jurjī, *Mukhtārāt Jurjī Zaydān*, 3 vols (Cairo: Maṭba'at al-Hilāl, 1919–1921).

Zaydān, Jurjī, *Tarājim mashāhīr al-sharq fī al-qarn al-tāsi' 'ashar*, 2 vols (Beirut: Dār Maktabat al-Ḥayāt, 1970).

Zaydān, Jurjī, *Tārīkh adāb al-lugha al-'arabiyya*, 2 vols (Beirut: Dār Maktabat al-Ḥayāt, 1984).

Zaydān, Jurjī, *Al-riḥla ilā Urubba*, ed. Qāsim Wahhāb (Abu Dhabi: Dār Al-Suwaydī, 2002).

Zayn al-Dīn, Naẓīra, *Al-sufūr wa al-hijāb: Muḥāḍarāt wa naẓarāt fī taḥrīr al-mar'a wa al-tajaddud al-ijtimā'i fī al-'ālam al-islāmi* (Beirut: Maṭābi' Quzmā, 1928).

Zayn al-Dīn, Naẓīra, *Al-fatāt wa al-shuyūkh: Naẓarāt wa munāẓarāt fī al-sufūr wa al-ḥijāb wa taḥrīr al-mar'a wa al-tajaddud al-ijtimā'ī fī al-'alām al-islāmī* (Beirut: al-Matba'a al-Amīrikiyya, 1929).

Zeldin, Theodore, *France 1848–1945: Politics and Anger* (Oxford: Oxford University Press, 1979).

Zenié-Ziegler, Wedad, *In Search of Shadows: Conversations with Egyptian Women* (London: Zed Books, 1988).

Zghal, Abdelkader, "The reactivation of tradition in post-traditional society", *Daedalus* 101/1 (1973): 225–237.

Ziadeh, Susan Laila, "A radical in his time: The thought of Shibli Shumayyil" (PhD dissertation, University of Michigan, 1991).

Zubaida, Sami, "Components of popular culture in the Middle East", in *Mass Culture, Popular Culture and Social Life in the Middle East*, eds Sami Zubaida and G. Stauth (Frankfurt: Campus Verlag and Boulder: Westview Press, 1987), 137–163.

Zubaida, Sami and Stauth, G. (eds), *Mass Culture, Popular Culture and Social Life in the Middle East* (Frankfurt: Campus Verlag and Boulder: Westview Press, 1987).

Zurayq, Qusṭanṭīn, *Al-wa'ī al-qawmī: Naẓarāt fī al-ḥayāt al-qawmiyya al-mutafattiḥa fī al-Sharq al-'Arabī* (Beirut: Dār al-Makshūf, 1925/1940).

Zurayq, Qusṭanṭīn, *Naḥnu wa al-tārīkh: Maṭālib wa tasā'ulāt fī ṣinā'at al-tārīkh wa ṣun' al-tārīkh* (Beirut: Dār al-'Ilm l'il-Malāyīn, 1963).

Zurayq, Qusṭanṭīn, *Fī ma'arakat al-ḥaḍāra: Dirāsa fī māhiyyat al-ḥaḍāra wa aḥwālihā fī al-wāqi' al-ḥaḍārī* (Beirut: Dār al-'Ilm li'l-Malāyīn, 1964).

Zwettler, Michael, *The Oral Tradition of Classical Arabic Poetry: Its Character and Implications* (Columbus: Ohio State University Press, 1978).

Index

Abbas, Ferhat, 250
'Abbas Pasha, 98
'Abbas II, 164
Abbasid caliphate, 36–9, 44, 48–9
Abbasid period, 23–4, 42, 55, 292
'Abbud, Marun, 253
'Abd al-Hafiz, Sultan, 88, 108
'Abd al-Jabbar, al-Qadi, 381
'Abd al-Karim, Khalil, 364
'Abd al-Malik b. Marwan, 364
'Abd al-Qadir, Emir, 88, 163, 164–5
'Abd al-Quddus, Ihsan, 359
'Abd al-Raziq, 'Ali, 35, 250, 262, 264, 293, 296, 302, 304–8, 315, 317–18, 324, 332–3, 335, 340, 383, 396, 422
'Abd al-Raziq, Mustafa, 229
'Abd al-Wahhab, Muhammad, 410
Abdelmedjid II, 334
'Abduh, Muhammad, 7, 88, 105, 107, 113–14, 119–21, 125–6, 129, 134–5, 141, 147–52, 163, 165, 185–90, 193–5, 197, 200–2, 205–7, 211, 213, 215–16, 218–22, 225, 230–1, 236, 247, 269, 287, 297, 305, 315, 317–18, 322, 329–30, 387, 396, 425
Abdülhamid II, 95–6, 104, 121–5, 153, 162, 165, 176, 196, 199–201, 226, 231, 241, 248
Abdülmecid III, 93, 94, 174
al-'Abid, Nazik, 137, 261, 265
Abraham, 295, 305, 361
abrogation (Muslim jurisprudence), 13, 65, 67, 176
absolutism, 15, 42, 113, 119
Abu Bakr, 296
Abu Hanifa, 62
Abu Nuwas, 292
Abu Shadi, Ahmad Zaki, 290, 305, 319
Abu Ya'la ibn al-Farra', 37, 38, 49
Abu Zayd, Nasr, 408–10
al-Abyari, Shaykh, 118
adab, 23–4
Adham, Isma'il, 289, 290, 297, 304
administration
  centralisation of, 73
  hierarchical structures, 196–7
  municipal, 72–3
  and rationality, 90, 92, 182
  reform of, 86–96, 121, 143–4, 167–8, 182
  religious, 54–6
  state, 1, 2, 15, 71–3, 81, 86–96, 121, 143–4, 153–60, 167–8, 182, 196–7, 245
  Turkification of, 167–8
Adonis, 358–9, 402, 403, 445
'Adud al-Dawla, 36–7, 44
adultery, 216, 272, 284–5
advice texts, xlvii, 41
aether, 313–14
Afāq, 373
al-Afghani, Jamal al-Din, 114, 186–7, 189–92, 194–5, 198–201, 207, 213, 228–33, 243, 338, 425
'Aflaq, Michel, 311, 343, 344–5, 353, 390, 421, 424
Aga Khan, 156
Ahmed, Hocine Ait, 391
Ahmet Cevdet Paşa, 106
al-Ahrām, 107, 163, 264
'A'isha, 216
Alaoui sultanate, 86
Albrecht V of Bavaria, 17
alchemy, 20, 228
alcohol, 63, 64, 88, 149, 152, 175, 387, 408
Aleppo, 47, 72, 86, 106, 156, 234, 251, 265, 302, 303, 341, 344
Alexandria, 72, 132, 162, 198–9
Alfieri, Vittorio, 208
Algeria
  and the Arab Revolt, 172
  Association of Muslim Ulama, 111, 247–8, 249, 347–8
  Berbers, 110, 111, 145, 348, 391
  family endowments, 146
  Étoile Nord-Africaine, 249–50
  Fédération d'élus musulmans, 249
  French colonisation, 88, 109, 110–12, 144–5, 163, 247, 347–8, 390
  independence, 390
  Islamic Conference, 348
  Islamic reformism, 247–8

Algeria (*cont.*)
- Islamism, 390–1, 407, 434
- Judaism, 110
- legal reform, 144–5, 271, 273
- Movement for the Triumph of Democratic Liberties, 348
- National Liberation Front, 249, 348–9, 390–1
- nationalism, 111, 347–9, 390–1
- religious education, 389
- Salafism, 347
- secular courts, 145
- secular intellectuals, 109, 110–12
- secular law, 144–5, 271, 273
- state reforms, 88, 93, 249
- status of women, 261, 380
- women's employment, 380
- Young Algerians movement, 110

Algerian Islamic Conference, 348
Ali, Jawad, 362
Ali Clay, Muhammad, 449
Ali ibn Abi Talib, 47
'Ali ibn Hussein, 174
Ali Mubarak, 98, 107
alienation, xxxviii, xxxix, 4, 366–7, 427
Almohad period, 416
Almoravid periods, 416
alt-right, xii
al-Alusi, Muhammad Shukri, 223
'Amara, Muhammad, 307
American Association for the Advancement of Atheism, 304
American University of Beirut, 398
Amin, Ahmad, 138, 252, 258, 259, 308, 309, 312, 319, 321, 345
Amin, Hussein Ahmad, 282
Amin, Qasim, 104, 133, 134, 135–6, 197
amputation (as punishment), 88, 139, 282
analogy (*qiyās*), 13, 62–5, 78, 213
anarchism, 369
Anatolia, 73, 86, 91–2, 98, 121, 131, 160, 161, 169, 173, 175, 177
Anglican church, 8, 18
Anglo-Egyptian Treaty, 337
Anglo-Ottoman Treaty, 140
'Anhuri, Salim, 162, 217, 232–3, 243
Ankara, 173–4, 175
Ankara University, 394
anthropology, xxviii–xxix, xxxi, xliii, xlv, xlvii, 133, 287, 363, 367, 448
anti-clericalism, 32, 227, 317
anti-Communism, xiv–xv, xxvii, xxxvii, 324–5, 344, 382–3, 394, 395, 442–3
anti-Enlightenment discourses, xxvii, xxviii, xxix, xxxvii
anti-modernism, xxii–xxv, xxvii–xxx, xxxviii, xlvii, 311, 404, 412–13
anti-secularism, xii, xvi, xvii, xix, xxii, 2–3, 102, 176, 383, 404, 412–22, 439, 443, 445
Antun, Farah, 7, 162, 190, 237, 238–40, 241
Antun, Rose, 132
apologetism, xviii, xx–xxi, xxii, xxx, xlii, xlvii–xlviii, 224
apostasy, 139, 151–2, 155, 284, 296, 298, 383, 405, 409
apostasy wars (*Ridda*), 296
apt performance, xlv–xlvi, xlix
'Aql, Said, 355
al-'Aqqad, Abbas Mahmud, 254, 258, 288, 308, 310–13, 315, 321–4, 333, 398
Aquinas, Thomas, 14
Arab associations, 165–6
Arab caliphate, 164–5, 170–1, 172–3
Arab League, 443
Arab nationalism, xxvii, 3, 162–7, 169–73, 174, 190, 200, 251, 311, 339–44, 382–3, 390–1, 398, 415, 420–31, 435, 437–8, 441–2
Arab Renaissance Society (Jam'iyyat al-Nahḍa al-'Arabiyya), 165
Arab Revolt, 168, 170, 171–3, 178
Arab Revolutionary Workers' Party, 374
Arab Spring, xxi, 272
Arabic language, 7, 59, 77–8, 103, 122, 166, 176, 255, 330, 347–8, 381, 391, 394
Arabic literature, 81–2, 233, 254–5, 291–2, 294, 355–60, 410
Arabic sultanic schools, 167
al-'Arabiyya al-Fatāt, 166
architecture, 24, 337
aristocracy, 17, 18, 23, 33, 44, 52; *see also* social class
Aristotle, 325
armed forces *see* military
Armenia, 160, 168
Armenian Church, 155
Arslan, Shakib, 249, 337
al-Arsuzi, Zaki, 287, 292, 343, 344, 424
art, 24, 337, 354, 375
artificial insemination, 387
al-'Arusi, Shaykh, 119
Asad, Talal, xxiii, xxiv, xxv, xxxi, xxxvi, xxxvii, xxxix, xlii–xlix
al-Asali, Shukri, 165
'Ash'ari theology, 48, 209, 211, 288, 312, 416
al-'Askari, 'Abd al-Halim, 303

Index

al-Assad, Hafez, 385–6
Association for Awakening of Young Arab Women, 137
Association of the Coptic Nation, 336
Association of Muslim Ulama, 111, 247–8, 249, 347–8
astrology, 43
astronomy, 19, 21–2, 227–8; *see also* cosmology
Atatürk *see* Kemal, Mustafa
atheism, 19–20, 28–9, 33, 132, 175, 231–2, 234–6, 287–90, 298–9, 301–5, 321, 331–2, 338, 369, 370, 400–1, 403, 443, 445
Augustine, Saint, 355
Augustinian Order, 15
authenticity, xxix, xxxviii, 3, 4, 56, 61–2, 79, 193, 327, 427–30, 433, 435, 436, 441
authoritarianism, 121, 168, 178, 182, 196–8, 255, 352, 353, 371, 378, 382, 397–8, 403, 446, 449
authority
  and the caliphate, 36–43, 307
  and charisma, 42, 44, 45, 47, 48, 49, 56
  delegation of, 36–41
  and education, 57–9
  family transmission of, 51–2
  ideological, 77–8
  political, 12, 13, 23, 30, 36–42, 50, 81, 94, 307
  religious, 8, 10, 12, 15, 23, 30, 36–42, 49–52, 56, 94, 183, 219, 240, 245, 297, 301, 307, 436
  secular, 108, 173, 297, 316
  and shari'a, 62, 64, 65, 66–7, 76–80
  and the state, 56, 108, 408
  and the ulama, 49–52, 61–2, 78, 219
avant-gardism, 178, 180, 236, 242–3, 290, 366, 371–2, 381, 399
'Awad, Louis, 325, 381, 410
'Awda, Abd al-Qadir, 284–6
Awlād ḥāritnā (Mahfouz), 387
awqāf see *waqf*
'Ayyad, Muhammad Kamil, 303
Ayyubid period, 47, 56
al-Azhar, 53, 98, 99, 118–21, 148–9, 250–3, 280, 297, 301–2, 305–7, 317–18, 321–2, 325, 329–36, 352, 380, 381, 386–90, 395, 409–11
al-'Azm, Rafiq, 165, 166, 197
al-'Azm, Sadiq, 368, 372, 377, 382–4, 399, 422, 444–5
al-'Azmah, Bahira, 265
al-'Azmah, Yusuf, 137
al-Azmeh, Aziz, xxxiv, li
Azmi, Mahmud, 302
'Azuri, Najib, 162–3, 339

Ba'albaki, Laila, 359–60, 381
Baath Party, 271, 287, 311, 343, 344, 385, 389, 390, 400, 424, 442
Babi creed, 216
Bach, J. S., 24
backwardness, historical, 4, 5, 32, 103, 180, 239, 246, 272, 347, 360, 368, 372, 375, 403, 441, 444–5
Bacon, Francis, 205, 319
Baghdad, 36, 43, 44, 47, 52, 55, 74, 77, 191, 362
Bahaism, 216
Bahrain, 395
Bakhit, Shaykh Abd al-Hamid, 387
Bali, xxxii, xlv
Balkan nationalisms, 177
al-Banna, Hassan, 260, 280, 287
Banu 'Abd al-Muttalib clan, 364
Banu Hanifa tribe, 364
baptism, 13, 16
Barjīs Bārīz, 155
Barquq, Sultan Abu Sa'id, 38
Bashear, Suliman, 363–4
Bashshar b. Burd, 227
Basra reform Association (Jam'iyyat al-Baṣra al-Iṣlāḥiyya), 166
Bayhum, Ahmad Mukhtar, 137
Bayhum, Muhammad Jamil, 261, 270
Bayram, Muhammad, 150
Baz, Jirji, 132
al-Bazzaz, 'Abd al-Rahman, 421
beginnings *see* origins
Beirut, 86, 102–3, 115–16, 128, 132–4, 137, 166, 169, 191, 242, 253, 265, 354, 377, 383–4, 412–13, 442
belief, xix–xx, 8–9, 201–2, 240, 286, 288, 300, 393
Ben Achour, al-Fadl, 393
Ben Ali, Zayn al-'Abidin, 393
Benedict, Ruth, xxix
Benjamin, Walter, xxviii
Berbers, 110, 111, 145, 345, 347, 348, 391
Bergson, Henri, 343, 344, 424
Berque, Jacques, 261
Bey, Ahmad Arif Hikmet, 94
Bible, xli, 9, 15–16, 20, 24, 26–7, 97, 216, 217, 234, 292, 355, 365–6, 414
Bildungsbürgertum, 118, 177, 197, 336, 351
Bildungsroman, 303, 401

Bishāra, ʿAzmī, xv
al-Bishri, Salim, 330
blasphemy, 29, 30, 227
bloodwit, 141, 274
Blunt, Wilfred, 170
Boas, Franz, xxix
Bonald, Louis de, 224
Bouhajib, Salem, 202
Bouhdiba, Abdelwahab, 393
Boumedienne, Houari, 391
bourgeoisie, 3, 16, 23, 31, 114, 116–18, 132, 153, 169, 198, 345–6, 374, 378, 394–5, 425; *see also* social class
Bourguiba, al-Habib, 248, 261, 349, 370–1, 393, 449
Boyle, Robert, 20
Britain
  Anglican Church, 8, 18
  and the Arab Revolt, 170–2
  Civil War, 18
  colonialism, 85, 89, 100, 115–16, 137, 164, 337
  death penalty for blasphemy, 29
  defeat at Gallipoli, 173, 179
  dissolution of monasteries, 17–18
  Freemasonry, 115–16
  and the Kemalist Revolution, 173–4, 179
  law, 144, 277
  pressure exerted on Ottoman state, 155, 156, 157, 158–9, 168
  Protestant Reformation, 15–16
  rate of religious belief, 9
  religious tolerance, 30, 155
  royal absolutism, 15
  scientific societies, 24
  Scottish Presbyterianism, 16
  secularisation, 16, 29–30, 33
  utilitarianism, 114
  Whig politics, 107
  women's suffrage, 176
Bruno, Giordiano, 21
Büchner, Ludwig, 231, 235
Buddhism, xi–xii, xliv
Buddhist nationalism, xi–xii
Buhajib, Salim, 105, 109
al-Bukhari, Muhammad, 46, 60–1, 118, 215
Bultmann, Rudolf, 28
Burke, Edmund, xxvii
al-Bustani, Butrus, 103, 162, 242, 415
Byzantine Christianity, 10, 11–12, 74–5

Cairo, 72, 77, 86–7, 89, 93, 98, 100, 103–4, 115–16, 128, 130, 166, 191, 196, 198–9, 235, 265, 337, 367, 382, 443
Cairo University, 253, 409
calendars, 127–8, 320
caliphate
  Abbasid caliphate, 36–9, 44, 48–9
  abolition of Ottoman caliphate, 174, 180, 255–6, 335
  adoption of theological doctrines, 48–9
  advisory council established, 174
  Arab caliphate, 164–5, 170–1, 172–3
  charismatic dimension, 42, 44, 45, 48, 49
  continuity of, 49
  as convergence of politics and shariʿa, 48–9
  delegation of authority, 36–41
  distinction from sultanate, 41–2
  Fatimid caliphate, 208
  Fouad I's candidacy, 334–5
  and Islamic jurisprudence, 296
  juridical functions, 38, 42–3
  and power, 36–44, 307, 335
  provisions on in Turkish constitution, 175
  Rightly-Guided Caliphs, 175, 206, 392
  separation from sultanate, 175
  and shariʿa, 47–9
  Shar'ist caliphate, 45
  as temporal rulers, 7, 38, 41–3, 307, 335
  Umayyad caliphate, 364
Calvinism, xlviii, 16, 17
Canning, Stratford, 155, 157
canon law, 13–14, 82, 154, 373
capital punishment, 29, 30, 143, 151, 169–70, 284–5, 320
capitalism, xxxix, 1–2, 5, 14, 25, 85, 129, 140, 157–8, 181, 226, 273, 404–5, 423, 432, 448
Capitulations, 86, 87, 140–1, 156, 157, 169
Carlyle, Thomas, xxvii, 323
Casanova, José, xxxix–xli, xlv
casuistic stratagems (*hiyal*) (Muslim jurisprudence), 67, 69–70
Catherine, Empress of Russia, 160
Catholicism, xxxix, 8, 11, 14–20, 24, 30–2, 117, 127, 155, 159, 224, 252–3, 311, 373, 385, 438
causality, xi, xliv–xlv, 22, 63–4, 66, 232, 237, 424
censorship, 122, 241, 381, 410–11
Central Intelligence Agency (CIA), 399
centralisation, 1, 14, 15, 16, 18, 73, 76–7, 168, 246, 436
Centre for Arab Unity Studies, 412–13, 428
charisma, 42, 44, 45, 47, 48, 49, 56
Charlemagne, 12
chastity, 64, 133
Chehab, Fouad, 405

Index

Christ *see* Jesus
Christendom, 14
Christianity
  and Arab nationalism, 342, 343
  and the aristocracy, 17, 18
  Armenian Church, 155
  Byzantine Christianity, 10, 11–12, 74–5
  and calendars, 127–8
  canon law, 13–14, 82, 154, 373
  common cultural features with Islam and Judaism, 82–3
  confessional conflicts, 16–19, 155–6, 158, 160–1, 336–7, 405
  confessional uniformity, 16–17, 160–1
  Coptic Christianity, 97, 100, 141, 147, 158–9, 161–2, 250, 324, 333, 336, 415
  Counter-Reformation, 16
  critical study of, 26–9, 31, 365–6
  cultural similarities between Arab Christianity and Islam, 415–16
  and Darwinism, 28, 30, 232–3
  days of rest, 127–8
  dialogue with Islam, 382
  dissolution of the monasteries, 17–18
  and dress, 130
  and education, 15, 19, 31, 100–2, 252
  emergence of Christendom, 14
  food practices, 126
  and heresy, 14, 16–17, 18–19
  historical contexts, 9–34
  jurisprudence, 13–14
  and literature, 23–4, 253, 355–60
  Maronite Christianity, 82, 127, 154, 155, 161, 162, 227, 233, 242, 251, 253, 373
  marriage practices, 13, 31, 127
  and morality, 17, 27
  and nationalism, 160–2
  Orthodox Christianity, 104, 154, 155, 159, 162, 373
  and the Ottoman *millet* system, 154, 155–60
  Papacy, 10, 13, 17, 19–20, 30, 31–2, 104, 117
  polemics against Islam, 155–6
  and power, 12–13
  progressive movements, 373
  Reformation, xliv, xlv, xlviii, 14, 15–16, 201, 204
  relationship to law, 11–14, 25, 30
  relationship to the state, 11–19, 29–34, 240, 333, 414–15
  religious festivals, 15
  religious orders, 14, 17–18, 19–20
  resistance to secularisation, 29–32, 156–7, 253, 352
  and science, 19–23, 27–8, 202–3, 224–5, 229, 235–6
  and secessionism, 160–2
  secularism as Christian theological category, xl–xli, 414–15, 419
  secularism as post-Christian, xxxvii–xxxviii, xl
  and social change, 252–3
  and social solidarity, 11
  status of women, 126–7, 133
  taxation of the Church, 17, 30
  and the three-stage theory of history, 186
  see also Anglican Church; Bible; Calvinism; Catholicism; Presbyterianism; Protestantism; religion
cinema, 152, 261, 353–4
citizenship, 11, 18, 90, 96, 140, 145, 153, 155, 157, 160, 162, 167, 169, 240, 241, 405–6, 438
civil society, xxi, 26, 404–5
civilisational trajectories, xxxix–xl
clan networks, 89
Clot, Antoine, 131–2
Code of Justinian, 12
cognitive relativism, xxiii, xxvi, xxix
Cold War, xiv–xv, xvii, xxi, xxiii, xxvi, xxvii, xxxvii, 382–3, 392, 394
colonialism
  British, 85, 89, 100, 115–16, 137, 164, 337
  colonisation of Algeria, 88, 109, 110–12, 144–5, 163, 247, 347–8, 390
  colonisation of Morocco, 145, 247, 347
  colonisation of Tunisia, 88, 93, 109–12, 121, 144–5, 247, 261, 347, 349
  and the creation of Israel and Pakistan, 394
  cultural, 398, 445
  Dutch, 85, 100
  French, 88, 93, 100, 109–12, 121, 144–5, 247, 261, 302–3, 347–9, 390
  occupation of Egypt, 100, 115–16, 120, 137, 164, 337
  and the Ottoman state, 86, 158, 241–2
  as representing a fall from grace, xvi, xxxii, 412, 432–3
  and social Darwinism, 188
  Spanish, 85
  see also post-colonialism
commercial law, 69–71, 106, 139–41, 142–3, 144, 149–51
Committee for Union and Progress (CUP), 125, 162, 163, 165–7, 169, 170, 171, 177–8, 241

commodity fetishism, xxxix
communications, xvii, 14, 15, 73, 77, 81, 181, 199, 221, 246, 351
Communism, xiv–xv, xxvii, 175, 324–5, 344, 370, 376, 382–3, 394, 395, 400, 403, 434, 442, 443
Compagnon, Antoine, xxix
comparative law, 275–7, 279
comparative religion, 330
Comte, Auguste, 30–1, 92–3, 106, 185, 286, 287
concubinage, 268
Condillac, Étienne Bonnot de, 205
confessional conflicts, 16–19, 155–6, 158, 160–1, 239, 336–7, 405
confessional uniformity, 16–17, 160–1
Congress for Cultural Freedom, 399
consensus (*ijmā'*), 61, 212
conservatism, xviii, xxiii, 159, 198, 202, 234, 245, 254–5, 257, 266–7, 361, 391, 395, 442–3
consociational state, 404–6
conspiracy theories, 113, 413
Constantine, 12
Constantinople, 12, 148, 154, 155, 160; *see also* Istanbul
constitutionalism, 153, 162, 165, 168, 206, 207–9, 248
constitutions
- attempted constitution in Morocco, 108
- Egypt, 329, 331–2, 334, 336, 337, 387
- France, 32
- Ottoman state, 95–6, 115, 121, 122, 125–6, 153, 162, 208
- Sudan, 449
- Syria, 339–40, 385–6
- Tunisia, 385
- Turkey, 175–6
- United Arab Republic, 385

constructivism, xxv–xxvi, xliv–xlv, 311
contemporaneity, 428, 438
continuity, historical, 49, 50–2, 81, 192, 267, 402–5, 419, 420, 422–6, 429–30, 435, 446–7
contraception, 268–9
contract law, 67, 149–50, 278
Copernicus, Nicolaus, 19
Coptic Christianity, 97, 100, 141, 147, 158–9, 161–2, 250, 324, 333, 336, 415
correlation, legal indices of (*'illa*), 63–5, 78
corporal punishment, 140, 268, 274, 380, 408
cosmology, 22–3, 41, 189, 221, 227–8, 299; *see also* astronomy
cosmopolitanism, 77–8, 86
Council of Nicaea, 12
Council of Trent, 16, 20
Counter-Reformation, 16
counter-revolution, xxvii, xxix, 192
courtly society, 77–8
courts
- *mazālim* courts, 71, 72, 74
- Mixed Courts, 140, 278
- secular courts, 71, 72, 74, 139–41, 145, 148–9, 275, 278, 385, 408
- shari'a courts, 71–3, 141, 173, 256, 301

craft guilds, 90, 91, 153–4, 155
Critique of Religious Thought (al-Azm), 372, 382–4
Cromer, Evelyn Baring, Lord, 100, 112, 120, 151, 163
cross-confessional marriages, 373
crowd psychology, 310, 321, 324, 325–7
cultural anthropology, xxviii–xxix
cultural colonisation, 398, 445
cultural hegemony, 96, 247, 384, 392, 433
cultural homogenisation, 81–2, 246, 329
cultural nationalism, xli, 188
cultural reform, 89–90, 181–2
cultural revival, 4, 377, 429
cultural translation, xlii–xliii
culturalism, xxviii–xxix, xxx–xxxiv, xl–xli, xlv
Cyril V, 162

Dadaism, 369
Daesh, 268, 285–6, 427
Dahir, 'Adil, xv–xvi
Dahrism, 231–2
Dallal, Jibra'il, 234
al-Damanhuri, Shaykh Ahmad, 99
Damascus, 51, 55–6, 72, 74, 86, 102–4, 106, 115, 123–5, 127, 129–30, 134, 137, 153–4, 159, 163, 169, 247, 251–2, 260, 265, 303
Damascus Spring, xxi
Dar al-Ṭalī'a, 377, 383, 384
Dār al-'Ulūm institution (Cairo), 98, 252, 253, 331, 332, 409
Darülfünun university, 98, 104
Darwaza, Muhammad Izzat, 343–4
Darwin, Charles, 133, 188, 286
Darwinism, 30, 132–3, 184–8, 228, 232–3, 235, 237
al-Da'uq, Bashir, 383–4
days of rest (weekly), 127–8
death penalty, 29, 30, 143, 151, 169–70, 284–5, 320

decadence, xxvii, 89, 299, 308–9
decisionism, xxx, xlii, 417–18, 426–7, 439
deism, 227–8, 312–13
delegation, 36–41
democracy, xxi, 1, 14, 23, 25, 93, 122, 153, 160, 324–5, 417–18, 420, 436, 439–41, 447, 449–50
Democratic Party, 324
dervishism, 310
Descartes, René, 21, 26, 299, 319
destiny (historical), xvi–xvii, xxvi, xxx–xxxv, xli, 419, 420, 424
Destour Party, 248
D'Holbach, Paul-Henri Thierry, Baron, 28, 231, 236
differentiation (cultural), xiv, xv, xix–xx, xxxvii, xli, xlix, 138
Dirāsāt 'Arabiyya, 354, 377
dirigisme, 4–5, 96, 247
discretion (legal), 68–70, 139, 142, 214, 275, 283
disenchantment (historical), xix, xxvii, xxxix, xlii
dissolution of the monasteries, 17–18
divine providence, 21–2, 187, 190, 210, 312–13
divine right of kings, 13, 18
division of labour, 266–7, 438
divorce, 65, 72, 127, 147–8, 176, 216, 260, 263, 267, 269–73
Diyanet, xviii
Dominican Order, 14
drama, 130, 197, 255
dress, xii, xvii, 42, 53, 57, 106–8, 112, 126–7, 129–30, 154, 176, 181, 196, 256–7, 354, 378, 396, 444; *see also* personal appearance; veiling
drinking, 63, 64, 79, 88, 149, 152, 175, 408
Dugin, Alexander, xxxiv
Dühring, Karl, 235
al-Dukkali, Abu Shu'ayb, 88, 248
Dunyā al-dīn fī aḍir al-'arab (al-Azmeh), li
Durkheim, Émile, 294

East/West dichotomy, 308–10, 326–8
economics, 25–6, 28, 77, 85–6, 266–7, 370–1, 375
Edib, Halide, 134, 160
Edict of Nantes, 16
education
Arabic sultanic schools, 167
and authority, 57–9
and cultural homogenisation, 246, 329
curricula, 99, 119–20, 121, 125, 248, 252, 253, 330, 388–9, 398
educational books, 102, 122
engineering schools, 86, 97
hadith colleges, 56
in Islamic jurisprudence, 330
kuttāb schools, 100, 251–2
language schools, 97, 98, 100
in literature, 253
madrasas, 52, 53, 56–9, 74, 388
for the masses, 327
medical schools, 97
military schools, 98, 106, 122
missionary schools, 100–2, 131, 252
and modernity, 1, 23–4
pedagogical techniques, 57–9
primary education, 97, 98, 100, 109, 251–2, 332
private schools, 98, 345
reform of, 87, 90, 97–105, 109, 118–21, 156, 167–8, 173, 176, 181, 251–2, 329–31, 386
and religion, 15, 19, 31, 52, 54–9, 74, 98–102, 125, 173, 198, 246, 251–2, 299, 329–32, 388–9, 394
repudiated by Islamic reformists, 193, 194, 199
secondary education, 97, 251
secular education, 30, 31, 32, 97–100, 103–5, 106, 109, 242, 251–3, 386
and the state, 5, 30, 31, 32, 97–100, 106, 109, 176, 251–3, 329–32
teacher training, 98, 109, 134
Turkification of, 167–8
universities, 24, 98, 104, 252, 253, 329–32, 386, 394, 398, 409
for women, 100, 103, 126, 131–2, 133–6, 258, 259, 267
Egypt
abolition of slavery, 152
abolition of *waqf*, 273
administrative structures, 87, 92, 94–5
adoption of Gregorian calendar, 128
anthropological study of, 367
anti-Communism, 395
Arab nationalism, 339
atheism, 304, 331–2, 401
al-Azhar, 53, 98–9, 118–21, 148–9, 250–3, 280, 297, 301–2, 305–7, 317–18, 321–2, 325, 329–36, 352, 380, 381, 386–7, 389–90, 395, 409–11
banquet massacre (Cairo), 87

Egypt (*cont.*)
British occupation, 100, 115–16, 120, 137, 164, 337
Capitulations, 140–1
Christianity, 158–9, 161–2, 250, 324, 333, 336, 405, 415
cinema, 354
citizenship, 405–6
Civil Code, 128, 143, 274, 276–8, 279–80
Commuinism, 434
confessional conflicts, 336–7, 405
consociational state idea, 405–6
constitutions, 329, 331–2, 334, 336, 337, 387
criminal law code, 274
Democratic Party, 324
dress, 129, 256–7, 396, 444
economy, 444
educational book publishing, 102
educational reform, 87, 97, 98–100, 104, 118–21, 251–2, 329–31
family endowments, 146
family transmission, 51
Fouad I's caliphal candidacy, 334–5
Free Constitutionalist Party, 250
Freemasonry, 113–16
fundamentalism, 395
hierarchies of religious scholars, 53
hyper-pietist practices, xliii, xlvi
Islamic reformism, 197–9, 298, 308, 318–20, 326, 396
Islamisation, 444
Islamism, 336, 345, 387, 395, 405, 407, 408–11, 431–2, 434, 443–4
journal publishing, 103, 303
and Kemalism, 255–7
legal reform, 6, 140–1, 143, 144, 148–9, 271, 272, 273, 274, 276–8
Liberal Constitutionalist Party, 302, 331, 332, 333, 334–5, 338
Liberal Nationalist Party, 297
literature, 337–8, 359, 387, 411
medical dissection, 128
military, 87, 159
Ministry of Awqaf, 301, 386
missionary schools, 100–1, 131
Mixed Courts, 141
Muslim Brotherhood, xii, 260, 280, 284, 307, 317, 336, 345, 386, 387, 391, 408, 411, 434, 442
nationalism, 90, 92, 120, 137, 163–4, 336–9, 383, 423
Pan-Arabism, 338, 390
Pan-Islamism, 338
petro-Islam, 444
Pharaonic period, 291, 337–8
political reform, 90
polygamy, 269
populism, 432
primary education, 97, 98, 100, 251, 332
proportion of Muslims, 74
protest against literature, 381, 387
religious cultural production, 388–90
religious education, 388–9
religious office-holders, 53–5
Revolution (1919), 137, 250, 265, 337
Revolution (1952), 387
rural political networks, 334
Saadist Institutional Party, 280
secession from Ottoman state, 164
sectarianism, 372, 397
secular courts, 141, 148–9, 408
secular education, 97, 98–100, 104, 251, 253
secular intellectuals, 112–13, 118, 297–8, 301–29, 351, 397, 401
secular law, 140–1, 143, 144, 148–9, 271, 272, 273, 274, 276–8, 279–80
separatism, 161–2
shari'a, 273, 329, 387, 405, 408
shari'a courts, 256, 301
social class, 112
state reforms, 87, 89, 90, 92–3, 94–5, 182, 198–9
status of women, 131–2, 137, 260, 264–5, 266, 272
teacher training, 98
universities, 98, 104, 253, 329–32, 386, 409
'Urabi Revolt, 107, 108, 118, 158
Wafd Party, 250, 265, 280, 297, 326, 331, 332, 333, 334–5, 444
Wahhabism, 338–9, 395–7, 410
Westernisation, 112
women's associations, 137
women's conferences, 265
women's education, 131–2
women's movement, 264–5
women's suffrage, 266
Young Egypt movement, 336
Egyptian Academy for Scientific Culture, 303
Egyptian University, 104, 321, 330, 332
Einstein, Albert, 313–14
"end of history" discourses, xxi, xxvii
engineering schools, 86, 97
English Civil War, 18
Enlightenment, xxvii, xxviii, xxix, xxxvii, xl, xlii, 21, 114, 185–6, 201, 236, 246, 368

Epicureanism, 232
esoteric symbolism, 358–9
ethnic cleansing, 160–1, 169, 177
Étoile Nord-Africaine, 249–50
eucharist, 20
Eurocentrism, xli–ii
Europe
  citizenship, 241
  colonialism *see* colonialism
  concepts of economy and society, xxxvi–xxxvii
  consular protection by, 89 ,156
  critical study of religion, 26–9
  dress, 129–30
  economy, 25–6, 85
  fascism, 309, 325, 344, 437
  financial interests, 89, 122, 157, 161
  Freemasonry, 113–17
  and globalisation, 375
  Gregorian calendar, 127
  historical contexts, 4, 9–34
  influence of European ideas on Arab nationalism, 343, 344
  influence of European ideas on Islamic reformism, 192, 205–6, 223–4, 245–6, 286–90, 309
  irrationalism, xxviii, 343, 344, 425, 430
  Islam, xlviii, 16, 33
  jurisprudence, 13–14, 25
  literature, 23–4, 128, 253
  and Pan-Islamism, 340
  pressure exerted on Ottoman state, 86, 87, 155, 156–60, 168
  Protestant Reformation, 14, 15–16
  religious tolerance, 19, 30, 155
  Renaissance, 23–4
  right-wing thought, xi, xii, 188, 192–3, 324, 437
  science, 19–23, 27–8
  scientific societies, 24
  secular law, 14, 25, 30
  secularisation, xl–xlii, 3–4, 8–9, 16, 29–34, 414
  trade, 85
  universities, 24
  see also Christianity; *and individual countries*
Europeanisation *see* Westernisation
Evangelicalism, 233, 396
evolutionism, 28, 30, 184–92, 202, 231–3, 236–7, 245, 286–9, 360, 366–7, 422
exceptionalism, 415, 421–31
executions, 29, 30, 143, 151, 169–70
Fahmi, 'Abd al-Aziz, 332
Fahmi, Murqus, 134
Faisal, King of Saudi Arabia, 340
family endowments, 146–7
family law, 147–8, 270–4; *see also* personal status law
family transmission, 51–2
Faraj, Jurjis, 233
Farid, Muhammad, 114
Farouk, King of Egypt, 297
fascism, xxvii, 309, 324–5, 344, 437
al-Fasi, 'Allal, 119, 264, 269, 271, 281, 282–3, 287, 346–7
Fatimid caliphate, 208
Fatimid movement, 45
fatwas, 68, 94, 113, 128, 149–51, 172, 173–4, 253, 260, 334, 338, 380, 387
Faysal I of Syria, 339, 341, 372
Fédération d'élus musulmans, 249
female genital mutilation, 380
feminism, 258, 260, 262, 264–6, 359–60, 378–9
Ferry, Jules, 32
feudal society, 14–15
Feuerbach, Ludwig, 27–8, 29, 366
Fez, 54, 91, 108, 345
Fī al-shi'r al-jāhilī (Taha Hussein), 293–4, 305–7, 321, 332
Fichte, Johann Gottlieb, 343, 344
al-Fikr, 392
al-Fikr al-Mu'āṣir, 354
fiqh see Islamic jurisprudence
financial instruments, 150
First Arab Conference, 166
First World War, 130, 137, 147, 148, 164, 168, 169–72, 173, 176, 179
flogging, 140, 274, 408
Flood, myth of, 219, 288, 291
food practices, 126, 149, 154, 354
Forbidden Trinity, The (Bou 'Ali Yassin), 369
forced marriage, 263, 271
fornication, 64, 65, 139, 263, 285
Fouad I of Egypt, 269, 297, 330, 333, 334–5
Foucault, Michel, xxxvi, xliii, xliv–xlv, 445
foundation myths, 80–1
France
  Action Française, 437
  and the Arab Revolt, 172
  and Catholicism, 8, 16, 31–2, 224, 311
  colonialism, 88, 93, 100, 109–12, 121, 144–5, 247, 261, 302–3, 347–9, 390
  constitution, 32
  critical study of religion, 26–7, 29, 31

France (*cont.*)
death penalty for blasphemy, 30
Freemasonry, 115
French Mandate in Syria and Lebanon, 170, 251, 262, 278, 302–3
Gallicanist Church, 17, 21, 31
Huguenot Calvinism, 16
invasion of Syria, 137
and the Kemalist Revolution, 173
laïcité, 8
law, 140–1, 144, 152, 272, 276, 277, 282
nationalism, 440
Paris Commune, 31–2, 192
political economy, 25
Popular Front, 249
Protestant Reformation, 15–16, 224
rate of religious belief, 8
religious festivals, 15
religious tolerance, 30
revocation of Edict of Nantes, 16
Revolution, xxvii, xxxvii, 21, 22, 29, 30–1, 33, 107, 114, 192, 426
royal absolutism, 15
St Bartholomew's Day massacre, 17
science, 21
secular education, 30, 31, 32
secular rituals, 30–1
secularisation, 3, 8, 30–1, 33
separation of Church and state, 8, 32
sociology, 26
state formation, 440
taxation of the Church, 17, 30
universities, 24
Vichy regime, 32
women's suffrage, 176
Franciscan Order, 14
Frankfurt School, xxviii, xxxvii
Fraternal Arab Union (Jam'iyyat al-Ikha' al-'Arabi), 165
Frédault, Félix, 224
Frederick II of Prussia, 114
Free Constitutionalist Part, 250
freedom of expression, 332, 333
freedom of religion, 103–4, 116
Freemasonry, 113–17, 163, 243, 413
French Revolution, xxvii, xxxvii, 21, 22, 29, 30–1, 33, 107, 114, 192, 426
Freud, Sigmund, 222, 290
Fuat, Beshir, 231
Fuda, Faraj, 397, 410
fundamentalism, xviii, xli, xliv, 79, 124, 390, 391, 395, 449
futuwwa, 44, 47
Galileo, 19–20, 21
Gallicanist Church, 17, 21, 31
Gallipoli, 173, 179
gambling, 151
Garibaldi, Giuseppe, 344
Geertz, Clifford, xxxi–xxxii
genders, social mixing of, 256, 259, 262, 266, 303, 379
genealogies, 76, 79–81, 161, 193
geometry, 24
Georg, Stefan, xxviii
Germany
atheism, 29
Catholicism, 17
critical study of religion, 27–8, 29, 369
independence of states recognised in Treaty of Westphalia, 17
law, 276
music, 24
Nazism, xxx, 309, 425, 427, 437
Protestant Reformation, 15–16
vitalism, 424, 425, 430
secularisation, 16, 29–30, 33
universities, 24
Gezira Club, 115–16
Ghali, Boutros, 115
Ghannouchi, Rashid, 379, 449
al-gharāniq see Satanic Verses
al-Gharra' group, 344
al-Ghazali, 63, 65, 69, 299, 355
al-Ghazali, Muhammad, 307, 408, 448
al-Ghifari, Abu Dharr, 403
al-Ghitani, Jamal, 360
Ghurab, Mahmud Abd al-Hamid, 408
Gibran, Khalil, 355, 423
globalisation, xxvii, 2–4, 375–7
Gobineau, Arthur de, xxvii
Goethe, Johann Wolfgang von, 114
Gökalp, Ziya, 168, 172–3, 177, 188
golden age, 46, 208–9, 210
Golwalkar, Madhav Sadashiv, xxvii, 324
Gospels *see* Bible
Great Syrian Revolt, 339
Greece, 154, 155, 159, 160, 162, 173, 177, 266
Greek myths, 291, 295, 357
Gregorian calendar, 127–8, 320
Gregory, VII, 12
Grotius, Hugo, 25
guardianship
of children, 272
male guardianship of women, 267, 268

Guha, Ranajit, xxiv
Gülhaneh Edict, 87, 93, 94

Habash, Georges, 398
Haddad, Grégoire, 373
Haddad, Taher, 248, 260–1, 262–4, 269–70
al-Hadira, 109
hadith, 57, 59, 60–2, 65–6, 81, 148, 215–16, 219, 293, 316, 323, 362–3
al-Hadīth, 264, 302, 303
hadith colleges, 56
hadith criticism, 215–16
Hadj, Messali, 249, 348
al-Hafez, Yassin, 374–5
Hafsid period, 55
Hajj, 65, 371
al-Hakim, Tawfiq, 258, 321, 338
Hama, 433
Hamid, 'Ala', 411
Hanafi, Hassan, 367, 428
Hanafi school, 52, 63, 66–9, 70, 74, 105, 106, 124, 142–3, 149, 270–1, 279
Hanbali school, 48–9, 66, 69, 72, 74, 148, 212, 218
Harb, Tala'at, 136
Hashemites, 171–2, 178
al-Ḥasnā al-Bayrūtiyya, 132
hats, 129, 256–7
al-Haurani, Ibrahim, 233
Hawi, Khalil, 357–8
al-Ḥayāt, 442
Ḥayāt Muḥammad (Haykal), 314–17
Haykal, Muhammad Hussein, 254, 287, 297, 299–300, 308, 310, 312–17, 321, 324, 338, 365, 431
Hedgewar, K. B., 324
Hegel, G. W. F., 26, 76, 426
Heidegger, Martin, xxviii
Henry VIII of England, 16, 17–18
Herder, Johann Gottfried, xxvi, xxvii, xxix, xxxvii, 192, 425
heresy, 14, 16–17, 18–19
heritage, 3, 5, 61, 361, 366, 381, 402–4, 419, 428–9, 435, 437
heroism, 310, 323, 377, 401
hierarchies
  of the cosmos, 41
  in education, 56–7
  of power, 40–2
  socio-economic, 266–7, 325–7
  in state administration, 196–7
  of the ulama, 53–4
higher education *see* universities
Hijaz, 92, 171–2, 174, 247
Hijra calendar, 127, 131, 320
al-Hilāl, 103, 132, 163, 257, 303
Hindu nationalism, xi–xii
historical contexts
  Christianity, 4, 9–34
  Islam, 4, 34–83, 292–7, 307
historism, xxvi–xxxv, xxxviii, xli–xlii, xlvi, 76–7, 404, 421 ,425
Hitler, Adolf, 344, 389
Ḥiwār, 399
Ḥizb al-Lamarkaziyya, 166
Ho Chi Minh, 344
Hobbes, Thomas, 26
Holy Roman Empire, 12, 17
homicide, 71
Homs, 434
honour, 258, 261, 272, 353, 379, 446
honour crimes, 272, 353
Hubaish, Youssef, 227
al-Hudaibi, Hasan, 280
Hugo, Victor, 234
human interest (*maṣālih mursala*), 25, 65, 69, 204, 212–15, 281, 283, 284
human rights, 320
humanism, 23, 103, 427
Hume, David, 185, 236, 237, 312
Ḥunafā, 234
Huntington, Samuel P., xxxiii, xxxiv
al-Husain ibn 'Ali, 47
al-Husri, Sati', 7, 168, 310–11, 340, 341, 342, 421, 422
Hussein, Prince of Egypt, 164
Hussein, Saddam, 390, 434
Hussein, Taha, 250, 252–5, 258, 266, 293–5, 297–9, 305–10, 313, 315, 319, 321–8, 330–3, 338, 360, 369, 383, 387, 396, 413, 422, 431
Hussein ibn 'Ali, Sharif of Mecca, 170–2, 174, 334, 339
hyper-nationalism, 422, 440, 442
hypnotism, 222, 312

Ibn 'Abidin, Muhammad Amin, 143
Ibn al-Farid, 355
Ibn al-Jawzi, Abu al-Faraj, 36–7, 43
Ibn al-Khatib, 79
Ibn al-Rawandi, 227
Ibn 'Arabi, 123, 213, 410
Ibn Badis, 'Abd al-Hamid, 111, 178–80, 211, 213, 247, 255, 261, 268–9, 347
Ibn bint al-A'azz, 53–4
Ibn Hajar, 216

Ibn Hanbal, Ahmad, 41, 44–5
Ibn Hazm, 213
Ibn Jamaʿa, Badr al-Din, 54
Ibn Khaldun, 3, 41, 42, 45, 49, 57–8, 60, 79, 106, 190, 216, 217, 228, 294, 403
Ibn Khallikan, 53
Ibn Qusayy, 45
Ibn Rushd, 24, 65, 403
Ibn Saʿd, 363
Ibn Saud, Abd al-Aziz, 174, 337, 340
Ibn Sina, 403
Ibn Taymiyya, 46, 47–8, 49–50
Ibrahim, Hafiz, 163
al-Ibrahimi, Bashir, 247–8
identitarianism, xxii, xxvi, xxx, xxxiii, xxxv, xlviii–xlix, 187–8, 347, 377, 429, 433, 435, 440
ideological authority, 77–8
idols, 186, 291, 292
Idris, Yusuf, 359
Idriss, Suhayl, 359
ijmāʿ see consensus
ijtihād, 67, 76, 124–5, 165, 204, 213, 281–2, 449
ikhwanisation, xii, xlvii
ʿilm see knowledge
ʿilmāniyya, 7, 307
imamate, 38, 42, 124, 335, 403
imperialism *see* colonialism
imprisonment, 140, 234
Independence Party, 346
independent legal judgment *see ijtihād*
India, xxii, xxvii, xxxvi, 37, 129, 174, 228, 247, 324, 344, 394
Indonesia, xiv
infanticide, 378
inheritance, 60, 70, 146–7, 171, 214, 260, 266, 267, 268, 270, 271, 274, 277, 380
Inönü, Ismet, 177
Inquisition (Catholic), 16
instinct, 187, 290, 308
intended meaning (jurisprudence), 220, 281–2
inter-confessional dialogue, 382
intercultural transfer, 205, 248
interest, 48, 67, 69, 151, 387; *see also* usury
International Declaration of Human Rights, 320
Iran
  Arab occupation, 75
  family transmission, 51–2
  Islamic Republican Party, 448
  Islamism, 422, 435
  nationalism, xxvii, 422
  proportion of Muslims, 74
  Revolution, xxv, xxvii, 428, 441, 445, 448
  shariʿa, 285
  violence of founding of state, 434, 448
  Zoroastrianism, 10
Iran–Iraq War, 390
Iranian Revolution, xxv, xxvii, 428, 441, 445, 448
Iraq
  Arab nationalism, 166–7, 339–41
  and the Arab Revolt, 172
  Baath Party, 271, 389, 390
  becomes independent Arab state, 170
  Christianity, 161
  Civil Code, 275, 279
  Communism, 370, 434
  consociational state, 404
  family transmission, 51
  French Mandate, 170
  Islamism, 434
  jurisprudence, 62, 74
  occupation of Kuwait, 390
  Ottoman territories, 92, 123
  polygamy, 272
  secular law, 270–1, 272, 275, 279
  Shiʾism, 434
  state paternalism, 353
  US invasion, 271
  women's conferences, 265
Ireland, 438
irenicism, 391, 413, 420, 431, 447
irrationalism, xxviii, 308–16, 322–5, 343, 344, 424–7, 430
al-Isfahani, Abu al Majd, 233
Ishaq, Adib, 107, 162, 238, 243
Ishmael, 216–17, 295, 305, 306, 361
Islam
  administrative structures, 54–6
  analysis of historical sources, 362–6
  and Arab nationalism, 164–5, 170–3, 251, 339–44, 390–1, 420–31, 435, 437–8, 441–2
  and calendars, 127–8, 320
  caliphate *see* caliphate
  Christian polemics against, 155–6
  claim for absence of clergy, 319, 399, 413–14
  common cultural features with Judaism and Christianity, 82–3
  confessional conflicts, 239, 336–7, 405
  critical study of, 287–307, 317–18, 362–9
  cultural homogenisation, 81–2

cultural similarities with Arab Christianity, 415–16
and Darwinism, 232–3
days of rest, 127–8
delegation of authority, 36–41
dialogue with Christianity, 382
discursive traditions, xliv, xlv–xlvii, xlviii, 58–9
as distinct from Muslims, 319
and dress, xii, xvii, 126, 127, 129–30, 396, 444
and education, 52, 54, 55, 56–9, 74, 98–100, 251–2, 329–32, 388–9
in Europe, xlviii, 16, 33
food practices, 126, 149
foundation myths, 80–1
and fundamentalism, xviii, xliv, 79, 124, 390, 391, 395, 449
golden age, 46, 208–9, 210
hierarchies of power, 36–42
historical contexts, 34–83, 292–7, 307
and historical destiny, xxx–xxxv, xli, 419, 420
and human rights, 320
as imaginary concept, 436–7
increased centrality of in Arab World, xii–xix, 353, 407–50
jurisprudence *see* Islamic jurisprudence
links with Judaism, 295
and literature, 226–7, 253, 254–5, 354–60, 381
marriage practices, 60, 126–7, 147–8, 176, 263, 267–73, 408
and the media, 388, 396, 408, 411–12, 444
and modernity, xli, 202–14, 319
and morality, 68, 188, 254, 318, 368
and myth, 361–2, 363, 365, 437
names of God, 292, 361–2
Paleo-Islam, 10, 35
Pan-Islamism, 170, 200, 338, 340, 392, 440
petro-Islam, xvii, 353, 383, 444
political use of, 250, 251, 301, 302, 326, 336–7, 352, 372
Protestantisation of, xliii–xliv, 319
and reactionism, 121–5, 200
and reason, 186, 201–3, 215–16, 218–25, 238–40, 300, 319, 368–9
referenced in literature, 226–7
reformism *see* Islamic reformism
relationship to law, 67–8, 270–86, 306–7
relationship to the state, 42, 48–9, 52, 94–5, 240–3, 302, 329–40, 353, 384–406, 407–15, 440–1
religious festivals, 127
religious infrastructure, xvii–xviii, 4, 50–6
resistance to secularisation, 126–30, 137–9, 148–9, 156–7, 181, 253–61, 298–308, 352, 383
"return of religion" theories, xvi–xviii, xxvi–xxvii, xxxix, 10, 431, 435, 436–7
and science, 104–5, 199, 202–3, 218–25, 229, 235–6, 239, 240, 298–300, 304, 311–17, 368, 383, 396
shari'a *see* shari'a
and social change, 126–37, 251–4
and social structure, xlv–xlvi, xlix, 41–2, 436
status of women, 33, 126–7, 131–7, 257–70, 320, 369, 378–80
super-Muslims, xvi, xl, xlvi
and the three-stage theory of history, 186, 287
ulama *see* ulama
see also hadith; Islamism; Qur'an; religion; Salafism; Shi'ism; Sufism; Sunni Islam; Wahhabism
Islamic finance, 150, 444
Islamic jurisprudence (*fiqh*)
abrogation, 13, 65, 67
analogy, 13, 62–5, 78, 213
application of discretion and preference, 68–70, 139, 142, 214, 283
and the caliphate, 296
comparability with Western law, 13, 25
distinction between legal and religious liability, 67–8
and human interest, 25, 65, 69, 204, 212–15, 281, 283, 284
ijtihād, 67, 76, 124–5, 165, 213, 281–2
indices of correlation, 63–5, 78
and Islamic reformism, 149–52, 209–14, 319
legal causes, 63–4, 66
legal contradictions, 67, 201
and natural law, 126, 210–11, 214, 277, 283
and origins, 62–5, 75, 79
and the power of the caliphate, 43, 46
Principles of, 59, 62, 66, 68–9, 74, 75, 142, 151, 211, 277, 283, 330
and reactionism, 123–5
schools of, 42, 61, 66, 67, 72, 73–4, 91, 209, 213, 330
and secular law, 139, 141–3, 145–7, 149–52, 270–86, 319
talfiq, 147–8, 213
teaching of, 330
see also shari'a

Islamic League, 251, 335, 340
Islamic reformism
  and abandonment of tradition, xlvii–xlviii, 124–5, 213
  attitude to mass population, 326
  and constitutionalism, 206, 207–9, 248
  and Darwinism, 232–3, 235, 237
  decline of, 297–8, 308, 318–20
  division into political and educational tendencies, 200–1, 248
  division into secular and religious tendencies, 197–8, 203, 305
  and hadith criticism, 215–16
  and heritage, 402–3
  and *ijtihād*, 124–5, 204, 213, 281–2
  influence of European ideas, 192, 205–6, 223–4, 245–6, 286–90, 309
  and Islamic jurisprudence, 149–52, 209–14, 319
  in the Maghreb, 247–8
  and modernity, 5, 175, 198, 202–3, 204–14, 319
  and nationalism, 248
  opposition from religious reactionaries, 200
  opposition to Abdülhamid, 165
  and origins, 193–5
  and the Qur'an, 189–90, 206–7, 208–9, 216–23, 239, 281–2, 318, 383
  and para-nationalism, 199–200
  and reason, 201–3, 215–16, 218–25, 238–40
  repudiation of modern education, 193, 194, 199
  and science, 104–5, 199, 202–3, 218–25, 239, 240, 383
  and secular law, 280–6
  and secularism, 225–43
  and shari'a, 207, 210, 211–14, 248, 280–6
  and social Darwinism, 189–92
  and socialism, 354
  and the status of women, 134, 259–60, 262–3, 268, 380
  and the *Tanzimat* state, 196–9, 225, 226, 241–3
  and universalism, 183
  and utilitarianism, 192, 195, 201, 203, 205, 207, 225
Islamic Republican Party, 448
Islamic Socialist Front, 442
Islamic societies, xxxi, 412, 430, 432–3
Islamisation, xvii–xviii, xl, xlix, 391, 405, 444
Islamism
  and anti-Communism, xiv–xv, xxvii, 324, 382–3, 394, 443
  and anti-modernism, xxii–xxiii
  and Arab nationalism, 390–1, 420–31, 435, 437–8, 441–2
  ascendancy of in Arab World, xii–xv, xvii, xxi–xxiii, 376–7, 407–50
  and the Cold War, xiv–xv, xxvii, 382–3, 392, 394
  concessions made to, 392, 399–400, 413, 418–20, 444, 447
  constructed as solution, xiii, 417–18
  and cultural hegemony, 392
  discourses internalised by adversaries, xxi, 412, 419
  and exceptionalism, 421–31
  and heritage, 404, 419
  infiltration of the state, 407–12
  interpretation of the Qur'an, 34–5
  interpretation of shari'a, 124, 284–6
  and the media, 408, 411–12, 444
  and moralism, 255, 391, 410
  and nationalism, 344–7, 412–13, 440, 447
  and oil revenues, 395
  in opposition to secularism, xiv–xv, xxx
  and para-nationalism, 200, 440
  political parties, xvii, xxii, 184–5, 411, 431
  and polygamy, 269
  and religious symbolism, 401
  resistance to legal reform, 279–80
  Sadat's support for, 387, 434, 443–4
  and the status of women, 261, 263, 264, 269, 379
  and violence, 336, 344–5, 407, 410, 427, 434–5, 448
Islams and Modernities (al-Azmeh), xxxiv
Isma'il Pasha, 87, 95, 98, 101, 114, 119, 141
Isma'iliyya, 156
Israel, 372, 382, 394
Istanbul, 12, 77, 86–90, 93, 95, 98–9, 103–4, 106, 112, 122, 125, 129, 131, 134, 153, 165–7, 173, 191, 196, 198, 229, 339; *see also* Constantinople
istiḥsān see legal preference
Italy, xiv, 17, 23–4, 173, 443, 440
Izmir, 173, 198

Jabbur, Jibra'il, 304
al-Jabiri, Ihsan, 251, 303
al-Jabiri, Muhammad 'Abid, 391, 402, 403
al-Jabiri, Sa'adallah, 251
Ja'fari school, 74, 148, 271

Jahiliyya, 292
al-Jami'a, 239
al-Jam'iyya al-Qaḥṭāniyya, 166
Jam'iyyat al-Baṣra al-Iṣlāḥiyya, 166
Jam'iyyat al-Ikha' al-'Arabi, 165
Jam'iyyat al-Iṣlaḥ, 166
Jam'iyyat al-Nahḍa al-'Arabiyya, 165
Jansenism, 21
Japan, xliv, 103, 199
al-Jawā'ib, 134, 142
Jawhari, Shaykh Tantawi, 223, 233
Jawish, Abd al-Aziz, 213, 215
al-Jaza'iri, Tahir, 198
Jesuit Order, 19–20, 21, 30, 252
Jesus, 9, 27, 31, 45, 291, 355–6, 368
jihad, xii, 124, 172, 190, 448
jinn, 43, 218, 318, 361, 388
al-Jisr, Basim, 384
al-Jisr, Shaykh Husayn, 105, 123, 222, 223, 233, 311
al-Jizawi, Abu'l Fadl, 334
jizya, 159, 409
Jordan, 174, 270–1, 405, 442
Journal des Débats, 229–30
journals, 103, 105, 107, 109, 132, 155, 163, 182, 189, 200–1, 235, 297, 302–4, 324, 353–4, 392; *see also* magazines; newspapers; *and individual journals*
Jubran, Jubran Khalil, 227
Judaism
  assimilation in colonial Algeria, 110
  common cultural features with Islam and Christianity, 82–3
  conspiracy theories about, 413
  food practices, 126
  links with Islam, 295
  myth of Ishmael, 216–17, 295
  and the Ottoman *millet* system, 154, 155
  reform Judaism, xliv
  religious tolerance for in Europe, 30, 155
  and social solidarity, 11
  and the three-stage theory of history, 186
  see also Torah
jurisprudence
  comparative, 275–7, 279
  European, 13–14, 25
  Islamic *see* Islamic jurisprudence
  see also law; shari'a
Justice and Development party, xxii

Kaaba, 80, 295, 362
Kamil, Mustafa, 115, 163, 164
Kant, Immanuel, 439
Karama, Butrus, 226–7
Kashf al-qinā' 'an i'tiqād ṭawā'if al-ibtidā' (Sultan 'Abd al-Hafiz), 88
al-Kawakibi, 'Abd al-Rahman, 132, 164, 170, 174, 208
al-Kayyali, Sami, 303
Kemal, Mustafa, 122, 173–4, 177–80, 255–6, 389
Kemal, Namik, 115, 188, 192, 198–9, 205, 208, 211, 231
Kemalist revolution, 5, 122, 169, 173–4, 178, 241, 242, 255–6
Khalafallah, Muhammad Ahmad, 318, 409, 432
Khaldouniyya association, 109, 202
Khalid, Khalid Muhammad, 317–18, 333, 378
Khalid b. al-Walid, 256
al-Khalidi, Ruhi, 234
Khan, Sir Sayyid Ahmad, 217
Kheireddine Pasha, 95, 105, 109
Khemiri, Taher, 290
Khodr, Georges, 365
Khomeinism, 188, 285
al-Khuli, Lutfi, 409, 431–2
Khouri, Ra'if, 301, 304
Khurasan, 51–2, 70, 74
al-Khuri, Faris, 344
Kishk, Muhammad Jalal, 442
Kitchener, Herbert, Lord, 115, 170
Klages, Ludwig, xxviii
knowledge
  'ilm, 52–3, 58, 80–1
  religious knowledge, 51–3, 57–9, 80–1, 297–9
  scientific knowledge, 20, 24, 28, 221, 298–300
  secular knowledge, 99–107, 217–25, 286–329
  transmission of, 51–3, 57–9
  see also education
al-Kulliya, 264
Kurd Ali, Muhammad, 197, 264, 300, 309, 345
kuttāb schools, 100, 251–2
Kuwait, 275, 390, 395

labour, 1, 98, 127–8, 158, 266–7, 270, 379–80, 389
laïcité, 8
laissez-faire economics, 25
Lamarck, Jean-Baptiste, 188
Lammenais, Hugues Felicité Robert de, 224

land ownership, 96, 140, 146–7, 175, 278
language schools, 97, 98, 100
Laplace, Pierre Simon, 22
Laroui, ʿAbdallah, 184, 346, 375–6, 391, 416–17
Latin alphabet, 176–7, 255, 256
law
and the caliphate, 38, 42–3
canon law, 13–14, 154, 373
codification of, 106, 139–43, 147–8, 270–86
commercial law, 69–71, 106, 139–44, 142–3, 144, 149–51
comparative law, 275–7, 279
contract law, 67, 149–50, 278
courts *see* courts
English law, 144, 277
family law, 147–8, 270–4
French law, 140–1, 144, 152, 272, 276, 277, 282
German law, 276
inheritance law, 60, 70, 146–7, 214, 260, 266, 267, 268, 270, 271, 274, 277, 380
jurisprudence *see* Islamic jurisprudence; jurisprudence
reform of, 5, 6, 87, 90, 91, 94, 138–52, 156–7, 173, 176, 181, 269–86
natural law, 21, 25, 65, 106, 126, 210–11, 214, 277, 283
personal status law, 73, 144, 145–8, 259, 266–7, 269–74, 302, 385, 387, 409
and punishment *see* punishments
relationship to religion, 11–14, 25, 30, 67–8, 270–86, 299, 306–7
Roman law, 11, 12, 25
secular law, 14, 25, 30, 71–3, 91, 94, 138–48, 176, 270–86, 302, 319, 347, 384, 385
shariʿa *see* shariʿa
and the state, 14, 25, 30, 71–3, 91, 94, 138–48, 175, 176, 270–86
Turkish law, 175, 176
Lawrence, T. E. (Lawrence of Arabia), 172
Le Bon, Gustave, xxvii, 310–11, 325
League of Nations, 163
Lebanon
atheism, 304
Christianity, 127, 155, 160–1, 162, 227, 242, 251, 343, 373
civil wars, 160, 161, 373, 425
collapse of Shihab emirate, 161
Communism, 370
connection between religion and politics, 371–2
consociational state, 404–5
French Mandate, 251
intellectual exiles in, 372, 384
Islamo-Christian dialogue, 382
marriage practices, 127
missionary schools, 101
Mutasarrifiya system, 161
nationalism, 373, 423
Phalange party, 398
protest against literature, 381, 382
publishing sector, 372
sectarianism, 371, 382
secular education, 103–4
secular law, 272
separatism, 101, 160–1
status of women, 272
universities, 398
women's conferences, 265
left-wing thought, xxiii, 29, 192, 336, 364–6, 371, 373–4, 397–403, 412, 428, 431–2, 441; *see also* Marxism; socialism
legal capacity, 70, 143, 279
legal causes, 63–4, 66
legal contradictions, 67, 201
legal preference (*istiḥsān*), 69–70, 214
legal reform, 5, 6, 87, 90, 91, 94, 138–52, 156–7, 173, 176, 181, 269–86
legal witness, 262, 269, 270, 274
legitmacy, xiii, 34–5, 395
Leibniz, Gottfried, 22
Leo II, 12
Liberal Constitutionalist Party, 302, 331, 332, 333, 334–5, 338
Liberal Nationalist Party, 297
liberalism, xxiii, xxvii, 5, 32, 108–11, 287, 297–8, 324–8, 336–9, 344–7, 352, 376, 412–13, 418–21, 427, 435, 441
lineages *see* genealogies; heritage; origins
literacy, 97, 112, 326
literal interpretations (of scripture), 201, 207, 218–20
Literary Club (al-Muntadā al-Adabī), 166
literary salons, 234
literature
Arabic literature, 81–2, 233, 254–5, 291–2, 294, 355–60, 410
avant-garde literature, 290, 381, 399
censorship and confiscations, 381, 410–11
and Darwinism, 233
depictions of women, 359–60
drama, 130, 197, 255

and educational curricula, 253
emigré Arabic poets, 254, 355
Egyptian literature, 337–8, 359, 387, 411
European literature, 23–4, 128, 253
as indicator of development, 375
and moralism, 197, 255
novels, 24, 128, 197, 255, 261, 303, 359–60, 381, 410, 411
and origins, 79
and Pharaonism, 337
Persian literature, 82
pre-Islamic poetry, 57, 253, 305
and religion, 23–4, 226–7, 253, 254–5, 354–60, 381
and religious symbolism, 226–7, 354–60
and secularism, 5, 226–8, 233, 303, 354–60, 381
short stories, 259, 381
liturgical music, 24
Llosa, Mario Vargas, 410
Locke, John, 19, 25, 26, 205
Louis XI of France, 86
Luther, Martin, 15–16, 195, 201, 204
Luxemburg, Rosa, 369
Lyautey, Hubert, 247

al-Ma'arri, 82, 227, 228, 295
madaniyya, 7, 307
madrasas, 52, 53, 56–9, 74, 388
magazines, 103, 107, 132; *see also* journals; newspapers
al-Maghribi, Shaykh Abd al-Qadir, 261–2
magic, 20–1, 43, 45, 48, 57, 120
Mahdi, 89
Maher, Ahmad, 280
Mahfouz, Naguib, 360, 387, 410
Mahmoud, Mustafa, 380
Mahmoud, Saba, xliii, xlvi–xlviii
Mahmud II, 94, 106
Maistre, Joseph de, xxvii, xxxvii
al-Majalla al-jadīda, 303
Makhzen, 88, 145, 347, 416–17
Malaysia, xiv
Malebranche, Nicolas, 312
Maleschott, Jacob, 29, 235
Maliki school, 51, 66, 68, 74, 105, 268, 271, 416
Mamluk period, 37–8, 47, 53, 55–6, 70
al-Ma'mun, 45, 48
al-Manār, 212, 247, 248
al-Maraghi, Shaykh Muhammad Mustafa, 316, 330
market inspection (*hisba*), 72, 74
market inspector (*muḥtasib*), 53, 72, 74
Maronite Christianity, 82, 127, 154, 155, 161, 162, 227, 233, 242, 251, 253, 373
Marrash, Francis, 107, 162, 187, 223, 224, 311
Marrash, Maryana, 234
marriage, 13, 31, 60, 126–7, 147–8, 154, 176, 216, 256, 260, 263, 267–73, 373, 380, 408; *see also* adultery; divorce; forced marriage; polygamy
marriage age, 256, 272
Marx, Karl, xxxix, 26, 28, 29, 201, 369
Marxism, xxxvii, 32, 303–4, 324, 352, 366–7, 370–2, 374, 376, 382, 402–3, 422, 427, 431, 442, 445; *see also* left-wing thought; socialism
Mashaqa, Mikhail, 234
mass media, 325, 388, 396, 408, 411–12, 443–4
mass population, 19, 112, 231, 325–7, 335–6, 431
materialism, 28–9, 189, 227, 231–7, 241, 287–8, 298–9, 308–9, 311, 324–5, 368, 382, 401, 402
Maturidi theology, 209
Mauss, Marcel, xxiii
Mawāqif, 354
al-Mawardi, Abu al-Hasan 'Ali ibn Muhammad, 37, 38, 43, 47–8, 67
Maysalun, Battle of, 137
mazālim courts, 71, 72, 74
Mazhar, Isma'il, 262, 270, 286–9, 291–3, 302, 303, 311, 322, 324, 335, 338
Mead, Margaret, xxix
Mecca, 80, 81, 168, 170–2, 174, 294, 295
Mecelle, 106, 142–3, 149, 278, 279
media *see* journals; mass media; newspapers; radio; social media; television
medical dissection, 128
medical schools, 97
Medina, 10, 55, 62, 74, 294
Mehmet, Çelebi, 86
Merinid period, 55
Mesopotamia, 154
Michelson–Morley experiment, 313
Midhat Paşa, 115, 122, 126, 162
military, 38, 86, 87, 159, 168, 177, 245
military power, 12–13, 382
military schools, 98, 106, 122
millet system, 153–60, 169, 178
Min hunā nabdā' (Khalid), 317–18, 333
Mina, Hanna, 359
al-Minyawi, Muhammad Faraj, 334

miracles, 22, 44–5, 221–2, 236, 311, 312, 315
Miṣr, 161
al-Misri, Shafiq Mansur, 102
missionary schools, 100–2, 131, 252
modernisation, xxxiii, 1–2, 73, 92, 93, 249, 250, 326, 346
Montesquieu, 114, 205
Monteverdi, Claudio, 24
moralism, 190, 197, 255, 391, 410, 442, 444
morality, xlvii, 17, 27, 34, 68, 135, 188, 199, 212, 237, 246–7, 254, 263, 292, 300–1, 308–9, 318, 368
Morocco
 Alaoui sultanate, 86
 anthropological study of, 367
 and the Arab Revolt, 172
 attempted constitution, 108
 Berbers, 145, 345, 347
 Egyptianisation, 391
 French colonisation, 145, 247, 347
 independence, 347
 Independence Party, 346
 Islamic reformism, 248, 391, 416
 Islamism, 345–7, 392
 Justice and Development party, xxii
 legal reform, 145
 Makhzen, 88, 145, 347, 416–17
 modernisation, 346
 Mudawanna, 271, 281
 National Action Bloc, 345
 National Party for the Achievement of Reform, 345
 nationalism, 345–7
 paganism, 416
 private schools, 345
 religious education, 389
 religious history, 416–17
 Salafism, 88, 248, 345, 416–17
 secular law, 145, 271, 281, 282–3, 347
 shariʿa, 347
 state reforms, 88, 108
 universities, 386
Morsi, Muhammad, xii
Mount Lebanon, 73, 87, 134, 154, 161, 162, 365
Movement for the Triumph of Democratic Liberties, 348
al-Muʾayyad, 115, 163, 269
Mubarak, Hosni, 408
Mughayzel, Joseph, 383
Muhammad, Prophet, 45–7, 61, 127, 215–16, 218, 222, 293, 314–16, 323–4, 342–4, 355–6, 363–4, 389
Muhammad V, Sultan of Morocco, 346
Muhammad Ali Pasha, 87, 92, 93, 95, 98, 131–2, 140, 182, 260
Muhammad b. Ahmad, 223
Muhammad b. al Hanafiyya, 364
Muhammad Bay, 87, 93, 144
Muhammad Sadiq Bay, 93
Muhammad Qadri Pasha, 143
Muhammadan Union party, 125
multiculturalism, xli–xlii, 157, 180
multiplicationism (conceptual), xxxiii–xxxvii
al-Munajjid, Salah al-Din, 442, 443
municipal administration, 72–3
al-Muntadā al-Adabī, 166
Müntzer, Thomas, 16, 365
al-Muqaṭṭam, 165, 264
al-Muqtaṭaf, 103, 105, 132, 165, 200, 233, 264, 303, 304
Muruwwa, Hussein, 402
Musa, Salama, 234–5, 257, 268, 288–9, 291, 303, 320–1, 326, 330, 337
music, 24, 119, 410
Muslim Brotherhood, xii, xvii, xxvii, 197, 260, 280, 284, 307, 317, 336, 345, 386–7, 391, 408, 411, 422, 434, 442–3, 448, 449
Muslim ibn al-Hajjaj, 46, 60
Mussolini, Benito, 344
al-Mustaqbal, 235
Mutasarrifiya system, 161
al-Muʿtasim, 48
Muʿtazilism, 48–9, 64, 65, 187, 202, 210–22, 319, 381, 402, 410
Müteferrika, Ibrahim, 86
al-Mutiʿ, Caliph, 47
Mutran, Khalil, 163, 264, 342
mysticism, 52, 82, 342, 358–9, 403, 423
myth, 27–8, 80–1, 154, 177, 291–2, 295, 314–15, 318, 357, 361–2, 363, 365, 368, 382, 437
Mzali, Muhammad, 392

al-Nabulsi, ʿAbd al-Ghani, 123
al-Nadim, ʿAbdallah, 107, 163
Nafir Suriyya, 242
nahḍa, 184–8, 192–6
Nahda party, xxii, 184–5
Najd, 89, 152
nakba, 372
naming (in history), 81, 419, 430–1, 432
Napoleon, 22, 31, 92, 147, 153, 389
Napoleon III, 164
Naploeonic wars, 22

narcissism, 374, 377, 430
naṣīḥa (advice) texts, xlvii
al-Nasir li-Din Allah, 44
Nasr, Syed Hossein, 399
Nassar, Nassif, 373–4
Nasser, Gamal Abdel, 266, 284, 339, 381, 386–7, 388, 389, 390, 401, 420, 432, 442
National Action Bloc, 345
National Liberation Front (FLN), 249, 348–9, 390–1
National Party for the Achievement of Reform, 345
nationalism
  Algerian nationalism, 111, 347–9, 390–1
  and anti-modernism, xxiii
  Arab nationalism, xxvii, 3, 162–7, 169–73, 174, 190, 200, 251, 311, 339–44, 382–3, 390–1, 398, 415, 420–31, 435, 437–8, 441–2
  Armenian nationalism, 160, 168
  Balkan nationalisms, 177
  Buddhist nationalism, xi–xii
  and Christianity, 160–2
  cultural nationalism, xli, 188
  Egyptian nationalism, 90, 92, 120, 137, 163–4, 336–9, 383, 423
  French nationalism, 440
  Greek nationalism, 159, 160
  Hindu nationalism, xi–xii
  hyper-nationalism, 422, 440, 442
  Indian nationalism, 394
  Iranian nationalism, xxvii, 422
  Irish nationalism, 438
  and Islamic reformism, 248
  and Islamism, 344–7, 412–13, 440, 447
  Italian nationalism, 440
  Lebanese nationalism, 373, 423
  Moroccan nationalism, 345–7
  Ottoman nationalism, 90, 166, 168, 198–9
  para-nationalism, 188, 191, 199–200, 340, 440
  and populism, 439, 441
  reprobation of liberalism, 397–8
  and Salafism, 345–7
  and secularisation, 249, 251, 352–3, 371
  Syrian nationalism, 162, 251, 255, 345, 373, 383, 423
  Tunisian nationalism, 110, 111, 248–9, 349, 371
  Turkish nationalism, xxvii, 166, 167–9, 173, 188, 190, 200, 341
nativism, xi–xii, xxiii, xxix, xxxv, xlii, xlv, 172, 180, 191, 440, 442
natural law, 21, 25, 65, 106, 126, 214, 277, 283
natural religion, 22, 28–9, 114, 116, 201, 205
natural selection, 188–9
nature, laws of, 26, 210–11, 289–90, 311–13
Nazism, xxx, 309, 425, 427, 437
necrophilia, 285
'neo-Baath' coup, 385, 400
Neo-Destour Party, 248, 442
neo-liberalism, xxi, 353, 370, 429, 444
Netherlands, 9, 16, 17, 85, 100, 409
New Testament *see* Bible
New Zealand, xlv
newspapers, 103, 107, 109, 115, 134, 161–3, 165, 193, 197, 200–1, 297, 302, 324, 351; *see also* journals; magazines
Newton, Isaac, 19, 20–2, 116
Nietzsche, Friedrich, xxviii, 343, 344
Night of Destiny (*laylat al-qadr*), 127, 393
Nimr, Faris, 233
9/11 attacks, xxiii
Nishapur, 51–2
Noah, 219
non-governmental organisations (NGOs), 420
nostalgia, xxix, xxxi, xxxviii, 3, 204, 404
novels, 24, 128, 197, 255, 261, 303, 359–60, 381, 410, 411
al-Nu'aimi, Slawa, 360
Nu'ayma, Mikha'il, 310
al-Numeiri, Ja'afar, 448–9
al-Nuqrashi, Mahmoud Fahmy, 280
Nūr al-islām, 302

obscurantism, xxiii, xlvii, xlviii, 328, 343
occultism, 117, 311–12
office-holders, 53–5, 106, 307
oil revenues, 395; *see also* petro-Islam
Old Testament *see* Bible
On Heroes, Hero Worship and the Heroic in History (Carlyle), 323
One Thousand and One Nights, 44, 360
oral tradition, 56, 57
Ordinances of Government (al-Mawardi), 47
organismic metaphors, xxv, xxxi, xxxiii, xlvii, 191–2, 424–5, 441
Orientalism, 77, 309–10, 324, 362
origins, xv, xxxii–xxxiv, xlv, 10, 28, 35, 56, 58–9, 62–5, 75, 78–81, 193–5, 202, 366, 420, 429, 435, 446–7
Orthodox Christianity, 104, 154, 155, 159, 162, 373

Ottoman conquest, 12
Ottoman Penal Law, 139, 141
Ottoman Nationality Law, 140
Ottoman period, 5, 47, 53, 54, 55–6, 70
Ottoman state
  administrative structures, 72–3, 86–96, 121, 153–60, 167–8, 197–8
  Arab nationalism, 162–7, 169–73, 415
  Arab Revolt, 168, 170, 171–3, 178
  Capitulations, 86, 87, 140–1, 156, 157, 169
  Christianity, 154, 155–60, 162, 169, 198
  citizenship, 90, 96, 140, 153, 157, 160, 162, 167, 169, 241
  Committee for Union and Progress, 125, 162, 163, 165–7, 169, 170, 171, 177–8, 241
  communications, 73, 199
  constitution, 95–6, 115, 121, 122, 125–6, 153, 162, 208
  Constitutional Revolution, 125, 239
  craft guilds, 90, 91, 153–4, 155
  cultural reform, 89–90
  dress, 129, 154, 176, 196
  economy, 158, 169, 199
  educational book publishing, 122
  educational reform, 87, 90, 97–8, 104, 121, 156, 167–8, 173, 329
  ethnic cleansing, 169
  ethnic groups, 90–1, 153–5, 158, 168–9, 198
  European pressure exerted upon, 86, 87, 155, 156–60, 168
  executions of Arab nationalists, 169–70
  fall of empire, 173
  family endowments, 146
  financial calendar, 127
  Freemasonry, 113–15
  Islamic reformism, 196–204, 241
  Judaism, 154, 155
  Kemalist Revolution, 5, 122, 169, 173–4, 178, 241, 242, 255–6
  labour market, 158
  Law of Family Rights, 147–8
  legal reform, 87, 90, 91, 94, 138–40, 142–3, 144–8, 156, 173
  Mecelle, 106, 142–3, 149, 278, 279
  military, 86, 159
  millet system, 153–60, 169, 178
  Muhammadan Union party, 125
  municipal administration, 72–3
  nationalism, 90, 166, 168, 198–9
  Nationality Law, 140
  parliament, 95
  Penal Law, 139, 141
  political reform, 89–90, 94–6
  primary education, 97
  printing, 128
  Public Debt Administration, 122
  reliance on Ash'ari theology, 49
  religious reactionism, 121–5, 200
  resistance to colonialism, 86
  secular courts, 71, 72, 74, 139–40
  secular education, 97–8, 104
  secular intellectuals, 93, 96, 106, 112, 246
  secular law, 71–3, 91, 94, 138–40, 142–3, 144–8
  separatism, 122, 160–2, 168
  şeyhulislam, 55, 71–3, 75, 94, 96, 104, 126, 136, 155, 173, 198, 229, 256
  shari'a, 74–5, 124, 125, 173
  social class, 112
  state reforms, 86–97, 121–3, 153–60, 162, 167–8, 172–3, 181–2, 196–9, 226, 241–3, 329
  status of women, 131
  Tanzimat, 87–94, 96–7, 106, 108, 112, 122, 138–9, 153, 157, 160, 162, 167, 173, 182, 192, 196–9, 203–4, 207, 225, 226, 241–3, 246–7, 327, 329, 351
  teacher training, 98
  trade, 158, 169, 198
  Turkish nationalism, 166, 167–9, 173
  universities, 98, 104
  Westernisation, 112, 199
  Young Ottoman movement, 115, 183, 188, 197–200, 208, 240, 425

paganism, 10–11, 12, 155, 298, 355, 357–8, 416
Pakistan, 394, 448
Paleo-Islam, 10, 35
Palestine, 265, 372
Pan-Arabism, 338, 340, 385, 390, 420, 428, 434, 435, 442–3; *see also* Arab nationalism
Pan-Islamism, 170, 200, 338, 340, 392, 440
Papacy, 10, 13, 17, 19–20, 30, 31–2, 104, 117; *see also individual popes*
Paradise, 222, 269, 411
paramilitary organisations, 336
para-nationalism, 188, 191, 199–200, 340, 440
Paris, 24, 30–2, 155, 166, 191, 196, 224
Paris Commune, 31–2, 192
Paris Peace Conference, 265

parody, 81–2, 227, 239, 411
Party for Decentralisation (Ḥizb al-Lamarkaziyya), 166
Pascal, Blaise, 21
paternalism, 297, 352, 353
patriarchy, 257–8, 266, 267, 270, 367, 374, 377, 378
Peace of Augsburg, 15
peasant revolt, 16
pedagogical techniques, 57–9
Persian literature, 82
personal appearance, xii, xvii, 129–30, 131, 354; *see also* dress
personal conduct, 16, 17, 46
personal hygiene, 131
personal status law, 73, 144, 145–8, 259, 266–7, 269–74, 302, 385, 387, 409
perspective, 24
pessimism, xxviii, xxix, xlvi
petro-Islam, xvii, 353, 383, 444; *see also* oil revenues
Phalange party, 398
Pharaonism, 337–8
Philby, Harry St. John (Philby of Arabia), 174
philology, 27, 34, 409, 410
photography, 152
pilgrimage, 65, 80, 81, 371, 394
Pius IX, xxvii, 22, 32
poetry *see* literature
Poland, xiv, 443
political authority, 12, 13, 23, 30, 36–42, 50, 81, 94, 307
political economy, 25–6
political participation, 89, 107, 112, 114
political parties, xvii, xxii, 1, 184–5, 297, 326, 333, 352, 444, 448
political power, 12–13, 18, 36–42, 123
political reform, 89–90, 94–6, 157
political thought, 5, 90, 187–93, 203
polygamy, 126–7, 147–8, 176, 263, 269, 271, 272, 282, 408
Ponsot, Henri, 264
Popular Front, 249
populism, xxi, xxiii, 411, 420, 431–2, 437, 439, 441, 450
positivism, xxvi, 29, 31, 92–3, 116, 182, 184–6, 201, 203, 223, 235, 286, 290, 311, 360, 366–7, 422–3, 425
post-Christianity, xxxvii–xxxviii, xl
post-colonialism, xviii, xxii, xxiii–xxv, xxx, xxxvi–xxxvii, xli–xlix, 327, 375, 377, 430
postmodernism, xxii, xxiii–xxiv, xliv–xlv, 377, 430
power
  and the caliphate, 36–44, 307, 335
  and the Church, 12–13
  delegation of, 36–41
  hierarchies of, 40–2
  military power, 12–13, 382
  political power, 12–13, 18, 36–42, 123
  see also authority
pre-Islamic poetry, 57, 253, 305
prelapsarian discourses, xxviii, xxix, xxxii, xxxviii, 437, 440
Presbyterianism, 16
primary education, 97, 98, 100, 109, 251–2, 332
printing, 128
private schools, 98, 345
probability, 289, 290
production, 1, 28, 181, 266–7
progress, xl, 103, 107, 108, 114, 171, 184–7, 199, 299, 327–8, 360, 371, 374–7, 422, 427
proletariat, 33, 376; *see also* mass population; social class
propaganda, 45, 92, 156, 160, 171, 176, 216, 333, 407–8, 415
property rights, 96, 140, 146–7, 278
proportional representation, 385
Protestantism, xliv, 8, 14–19, 30, 100–1, 155, 156, 204, 206, 216, 224, 227, 234, 373
psychoanalysis, xxiv, 290, 377
public baths, 130–1
public humiliation, 140
public interest *see* human interest
punishments, 29, 30, 65, 71, 88, 124, 139–40, 143, 213–14, 272, 274, 282, 284–5, 317, 320, 380, 408, 448–9

al-Qabbani, Abu Khalil, 130
al-Qadir Billah, 48–9
al-Qaeda, 427
al-Qaradawi, Yusuf, 449
al-Qarawiyyin Mosque, 88, 386
Qarawiyyin University, 386
al-Qasimi, Jamal al-Din, 198, 213, 223
al-Qawuqji, Fawzi, 338
al-Qimni, Sayyid, 364, 381
qiyās see analogy
Qom, 191
Quesnay, François, 25
Qur'an
  and Arab nationalism, 421
  and authority, 57
  authorship, 324

Qur'an (*cont.*)
and the biography of Muhammad, 315–16
collection into book form, 293, 363
on concubinage, 268
creation in time, 48
critical study of, 293–5, 306, 318, 362–3, 365, 409
as forerunner of materialism, 401
historic interpretation, xlvii, 293–5, 362–3
inimitability of, 292, 381
and intended meaning, 220, 281–2
and Islamic reformism, 189–90, 206–7, 208–9, 216–23, 239, 281–2, 318, 383
Islamist interpretations, 34–5
literal interpretations, 201, 207, 218–20
magical uses of, 120
memorisation and recitation of, 97
and miracles, 45
and morality, 318
mysterious letters, 294, 396
and myth, 361–2, 363
notion of religion, xliv, xlviii
parallels with Old Testament, 292
parodies of, 82, 239, 411
prohibition on printing of, 128
on punishment of wives, 268
reconceived as guidance text, 150, 318
referenced in literature, 226–7
scientific interpretations, 218–23
as source of shari'a, 60, 62, 65, 279–80
traditional interpretations, 315–16, 363
translation into Turkish, 176, 179–80
on veiling of women, 264
Quraysh, 171, 172, 295, 306, 364
Qutb, Sayyid, 214, 255, 430

Rabbath, Edmond, 303, 341, 383–4
al-Rābiṭa al-Qalamiyya, 355
radio, 325, 388
al-Rafi'i, 'Abd al-Rahman, 256
al-Rafi'i, Mustafa Sadiq, 292, 305, 337
al-Raghba al-Ibāḥiyya, 369
Rahmanism, 424–5
Ramadan, 127, 171, 371, 387, 393
Rashtriya Swayamsevak Sangh (RSS), xxvii, 324
rationality, 1, 3, 22–3, 78, 90, 92, 101, 103, 107, 112, 182, 368–9, 371, 382, 403, 418, 420; *see also* reason
al-Rayyan Investment Company, 409
al-Razi, Fakhr al-Din, 60–1
reactionism, 100, 107, 121–5, 200
reason, xlvi–xlvii, 1, 30, 114, 186, 201–3, 215–25, 238–9, 291, 300, 311, 319, 328, 368–9, 371, 374–7; *see also* rationality
recognition, politics of, xxxiii, xxxviii, xlix
Red Star association, 137
reform
adminstrative, 86–96, 121, 143–4, 167–8, 182
at al-Azhar, 118–21, 252, 329–31, 386
cultural, 89–90, 181–2
educational, 87, 90, 97–105, 109, 118–21, 156, 167–8, 173, 176, 181, 251–2, 329–31
Islamic *see* Islamic reformism
legal, 5, 6, 87, 90, 91, 94, 138–52, 156–7, 173, 176, 181, 269–86
political, 89–90, 94–6, 157
and the state, 4–5, 85–180, 181–2, 196–9, 226, 241–3, 245–51, 329, 351
Reform Association (Jam'iyyat al-Iṣlaḥ), 166
Reformation, xliv, xlv, xlviii, 14, 15–16, 201, 204
relativity, theory of, 313–14
religion
administrative structures, 54–6
and authority *see* religious authority
and calendars, 127–8, 320
and the Cold War, xiv–xv, xvii, xxvi, xxvii
comparative religion, 330
confessional conflicts, 16–19, 155–6, 158, 160–1, 239, 336–7, 405
critical study of, 26–9, 31, 287–307, 317–18, 362–9, 382–4
and Darwinism, 28, 30, 232–3, 235, 237
days of rest, 127–8
differentiation of, xiv, xix–xx, xxxvii, 138
and dress, xii, xvii, 126, 127, 129–30, 396, 444
economic effects of, 370–1
and education, 15, 19, 31, 52, 54–9, 74, 98–102, 125, 173, 198, 246, 251–2, 299, 329–32, 388–9, 394
evolutionist theories of, 185–8, 231, 236–7, 286–9, 366–7
and Freemasonry, 113–14, 116–17
and food practices, 126
and fundamentalism, xviii, xli, xliv, 79, 124, 390, 391, 395, 449
increased centrality of in Arab World, xii–xix, 353, 407–50
infrastructure *see* religious infrastructure
as instinctive, 187, 237, 290, 308
and literature, 23–4, 226–7, 253, 254–5, 354–60, 381

Marxist theories of, 366–7, 370–1
and marriage practices, 13, 31, 60, 126–7, 147–8, 176, 263, 267–73, 408
and the media, 388, 396, 408, 444
and modernity, xli, 202–14
and morality, 17, 27, 68, 188, 237, 254, 300–1, 318, 368
and music, 24, 119, 410
and myth, 361–2, 363, 365, 368
natural religion, 22, 28–9, 114, 116, 201, 205
and personal belief, xix–xx, 8–9, 240, 286, 288, 300, 393
political use of, 250, 251, 301, 302, 326, 336–7, 352, 372
as the product of fear, 187, 236, 288, 289, 366
as providential, 187
and reactionism, 100, 107, 121–5, 200
and reason, 186, 201–3, 215–16, 218–25, 238–40, 291, 300, 319, 368–9, 371
relationship to law, 11–14, 25, 30, 67–8, 270–86, 299, 306–7
relationship to the state, xiv, 5, 11–19, 29–34, 42, 48–9, 52, 94–5, 240–3, 273, 302, 317–18, 329–40, 353, 384–406, 407–15, 440–1
resistance to secularisation, 29–32, 126–30, 137–9, 148–9, 156–7, 181, 253–61, 298–308, 352, 383
"return of religion" theories, xvi–xviii, xxvi–xxvii, xxxix, 10, 431, 435, 436–7, 440
and science, 19–23, 27–8, 104–5, 199, 202–3, 218–25, 229, 235–7, 239–40, 253, 287, 290, 294, 298–300, 304, 311–17, 368, 371, 383, 396
separation from cultural and social activity, 354–5
separation from the state, xiv, 7, 8, 32, 94–5, 240, 317–18
and social change, 126–37, 251–4
and social control, 19
as social necessity, 187–8
social practice of, xix–xx
and social solidarity, 11
sociology of, 367
state regulation of, 273
and the three-stage theory of history, 186, 287
and violence, 17, 158, 160–1, 237, 294, 336–7, 344–5, 407, 448
see also Buddhism; Christianity; Hinduism; Islam; Judaism; paganism; Roman religion; Zoroastrianism
religious authority, 8, 10, 12, 15, 23, 30, 36–42, 49–52, 56, 94, 183, 219, 240, 245, 297, 301, 307, 436
religious festivals, 15, 127
religious freedom, 103–4, 116, 332
religious infrastructure, xvii–xviii, 4, 50–6
religious knowledge, 51–3, 57–9, 80–1, 297–9
religious orders, 14, 17–18, 19–20
religious solidarity, 129, 164, 188, 190–1, 237
religious symbolism, 12, 226–7, 354–60, 401
religious tolerance, 19, 30, 155, 239, 240
Renaissance, 23–4
Renan, Ernest, 31, 229–30, 234
Reşid Paşa, 92–3, 106, 115
re-socialisation, xvii, xliii, xlix
resurrection, 235–6, 357–9, 424
"return of religion" theories, xvi–xviii, xxvi–xxvii, xxxix, 10, 431, 435, 436–7, 440
revisionist historiography, xxvii, 161
revisionist sociology, xviii–xix
revivalism, xxxii, 374, 377, 424–7, 429, 437, 440, 441, 444, 446–8
Richelieu, Cardinal, 18
Rida, Muhammad Rashid, 50, 101, 105, 113, 120, 129–30, 148–52, 165, 170–1, 197–8, 200, 205–6, 210–16, 218, 220, 222, 229–30, 247, 253, 255–6, 259–60, 267–9, 284–5, 302, 305, 307, 312, 314–16, 318, 337–40, 387, 398
right-wing thought, xi, xii, xxvii, 188, 192–3, 324, 437
Rightly-Guided Caliphs, 175, 206, 392
al-Rihani, Amin, 264, 304, 339
al-Risāla, 324
Al-risāla al-ḥamīdiyya (al-Jisr), 123, 223, 224
Risālat al-tawḥīd ('Abduh), 186, 201–2
Risorgimento, 440
ritual, 10–11, 30–1, 80, 81, 127, 155, 362, 415
Robespierre, Maximilien, 30
Rodinson, Maxime, 363
Roman law, 11, 12, 25
Roman religion, 10–11
Romanticism, xxvii–xxviii, xxxviii, 117, 192, 423–7
romanticism, 188, 323, 344, 392, 402–3, 423–4, 441
Rousseau, Jean-Jacques, 26, 30, 192, 205, 346, 441
royal absolutism, 15
Royal Society, 24
al-Rusafi, Ma'ruf, 124, 264, 290, 295
Rushdie, Salman, xvii, xlviii, 422

Russia/Soviet Union, xxvii, 32–3, 86, 104, 394, 442, 443, 446, 448
Russian Revolution, xxvii, 448

Sa'ab, Hassan, 399
Saadeh, Antoun, 292, 343
Saadist Institutional Party, 280
Sabri, Mustafa, 136–7, 256, 312, 315, 323
Sadat, Anwar, 225, 260, 308, 387, 388, 395, 434, 443–4
al-Sa'dawi, Nawal, 377
Sadikiya College, 98, 105, 109, 248
Safi, Shaykh Uthman, 384
Sa'id of Egypt, 101
al-Sa'idi, 'Abd al-Mit'al, 317
St Bartholomew's Day massacre, 17
Saint Joan (Shaw), 253
Saint-Simonian movement, 31, 93, 182
Saladin, 37, 389
Salafism, xii, xlix, 46–7, 56, 88, 124, 197, 203–4, 207, 248, 305, 316, 323, 345, 347, 389, 395, 416–17
Saliba, Jamil, 303–4
al-Samman, Ghada, 359–60
al-Sanhuri, Abd al-Razzaq, 6, 144, 274–7, 279–80, 300, 338
Sannu', Ya'qub, 243
al-Sarakhsi, Muhammad b. Ahmad, 70, 143, 284, 285
Sarruf, Fouad, 303
Sarruf, Ya'qub, 116, 233
Satan, 288, 361, 382
Satanic Verses (*al-gharāniq*), 215–16, 316
Saudi Arabia
  abolition of slavery, 152
  adoption of Gregorian calendar, 127
  clan networks, 89
  conservatism, 395, 442
  family transmission, 51
  Islamism, 395
  Muslim Brothers take refuge in, 443
  naṣīḥa texts, xlvii
  oil revenues, 395
  polygamy, 408
  reform movements, 89
  shari'a, 285
  ulama, 329
  violence of founding of state, 434, 448
  Wahhabism, xvii, xxi, xlvii, 89, 171, 174, 395
Savigny, Friedrich Carl von, xxvii
Sayigh, Tawfiq, 356–7, 399
al-Sayyab, Badr Shakir, 355–7
al-Sayyadi, Shaykh Abu al-Huda, 123–5
al-Sayyid, Ahmad Lutfi, 164, 259, 297, 325
al-Sayyidāt wa'l-Banāt, 132
scepticism, 20, 26, 123–4, 224–5, 227–8, 290, 295
Schmitt, Carl, xxx, xxxvii
Scholastic philosophy, 19
School of Shari'a Justice, 329, 330, 331
Schütz, Heinrich, 24
science, 19–23, 27–8, 99–105, 109, 122, 182, 199, 202–3, 218–25, 229, 235–7, 239, 240, 245, 253, 286–7, 290, 294, 298–300, 304, 311–17, 360, 368, 371, 377, 383, 396, 401
scientific knowledge, 20, 24, 28, 221, 298–300
scientific reason *see* rationality; reason
scientific societies, 24, 102–3, 109
Scotland *see* Britain
secessionism, 160–2, 168, 170–2, 415–16; *see also* separatism
secondary education, 97, 251
sectarianism, 101, 103, 160–1, 242, 302–3, 304, 336, 344, 371, 372, 382, 397
Secular Age, A (Taylor), xxx, xxxviii
secular authority, 108, 173, 297, 316
secular courts, 71, 72, 74, 139–41, 145, 148–9, 275, 278, 385, 408
secular education, 30, 31, 32, 97–100, 103–5, 106, 109, 176, 242, 251–3, 386
secular intellectuals, 5, 93, 96, 102–21, 182, 242–3, 246, 286–329, 351, 397
secular knowledge, 99–107, 217–25, 286–329
secular law, 14, 25, 30, 71–3, 91, 94, 138–48, 176, 270–86, 302, 319, 347, 384, 385
secular rituals, 30–1
secularisation
  of daily life, 126–52, 181
  and dress, 106, 107–8, 112, 129–30, 176, 181, 196, 256–7
  of education, 30, 31, 32, 97–100, 103–5, 106, 109, 176, 181, 242, 251–3, 386
  in Europe, xl–xlii, 3–4, 8–9, 16, 29–34, 414
  of the law, 14, 25, 30, 71–3, 91, 94, 138–48, 176, 270–86, 302, 384, 385
  and literature, 5, 226–8, 233, 303, 354–60, 381
  and morality, 34, 246–7
  and nationalism, 249, 251, 352–3, 371
  as objective historical process, xv, xxxvi, 3–4, 418
  and politics, 329–49
  and publishing, 128–9

religious resistance to, 29–32, 126–30, 137–9, 148–9, 156–7, 181, 253–61, 298–308, 352, 383
and social change, 126–37, 251–67
social and cultural dynamics of, 353–384
and the status of women, 126–7, 131–7, 257–73, 378–80
as subtraction of religion, xxxviii–xxxix
and temporal regimes, 127–8
of thought, 5, 102–21, 286–329
and Westernisation, 253–4
sécularisme, 8
segregation (of women), 126
self-censorship, 324
self-help books, 129
Selim III, 86–7, 106
Seljuk period, 52, 55, 74
Senoussi, 89
sentimentalism, xxiii–xxiv, xxix, xlii, 204, 281, 310, 315, 343, 435
separatism, 101, 122, 158, 160–2, 168; *see also* secessionism
sexuality, 258, 259, 285, 290, 360, 362, 369, 379; *see also* chastity; fornication
şeyhulislam, 55, 71–3, 75, 94, 96, 104, 126, 136, 155, 173, 198, 229, 256
Sfar, Bashir, 105, 109
Sfax, 433–4, 435
Sha'an al-shāh, 363
al-Sha'b, 410
Shabāb Muḥammad, 336
al-Shabbi, Abu'l-Qasim, 248, 291–2
al-Shafi'i, 62
Shafi'i school, 52, 66, 69
Shahādat al-ṭabī'a fi wujūd allāh wa al-sharī'a (Marrash), 223
al-Shahbandar, Abd al-Rahman, 165, 287, 300, 303
Shahin, 'Abd al-Sabur, 409
Sharabi, Hisham, 374
Sharara, Waddah, 184
Sha'rawi, Huda, 264–5, 268
Sha'rawi, Muhammad Mutawalli, 444
al-Sharbini, Abd al-Rahman, 330
shari'a
abolished in Turkish Republic, 174, 176, 256, 274
and authority, 62, 64, 65, 66–7, 76–80
basis of judgments, 62–6
and the caliphate, 47–9
and hadith, 60–2, 65–6
history of, 59–62, 73–6
and ideology, 76–82
and Islamic reformism, 207, 210, 211–14, 248, 280–6
Islamist interpretations, 124, 284–6
and modernity, 210, 211–14
multiplicity of legal institutes contained by, 75–6
and origins, 62–5, 75, 78–80
and politics, 47–8
punishments (*ḥudūd*), 65, 124, 139, 213–14, 282, 284–5, 317, 408, 449
and reactionism, 124, 125
realities of legal practice, 66–71
and secular law, 141–3, 149, 273, 276–86
sources of, 59–62, 74, 75, 213, 214, 279–80
and the status of women, 259, 260–1, 262, 263, 320
and tradition, 59–62, 66–8, 76
training in, 329, 330, 386
and the ulama, 60, 61–2, 78
see also Islamic jurisprudence; law
shari'a courts, 71–3, 141, 173, 256, 301
Shar'ist caliphate, 45
Shar'ist politics (*siyāsa shar'iyya*), xliv, 41, 47–8
al-Sharqawi, 'Abd al-Rahman, 401
al-Shatibi, Abu Ishaq Ibrahim ibn Musa, 65, 69–70, 212–13
Shaw, George Bernard, 253, 289
Shawkat, Sami, 341
Shawqi, Ahmad, 163, 256
al-Shidyaq, Ahmad Faris, 107, 134, 138, 142, 162, 217, 227, 240
al-Shihāb, 178–9
Shihab, Amir Bashir, 227
Shihab emirate, 161
Shihata, Shafiq, 274, 277
Shi'ism, 42, 47, 49, 74, 148, 271, 359, 434
al-Shishakli, Adib, 385
short stories, 359, 381
Shubra al-Khaima, 434
al-Shumayyil, Shibli, 132–3, 185, 191, 231, 233, 234–42, 287–8, 415
al-Siba'i, Muhammad, 323
al-Siba'i, Mustafa, 442
Sidi al-Akhdar mosque, Algeria, 248
Simon, Richard, 27
Six-Day War, 329, 372, 377, 382, 383, 384, 390, 395, 425, 444
al-Siyāsa, 229, 302, 307, 324, 338
al-Siyāsa al-Islāmiyya fi 'ahd al-nubuwwa (al-Sa'idi), 317
slavery, 89, 105, 124, 150, 152, 209, 213, 268, 320, 409

Smith, Charles Lee, 304
social change, 126–37, 181, 183, 251–67, 394–5
social class, 112, 127, 177, 366–7, 369–71, 394–5; *see also* aristocracy; bourgeoisie; proletariat
social control, 19, 219
social Darwinism, xxi, 32, 188–92
social differentiation, xiv, xv, xix–xx, xxxvii, xli, xlix, 138
social engineering, xii, xviii, xxv, 33, 79, 90, 96, 182, 241, 385, 446
social media, xx–xxi
social solidarity, 11, 190–1
social structure, xlv–xlvi, xlix, 41–2, 89, 96, 153–5, 367, 436
socialism, 1, 5, 19, 111, 303–4, 354, 374, 378, 382–3, 389, 397–401, 442–4; *see also* left-wing though; Marxism
sociology, xxx–xxxii, xxxiv, xxxix–xlii, 26, 127, 287, 367
solidarity *see* religious solidarity; social solidarity
Soviet Union *see* Russia/Soviet Union
Spain, 15, 16, 17, 49, 85, 437
Spencer, Herbert, 185, 288
Spengler, Oswald, xxx, xxxiii, xxxiv, 344, 424
Spinoza, Baruch, 26–7, 367
spiritualism, 117, 222, 311–12, 355
spirituality, 44, 308–10, 324
state, the
  administration, 1, 2, 15, 71–3, 81, 86–96, 121, 143–4, 153–60, 167–8, 182, 196–7, 245
  and authoritarianism, 182, 196–8, 352, 353
  and authority, 56, 108, 408
  centralisation, 1, 5, 15, 16, 18, 73, 76–7, 168, 246, 436
  communication and information systems, 246
  consociational state, 404–6
  and democracy, 439–40, 441
  dirigiste state, 4–5, 96, 247
  and education, 5, 30, 31, 32, 97–100, 106, 109, 176, 251–3, 329–32
  infiltration of Islamism, 407–12
  and law, 14, 25, 30, 71–3, 91, 94, 138–48, 175, 176, 270–86
  and paternalism, 297, 352, 353
  promotion of myths, 382
  recession of cultural and social direction, 353
  and reform, 4–5, 85–180, 181–2, 196–9, 226, 241–3, 245–51, 329, 351
  regulation of religion, 273
  relationship to religion, xiv, 5, 11–19, 29–34, 42, 48–9, 52, 94–5, 240–3, 273, 302, 317–18, 329–40, 353, 384–406, 407–15, 440–1
  relationship to society, 440–1
  separation of state and religion, xiv, 7, 8, 32, 94–5, 240, 317–18
  shaykhification of, 397, 443
  state formation, 160–1, 169, 177, 434–5, 440, 448
  and violence, xxv, 404, 434–5, 440, 441, 448
Stein, Lorenz von, xxvii
stock markets, 151
stoning, 65, 124, 139, 284–5
Strauss, David Friedrich, 27
Su'ād (al-'Askari), 303
Subaltern Studies, xxiv
Sublimity, xxix
subtraction thesis (of secularisation), xxxviii–xxxix
Sudan, 89, 152, 370, 407, 434, 448–9
Sufi fraternities, 54–5, 88, 91, 123, 172, 176, 248, 315, 416
Sufism, 42, 44, 47, 54–5, 88, 91, 123, 163, 172, 176, 195, 248, 290, 311, 312, 315, 355, 403, 416
suffrage, 176, 266
al-Suhrawardi, Shihab al-Din Abu Hafs, 44
Sunna, 47, 62, 207, 213, 217, 279–80, 319, 365
Sunni Islam, 64, 67, 74, 75, 229, 271, 358, 383, 403
super-Islamisation, xvi, xl, xlvi
Surrealism, 369–70
Swedenborg, Emanuel, 117
Switzerland, 20, 176, 266, 276
Sykes, Mark, 170
Syllabus of Errors (Pius IX), xxvii, 22
Syria
  Arab nationalism, 162–3, 166–7, 339–44
  Arab occupation, 75
  and the Arab Revolt, 172
  Baath Party, 287, 343, 385, 389, 400
  Christianity, 155, 159, 162, 163, 172, 234, 339, 344, 385, 415
  Civil Law code, 274–5, 278–9, 280
  Civil War, 433
  Communism, 370, 434
  consociational state, 404

constitutions, 339–40, 385–6
dissolution of *waqf*, 273
dress, 129, 130
educational book publishing, 102
family transmission, 51
Freemasonry, 113, 115
French invasion, 137
French Mandate, 170, 251, 262, 278, 302–3
Great Syrian Revolt, 339
hierarchies of religious scholars, 53
independence, 170, 385
Islamic reformism, 197–8
Islamism, 344–5, 385, 407, 433, 434
journal publishing, 103, 108, 303–4
jurisprudence, 62
kuttāb schools, 251
legal reform, 139, 270–1, 273, 274–5, 278–9
madrasas, 56, 388
Ministry of Awqaf, 388
missionary schools, 101–2, 252
Mixed Courts, 278
Muslim Brotherhood, 345, 434, 442–3
nationalism, 162, 251, 255, 345, 373, 383, 423
'neo-Baath' coup, 385, 400
Ottoman Syria, 92, 94, 98, 101–2, 113, 115, 121, 123, 125, 129, 132, 155, 159, 160, 162, 415
Pan-Arabism, 385, 434
Penal Law code, 274
polygamy, 269
primary education, 251
proportion of Muslims, 74
proportional representation, 385
public support for independence, 163
religious education, 389
religious office-holders, 53
scientific societies, 102–3
secession from United Arab Republic, 442
sectarianism, 302–3, 304, 344
secular courts, 139, 278, 385
secular education, 98, 100, 106, 251, 252
secular intellectuals, 246, 287, 301–4
secular law, 139, 270–1, 273, 274–5, 278–9, 280, 385
shari'a, 273, 385
Shi'ism, 47
state paternalism, 353
status of women, 260, 261–2, 264–6, 380, 389
Syrian Social Nationalist Party, 343, 423
universities, 104, 386
women's conferences, 265
women's education, 132, 133–4
women's employment, 380, 389
women's movement, 264–6
women's suffrage, 266
Syrian Protestant College, 101, 103, 116, 132, 233
Syrian Scientific Society, 102–3
Syrian Social Nationalist Party (SSNP), 343, 423
Syrian University in Damascus, 104, 386

al-Tabari, 216
tafarnuj see Westernisation
tafwīḍ, 218, 219, 220
al-Tahtawi, Rifa'a Rafi', 92, 99, 106, 135, 141, 205, 209, 210–11, 213
al-Ta'i', 36–7, 44
Takhlīṣ al-ibrīz fī talkhīṣ Bārīz (al-Tahtawi), 205
Talat Paşa, 166
talfiq, 147–8, 213
al-Ṭalī'a, 303–4, 354, 431
al-Talimsani, 'Umar, 448
Tammuz, 355, 357–8
Tangiers, 108
Tanzimat, 87–94, 96–7, 106, 108, 112, 122, 138–9, 153, 157, 160, 162, 167, 173, 182, 192, 196–9, 203–4, 207, 225, 226, 241–3, 246–7, 327, 329, 351
Taqla, Salim, 163
Tarabishi, Georges, 377
Tawfiq Pasha, 115
taxation, 17, 30, 33, 54, 70, 90, 153, 245
Taylor, Charles, xxx, xxxiii, xxxviii, xxxix–xl
Taymur, Ahmad, 197
Taymur, Mahmud, 354
teacher training, 98, 109, 134
technologies of the self, xliii
technology, 199
telegraph, 73, 221
television, 388, 396, 411, 444
temporal Balkanisation, 3, 438
temporal regimes, 127–8, 320
al-Tha'alibi, Abd al-Aziz, 248
theatre, 130, 197, 255, 303
theosophy, 310–12
Thessaloniki, 177–8
three-stage theory of history, 185–6, 287
al-Tirmidhi, 60
Tizini, Tayyib, 402

Torah, 216, 217, 295, 355, 362
Trabulsi, Nawfal Nawfal, 102
trade, 70, 77, 85, 158, 169, 198
tradition, xxxi–xxxiii, xlv–xlvii, xlix, 59–62, 66–8, 76, 154, 204, 213, 218, 241, 267, 313–16
Transjordan *see* Jordan
transubstantiation, 20
Treaty of Sèvres, 173
Treaty of Westphalia, 17
tribal structures, 13, 143, 153, 353
Trotskyism, 369
Truman Doctrine, 383, 394
Trumpism, xii
truth, xxvi, xxxvi, 1, 27, 240
al-Tufi, Najm ad-Din, 212
Tunis, 86, 87–8, 89, 95, 105, 109, 121, 248, 265, 389, 433
al-Tunisi, Khayr al-Din, 207, 213
Tunisia
- abolition of slavery, 152
- agricultural cooperatives, 442
- conservatism, 442
- constitution, 385
- Destour Party, 248
- education in French schools, 248–9
- educational reform, 98, 109, 121
- French colonisation, 88, 93, 109–12, 121, 144–5, 247, 261, 347, 349
- Fundamental Law, 93
- independence, 248–9, 370–1, 386
- Islamic reformism, 248
- Islamism, 379, 433–4
- journal publishing, 109, 392
- *kuttāb* schools, 252
- legal reform, 144–5, 271–2
- Nahda party, xxii
- nationalism, 110, 111, 248–9, 349, 371
- Neo-Destour Party, 248, 442
- Pledge of Security (*'Ahd al-Amān*), 93
- primary education, 109, 252
- religious education, 389
- scientific societies, 109
- secular education, 98, 109, 386
- secular intellectuals, 105, 109–12
- secular law, 144–5, 271–2
- socialism, 442
- state reforms, 87, 88, 93, 95, 249
- status of women, 260–1, 272, 378–80, 449
- teacher training, 109
- universities, 386
- women's employment, 380
- Young Tunisian movement, 109, 110, 121, 248, 249
- Zeitouna, 105, 109–10, 111, 121, 248, 260–1, 330, 386

Tunisian University, 386
al-Turabi, Hasan, 449
Turgot, 25
Turkey
- abolition of shari'a, 174, 176, 256, 274
- atheism, 304
- constitution, 175–6
- declaration of Republic, 174
- Diyanet, xviii
- dress, 256–7
- educational reform, 176
- establishment of secular state, 158, 174–80
- ethnic cleansing, 177
- ethnic groups, 177
- Kemalist revolution, 5, 122, 169, 173–4, 178, 241, 242, 255–6
- legal reform, 176
- military, 177
- National Assembly, 173–4, 175
- nationalism, xxvii, 166, 167–9, 173, 188, 190, 200, 341
- Ottoman conquest, 12
- religious education, 394
- secular education, 100, 176
- secular intellectuals, 5, 106, 246
- secular law, 175, 176
- social class, 394–5
- status of women, 134, 176, 262, 266
- universities, 394
- women's education, 134
- women's suffrage, 176, 266
- Young Turk movement, 122, 241

Turkish Association for the Propagation of Atheism, 304
Turkish language, 8, 92, 122, 176, 177, 179–80
Tusun, Prince Umar, 260, 334
tyranny, xiii, 170, 207, 208–9, 229, 239, 240, 318, 353, 403

ulama
- and authority, 49–52, 61–2, 78, 219
- and continuity, 50–2
- distinguished from other office-holders, 53–5
- and Freemasonry, 116–17
- hierarchies of, 53–4
- and knowledge transmission, 51–3
- miracles performed by, 44–5

mockery of, 138
and religious authority, 49–52
resistance to secularisation, 127–8, 137–9
role as legatees, 49–50
and secular intellectuals, 106, 107, 109–10, 111, 118–21
and shari'a, 60, 61–2, 78
Ultramontanism, 17, 30, 31
'Umar ibn al-Khattab, 364
Umayyad caliphate, 364
Umm al-qurā (al-Kawakibi), 164, 170, 174
unemployment, 98, 394–5
United Arab Emirates, 275
United Arab Republic, 385, 442; *see also* Egypt; Syria
United States
alt-right, xii
anti-Communism, 383, 394, 442
Central Intelligence Agency, 399
cultural anthropology, xxviii–xxix
emigré Arabic poets, 254, 355
Evangelicalism, 233, 396
fundamentalism, xviii
invasion of Iraq, 271
9/11 attacks, xxiii
post-colonial scholarship, xxiii–xxv
rate of religious belief, 9
Truman Doctrine, 383, 394
Trumpism, xii
universalism, 76, 78, 111, 183, 245–6, 248, 327–8, 358–9, 368, 377
Université Saint Joseph, 253
universities, 24, 98, 104, 252, 253, 329–32, 386, 394, 398, 409
al-Uqbi, Tayyib, 247–8
'Urabi Revolt, 107, 108, 118, 158
al-'Urwa al-Wuthqā (association), 195, 197, 200, 398
Al-'Urwa al-Wuthqā (journal), 105, 189–90, 193–4, 195–6, 425
Usul el-hikem fi nizam el-ümem (Mehmet), 86
al-'Uṣūr, 300, 303, 304
usury, 13, 69, 151; *see also* interest
'Uthman, 293, 316, 323
utilitarianism, 3, 29, 114, 116, 182, 192, 195, 201, 203, 205, 207, 225, 229, 245, 372
utopia, xxxviii, 74, 204, 241, 284, 296

Vatican *see* Papacy
veiling, xii, 100, 126, 127, 131–3, 135, 136, 176, 256, 259–66, 304, 407, 411, 415, 446
Vietnam, 374
violence
and colonialism, 111, 145
confessional conflicts, 16–19, 155–6, 158, 160–1, 239, 336–7, 405
and ethnic cleansing, 160–1, 169, 177
and Islamism, 336, 344–5, 407, 410, 427, 434–5, 448
and religion, 17, 158, 160–1, 237, 294, 336–7, 344–5, 407, 448
and revolution, 29, 169
and state formation, 160–1, 169, 177, 434–5, 448
state violence, xxv, 404, 441
against women, 260, 262, 380, 407
virgins of Paradise (*houris*), 222, 269
vitalism, xxv–xxvi, xxix, xxx–xxxv, xxxviii, xli–xlii, xlviii, 191–3, 424–5, 430, 441, 442
Vogt, Karl, 29
Voltaire, 19, 114, 116, 192, 205, 234, 346
voluntarism, 376, 403–4, 439

Wafd Party, 250, 265, 280, 297, 326, 331, 332, 333, 334–5, 444
Wahhabism, xvii, xxi, xlvii, 89, 124, 151–2, 171, 174, 210, 305, 339, 388–9, 395–7, 410
Wajdi, Muhammad Farid, 302, 306, 311–12
Wannus, Sa'd Allah, 397
al-Waqā'i' al-Miṣriyya, 107
waqf, 53, 95, 98, 146, 167, 173, 174, 176, 273, 387, 388
al-Waqidi, 217
Waraqa ibn Nawfal, 234
al-Waṭan, 161
Weber, Max, xix, xxxvi
Wells, H. G., 289
West/East dichotomy, 308–10, 326–8
Westernisation, 4, 112, 128, 129–30, 199, 253–4, 257, 324, 433
Westtoxification, 427
Whig politics, 107
witch trials, 17
women
attitudes towards, 132–6, 258–68
in the civil service, 131
and contraception, 268–9
and dress, 378, 396; *see also* veiling
education, 100, 103, 126, 131–2, 133–6, 258, 259, 267
employment, 267, 270, 272, 379–80, 389

women (*cont.*)
feminism, 258, 260, 262, 264–6, 359–60, 378–9
guardianship of children, 272
and honour, 258, 261, 272, 353, 379, 446
hyper-pietist practices, xliii, xlvi
and inheritance, 147, 171, 214, 266, 267, 268, 270, 271, 380
and Islamic reformism, 134, 259–60, 262–3, 268, 380
and Islamism, 261, 263, 264, 269, 379
and legal witness, 262, 269, 270
and literature, 359–60
and male guardianship, 267, 268
and marriage practices, 126–7, 147–8, 260, 267–73, 380
movement in public space, 91
physical punishment by husbands, 268, 380
psychological study of, 377
in public office, 134
and secular law, 270–3
and secularisation, 126–7, 131–7, 257–73
segregation, 126
and sexuality, 258, 259, 360, 369, 379
and shari'a, 259, 260–1, 262, 263, 320
social mixing of genders, 256, 259, 262, 266, 303, 379
status of, 2, 33, 126–7, 131–7, 257–73, 320, 369, 378–80, 389, 446, 449
suffrage, 176, 266
as symbolic of national sovereignty, 261
veiling, xii, 100, 126, 127, 131–3, 135, 136, 176, 256, 259–66, 304, 407, 411, 415, 446
violence against, 260, 262, 380, 407
women's associations, 137
women's conferences, 265
women's movement, 264–6, 378–9
Women of the East (Fahmi), 134
World Bank, 89

Yakan, Wali al-Din, 163
Yassin, Bu Ali, 369
al-Yaziji, Nasif, 162
Yemen, 82, 92, 152, 272, 400
Younan, Ramses, 369–70
Young Algerians movement, 110
Young Arab Society (al-'Arabiyya al-Fatāt), 166
Young Egypt movement, 336
Young Ottoman movement, 115, 188, 197–200, 208, 240, 425
Young Tunisian movement, 109, 110, 121, 248, 249
Young Turk movement, 122, 241
Yusuf, 'Ali, 163, 186, 192
Yusuf, Hassan, 114-5

Zaghloul, Sa'd, 104, 114, 197, 265, 329, 330, 337
Zaghloul, Safiyya, 265
al-Zahawi, Jamil Sidqi, 123–4, 227–8, 264, 269, 289, 302, 356
al-Zahrawi, 'Abd al-Hamid, 167, 169–70, 190, 340
Zahiri school, 213, 416
al-Za'im, Husni, 278, 280
Zai'ur, Ali, 377
Zakaria, Fouad, 397
Zakariyya, Ahmed, 304
al-Zarqa, Mustafa, 283
al-Zawahiri, Muhammad, 330, 334
Zaydan, Jurji, 116, 126, 133, 163, 229–30, 237, 303, 335
Zayn al-Din, Nazira, 258, 260, 262–4, 268
al-Zayyat, Hassan, 324
Zeinab bint Jahsh, 216
Zeitouna, 105, 109–10, 111, 121, 248, 260–1, 330, 386
Zola, Émile, 231
Zoroastrianism, 10, 75
Zubdat al-ṣahā'if fi uṣūl al-ma'ārif (Trabulsi), 102
Zurayq, Constantine, 304, 342, 372, 376, 398, 422, 424
Zwingli, Huldrych, 20

EU representative:
Easy Access System Europe
Mustamäe tee 50, 10621 Tallinn, Estonia
Gpsr.requests@easproject.com

www.ingramcontent.com/pod-product-compliance
Lightning Source LLC
Chambersburg PA
CBHW052053300426
44117CB00013B/2099
* 9 7 8 1 4 7 4 4 4 7 4 7 8 *